American State and Local Politics

American State and Local Politics

Jeffrey M. Stonecash

Department of Political Science
Maxwell School, Syracuse University

HARCOURT BRACE

Harcourt Brace College Publishers

Fort Worth   Philadelphia   San Diego   New York   Orlando   Austin   San Antonio
Toronto   Montreal   London   Sydney   Tokyo

Publisher	Ted Buchholz
Senior Acquisitions Editor	David Tatom
Developmental Editor	J. Claire Brantley
Senior Production Manager	Ken Dunaway
Cover Design	Scott Baker
Production Management	Impressions, a Division of Edwards Brothers
Text Design	Jane Tenenbaum/Tenenbaum Design

Library of Congress Cataloging-in-Publication Data
Stonecash, Jeffrey M.
    American state and local politics / Jeffrey M. Stonecash.
      p. cm.
    Includes bibliographical references and index.
    ISBN 0-15-500368-2
    1. State governments—United States. 2. Local government—United States. 3. Political participation—United States. I. Title.
    JK2408.S855   1995
324′.0973—dc20   94-37687
                                                 CIP

Printed in the United States of America

ISBN 0-15-500368-2

5 6 7 8 9 0 1 2 3 4 039 9 8 7 6 5 4 3 2 1

To

My mother, who always encouraged me to understand
the views of others. Her advice has been invaluable for
understanding politics, and for life in general.

My father, who taught me the work ethic necessary
to complete this and other projects.

Preface

Almost fifty years ago, V. O. Key presented two fundamental propositions about politics: first, that the enduring conflicts in politics revolve around class issues; second, that the way political processes "work" affects who wins and loses. Processes can differ, and those differences can bias the process toward one group or another. *American State and Local Politics* approaches politics with a particular perspective—one that may be particularly valuable at a time when evidence suggests that class divisions in our society are increasing. Whether such divisions actually emerge as political conflicts is an intriguing question and one of the prime concerns of this textbook.

Conflict is pervasive in American society. There are conflicts over environmental policies, abortion rights, gay rights, and many other issues, none of which are based on class. But the enduring conflicts have been between the haves and have-nots. The political process is our means of trying to respond to and resolve differing concerns as we formulate public policies.

This textbook argues that the political process is not neutral. The theme that runs through this book is that the political process shapes who wins and who loses in the pursuit of public policy. Variations in process affect how the haves and the have-nots fare. The broad questions pursued throughout this book are how the process shapes who gets represented, what kinds of concerns become dominant on the agenda of politicians, and whose interests get priority when decisions are made.

Societal conflicts persist because citizens face enduring differences of opportunities. Conflicts also emerge because of our culture. American society places great importance on equality of opportunity. The persistence of inequality of condition raises questions of whether opportunity really exists for all citizens and whether we should change public policy to create or enhance equality of opportunity.

American State and Local Politics is organized in a fairly conventional fashion. In general, chapters on representation are followed by chapters on institutions and decision making. This textbook, however, does do some things differently.

The State and Local Question

Many textbooks provide separate coverage of state and local politics. The presumption of this textbook is that the important questions of politics apply equally to both levels and that more is gained from analyzing them together than from doing so separately. For example, in considering whether politicians are able to effect change once in office, the question of whether an executive has a political agenda and the formal power to achieve that agenda applies equally to governors, county executives, and mayors. When the two levels need to be considered separately, I have done so.

Constitutional Rules

Some textbooks have a chapter on constitutions. Although this book does not, constitutional issues are not neglected. They are considered in the subject chapters when a legal principle is relevant. The hope is that this more specific use of constitutional issues will make "the rules of the game" more relevant. The legal relationship between states and their local governments is considered in the chapter on state and local relations (Chapter 4). The legal power of executives in the decision-making process is considered in the chapter on executives (Chapter 9).

This textbook also includes chapters on the sources of conflict in state and local politics. Public opinion, conflicts between the state and its local governments, and disputes about taxes are covered. My teaching experience indicates that many students are not aware of what all the squabbling is about in American state and local politics. I hope these chapters provide that background.

Literature

There are always questions about the timeliness of a new book. I have drawn on recent publications whenever possible, but I have also drawn on publications that are somewhat "older." Older publications often contain important insights and should not be discarded simply because of their publication date. I have also drawn upon as wide a range of publications as possible.

I have always felt that state and local politics should be treated as part of national politics. Many of the concerns relevant to American national politics are also relevant at the state and local levels. For example, whether parties play a role in organizing political debates is relevant at all levels. For that reason, I draw on literature about American national politics where it is appropriate.

Accumulated Political Conditions

I have long thought that academic studies are often too preoccupied with finding the effect of some political condition in isolation from other conditions. My argument is that it is the combination of conditions (the party bases of gubernatorial and legislative parties, and their relative power over each other, for example) that determines what policies are adopted. To address the importance of such combinations, Chapters 8 and 12, which follow the sections on representation and decision making, address the cumulative effect of certain conditions. I hope this material contributes to an overall understanding of politics.

An Instructor's Manual is available upon request to instructors using *American State and Local Politics*. This ancillary includes chapter overviews, suggestions for how to use text materials, a listing and definition of key concepts, and test items for student exams.

As with any textbook project, I owe an enormous debt to the scholars who have produced so many studies of American politics. I am particularly indebted to the work of V. O. Key in *Southern Politics*. I read this work at a time when I was uneasy about the quantitative studies that have dominated the analysis of state politics. Key's book was a revelation and continues to be a model for other research. He focused on what he termed the enduring questions of politics: How much should the government tax? Who should bear the burdens? How much, and for whom, should the government spend? and How do the workings of the political process shape who wins and loses? Key gathered politically relevant quantitative *and* qualitative information in an attempt to capture how the process works. He also had an intuitive sense of how to use and present that information. I greatly appreciate having this work to guide my thinking in how to analyze politics.

I have been fortunate to be engaged in polling, consulting, and targeting analysis for candidates in my region as well as in campaign planning. I have learned an enormous amount from these experiences and am indebted to many people for my political education.

I have also had the good fortune of working with the New York Assembly Intern Committee as Professor-in-Residence for a number of years. Legislators, staff, and journalists have all added to my education on politics.

I have found the Maxwell School at Syracuse University a wonderful place to balance academic studies with more applied learning. My colleagues have been supportive of my efforts, and I thank them for their encouragement.

Several reviewers provided helpful feedback as I completed this manuscript. My thanks go to Gerald Benjamin, State University of New York at New Paltz; Thad Beyle, University of North Carolina at Chapel Hill; Pat Freeland, University of Tennessee; Russ Getter, University of Kansas; William Lammers, University of Southern California; Morris Levitt, Howard University; Sarah McCauly-Morehouse, University of Kentucky; David Ringsmuth, California State University at Northridge; William Winter, University of Colorado; and Joseph Zimmerman, State University of New York at Albany.

I asked several faculty members from other schools to help me categorize legislative districts in their state. Their generosity has been invaluable. They are James Carter, Sam Houston State University; Susan MacManus, University of South Florida; and William K. Muir, University of California at Berkeley. My thanks also to Gerald Wright, Indiana University, and Robert Brown, University of Mississippi, for allowing me access to their files of survey data on public opinion in the states. Edward Jennings at the University of Kentucky was kind enough to let me use the original data from his study on Louisiana and Virginia.

This textbook would not have come about without the support of several people at Harcourt Brace College Publishers. Sales representative Deborah Van Patten persisted in asking me if I was interested in writing a textbook and convinced David Tatom, the acquisitions editor, to listen to my ideas. I appreciate both Deborah's faith and David's support and encouragement. Claire Brantley, the developmental editor who helped push the project along, has always been supportive and a delight to talk with. I thank all of them.

Finally, my family has been enormously patient with the demands of this book. I greatly appreciate their faith and understanding.

Contents

1 **Studying State and Local Politics: Perspective and Theme** 1

Diversity, Conflict, and Politics 2
The Importance of Process 3
The Significance of Process: Examples 9
The Broader Debate about Process 13
The Plan of the Book 14

2 **Federalism and the States: The Issue of Autonomy** 19

Introduction 20
The Formation of Federalism 21
Federalism and the States 24
The Move to a More Activist National Government 42
Centralization and the Courts 60
The Resulting Position of the States 63

Overview I

Political Conflict and Representation 69

3 **The Sources of Political Conflict** 71

Conflict: The Driving Force of Politics 72
Individual Situations as Sources of Conflict 73
Group Identities and Political Conflict 80
The Importance of Geography: Conflicts between Areas within States 83
The Importance of Geography: Conflicts within Localities 86
Change as a Source of Conflict 90
Moderating Conflict 96

4 **Political Conflict, States and Their Local Governments, and Taxes** 101

The Role of the State: The Debate 102
The Role of the State: Change amid Continuing Diversity 110
Paying for Government: Issues of Raising Money 118
Paying for Government: Tax Burdens 124

5 **Political Parties, Elections, and the Representation of Political Concerns** 137

Political Parties and Representation: The Ideal 138
An Example: Politics in New Jersey 141
The Criticism of Political Parties 144
Reforming Political Parties: The State Level 148
Reforming Political Parties: The Local Level 151
The Consequences of Anti-Party Attitudes 153

The Persisting Role of Political Parties: Organizing the Electorate   158
The Unclear Role of Local Parties   169
The Intrusion of National Politics   172
The Persisting Role of Parties: Representing Different Concerns   173
Party Competition in the States   176
Summary   176

6 **Political Participation and Representation   185**

The Significance of Participation   186
The Reasons for Low and Declining Turnout   188
Who Participates and Why   192
The Consequences of Differences in Participation   195
Changing the Conditions and the Rates of Participation   198
Changes in Political Involvement over Time   202
State Turnout Differentials   206
Alternative Means of Representation: Referenda,
    Initiatives, Polls, and Protests   207
Representation and District Elections   210
Summary: The Effective Public   216

7 **Interest Groups and Representation   221**

The Role of Interest Groups   222
Who Belongs to Interest Groups   223
Which Interests Are Organized   225
Interest Groups and Electoral Influence   227
Interest Groups and Persuasion   229
Variations in Interest Groups from State to State   234
Assessing Interest Group Influence   235
Public Efforts to Restrain Interest Groups   245

8 **Representation: The Effects of Political Conditions   255**

Political Processes and Differences in Representation   256
The Difficulty of Forming Expectations of the Impact
    of Different Processes   259
Whose Concerns Get Attention: Evidence from the States   260
Whose Concerns Get Attention: Evidence from Local Politics   264
What Policies Are Enacted: Evidence from the States   267
What Policies Are Enacted: Evidence from Local Politics   272
Summary   274

Overview II

Institutions and Decision Making   279

9 **Executives and Policy Pursuits   285**

Governors and Mayors: Defining and Pursuing Agendas   286
Pursuing Agendas: The Formal Power of Governors and Mayors   298

Pursuing Agendas: The Informal Power of Governors and Mayors   308
The Mix of Constituencies and Power   312
Summary   316

10 Legislatures and Policy Pursuits   321
The Role of State and Local Legislatures   322
Political Representation: Careerism and the Issue of
   Motivations in State Legislatures   323
Political Representation: Careerism and the Issue of
   Motivations in Local Legislatures   327
Policy Pursuits: Legislators and Political Coalitions   329
Organizing to Act: The Formal Process of Enacting Legislation   332
Organizing to Act: Staff and the Professional Legislature   337
Organizing to Act: Informal Practices for Reaching Decisions   338
Political Parties and Building Majorities   340
Case Studies of Legislative Agendas   348
Legislative Agendas and Power   350
The Public and Legislatures   352

11 Courts and the Agendas of Politicians   357
The Argument for the Third Branch   358
Arbitrating Disputes over the Political Process   359
The Role of Cases: Issues of Access and Representation   360
Structures, Jurisdictions, and Process   366
Selecting Those Who Preside   369
Treatment of Cases   373
The Effects of Court Practices and Rulings:
   Shaping Agendas and Altering Policy   379

12 Political Control and Public Policy Decisions   387
Expectations of Impacts   388
The Significance of Party Control   392
Factors Affecting Party-Control Impact   397
Divided Party Control   406
Public Involvement in Decision Making   409

**13 Trying to Change Social Conditions:
The Design and Impact of Public Policy   417**
Introduction   418
Pursuing Public Policy: Alternative Methods of
   Achieving Policy Goals   419
Government Provision of Services   420
Regulating Private-Sector Practices and Behaviors   431
The Impact of Policy: The Expectations Problem   436
Problems of Policy Impacts   439
The Persistence of Efforts to Affect Social Conditions   444

Appendix A: Electoral Allegiances and Party Composition   449

Appendix B: The Constitution and the States   459

Index   483

1

Studying State and Local Politics: Perspective and Theme

PREVIEW

Diversity of population, issues of inequality, and the conflicts that ensue are persistent in states and localities. The political process is our means of resolving these conflicts. This chapter explains the focus taken in this text to analyzing the political process. The text focuses on one of the most enduring conflicts in American society, that between the haves and the have-nots. This chapter is concerned with how conflict emerges and how varying political processes shape the relative chances of the haves and the have-nots in public policy battles.

Politics generally comes down, over the long run, to a conflict between those who have and those who have less. In state politics the crucial issues tend to turn around taxation and expenditure.[1]

Diversity, Conflict, and Politics

There are vast differences in people's economic situations throughout states and localities. People differ in wealth, education, and the kinds of jobs they hold. This affects the health care they receive, the quality of the food they eat, and the opportunities they have in life. Children come from families with very different resources and live in communities with very different tax bases, which affects the kinds of schools children attend and the opportunities they have. These differences lead to disputes about inequality and whether government should do anything about inequality. Should state and local governments try to address these differences? Should welfare levels be higher to provide minimal income levels? Or should welfare be limited and participation in work programs required so people are encouraged to get off welfare? Should efforts be made to equalize school finances? How should money be raised to pay for such government programs? Should the wealthy pay more because they have a greater ability to pay? Or should the wealthy not have to pay more because it discourages initiative and drives people out of areas that tax the wealthy more? There is no end to the specific disputes that flow from debates about inequality.

People's values vary as greatly as their economic situations. There is much debate over the extent to which individuals should be responsible for their own lives. Liberals think social conditions affect what happens to people. Conservatives think individuals should be primarily responsible for their lives. Such differences of opinion lead to battles over whether and to what extent government should take an active role in providing food stamps, job training, and public housing. Differences in religious beliefs also lead to conflicts over abortion rights. Some people support the right to have abortions and others believe it is a criminal act.

Just as there are differences and conflicts among people, there are also differences and conflicts between communities. Some have wealthy tax bases while others have relatively poor tax bases. This revenue discrepancy leads to disputes over the distribution of school aid. Central cities and suburban areas generally differ in the percentage of minorities present, a situation that leads to arguments about segregation and open-housing practices.

Such disputes prompt questions as to whether (and which) government should be actively involved. Should we rely on local governments, which may differ in tax bases and in the values, beliefs, and education of their populations, and, therefore, possibly produce very different outcomes across localities? Or should the state take an active role and try to create some minimal set of standards across communities?

Diverse populations, issues of inequality, and the conflicts that follow from these conditions are persistent in American society. Differences in wealth, opportunity, and beliefs about individual responsibility and the role of government have been with us since the founding of the country, and, as a result of immigration within the last two decades, cultural diversity within the United States may even be growing.

The Role of Politics

The fundamental challenge of a democratic society is to find some way to respond to this diversity and to resolve conflicts so that public policies can be established. We rely on the political process to do so. Politics is the sum of activities by which we draw out these diverse concerns and then make policy decisions. In this process, we first encourage people to express their concerns so that they are represented. We choose decision makers who we hope will listen to those concerns. We create institutions with decision-making rules to make choices about policy directions.

The political process is the means by which we make value choices. We choose to recognize some concerns and not others. We grant importance to some problems and opinions and not to others. We impose burdens and benefits on some and not others. We allocate resources to some programs and cut others. Politics is our means of deciding which activities to support and which to discourage.

The Importance of Process

How this process works is crucial. The political process is not neutral. It is a process that can amplify some concerns and downplay others.[2] It is a process that can systematically allocate more burdens and benefits to some but not to others. How the process works ultimately affects who wins and loses.

This text revolves around two propositions. First, that the enduring conflicts in American politics are between the haves (those with money and better jobs) and the have-nots (those not as well off). These broad conflicts occur at the national level as well as at state and local levels. Resolving these conflicts is one of the most important challenges our society faces because these conflicts involve the issues of equality and equality of opportunity. Our society attributes enormous importance to the existence of equality of opportunity, and we must continually address the issue of whether equality of opportunity is decreasing or increasing.

This is not to argue that all conflicts in American society are class conflicts. Issues come along periodically (environmental concerns, abortion rights) that do not revolve primarily around class conflict. It is also possible that issues with the potential to divide people by class never emerge as class conflicts. Access to health care may differ dramatically according to an individual's income level, but interest groups may be successful in defining the health-care issue as a battle over the wisdom of government regulation of doctor–patient relations. The argument in this text is that battles between the haves and have-nots endure, that they are fundamental to our society, and that many issues become entangled in this basic conflict.

The second proposition is that the political process, which attempts to resolve conflicts, affects the relative success of the haves and the have-nots. It determines whose interests become part of the public agenda and whose do not. This process varies across states and localities. These variations affect how much lower-income and upper-income concerns become part of political debates and to what extent these concerns dominate decision making. The process affects the policy choices that are made. This text is concerned with the reasons the process varies and the consequences these variations have for the haves and have-nots.

The Argument of V. O. Key

This text relies heavily on the arguments of V. O. Key. He was a prominent political scientist whose major works were published from the 1940s through the 1960s. Key offered a particular perspective on state and local politics in his book *Southern Politics* (1949). His concern was with the way process affects outcomes. That work had a major influence on much of the research that has been done in state politics.[3] The concern with the ways political institutions and process affect who wins and loses in politics has also dominated much of the interpretation of urban politics.[4]

Views such as Key's, of course, are not the only ones that might be drawn upon for a text. Diverse perspectives and concerns shape political research,[5] and textbooks have been written around very diverse perspectives.[6] But V. O. Key provided perhaps the most engaging and enduring set of questions about democracy and the political process. In *Southern Politics*, Key presented a detailed argument about politics and the importance of *how* the political process works. He presented some fundamental propositions about politics and about what we should focus on if we are to understand how the process affects what happens—who wins and who loses.

While some people presume that politics should work to find the public interest or that particular set of policies that are good for everyone, Key largely rejected that perspective. He argued that politics is about groups seeking to get their concerns addressed, an activity that puts them in conflict with other groups. He argued that "Politics generally comes down, over the long run, to a conflict between those who have and those who have less. In state politics the crucial issues tend to turn around taxation and expenditure."[7] The important question is not whether government does more or less, but more or less for whom. The broad and enduring issues of politics revolve around the extent to which government will intervene in society to enhance equality of opportunity and to try to alter conditions of inequality.

These broad political battles encompass many specific political questions. For example, how much should the state tax personal income or sales of goods, and to what extent should tax burdens differ by economic class? Should the state rely on local tax bases (which vary dramatically) to fund local (elementary and secondary) schools with the consequence that families in well-to-do communities have access to better public schools? Or should the state tax individuals through state income and sales taxes and distribute state aid to local districts in a way that reduces differences in local education budgets? Should the state impose higher taxes to pay higher welfare and unemployment-compensation benefits? And who should pay such taxes? Should the state subsidize tuition at state universities to increase educational opportunities for children from lower-income families? Or should the state expect students to find their own sources of money to pay for education? Or should state loan and grant programs be established? All these issues involve using the power of the state to take private wealth and use it to enhance the opportunities of those with fewer resources.

There is also the persistent question of what role state and local governments should play. If programs to increase equality or equality of opportunity are to be attempted, should the money come from local property-tax bases, which vary considerably, or should the state raise and distribute funds? Should we rely on local tax bases to deal with inequities in school finance, or will the state provide funding? Should welfare be locally funded and administered, or should the state handle this responsibility? If relying on local governments contributes to inequality, then decentralization becomes an issue, and there may be pressures to have state government play a greater role.

Key then proposed a general argument about the way variations in the democratic process affect decisions about such issues.[8] He argued that different political processes are not just a matter of taste and preference. Political practices shape who wins and who loses in battles over public policy.

The crucial matter for Key was how the process shapes the ways in which issues of inequities emerge in political debates. Societies inevitably contain inequities in the distribution of wealth and opportunities in society. The have-nots generally seek changes in public policy and programs to address inequities. They want issues of inequity to be a part of political debate. The goal of the haves is generally to obstruct change because change is likely to involve taking their wealth and using it to fund programs for the have-nots. The have-nots possess fewer political resources in this battle and are likely to lose unless they find a means to make their issues more prominent and part of public debate. If they can find a way to present their plight as an issue in political campaigns, the have-nots have a chance that politicians will feel obligated to respond.

If the have-nots can organize, they may be able to mobilize constituencies to vote. That may result in the election of politicians responsive to the have-nots. Those politicians can then articulate the concerns of the have-nots and attempt to focus debate on and around problems of inequality. If these politicians are skilled, they can present their argument for programs in a way that makes other politicians feel pressure to respond.

The impact of these arguments is affected by the culture of American society. Our culture emphasizes individual effort and achievement and the right of individuals to keep what they have achieved. This can lead to political debates in which the emphasis is on individual responsibility and on creating conditions favorable to individual entrepreneurs in business. But there is also concern in our society with the individual's opportunity to achieve and with equality of opportunity.[9] Many politicians argue that there is not much equality. Their goal is to focus public attention on such problems and make other politicians, who represent the haves, feel uneasy about appearing unconcerned about creating some minimal equality of opportunity in society.

For the have-nots to get a response from politicians, they must create pressure on politicians to worry about equality of opportunity. The crucial issue in politics is the extent to which the have-nots are politically organized to do battle with the haves about these issues. Key argued that the *primary* means for have-nots to mobilize people to work for their concerns is through political parties. Parties mobilize large groups of individuals around basic concerns such as inequality. They organize people behind common goals. They elect politicians sympathetic to them, who call attention to their problems. The have-nots lack money. They can, however, organize their numbers to get the attention of politicians and to have an impact.

For the have-nots to get their arguments on the agenda they need a political party which represents their interests. For most of American history, in most states this has been the Democratic party. This party has traditionally drawn its support, its electoral base, from the have-nots and those sympathetic to their concerns. That base differs from that of the Republican party. For the have-nots to get their concerns on the agenda, their party must be cohesive so it will present coherent policies and be able to enact those policies. A political process that does not have a strong, competitive party representing the have-nots is likely to be one in which their concerns are not a part of the ongoing public debate over public policy. Without such organization, politicians concerned more with the haves will feel less pressure to respond to the concerns of the have-nots. They will feel less obligation to raise taxes and establish programs that will benefit the have-nots. The status quo is more likely to persist, and the haves to do better.

The essence of Key's argument is that the democratic process is not a neutral mechanism that just conveys public opinions. Differences in the political process do not just produce more or less policy. They produce differences in policy winners and losers. A political process can work to produce relatively equal expression of the concerns of the haves and the have-nots. But it can also work to neglect the concerns of some groups.

A summary of Key's argument is presented in the accompanying box. The argument is complicated, and we are only concerned about the broad argument and its implications now. We will return to different aspects of it throughout the text.

Restating Key

The argument of V. O. Key has broad implications. It is important to make sure the nuances of his argument are clear. It is also important not to suggest that Key was trying to explain everything about politics. To do that would be too heavy of a burden for any argument.

Key did not argue that all conflicts in society revolve around class. Indeed, a crucial aspect of his argument is that there are situations in which other issues divide the electorate and class issues become submerged. These are the interesting situations in which the "organization" of the electorate into the haves and the have-nots does not occur and response to have-not concerns is reduced. In the South, for example, for many years lower-income whites were more concerned

V. O. Key on the Role of Parties

Key's argument is an important statement about what affects winners and losers in state politics. What follows is a summary of his argument from *Southern Politics,* using his statements.

The question: Who wins when no parties exist to furnish popular leadership? (p. 299)

Presumptions about fundamental conflicts: Politics generally comes down, over the long run, to a conflict between those who have and those who have less. In state politics the crucial issues tend to turn around taxation and expenditure. (p. 307)

Presumptions about conditions which affect this battle: The significant question is who benefits from political disorganization? . . . It follows that the grand objective of the haves is obstruction . . . Organization is not always necessary to obstruct; it is essential, however, for the promotion of a sustained program in behalf of the have-nots. . . . It follows . . . that over the long run the have-nots lose in a disorganized politics. (p. 307)

Argument I: Those states with loose factional systems usually also have factional groupings of the most transient nature. Cleavages among voters form and reform from campaign to campaign depending on the issues and candidates involved. This . . . contrasts markedly with the stability of electoral loyalty and the continuity of leadership of true political parties. (p. 301)

Argument II: Discontinuity of faction both confuses the electorate and reflects a failure to organize voters into groups of more or less like-minded citizens with somewhat similar attitudes toward public policy. (p. 303)

Argument III: The lack of continuing groups of "ins" and "outs" profoundly influences the nature of political leadership. Free and easy movement from loose faction to loose faction results in there being in reality no group of "outs" with any sort of corporate spirit to serve as critic of the "ins" or as a rallying point around which can be organized all those discontented with the current conduct of public affairs. . . . When two distinct groups with some identity and continuity exist, they must raise issues and appeal to the masses if for no other reason than the desire for office. . . . In states with loose and short-lived factions campaigns often are the emptiest sorts of debates over personalities. . . . (p. 304)

Argument IV: They [the have-nots] have no mechanisms to act and their wishes find fitful rebellions led by transient demagogues who gain their confidence but often have neither the technical competence nor the necessary stable base of political power to effectuate a program. (p. 307):

Argument V: A loose factional system lacks the power to carry out sustained programs of action . . . This negative weakness thus rebounds to the benefit of the upper brackets. (p. 308) with restraining the influence of blacks than they were with opposing wealthy whites. Lower-income whites tended to form an alliance with upper-income interests, a situation which stifled discussions of class interests. In the current political world there are often divisions which revolve around region, race, religion, or ethnicity. Debates are then not about equality of opportunity, but about upstate versus downstate interests, about minority versus Caucasian issues, about fundamentalist versus nonfundamentalist beliefs, about Italian versus Irish cultural conflicts.

All conflicts, then, are not about haves versus have-nots. But situations where the electorate divides itself differently are *not* just exceptions to Key's argument: They are of fundamental interest. Key's argument is that class conflict persists, but for many reasons class divisions and debates do not always dominate the political agenda. The contrast between the situations where class conflict does and does not persist and the consequences that flow from such different divisions were of interest to Key. These situations are of central concern to this text.

Key's argument may be too imprecise for many. There is the problem of where we draw the line to distinguish the haves from the have-nots. Many people do not regard themselves as belonging to the lower class, even though their income level would appear to put them among the lower class. Key never provided a precise dividing line. His lack of a dividing line may seem to render his perspective too sloppy to be of value. But his argument does not require a precise line. The crucial matter to Key was not whether people had incomes above or below a specific line, but whether they divided themselves politically along class lines because they felt such a division was relevant to their lives. Sometimes that division occurred and sometimes it did not. The effects of the presence or the absence of that division becomes the interesting political matter.

Finally, we should not presume that class divisions explain everything. Not everything that states and localities do is driven by class divisions. The amount of wealth available for public programs plays a role. States and localities with more money spend more money. Those with less money spend less. It has long been established that greater levels of wealth make higher public policy spending levels possible.[10] Key's argument does not dispute that. His argument is most relevant as an explanation of why states with the *same* wealth do not necessarily do the *same* for the have-nots.

Political culture also affects policy choices. Culture refers to the set of beliefs and views about society that a group of people have. These views and beliefs shape how people see their world and how they react to events. Some views stress the obligation of people to contribute to the overall condition of society and the belief that government can be a positive contributor. Other views stress that individuals should be responsible for themselves and that government has no obligation to assist. Some states are dominated more by a community focus than by individualistic views of the world.[11] States in which the individualistic culture dominates do less for the have-nots across a broad array of programs than other states do.[12]

But even with all these qualifications about the role of class, the argument of this text is that class issues do persist in American politics.[13] Class issues may come and go as the dominant focus, but the enduring, recurring battles involve class issues. Debates about equality-of-income distribution, about equality of opportunity, about how much to help the poor or how much to reward hard work, all involve—either explicitly or implicitly—issues of class. We may not discuss them as "class conflict" in American politics, but class is always relevant to those debates. Within states and localities, we continually grapple with issues of whether to respond to metropolitan school and housing segregation and whether to do more to equalize school finance. These debates often involve issues of race, but race and class have been intertwined for a long time in American politics, so class issues still emerge. Again, class is not everything in American state and local politics, but it persists and is fundamental to much of the conflict we must grapple with.

The Significance of Process: Examples

Key argued that the way the political process works affects whose interests dominate. The example that follows presents an illustration of Key's ultimate concern: which topics become part of political debate within the political process. In this example, a crucial political topic became part of political debate in one state while it was excluded in another. The case is interesting because it involves two very similar states with quite different processes, and has produced two different outcomes.

New Hampshire and Vermont

Richard Winters, who teaches at Dartmouth College in New Hampshire, has long observed politics in the two states. He found that many characteristics of both New Hampshire and Vermont, such as the attitudes and the average wealth of the population, were very similar. Winters also found, however, several significant differences between the states in the way political issues were handled. In particular, he found a significant difference in the way issues of taxation could be discussed.[14] Winters argued that this difference derived from the nature of the news media and from the way the media affected candidates for governor. Ultimately this difference affected the taxes adopted in each state.

News Media

In Vermont there is no single statewide newspaper, and the newspapers that exist are not dominated by any particular philosophy. In New Hampshire, things are considerably different. In that state, the *Manchester Union Leader* is the only newspaper with statewide circulation, and this paper has been dominated for some time by the philosophy of William Loeb. From 1946 to 1981, when he died, Loeb was the owner and publisher of this paper, and he used his newspaper to push his personal conservative philosophy that government should not grow in size. He pursued this by attacking any candidate who advocated or supported tax or spending increases. He also made sure that any politician endorsing such policies was prominently and negatively covered in the newspaper. Politicians in New Hampshire were "crucified" for endorsing taxing and spending. By using the newspaper to pursue his own political preferences, Loeb made it very difficult for candidates to support state taxes such as the income tax. After he died in 1981, his wife took over and maintained the same practices.

In Vermont, politicians found it easier to support state taxes. They did not have to be relentlessly negative toward taxes, and they were not subject to harsh criticism from the press for supporting taxes. Winters concluded that the attacks Loeb unleashed in New Hampshire made it difficult for a politician to endorse spending programs that required taxes, while in Vermont politicians found it somewhat easier to do so.

Candidate Strategies

These conditions affected the approaches of statewide candidates for positions such as governor. In Vermont there has been considerable competition for this position, and the competition for electoral votes often took the form of offering new programs, which led to greater expenditure. Governors were also more inclined to bring in top-level administrators from outside the state, who were more inclined to advocate new programs. In New Hampshire, candidates for the governorship had to avoid antagonizing Loeb. The power of Loeb was widely acknowledged, and it was common practice for gubernatorial candidates to have to come to editorial board meetings and take "the oath," which was a commitment not to propose or support an income tax while in office. Without the revenue from taxes, no gubernatorial candidate could propose programs requiring significant expenditures.

Tax Systems

These differences in the ability to discuss taxes are reflected in the tax systems of the two states. Vermont has a progressive state income tax, while New Hampshire relies on a combination of property, sales, and miscellaneous taxes and charges. The difference between these two tax systems is significant. A progressive income tax system tends to be "elastic," which means that as the population's income increases, state tax revenues increase by an equivalent or greater proportion. As individual incomes increase, individuals move into higher tax brackets, a greater proportion of their income is taken as taxes, and the state receives more revenue. New Hampshire, on the other hand, relies on taxes that do not produce significant increases in tax revenue as income increases.

Because of its tax system, Vermont has received a continual flow of more revenue, while New Hampshire has not. As a result, Vermont has been able to establish new programs more easily, without explicitly raising taxes.

The cumulative impacts of these conditions in each state are important. New Hampshire's political process has made it difficult for politicians to advocate taxes and programs while in Vermont the political process makes it easier for taxation and expenditure issues to be discussed. Politicians in Vermont have found it easier to propose both programs that require expenditure and the taxes necessary for those programs.

The consequences are significant. Figure 1.1 presents the tax effort in the two states from 1950 to 1990. Tax effort is defined as the total amount of state taxes divided by the total personal income of residents of the state. The graph indicates the general inclination of politicians to tax individuals. Over time Vermont

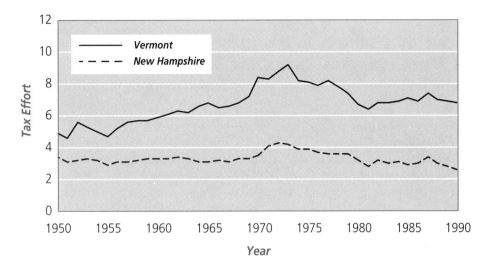

Figure 1.1

Comparison of Tax Effort in New Hampshire and Vermont, 1950–1990

has consistently taken a larger proportion of people's income than New Hampshire has. Vermont has also increased its net tax effort over time (with some erratic movements) while tax effort in New Hampshire has dropped since the early 1950s. This greater effort by Vermont developed even though the two states had nearly identical wealth bases across this time period. The average income in Vermont was $13,175 in 1987; in New Hampshire, it was $15,457. Vermont taxed more of its wealth base for government spending than New Hampshire. In 1987, Vermont, with a somewhat lower wealth base, spent $2,747 per person on government programs. In the same year, New Hampshire spent only $2,238 per person on such programs.

The differences in tax effort also translate into differences in the willingness to spend money on welfare. New Hampshire, with its lower tax effort, spent an average of $20 per person on welfare. Vermont, with a higher tax effort, spent $34 per person on welfare. The inability to generate more tax revenue in New Hampshire meant the have-nots did not do as well in that state. Conservative views shaped the terms of political debate, stifled discussions of taxes, and restrained benefits.

Patterns across the States

Vermont and New Hampshire have different political processes, and they tax and support welfare differently. They suggest a pattern, but they represent only two states. Is there evidence that this pattern exists across more states?

Table 1.1

Comparison of State and Local Tax Effort to Welfare Expenditure Per Capita, 1991

State	Tax Effort	Per Capita Welfare Expenditure ($)	State	Tax Effort	Per Capita Welfare Expenditure ($)
Alaska	18.7	53.33	Massachusetts	10.4	50.20
New York	14.9	32.89	Ohio	10.4	29.46
Wyoming	13.4	22.45	Idaho	10.4	15.33
Hawaii	12.8	27.98	South Carolina	10.3	17.69
Minnesota	12.4	26.50	Delaware	10.3	21.43
Wisconsin	11.9	37.45	Colorado	10.3	17.45
Montana	11.9	27.94	North Carolina	10.3	15.66
New Mexico	11.9	21.07	North Dakota	10.3	31.70
Arizona	11.8	17.28	Kansas	10.3	20.80
Vermont	11.5	34.49	Oklahoma	10.2	25.70
Maine	11.5	41.70	New Jersey	10.1	24.17
West Virginia	11.4	26.58	Kentucky	10.0	26.43
Michigan	11.3	43.36	Pennsylvania	10.0	31.45
Oregon	11.3	20.52	Mississippi	10.0	20.65
Washington	11.3	31.25	Nevada	9.9	13.70
Utah	11.2	22.98	Texas	9.9	15.35
Iowa	10.9	26.61	Indiana	9.7	18.98
Louisiana	10.9	22.71	Virginia	9.6	13.30
California	10.8	19.29	Florida	9.5	15.84
Rhode Island	10.8	47.46	South Dakota	9.1	20.17
Connecticut	10.7	32.54	Alabama	9.0	15.31
Georgia	10.7	20.62	Arkansas	9.0	22.53
Nebraska	10.6	24.72	Tennessee	8.9	23.85
Illinois	10.5	31.02	Missouri	8.1	20.93
Maryland	10.4	30.54	New Hampshire	8.1	20.25

Source: Advisory Commission on Intergovernmental Relations, Significant Features of Fiscal Federalism, 1992 *(Washington, DC, 1992)* xix; and Government Finances, 1990–1991.

Table 1.1 presents information on tax effort and welfare expenditures per capita for all states for 1991. First, tax effort varies considerably across the states. There is something happening across the states that produces varying inclinations to tax the public. Second, per capita (average) welfare expenditure also differs across the states. Support for welfare spending differs across the states. Third, these two indicators of state activity—tax effort and welfare expenditure—are positively associated. States that are inclined to tax wealth more are also inclined to spend more on welfare. There are exceptions, but the association is positive.

At this point, we do not know why these patterns exist. Key has provided one possible explanation of why some states tax their populations more and provide more welfare support. We will assess the evidence for his argument as we proceed.[15]

The Broader Debate about Process

The example of New Hampshire and Vermont represents a relatively limited difference in political processes: A major media outlet in one state approached coverage in ways that affected candidate discussions of income taxes. This text will review a broad array of differences in political processes. States and localities differ considerably in their rules and institutional arrangements. While Key's argument focused primarily on political parties, his argument has much broader implications: Varying the rules and changing institutions and political practices can affect who wins and who loses in politics. The possibility of such change has been an enduring concern in American politics.

The connection between process and outcomes has preoccupied many groups. Reform efforts have regularly been sought to change rules of procedure because it is presumed the result of such efforts will be better processes or outcomes. Some groups have sought a process that would focus more on the public interest. Others have sought reforms to alter the relative success of certain groups (ethnics, blacks) in the process. The goals may vary, but the concern with varying political practices to affect results has been persistent in American politics.

In urban politics, for example, there has been a debate since at least the early 1900s about how to change institutions in order to shape the ways issues are dealt with. Many reformers have argued, for example, that party politics are detrimental to the political process. They have tried to diminish the role of partisan identification of candidates in elections or sought to replace partisan arrangements with nonpartisan elections. On a more general level, reformers have sought to make it easier for voters to operate in elections without being attached to parties. In administrative matters, reformers have sought to reduce the extent to which patronage (which is seen as heavily tied to partisan politics) is relied on as a means to appoint government officials. They have sought to replace patronage with merit appointment of government workers. Though the initial concern in these efforts may not have been on altering the influence of different classes, these reforms ultimately affect the relative success of the haves and have-nots.[16]

There has also been concern at the state level with how to change political arrangements. Reformers have sought to reduce the role of party insiders in selecting party candidates and have lobbied for the use of direct primaries. They have fought to introduce the referendum, which allows citizens to vote on policy decisions. They have also tried to make political institutions more effective. Some reformers have argued to give governors more power to run state government and to make legislatures and legislators more professional.[17] Other reformers argue that we have too many professional politicians and that there should be limits on the number of terms legislators can serve.[18]

All these efforts at reform share a common theme. They are based on the presumption that the way in which we structure the process affects which decisions result. Most of these reforms were based on the presumption that they will produce a better "quality" process, and better decisions.

There is considerable evidence, however, that the primary effect of reforms is upon who does well in the process. Changes in political rules—who can vote, how elections take place—and in political practices—how much the electorate is attached to political parties, how much power governors and legislatures have—are relevant to the extent that they affect the winners and losers in the process. Again, the goal of those introducing reforms may not have been to change winners and losers. But reforms often have such an impact, and these effects will be discussed throughout. The effect such reforms have on the haves and have-nots will receive particular attention.

The Plan of the Book

The activities that comprise the political process are considerable and complicated. In Chapter 2, we will begin with federalism. This basic political arrangement of our society establishes the context within which state and local politics play out. Federalism defines how much power the national government has and how much autonomy states and localities have in American politics.

We then move to the study of state and local politics. To understand what political battles here are about, we first need to know the major sources of conflict in states and localities. Chapter 3 focuses on the opinions, beliefs, and experiences of individuals and how these lead to conflict. How opinions shift over time is also discussed.

Chapter 4 focuses on more specific conflicts that flow from population differences. The debate over whether government should do more in society leads to disputes about what means government should use to raise money, what level of government should raise money, and what level of government should take responsibility for any programs established. Should general taxes like the state income tax be used to support government programs or should local property taxes be used for this funding? Understanding these debates is fundamental because different income classes pay different tax rates under each tax. States and localities must also decide whether a program will be administered by the state, or through the multitude of local governments. Administration by the latter creates the possibility of variation in implementation if local governments vary in their commitment to a program. Many oppose administration by locality, and many support it.

We will then focus on representation, or on all those activities that put the concerns of the public on the public agenda. Our primary concern is what affects whose concerns get on the agenda and whose concerns do not get on the agenda.

Chapter 5 focuses on political parties, which play a fundamental role in organizing and representing the conflicts that exist in society. The role of parties has changed greatly over the years, but they still provide one of the main ways of bringing group concerns together to push for broad policies.

In Chapter 6, we discuss the effect of mass participation on the political process. Individuals engage in voting, writing letters, signing petitions, and contributing to campaigns. These activities either provide politicians with support or do not provide sufficient electoral bases for parties to win. The sources of voting activity, differences among groups, and the impact of these differences on whose issues get represented will be reviewed. Particular attention will be given to the role of the media in presenting issues and political information to the public.

This will be followed in Chapter 7 by an analysis of the role and impact of interest groups. Interest groups serve as an alternative means of representation for individuals and groups. Lobbyists and their group bases are of fundamental importance in politics.

Representation is important because it affects whether concerns of the public and conditions within states and localities are brought to the attention of decision makers. The activities of parties, mass participation, media attention, and interest groups affect which concerns become issues and which concerns politicians pay attention to. The cumulative nature of these influences will be assessed in Chapter 8.

Once issues become part of political discussion, politicians must make some decisions. It is at this stage that we become concerned about the major institutions of decision making, the executives, the legislatures, and the courts. Section II of the text will focus on decision making. We will be concerned here with the motives of decision makers and their formal and informal authority to achieve their goals. Chapter 9 will discuss executives, how their political agendas are formed and how institutional powers affect their ability to achieve their agendas.

Chapter 10 will discuss legislatures. The focus will be similar to that of Chapter 9. We will discuss what shapes the agendas that emerge in legislatures, and how institutional power affects the ability to achieve those agendas.

In Chapter 11, we will review the role of the courts and the potential the courts have to be involved in decision making. We will discuss the extent to which the courts do get involved and what shapes their inclinations to do so.

In Chapter 12, we will focus on how these institutions interact to determine the policies adopted. The focus will be on the way combinations of political conditions affect decisions.

Finally, there is the question of how government goes about trying to achieve the goals desired and whether public policies have the impact we expect. In Chapter 13, we will examine the ways government seeks to have an effect. There is considerable debate about whether policies have the impact expected, and we will review the evidence on their impact.

For Further Reading

There are perpetual debates about what perspective to take in studying state and local politics. The following works provide some examples of different approaches, or discuss the kinds of approaches taken at different times.

State Politics

Key, V. O. *Southern Politics*, Chaps. 1–14 New York: Knopf, 1949. An emphasis on conflict and how varying political processes affect who is responded to.

Davidson, Chandler. *Race and Class in Texas Politics.* Princeton: Princeton University Press, 1990. An analysis of Texas politics in the V.O. Key tradition.

Wright, Gerald C., Robert S. Erickson, and John P. McIver. "Public Opinion and Policy Liberalism in the American States" *American Political Science Review* 31 (1987): 980–1001. A focus on explaining variations in expenditures at one time across states using differences in public opinion across states; conflict within states is not addressed.

Osborne, David, and Ted Gaebler *Reinventing Government.* Reading, Mass: Addison–Wesley, 1992. An argument that in order to improve efficiency and effectiveness we should focus not on what should be done (what policies should be formulated) but on how services are delivered.

Local Politics

Fuchs, Ester. *Mayors and Money.* Chicago: University of Chicago Press, 1992. An emphasis on the ability of political systems to restrain overall public demands.

Judd, Dennis R., and Todd Swanstrom. *City Politics.* New York: HarperCollins, 1994. Harrigan, John J. *Political Change in the Metropolis.* 5th Ed., New York: HarperCollins, 1993. An emphasis on how different types of local political processes and the creation of multiple local governments affect winners and losers in politics.

Savas, E. S. *Privatization: The Key to Better Government.* Chatham, N.J.: Chatham House, 1987; and Morgan, David R. *Managing Urban America.* 3d Ed. Pacific Grove, Calif.: Brooks/Cole, 1989. Focus on efficiency and reducing costs of government.

Suggestions for Analysis in Your Own State and Locality

1. What have been the major conflicts in your state in the last several years? What conflicts exist in your local area?

2. What issues exist in your state and locality that involve conflicts between haves and have-nots? Have there been conflicts about welfare reform, public housing, equality of local school finance, or access to higher education?

3. What tax levels prevail in your state and local area? How do those tax levels compare with national averages? Have there been disputes about levels of taxation or about who bears the burden of state and local taxes?

Notes

1. V. O. Key, *Southern Politics* (New York: Knopf, 1949), 307.

2. E. E. Schattschneider, *The Semisovereign People* (New York: Holt, Rinehart, and Winston, 1960).

3. For a review of that impact and the research it generated, see Jeffrey M. Stonecash, "Inter-Party Competition, Political Dialogue, and Public Policy: A Critical Review," *Policy Studies Journal* 16, no. 2 (winter 1987–88): 243–62.

4. See such textbooks as John J. Harrigan, *Political Change in the Metropolis*, 5th ed. (New York: HarperCollins, 1992); and Dennis R. Judd and Todd Swanstrom, *City Politics* (New York: HarperCollins, 1994).

5. For examples of the diverse questions political scientists address, see Thomas R. Dye, "The Independent Effect of Party Competition on Public Policy," in *State Politics*, ed. Robert Crew (Belmont: Wadsworth Publishing, 1968); Samuel C. Patterson and Gregory Calderia, "The Etiology of Partisan Competition," *American Political Science Review* 78, no. 3 (1984): 691–707; and, Gerald C. Wright, Robert S. Erickson, and John P. McIver, "Public Opinion and Policy Liberalism in the American States," *American Journal of Political Science* 31 (1987): 980–1001. Reviews about what might be studied and what has been studied are contained in such papers as Malcolm Jewell, "The Neglected World of State Politics," *Journal of Politics* 44 (1981): 638–57; Malcolm Jewell, "The State of State Legislative Research," *Legislative Studies Quarterly* 6 (1981): 1–26; and Carol S. Weissert, "The Neglected World of State Politics Revisited," presented at the 1991 Annual Meeting of the American Political Science Association, Washington, DC.

6. Some textbooks focus primarily on comparing states. For good examples of such texts, see Thomas R. Dye, *Politics in States and Communities*, 7th ed. (Englewood Cliffs: Prentice–Hall, 1991); Virginia Gray, Herbert Jacob, and Kenneth Vines, *Politics in the American States*, 5th ed. (Boston: Little, Brown, 1989); and Norman R. Luttbeg, *Comparing States and Communities* (New York: HarperCollins, 1992). Other writers have chosen to focus on change in American society and policy: Richard D. Bingham and David Hedge, *State and Local Government in a Changing Society*, 2d ed. (New York: McGraw–Hill, 1991); Others focus on the consequences of population mobility among state and local governments: Virginia Gray and Peter Eisinger, *American States and Cities* (New York: HarperCollins, 1991). Others focus on how entangled state and local politics are in intergovernmental relations: Richard Lorch, *State and Local Politics: The Great Entanglement*, 4th ed. (Englewood Cliffs: Prentice–Hall, 1992); finally, others have focused on the changes in state and local government institutions and their capabilities over time: Ann O'M Bowman and Richard C. Kearney, *The Resurgence of the States* (Englewood Cliffs: Prentice–Hall, 1986).

7. V. O. Key, *Southern Politics*, 307.

8. Key, *Southern Politics*, chap. 14.

9. For an example of this concern, see Jonathon Kozol, *Savage Inequalities* (New York: Crown, 1991).

10. Thomas R. Dye, *Politics, Economics, and the Public. Policy Outcomes in the American States*. (Chicago: Rand McNally, 1969).

11. Daniel Elazar, *American Federalism: A View from the States*, 2nd ed. (New York: Thomas Crowell, 1972).

12. Gerald C. Wright, Robert S. Erikson, and John P. McIver, "Public Opinion and Policy Liberalism in the American States," *American Journal of Political Science* 31 (1987): 980–1001.

13. John J. Harrigan, *Empty Dreams, Empty Pockets: Class and Bias in American Politics* (New York: Macmillan, 1993).

14. Richard Winters, "Political Choice and Expenditure Change in New Hampshire and Vermont," *Polity* 12, no. 4 (summer 1980): 598–621.

15. The academic literature that seeks to assess the impact of political conditions is extensive. It is also a literature plagued by numerous disputes about how well or appropriately the research was done. Some studies are criticized because scholars argue that the data used was not appropriate. Other studies are criticized because scholars argue that the way the question was asked is not appropriate. An example of the problems with academic studies in the area of inter-party competition is presented in, Jeffrey M. Stonecash, "Inter-Party Competition, Political Dialogue, and Public Policy: A Critical Review," *Policy Studies Journal* 16, no. 2 (winter 1987–88):

243–62. This is just one example of a disputed area of research. Others will be discussed throughout the text.

16. Richard Hofstader, *The Age of Reform* (New York: Knopf, 1956); Edward Banfield and James Q. Wilson, *City Politics* (Cambridge: Harvard University Press, 1961); and Dennis R. Judd, *The Politics of American Cities* (Glenview: Scott, Foresman/Little, Brown, 1988).

17. Advisory Commission on Intergovernmental Relations, *The Question of State Government Capability* (Washington, DC: U.S. Government Printing Office, 1985), 127–141.

18. Alan Ehrenhalt, *The United States of Ambition* (New York: Times Books, 1991).

2

Federalism and the States: The Issue of Autonomy

PREVIEW

Studying states and their political choices is relevant only if the states have some autonomy to make their own decisions. This chapter analyzes federalism, the political arrangement that affects their independence.

The chapter focuses on three broad concerns. The first concern is the formation of federalism. Federalism was created as a product of two conflicting concerns: fear of strong, centralized government, and anxiety about having an ineffective government.

The second concern discusses how these fears shaped the nature of federalism and the extent to which this affects the states. The compromise reached created a system that tends to restrain national government, but allows national action when there is a consensus. The primary result is considerable state autonomy in policy making.

Finally, the chapter will discuss the changes that have brought about a more activist government. While the system favors restrained government, national intervention has grown in recent years as consensus has emerged that minimal policy uniformity should prevail in certain policy areas. Despite the changes, states retain considerable discretion in the policy choices they can make. The states continue to play a major role in American politics and in policy choices.

Introduction

Our newspapers are filled with stories that suggest that state and local policy is dominated by frequent and widespread federal-government intervention. The *New York Times* reported in 1992 that even under Republican presidential administrations—supposedly opposed to imposing mandates on states and local governments—the "U.S. Adds Programs with Little Review of Local Burdens."[1] This article listed many policies that the national government requires state and local governments to adopt. The national government is involved in the determination of allowable pollution levels, the proper construction of street-corner curbs suitable for wheelchair users, speed-limit levels, and legal drinking ages. The national government provides billions of dollars of aid to state governments. This revenue distribution creates dependency on federal funds and gives national officials leverage to require programs and standards.

It would appear that state and local governments have become subordinate political bodies that no longer have much influence in the American political system. It also would appear that the states have little autonomy in making policy choices. If what the state and local governments do is largely dictated by the national government, there may not be much variation in the policies they pursue. If there is little variation in policy, there may not be much reason to study state and local governments—and little of interest to study.

This impression of the influence of the national government is inaccurate, however. Both state and local governments retain substantial autonomy in their political processes and policy choices. This autonomy is a product of federalism. To understand the position of the states, it is necessary to understand federalism. Federalism is a complex political arrangement that creates and maintains the state autonomy that does exist. A more developed definition will follow later in this chapter. We will explore the political conditions that led to the existence of federalism, its current nature, and the resulting position of the states in the system. The argument will be that states retain considerable autonomy.

Yet, while the states continue to have considerable autonomy, it is also true that there are more federal interventions in state and local government now than fifty or one hundred years ago. There is greater national influence on the states now than there used to be, and explaining that change is essential for understanding the position of the states.

We will need to explain both how the nature of federalism continually favors decentralization (and thus the autonomy of the states), and at the same time, why, if the above is true, there has been a gradual, cumulative drift toward a more activist national government. The concern is to understand the enduring autonomy of the states, while also understanding the gradual drift toward a greater role for national government. To do this, we need to understand federalism and the change that is occurring within the system.

The Formation of Federalism

The Political Compromise Creating Federalism

Political arrangements reflect choices made by individuals operating within a particular historical context. Institutions are created in response to problems of particular eras. Those creating institutional rules seek to avoid the problems that are prominent in that era. Federalism is no different. It emerged in an era in which specific concerns dominated political discussions.

We can first approach federalism by providing a rough definition of it. Federalism is an institutional arrangement that creates two separate levels of government. In the United States, this arrangement also places heavy reliance on politicians elected to the national government (Congress) to represent the interests of their states and districts. This representation should lead to the expression of diversity. When diversity among areas of the country is great, opposition to the imposition of national, uniform policies upon states and localities should result. When conflict exists, the national government should be restrained because of these differences. The process by which this happens is complex.

Definitions of federalism, however, rarely capture the *dynamics* of political behavior the system creates. Federalism is perhaps best approached and explained in terms of the conditions that create these behaviors and the restraint that results from these behaviors. We need to start with the historical setting that led to the creation of the institutional arrangements.[2]

The Legacy of the Revolutionary War

The American states were once the colonies of England, and living under English rule had a profound impact on the colonists' concept of a desirable government. These first settlers experienced an English government that did not respect the individual rights and liberties of the colonists. Colonists also believed that the imposition of uniform practices across the colonies ignored the diversity of needs and conditions among the colonies.[3]

As a result, the primary concern of many colonists after the American Revolution was to limit the ability of government to intervene in the affairs of the states. They also wanted to preserve individual liberties. To ensure this, representatives from the states drew up the Articles of Confederation in 1777. This was an agreement among the states to meet regularly to discuss and work on common problems. The crucial trait of the Articles of Confederation was that the ability to form national policy was very limited. Each state got one vote. To adopt a policy, nine of the thirteen colonies had to agree to take action on that policy. To adopt taxes, unanimous agreement was necessary. Even policies that were adopted were only voluntary. There was no means of forcing compliance. Tax obligations could be, and regularly were, avoided, with the consequence that the new nation could not pay its debts from the Revolutionary War. Each state also issued its own currency, a situation that created problems because some states would not accept the currency of other states.

The system soon proved unworkable. There was no national government to perform common activities such as defense. No national government existed to ensure that adopted policies were implemented. Many of the states simply ignored the policies passed at the meetings of the state representatives. There were problems with resolving trade disputes among the states and with establishing a national army to defend the country and to handle internal rebellions.

The experience with England led to a desire to have a decentralized form of government in which central intrusion abilities and powers were limited. This decentralization was accomplished by the Articles of Confederation. But this experience created another preoccupation: how to create a stronger national government to handle common concerns. The two experiences pulled individuals in opposite directions. Some sought a system that would recognize and respect varying state conditions and needs, and be restrained in imposing national laws. Others sought to create a national government with at least the potential to handle "national" problems.

This battle over the kind of government necessary was played out in the Constitutional Convention of 1787. The battle was between the "localists," who wanted a government that was based on states and served "local" concerns, and the "centrists" who wanted a national government that was more effective.[4]

The result was a political compromise that resulted in the unique and creative system of government that we call federalism. This federal system of government was designed to avoid the drawbacks, and retain the benefits of the Articles of Confederation. The system could both disperse and unify political power. The features require some detailed explanation.

On the simplest level, federalism is a division of power between two levels of government in order to disperse and restrain power. The Constitution created two levels of government (the national government and the state governments) and guarantees the continued existence of each. Neither has the power to dissolve the other. The Constitution also assigns each level of government different responsibilities. This is a "structural" or "division-of-labor" perspective on the system. It suggests a system that restrains power by having two distinct and independent levels of government in which state concerns about intrusion should lead state governments to fight off national interventions.

Ideally, each level would have its own tasks and concerns and operate largely independently. It was expected, for example, that the national government would handle defense problems and the states would handle police and fire responsibilities. Having exclusive responsibility for a certain activity would allow each level to operate independently in its "own" area. State concern for managing its responsibilities would lead states to fight any tendency of the national government to take over state activities. The Tenth Amendment was added to the Constitution several years after the convention to insure this independence. The Tenth Amendment states: "The powers not delegated to the United States (the national government) nor prohibited by it to the states, are reserved to the states respectively, or to the people." The clause makes the division of powers sound rather clear, simple, and set.

While divisions of responsibility are important, the essential source of restraint on national government does not stem from a fixed administrative assignment of responsibilities to different levels. The essential source of restraint stems from the behaviors of representatives elected to the national government from states and localities. As James Madison and others conceived the political process, legislators would be concerned with making sure the uniqueness of their area was considered when "national" laws were being formulated. To the extent diversity of state and local needs persisted, these politicians would continually fight against national laws that imposed uniform practices on diverse populations.

The goal of restraining the national government was not to be achieved by any constitutional guarantee of specific autonomy. The belief that national intrusions would be limited was based on the faith that diversity would lead politicians to fight uniform national policies. The premise was that ambitious politicians would seek to defend their constituents, or they might lose reelection. The compromise did not focus on legalistic guarantees, but on creating a representation system in which the ongoing, perpetual, political concern of each politician would be to approach policies in terms of the benefit or harm for that local area. To the extent that a consensus over national policy would be difficult to achieve because of the diversity of needs among the states and localities, the enactment of national policy would be limited.

This emphasis on the representation system was the concession to those who were reluctant to establish a strong national government because of their experience under British rule. Madison and others consistently presented the argument that such a representation system would make it unlikely that an activist national government would emerge to dominate the states.

Those wanting a stronger national government also won something. The very creation of a national government with a President, Congress, and Supreme Court was a major victory. These institutions were permanent and had the constitutional authority to take action if there was political inclination to do so. There had not been such a continuing national government before, so national action had not even been possible. It now was.

The pro-national government groups were also able to insert various vague phrases in the Constitution which created the potential for a more activist government in the future. The Necessary and Proper Clause (Article I, Section 8) states: "The Congress shall have Power to lay and collect Taxes, Duties, Imposts and Excises, to pay the Debts, and provide for the Common Defence and General Welfare of the United States." In that same section, the Constitution states that Congress has the power "To make all laws which shall be necessary and proper for carrying into execution the foregoing Powers. . ." Finally, in Article VI the Constitution states: "This Constitution, and the Laws of the United States which shall be made in Pursuance thereof; and all Treaties made, or which shall be made, under the Authority of the United States, shall be the supreme Law of the Land; and the Judges in every state shall be bound thereby, any Thing in the Constitution or Laws of any State to the Contrary notwithstanding." These clauses provided the basis for the legitimacy of an activist national government. They did not require national activity, but made such activity legitimate.

Finally, the very existence of a national government with the authority to make decisions created an arena in which "national" issues could be considered and *perhaps* acted on. That possibility had not existed before. The new constitution created the *potential* for national action *if* it was desired. If common concerns and perspectives developed, something could be done by a national government.

The Constitution and federalism were products of compromise.[5] Each side got some—but not all—of what it wanted. The compromise resulted in a system with political protections for the states. It also resulted in a system with the potential for a more active national government.

The Enduring Traits of Federalism

The basic political dynamics of federalism have persisted: Diversity is strongly reflected, and "national" policy emerges only when some minimal consensus can be formed. Much of the separation of responsibilities for activities has gradually given way to a high degree of interdependence among levels of government. This increasing interdependence will be discussed later. The important matter about federalism, however, is the persistence of a representation system that continues to give the states considerable importance. The continuing importance of this representation system and its consequence for the position of the states will be discussed next.

Federalism and the States

The Main Actors of Federalism: Politicians

The important national decision makers for the states are their Senators and Representatives. The President may dominate national attention, but his proposals must be passed by Congress. Congress is made up of politicians from states and localities. It is a body concerned about state and local needs.[6] This does not always mean politicians are concerned about state and local governments. Politicians worry about constituents because constituents elect them. Sometimes state and local officials become just another set of constituents. Together, the members of Congress have fundamental influence upon the nature of national legislation that may affect the states. The concerns of members of Congress dominate the kinds of legislation passed.

The role of American political parties on the behavior of politicians is also significant because parties shape the inclinations of politicians. It is often assumed that American political parties are "national" bodies, because the actions of their members are directed by the national party. The reality is just the opposite. American parties are highly decentralized.[7] "National" parties are just collections of "local parties" which pursue their own agendas and have their own electorates and concerns. As Tip O'Neill, a former Speaker of the House of Representatives, is alleged to have said: "All politics is local."

Presidential elections and fund raising are somewhat more national. But even in presidential elections, candidates must cater to state electorates. The constitution created the electoral college for controlling the way presidential elections take place. Each state is given a certain number of electoral-college votes. That number is based on the number of Senators and Representatives representing that state. Presidential candidates win or lose all the electoral votes for a state (a "winner-take-all" system). This prompts candidates to focus on state concerns in order to win a state. The national parties create rules for the conduct of presidential primaries in the states and for the selection of delegates to national conventions, but the conduct of presidential races is heavily influenced by local electorates because of the electoral college.

State governments and parties are also the major actors in defining the conditions of congressional elections. States and localities are responsible for nomination processes in the contests for the Senate and the House. They determine the dates and many of the conditions for party nominations.

There may be pressures from outside the district because of the need to raise money. There is evidence that more congressional-campaign money is coming from groups with offices outside the district and from individuals with home addresses outside the district.[8] This money has its dangers, however, and politicians must be very careful whom they take money from and how they vote on issues. Politicians who are portrayed as heavy recipients of outside funds run the risk of being labelled "pawns" of outside influences. This problem restrains outside fund raising somewhat and makes members of Congress careful of their voting records. Members of Congress must still focus on cultivating the support and resources of local organizations or groups.

The fundamental factor shaping the behavior of the members of Congress, though, is the electorate in their state or district. It is this population that controls their fate. Although members of Congress may benefit from the endorsements of outside groups or from the President, it is the local constituency that really matters if reelection is to be assured.

The crucial matter for politicians is that it is unusual in this country for there to be a broad, uniform, across-the-nation vote for or against Republican or Democratic candidates for Congress.[9] Such votes do occur, they but are unusual. In 1974 there was a general tendency to vote against the Republican party because of Watergate. In that year, many Republican candidates lost simply because they ran on the Republican ticket. In those cases, party candidates find their local bases of support overwhelmed by reactions to national events. Most of the time, however, this does not happen. Local conditions, issues, and personal images usually dominate. This allows candidates to devote their attention to local concerns as a means of getting elected and reelected.

This necessity of pleasing the local constituency has significant and consistent effects on members of Congress. Morton Grodzins argues that "national" politicians in Congress are really local politicians representing local interests.[10] Even though Congress makes national policy, which affects all states and localities, the concern of members is primarily to serve the local constituency.

Occasionally, a member of Congress will pursue a national issue. The ability of the United States to export its goods to other countries, for example, is a national issue. It is in the best interest of the United States to maintain a level of exports higher than imports. If we buy more than we sell, we are in debt to other countries. Interest in this issue, however, is likely to come from districts where international trade is important. Politicians who represent other districts will be concerned with it only as an abstract issue. The issue will have low relevance to their constituency and to their reelection chances. The motivation of the politicians, then, is to focus on local problems and not on national concerns unless those concerns touch the local constituency. To the extent that "local" problems are widely shared, they become "national" problems.

Diversity and Conflict among the States

The preoccupation among members of Congress with the needs of local electorates means local (parochial) concerns have considerable influence over "national" policy formation. Legislators represent diverse districts and recognize that other members also do. Because of the diversity of needs among states, legislators realize that on any proposed legislation, the ends they seek for their constituency might differ from those sought for other states. Legislators have developed a set of decision-making practices which they routinely rely on when trying to formulate policy. Legislators are receptive to bargaining and compromising as a means of formulating legislation. To come up with a proposal acceptable to enough legislators to win a majority, legislators must be willing to compromise.

A review of some examples of state diversity on specific policy concerns may help in understanding this situation. Table 2.1 presents the diversity among states for certain important conditions. The conditions included are population change, poverty, unemployment, farm and fuel production, federal land ownership, and political preferences. The following discussion illustrates how differences in these areas cause conflict in Congress.

Population Change

During the last thirty years, there has been a substantial shift in population from the Northeast and North Central states (the Frostbelt) to the states in the South and

Table 2.1
Diversity among the States

State	Population Change (%) 1970–1980	Population Change (%) 1980–1988	Families Below Poverty (%) 1990	Unemployed (%) 1993
Alabama	13.1	5.4	19.2	7.3
Alaska	32.8	30.5	11.4	6.8
Arizona	53.1	—	13.7	5.8
Arkansas	18.9	4.7	19.6	6.1
California	18.5	19.6	13.9	9.4
Colorado	30.8	14.2	13.7	5.7
Connecticut	2.5	4.0	6.0	6.2
Delaware	8.4	11.1	6.9	5.4
District of Columbia	−15.6	−3.4	21.1	7.3
Florida	43.5	26.6	14.4	6.4
Georgia	19.1	16.1	15.8	4.5
Hawaii	25.3	13.8	11.0	4.2
Idaho	32.4	6.2	14.9	6.0
Illinois	2.8	1.6	13.7	8.5
Indiana	5.7	1.2	13.0	4.7
Iowa	3.1	−2.7	10.4	3.4
Kansas	5.1	5.6	10.3	4.6
Kentucky	13.7	1.8	17.3	6.5
Louisiana	15.4	4.8	23.9	6.9
Maine	13.2	7.2	13.1	7.7
Maryland	7.5	9.6	9.9	6.3
Massachusetts	0.8	2.7	10.7	7.2
Michigan	4.3	−0.2	14.3	6.7
Minnesota	7.1	5.7	12.0	4.9
Mississippi	13.7	—	25.7	5.4
Missouri	5.1	4.6	13.4	5.6
Montana	13.3	2.3	16.3	5.6
Nebraska	5.7	2.1	10.3	2.5
Nevada	63.8	31.7	9.8	7.2
New Hampshire	24.8	17.9	6.3	6.0
New Jersey	2.7	4.8	9.2	7.7
New Mexico	28.1	15.6	20.9	7.2
New York	−3.7	2.0	14.3	7.1
North Carolina	15.7	10.3	13.0	4.2
North Dakota	5.7	2.2	13.7	4.1
Ohio	1.3	0.5	11.5	7.3
Oklahoma	18.2	7.2	15.6	5.9

continued

Table 2.1 (continued)
Diversity among the States

State	Population Change (%)		Families Below Poverty (%)	Unemployed (%)
	1970–1980	*1980–1988*	*1990*	*1993*
Oregon	25.9	5.1	9.2	7.5
Pennsylvania	0.5	1.2	11.0	6.9
Rhode Island	−0.3	4.8	7.5	6.9
South Carolina	20.5	11.2	16.2	6.9
South Dakota	3.7	3.2	13.3	3.6
Tennessee	16.9	6.6	16.9	5.6
Texas	27.1	18.4	15.9	6.6
Utah	37.9	15.7	8.2	3.3
Vermont	15.0	9.0	10.9	4.8
Virginia	14.9	12.5	11.1	5.3
Washington	21.1	12.5	8.9	8.2
West Virginia	11.8	−3.8	18.1	9.3
Wisconsin	6.5	3.2	9.3	4.3
Wyoming	41.3	—	11.0	4.9

State	Value Farm Production (in millions of dollars) *1988*	Fuel Production (in millions of dollars) *1980*	Land Federally Owned (%) *1986*	Clinton Vote (%) *1992*	Percent of Population Liberal
Alabama	2,400	1,994	3.5	41.2	16.1
Alaska	30	9,498	87.1	31.6	—
Arizona	1,959	2,476	43.6	37.1	17.8
Arkansas	3,974	787	10.1	53.5	18.2
California	16,598	10,483	46.2	46.7	24.9
Colorado	3,692	2,544	36.4	40.5	22.1
Connecticut	382	66	0.4	42.5	24.5
Delaware	592	2	2.4	43.8	19.3
District of Columbia	—	—	27.8	—	—
Florida	5,811	2,317	12.3	39.3	19.4
Georgia	3,544	771	6.2	43.7	18.0
Hawaii	568	60	6.7	48.6	—
Idaho	2,291	522	63.8	29.1	13.4
Illinois	6,461	2,770	1.4	48.3	20.9
Indiana	4,117	1,106	1.9	37.0	17.8
Iowa	9,074	265	0.4	43.6	20.0
Kansas	6,594	2,740	1.1	33.8	19.3
Kentucky	2,530	4,498	5.5	44.6	18.5

State	Value Farm Production (in millions of dollars) 1988	Fuel Production (in millions of dollars) 1980	Land Federally Owned (%) 1986	Clinton Vote (%) 1992	Percent of Population Liberal
Louisiana	1,885	16,396	4.1	46.4	16.3
Maine	404	37	0.8	38.8	19.0
Maryland	1,226	293	3.1	50.0	24.0
Massachusetts	402	91	1.6	47.8	25.5
Michigan	2,670	2,587	9.7	43.5	20.5
Minnesota	6,107	1,782	6.8	43.6	20.5
Mississippi	2,341	1,150	5.6	41.0	15.3
Missouri	3,826	1,172	4.7	44.2	17.2
Montana	1,386	1,331	30.3	38.1	24.8
Nebraska	7,979	272	1.5	29.5	19.3
Nevada	229	408	85.1	38.1	30.8
New Hampshire	137	25	12.8	39.3	18.7
New Jersey	642	149	3.1	43.0	26.2
New Mexico	1,272	4,789	33.3	46.0	19.4
New York	2,605	557	4.8	49.8	25.9
North Carolina	4,173	380	7.1	42.8	16.4
North Dakota	2,423	801	4.4	32.4	10.5
Ohio	3,629	2,390	1.2	40.4	21.7
Oklahoma	3,410	7,336	2.0	34.1	14.3
Oregon	2,096	152	48.8	42.8	22.9
Pennsylvania	3,284	3,736	2.2	45.4	21.9
Rhode Island	78	6	0.7	47.9	23.9
South Carolina	1,078	195	6.0	40.1	15.7
South Dakota	2,911	250	5.6	37.3	12.4
Tennessee	2,046	674	7.4	47.3	18.9
Texas	10,281	34,710	2.0	37.4	16.7
Utah	687	1,661	63.7	25.9	13.2
Vermont	405	43	5.4	46.1	24.4
Virginia	1,886	1,708	9.6	40.9	17.8
Washington	3,287	207	29.2	44.2	21.1
West Virginia	248	4,860	7.6	48.6	22.2
Wisconsin	5,048	152	5.4	41.4	20.6
Wyoming	730	5,133	50.4	34.2	22.3

Sources: Population change, farm and fuel production, and federal ownership of land: U.S. Bureau of the Census, Statistical Abstract of the United States, 1991, 111th Ed. (Washington, DC, 1991); Unemployment: U.S. Department of Labor, Bureau of Labor Statistics, Employment and Earnings, 40, no. 11 November 1993, 130–34; Poverty: U.S. Bureau of the Census, Current Population Reports, Poverty in the United States: 1990, Series p-60, no. 175 (Washington, DC, 1991); Clinton vote: Newspaper reports, November 1992; Political liberalism: Gerald C. Wright, Robert S. Erickson, and John P. McIver, "Measuring State Partisanship and Ideology with Survey Data," Journal of Politics 47 (1985): 469–89.

Southwest (the Sunbelt). The stagnation of population experienced by Pennsylvania, New York, and Rhode Island from 1970–1979 and from 1980–1988 resulted in no growth in their tax bases. Frostbelt states found themselves without tax revenues sufficient to support current levels of public services and to repair and replace aging capital equipment, such as sewer and water systems. Frostbelt states also began losing businesses to the Sunbelt states. Conditions were quite different for states such as Colorado, New Mexico, and Texas, which experienced significant population increases. In these states, cities grew, businesses moved in, and new supporting public facilities (utilities, sewers, roads) were needed.

These population shifts led to the need for federal aid in all the states, but for different purposes. Representatives of the Frostbelt states seek different programs than those of the Sunbelt states. The former group would like to see legislation passed to allot federal funds for the repair and replacement of existing facilities, along with subsidies to attract business. The latter group seeks the allotment of federal money for the building of new facilities and has no need for business subsidies.

Poverty

Varying levels of poverty within states are also a source of policy disagreement in Congress. States with a higher percent of their population below the poverty level and with lower tax bases—Mississippi, Georgia, Florida, Alabama, Arkansas, and North Carolina—need money to provide welfare payments, training programs, and housing assistance. Yet, because of the number of poor people in these states and because most federal programs require some form of state contribution, giving substantial aid to everyone in need would require raising large amounts of state revenue. These states, therefore, seek programs that give them access to the needed funds without requiring them to serve the large numbers of people eligible or to provide high levels of aid.

Political dispositions in states also matter. Southern states as a whole are more conservative politically (see Table 2.1, the vote for Clinton, who was more liberal than Bush, in 1992) and are not as supportive of higher welfare payment levels as other states. On the other hand, many northern states, with much smaller proportions of their populations below the poverty line and with wealthier tax bases, can afford to pay higher benefit levels to a greater proportion of poor individuals. These states also tend to be more liberal and willing to support higher payments. Consequently, wealthier states such as Connecticut, New Jersey, and New York, which pay high benefit levels, would prefer to have federal aid programs fund a large proportion (for example, 75 percent) of the money given to each recipient who is eligible. These states might also seek to broaden the criteria of who is eligible for federally supported welfare. This would allow the state to be generous with less burden on the state. Southern states might be reluctant to fund welfare at high levels. They want to contain these expenditures, so they seek a 50 percent federal reimbursement with a limit on the maximum which can be reimbursed. This limit should create a reluctance to raise benefits because the cost will not be reimbursed after a certain point. The result is conflict in Congress over the ways federal aid formulas to help states should be structured.

Unemployment

Average levels of unemployment, and the extent to which people are concerned with unemployment problems, also differ among the states. California, Illinois, and Massachusetts, for example, have recently had higher rates of unemployment. Such states desire programs to provide extensive unemployment benefits. Such programs are not likely to be supported as much, however, by representatives from Iowa and Nebraska, where unemployment difficulties are less prevalent.

Farm Production

In states whose economies depend heavily upon agriculture—California, Illinois, Iowa, Minnesota, Nebraska, and Texas—representatives are likely to desire government programs that include the federal purchase of surplus production and federal support for minimum prices for farm products. Because such programs cost money and raise the prices of farm products, they are likely to conflict with the desires of legislators from Rhode Island, Alaska, and other states with much less economic dependence on agriculture.

Fuel Production

The primary fuel production in the U.S. involves oil. The production of oil is largely confined to Alaska, California, Louisiana, Oklahoma, Texas, and Wyoming. These states are very concerned that government programs support oil production. They want legislation that allows companies generous deductions from their corporation income-tax obligations for the costs of drilling for oil. Residents of other states, who see their heating oil and gasoline prices increasing, also want to see oil production increased. They are opposed, however, to subsidies for oil exploration and would like to see some sort of constraint on the price of oil and gas.

Federal Land Ownership

The federal government owns a large proportion of land in western states. The federal government has appropriated land over the years for national forests and parks, defense facilities, and Native-American use. Some of this ownership dates from the early days of the country when most land in the West was owned by the national government. Land is owned by the Forest Service, the Department of Defense, the Department of Energy, the Bureau of Indian Affairs, the Bureau of Land Management, the Fish and Wildlife Service, and the National Park Service.[11] The federal government controls much of the land in Alaska, Arizona, California, Idaho, Nevada, Oregon, Utah, and Wyoming. Although representatives from outside these states see this land as a national resource to be enjoyed by everyone, including their own constituents, legislators in the West receive considerable pressure from their constituents to reduce federal restrictions that limit economic development of the land. The result is conflict in Congress over continued federal ownership and the tight restrictions that go along with that ownership.

Political Preferences

Finally, states differ in the extent to which their populations tend to be liberal or conservative. This is indicated in the voting patterns of state populations regarding Presidential candidates. The 1992 election was complicated by the presence of a third party candidate, but Clinton clearly represented the liberal option. The states differ in the extent to which their populations voted for him. As Table 2.1 indicates, Clinton did better in northern states like New York, Pennsylvania, and Rhode Island. He did not do nearly as well in states with a reputation for being conservative, such as Utah, Wyoming, North Dakota, and Nebraska. A state's response to a candidate for the presidency depends on several things, but the general political dispositions of the voting public, whether liberal or conservative, play a significant role.

Another indication of the dominant political views within the states comes from national surveys of the public. The last column in Table 2.1 presents the proportion of the public in each state that identifies itself as liberal.[12] The consistency of state reactions is shown in that the lower the proportion of liberals in a state, the less well Clinton generally did in the 1992 election.

These liberal and conservative dispositions within the states come into play in legislative issues in Congress. Legislators tend to take policy positions that reflect the general opinion of their constituencies.

Diversity and Policy Compromise among the States

These differences affect the willingness of legislators to take up state issues and the way in which they go about forming "national" policy when they do take up an issue. As a first principle, Congress often does nothing in a state or local policy area when a problem is too controversial. This is likely to occur when differences among the states are great and when any attempt to impose some national standard will alienate significant proportions of local constituents. The distribution of educational aid within a state is one important, but controversial, area in which Congress does not attempt to make any policy decisions. Because the localities represented have very different financial needs and tax bases, any action to create national distribution requirements would anger substantial numbers of constituents. The best political position for a member of Congress is to avoid the issue. Congress also stays away from state labor law, property-assessment practices, and apportionment of legislative districts.

When Congress does decide to intrude on a local concern, there is a fairly predictable pattern to its actions. Because of diversity, compromise results in a policy in which no group gets everything it wants. To obtain national environmental laws, for example, legislators who wanted strong national standards agreed that the initial policy goals would be somewhat vague. Otherwise, opposing states would have fought any environmental policy.[13] This appeased legislators who were not yet in favor of imposing clear national standards.

Compromise can also take the form of broadening eligibility for a policy so that more states and localities can participate. A program will be politically more appealing if written to make more districts eligible to receive benefits. This is a tactic used by the President to accommodate the locally focused interests in Congress.

Rather than pass legislation that the President has aimed at specific problem areas, legislators will often hold out for a revised proposal that will benefit their own districts. Democratic presidents have submitted proposals aimed at helping declining inner cities. President Carter did so early in his administration. He wanted to direct aid toward cities with high unemployment rates and declining tax bases. This originally involved approximately fifty-five cities located largely in the older areas of the Midwest and the Northeast. Many members of Congress indicated, however, that they would not vote for the proposal unless more cities were included. To acquire the necessary support for his proposal, Carter then agreed to change the criteria to ensure that each state had at least one city that qualified for aid. He also increased the amount of funding the program would receive so each qualifying city would be able to receive some minimal amount of funds. Carter did this because he realized that in a federal system, he would not be able to get his legislation passed unless he increased the number of representatives (and states and localities) that would benefit from the program. In this case, federalism resulted in a dilution of the program and a wider and less focused distribution of federal funds. All presidents have to engage in these practices. Such changes in legislation illustrate the bargaining legislators do to benefit their own districts and the impact this negotiation has on the formation of legislation. Such motives on the part of legislators have several other effects that are important.

At times, members of Congress will devise legislation that is simply a collection of individual unrelated projects, the sole intent of which is to benefit individual states or districts. This practice is called "pork-barreling," and legislative acts carrying out such practices are often characterized as "Christmas trees," a name referring to the different "trinkets" tied to the legislation. At other times, legislators will make an investment in the future interests of their state or locality by "logrolling." This is a practice of voting for a policy that does not directly benefit a representative's constituents (but does benefit those of other representatives) in exchange for a similar sacrifice from other legislators in the future. President Reagan participated in a form of this vote trading in 1981, when, in order to gain support for his tax cut, he allegedly promised undecided legislators his support for their program preferences at some future time. Clinton supported special projects for members in 1994 when he sought support for NAFTA, the North American Free Trade Agreement.

This relentless bargaining revolves around state and local concerns. As a result, "national" government policy is not really formulated by some entity separate and distinct from the states and localities. National policy is, and will continue to be, a composite of state and local concerns. Whenever there are differences among states and districts, national policy generally ends up being a compromise among state interests. The structure of federalism, and specifically the representation system, allows the states considerable influence over the formation of policy that affects them.

Congress and Policy Implementation

The impact of federalism on the states does not cease with the passage of legislation in Congress. Because of the local orientation of legislators, there is continual

Attempting to Change Federal–State Relations: A Lesson in the Nature of Federalism

The preoccupation with local interests also affects the reaction of legislators to proposed changes in programs for the states. If a change will adversely affect a large number of states, then the legislation is unlikely to pass. An example is provided by the treatment given to President Reagan's proposed "New Federalism." Reagan felt that federalism could be improved (or "restored," in his words) if some shared functions were made either exclusively federal or state. He believed that this change would increase separation between the levels and give the states more autonomy in the programs they conducted. Reagan proposed to swap a large number of functions to achieve this. The federal government would take over responsibility for food stamps, and the states would take over financial and administrative responsibility for many other welfare programs. The federal government would set up a trust fund (that would be eliminated in about five years) to provide temporary assistance to the states for the programs picked up by the state governments. The fund would smooth the transition to state assumption or complete financial responsibility for these programs.

There were arguments against this swap. Having welfare programs funded by states with varying tax bases would produce greater inequality among the states in benefit levels (there is considerable inequality now). The primary reaction of legislators, however, was immediate concern over which states would be winners and losers in the swap. How much would each state gain from the costs it would no longer have to pay, and how much would each state lose in costs it would have to pick up from programs the federal government had been subsidizing? The Reagan administration floundered initially because it could not provide any estimates of funding differences. Although the administration tried to downplay the benefits to individual states while emphasizing the overall benefits of the program changes, the concern of legislators in Congress remained the same. Once a table of net effects (taking into account the costs and gains to each state) was produced (a table that was not regarded as accurate by everyone), the program was essentially "dead." Representatives became aware there would be many initial losers, and that with the eventual demise of the trust fund, all states would probably be losers. The proposal for this change was largely ignored by Congress after that, and the Reagan administration faced up to the realities of dealing with "local" legislators and stopped devoting much attention to its proposal.

concern with whether legislation imposes policy requirements on states and localities. Rather than demand participation in specific ways in national programs, Congress prefers to pass legislation that induces the states to participate and allows state and local governments to negotiate many of the details of participation. This avoids alienating local officials and gives localities maximum flexibility in determining how they participate.

If Congress were to mandate that each state or local jurisdiction provide a certain program, many jurisdictions (given the diversity of our society) would be opposed to the program and would resist establishing a program that would run contrary to the predominant political attitudes within their areas. Unless the program were funded completely by the national government, local jurisdictions would have to allocate some of their own tax revenues to a program disliked within the district. Local officials and constituents are likely to feel considerable hostility if Congress regularly engaged in mandating programs and the allocation of local revenues. This hostility would be directed at Congress in general, but particularly at the legislators from that district or state, if they voted for the legislation.

How national programs are administered is also handled carefully by Congress. Congress might elect to set up offices of the national government in each jurisdiction for the administration of national programs. This approach is also likely to create local hostility for two important reasons. First, it would deny local control of programs, and it would offend many individuals who wish to control the effect of government activity within their community. Secondly, it would deny state and local officials the ability to claim credit for local jobs. Since local officials must run for office, they want to be able to control programs and the distribution of local job opportunities. If local officials control the programs, they can claim credit for the programs and the jobs that result, and they can reward (and create) supporters whenever possible.

For all of the prior reasons, Congressional legislators generally prefer not to mandate state or local participation in a program. They may wish to establish national programs, but they do not want to force their own constituents to adopt policies unless there is enormous national political pressure to do so. Nor do they wish to force their colleagues' constituents to adopt policies, since their colleagues may retaliate at a later date.

The most common approach in trying to induce state participation is to have the national government pay a set proportion of all program costs, as was done with the Medicaid program. To get states to provide coverage of health care for low-income individuals, Congress knew that the national government would have to pay a proportion of the costs. Congress also knew the national government would have to offer more money to states with less wealth because the poorer states would find it more difficult to participate. Poorer states also tend to be more conservative and less inclined to participate.

As a result of these considerations, the program was designed so that the national government would pay 50 percent of all costs for wealthier states, like New York and California, and up to almost 80 percent for poorer states like Alabama and Mississippi. Table 2.2 indicates the variation in 1989 reimbursement rates paid to different states if they participated in the Medicaid program. The medicaid reimbursement rate is also used by states as the reimbursement rate for the AFDC (Aid to Families with Dependent Children) program. The states in Table 2.2 are ranked by reimbursement rate, from the highest to the lowest.

States respond very differently to reimbursement incentives. Table 2.2 also presents the variation among the states in AFDC benefit levels. This program is financed in part by the national government, with federal contribution varying from

Table 2.2

State Reimbursement Rates for Medicaid and AFDC and AFDC Payments for a Family of Four, 1989

State	Reimbursement Rate (%)	AFDC Payments ($)	State	Reimbursement Rate (%)	AFDC Payments ($)
Mississippi	79.6	118	Ohio	59.1	314
West Virginia	74.8	253	Wisconsin	58.9	461
Arkansas	74.2	193	Wyoming	58.0	307
Utah	73.7	352	Pennsylvania	57.3	356
South Carolina	73.5	208	Texas	56.9	168
Alabama	73.3	114	Michigan	56.5	480
Kentucky	72.3	223	Rhode Island	55.8	483
New Mexico	71.5	225	Florida	55.4	253
Tennessee	70.6	170	Kansas	55.2	349
Idaho	70.5	251	Minnesota	54.0	523
South Dakota	70.4	271	Hawaii	53.7	546
Montana	69.4	356	Washington	53.2	449
North Carolina	68.7	238	Delaware	51.9	283
Louisiana	68.3	167	Virginia	51.3	260
Maine	67.1	408	Nevada	50.2	277
Vermont	66.2	500	Alaska	50.0	619
North Dakota	64.8	366	California	50.0	620
Georgia	63.8	261	Colorado	50.0	324
Indiana	63.7	263	Connecticut	50.0	534
Oklahoma	63.3	288	Illinois	50.0	320
Iowa	62.7	360	Maryland	50.0	356
Arizona	62.1	271	Massachusetts	50.0	559
Oregon	62.1	361	New Hampshire	50.0	417
Nebraska	59.7	333	New Jersey	50.0	357
Missouri	59.3	272	New York	50.0	530

Sources: Reimbursement rates: Robert J. Dilger, National Intergovernmental Programs *(Englewood Cliffs: Prentice–Hall, 1989), 20, 47, 63; AFDC rates: U.S. Statistical Abstract, 1991.*

50 to 79.6 percent. Each state has considerable control over the eligibility standards and benefit levels, and the variation that exists is a result of this discretion. Table 2.2 indicates that providing high federal support through generous reimbursement does not automatically translate into the state providing high benefits. The national government seeks to induce participation, but each state retains the right to determine what is an appropriate benefit level. A state like Mississippi, for example, receives almost 80 percent reimbursement, but paid only $118 per family in 1989. New York, while receiving 50 percent reimbursement, paid $530 per family that same year. State politics has more to do with determining benefit levels than federal reimbursement rates do.

Other programs use varying federal payment arrangements to make programs more attractive to states. A few of these programs and the percent of costs the national government will reimburse are presented in Table 2.3. The national government pays much of the cost of national programs but allows state and local negotiation of the conditions of participation in those programs.

The states play an enduring role in policy formation in America. The source of this state role is federalism. Federalism continues to give the states influence over the formation and pursuit of policy in United States politics. Policies emerge from our "national" Congress, but they are shaped by the "local representatives" who comprise Congress. The influential role of the states stems not from legal protections in the Constitution but from political representation of the states within the federal system.

Table 2.3

Reimbursement Rates for Various National Programs

Program	Reimbursement Rate (%)
Variable Rate Reimbursement	
Medicaid	50–83*
Aid for dependent children	50–79
Public library construction	33–66
Watershed protection and flood prevention	50–100
Air pollution control	50–75
Single Rate Reimbursement	
Elementary and secondary schools: Programs for the handicapped	100
Community development	100
Low-Income housing assistance	100
Interstate highway construction	90
Headstart	80
Urban mass transit	
capital improvements	75
Health services: Programs for the homeless	75
Historic preservation	70
Interstate meat and poultry inspection	50
Gas pipeline safety	50
Cooperative extension service	27

Sources: Advisory Commission on Intergovernmental Relations, Characteristics of Federal Grant-in-Aid Programs to State and Local Governments *(Washington, DC, 1992) M-182; and Robert Dilger,* National Intergovernmental Programs *(Englewood Cliffs: Prentice–Hall, 1989), table 2.1.*
*The range in reimbursement rates represents the minimum and maximum the federal government will pay, depending on some designated criterion such as per capita income.

Implementation of "National" Policy in the States: State Leverage

Once programs are established, another phase of state leverage begins. It often appears from news stories that the states are in a subordinate position. Sometimes an agency of the executive branch has indicated to the states that they must comply with a federal regulation or face losing the funds they are receiving from the national government. Federal bureaucrats in Washington appear to have power to dictate to the states the terms of compliance. This power, however, is not as great as it seems.

Bureaucratic Dependence on Congress

Federal bureaucracies have considerable influence over programs affecting the states. Federal agencies do have the authority to establish and "clarify" many of the requirements for participation in federal programs once those programs are under way. Agencies can also determine whether state programs are meeting national policy goals. There is, however, one significant constraint upon this influence. If a particular bureaucracy is to survive and grow (both of which most bureaucrats desire), it must receive funds through congressional authorization. The federal budget is put together and passed once a year. As a part of passing this budget, the committees of the House of Representatives and the Senate have the right to request that the directors of each agency appear before Congress to justify their budget request. This gives members of Congress a chance to question directors and to seek justifications for policy decisions. This situation also gives legislators a chance to voice their complaints about the treatment their states receive.

Legislators, though, are not limited simply to voicing criticism of a bureaucratic agency. The most significant action they can take against a bureaucratic agency is to threaten its budget. Because budget limits prevent agencies from growing and gaining prestige, bureaucrats often seek to avoid antagonizing legislators. They may even seek to support the proposals of key legislators in the hope that this support will be reciprocated when the agency's budget comes up for review. To maintain a good relationship with Congress, then, administrators in federal agencies generally remain sensitive to the positions of individual states and are reluctant to "push" a state more than necessary.

The Ability of States to "Stall"

In addition to the influence of Congress over federal agencies, states also exert much influence. Programs are usually set up such that states maintain control over the administration and implementation of policy requirements that might be imposed on state and local government. To enhance their support among their constituents, members of Congress prefer to allow local officials to have control over the money and jobs that accompany programs. Most national policy is not administered by autonomous branches of federal bureaucracies in local jurisdictions. Rather, state and local officials administer these programs. This control over these programs gives local officials considerable influence over how programs are implemented.

When a state or locality enrolls in a federal program, there is usually a commitment to the federal agency to implement programs according to a specific plan worked out between the state and the federal agency. The states, however, have considerable freedom to interpret (or misinterpret) this plan and to determine the best way to attain federal goals. Even though federal agencies might believe the state's interpretation is not sincere or might disagree with its determination of what the program requires, federal agencies are cautious about ruling in advance of program implementation that such implementation will be a failure. It is also difficult for federal agencies to thoroughly assess state and local program proposals because they often lack the staff resources this requires.

Because of this situation, state and local governments usually have some freedom to implement a program first and to argue with a federal agency later over whether the program's requirements have been met. This sequence of events gives states the possibility of implementing a program the way they wish and then stalling about changing it while the argument proceeds. This ability to stall and argue is enhanced by the tendency of Congress to indicate only general and vague goals when forming policy. Federal programs without precise expectations or goals create an ambiguity that allows a state room to argue over what was and is the intent of the program.

Limits on Withdrawing Federal Support

Finally, federal agencies are reluctant to wield their power and actually withdraw funds designated for a state. Federal bureaucrats generally want to see that people who need benefits receive them. Federal grants are crucial to the maintenance of benefit programs. Federal agencies could exert influence by threatening to withdraw funds from state or local governments for failure to execute a program as the agencies wish. While the threat may be suggested occasionally, funds are seldom actually withheld. Withdrawing funds would antagonize state and local officials and program beneficiaries who would convey their displeasure to congressional legislators, who in turn might seek reprisals against the agency. The individuals who would be hurt the most, moreover, are those at whom the program is aimed, and the agency will have achieved nothing in terms of its goals. Finally, a federal agency with programs that are not being executed by state and local governments is in effect an agency with no programs, a situation that is difficult to justify before Congress. For all these reasons, federal agencies are reluctant to invoke the ultimate penalty of withdrawing funds. The ability of the states to remain semi-autonomous and to pursue programs in their own ways is strengthened.[14]

The Reluctance to Intrude

Even after numerous battles over "improper" state action, federal officials are still reluctant to intrude. Federal intrusion creates the unpleasant image of officials from Washington taking over local programs and pushing aside local officials. One of the most intense conflicts in American politics was over the registration of blacks in the South in the 1960s. In the late 1950s, very few blacks were registered to vote in Southern states, and there was enormous media coverage of the resistance of Southern registrars to register black voters. Congress finally passed legislation requiring federal registrars to go into Southern counties and take registration duties away from local officials. Despite the enormous publicity that accompanied passage of the legislation and the stories about federal registrar activities, the national officials went about implementation of the legislation in a restrained manner. From 1965 to 1980, federal registrars entered only 60 of the 533 counties covered by the Voting Rights Act of 1965. Even then federal registrars interfered only if the local official flagrantly opposed registering blacks.[15] The inclination to be careful in taking over local activities is strong.

Defying Federal Policy Changes: Other Examples

Not only do the states have the capability to shape how new programs are implemented, they can also resist changes in existing policies. When the Reagan administration assumed power in 1981, one of its first acts was to go after programs that the administration believed contained significant waste. One of its first targets was the Social Security disability program. A 1980 federal law required that recipients be reexamined every three years to see if they were still disabled and still deserving of assistance. Since the Reagan administration controlled the federal bureaucracy, it had the power to redefine eligibility standards. The administration made eligibility standards much more difficult to meet. From March 1981 to September 1983, 374,000 of 3.9 million people were removed from the eligibility rolls. These removals were done by state offices (the implementation of this program is done by the states, using eligibility criteria supplied by the federal government). By early 1983, there were repeated reports of people being removed who had no capability to work. The subsequent publicity created questions as to whether the new rules were fair and whether the pursuit of savings had gone too far. The public reaction had its effect on state governments because it was at that level that the decisions to remove individuals had to be made and announced. The governors of the states began to oppose any further removals (and some even sought reinstatements of recipients). By mid-1983 several governors moved to outright defiance of the new federal rules. Some states, such as Massachusetts, filed lawsuits against the new rules, claiming they violated court rulings. Other states, such as North Carolina, New York, West Virginia, Arkansas, and Kansas, declared a moratorium on removing anyone else from eligibility.

The importance of these activities by the states is that they were not met with any punishment or penalties from the federal government. Sensing growing opposition to eligibility changes among state representatives in Congress, the administration began to moderate its demands for removals. There were continued directives to remove recipients, but at a slower pace. The directives had no impact, however, and the administration agreed that the courts should settle the matter. The states retained control over policy, and the federal government was unable to force any further policy changes until the courts or Congress resolved the matter. The courts eventually ruled against the Reagan administration.

Such defiance can also occur on a less grand scale. Since the mid-1970s, states have been required to have a 55 mph speed limit or lose transportation funds. Montana, with great stretches of open land to cover in order to get anywhere, has never been happy with this limit. State efforts to monitor speed levels and to ticket violators were initially very lax in Montana and other states. To counter this, the national

Federal Pressures on a State: An Example

All the restraints on federal action result in states having a lot of room to maneuver. This relationship between federal "national" goals and state action is illustrated very well by the relationship between the federal government and the state of Massachusetts from 1936 to 1967 in the area of public welfare, specifically in the Aid for Dependent Children program. At one time, each state in the United States administered its own welfare program. In 1935, Congress passed legislation to assist the states and to establish a national program of welfare. Among other things, this program was to provide aid for families with no parent available to earn sufficient income. In this part of the program, Congress sought uniformity in the amounts of aid provided by each state. Congress, though, knew that national, uniform levels of benefits would be impossible because of the variation in programs existing among states before Congress intervened. Congress settled for seeking uniformity just within each state. The original legislation left some ambiguity in program goals. The original language called for a plan from each state for administering a welfare program that would be "in effect in all political subdivisions of the state, and if administered by them, be mandatory upon them."[16] Federal administrators interpreted this statement to mean that like cases were to be treated alike.

This interpretation contrasted with the program in effect at the time in Massachusetts, and an extended conflict ensued between that state and the federal government. When federal administrators began reviewing the Massachusetts program, they decided that, according to their interpretation of the program's intent, eligibility standards and payment levels had to be the same in each local jurisdiction. The state of Massachusetts, however, had a long tradition of local autonomy in the area of public welfare, and the state was reluctant to accept an interpretation that the program should be administered at the state level. Conflict continued for thirty years between the federal government and the state over what constituted proper administration of this program. Federal officials threatened several times to cut off funds for noncompliance because the state would not centralize administration. Each threat was countered by an appeal by the state to its representatives in Congress to intervene and reduce this pressure. The result was a cycle of pressure, controversy, slight reductions in local discretion, and reduced pressure. Eventually, the federal government succeeded in convincing the state of Massachusetts to assume control over a program that would include similar standards and payment levels across the state. The important matter is that the federal administrators were unable to achieve this change until 1967. This pattern exists in numerous policy areas. The federal government is capable of inducing change, but change is gradual, and the states have the means to resist.[17]

government required that states do more to regulate speed on highways. Montana complied, but made its scorn for the law very clear. Anyone caught speeding in Montana received a five dollar fine, regardless of the speed level. The ticket also did not result in any penalty points on licenses. Drivers could accumulate as many speeding tickets as they wished. The policy was very clear. The state government formally complied with the national government requirement, but made its unwillingness to enforce the law very clear. The result was that Washington agencies and Montana officials were continually arguing about whether this was "real" compliance.

The Persisting Significance of the States

The original intent of the creators of American federalism was to establish a system that dispersed and restrained power. One means of achieving dispersal was to structurally divide power between a national government and the states. This division was accomplished through the creation of separate levels of government and the assignment of different responsibilities to the two levels. The creation of a representation system making the states the source of representation was intended as a means to restrain the power of the national government. While many aspects of American society and politics have changed since the formation of American federalism, this system of representation has continued to give the states a great deal of influence over the formation and implementation of policy in our society. State needs from federal programs vary, as do state inclinations to participate in such programs. These differences are reflected in Congressional debate and lead to national policies that grant states some autonomy in program implementation.

The Move to a More Activist National Government

Indicators of Change

While federalism as a political process has endured, some things have clearly changed. The division of labor between the national government and the states has changed considerably since 1800. The national government now requires more of the states, funds more of their activities, and is more intrusive in state affairs. The political process may have endured, but the results of this process have clearly changed. This section addresses the ways in which the federal system has changed, the causes of that change, and the resulting position of state and local governments.

Nature of Change

The national government is much more involved in the practices and policies of state and local government. American public policy in 1800 was a result of highly decentralized decision-making. Policy matters were left almost completely to state and local governments. Now the national government is much more involved in state and local affairs. Congress attempts to create many relatively uniform policies and to affect local policy implementation from Washington. Although these efforts may not always be highly coercive, the trend towards greater national activism is real. There are national attempts to prompt more government activity in the states and to alter existing state policy practices. There are attempts to establish common programs in all the states and to reduce variations in policies across the states. These changes have not come about smoothly. We have passed through different eras of federal–state relations to arrive at the current situation.[18] Much of our early history has been characterized as dual federalism. National and state governments had their own separate responsibilities, and they did not interact much. Cooperative federalism emerged during the 1930s. This era involved much more joint cooperation between the national and state governments to achieve policy goals. While there are many labels we might use to classify the phases of relationships between National government and state and local governments, there is no dispute that change has occurred.

This shift of influence over policy is evident in several aspects of government. First, the federal government raises much more of all tax revenues than it did in the past. These changes are summarized in Table 2.4. Table 2.4 presents the proportion of all tax revenues (such as tax revenues from income, sales, property) raised by different levels of government across time. In 1902, the majority of all government revenues were raised at the local level. By 1990 only 17 percent was raised by local governments. The federal government was raising the major portion of government funds. Though federal dominance has characterized the last forty years, the federal role has declined somewhat since the 1960s, and state governments have come to play a larger role. This change will be discussed later.

Table 2.4
The Federal Role in Raising Government Tax Revenue (Selected Years)

Year	Proportion of All Taxes Raised by (%)		
	Federal	State	Local
1902	37	11	51
1922	46	13	42
1929	34	20	46
1939	44	20	36
1959	68	16	17
1969	66	19	16
1979	61	24	15
1984	56	27	17
1988	56	27	17
1990	56	27	17

Sources: 1902–1922: Historical Statistics on Governmental Finances and Employment, Census of Governments *(1962), tables 3 and 4; 1929–1939:* Significant Features of Fiscal Federalism, *1988 ed., vol. 1, tables 2 and 3; 1959–1988:* Significant Features of Fiscal Federalism, *1990 ed., vol. 1, table 57; and* Government Finances, 1989–90 *(Washington, DC, 1991), GF-5*

These national tax revenues are used to provide more intergovernmental aid to state and local governments for the support of various programs. States and localities have become much more financially dependent on federal revenues. This change is shown in Table 2.5. While dependence has increased, it is important to note that this dependence is by no means total. As we will examine later, states still have considerable autonomy in deciding their own tax levels and how those taxes are imposed. This revenue dependence does not make the states subservient to the federal government. It does, however, place state governments in a situation where there are significant pressures to reasonably satisfy the policy goals of a program, if the state or local government wishes to continue to receive federal aid. State and local autonomy has been reduced.

It is also important to note that this dependence on federal revenue has not continually increased over time. Dependence peaked in 1978, and it has been declining since, largely because of a decline in aid to local governments. The reasons for this shift will also be discussed later.

Finally, the greater revenue raised by the national government has not gone just to support state and local governments. The national government is transferring much of this money to state and local governments, but it is also retaining and directly spending much of this revenue. Although much of this expenditure, to be sure, goes toward national defense programs, most of this expenditure is for

Table 2.5

The Dependence of State and Local Governments on Federal Aid: Federal Aid as a Proportion of State–Local Revenue (Selected Years)

Year	Proportion of State–Local Revenue from Federal Aid (%)
1902	0.7
1913	0.6
1927	1.7
1934	12.7
1940	9.2
1957	10.1
1967	16.4
1974	20.6
1979	24.9
1984	17.9
1988	16.2
1990	16.1

Sources: 1902–1979: Historical Statistics on Governmental Finances and Employment, *Census of Governments, tables 3 and 4; 1984:* Government Finances, 1986–87 *(Washington, DC, 1988), GF-87-5, table 5; 1988:* Significant Features of Fiscal Federalism, *1990 ed., vol. I, table 51; and* Government Finances, 1989–90, *(Washington, DC, 1991), GF-5.*

domestic matters. Table 2.6 indicates the proportion of all funds spent directly by federal, state, and local governments. Funds that are transferred to state or local governments are not included in the federal proportions, since these funds are ultimately spent directly at the state or local level. The changes in proportions over time provide another indication of changes in national–subnational relationships. Since the beginning of this century there has been a significant rise in direct expenditure activity by the national government. In fact, the federal budget is now so large that the predominant congressional debate revolves around the size of the federal budget.

Changes in this century have been significant. The national government now raises a larger proportion of all taxes collected by government. It now also engages in more direct expenditure than it used to. The national government, despite some fluctuations, has come to play a major role in American politics.

The federal government has also gained considerable influence through several non-monetary means. The federal government affects states and localities through laws, directives, and regulations.[19] For example, to assure that citizens in each state have the same rights, Congress has passed numerous national civil rights laws. Federal laws have been passed that create directives for state and local governments to adopt common provisions for accessibility to facilities by the handicapped. The federal government has used regulations to push for more uniform standards of allowable pollution levels. Many federal laws that preempt (replace) state and local laws have also been passed.[20] It is clear that federal actions now have a significant effect on the activities and policies of the states and localities.

Table 2.6

The Federal Role in Government Expenditures (Selected Years)

Year	Federal (%)	Proportion of Funds Spent by State (%)	Local (%)
1902	34	8	58
1929	25	21	54
1939	46	17	38
1959	60	14	26
1969	52	18	30
1979	48	20	32
1988	52	19	29
1990	51	20	29

Sources: 1902 and 1929: Historical Statistics on Governmental Finances and Employment, *Census of Governments, tables 10, 13 and 14. 1939:* Significant Features of Fiscal Federalism, *1988 ed., vol. 1, tables 2 and 3; 1959–1988:* Significant Features of Fiscal Federalism, *1990 ed., vol. 1, table 40; and* Government Finances, 1989–90 *(Washington, DC, 1991), GF-5.*

The Movement away from Decentralization

The original federal arrangement was established at a time when protecting the liberty of individuals was a major concern. The prime concern was freedom from government. The resulting system was based on the dispersal of power achieved by creating three branches of government (executive, legislative, and judicial), and by decentralizing the determination of policy through federalism. States and localities had enormous discretion in adopting policy.

The intriguing question is why a society would make such a significant change from this highly decentralized system to one in which the direction of policy is much more centralized and the national government much more active. What is it that would prompt such change? There appear to be two general factors prompting this shift: changes in the economic system and changes in society conceptions of the responsibility of the central government to affect social conditions and relevant state and local policies. These changes explain shifts within our federal system. They also illustrate the role and connections between economic change and political ideas.

Economic Change and Its Effects

When the federal arrangement was first established, the American economy was almost entirely agrarian. Most people worked on small farms. Industrial firms as we know them now were nonexistent. Since that time we have undergone the Industrial Revolution of the 1800s, and we continue to experience economic and technological change. The change from an agrarian to an industrial and service economy has altered the nature of economic activity. As we shall see, as a consequence of these changes, government has shifted from an institution that threatened our freedom to one that many see as an instrument to protect us from social change. Government now provides unemployment compensation to those who lose their jobs. Medicaid is a national health-insurance program designed to help those low-income individuals without health insurance. We have job training programs to help people adapt to changing labor markets. In very general terms, we have altered the structure of political authority in response to changes in our economic structure.

Three specific kinds of economic change have been particularly important in prompting change in the role of the national government. They are changes in interdependence, scale, and externalities.[21] While these changes overlap, we will discuss them separately here for purposes of clarity.

Interdependency

As production increased with economic growth, production also became more specialized. Complete goods had once been produced in one spot by one firm. The item was constructed in one site. Individual firms began to specialize in producing just one of the items that make a finished product. Firms specialized because they could make the one item cheaper and then sell it to another firm that would assemble the parts. The tires, glass, radios, upholstery, and other parts of a car, for example, are all produced by different firms. Firms came to depend on each other for products and employment. Firms became dependent on other firms and on production in other areas of the country. Economies and communities became linked to each other, these linkages also created more interdependency and vulnerability. When the Chrysler Corporation was threatened during the late 1970s with economic collapse, the threat of unemployment reached beyond the auto industry to the steel, glass, rubber, and electronics industries, to name only a few. The possible breadth of this impact was such that the Chrysler situation became a political issue. No politician wished to see his or her constituents experience such dislocation, and no government wanted to lose the taxes derived from these economic activities.

The inclination was to turn to the national government to deal with the problem. Because of the extensive interdependency among corporations, almost any problem of this nature would affect industries in many states, making it impossible for any one state to impose a solution. The issue of bankruptcy at Chrysler was thus taken up by the President and Congress, a decidedly more centralized approach to deciding policy. The same pattern has occurred for numerous policy issues, such as those concerning antitrust laws (laws preventing the collaboration of firms for the purpose of restraining free trade in a product area), and "nationwide" strikes (such as in the coal or trucking industry). When savings and loan banks were threatened with bankruptcy during the 1980s, Congress stepped in to provide a "bail-out" because large failures would have negative economic effects across many states. In each case, the interdependency of businesses made it difficult for individual states or groups of states to handle the problem and necessary for the national government to step in.

Scale

In our early, predominantly agrarian, society, most economic enterprises were limited in size. Having few workers, small production volumes, and a limited geographical market, most businesses were not large enough to dominate an entire city or rural area. The situation changed considerably, however, with the arrival of the Industrial Revolution. As specialization continued, industries grew to the point of dominating entire areas, and some of our larger corporations, such as General Motors, have in fact grown so large that their gross sales exceed the total income from production (the gross national product) of many states and nations. These firms are so large that often they can dictate the terms of business activity to other firms and the terms of employment to employees.

The sheer size of these emerging businesses created the potential for considerable abuse, which individual states were often not capable of, or not willing to, oppose. Business creates jobs and income and, consequently, strengthens an area's tax base. In a decentralized system in which states must raise their own tax revenues and establish strong tax bases, state and local governments often prefer not to antagonize businesses.[22] Some of the activities of these large-scale firms resulted in calls for regulation, a task for which individual states were not well suited. A gradual consensus emerged that much of the regulation of business would have to take place at the national level. As the power of corporations increased, efforts to conduct regulatory activity began to shift to the national level. This resulted in agencies such as the Federal Trade Commission and the Interstate Commerce

Commission. The formation of these federal agencies shifted some of the responsibility for regulation to the national level and increased national activism.

Externalities

Another major influence upon centralization has been the increase in the existence and recognition of externalities. Externalities is a term used by economists to refer to a situation in which two or more parties are engaged in a market transaction, during the course of which costs or benefits are experienced by individuals other than the parties of the exchange. For example, a factory produces a product, which it sells to its customers. While this transaction is taking place, the factory may also produce air and water pollution, which is released into the immediate environment. This pollution reduces the value of property in the surrounding area and harms the health of those residents. Nearby individuals suffer costs that they cannot recoup.[23]

When these externalities spread across state and local lines, there are significant problems for federalism. For example, the Midwest industrial states of Illinois and Ohio produce considerable air pollution, which is released into the air and caught up in the jet stream, which blows west to east. This pollution falls on eastern states in the form of "acid rain," which destroys vegetation and trees. Within the federal system, New York and Ohio are equals, so the attempts of New York to change policies in Ohio are likely to be limited in effect. Because of this, many problems that involve externalities (negative in most cases, since costs are imposed) are handled at the national level. Resolution is much easier at this level.

In some regards, centralization of this nature has resulted because economic change has increased the scale of economic activity such that the externalities involved cover a larger geographical area. Larger factories produce more air and water pollution. Some of this centralization, however, has come about because of increased recognition of externalities. In the area of health, for example, it is now recognized that diseases such as AIDS are communicable across jurisdictions, and failure to handle health problems at one level will impose costs on populations in other states.

The Political Process and Response to Change

The nature of the American economy has changed since the inception of federalism. The role of the national government has increased in response to that change. The division of responsibilities in American politics is not a fixed institutional arrangement. It is an ongoing decision made through the political process. Federalism shapes how those decisions are made, and there is no set or "proper" division of labor. The division changes as political judgments change.

This increase in the federal role is not, however, an automatic, mechanical adjustment. Each time a decision is made to have the national government play a more activist role, a problem that was not regarded as a national policy concern must be redefined as a national concern. This often means redefining individual freedoms and obligations in society, a change that creates political conflict. If the mine workers have their ability to strike limited because of the national impact such a strike would have, their freedom to strike is reduced for the sake of the society as a whole. If factories are required to "clean" their polluted exhaust before releasing it, costs that they previously did not bear are imposed on them. If apartment owners are no longer allowed to arbitrarily exclude minorities from housing, their freedom is limited in order to protect the freedoms of another group. The groups whose freedoms are restricted generally lobby heavily to prevent this restriction, and the resulting conflict creates serious debates about the rights of individuals, the threats to individual liberty, and the proper degree of activism of the national government. The changes discussed thus far have not come about without conflict, and it is inevitable that conflict will continue to occur. Changing the allocation of authority within federalism changes the ability of groups to be free from national scrutiny. This change is rarely accepted without a fight.

Amid these changes, however, the essential features of the political process of federalism remain unchanged. Representatives still come from the individual states, and throughout the debates on these changes, representatives fight for the views of their constituents and for the best possible terms for their states and localities. While this debate goes on, the representation system organizes discussions of change. New policies are discussed, agreed upon, and enacted. The representation system provides a means for dissent by the states and for the eventual (if at all) emergence of some minimal consensus about change. As Deil Wright, a political scientist who studies federalism, has stressed, it is people, not vague "economic forces," that perceive, debate, and institute change.[24]

Changing Attitudes and the Changing Role of Government

While economic change has played an important role in the changes in governmental responsibilities, it is not the only source of change in our society. We have debated the appropriate nature and validity of national activism and changed the role of the national government because we have changed our conception of the role government should play in our lives. There have been profound changes in our *ideas* about the role of government and its responsibilities in society. These intellectual changes have not proceeded without resistance, and this halting, jerky progression has produced some of the great impassioned debates in our society about our obligations to our fellow human, the nature of freedom, and the definition of a just and fair society. We will examine examples of those debates as we proceed.

The change in our ideas can be seen in terms of the succession of three sets of ideas that have successively come to dominate and partially replace over time previously dominant ideas in our society. None of these successive replacements has been complete, but they have been pervasive enough to lead to changes in the role of the national government. These three changes involve: our notions of what causes individuals to vary in their success; our notions of the possible ways in which government can positively shape society; and our commitment to equality and its implications. Each of these changes and the subsequent impacts illustrate the importance of ideas in our society and the ways in which dominant ideas can vary over time.[25]

Attitudes in Early American Society: Theistic Beliefs

The nature of the changes that have transpired in our society can be more easily recognized by first clarifying the situation when the federal arrangement was established. Several aspects of American society and politics were particularly important and affected the legitimacy of a decentralized federal system. One of the important characteristics of that society was a relatively pervasive (and sometimes vague) view among the population that God had a significant impact on the lives of individuals. People believed that, to a large extent, God influenced the fate of individuals. Although some groups felt that an individual might be able to actively influence this fate by performing good works, a person's fate was generally felt to be heavily influenced by God. This belief had indirect but significant political implications. It meant that even if government efforts (as we know them today) were made in order to offset the lives of individuals, these efforts were not perceived as likely to affect the overall fate of those individuals. The primary source of influence was God. This belief led to a relatively passive view of the ability of society to alter the conditions of its members. Government action would have no lasting impact. If some individuals were poor, it was perhaps tragic, but the situation was to be accepted as reflective of God's intent.

This passive view of government activity was reinforced by the pervasive view that strong government was a threat to liberty and something to be feared. The experience with British rule prompted worry about government having too much power. Much of the political thought of that era was dominated by a concern for restraining government action and worry about the dangers of central power. These attitudes provided considerable support for a limited government.

One idea that might have played a crucial role in affecting government action was notable by its absence. That idea was equality of opportunity. Equality was only an emergent and vaguely formed idea in the early republic, the implications of which had not been fully explored. There was not yet strong concern with equality. No one was arguing that conditions of life should be similar among people or across the states. Since social conditions were not perceived as the source of individual differences, there was no reason to worry about equality of individual conditions, much less equality across the states.

Together, these ideas provided a justification for a limited government and a decentralized federal system. It was perceived as appropriate to have a government that was not very active, since such activity would do no good and was to be feared. In addition, having a decentralized system of policy enactment was thoroughly acceptable, since there was no pressure to have equality of policy. Indeed, it was argued that one of the great merits of federalism was that different states could vary their policy responses as they desired.

The Industrial Era and Individualism

Since that time, there has been considerable change in the ideas dominating our society. The changes have been profound, and they have had significant implications for the structure of our political system. The first noticeable changes occurred in the Industrial Era of the 1800s. During the nineteenth century, attitudes toward individual success, government involvement, and the concept of equality all changed. First, there was a decline in the extent of attachment to religious views.[26] There was less of a popular conviction that God determined the fate of individuals. With the rise of laissez-faire economic doctrines, there was a greater emphasis on the virtues of the free market as a means of making economic allocation decisions. This change was accompanied by an increased emphasis upon individual will and initiative as a source of individual differences. But this change was subtle in its impact. On the one hand, there was still no justification for government activity to affect individuals, since the source of individual motivation and will was perceived to be internal. But this transition had profound implications, because it suggested that humans, not God, controlled the fate of the individual.

This change in belief also indirectly affected views of government. These changed views had the subtle implication that perhaps humans could direct events in a society. As a part of the Industrial Revolution and the development of the American West, many people felt that government could be used to create conditions favorable to the development of the American economy. This belief led to national government activity to fund or encourage water projects, development of railroads, building of roads, and many other projects that would make economic development easier.[27] The significant aspect of these activities is that they involved viewing government as a positive force in society. The role that government played was still limited. There were no programs to affect individual lives directly, but there was a view that government could play a positive role. These two changes, from a religious interpretation of individual fate to an individual-centered view, and from support for a highly decentralized national government to belief in a government that could play a limited but positive role, were a crucial transition in American politics. They provided the basis for a more activist government at all levels of politics.

At the same time, there was an important change taking place with regard to the idea of equality. During the nineteenth century, there was a slow but gradual increase in concern with equality, even as a vague concern. In the 1830s, President Andrew Jackson advocated more legitimacy for the "common man" and less deference to traditional elites. One of the most important events with regard to equality was the Civil War, which raised the fundamental question of who had equal rights in American society. While the Civil War did not result in equality for blacks, the issue was nonetheless raised, and it was not easy to bury.[28] The changes in the nineteenth century resulted in a transition to a society that held a somewhat more active view of government and a somewhat greater concern with equality. The changes were not great, but were sufficient to provide a basis for more significant changes later.[29]

The "Modern" World and Social Science Views

The twentieth century saw further changes in ideas. These changes also had significant implications for the division of labor in American federalism. Perhaps the most important change has been the growing belief that individuals are not entirely in control of their fate, but that they are heavily influenced by the socioeconomic environment they grow up in. This environment is presumed to affect individual self-esteem, motivation, sense of efficacy, intellectual skills, and personality, among other factors. These characteristics of individuals affect the chances of those individuals to succeed and, ultimately, affect the distribution of wealth in society. Put more directly, the view that socioeconomic environments affect us means that children born into relatively poor families are likely (though not necessarily destined) to remain relatively poor as adults. Thus, the distribution of opportunities and wealth in society may not be entirely a result of differences in effort and innate talents, but may be heavily influenced by background.

The emergence of these beliefs cannot be attributed to any single factor, although it is partly traceable to the rise of social science and the resulting studies of the sources of individual variations. These studies often found that background played a significant role in affecting the "fate" of individuals. These findings contributed to the decline of individualistic interpretations which stressed the will and innate attributes of individuals.

In addition, cataclysmic events such as the Great Depression played a role. During the 1930s at least one-third of the population was unemployed, and another large proportion was employed only part-time. In the face of such massive unemployment, it became very difficult to argue that these individuals were unemployed because of personal failings. This further undermined the individualistic thesis that individuals are in control of their own fates. This crisis coupled with the emerging idea that the government could affect the national economy through government regulation and spending resulted in an increase in government activity and programs.[30]

The acceptance of social science views of the world had at least two effects. First, if background is a source of variations in success and the distribution of wealth, then there is some question as to whether the inequality in the distribution of wealth in society is thoroughly justifiable. It became harder (though not impossible) to argue that individuals "earned" their differences in wealth. The heirs of the Rockefeller fortune were only the most obvious case used in this argument. Acceptance of the effects of the socioeconomic environment led to increased concern with equality and equality of opportunity in society.

Second, if socioeconomic environments and background affect individuals, then there is strong justification for changing the direction of social welfare policies. When it was presumed that poverty was due to personal limitations, social workers sought to correct the personality deficiencies and work habits of the poor. If, however, these differences are due to environmental variations, then the focus is more logically upon correcting the environments of individuals.[31]

In this change we see the roots of the greater national role of the last fifty years. When it was presumed that environmental conditions did not affect individuals, there was really no reason for government to worry about establishing extensive social welfare programs to affect individual "environments." If the backgrounds of individuals do matter, then it is appropriate for government to have education, nutritional, and financial support programs. This provided a logical basis for government programs as a means of attempting to reduce inequality of individual situations.

This change, coupled with concerns for equality, had profound implications for the role of the national government. Concern for background influences prompted concerns with equality. American society had become more concerned with equality. The focus on the ways in which individual background affected wealth distribution prompted a growing focus on equality of conditions. If there is to be equality of opportunity, and if government policies can affect the socioeconomic environments of individuals, then the (unsettling, for some) implication for federalism is that there ought to be some similarity of opportunities (and government policies) across the states. For example, if blacks are to be legitimate members of American society, then shouldn't they have the same rights in each state? If medical benefits to the poor are to be provided, shouldn't these benefits be available to the poor regardless of the state they live in?

This debate about what values should be dominant became particularly intense during the 1960s, when blacks and the poor of our society began to push harder for greater equality of opportunity. At the same time, the widespread diffusion of mass media, and particularly television, heightened awareness of the inequalities in our society. During the early 1960s, for example, people watched while Sheriff "Bull" Connor ordered police to attack with hoses and dogs the blacks marching through the streets of Birmingham, Alabama in a protest to obtain equal rights. This image of inequality of treatment was powerful and unsettling to many who believed that the United States was the land of opportunity. The effect of media communication of such events throughout our society was to create more support for national action to protect individual rights across all states.[32] Other groups, such as women and the handicapped, have created further pressures for guarantees of rights across the states since the 1970s. Taking action to produce these rights means reducing the autonomy of individual states to select the policies they wish.

In addition to the change in ideas, there have also been arguments that the diversity among states in ideas and conditions has declined. This change should result in less conflict within society and in Congress about what policies to adopt. It has been argued that we are now more of a nationalized society.[33] The economies of states and localities have become more alike.[34] We all receive similar messages through the national media.[35] While many scholars disagree with this thesis and the evidence for it,[36] the argument is that with less diversity, legislators find themselves in less conflict with others. Reaching a consensus becomes easier, and national action more likely.

A Recapitulation

The changes just discussed are complicated, and a restatement may help. Belief has gradually grown that government can be a positive force in our society. This view is not unanimous by any means, but beginning with President Roosevelt and the New Deal of the 1930s, action by the national government has become more acceptable and desired. Individuals began to see positive benefits from government activity. Some even began to perceive government as a mechanism to help people achieve liberty from oppression in the private sector (job discrimination, for example). While our society began with concern with liberty *from* government, we have broadened the perceived range of aspects of life that threaten liberty. Many people

Changing Views of the Role of Government: The Responsibility for Unemployment as an Example

In a capitalist society such as the United States, one of the areas where notions of individual responsibility have been most important has been the debate over unemployment. This is also an area where there has been enormous change in beliefs about government responsibilities over the last sixty years.

Prior to the 1930s, United States economic thought was largely dominated by what is known as classical or free-market economics. This set of ideas argues that unemployment is due largely to the unwillingness of workers to adjust their wage or work expectations when the economy goes through growth and decline cycles. The more popular form of this theory held individuals responsible for their own unemployment. Government had no responsibility to cope with unemployment problems. Indeed, it was considered detrimental for the government to intervene because such intervention would discourage individual adjustment to changing markets.

In the 1930s, a significant change in these views began. During the Great Depression one-third of the labor force was unemployed. Despite this serious situation, most businessmen and economists testifying at Congressional hearings argued that the solution to this problem was for the government to stay out of the economy and allow it to correct itself.[37] Amid this debate, the one significant change that emerged was that it became difficult to blame the unemployed for their situation, since this situation was shared by one-third of the labor force.

During the 1930s, British economist John Maynard Keynes published a major book that argued that government could affect the overall level of unemployment by varying the total demand for goods and services. The book was highly controversial because it presented the argument that government could take a positive role to affect unemployment.[38] The book initially met with considerable resistance, but these ideas and other external events eventually led Congress to enact the Full Employment Act in 1946.[39] This act declared for the first time that it was the responsibility of government to affect unemployment levels.

Ideas change slowly, however, and throughout the 1950s, President Eisenhower resisted this responsibility. To a considerable extent, he was able to avoid being held accountable for unemployment levels. This avoidance was possible largely because the view that government was responsible for unemployment was not yet widely accepted.

A major change occurred in the 1960s when President Kennedy proposed a major tax cut to boost demand in the economy. When finally enacted, the tax cut resulted in a marked increase in economic activity and a reduction in the level of unemployment. Once this impact was demonstrated, the notion that government could affect unemployment levels became an important part of political discourse, and politicians generally perceived themselves as responsible for dealing with unemployment levels.

The Reagan administration advocated supply-side economics, which put the emphasis on reducing government intrusion and freeing up individual action and income. This approach, which was by no means widely accepted, still assumed that government actions have a significant impact on unemployment. The debate was over which kinds of policies the government should use.

Through these protracted debates, American society underwent a change in the perception of the relationship between politics, the national government, and the economy. At one time, it was presumed that unemployment was largely an individual failing. Now government action is viewed as the primary influence on levels of unemployment.[40]

worry about how social conditions are harmful to people, and government is now viewed as a possible creator of liberty. There are still those who stress the potential negative effects of a strong national government, but their ideas are not as dominant as they were fifty years ago.

The transition has not always been smooth. There was optimism in the positive impact of government during the 1960s. The experiences of Vietnam and Watergate, however, convinced many Americans that government and politicians were not to be trusted. These events resulted in a marked drop in trust in government during the 1970s. The 1980s, however, saw a resurgence of trust in government. There is no certainty what trends will emerge in the future, but the current pattern suggests that the levels of distrust are not as high now as they were fifteen years ago.

The Rise of Federal Programs: Grants-in-Aid, Mandates, and Federal Preemption

The result of all this debate about the impact of social conditions has been the enactment of federal legislation that establishes a wide range of programs intended to improve the environments of individuals. Such legislation has taken different approaches, all of which have affected the autonomy of states. In some cases, federal legislation has sought state participation in federal goals by providing grants-in-aid to support state efforts. In other cases the national government has mandated minimal state policies, often without providing any aid. Finally, in other cases, the federal government has preempted state action, or taken over responsibility for policies once handled by states.

In 1960, there were 132 federal grant-in-aid programs. By the late 1980s, there were 435 such programs.[41] Programs have focused on school lunches, preschool programs for children, medical benefits for the poor, community health programs, job training programs, low-income housing, aid for dependent children, the blind, access for the handicapped, and an endless number of other programs. All of these programs reflect a desire to help individuals and to improve their chances in life, while also trying to ensure that these chances are somewhat similar across the states.

These grant-in-aid programs define general national goals. If states agree to meet minimal standards, they receive federal assistance to support state efforts in these areas. States generally must provide some matching funds. As noted before, state interests are considered in defining what minimal standards must be met, and states have some ability to negotiate the terms of participation. Nonetheless, these programs do push states somewhat toward common national standards and do reduce state autonomy. Once a state becomes dependent on federal funds, it has difficulty walking away from those funds. States may also find that these programs create unexpected fiscal restraints. Many of these programs are "entitlement" programs, in which anyone who meets certain criteria (income below a certain level) is entitled to benefits. When recessions emerge, more people qualify, and states find themselves obligated to find the matching funds. While states initially choose to participate, involvement in such programs subsequently create constraints for states.

In other areas Congress and the President have chosen to impose mandates or minimal policies on states.[42] With this approach the federal government specifies some minimal policy that the states must meet. If states do not meet set minimal standards, national officials can intrude and impose their own standards. States are also free to impose more demanding standards. This approach has been relied upon to deal with many environmental concerns. It resulted in the Water Quality Act of 1965 and the Clean Water Act of 1977, along with several acts amending these laws. In other areas the federal government has entirely preempted the right of states to enact policy. This occurred, for example, with the Bus Regulatory Reform Act of 1982, which deregulated that industry and stipulated that there could be no state economic regulation of that industry. The federal government also sometimes mandates that states enact policies. The Equal Employment Opportunity Act of 1972 required that states comply with federal laws by enacting state equal-opportunity laws or face the threat of civil or criminal penalties.[43]

Most of this legislation was designed to shape state public policies that ultimately affect people. The increases in federal enactments reflect changes in public attitudes. We have changed from a society in which individual environments were not deemed relevant to individual success to a society in which environments are regarded as highly important. We have also become much more concerned with equality of opportunity. These two changes together create a logical justification for government policies that affect these environments and for policies that attempt to make the environments of individuals roughly comparable. Government is now perceived as more of a positive force than it was seventy years ago. All of these changes have resulted in more efforts to standardize social policies through centralization. Centralization is not so much desired as it is perceived as a means to achieve these goals.

These changes are dramatic when viewed over time, and they represent a profound transition in American thought. The changes also illustrate the vital importance of ideas in our society in affecting political structures and activity. We have changed our structure to reflect a changing consensus on the roles and impacts of society and government.

The Persisting Opposition

Despite all these changes, increasing the role of the national government has encountered significant opposition, and that opposition will continue. There are several sources of this opposition. First, restructuring the distribution of political authority in society changes winners and losers in politics. Those who stood to lose autonomy strongly opposed (and still oppose) such changes. Air and water polluters, business groups, and groups unsympathetic to minorities felt their chances of political success were greater at state and local levels and did not want to see conflicts resolved at the national level through uniform national policies.

Second, opponents have argued against uniform policies across the states because they believe problems are often unique. State and local officials know these problems better than anyone else and are also best equipped to respond to their own problems. They argue that centralized policies will destroy the ability of a federal system to be flexible in its response to varying state needs. This conflict has produced a great deal of argument that states should be given more autonomy to respond to problems. The argument is that national efforts should be restrained and should occur only after all else fails.

Third, some have opposed centralization for general philosophical reasons. Opponents feel a move toward a greater national role will create the potential for abuse of power. Conservatives tend to fear centralized power and believe in the virtues of diversity of response. Change and centralization have been generally opposed, and they will continue to be.

Fourth, opponents have opposed national programs because they believe they undermine individual initiative and cost too much money.[44] The administration of Ronald Reagan, in particular, felt that federal welfare programs were wasteful and counterproductive because of their effects on individual effort. Reagan consistently sought to reduce the amount of money devoted to such efforts and to grant states more autonomy in their practices.[45]

Finally, the late 1970s and the 1980s saw a general decline in the perception that government programs were achieving as much as they should. Arguments relying on this perception received more attention in the late 1970s and 1980s when the society already believed that taxes were too high. The sense was that many programs were wasteful and unnecessary. Many people also argued that major differences in the treatment that individuals received across the states had declined, so it was not as necessary for the national government to intervene in the affairs of state and local governments. Ronald Reagan appealed to all of these concerns in his election campaigns in 1980 and 1984. George Bush made similar arguments in 1988, but Reagan probably stands as the most articulate and most respected opponent of an activist national government.

Reagan was committed to the belief that centralized policy guidance restricts initiative in the states and indicates distrust of political jurisdictions (states and localities), which do not deserve such a judgement. His most sustained criticism was that this consolidation of power is an unwarranted and counterproductive intrusion into state and local prerogatives. His views stemmed from a belief that there is not as much inequality in America as many argue, and that the redistribution efforts of the last forty years have gone so far that they discourage private initiative.

Reagan reversed some of the prior centralization. He did this by reducing the state policy requirements attached to federal grants. He reduced the amount of federal aid to local governments. The amount of federal aid going directly to the local governments had already begun to decline, and Reagan pushed that trend along. He believed states themselves were best equipped to decide how money should be allocated, and he wanted funding to go directly to the state.[46] (The overall change is shown in Table 2.5, earlier in this chapter.) Reagan also reduced the extent of regulations imposed by federal bureaucrats. An example of this is provided in Table 2.7. This table shows the changes in funding and staffing for EPA (Environmental Protection Agency) activities from 1981 to 1984. The figures show a significant decline in funding and staffing in almost all areas by 1984. The changes did not occur simply because Reagan directed them. He proposed the changes to Congress and legislators enacted them because they sensed a decline in public support for federal regulatory activity. Similar changes took place in other areas, such as housing.

President Bush continued these efforts to give the states a major role in responding to policy problems. Early in his administration, he held a national conference on local education problems. His administration urged that the problems be addressed largely through state and local standards and that the financing come from state and local sources. He also held a national conference on the need to maintain and upgrade the "infrastructure" (roads, bridges, and tunnels) of the

Table 2.7

Reductions in Funding and Staffing for the Environmental Protection Agency 1981–1984

	1981	*1984*	*Percent Change 1981–1984*
Funding (in billions of dollars)			
Water quality	341	138	−59
Air quality	252	175	−31
Hazardous waste	151	100	−34
Toxic waste	100	61	−40
Staffing (number of employees)			
Water quality	2781	1663	−40
Air quality	1754	1351	−23
Hazardous waste	726	626	−14
Toxic waste	716	606	−15

Source: Paul Portney, "Natural Resources and the Environment," in John Palmer and Isabel Sawhill, The Reagan Record *(Cambridge: Ballinger, 1984), 148.*

society, but he again urged that state and localities play a major role in raising those funds. Like Reagan, Bush was not in favor of the national government taking on additional responsibilities.

Both Reagan and Bush wanted to restrain national efforts to impose new environmental regulations. Their attempts to ease environmental protection efforts, however, ran into some of the changing public views we have been discussing. Public opinion changes continually, and it had continued to change in this area. While Reagan wanted to drastically reduce efforts in this area, public opinion polls indicated rising support for such efforts. The rise in this support is shown in Figure 2.1. Faced with the clear emergence of a consensus in Congress in favor of strong environmental efforts, the Reagan administration ceased its efforts to cut environmental programs any further. The Bush administration recognized this shift of opinion and was more cautious in trying to ease environmental regulations.

The point of this example is that there is no inevitable drift toward greater national activism, and consensus is often difficult to detect. For a while politicians in Congress thought the consensus in favor of environmental protection efforts had collapsed. Reagan acted on that belief, but support subsequently clearly grew. Debates over the merits and demerits of centralization are likely to continue. People change their minds and change their assessments of the need for and efficacy of federal programs. The past trend of centralization is not destined to continue. Different eras are dominated by different ideas, and only time will indicate the subsequent drift.

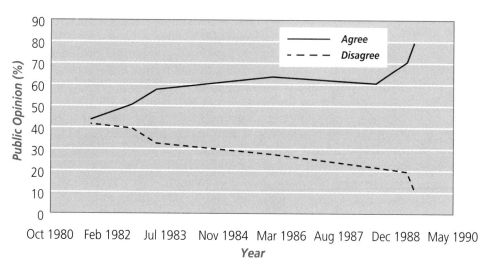

Question: *Do you agree or disagree with the following statement: Protecting the environment is so important that requirements and standards cannot be too high, and continuing improvements must be made regardless of cost.*

Figure 2.1

Public Opinion on Importance of Protecting the Environment, 1981–1989
Source: New York Times, *2 July 1989, A1.*

The Clinton administration suggests another turn in the role of the national government. In his campaign for the presidency, Clinton supported a more activist government. Once in office he soon discovered he had to adjust his priorities. The U.S. government was consistently running deficits of over $300 billion when he took office. This meant the government was spending more than it received in revenue, and having to borrow the difference. There was strong support in Congress for making deficit reduction a high priority. This led to efforts to lower spending and to increase taxes in order to reduce the deficit. The efforts to reduce spending left little money for new initiative to fund new programs. As a consequence, the Clinton administration has found that its primary means of having some impact on intergovernmental relations is to change federal regulations imposed on the states.

Centralization and the Courts

The changes in the economy and in attitudes, which we have just reviewed, have resulted in actions taken largely through Congress. When the economy changed, the public and politicians reacted to this change, sometimes with long lags. Congress enacted legislation that resulted in national standards for different policy areas. Gradual changes in public attitudes have also been registered through Congress.

Another major actor in this process of change has been the court system. The courts play the role of "umpire" in our political system. It is their responsibility to rule on disputes brought to the courts about the rights of the federal government to intervene in state policy. Despite some eras of resistance, over the long run the courts have accepted the general trend toward a greater role for national government. The Supreme Court has been very important in this trend because, as the highest court in the country, its decision to accept or confirm a change toward national intervention gives that change legitimacy.

Opinions on the Supreme Court do not always coincide with political changes. Sometimes the Court lags behind the political action of the federal government, and at other times the Court leads.[47] The members of the Court may lag behind because they are appointees from prior administrations and were chosen because they had a record of relatively liberal or conservative rulings. The individual views of the justices may also diverge because their views evolve while they are on the court. Sometimes their views reflect ideas from a prior era. At other times their views run ahead of current dominant views in the society.

In the 1930s, the Supreme Court was composed of justices with the average birth year of 1864. When Roosevelt proposed increased federal action in society, the Court nullified his proposals. It was only through a threat of "packing" the Court (adding more justices to raise the total beyond nine) that members of the Court eventually changed their minds and ratified some of his policies.

Another area where the Supreme Court was reluctant to intervene was in apportionment problems in the states. In many states, the voting districts for state legislatures had been drawn up in the early 1900s. As the population moved from rural to urban areas, a situation developed where some districts held ten times as many constituents as other districts. This led to court suits that claimed that urban areas were being underrepresented. Even though these problems of representation began around 1900, the Court was unwilling to intervene and impose national standards of population per district until the 1960s. The Court then ruled that states had to have equal population in legislative districts (the "one man–one vote" rule). This ruling required massive reapportionment in the states.

In other areas the courts have led public opinion. In the famous 1954 *Brown v. Board of Education* case, the Supreme Court ruled that separate but equal educational facilities for blacks and whites were unconstitutional. This opinion, favoring national rights in this area, was far ahead of public opinion in the country.

While the Supreme Court sometimes lags and sometimes leads changes in the role of the national government, over the long run the Court has generally been respectful of policy decisions made through the federalist political process. The Court's current view on this is perhaps best expressed in their decision on *Garcia v. San Antonio Transit Authority*.[48] In this case, the issue was whether Congress could impose federal wage and hour regulations on a local government. The Court ruled this could be done. The Court also stated it was not appropriate for the Court to assess each federal intrusion to decide if it is allowed within the federal arrangement. The Court argued that

> the states' continued role in the federal system is primarily guaranteed not by any externally imposed limits on the commerce power, but by the structure of the federal government itself. . . . The political process ensures that laws that unduly burden the states will not be promulgated.[49]

The logic of the Court was that states use their political representation to fight imposed policy rules. If that political process results in a shift of policy authority from the states to the national government, then that shift should be accepted as a legitimate political choice. The decision drew considerable criticism because many people do not accept the notion that federalism is a flexible political representation system that leads policy wherever the political consensus leads. There is still considerable support for the idea that federalism is a fixed distribution of responsibilities.[50]

While the role of the courts is important, it is also important to recognize that not all court decisions have a binding effect on state and local policies. Federalism is a system in which most policy administration takes place at the state and local level. Control over administration means that state and, particularly, local governments can pursue their own priorities and not honor a court ruling. This ability limits the significance of court rulings. Recognition of this possibility also makes the courts reluctant to intrude in too many areas where they suspect their rulings will be ignored and respect for the courts and the law eroded.

Almost forty years have passed since the courts ruled that integration of schools must proceed with "deliberate speed." That integration has not been achieved because many local jurisdictions have resisted it. It is also the case that the courts cannot control population mobility patterns, which affect where whites and blacks live. Many whites have moved to suburbs. This mobility pattern has resulted in higher concentrations of black students in city schools and white students in suburban schools, creating segregated school systems. The courts have been very reluctant to try to influence these mobility patterns. In the 1950s the courts also ruled that official school prayer was unconstitutional. Yet studies in the 1980s showed that school prayer was still widespread in many areas of the country, particularly the South. Finally, the courts have ruled that women have a right to abortions. Despite that ruling, the availability of abortion varies tremendously across the country. Figure 2.2 indicates differences in the availability of abortions across the states. In some states abortion is widely available. Women in other states, however, must leave the state to obtain abortion. [51] Local doctors, hospitals, and clinics ultimately make the decision about whether abortion will be available, and many of them have been very restrictive about this right. The Supreme Court justices may rule on what the law is, but that "law" may not apply to everyone.

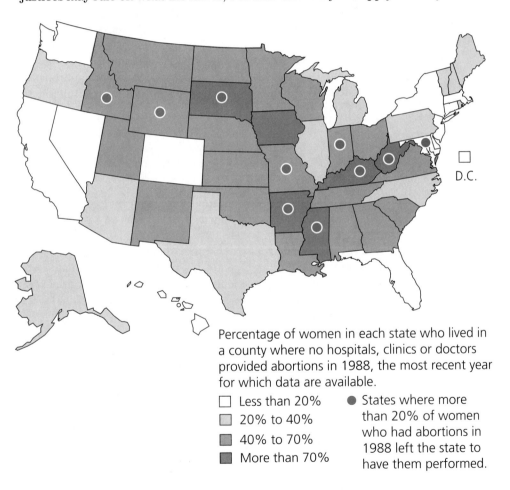

Percentage of women in each state who lived in a county where no hospitals, clinics or doctors provided abortions in 1988, the most recent year for which data are available.

☐ Less than 20%
☐ 20% to 40%
■ 40% to 70%
■ More than 70%

● States where more than 20% of women who had abortions in 1988 left the state to have them performed.

Figure 2.2
Abortions: Legal but Less Available
Source: *New York Times, 15 March 1992, p.18*

The Resulting Position of the States

Although there has been a gradual increase in national intrusion in our society, it is crucial to understand that state and local governments are still very important parts of our political system. Their autonomy is less than in 1800, or 1900, or 1930, but their importance as bases for representation, as implementors of federal policy, and as independent creators of policy is still considerable within the federal system.

On one hand, states are now more dependent on federal aid. There are more federal regulations now than there were thirty years ago. On the other hand, states remain the place where legislators get elected to Congress. State and local majorities are the bases from which representatives make "national" policy. Representatives face strong incentives to enact permissive policy requirements for the states and to set up the implementation of policies such that implementation is left in the hands of state officials. Representatives are also reluctant to have the national government intrude on certain areas of state and local policy, with the result that the states are largely autonomous in those areas.

It is very difficult to present a simple image of the degree to which the states remain significant and independent in the federal system. A general idea of this emerges from examining the data shown in Table 2.8. This table shows the relative importance (measured by expenditure) of certain government activities in our society and the levels of government responsible for them.

The left side of the table lists the major government program areas that involve expenditure. The first column of figures shows the total amount of expenditure by all levels of government in each area. The next two columns show the proportion of expenditure by the federal government and by the state and local governments combined. Expenditure is classified by the level of government that finally delivers the service, not the level of government that initially raises the money. This classification is important because for some programs, such as welfare, the federal government raises and distributes to the states a considerable proportion of the funds, but state and local governments ultimately spend the money and "deliver" the service. As these figures show, the federal government has primary responsibility for national defense matters, natural resource programs, and housing and urban renewal. In all other areas, the primary responsibility lies with state and local governments. The last column indicates the extent to which federal funds are the sources of state and local expenditures. These figures also show that for most programs, the primary source of funds is the revenue raised by state and local governments.

The point is simple but important. While national influence has increased, and while national policy debates draw most of our attention, state and local governments remain fundamental components (some would say the foundation) of our political system. State and local governments still have considerable autonomy. This fact alone (in addition to any simple curiosity you might have) is sufficient to justify studying the workings of state and local political processes. It is to the workings of these processes that we now turn.

Table 2.8

Relative Responsibility for Certain Domestic Expenditures by Level of Government 1990 Fiscal Year

Policy Area	Total Expenditure (in billions of dollars)	Spent by Federal (%)	Spent by State–Local (%)	State–Local Expenditure from Federal Aid (%)
National defense	344	100.0	—	—
Postal service	39	100.0	—	—
Local and higher education	306	–0–	100.0	7.9
Public welfare	141	23.7	76.3	54.7
Hospitals	59	14.3	83.7	0.1
Health	34	27.7	72.3	26.5
Highways	62	1.4	98.6	23.3
Air transportation	11	41.0	59.0	18.6
Fire	13	—	100.0	–0–
Police	36	14.8	85.2	1.1
Corrections	26	6.1	93.9	0.5
Natural resources	81	84.8	15.2	17.9
Parks and recreation	16	10.5	89.5	0.5
Housing and community development	32	52.3	47.7	79.6

Source: Government Finances, 1989–90 *(Washington, DC, 1991), GF-90-5, tables 8 and 10.*

For Further Reading

Advisory Commission on Intergovernmental Relations. *The Condition of Contemporary Federalism: Conflicting Theories and Collapsing Constraints*, A-78. Washington, DC, August 1981.

Advisory Commission on Intergovernmental Relations. *State and Local Roles in the Federal System*, A-88. Washington, DC, April 1982.

Advisory Commission on Intergovernmental Relations. *The Transformation in American Politics: Implications for Federalism*, A-106. Washington, DC, August 1986.

Anton, Thomas J. *American Federalism and Public Policy: How the System Works.* New York: Random House, 1989.

Dilger, Robert Jay. *National Intergovernmental Programs.* Englewood Cliffs: Prentice–Hall, 1989.

Elazar, Daniel. *American Federalism: A View from the States.* 3d ed. New York: Harper and Row, 1984.

Henig, Jeffrey R. *Public Policy and Federalism.* New York: St. Martin's, 1985.

Kelley, E. W. *Policy and Politics in the United States: The Limits of Localism.* Philadelphia: Temple University Press, 1987.

Ketcham, Ralph. *The AntiFederalist Papers and the Constitutional Convention Debates.* New York: Mentor, 1986.

Kramnick, Isaac, ed. *The Federalist Papers.* New York: Penguin, 1987.

Wood, Gordon. *The Creation of The American Republic, 1776–1787.* New York: W. W. Norton, 1972.

Suggestions for Analysis in Your Own State and Locality

The State's Position in Congress

1. Does your state have particular concerns that become important when national policies are adopted? Are there specific industries or economic sectors that are more important than others within the state?

2. Do Representatives and Senators from your state generally have liberal or conservative voting records in Congress? *Congressional Quarterly* and *The Almanac of American Politics* publish interest group ratings of legislators, which you can use to assess voting records.

The State's Relationship with the Federal Government

3. Are there federal policies that are particularly important to your state?

4. How much federal aid does your state receive? What proportion of the total state budget comes from this source? How much federal aid do local governments in your area receive? What kinds of programs receive the greatest support?

5. For many federally supported programs, states have the option to choose the extent to which they will participate. What has your state chosen to do about program options with the Medicaid program? What has your state chosen to do about environmental enforcement efforts, and how much federal assistance does the state get to support these efforts? To support other policy areas?

6. Are there controversies within the state about the level of support the state gives certain programs? For example, do some groups want more state support for Medicaid, and do other groups want less support?

Notes

[1] Michael deCourcy Hinds, "U.S. Adds Programs with Little Review of Local Burdens," *New York Times*, 24 March 1992, sec. A1.

[2] For a good review of this era, see *The Federalist Papers* ed. Isaac Kramnick (New York: Penguin, 1987), 11–82.

[3] A history of this situation is provided by Gordon S. Wood, *The Creation of the American Republic, 1776–1787* (Chapel Hill: University of North Carolina Press, 1969).

[4] Charles L. Mee, *The Genius of the People* (New York: Harper and Row, 1987), provides a lively account of the convention.

[5] John P. Roche, "The Founding Fathers: A Reform Caucus in Action," *American Political Science Review* no. 4 (December, 1961); 799–816. These multiple goals in the construction of federalism are also presented by Martin Diamond, "What the Framers Meant by Federalism," in R.A. Goldwin, *A Nation of States*, 2nd ed. (Chicago: Rand McNally, 1974), 25–42; William S. Livingston, "A Note on the Nature of Federalism," in Aaron Wildavsky, *American Federalism in Perspective* (Boston: Little, Brown, 1967), 33–50; and Martin Diamond, "The Ends of Federalism," *Publius* 3, no. 2 (fall 1973), 129–52.

[6] For arguments that members of Congress focus on local concerns to the exclusion of "larger" concerns, see David R. Mayhew, *Congress: The Electoral Connection* (New Haven: Yale University Press, 1974); and Morris Fiorina, *Congress: Keystone to the Washington Establishment*, 2d ed., (New Haven: Yale University Press, 1989).

[7] Samuel Eldersveld, *Political Parties in American Society* (New York: Basic Books, 1982), 91–157; Malcolm E. Jewell and David M. Olson, *Political Parties and Elections in American States*, 3d ed. (Chicago: The Dorsey Press, 1988); and David R. Mayhew, *Placing Parties in American Politics* (Princeton: Princeton University Press, 1986).

[8] Frank J. Sorauf, *Inside Campaign Finance* (New Haven: Yale University Press, 1992), 46–48.

[9] Donald E. Stokes, "Parties and the Nationalization of Electoral Forces," *The American Party Systems*, eds. William N. Chambers and Walter D. Burnham (New York: Oxford University Press, 1967); William Claggett, William Flanigan, and Nancy Zingale, "The Nationalization of the American Electorate," *American Political Science Review* 78 (1984):77–91; and Sadafumi Kawato, "Nationalization and Partisan Realignment in Congressional Elections," *American Political Science Review 81*, no. 4 (December 1987): 1235–50.

[10] Morton Grodzins, *The American System* (Chicago: University of Chicago, 1966), 249–52.

[11] Richard Conniff, "Federal Lands," *National Geographic* 185, no. 2 (February 1994), 2–39. A map is included for those who wish to gain some idea of the magnitude of the land owned by the federal government.

[12] Gerald C. Wright, Robert S. Erikson, and John D. McIver, "Measuring State Party Identification and Ideology Using Survey Data," *Journal of Politics 47*, (May 1985): 445.

[13] Charles Jones, *Clean Air*, (Pittsburgh: University of Pittsburgh Press, 1975).

[14] Jeffrey Pressman, *Federal Programs and City Politics*, (Berkeley: University of California Press, 1975), chap. 5.

[15] Earl Black and Merle Black, *Politics and Society in the South* (Cambridge: Harvard University Press, 1987), 135.

[16] Martha Derthick, *The Influence of Federal Grants* (Cambridge: Harvard University Press, 1970), 71.

[17] Ibid., 193–218.

[18] Morton Grodzins, *The American System* (Chicago: University of Chicago, 1966), 19–57; Deil Wright, *Understanding Intergovernmental Relations.* 2d ed., (Monterey, California: Brooks/Cole, 1982), chap. 3.

[19] Donald F. Kettl, *The Regulation of American Federalism* (Baltimore: Johns Hopkins University Press, 1983).

[20] Advisory Commission on Intergovernmental Relations, *Federal Statutory Preemption of State and Local Authority: History, Inventory, and Issues* (Washington, DC, September 1992), A–121.

[21] Samuel Beer, "The Modernization of American Federalism," *Publius* 3, no. 2 (fall 1973): 49–96; and Robert H. Wiebe, *The Search for Order, 1877–1920.* (New York: Hill and Wang, 1967).

[22] Paul E. Peterson, *City Limits* (Chicago: University of Chicago Press, 1981).

[23] An excellent study of how the roles of government changed in the area of pollution is Charles Jones, *Clean Air* (Pittsburgh: University of Pittsburgh Press, 1975).

[24] Deil Wright, *Understanding Intergovernmental Relations* 2d ed. (Monterey, California: Brooks/Cole, 1982), 11.

[25] This section draws on the ideas of Robert Wuthnow, *The Consciousness Reformation* (Berkeley: University of California Press, 1976), 82–135.

[26] James Turner, *Without God, Without Creed: The Origins of Unbelief in America* (Baltimore: Johns Hopkins University Press, 1985).

[27] Daniel Elazar, *The American Partnership* (Chicago: University of Chicago, 1962); and Frank Bourgin, *The Great Challenge: The Myth of Laissez–Faire in the Early Republic* (New York: Harper and Row, Perennial Library, 1989).

[28] Gary Wills, *Lincoln at Gettysburg: The Words that Remade America* (New York: Simon and Schuster, 1992).

[29] J. R. Pole, *The Pursuit of Equality in American History* (Berkeley: University of California Press, 1978), 112–78.

[30] On the extent of the crisis, see Robert Higgs, "The Great Depression: 'An Emergency More Serious Than War,'" in Robert Higgs, *Crisis and Leviathan: Critical Episodes in the Growth of American Government* (New York: Oxford, 1987), 159–195. On changing ideas of the role of government in the economy, see Walter S. Salant, "The Spread of Keynesian Doctrines and Practices in the United States," in *The Political Power of Economic Ideas,* ed. Peter A. Hall (Princeton: Princeton University Press), 87–106; and Peter A. Gourevitch, "Keynesian Economic: The Political Sources of Economic Policy Choices," in *The Political Power of Economic Ideas,* ed. Peter A. Hall (Princeton: Princeton University Press), 27–51.

[31] Walter I. Trattner, *From Poor Law to Welfare State: A History of Social Welfare in America,* 4th ed. (New York: The Free Press, 1989).

[32] A good review of the civil rights movement is provided by Robert Weisbrot, *Freedom Bound: A History of America's Civil Rights Movement* (New York: Penguin, Plume Books, 1991).

[33] For a summary of these arguments, see John Agnew, *Place and Politics* (London: Allen and Unwin, 1987), 62–107.

[34] Advisory Commission on Intergovernmental Relations, "Regional Economic Convergence and the Geographic Dispersion of Economic Activity," in *Regional Growth: Historic Perspectives* (Washington, DC, 1981), 9–30.

[35] Advisory Commission on Intergovernmental Relations, "Mass Media, National Politics: Political Communication and American Federalism," in *The Transformation of American Politics,* (Washington, DC, 1986), 163–205.

[36] See Agnew, *Place and Politics,* 62–107.

[37] Arthur Schlesinger, Jr., *The Coming of the New Deal* (Boston: Houghton Mifflin, 1959).

[38] John Maynard Keynes, *The General Theory of Employment, Interest, and Income* (London: Harcourt, Brace, and World, 1936).

[39] Stephen K. Bailey, *Congress Makes a Law: The Story Behind the Employment Act of 1946* (New York: Columbia University Press, 1950).

[40] For a review of relationships between politics and the economy, see Douglas Hibbs, *The American Political Economy: Macroeconomics and Electoral Politics* (Cambridge: Harvard University Press, 1987), 213–326.

[41] Robert J. Dilger, *National Intergovernmental Programs* (Englewood Cliffs, N.J.: Prentice–Hall, 1989), 7.

[42] For a history of federal actions in preemption, see Joseph F. Zimmerman, *Federal Preemption: The Silent Revolution* (Ames: Iowa State University Press, 1991).

[43] U.S. Advisory Commission on Intergovernmental Relations, *Federal Statutory Preemption of State and Local Authority: History, Inventory, and Issues* (Washington, DC, September 1992), A–121.

[44] Charles Murray, *Losing Ground: American Social Policy, 1950–1980.* (New York: Basic, 1984). For a view opposing Murray's, see John E. Schwarz, *America's Hidden Success: A Reassessment of Public Policy from Kennedy to Reagan,* revised. (New York: Norton, 1988).

[45] Richard P. Nathan, Fred C. Doolittle, and associates, *Reagan and the States* (Princeton: Princeton University Press: 1987).

[46] Jeffrey M. Stonecash, "State Responses to Declining National Support: Behavior in the Post–1978 Era," *Policy Studies Journal*, 18, no. 3 (spring 1990), 214–26.

[47] William Mishler and Reginald S. Sheehan, "The Supreme Court as a Countermajoritian Institution: The Impact of Public Opinion on Supreme Court Decisions," *American Political Science Review* 87, no. 1, (March 1993), 87–101.

[48] *Garcia v. San Antonio Metropolitan Transit Authority*, 469 US 528 (1985).

[49] Advisory Commission on Intergovernmental Relations, *Reflections on Garcia and Its Implications for Federalism*, (Washington, DC, 1986), 3–4.

[50] See the criticism contained in John C. Pittenger, "Garcia and the Political Safeguards of Federalism," *Publius* 22, no. 1, (winter 1992), 1–19.

[51] "Hurdles Increasing for Women Seeking Abortion," *New York Times*, 15 March 1992, A1 and A18.

Political Conflict and Representation

Democracy entails a commitment to having the concerns and the needs of the public play a fundamental role in determining public policy. The faith and hope of a democracy is that if people feel their concerns are represented and listened to, they will be more likely to accept the decisions made. They will accept the political process as legitimate.

Achieving representation, however, is not a simple matter. It is not always easy to find out what the public wants. There are also differences of opinion about what we should be trying to represent. People differ in their opinions about the conflict in society. Some people believe there is a public interest, which unites all of us, while others believe there are inherent fundamental differences in society.

These presumptions about the extent of conflict also affect people's notions about the way the representation process should work. There is little disagreement in American politics that representation should take place. The issue is whether to presume conflict and rely on mechanisms of representation that bring out differences, or to presume some sort of unity and rely on mechanisms that emphasize the expression of general concerns. Those who presume that conflicts exist and that a democracy must represent those conflicts place a strong emphasis on the importance of political parties. These people, like V. O. Key, see parties as mechanisms to bring differences of opinion to the political arena for discussion and debate. Given the presumption that conflicts exist, interest groups and lobbyists become another important and legitimate means to make sure the specific concerns of groups are represented.

Those who presume a public interest are much less positive about political parties and special-interest groups. They see such mechanisms as self-serving. They see interest groups as focused on narrow interests and unconcerned about the larger needs of society. They think party politicians distort public debates because party leaders are preoccupied with criticizing the opposing party and claiming the superiority of their own policy proposals. These critics distrust parties. They stress other routes of public expression, such as non-partisan elections, public referenda, and the right of citizens to use the initiative process to get items on the ballot. Their concern is to bring out general views and to reduce the extent to which that commonality is fractured by smaller conflicts.

Finally, understanding debates about the way politics should work is made difficult (and challenging) because people often use and exploit the above arguments to serve their own self-interest. A lobbyist may support the initiative and referendum process, for example, because he or she thinks this means of making decisions will best serve the interests of his or her group. The argument he or she makes for this approach, however, will focus on the way the overall process will be improved. It is publicly damaging to indicate that the reason for support of a particular political process is simple self-interest. The existence of these "hidden" motives makes disentangling the debates about the way representation should take place very complex. It is not always clear whether a group's argument for an approach is because of a general conviction that it will be good for democracy or because the members think it will serve their own self-interests. It is always worth considering that there may be concealed motives for supporting a change in the political process.

But what difference does it make whether strong political parties exist? Whose interests are served by having strong or weak parties? What difference does it make if referenda are relied on to make decisions? Who participates in politics and what difference does this make? The representation process exists to convey the concerns and needs of citizens to their public officials. The important question in this section is whether this process is neutral in conveying opinions, or whether different arrangements affect whose interests receive more attention.

As discussed in Chapter 1, a primary concern in this text is the way different political practices affect whose interests get greater representation. If we assume a consensus exists in society, we might ask how different arrangements improve the representation of that consensus. But the presumption of this text is that conflict is extensive in American politics. The initial concern, therefore, is to outline the primary conflicts that dominate state and local politics. These conflicts revolve around differences in economic situations, conflicts among communities, and disputes about the role that state governments should play relative to local governments in responding to problems. Many of these issues involve conflicts between the haves and the have-nots. Given these conflicts, the main issue is whether the representation process favors the concerns of the haves or have-nots.

This section focuses on the way these means of representation benefit the haves and have-nots. The chapters in this section review the sources of conflict in society and the main ways in which representation takes place: political parties, individual participation, and interest groups. Chapters 5 through 7 review the debate about what role political mechanisms should play, then discuss what we know about the way each of these mechanisms contributes to representation, and, finally, assess the effects of each mechanism.

After reviewing the separate means of representation in Chapters 5 through 7, in Chapter 8 we will discuss the impact of combinations of conditions and the ways these combinations affect representation.

3

The Sources of Political Conflict

PREVIEW

Conflict originates because people differ. They differ in income level and in their beliefs about the values society should support and the policies government should adopt. They form attachments to groups. People identify with others of their race, gender, sexual preference, heritage, and occupation, and they clash with others who are not sympathetic to their group. They identify with the area they live in and its population, and they see themselves as in conflict with those in other areas (central city versus suburb, rural areas versus urban areas, or downstate versus upstate).

Mobility in and out of areas and states also generates conflict. Movement erodes tax bases in some areas and creates new demands in other areas. Changes in federal aid programs and new ideas prompt new conflicts. This chapter discusses all of these potential sources of conflict.

Conflict: The Driving Force of Politics

Politics exists because conflict exists. Democratic political processes are a means to mediate conflict arising from the variety of values and interests within society. People continually attempt to protect their interests and to impose their values while, at the same time, attempting to deny such action to others. For example, those opposed to abortion believe it is wrong to legitimize abortion by legalizing it and using government funds to pay for abortion counseling and abortion services. Those in favor of the right to abortion want the government to guarantee that right. Many proponents also believe that the government should provide funds that would allow low-income women equal access to abortions.

Such conflicts are pervasive. Environmentalists want laws imposing deposits on returnable bottles so people will be motivated to return them. Beverage industries oppose such measures because they believe "bottle laws" will make their products more expensive, thus decreasing sales. Companies and labor groups producing glass bottles also oppose such measures on the grounds that bottle laws will result in less demand for new bottles and will necessitate job cuts. Again, politics is the means for resolving this conflict.

These conflicts derive from multiple sources. People differ in the values instilled during their upbringing, in their economic situations, in the neighborhoods they live in, and in many other ways. These differences cluster into group differences and form the bases for enduring group conflicts. Blacks have suffered social, racial, and economic discrimination and, consequently, are poorer (on average) than the rest of the population. As a result, blacks as a group tend to favor programs that use public resources to increase their opportunities and provide some redistributive benefits. Conversely, business executives, who often earn large salaries, tend to oppose redistributive taxes and programs. Suburban residents are generally (though not entirely) white and of higher income levels than central city residents. Residents of the two areas consistently have different interests and can be expected to support opposite sides of many policy issues.

State and local communities are complex collections of different values and interests. These differences are the raw material, the grist, of state and local politics. Differences may be explicit, or they may be dormant, waiting for some event to serve as a catalyst to bring the conflict to the surface. These conflicts shape the politics of every state and community. They also affect the kind of political process engaged in, the kinds of issues that persist year after year, the nature of partisan divisions, and the kinds of policies adopted.

Not all potential conflicts however, become actual conflicts. While some might support a policy and others oppose it, sometimes these differences do not result in political divisions.[1] Individuals may have other pressures that pull them in other directions and leave them ambivalent about certain issues. The political process may end up repressing or ignoring a certain issue.[2] The factors that *limit* conflict should be examined as closely as the sources of conflict.

This chapter focuses on the primary differences in the ways and extent to which groups differ, the reasons for these differences, and the ways these differences create or affect political conflict.

Individual Situations as Sources of Conflict

Economic Position and Self-Interest

Economic situations have a major impact on individual political interests. People who earn more money are generally concerned with keeping it. People who do not earn much are often concerned about receiving some assistance from the government. The issues that are important here are fundamental and persistent in politics: How much income does an individual have a right to keep? How much will the government collect to distribute to other people? For what purposes will tax revenue be used? The questions of taxation levels and the uses of the resulting revenue are inseparable.

The general pattern is that individuals with higher incomes would prefer to pay less in taxes and usually favor cutting the level of taxation. Public opinion polls have regularly shown strong support among upper-income groups for lower taxes. The result is that politicians can generally assume (with some qualifications to be noted shortly) that proposals for increases in taxes will receive less support from upper-income constituents.

Income levels also affect attitudes toward progressive taxes. A progressive tax is one in which the proportion of income paid in taxes increases for higher-income brackets. This means that upper-income individuals not only pay a higher *total amount* of taxes (because they have more income to be taxed), but they also pay a higher *proportion* of their income in taxes. Progressive taxes are not strongly supported by higher-income groups. Many upper-income individuals prefer to have proportional taxes, a tax that takes the same proportion of income from everyone. Table 3.1 shows the opinions of different income groups about proportional taxes. Opposition to a proportional tax is greatest among those with lower incomes. Those who make less money clearly regard this tax as unfair. Politicians can usually anticipate more support for a proportional tax among upper-income groups, and much opposition to such a tax among lower-income groups.

Economic situations also affect attitudes toward government attempts to help low-income individuals. As discussed in Chapter 2, individualism has been, and is,

Table 3.1

Economic Status and Political Opinion on Proportional Taxes

Yearly Income Level (in dollars)	Favor (%)	Oppose (%)	No Opinion (%)
0–7,500	19	70	11
7,501 15,000	32	65	3
15,001–25,000	35	61	4
25,001–35,000	38	56	6
35,001 +	48	49	3

Source: Louis Harris poll, 21 September 1981.

a strongly held belief among Americans. Many individuals interpret individualism to mean that each person has an obligation to resolve his or her own economic problems and that government should not be heavily involved in assistance to low-income individuals. In this view, government should provide only minimal services in order to encourage individuals to achieve what they can. Not surprisingly, attitudes toward individualism and government programs for lower-income groups are shaped by a person's own economic achievement. The more a person has achieved, the greater the tendency to believe that others are capable of doing the same.

The association between ecomomic situation and attitudes toward government programs to help the poor can be seen in Table 3.2. The top part of the table shows the breakdown of individual responses to a question concerning government efforts to help the poor. Responses are presented by income levels. Prosperous people were less likely to believe that the government should do more, while the poor were much more likely to think so.

Table 3.2

Economic Situation and General Attitudes toward Government Programs for the Poor

Question: Do you think the government should do more to improve the conditions of the poor; that the government is doing about the right amount; or the the government has already done more for poor people than is good for them? [a]

Economic Situation	Do More (%)	Right Amount (%)	Too Much (%)	No Opinion (%)
Prosperous	28	42	23	7
Upper middle	35	38	20	7
Lower middle	44	36	12	8
Poor	57	27	7	9

Subjective Social Class and Support for Increased Funding of Specific Government Programs [b]

	Subjective Social Class		
Program	Working (%)	Middle (%)	Upper Middle (%)
Student loans	39	27	15
Food stamps	27	18	13
Child care	62	55	49
Elderly	83	72	68
Homeless	72	64	54

Source: [a] *Erickson et. al.* American Public Opinion *(New York: Macmillan, 1980), 154.*
[b] *Erickson et. al.* American Public Opinion *(New York: Macmillan, 1991), 170.*

Differences in opinions about specific programs are also linked to class. The second part of the table shows the percent of approval of increased spending on specific government programs, broken down by class identifications. Each of the programs listed provides more benefits to working-class individuals than to upper middle–income individuals. The support for each of these programs is greater among the working class than among more affluent groups.

The general attitude towards assisting the poor, reflected in Table 3.2, has implications for a large number of government programs. Upper-income groups tend to be less supportive than lower-income groups of a broad array of government programs. Upper-income individuals usually do not favor food-stamp programs, government subsidies for public housing, welfare payments, government subsidies of utility bills and insulation expenses, or government-subsidized day-care programs for low-income parents. Support for these programs is much higher among lower-income individuals.

Much of this pattern is due to simple self-interest. Those who benefit from these programs tend to favor them, and those who pay for the programs tend to oppose them. Immediate self-interest however, is not the only source of opposition. Those in higher income brackets often believe that effort and productivity should not be discouraged by excessive taxation or by providing too many benefits to those with low incomes. Those with low incomes disagree with this argument on the grounds that their incomes do not reflect a lack of effort. They argue that the number of economic opportunities available to individuals varies and that those with fewer opportunities tend to earn lower incomes. These different attitudes about government programs create political conflict. Since states and communities are composed of diverse income groups, there are continuing conflicts about what public policies to support.

Some Caution about the Effects of Economic Position

Political dispositions and attitudes are a product of more than our economic status. We are much more complicated creatures than that. First of all, many people do not define their status in life by their income level. Many people see themselves as middle class even though we might not define them as that based on their income level. Table 3.3 presents how people define themselves in terms of class. The table also presents the actual distribution of families by income groups. Even though there are significant differences in the actual distribution of income, most people identify themselves as middle class. This tendency for most people to see themselves as middle class has prevailed for several decades in the United States.[3] The consequence is that many people with relatively low incomes do not take positions that we associate with the lower class. Some relatively poor individuals are adamant defenders of individualism because they see themselves as middle class and believe they became so through individual effort. This tendency means that a potential class conflict might never become an actual conflict to the extent we might expect.[4]

It is also the case that many people do not assess policies in terms of how they will benefit from them, but on the basis of their perception of whether those policies will be good for society at large. Individuals in difficult economic situations

Table 3.3

Subjective Social Class versus Income Distributions

Social Class	Self-Definition (%)	Income Brackets	U.S. Families (%)
Upper	1	$100,000 plus	5.4
Upper middle	14	$50–$99,999	25.1
Middle	57	$25–$49,999	36.3
Lower middle	21	$15–$24,999	6.4
Lower	5	Under $15,000	16.8

Source: Derived from Census Bureau and Roper Poll, Newsweek, *2 March 1992, 34.*

may believe they are responsible for their difficulties and not be critical of government policies that do not do much for them. Other individuals might be doing well economically but see an increase in unemployment as the fault of government. They also may believe that government should be responsible for the collective good of society and, therefore, may be critical of government policies that do not address unemployment. Individual beliefs play an enormous role in affecting reactions to government policy.[5]

Individuals are also affected by educational and cultural experiences. These experiences produce reactions that temper how they react to economic situations. Education does not totally change people (ask any frustrated teacher), but the cumulative experience of education does affect the way people see the world. Education seems to increase appreciation for the complexity of life and awareness of the differences between individuals. As a result, education can lead to greater tolerance for the rights and ways of life of others.

The significance of this for politics is that individuals with more education are more likely to be liberal on what we call "social issues." Social issues involve the rights of others to choose their own values and beliefs. An indication of the impact of education is illustrated in Table 3.4, which shows the relationship between education level and "cultural intolerance." In this case, the index is a reflection of

Table 3.4

Education and Cultural Intolerance

Education Level	Cultural Intolerance (%)
Eighth grade	52
High school	39
Some college	28
College graduate	12

Source: Robert S. Erickson, Norman R. Luttbeg, and Kent L. Tedin, American Public Opinion, *4th ed. (New York: Macmillan, 1991), 197.*

unwillingness to allow expression of minority views, or of hostility toward allowing people to demonstrate in opposition of government policies.

Education generally makes individuals more liberal on tolerance issues.[6] People with higher education levels are more likely to support children's rights, gay rights, civil rights, abortion rights and the right to free speech. They are also more likely to oppose censorship laws and to support freedom-of-information laws. Education also affects attitudes toward the Equal Rights Amendment (ERA). This proposed amendment to the U.S. Constitution would have prohibited discrimination against people on the basis of sex. Those with higher education were much more supportive of the amendment. The variation in support by education for the issues of abortion and the ERA are shown in Table 3.5.

The impact of education also extends to areas of politics where understanding complex, often technical, issues is important. For example, it is often argued that support for environmental politics is based on middle-class desires to emphasize aesthetic standards to the exclusion of concerns about jobs and productivity. Although that may be partly true, support for restrictions on environmental abuse also stems from recognition of the ways in which chemicals and pollution interact to harm our environment, damage our health, and threaten future populations. Understanding of such complex issues is also furthered by education, and individuals with higher education levels tend to lend greater support to laws that protect the environment.

Cross-Pressures and Political Conflict

All of these differences among people might emerge as political conflicts. By compiling a profile of any state or community, we can gain an idea of the possible conflicts in that area. The larger the proportion of lower-income individuals, the more likely that state is to have conflict over redistributive policies. The larger the proportion of blacks, the more conflict there is likely to be about racial issues.

The emergence of actual issue conflict, however, is much more complicated than that. Each of us is a product of diverse experiences, and some of those

Table 3.5
Education and Support for Abortion and the ERA

| Education | Abortion | | ERA | |
| | Favor | Oppose | Favor | Oppose |
Level	(%)	(%)	(%)	(%)
Eighth grade	31	57	44	51
High school	37	53	51	43
College	58	34	55	43

Sources: Abortion attitudes from Gallup Opinion Index, no. 56 (December 1969), 19; ERA attitudes from Louis Harris Poll, 17 August 1981.

experiences are likely to have had conflicting impacts on our attitudes. Consider the impacts of education and income, for example. Higher incomes tend to make people more conservative and less willing to support redistributive programs. Individuals with higher incomes, though, also tend to have had more education, and this is likely to have an opposite effect on attitudes about redistribution. Education tends to create an awareness of the importance of early family background and the opportunities for later success a good background can offer. This awareness tends to make individuals with higher education levels more sympathetic toward policies attempting to provide those same opportunities to lower-income individuals. The interaction of family income and individual education level is shown in Table 3.6. The figures shown represent the proportion of individuals in favor of providing government aid to minorities. The table suggests how political attitudes can be affected by cross-pressures.

The results of this table should be read across single rows or down single columns. When row results are read, they show the effects of increases in education for those of the same income level. If column results are read, they show the effects of increases in income for those at the same education level.

Within any row, the results show that those with some college education are more supportive of aid for minorities than those who did not finish high school. The change as education levels increase is not smooth and constant, but there is an increase in support as education level increases. Income increases have the opposite effect. Within any column, as income increases from low to high, support for aid to minorities declines. The effects of education and income increases produce conflicting effects.

These conflicting effects are important because education and income tend to be associated. Those with higher incomes also tend to have more education. Those with low incomes tend to have less education. Individuals, for example, with high income and education are being pushed in opposite directions. When both income and education are high, support for aid to minorities is at 51 percent. Because higher income is usually accompanied by higher education, support for aid for minorities is not that much different from those with low income and low education. This

Table 3.6

Cross-Pressures: Separating the Effects of Education and Income on Support for Minority Aid

Family Income	Did Not Finish High School (%)	High School Graduate (%)	Some College (%)
Low	45	41	65
Medium	32	33	55
High	42	35	51

Note: The proportions are of those who hold some opinion.
Source: Erikson et al., American Public Opinion (New York: Macmillan, 1991), 172.

situation is one in which individuals are cross-pressured. One experience pushes people in one direction, but another pushes them in the opposite direction. Such cross-pressuring is quite common.

The importance of cross-pressuring can be seen in the way it affects the emergence of political conflict. People with more income might be presumed to oppose redistributive programs. Because of cross-pressuring, however, as a group they have about the same level of support as other groups. The extent of conflict between groups that might occur is restrained somewhat.

This cross-pressuring means politicians have to be careful about predicting political attitudes on the basis of just one trait of individuals. An individual with high income might be relatively liberal because of other experiences. An individual with low education might not be as conservative as expected. It is not always easy to anticipate the concerns of the public from simple profiles of the population. Data representing the proportion of people with high education levels may be misleading when anticipating their reactions to economic issues, unless it is also possible to know their income levels and their ethnic or religious heritage. Public opinion polls that present attitudes by only education or income levels may misrepresent the extent to which conflict actually exists.

Numerous other situations arise in which individuals experience cross-pressure. Skilled union workers sometimes have relatively high incomes, but do not attain high education levels. While the heritage of union situations may incline them to be liberal on economic issues, they may be inclined to be conservative because of their education and income levels. This cross-pressuring means it cannot be assumed that the proportion of union members in the society can be used as a simple indicator of support for traditional union positions in favor of redistribution. Many union members are shaped more by their level of education than by their economic situation.

Cross-pressuring occurs in other ways. An individual may have a low education level and be black. The former trait may incline him or her to adopt conservative views on some social issues and on government responsibility to individuals, but the experience of being black is likely to have a strong influence in prompting the person to be liberal on these issues.

Many Jewish individuals have high education levels because of the commitment to education in their culture. Many also have high incomes, and this affluence might normally produce conservative economic attitudes. The Jewish heritage of being liberal, however, may dominate and result in a tendency toward liberalism among Jews. To some degree, all people experience some kind of cross-pressuring. Many people end up being moderate because of that. Other people are heavily influenced by a few experiences, and they lean heavily in one political direction.

Coherence and Intensity of Political Attitudes

The likely emergence of political concerns is further complicated by other aspects of opinion holding. Not everyone in our society is equally interested in politics and forms political attitudes. Many people pay little attention to political concerns and have few political opinions. They may have a response if asked a specific question that provides alternatives, but they do not hold those views with any intensity. Thus, while we may presume that particular individual traits are associated with political views, that assumption is not true for much of the population.[7] Not only do individuals differ, but issues also differ in the amount of media attention they attract. Some get very little media attention. The combination of low personal interest in an issue and low media coverage of it may produce very weak public opinions about many issues.

The emergence of issues as sources of conflict is diminished by cross-pressuring and by sometimes limited individual interest in public issues and politics. Longtime politicians or sophisticated pollsters may be able to assess the impacts of these factors and anticipate the likelihood of issues emerging, but they need a thorough knowledge of the public to do that.

Group Identities and Political Conflict

Individual attitudes are not affected just by income and education levels. They are also affected by group identities and experiences. We are all social creatures. Whether membership in a group is voluntary or involuntary, group experiences shape us because we perceive ourselves as separate and distinct from others who also perceive and treat us as separate and distinct from themselves.

Race, Gender, and Sexual Preference

Many group characteristics are ones over which individuals have no control. To be black, Latino, or Caucasion, female or male creates a sense of belonging to a group different from other groups in American society. Individuals in one group are often treated differently by those outside that group, a situation that can heighten a sense of difference from others. If this sense of difference is accompanied by extensive interaction with others in the same group, a group identity is created. This experience can lead to individual political attitudes that are derived primarily from the group identity.

Despite changes in race relations in American society in recent decades, many blacks do not feel that they are given equal treatment. Blacks are very likely to interact with other blacks that share their perceptions. Whites are also very likely to interact with other whites that share their own perceptions. As a result, blacks and whites can form attitudes based on group identity and group experience. Table 3.7 shows significant differences in opinion between blacks and whites on several issues. These attitudes affect reactions to policy concerns. Given these differences in perception, whites as a group are less likely than blacks as a group to see the need for civil-rights commissions at the state or local level. They are less likely to see the need for open-housing laws and for affirmative-action laws. Blacks are more likely to support these policies and related programs such as job training.

Numerous groups in our society feel this sense of being different. This experience is likely to be true for the increasing number of Latinos in our society. Also, considerable evidence shows that women as a group support certain policies more

Table 3.7

Differences in Perceptions by Race of the Treatment of Blacks in American Society

Question: How well do you think blacks are treated in this community—the same as whites, not very badly, or badly?[a]

Race	Same (%)	Not Very Badly (%)	Badly (%)	No Opinion (%)
White	67	17	3	13
Non-white	35	41	16	8

Question: Do you believe that because of past discrimination against black people, qualified blacks should receive preference over equally qualified whites in such matters as getting into college or getting jobs?

Race	Should (%)	Should Not (%)
Whites	19	72
Blacks	48	42

Question: Is there enough legislation on the books to improve conditions for blacks in this country? Or is more legislation needed?[b]

Race	Enough Legislation (%)	More Legislation Needed (%)
Whites	53	35
Blacks	24	64

Source: [a] Gallup Poll, 5–8 December, 1980.
[b] Newsweek Poll, 23–25 April 1991, Newsweek, 6 May, 1991, 24–26.

than men as a group do. Women are more supportive of affirmative action, widows' rights to pensions, tougher child-support laws, and subsidized day-care programs than are men. Gays, too, are likely to perceive themselves as a distinct group and be very supportive of civil-rights laws.

Culture, Ethnic Heritage, and Religion

Individuals may also derive a sense of group identity from cultural, ethnic, or religious background. WASPs (White Anglo-Saxon Protestants) often perceive themselves as distinct within American culture. WASPs as a group do not wish to share power with groups of different ethnic backgrounds. The resulting conflict has been particularly visible in urban politics. Most immigrants to America settled first in urban areas, and the already established WASPs were not receptive to the Catholic Irish, Italians, Polish, and other ethnic and religious groups who came to dominate many cities. Because of this history of conflict, many groups in state and local politics form voting attitudes based on ethnic background. Such attitudes can affect the election chances of candidates. In many states, an Italian would not have a chance of being elected governor, while in a state like Rhode Island, which has a high proportion of individuals of Italian descent, an Italian candidate has a much better chance of being elected than a non-Italian opponent.

Religious heritage was particularly important in earlier eras, when American society was less tolerant of different religions. It is still an important factor in many states and communities, where a history of recognizing religious backgrounds, and playing to them politically, still exists. Many Eastern states have large proportions of Catholics and Jews. These groups often express quite different opinions from the dominant WASP groups in our society. WASP groups did not (and many still do not) want Catholics and Jews in their country clubs or their neighborhoods. This sense of separation has been particularly strong among Jews, especially among those whose families or friends experienced the Holocaust. This event contributed strongly to their sense of being different. This sense of separation combined with common identity often means that these groups will vote as a bloc either for or against a candidate based on his or her religion.

Occupations and Organizational Affiliations

One of the most obvious influences upon political attitudes is the occupational or organizational affiliation of an individual. Conflicts in state politics often derive from these affiliations. Jobs provide individuals with income, and people want the government to do nothing to harm that source of income. If possible, they want the government to improve their situation. A rather straightforward expression of group self-interest results.

These group experiences can also contribute to a sense of being different. Being part of a union can create such a feeling, especially if there is a strong sense of solidarity in the organization, or hostile reactions to the union from the employer. Teachers, particularly those in the public schools, may feel a sense of identity because of the common issues they face. Many other experiences create a sense of group identity with the possibility of group political attitudes and group support of specific policies. Owners of small businesses may feel neglected by state policies and forms groups to lobby to protect their interests. Police officers often feel unappreciated and seek policy changes that will give them more control over their jobs.

Police officers, firefighters, and teachers want the state to pass legislation giving them the right to organize and to strike. They push for laws that would make bargaining rules favorable to them. Public employees want the state to raise taxes so public employees will have higher salaries. They want more job security and more benefits. Doctors want legislation that limits their liability for malpractice suits. They want the state to create a fund that would provide reasonable malpractice insurance. Lawyers want laws extended that provide them with work. They are opposed to no-fault auto insurance, and they do not wish divorces to be settled without litigation. Union officials want laws that require employees to join unions, and employers, and sometimes employees, do not want such laws. Farmers want state programs that help them market their products. Small "mom-and-pop" groceries do not want laws that require returnable bottles because they do not want to use the small amount of storage space available for storing returned bottles. In general, any time legislation affects an occupation, members of that occupation will be very concerned about the changes that result and will be opposed to any that are not favorable to them.

This occupational concern is particularly evident when organizations are involved. All organizations are affected to some degree by state and local laws, and they do not wish to be adversely affected. Restaurant owners do not wish health and safety laws that impose numerous inspections because they believe such inspections will be costly and onerous. Churches, social clubs, charities, YMCAs, and private colleges do not want the state or city to tamper with their exemption from local property taxes. Utilities do not wish to be regulated too heavily. They believe state utility commissions should be more receptive to their rate-increase requests. Banks do not want laws that require them to loan money to low-income applicants, and they do not want any laws that require them to disclose the reasons for their decisions on individual applicants. Consumer groups and groups concerned that banks systematically discriminate against women, minorities, and low-income applicants lobby for such laws. Insurance companies do not want disclosure laws, but consumer groups do. Corporations do not want corporate income taxes. They do not want high personal income taxes in their state because they must pay higher salaries to compensate. State universities often do not want the state to legislate high tuition levels because they believe that high tuition reduces the ability of the university to attract students. The list of such concerns is as long as the list of organizations that exist in any state or local area.

The Importance of Geography: Conflicts between Areas within States

Needs and interests emerge from individual experience. But individuals ultimately locate somewhere, and geography is very important in American politics. People with similar concerns, incomes, and perspectives tend to cluster together. People within specific areas often see themselves as different in some way from people in other areas, and they generally see these differences as relatively enduring.

This geographic group identity sets up possible conflicts that often become real conflicts when representatives from specific areas differ in what they want from the political process. Individuals in different areas tend to look at politics in terms of whether "other" areas are getting more benefits than their own areas. This tendency prompts conflicts very much like those we reviewed in discussing federalism and the differences among the states. In state and local politics, the differences that emerge are often characterized as downstate-upstate or rural-urban or central city–suburban, or some other sectional conflict.

Urban and Regional Conflicts

Some of this conflict is easily anticipated because regions of states and localities differ in the actual composition and needs of their populations. The population of the city of Chicago and the surrounding Cook County is considerably different from the population of downstate Illinois. The Chicago population is more urban, more black, more Hispanic, more Irish, and more Polish than the population downstate (in Illinois, all of the population outside Chicago is called downstate, even though parts of "downstate" are north of Chicago).[8] In New York City, the population is also more urban, more black, more Jewish, more Latino, more Asian, and more Italian than the population upstate. Both Chicago and New York City also have large concentrations of low-income individuals, compared to other areas within each state.[9]

Many states have similar divisions between large cities and the rest of the state. These differences between large cities and the rest of the state create conflicting policy needs. Large cities have a greater need for funds for welfare, job training, and medical care. Crime rates are higher, and fires are more frequent in large cities, so there is an increased demand for funds to pay for these municipal services. Both New York City and Chicago have mass-transit systems that are costly, and residents of these cities want public subsidies for operating the systems. These cities also need more money for public housing, and they face more militant demands from large and powerful public labor unions. These cities place great demands on state government for state aid. Since large cities often constitute a significant proportion of a state's population, they elect many representatives to the legislature. All of these factors lead to conflict over the kinds of state policies adopted and the distribution of benefits.

Conflicts between areas go beyond simple demographics, however. Years of division between areas creates enduring identities. People in upstate New York cities see themselves as distinct from residents in New York City. They talk about how different New York City is, and they have an enduring sense of "us versus them." This sense of division may often be false. Central-city residents from upstate cities such as Rochester, Buffalo, and Syracuse have the same policy needs as residents in New York City. Nonetheless, the perception of difference is crucial.

This same kind of regional conflict exists in states like Illinois, Michigan, and California. Some politicians find it advantageous to appeal to this sense of difference. A conservative upstate politician in Michigan may wish to attack welfare payment levels or the total amount of money going to welfare in Detroit. Not wishing to argue openly for reducing payments to people in need, he may proclaim that upstate Michigan is being neglected because a disproportionate percent of the state welfare budget is going to Detroit (even though the city has a higher percent of poverty than other areas of the state). This politician may also hope to receive some credit for defending his constituents' concerns against those of Detroit.

This sense of differentiation between areas, and political appeals and conflicts based on it, is common in state and local politics. In states like Iowa, it takes the form of an rural-urban conflict.[10] This conflict may have originated with demographic or occupation differences, but it has become relatively enduring. Rural areas differ from urban areas in their needs and populations. Farming and agriculture-dependent communities often carry with them a strong belief that individuals should have primary responsibility for taking care of themselves. Government welfare is not strongly supported by such communities. People in small towns also have less experience with unions and are not supportive of them. When small-town residents read about expensive wage settlements with public unions (and the need for state aid to fund these settlements), they are not likely to be supportive of the funding. They also may not be in favor of state subsidies for urban convention centers or state grants for business development. Residents of rural areas are often more preoccupied with the maintenance of roads and the reduction of state interference in their affairs.

Rural-urban conflicts exist in almost all states. Some of the more completely rural states, such as Vermont, Mississippi, and Montana, have less of it, but conflict between big cities and small towns is common in most states.[11] The persistence of such differences over the years creates enduring conflicts. Residents and legislators of rural areas come to suspect (with or without evidence to back it up) that policy is continually made to their disadvantage. They presume that they must organize against urban interests.

These conflicts are often accentuated by the spatial concentration of groups. Urban poverty has become more of a black phenomenon over the years. Even though most poor people in most cities are not black, many people see poverty as an urban black issue. Table 3.8 presents the distribution of black and white poverty in the United States. Over 60 percent of poor blacks live in urban areas, while only 26 percent of poor whites do. This concentration of poor blacks in urban areas creates a sense that urban aid is going primarily to racial minorities, even though the actual number of poor blacks in a given urban area may be smaller than the number of poor whites in the same area.

Differences in Natural Resources and Economic Bases

Finally, conflicts result from differences in access to resources. California, for example, is a state with a large agricultural sector, particularly in the southern, drier part of the state. It is also a state with a rapidly growing urban population and

Table 3.8

Distribution of White and Black Poverty within the United States

Location	Proportion of Total Group Poverty	
	White (%)	Black (%)
Central cities	25.8	61.2
Suburbs	36.3	17.8
Non-Metropolitan	37.9	21.0

Note: Percentages sum down to 100.
Source: Andrew Hacker, "Playing the Racial Card," New York Review of Books, 24 October 1991, 14.

high urban water use. The difficulty is that agricultural southern California receives much less rainfall than northern areas of the state. In the northeastern part of the state, the average yearly rainfall is 110 inches, while the southeastern part of the state receives an average of 2 inches. If the agricultural sector in the southeast is to survive drought years and continue to develop, it must take water from the north. To build a water redistribution system on this scale, however, the state government would need to borrow (and pay back) large amounts of money. A great deal of conflict has resulted because residents in the northern part of the state are wary of an arrangement that will continuously and permanently take some of their water. They are also reluctant to be burdened with the cost of a large water redistribution system. Differences in natural resources can create much tension between areas of a state.[12]

This same kind of tension can emerge when areas have different economic bases. Areas of a state with different kinds of economic activity often want different state policies. In Montana, for example, the western part of the state has traditionally been heavily involved in mining and forestry, while the economy of eastern Montana is based on wheat farming. The different needs create policy conflicts over subsidies to farming, land-use issues, and other matters. Similar divisions and the resulting conflicts exist in most states.

The Importance of Geography: Conflicts within Localities

Demographically based geographic conflict is also important within metropolitan areas. Neighborhoods and areas differ in wealth, culture, race, and lifestyle. In cities, neighborhoods may also differ in the ethnic groups that dominate them. In many cities, some sections are predominantly Italian or Irish or Jewish or Polish.[13] This is particularly true in Northeast and Midwest cities, where ethnic groups first immigrated and established ethnic neighborhoods. More recently Latino groups have established neighborhoods in larger cities. The black population in America is also highly urbanized and is usually concentrated in certain areas of any city.

These clusterings affect representation and the policies desired. Blacks tend to see themselves as different from whites and other racial groups, and they would prefer to have black representatives. Jews tend to prefer Jewish representatives. Since blacks generally have lower incomes, they want black representatives on the city council who understand poverty and the black experience. Residents of white middle-class areas have little need for welfare-related city services, and they generally would prefer to have city funds devoted to schools, road maintenance, police, and support of local symphonies.

Conflicts also stem from cultural clashes. Many ethnic groups, such as the Italians, Irish, and Polish, have historically been urban residents. Over the years, a large proportion of these immigrant groups have experienced upward movement in American society without the benefit of government aid. They tend to believe that the same effort should be made by blacks and Latinos, and they are not, as a group, very supportive of arguments that government should step in and assist these newer urban groups.

Life-style differences between groups are another important source of urban conflict. Life style refers to the social behavior that a group regards as appropriate. Oliver Williams, a political scientist argues that some ethnic groups traditionally have a very family-centered life, with an emphasis upon traditional roles (the husband is dominant and children respectful and obedient). Upper middle–class families in which ethnic heritage has been dropped or never existed, view authority differently. They are generally more concerned with individual development and give their children a great deal more freedom to develop as they wish. This difference leads to conflicting pressures on educational systems.[14]

Many other aspects of life-style differences have consequences for urban politics. Middle-class groups generally place more emphasis on the neatness of homes. They devote more time and money to cleaning and landscaping their yards than lower-class residents do. The reason for this difference, however, is not simply a matter of taste—or the lack of it. Low-income residents have less money to spend on these matters, and because more of them rent, they see no value in such allocations of their income or their energy. Middle-class groups push for ordinances that regulate the storage and disposal of garbage, prohibit the right of people to park on their lawns, limit the height grass can to grow before it must be cut, set the standards sidewalks must meet, and determine the colors houses may be painted. They do not want taverns or bars located in their neighborhoods because they feel taverns engender disorderly conduct. Lower-income residents often find such ordinances financially burdensome.

The existence of neighborhoods with concentrated populations of one income level often results in the formation of group idenity. This resulting sense of difference alone is enough to serve as a basis for conflicts within cities. It also leads to concerns about whether some neigborhoods are treated differently from others. Is service delivery (response to crime calls, condition of parks, road maintenance, frequency of police patrols, quality of schools) the same across neighborhoods?[15]

Many of these differences within cities lead residents to move to the suburbs seeking a population with similar values and fewer neighborhood conflicts. People, of course, also move to the suburbs because they want bigger lots and newer houses. But the type of people residing in a particular suburb is an important factor in deciding whether to move there. This flight of middle-class groups from the city to the suburbs creates conflicts between suburban areas and central cities.[16] Suburban areas wish to zone their property so that housing is expensive, and only those with middle-class incomes (or above) can move in. Local governments do this by requiring, among other things, that lots and houses be large and that the best materials be used in their construction. Racial conflicts also prompt moves out of the city. Many of those who move to suburbs are white and are seeking to avoid minorities. Consequently suburan residents often support practices that make it difficult for minorities to move in.[17]

The consequence of the population movement from urban to suburban areas has been class and racial segregation.

Segregation by race has remained an enduring problem. Although segregation of school children declined in the late 1960s as formal school segregation was abolished, in recent years it has increased again as whites continue to move out of the cities.[18] Suburbs, which are predominantly white and more affluent than central cities, have wealthier tax bases. This difference in tax bases results in significant disparities in school funding between urban and suburban areas.[19] Table 3.9 shows the relationship between poverty in schools and black and Latino enrollment in school districts. Districts are first broken down by the percent of school enrollment that is black and Latino. The percent of students who are living below the poverty level in these districts is then determined. The first column, for example, represents districts with 0 to 10 percent black and Latino enrollment. In those districts, only 17.6 percent of districts have over 25 percent of students living below poverty. In contrast, in districts with 70 percent or more minority enrollment, 66 percent of the districts have 25 percent or more of students living below the poverty level. The percent of poor students in school districts is positively associated with black and Latino enrollment. The combination of class and race differences between urban and suburban areas reinforces the sense of difference and frequently results in strong group identity.

The differences between large central cities and their suburbs is not the same across the country. Differences are generally greater in older, Northeast and Midwest cities. In these areas of the country, states created limits on the boundaries of cities very early in their histories. The populations of these metropolitan areas were also very diverse, and there was more movement among affluent whites to the suburbs.[20] School racial segregation is the greatest in many of the Northeast and Midwest states, such as Illinois, Michigan, New York, New Jersey, Pennsylvania, and Connecticut.[21] In many, but not all, southern and western states, the differences are not as great because central cities in these areas of the country were granted the right to annex areas around them. Many of them used that power, and the annexation of surrounding areas prevented the development of central cities considerably different from their suburbs.[22]

Table 3.9

Relationship between School Poverty and Black and Latino Enrollment

American School Districts (Broken Down by Black and Latino Enrollment)									
Students Living below Poverty Level (%)	0–10 (%)	10–20 (%)	20–30 (%)	30–40 (%)	40–50 (%)	50–60 (%)	60–70 (%)	70–80 (%)	80–90 (%)	90–100 (%)
0–25	82.4	74.4	62.6	49.0	40.6	35.4	33.6	33.9	33.5	37.9
25–100	17.6	25.6	37.4	51.0	59.4	64.6	66.4	66.1	66.4	62.1

Note: Percentages sum down to 100.
Source: Adapted from Gary Orfield, "The Growth of Segregation in American Schools: Changing Patterns of Separation and Poverty Since 1968" (report of the Harvard Project on School Desegregation to the National School Boards Association, Cambridge, Massachusetts, Harvard University, December 1993), 22.

The differences between central cities and their suburbs for selected metropolitan areas of the country can be seen in Table 3.10. Cities in the East and Midwest show large differences, while those in the South and West show smaller ones.

Differences between central cities and suburbs within metropolitan areas cause continuing political conflicts. Central-city residents and politicians want commuters to pay city taxes to help support the services necessary for downtown workers. Central-city politicians argue that because of commuters, the city must spend more money on police and roads. Commuters argue that because they generate economic activity in the city they should not have to pay additional costs. Suburban residents do not want urban blight to spread to suburbs, and they oppose public housing in the suburbs because they believe that it will contribute to economic decline. These differences between areas make it difficult to achieve agreements on city-suburban coordination of water systems, waste disposal, and police services.

These differences within metropolitan areas also have a major impact at the state level when it comes to the distribution of state aid. Central-city residents feel

Table 3.10
A Comparison of Central Cities and Their Suburban Areas

Central City and Suburbs	White (%)	Minority (%)	Median Annual Household Income (in dollars)
New York City	60.7	45.1	13,855
Suburbs	89.0	8.0	23,740
Boston	69.9	28.8	12,500
Suburbs	96.6	3.1	20,469
Chicago	49.6	53.8	15,301
Suburbs	90.8	9.5	24,811
Baltimore	43.9	55.8	12,811
Suburbs	89.2	10.0	22,272
Indianapolis	77.1	22.7	17,279
Suburbs	98.3	1.5	26,854
Memphis	51.6	47.6	14,040
Suburbs	77.8	22.0	18,753
Dallas	61.4	41.7	16,227
Suburbs	92.2	9.2	21,301
New Orleans	46.2	55.3	11,834
Suburbs	85.4	12.6	19,678
Phoenix	84.0	20.0	17,419
Suburbs	89.4	12.6	18,085
San Diego	75.4	23.7	16,409
Suburbs	85.9	17.2	17,808

Source: New York Times, *28 February 1983, B8.*

that since they have a lower tax base, they should receive more aid per person. They need more money for schools, for police, and numerous other city services. Suburban residents, of course, feel that their needs are just as legitimate, and they do not wish to see state revenue derived from taxation of their income used to support central-city services.

Change as a Source of Conflict

Thus far the emphasis has been on the composition of state and local populations. Population distributions can create relatively stable political divisions. Amid this stability, however, population growth and decline have a major impact on the kind of issues that dominate a particular state or locality. Population change alters the need for public services. Changes in the composition or size of the population can dramatically alter political concerns. States often have little control over these changes.

Population Mobility

Mobility is continual in American society. Two patterns of mobility have been particularly important: the movement from central cities to suburbs, and the movement from northern and central states (the Frostbelt) to southern and western states (the Sunbelt).

The movement out of central cities began in the early 1900s and accelerated during the 1950s. Americans sought to escape the crime, blight, and high-density in cities. They desired houses in suburban settings with larger lots. The dominant white population also wished to get away from low-income groups (and their life styles) and to minimize their contact with minorities. Recent population movements out of cities are presented in Table 3.11. This table shows population change for several major cities and their suburban areas (grouped by region) between the years 1980 and 1989. With few exceptions, central cities have either lost more population than their suburbs or have not grown as much.

The pattern of declining central-city population and suburban growth shown here is very common to Northeast and Midwest cities over the last thirty years. These changes create political issues. As the population declines, there is less need for many urban government services, such as education and garbage pickup. City employees who deliver these services oppose cutting these services because they will lose their jobs. The population that moves is usually middle class, leaving lower-income families behind. With a poorer population, the value of city housing declines, and there is a smaller tax base to provide urban services. The declining population in the central city also prompts many businesses to move to the suburbs. Such a move further reduces the tax base. The conflict that emerges is not a pleasant one for city officials. Will cuts in taxes (and services) make the city a more attractive place to live and draw businesses and people back into the city, or will maintaining services (and raising taxes) make the city more attractive?[23]

Table 3.11

Population Change in Metropolitan Areas, 1980–1989

Metropolitan Area	Population Change (%)
North and East	
Chicago	− 7.9
Suburbs	+ 6.6
Detroit	− 17.0
Suburbs	+ 2.3
Cleveland	− 0.2
Suburbs	+ 4.0
Indianapolis	+ 4.0
Suburbs	+ 10.2
Baltimore	− 6.0
Suburbs	+ 14.2
Buffalo	− 9.1
Suburbs	− 8.3
South and West	
San Diego	+ 21.1
Suburbs	+ 28.9
Houston	+ 2.2
Suburbs	+ 27.6
Atlanta	− 7.8
Suburbs	+ 29.7
Miami	+ 3.3
Suburbs	+ 18.9
Denver	− 5.3
Suburbs	+ 18.4

Source: U.S Statistical Abstract *(Washington, DC, 1991).*

Large population increases in suburban areas create problems in those area. Money must be raised for new schools, more roads, and more government services. A large proportion of this money must come from higher property taxes. This increase will not please the original residents of the area. These same residents may also try to adopt laws that make it harder for new residents, particularly low-income and minority groups, to move in.

Cities in the Sunbelt, both central city and suburban, are the places where most of the recent population growth has occurred, and these areas must cope with the requirements of a greater population. In many cases, the result is controversy. The Houston metropolitan area grew by 29.2 percent in the central city and 71.2 percent in the suburbs from 1970–1980. By the early 1980s there was an enormous increase of commuter traffic coming into the downtown business district. The

traffic jams in the morning and evening became legendary, and occasionally commuters from nearby suburbs took four hours to get to work. Tempers flared, and
murders and assaults involving drivers took place during the traffic jams. Businesses began to worry about the impact of these transportation difficulties upon
current and future downtown business activity. The result was that the city administration reversed its longstanding opposition to mass transit. Finally, officials formulated plans for a mass transit system and submitted a grant to the federal government for partial funding. The resistance to dealing with transportation problems
was overcome only because of the sheer increase in commuters.

Population changes also alter political constituencies. Central cities that were
once Republican have become Democratic as the proportion of blacks and other
minority groups has increased. States that have experienced a major influx of Latinos, such as Florida, California, Texas, and New York, have new constituencies
worried about new issues like the right to bilingual education.

An example of change that surprised many took place in Houston during the
late 1970s and early 1980s. Houston, long regarded as the embodiment of the western cowboy life style, acquired a large gay community. Politicians originally
scorned the group and then discovered that the gay community registered and
voted heavily. The result was that politicians had to give gay issues serious consideration.

Change has also been important for Frostbelt cities. Cities in the Midwest and
Northeast have growing proportions of minorities, and political concerns in these
cities are changing. The 1970s produced a steady increase in the proportion of the
black population in Chicago, and Harold Washington, a black, was able to mount a
successful campaign for mayor as a result of this change. In 1983 he became the
city's first black mayor. By the 1980's, Boston, a city once famous for its domination
by Irish Catholics, had changed greatly. Irish males constituted only 10 percent of
the population. The city had lost 25 percent of its white population, and the black
and Latino proportion of the population changed from 19 to 33 percent. From 1970
to 1980, there was also a substantial influx of young college-educated professionals.
The result was that in the 1983 general election, this city, once polarized by racial
tensions, had its first black mayoral candidate (Mel King). The effectiveness of
appealing to the Boston electorate through racist campaigns had lessened.

Parallel changes exist for the states. During the last several decades there has
been a major movement of the population to the Southern and West from the Northeast and the Midwest. Changes in population within all states were discussed in
Chapter 2. Table 3.12 presents these changes for only a few states to illustrate the
extent to which the states vary in this regard.

Population decline in Frostbelt states has been accompanied by loss of jobs
and stagnant tax bases. These states have to deal with tax bases that either have
dwindled or have grown less than in prior eras. This decline in jobs puts pressure
on state politicians to listen to business pleas to cut taxes to make the state more
attractive for business.

The situation in Sunbelt states is quite the opposite. These states face
demands for more services of all types. There is a need to expand public-education
facilities at all levels to enable the greater number of students to attend school.

Table 3.12
Population Change in Selected States, 1980–1989

State	Change (Increase) in Population (%)
Sunbelt States	
Arizona	34.8
Florida	32.7
Nevada	50.1
New Mexico	16.3
Frostbelt States	
Illinois	0.1
Massachusetts	4.9
New York	2.5
Pennsylvania	0.1

Source: U.S. Statistical Abstract *(Washington, DC, 1991).*

Roads must be built. Many individuals who lost jobs in Frostbelt states migrate south, and Sunbelt states must decide whether or not they will provide these people with unemployment benefits and welfare. Local governments in these areas also demand more state aid to meet the greater demands placed upon them.

Population movements also affect the distribution of legislative seats within states. This shift in the location of the population over time is shown in Table 3.13. The data indicates that there has been a dramatic increase in the proportion of the population in the suburbs. As of 1988, a higher percent lived in those areas than anywhere else. As the population moved out of central cities to the suburbs, state legislatures were required to increase the number of districts in the suburbs. The population shift also resulted in a smaller number of representatives from central-city areas. This reduction affected the level of legislative concern with central-city problems.

Table 3.13
Spatial Distribution of American Population, 1950–1988

Year	Cities (%)	Suburbs (%)	Rural Areas (%)
1950	32.9	23.2	43.9
1960	32.3	30.6	37.0
1970	31.4	37.2	31.4
1980	30.0	44.8	25.2
1988	31.3	45.7	22.8

Source: New York Times, *11 September 1990, A20.*

Federal Actions

Actions of the federal government also create issues. Federal government interventions in the South in the late 1950s and 1960s, which increased black registration, changed the composition of the southern electorate, and the concerns of politicians who ran for office. Federally imposed restraints on economic activity in order to lower inflation reduce state and local tax revenues. Because states cannot run budget deficits, they are forced to decide what services to cut. Cuts in government aid to states and localities create political conflict over whether to cut programs or raise taxes.

Political Movements

There are also times when new political movements emerge that change the way government works and the kinds of public policies pursued. During the late 1800s, Populism swept through many states. The Populist movement was concerned with the needs of the common person. This movement led to policies more favorable to lower-income interests and changes in the political process that made mass participation in politics easier.

The Reform movement, which has had intermittent influence since the early 1900s, had a significant influence on the way politics works. Reformists believed that the political and administrative process could be made less partisan by more objective consideration of issues. The movement resulted in major alterations in government, many of which we will explore later.[24]

During the 1960s, all levels of government were affected by a rise in the belief that our society should do something about poverty and racial discrimination. The redistributive programs that followed were not just a reflection of the economic or education level of the people in favor of these programs. The beliefs these programs were based on derived from a more optimistic perspective about the potential of government to change society. Those beliefs declined during the 1980s.

Shifts in Public Opinion

Shifts in public opinion can also occur within very specific policy areas. Table 3.14 presents changes in public opinion for four policy areas across time. The first column indicates the proportion of people who think we spend too little on schools. The rise in concern with school funding corresponds to the emergence of commission studies in the early 1980s that argued that we were not doing enough for schools.[25] Apparently that debate led to or was part of greater concern about the efficacy of the education system. The last several decades have also seen more concern about crime rates. The second column in Table 3.14 shows the rise in the proportion of people who believe the courts are not harsh enough on criminals. The third column shows the proportion of the population who feel that too much is spent on welfare. This proportion rose during the 1970s and then fell dur-

Table 3.14

Long-Term Shifts in Public Opinion

Year	Education (%)	Treatment of Criminals (%)	Welfare (%)	Integration (%)
1942	—	—	—	30
1956	—	—	—	49
1963	—	—	—	63
1965	—	48	—	68
1970	—	—	—	74
1971	44	66	53	—
1973	49	73	51	—
1974	51	78	42	—
1975	49	79	43	—
1976	50	81	60	83
1977	48	83	60	85
1978	52	85	58	—
1979	53	—	57	—
1980	53	83	57	86
1981	56	77	52	—
1982	56	86	48	88
1983	60	85	47	—
1984	64	82	40	90
1985	65	84	45	92
1986	60	85	40	—
1987	62	79	44	—
1988	64	82	42	—

Responses above are proportions answering yes to questions below:

Education: Are we spending too little on the nation's education system?

Treatment of criminals: Do you think the courts are not harsh enough with criminals?

Welfare: Are we spending too much on welfare?

Integration: Do you think that white students and black students should attend the same schools?

Source: Richard G. Niemi, John Mueller, and Tom W. Smith, Trends in Public Opinion *(New York: Greenwood Press, 1989), 84, 89, 136, 180.*

ing the 1980s. The change corresponds to the rise and subsequent decline in real (adjusted-for-inflation) welfare benefit levels in that time period.[26] Our society has produced continual debate about race relations. Although progress in this area does not appear large, the last column of the table indicates there has been considerable change in the proportion of individuals who believe black and white children should attend the same schools. Public opinion may change slowly, but it does change.

"New Ideas"

People's opinions are not stable products of their education, income, or occupation. New ideas emerge, are embraced, and then may be partially or totally abandoned. This cycle occurred at the national level with an idea Ronald Reagan proposed. He sought to convince many blue-collar workers—traditionally Democratic—that he had a new way to improve the economy. He convinced many that there would be more job growth if government reduced its regulatory role, because this action would free the private sector to generate jobs. His "theory" became known as "supply-side economics." In retrospect this policy did not accomplish what was expected, and by the 1992 presidential election many of these blue-collar workers again voted for a Democrat. The short duration of the affect of Reagan's supply-side economics on the voting population is not important. What is important is that a president was able to effectively counter traditional political loyalties by convincing people that he had an idea that was new and that would solve their problems. New ideas come and go, and they often push people away from voting simply on the basis of their personal socioeconomic situation.

Moderating Conflict

States and localities are composed of groups and individuals with considerable potential for conflict: blacks versus whites, business groups versus labor unions, business groups versus environmental groups, suburbanites versus inner-city residents, pro-choice versus pro-life groups, to name just a few. The potential for conflict to be intense and for politics to be an ugly, divisive part of our lives appears to be high. Differences exist over the taxation of personal wealth, the expenditure of public funds, the subsidizing of certain activities but not others, the rights to jobs and living locations, the abortion issue, minority scholarships, and many other issues. Despite such potential for explosive conflict, conflict is generally somewhat restrained. Differences of opinion may sometimes become pronounced; protest marches may even take place. But conflict rarely leads to pitched battles in American society. Physical battles are unusual, and they become news when they do occur.

There are several reasons why conflict in American society remains relatively contained. The first derives from the cross-pressures discussed earlier in this chapter. Individuals have backgrounds that create contradictory attitudes. A wealthy individual opposed to redistributive programs because of the effect on his or her taxes may also have the educational background that makes him or her somewhat sympathetic to the plight of others who have not done as well. In this way, the political views of the individual become moderated. People are less likely to hold purist or dogmatic views, which are the basis for intense conflict.

Politicians also try to reduce conflict over specific issues. Politicians present themselves to voters as a collection of issue positions. Candidates hope all their issue positions will be considered by the electorate when they vote. Politicians hope voters opposed to their position on abortion will consider their positions on open housing, tax cuts, municipal aid, and other policies. Politicians hope that if the electorate considers multiple issues, disagreement on one issue will be offset by agreement on other issues. If a politician can satisfy a voter on the less emotional issues, the impact of the intense emotions accompanying highly divisive issues like abortion may be reduced.

Conflict is also contained because of the willingness of the public to abide by the outcome of the political process. Most Americans are supportive (to varying degrees) of the "rules of the game."[27] While differences on certain issues may be significant, the general presumption is that once a decision is reached, it should be accepted. This acceptance is based on the belief that decisions should be made through a democratic process, and that the outcomes of this process should be accepted as legitimate. If this belief were not widely accepted, chaos would ensue, and there would be no effective means of reaching decisions.

This belief in the democratic process and in the legitimacy of its outcomes is not strongly held by everyone, nor at all times. Public opinion polls show that many Americans hold this belief only in the abstract and are less respecting of the democratic process on specific issues.[28] Enough people do have strong commitment to this belief, however, to maintain the process. In addition, studies have indicated that elites in our society support democratic procedures. Elites generally refuse to indulge in attempts to undermine the process, even if they are currently losing a particular political battle.

Despite this general support, there are times when groups believe that the particular issue is so important and their influence so small, they must go beyond simple debate to active protest, civil disobedience, or vigilante action. Such action occurred in the 1960s over civil rights, and in the 1980s over the use of nuclear energy. Again, given all the potential conflicts that exist in our society, such actions are unusual.

For Further Reading

It is difficult to obtain information on the conflicts that dominate in particular states and localities. One source for the situation in states is the series of books being published on individual states by the University of Nebraska Press.

For each state there are usually books that provide overviews of political conflict within the state or within some of the major urban areas in the state. Other books may provide studies of specific conflicts. Check the local library to see what books exist about your state. Do not automatically eliminate books more than ten years old. Many conflicts persist for years. What do these studies tell you about conflict in your state or locality?

Kozol, Jonathan. *Savage Inequalities*. New York: Crown, 1991.

Suggestions for Analysis in your own State and Locality

1. Public opinion polls are major sources of information about political conflict in a state or locality. Is there any organization that conducts polls in your state or locality that then releases those polls to the public? If so, try to get a copy of a recent poll to see if the poll presents opinions by different groups. Are there differences by groups?

2. Differences of opinion also emerge when policy proposals are presented. Those proposals might be in the form of executive orders, or in the form of legislative proposals. Are there any that have emerged recently in your state or locality that drew responses from many groups and could provide indications of political conflict?

3. Much of the conflict within states and localities is geographically based. Areas differ in composition and have different policy preferences. You can try to assess differences in areas two ways. See if your state has a statistical abstract that provides demographic information by area.

   First, how much do areas of the state differ in demographic characteristics? How much do areas differ in average income, average value of homes, education levels, and racial composition? Make the same assessment for communities within your locality.

   Another way to assess differences is to examine the way areas react to a common choice, such as gubernatorial, state legislative, county executive, or mayoral candidates. That information is presented in public documents and is usually broken down by area. How much do areas differ in their votes for candidates?

Notes

[1] V.O. Key, Jr., *Public Opinion and American Democracy* (New York: Knopf, 1961), 263.

[2] Peter Bachrach and Morton S. Baratz, "Two Faces of Power," *American Political Science Review* 56 (December 1962): 947–952. See their discussion of non-decisions.

[3] Richard G. Niemi, John Mueller, and Tom W. Smith, *Trends in Public Opinion: A Compendium of Survey Data* (New York: Greenwood Press, 1989), 248.

[4] For an extended analysis of this issue, see Kay Lehman Schlozman and Sidney Verba, *Injury to Insult: Unemployment, Class, and Political Response* (Cambridge: Harvard University Press, 1979).

[5] Donald R. Kinder and Roderick Kiewit, "Sociotropic Politics: The American Case," *British Journal of Political Science* 11: 129–161; Donald R. Kinder and Roderick Kiewit, "Economic Discontent and Political Behavior: The Role of Personal Grievances and Collective Economic Judgments in Congressional Voting," *American Journal of Political Science* 23: 495–527; and Stanley Feldman, "Economic Self-Interest and Political Behavior," *American Journal of Political Science* 26, no. 3 (August 1982): 446–466.

[6] Robert S. Erickson, Norman R. Luttbeg, and Kent L. Tedin, *American Public Opinion*, 4th ed. (New York: Macmillan Publishing, 1991), 157.

[7] Jerry L. Yeric and John R. Todd, *Public Opinion*, 2d ed. (Itasca, Illinois: F.E. Peacock, 1989), 198–99.

[8] For an assessment of Illinois, see Peter F. Nardulli, ed., *Diversity, Conflict, and State Politics* (Urbana: University of Illinois Press, 1989).

[9] Gerald Benjamin, "The Two New Yorks," in *The Two New Yorks*, ed. Gerald Benjamin, (New York: Russell Sage, 1990); and Jeffrey M. Stonecash, "The City and Upstate," in, *New York State Today*, eds. Peter W. Colby and John K. White (Albany: SUNY Press, 1989), 41–49.

[10] Harlan Hahn, *Urban-Rural Conflict* (Beverly Hills: Sage, 1971).

[11] Frank Bryan, *Politics in the Rural States* (Boulder: Westview Press, 1981).

[12] Terry Christensen and Larry Gertson, *The California Connection* (Boston: Little, Brown, 1984), 24–25.

[13] Dennis R. Judd, *The Politics of American Cities*, 3d ed. (Boston: Little, Brown, 1988), 27–32.

[14] Oliver P. Williams, Harold Herman, Charles S. Liebman, and Thomas R. Dye, *Suburban Differences and Metropolitan Politics* (Philadelphia: University of Pennsylvania Press, 1965).

[15] The issue of differences in service delivery by neighborhood has been studied extensively. For examples, see Robert L. Lineberry, *Equality and Urban Policy* (Beverly Hills Sage, 1977); Peter F. Nardulli and Jeffrey M. Stonecash, *Politics, Professionalism, and Urban Services: The Police* (Cambridge, Mass.: Oelgeschlager, Gum, and Hain, 1981); and Kenneth R. Maldenka, "Citizen Demands and Urban Services: The Distribution of Bureaucratic Response in Chicago and Houston," *American Journal of Political Science* 25, no. 4 (November 1981): 693–714.

[16] Kenneth Jackson, *The Crabgrass Frontier* (New York: Oxford University Press, 1985).

[17] Michael Danielson, *The Politics of Exclusion* (New York: Columbia University Press, 1976).

[18] Gary Orfield, "The Growth of Segregation in American Schools: Changing Patterns of Separation and Poverty Since 1968" (report of the Harvard Project on School Desegregation to the National School Boards Association, Cambridge, Massachusetts, Harvard University, December 1993), 7.

[19] Jonathan Kozol, *Savage Inequalities: Children in America's Schools* (New York: Crown, 1991.

[20] Kenneth T. Jackson, *Crabgrass Frontier* (New York: Oxford University Press, 1985); and Robert Fishman, *Burgeois Utopia* (New York: Basic Books, 1987).

[21] Orfield, "The Growth of Segregation in American Schools," 12.

[22] John J. Harrigan, *Political Change in The Metropolis*, 5th ed. (New York: HarperCollins, 1993), 348–349.

[23] Paul Peterson, *City Limits* (Chicago: University of Chicago Press, 1981).

[24] Richard Hofstader, *The Age of Reform* (New York: Knopf, 1956).

[25] National Commission on Excellence in Education, *A Nation at Risk : The Imperative for Educational Reform* (Washington DC, 1983). One of most prominent of many studies released in the 1980s.

[26] Robert Pear, "Poor Mainly Silent After Welfare Cuts, State Officials Find," *New York Times*, 10 February 1982, A1.

[27] John L. Sullivan, James Piereson, and George E. Marcus, *Political Tolerance and American Democracy* (Chicago: University of Chicago Press, 1982), 203.

[28] Robert S. Erickson, Norman R. Luttbeg, and Kent L. Tedin, *American Public Opinion*, 4th ed. (New York: Macmillan, 1991), 107–112.

4

Political Conflict: States and Their Local Governments, and Taxes

PREVIEW

Differences of opinion within the public result in conflicts about what role government should play in society, how much state government should do, and how funds should be raised. Opponents stress the threat to liberty from dominant states, while supporters stress the problems that inequality creates. These arguments have affected the role of government within the states. Over time states have taken on more responsibilities. Despite this general trend, states have their own histories, and the role of state governments still differs across the country. These battles over the role of government inevitably lead to disputes over what taxes should be imposed, who should pay them, and the ways tax burdens are distributed. This chapter focuses on the sources of these battles, the ways these battles affect the role of the state, and the effects these battles have on state tax distribution and burden.

The Role of the State: The Debate

Different points of view in American society result in political battles over the enduring issues in American public policy: Should government get involved in trying to change conditions in society? Which level of government should undertake such activities? How should money be raised to pay for government? How should the burden of taxation be distributed to pay for such activities? These issues reflect conflicts between the haves and the have-nots. This chapter explains these conflicts as background for subsequent chapters. To understand what politicians, political parties, and interest groups are battling about, it is necessary to understand the policy choices they are arguing about. We also need to understand the consequences of different policies to know why politicians take the positions they do. Democrats in a state may advocate a progressive state income tax. This tax takes a higher percentage of income in taxes as income rises. Republicans are likely to oppose a progressive tax because of the effects of such a tax. This chapter will review the debate about the role of the state, the choices states have made, the debates about taxes, and the tax choices made by states.

The Legal Basis for State Action

If government decides to take action, the next question is whether action should be taken by the state, or by local government. Is it desirable to have the state create a relatively uniform statewide policy approach, or is this likely to result in unequal policies across the state that do not match the needs of local communities? Should resources be marshalled by the state to avoid inequalities due to differences in tax bases, or is it better to have local governments retain their own resources?

These questions are fundamental political battles between groups and areas. Their emergence is also pushed along because of the legal relationship between states and their local governments. Each state and its local governments constitute a unitary form of government and are legally regarded as a single, unified government. This doctrine evolved gradually in American society. The principle that the state is dominant relative to local governments was most forcefully articulated in the court ruling known as Dillon's rule, handed down in 1868. In that case, the courts ruled that local governments are the legal "creatures" of the state.[1] The state creates local governments, and the state may alter or abolish them. States themselves have the right to persist, and the national government cannot abolish them. But that same right does not exist for local governments. Local governments do not have any guarantee that certain government activities (police or fire, for example) are theirs to perform. Local governments may be altered, as may any of the responsibilities local governments have.

This court ruling did not definitively resolve the issue. Other court rulings have made Dillon's rule less absolute, and there have been periodic movements to give localities the right of "home rule" to make decisions in purely "local" issues (the right to be in charge of their own affairs). Over the long run, however, the argument that states are largely responsible for and legally superior to their local governments has prevailed.

This legal view of the role of state governments, however, is probably less relevant to the issue of state dominance than the roles of political ideas and local constituencies. On the state level, as on the national level, the idea has grown that significant differences in local wealth bases across the state create inequality of opportunity, which society should consider and perhaps act to remedy. Constituencies in areas with fewer resources have sought help from the state to respond to these inequalities. Local governments turning to state governments for help has become common. Even suburbs that are seemingly well off regularly seek state aid to help with their growth.

All these conditions have combined to make the relationship of the state to its local governments a basic issue of state and local politics. States have the legal power to act, many people believe that the state should act, and many local constituencies actively ask the state to act. There is, however, opposition to the state taking a greater role at the local level. The debate about what role state governments should play continues.

The Argument against State Involvement: Decentralization, Liberty, and Responsiveness

When a state decides to take action in some policy area, it chooses from an enormous range of available policy options. A state may assume responsibility for all funding and service delivery. It may make local governments responsible, but provide funding and guidelines as to how policy should be implemented. It may simply allow all policy decisions to be made at the local level without any direction or funding from the state. Each one of these broad alternatives draws strong support and strong opposition. People have firm convictions about the relative merits of these policy options. The issues raised are part of a continuing dialogue about what is a fair, responsive, and effective way to conduct governmental affairs. The divergence of opinion about these issues is remarkable.

The argument for a constrained national government also applies to a constrained state government. Many people see government as a mechanism with enormous potential to intrude upon and destroy individual lives. The opponents of centralized government argue that it should never be forgotten that strong central governments around the world have been a primary means (well-intentioned or not) of depriving people of their liberty. They argue that great concentrations of power present great opportunity for abuse, and that only the decentralization of power in a society can inhibit such possibilities.

According to those in favor of decentralization, responsiveness to the public is best engendered when local governments have significant control over government activities within their boundaries. If governments at the local level control important decisions, citizens at the local level are more likely to take local politics seriously. They are more likely to participate, and more likely to feel they can affect policy. This greater activism and the smaller size of government should produce more responsive governments. Government in a decentralized society will be more attuned to the needs and concerns of people, and citizens will be more involved in local issues. There is surprisingly little evidence supporting this belief, but the argument is a powerful one in American politics.[2]

Allowing each local government independently to decide policies will produce diverse policies. This diversity may allow different groups of people to construct sets of policies consistent with their desires. Not everyone wants the same policies, and multiple local governments can allow diversity to flourish.[3]

There is also a practical argument for decentralization. Decentralized government should be more efficient administratively. Local officials have intimate knowledge of their problems, and they are the best equipped to design a response or solution that will resolve the problem. Decentralization should produce a better fit between solutions and problems. Again, there is considerable assertion in this area, but not much evidence.

The intrusion of the national government and state governments into local affairs has increased tremendously in the last fifty years. We need to understand the impact of the resulting changes in local autonomy on citizen attitudes and policy administration, but we lack sufficient research in this area. These changes in local autonomy may have convinced the public that local governments are no longer the level at which significant decisions are made. The national government and its politics draw a great deal of attention, and it may be that in the current world, local politics simply does not generate much interest. Turnout is much lower for local elections than for other elections, and this may reflect public dismissal of local government. Some argue that only decentralization will restore citizen involvement.

The Argument for State Involvement: Concerns about Inequality

Beauty is always in the eye of the beholder. While some see virtues in decentralization, others see inequality. This difference of opinion is not minor. Although some see centralized (state) government as a threat to liberty and freedom, supporters of state action see local autonomy as the means by which local majorities deprive minorities of their rights. The history of civil-rights practices, in particular, gives the impression that local majorities tend to abuse the rights of minorities. Critics of local autonomy see arguments against centralized activity as an elaborate justification for those abuses. The have-nots, in particular, often see the defense of "local diversity" as a way to preserve inequality of benefits in society.

The composition of local majorities can result in varying policies.[4] Examples of the way composition of local majorities can affect policy choices are endless. The homosexual population is relatively large in cities like San Francisco and Houston, and politicians are more inclined to be responsive to gay and lesbian issues in these cities than they are to those same issues in cities like Boise, Idaho. Blacks and Hispanics are relatively more numerous in large cities, and politicians are more receptive to their concerns in these cities. Policies about affirmative action and public housing are generally pursued more vigorously in urban areas than they are in upper middle–class white suburbs. There are variations in economic dominance of large businesses across communities, and variations in community inclination to adopt policies favorable to business.

To critics of local autonomy, relying on local administration of state and federal programs is not a virtue. Local officials, influenced by local majorities, can make decisions that create differences in opportunities and affect implementation of programs. An instructive example is provided by Martha Derthick in her study of the welfare program in Massachusetts before and after the federal government forced the state to assume responsibility for administration.[5] Before the state centralized administration of the program, the determination of eligibility for welfare was done locally by non–civil-service employees. Those appointed to these positions were from the local area and were not uniformly "trained" in the kinds of conditions an individual had to meet to be eligible for aid. In addition, many of the funds for welfare were locally raised, and each jurisdiction had some control over the benefit level paid. After centralization of the welfare program, employees were gradually made state civil servants, and they were all given common instructions regarding eligibility criteria. More of the funds came from the state (and the federal government).

To assess the effects of these changes, Derthick examined whether cities with similar populations had similar proportions of their population on welfare before and after centralization. She found much more diversity in this proportion before centralization than after. Individuals in similar conditions were not uniformly eligible (or ineligible). She also examined benefit levels and found they varied much more before than after centralization. The determination of eligibility and the setting of benefit levels became much more uniform with more centralization.

Opponents of decentralization also argue that diversity and inequality of social conditions presents its own threat to liberty. Since populations with similar incomes cluster together, differences in tax bases and differences in public services result. These differences affect the lives of the citizens and can deprive them of equal opportunities in society.

This argument has been made by critics of decentralization of school finance. They argue that the greater the variation in tax bases, the greater the inequalities in resources and funding for schools. Inequalities among local tax bases are widespread in American society. The situations in New York, New Jersey, and Illinois, shown in Table 4.1, illustrate these differences. The table presents the variations in per student expenditure for selected school districts within the three states. The data shows enormous differences in the amount available per student across school districts within the same metropolitan area.

These inequalities exist even if poorer communities tax at higher levels. The inequalities also endure across time and create lengthy battles over what, if any, actions should be taken by the state to respond to the situation. Texas provides an example of the inequities that can exist and the length of time this battle can go on. Table 4.2 presents inequities in school finance in Texas during the early 1970s and in 1993. The first findings are from evidence presented as part of a lawsuit resolved in 1973 (*San Antonio Independent School District* v. *Rodriquez* (1973).) The plaintiffs (those claiming the existing system was illegal) presented information showing the variation in tax bases of school districts within the metropolitan area of San Antonio, and the variation in expenditure per pupil that resulted from the varying tax bases. The variation in tax base per student is shown in the first column. The

Table 4.1

Inequities in School Finance in Three States

School District	Average Student Expenditure (in dollars)
New York	
Manhasset	11,372
Jericho	11,325
Great Neck	11,265
Bronxville	10,113
Rye	9,092
Yonkers	7,399
Levittown	6,899
Mt. Vernon	6,433
Roosevelt	6,339
New York City	5,585
New Jersey	
Princeton	7,725
Summit	7,275
West Orange	6,505
Cherry Hill	5,981
Jersey City	4,566
East Orange	4,457
Paterson	4,422
Camden	3,538
Illinois	
Niles Township High	9,371
New Trier High	8,823
Glencoe (elementary and junior high)	7,363
Winnetka (elementary and junior high)	7,059
Wilmette (elementary and junior high)	6,009
Chicago (all grades)	5,265

Source: Jonathon Kozol, Savage Inequalities *(New York: Crown, 1991), 236–37.*

second column indicates the number of school districts involved. Tax effort, or percent of existing property values taxed by local school districts for school expenditure purposes, is shown in the next column. The last column shows the average amount of money raised per student by groups of communities with different tax bases. The results are clear. Those districts with smaller tax bases made a greater tax effort, but they still generated less revenue per student than the wealthy districts did. The plaintiffs lost this case, but other lawsuits in subsequent years continued to challenge the school finance system in Texas.

Table 4.2

Local Tax Bases, Tax Rates, and Education Finance in Texas School Districts

1970s Data

School Districts with Taxable Property per Child of:	Number of School Districts	Tax Rate per $100 (in dollars)	Tax Yield per pupil (in dollars)
above $100,000	10	0.31	585
$55,000–100,000	26	0.38	262
$30,000–49,999	30	0.55	213
$10,000–29,999	40	0.72	162
below $10,000		0.70	60

1993 Data

District Category	Average Local Wealth Per Student (in dollars)
The ten poorest	19,457
The middle ten	102,938
The ten wealthiest	1,969,319

Sources: The 1970s data: Robert L. Lineberry and Ira Sharkansky, Urban Politics and Public Policy, *3d ed. (New York: Harper and Row, 1978), 314; the 1993 data: Lists prepared by the Equity Center, Austin, Texas, 1993.*

By 1993 this issue had still not gone away because inequities in school financing still existed. The Equity Center gathers data on the average wealth each school district has available to tax in order to raise funds for schools. The bottom of Table 4.2 presents information on the differences among the 1042 school districts in Texas. Three categories of school districts are presented. The first category comprises the ten districts with the lowest average wealth per student, followed by the ten districts in the middle relative to others in the state, followed by the ten with the highest wealth per student. The differences are huge and have been a source of persistent conflict in Texas. We will return to this specific conflict later in the text.

Other states also have disparities across districts in the wealth available to school districts. These disparities create a continuing debate about whether the state should intervene to play a role. The issue persists because people believe that differences in schooling lead to inequities in opportunity in society and perpetuate class differences in that society.[6]

These inequalities have become the basis for numerous lawsuits in the states. Critics of existing school-finance situations argue that states are aware of these differences and have played a role in their emergence. By allowing the financing of education through the property-tax system, the state has created this inequality. The consequence of this system is often an enormous difference in the education received by students across the state, a difference related to where they live.

To critics of local autonomy, diversity of educational-finance conditions does not create more responsiveness, but variance in rights and liberties across communities. Allowing local autonomy in policy choices is seen as a way of allowing the wealthy to separate themselves from lower-income areas and to create greater opportunities for themselves and their children. These critics argue that the state grants the right for municipalities to exist and to zone property. This municipal authority is often used to exclude certain income groups.[7] Thus the state is ultimately responsible for inequality. In addition, some state constitutions make vague references to the obligation of the state to make sure that all students receive an adequate education. This apparent state responsibility for any inequalities across localities frequently leads to lawsuits.

New Jersey, for example, has faced two significant lawsuits over education finance in the last twenty years. Papers filed as a part of these lawsuits documented large differences in per capita expenditure, availability of computers for students, and availability of foreign language programs. The state lost both lawsuits. The court ruling stated that "financing school by relying on local property taxes was fundamentally unequal."[8] This decision forced the state to play a greater role in school finance.

Education finance and equity concerns have become major issues in the states. As of 1991 there were twenty-two states facing lawsuits over inequalities in school finance.[9] In a number of states, the state courts have ruled that the existing finance system is unconstitutional and in need of change.[10] This issue inevitably brings up the question of the role of the state. The lawsuits are directed at the state because the only practical way to find funds to correct these inequities is to have the state raise revenue to redistribute among school districts. The state becomes the solution because only the state has the authority to raise sufficient resources to engage in this redistribution.

Proponents of state involvement see the state role as relevant in other areas where equity issues emerge. Consumers, for example, are often seen as helpless without the leverage of government. Many public employee groups feel that without state mandates, local governments will not negotiate with them and that they will receive lower wages and benefits. To remedy that, public employees have worked to pass state laws that require local governments to bargain with them and to set the terms of the negotiations. Without such mandates, a local government or school district may refuse to recognize an employee group or to negotiate with that group. The states vary in the mandates they impose on their local governments, and studies of the effects of state mandates have shown that the more a state issues and supports these mandates, the better local employee groups do in obtaining salary and benefit increases.[11]

Again and again we see that while some groups see the state government as detrimental to liberty, others see it as the means to create a response to their needs. Some fear centralized government, while others see it as essential to individual liberty.

The Battle over the Role of State Government

These debates about the role of the state are persistent. They show up in public opinion surveys. Table 4.3 presents an example. Individuals were asked who they thought was responsible for racial inequality and poverty. They were also asked

Table 4.3

Perceptions of Individual versus Society Responsibility for Causes and Solutions to Racial Inequality and Poverty

| | Racial Inequality | | Poverty | |
| | Perceived Responsibility for Solution | | | |
Perceived Responsibility for Cause	*Individual (%)*	*Society (%)*	*Individual (%)*	*Society (%)*
Individual	63	37	64	36
Society	27	73	32	68

Note: Percentages sum across for each problem area.
Source: Shanto Iyengar, "How Citizens Think about National Issues: A Matter of Responsibility," American Journal of Political Science, 33, no. 4 (November 1989): 887.

who they thought should take responsibility for solving these problems. Those who regarded society as responsible are likely to seek solutions from society. To these individuals, state governments are crucial mechanisms to respond to problems. Those who think individuals cause their own problems see no need for the state to remedy problems of the individual. Indeed, they believe that involvement by the state provides individuals with benefits they do not deserve and that may undermine their resolve to get out of their situation.[12]

These divisions of opinion persist in our society, and they are often very intense. With some exceptions, the arguments for decentralization are usually put forth by conservatives, while the arguments for centralization are articulated by liberals. These arguments are likely to persist. There is no objective basis for selecting one line of reasoning as the true one, or for saying that one way of implementing policy is better. As with so many other aspects of politics, the relative truth of either argument is heavily dependent on the experiences of the individual. Those who have found their local governments responsive, and who are not frustrated over a lack of opportunities in society, find the argument for decentralization persuasive. Many middle-class and upper-class whites in our society fall into that situation, and they are staunch advocates of local autonomy. Those who have found local governments unresponsive to their needs find little merit in the argument for decentralization.

These debates are reflected in the positions that politicians take on issues. Democrats are usually more in favor of state mandates, a greater state role in funding of education, and state aid formulas that distribute state aid to low-income communities. Republicans often see little need for these policies and many dangers in them. These decisions about whether, and which level of, government should be involved become political issues. While it may seem logical to implement policy in a way that is rational, efficient, and effective, the definition of what is "best" becomes political, or subject to debate within the political process. Each group sees its own policy as rational and uses that rhetoric to describe its proposals. But what is involved is a political debate about the way power and responsibilities in society should be distributed. Groups see varying benefits from different distributions and fight over changes in these arrangements.

The Role of the State: Change amid Continuing Diversity

Political debates over the role of state government have political consequences. They affect the role state government plays. They affect how much the state does and how much it intrudes in local affairs. These debates about what role state and local governments should have play out differently in each state. States have different histories and traditions, and these contexts shape how these debates evolve. Some states have a long history of decentralization. Any argument about the state playing a greater role in those states means that considerable change will have to take place. Such changes are not always easy to bring about. In some states, as discussed in Chapter 2, the population is conservative and not receptive to change. In other states the population is liberal and more inclined to support change. The effects of these debates depend on the situation that exists when the debate occurs.

To understand the significance of state histories, we first need to know the kinds of local governments that exist, how their relationship to state governments has changed over time, and the current situation that prevails in the states. This information will provide the background against which these debates about the role of state governments play out.

Local Governments and Relations with the State

Decentralization begins with local governments. The more local governments there are, the more possibilities for having many different political processes with varying populations and wealth bases making policy choices. Local governments are given their right to exist by the state, and there are several different types of local governments the states have created. All of them were created to cover specific geographic areas and to be responsible for certain governmental activities in their area.

Some local governments are described as general purpose because they are responsible for several functions.[13] County governments are general-purpose governments that were created to serve as basic governmental units over geographic divisions of the state. These governments were created to ensure that each area of the state, no matter how rural, was covered by a local-government unit. In some cases these county governments are now in heavily urban areas and are responsible for many activities and large sums of money.[14]

The other major general-purpose government is the municipality. Municipalities are formed when people wish a general-purpose government to make decisions about matters in their area. Municipalities are almost always smaller than counties. Most counties in urban areas encompass many different municipalities.

Some areas of the country have other general-purpose governments. In the Midwest, most states have created townships or subdivisions of counties. Townships assume local responsibility for the functions that the county handles. In New England there are also "towns," jurisdictions smaller than counties. These jurisdictions cover the entire state and ensure that each area has some general jurisdiction government.

In addition to these governments, there are are also special-purpose (single-purpose) governments, which handle only one responsibility. The most prominent of these is the school district. The only responsibility of such districts is to manage schools. They raise money through property tax or they receive aid from the city, county, and state. The other type of single-purpose government is a special district, created by the state legislature to handle one problem within a set geographic area. A single-purpose government is generally designed to handle a problem that encompasses an area larger than a municipality or a county, or an area different from them. The district is often created because the individual governments of the area find it difficult to coordinate their activities for a specific problem. An example of special districts is one set up for mosquito abatement. No single local government can establish a program that will control mosquitoes (since they are so mobile), so a government that covers the entire affected region is created to coordinate mosquito control. Such districts are also created for soil-conservation programs and for supplying water to residences, businesses, and other sites.

There are an enormous number of these local governments in America.[15] Table 4.4 presents the types of local governments that exist and the number of each type. These local governments create decentralization of policy pursuance within the states.

The number of local governments, however, is only a starting point for understanding the degree of centralization in a state. Local governments are the legal creatures of the state, and there are many different ways that states can treat their local governments. The state controls the ability of local governments to raise revenue. The state controls the kinds of taxes that can be used, the level of taxation allowed, the amount of money that can be borrowed, and the ways in which it is borrowed.[16] The state can also mandate the policies pursued by local governments,

---

Table 4.4

Types of Local Governments in the United States, 1987

Type	Number	Percent
County	3,042	3.7
Municipal	19,200	23.1
Township	16,691	20.1
School districts	14,721	17.7
Special districts	29,532	35.5
TOTAL	83,186	

Source: U.S. Bureau of Census, Census of Governments, 1987, *vol.1, no. 1.*

covering such matters as the hours and shifts that police and fire personnel work, the number of days schools must meet, the requirements for being a teacher, the books that must be used in the classroom, the use of local zoning ordinances, the procedures that must be used in bargaining with local public employees, the local assessment practices, and a host of other matters. Some states use this power regularly, while others are more restrained.[17]

Who spends the money, however, does not tell us who provides the funds. Local governments do raise funds from local tax bases, but states also provide state aid to local governments. The state faces a decision of the degree of autonomy to allow local governments in the use of those funds.[18] State politics has come to be dominated by questions over the amount of aid the state will provide and what restraints will be placed on this aid.

State funds can be distributed through formula or project grants. About 85 percent of all state aid is distributed through these two grants. Formula grants distribute funds according to certain criteria, such as the size of the population in the locality, or its per capita income. For example, the amount a community receives can be determined by multiplying a set amount times the population. Project grants are funds awarded for a specific project. The funds cover only that project and are a onetime award. The aid may be granted in order to rebuild a bridge, to renovate buildings, or to subsidize the building of an office complex that is supposed to attract business to an area. To obtain such funds a state or local government must file an application with a federal or state government agency justifying the request. This justification usually involves indicating the positive benefits that will accompany the project and demonstrating the capability of the local government to conduct that project.

These forms of intergovernmental aid generate different local concerns. The existence of project grants promotes a focus on trying to sell state and federal agencies on specific local projects, such as convention or sports complexes. Formula grants, on the other hand, encourage strong political lobbying efforts to try to alter or to maintain the terms of formulas for distributing local aid. One central battle is over the distribution of education aid. Suburban schools find that most of their students show up regularly for class, and they would like to see aid distributed on the basis of actual pupil attendance. Inner-city schools have problems with truancy, and they would like to see aid distributed on the basis of the number of students enrolled in the school (many of whom do not show up on a regular basis).

The primary focus of these battles is the redistributive impact of these formulas. Some legislators try to promote redistribution from wealthier cities to those with lower wealth bases, while other legislators (usually from well-to-do areas) try to minimize such redistribution.

State-Local Fiscal Relations and Change

The relationship between state and local governments is a product of the political process. This relationship is affected by larger political debates about differences in tax bases, issues of local discretion, and equity issues. In recent decades the debates over whether the state should play a greater role have been resolved largely in favor of such a role, and over the last several decades states have come to play a much greater role.[19] Some of this increase has occurred because the federal government has pressured states to assume the responsibility for the delivery of services such as welfare.[20] But much of the change is because advocates within the state of having state governments play a greater role have been influential.

Figure 4.1 presents summary figures on how the relative role of the state has changed over the years. The figure presents the percent of all state-local taxes raised by the state, the percent of all state-local expenditure conducted directly by the state, and the percent of local revenue derived from state governments. There has been a significant increase in the role of the state in raising and spending money, and in providing aid to local governments. In recent decades these changes have been the greatest in the East and the West.[21] Government in these regions was more decentralized forty years ago, and the data reflects the move toward centralization. As a result of the changes, over the years state-local relationships have become more similar across the states.

Current State-Local Relations in the States

Despite all this change, state governments still differ enormously in the roles they play in raising money, directly delivering services, and providing aid to local governments. The variations in practices are significant. In Table 4.5, the states are

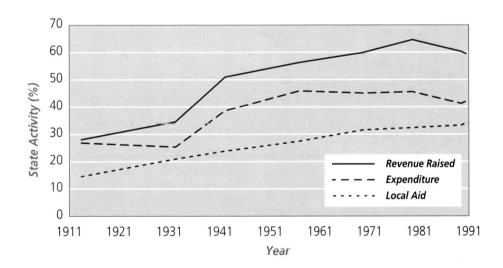

Figure 4.1

Fiscal Centralization across the States

Sources: Jeffrey M. Stonecash, "Fiscal Centralization in American States: Similarity and Diversity," Publius, *13, no.4;* Governmental Finances in 1989–1990 *(Washington, DC, 1991) GF/90-5; and,* Government Finances: 1990–1991, *Preliminary Report (Washington, DC, 1993), GF/91-5p.*

Table 4.5
The Role of State Government

	Revenue Raised by State (%)	Revenue Spent by State (%)	Local Reliance (%)
Minimal state role:			
Colorado	31.9	35.5	25.1
Florida	37.7	32.6	29.2
New Hampshire	22.4	44.2	12.5
Nebraska	34.4	41.8	19.6
New York	37.7	33.6	32.5
Oregon	34.2	41.3	24.5
Texas	35.6	34.4	24.2
Limited state role:			
Arizona	43.6	39.2	35.5
Georgia	42.1	39.3	28.3
Illinois	40.9	40.9	26.8
Indiana	43.8	43.2	37.3
Iowa	43.3	44.9	33.2
Kansas	40.0	40.2	25.9
Michigan	42.4	42.5	32.3
New Jersey	39.8	41.1	31.5
Ohio	42.0	40.0	33.0
Pennsylvania	43.7	40.4	32.2
South Dakota	32.8	53.3	22.0
Virginia	40.0	42.9	30.4
Wyoming	32.2	41.5	38.8
Moderate state role:			
Alabama	43.9	49.5	35.4
Alaska	28.0	63.6	36.9
California	44.8	32.0	43.0
Louisiana	37.5	47.9	32.3
Maryland	44.6	45.0	26.9
Montana	39.5	48.9	29.8
North Dakota	39.1	56.0	35.9
Tennessee	41.5	44.6	44.0
Utah	42.7	50.2	35.6
Vermont	41.5	58.5	28.9
Significant state role:			
Arkansas	52.1	51.4	41.4
Connecticut	47.3	52.3	28.5
Delaware	49.8	64.2	44.5
Hawaii	53.8	77.8	8.0
Idaho	49.4	47.0	39.4

Table 4.5 (continued)
The Role of State Government

	Revenue Raised by State (%)	Revenue Spent by State (%)	Local Reliance (%)
Significant state role:			
Kentucky	53.4	54.0	40.6
Maine	47.4	51.8	33.2
Massachusetts	49.9	53.5	37.9
Minnesota	45.9	35.7	38.7
Mississippi	46.1	40.9	39.5
Missouri	45.2	41.1	28.2
Nevada	45.4	34.3	37.3
New Mexico	46.1	48.9	50.1
North Carolina	50.3	39.9	41.8
Oklahoma	47.1	47.1	33.8
Rhode Island	45.4	59.1	28.8
South Carolina	48.6	49.0	36.4
Washington	50.5	46.3	39.0
West Virginia	55.4	55.3	42.1
Wisconsin	46.5	37.2	42.0

Source: U.S. Department of Commerce, Bureau of the Census, Government Finances, 1989–1990 *(Washington, DC, 1991), GF-5.*

grouped to distinguish different levels of state participation. The first group of states are those in which the state plays a minimal role, relative to the activity levels of local governments. Compared to other states, in New Hampshire and Oregon, the state government essentially leaves raising money and the making of policy to local governments. In these states, an average of 61.7 percent of school funds come from locally raised revenues, and there are continuing debates about whether the state should do more to provide aid to schools. This reliance on local revenues is much higher than in other states.

At the other extreme, in the last group of states, which includes Delaware, New Mexico, and West Virginia, the state plays a significant role in raising, spending, and providing money. In this group of states, the average proportion of school funds that are locally raised is only 36.3 percent. In these states, the state government is already heavily involved in school finance, and probably in schools in general.

Within this last group, Hawaii provides an example of a state where most services are handled directly by the state, and local governments are responsible for only about 20 percent of all direct expenditure.

Arkansas and West Virginia are similar to Hawaii in that the state government is a dominant and direct provider of services, but both of these states also provide about 50 percent of local revenue. In such situations government is also very centralized. Other states have taken quite different approaches to the issues of fiscal responsibilities. New York, Minnesota, and North Carolina present situations where the state does not play a dominant role as a direct provider of services, but it does provide relatively high levels of local government revenues. While this is a less centralized situation than those just discussed, the state and its local governments are heavily tied together by the reliance of local governments on the state, and by the recognition by state politicians that a major part of the state budget goes for "local" (or at least locally administered) programs.

Finally, we have states, such as Ohio, Montana, and Virginia, where the state plays a moderate role in directly providing services and local funds. These are states in which the combined delivery of government programs by state and local governments is relatively decentralized.

These variations provide us with only a rough idea of the different approaches the states have taken toward the centralization of policy within their confines. These variations indicate the general tendency within the state regarding who will be responsible for decisions, financing, and implementation. There are also significant differences within each policy area. States differ in the role the state plays in funding such areas as mass transportation and public welfare. States differ in the degree to which they mandate local activities. The indicators are also just relative. A state government that appears to play a minimal role may still do a great deal within the state, but less relative to some other state governments.

These fiscal relations create situations that are the background for political debates in each state. Where policy decisions are generally made through local political processes that use local resources to solve problems, there is usually a presumption that a local approach is the norm. If a group or political party wishes to change that, they must mobilize great support. Tradition creates a presumption that the usual way of doing things should continue. Change is by no means impossible in such a situation, but a strong case for change has to be presented, or something has to go wrong with the existing approach. Changing the role of the state in Texas or New Hampshire, for example, would be very difficult because it would require a significant rearrangement of responsibilities.

In other states, state government has been heavily involved in local affairs for some time, and the question of state government involvement is not a major issue. The governor and the legislature are active in deciding local matters, and local officials (often with some grumbling) expect state intervention in their affairs. Indeed, many local officials regularly focus on lobbying state officials regarding "local" matters because the state generally makes final decisions on such matters.

Local Consolidation Battles

Efforts to change governmental relationships have also occurred at the local level. As noted in Chapter 3, American suburbs have continually expanded. This development of a "fragmented" metropolis (multiple governments with differing tax bases and separate provision of services) has not proceeded without criticism. Many groups argue that the arrangement has led to duplication of services and inefficiency. Others argue that it has led to segregation of populations and tax bases in ways that create inequality within metropolitan areas.

In many metropolitan areas, reform groups have pushed for changes to respond to this fragmented metropolis. In most cases, advocates for change have argued that either some services, or all local governments, should be consolidated into a single metropolitan government in order to have a more coherent and efficient government arrangement. Often reformers have pushed for and obtained public referenda on the question of whether local governments should be consolidated into a single county or metropolitan government. These efforts have usually been strongly opposed by suburban residents who do not want a common government shared with central-city residents.

Most efforts at forming consolidated metropolitan governments have failed because of this opposition. State laws usually require that majorities of both central-city and suburban residents approve such change, and suburban areas usually vote against consolidation.[22] Metropolitan areas with many different local governments, very diverse tax bases, and large population diversity continue to exist.

Change, however, has occurred. While complete consolidation has encountered considerable opposition, two changes have altered metropolitan government arrangements. First, there has been a quiet and gradual transfer of some functions from local governments to county governments.[23] Counties have taken on responsibility for police-dispatch services, water and sewage services, and such areawide services as sports stadiums. These changes usually occur gradually and are presented as isolated changes.[24] Over time many counties have assumed many more responsibilities, and many play a significant role in decision making in their jurisdictions.[25]

Second, even though local municipalities often resist consolidating or transferring responsibility for a service, many are willing to enter into cooperative arrangements with other local governments to share equipment and information and to coordinate their activities to form a quasi-metropolitan approach to service delivery.[26] In many metropolitan areas library books are shared so that each library does not have to buy its own inventory. Police-dispatch services are coordinated. Planning and demographic information are shared. The lack of consolidation of local governments frustrates many critics, but cooperation does represent coordinated action that might otherwise not occur.

The consequence is that over time county governments have come to play a much bigger role than they did several decades ago.[27] They now have much bigger budgets and are acknowledged to be major actors in decision making. They also impose more taxes. While there is still intense opposition to complete consolidation, counties have come to play a greater role in providing a forum for metropolitan decision making. Much as with states, this role varies considerably from area to area and state to state.

Paying for Government: Issues of Raising Money

When state governments take action, that action almost always costs money. Some costs involve direct payments to individuals, such as with welfare or college financial aid. Other costs involve personnel to manage programs. Regardless of how the money is spent, revenue must be found. How to raise money is a major and continual decision for politicians.

Money can be raised from a number of sources, and each of these sources raises a political issue. Politicians can impose income or sales taxes, or they can charge fees for using services. Funds can also be raised by borrowing money, by charging fees, or by seeking intergovernmental aid. Each of these sources generates political opposition and political support. Each of them also raises issues of whether they are fair or unfair. Choosing among the alternatives is never an easy task for politicians.

Paying for Facilities and Services

Many projects require large initial expenditures, but much less expenditure for maintenance. Government may be considering constructing a sports stadium, a new park, or an arts facility. These projects are expensive, and it is usually impossible to pay the up-front costs of such projects out of current revenues. The state must borrow. The question that emerges is how the money should be paid back. Should funds be taken from general revenues with the presumption that the general public benefits, or should the users of the particular facility pay? If an arts facility is constructed and used primarily by the more affluent, shouldn't users pay additional costs each time they visit? If a sports stadium is built, should the costs be recouped from the team and the fans involved? The issue of whether government should provide general support for facilities that are used by one segment of the population is difficult to resolve. Some believe such facilities help an entire area, while others want the group benefitting most to pay.

There is also the question of whether the way in which facilities and services are paid for affects our tendency to use them. Economists have been particularly concerned with this matter. Government services can be regarded either as generally available to everyone or as a service consumed by specific individuals. When a service is intended to be available to everyone, we regard it as a collective good, or one that everyone enjoys. The common example of such a good is individual education, which is presumed to benefit the entire society. In contrast, other goods are used and enjoyed only by the specific individuals using them. People whose houses do not catch fire might never use fire departments. Individuals who do not water their lawns (or have no lawns to water) use less water. People who do not go to parks do not benefit from them.

This difference in usage leads many people to argue that there should also be a difference in the way services are paid for. Goods consumed by individuals should be paid for by those individuals. If this is not done, users have no idea of the cost of services, and consumption will bear no relationship to the cost of providing the services. This idea of payment may lead to a significant distortion of the provision of government services.

The argument generally put forth is that when services are presented to the public in a way in which the costs are not clearly tied to usage, there is a tendency toward over-usage of those services, compared to what would happen if people had to pay for what they actually used. There is evidence to support this proposition. Most of us perceive no direct personal cost when we use roads to transport ourselves. We think about the cost of our car, not about the costs of road construction and maintenance. As a result, our society is very dependent on cars. We probably consume larger quantities of "road usage" than we would if we had to pay for roads to the degree that we use them. We generally do not pay for park facilities, and there are many people who argue that our parks are overcrowded as a result of that. The proposed solution has been to impose fees that cover the actual costs of maintaining the parks.

Governments are also affected by the prices they face. Studies of overcrowding in prison facilities found that most overcrowding was due to the structure of costs facing local governments.[28] In Illinois, local courts have the option of sending convicted criminals to county jails or to state prisons. If they send them to county jails, the county pays for the cost of imprisonment. If the individual is sent to a state prison, the state pays for it, and the county bears no costs. During recent years, there has been a significant increase in the state prison population. This increase is much greater than the rise in crime across the state, and it appears that the reason for the increase is linked to the cost of confinement in county jails. Counties do not pay state imprisonment costs, so county courts tend to overconsume state prison space.

In this particular case, the outcome may be an unintended consequence of the pricing policies. In many cases, though, this "overconsumption" is not unanticipated or undesired. States price the cost of education at community colleges, junior colleges, and state universities lower than the real cost because they want more individuals to pursue education. The presumption is that the education of the individual is a general benefit to society. Since everyone in the society will benefit, everyone should share the cost. That same argument is the basis for everyone in a community paying for elementary and secondary education. In many policy areas, the public appears to accept the idea of "underpricing" user costs so that usage will be greater. Most people would like to have many more services provided in this manner.

This argument over collective versus individual benefits and over pricing policies for government services emerges frequently in political debates. Some groups consistently emphasize the collective benefits that follow from the promotion of education, parks, and road systems, while others place their emphasis on the importance of individuals being aware of the costs of the services they consume. The latter group often argues there is too much government and too much consumption because of these pricing policies.

Conservatives usually line up on the side of creating more cost consciousness, while liberals are inclined to think of the collective benefits that follow from public usage of government services. There are exceptions, of course, and many liberals have become more interested in pricing policies, but this division between liberals and conservatives is unlikely to disappear.

These debates have also affected decisions about ways to raise revenue. During the last two decades, state and local governments have received less federal aid and and have seen greater resistance to taxes. Many states and localities have imposed charges and fees as a way to raise more money and to make users pay more of the costs of services. In 1952, such charges and miscellaneous revenue accounted for 14.3 percent of all state and local general revenue. By 1989, they had grown to 24.3 percent.[29]

Raising Taxes

The most common way for state and local governments to raise money is to impose taxes. The question is who (or what) should pay taxes. Should it be corporations, or should it be individuals? Some people feel that corporations should pay because they make money from their presence in a state or community, and because they generally are more able to afford taxes. Others argue that these moral arguments have little meaning because corporations ultimately pass along their tax burdens to individuals by raising their prices by an amount equivalent to the taxes paid, thus "shifting" the tax obligation to consumers. There is, of course, dispute over the extent to which business can shift taxes to consumers.

If the decision is made to tax individuals, there are still the issues of whom to tax and the way that tax should be applied. These debates are shaped somewhat by tradition. The property tax is generally regarded as a local-government tax. The sales tax is usually imposed and collected by the state, though some states allow their local governments the option of adding percentage points to the state sales tax. The locally added percent is collected by the state and then returned to local governments. The personal income tax, however, is used almost exclusively by state governments.

The crucial issues revolve around which taxes should be imposed and how they should be structured. Should an income, sales, or property tax be applied? Should individuals be taxed on the basis of their current income (the income tax), on the amount they spend (sales tax), or on the value of the property they own (property tax)? Each of these is a different manifestation of wealth, and an individual may register high in one but not in another. Someone might have an expensive home, but not a high income. This is often the case for young couples who have just bought a home, and for retired individuals, who have a house that is worth more than they now earn. These arguments lead to criticism of the property tax. For twenty years, the Advisory Commission on Intergovernmental Relations has commissioned annual polls on the taxes regarded as most unfair. The property tax regularly is first or second in that category.[30] Others argue that taxing consumption is not fair because it means taxing people for buying necessities, such as food, clothing, furniture, and cars. If an income tax is used, will it be progressive? The argument is generally made that those who earn higher incomes are able to pay more in tax. Those who earn more are not in favor of such an approach. They will pay a higher percentage of their income in taxes, and they argue that such taxes added on to the federal tax is a disincentive to work.

Taxes and Economic Growth

While much of the concern over taxation revolves around its effects on individuals, an enduring issue of tax policy is how it affects business organizations. States and localities derive the bulk of their revenue from taxes raised within their jurisdictions. To raise revenue they must have a strong economic base. States and localities must continually seek to attract and retain economic activity. This effort results in business activity that can be taxed. More business revenue increases sales tax revenue. Greater economic activity generates new jobs. Employed individuals have income that can be taxed, and they purchase new homes, generating property tax revenue.

In our federal system, each state and locality is on its own in attracting economic activity.[31] This separateness creates competition between and across regions. Governments become wary of establishing tax policies that could create an unfavorable business "climate." This general concern about the treatment of economic activity usually emerges in two forms. First, are taxes on corporations too high relative to other states? Second, are taxes on upper-income people too high? The anxiety is that high taxes in either regard will drive economic activity out of the state.

The question for policy makers is the degree to which taxes affect the inclination of businesses to stay in a state, to move to another state, and to survive. Despite all of the concern with this matter, there is considerable disagreement over the impact of taxes.[32] At first glance, there appears to be strong evidence that taxes do affect the location of economic activity. Over the last thirty years, taxes have been higher in northern states than in the Sunbelt states. During those years northern states have had many businesses fail or move to Sunbelt states. Northern states have experienced population loss as people moved south. It seems plausible to conclude that taxes prompted these shifts. It also seems plausible to conclude that higher taxes make areas less attractive to businesses.

While this conclusion may seem obvious, it is not so clear that business relocation is just a function of tax levels. Much of the decline in economic activity in northern states in the last twenty years has been because of general declines in "heavy" industries (cars, steel, machinery) in the United States. Foreign competitors can produce these products at lower prices, and the number of American industries in these areas has shrunk. It is not so much these industries moved elsewhere, as that they "died." Since these heavy industries were originally located in northern states, the greatest decline in economic activity should be in those states.

It is difficult to tell how much state tax levels influenced this decline. Tax levels were high in many of these states because these states had (and still have) a highly diverse population that makes many demands on government for services. But tax levels may not have driven industry out. Many analysts argue that taxes are only one of many matters that businesses consider when deciding where to locate.

Businesses also consider where raw materials are, what transportation costs will be to move raw materials, how good transportation systems (roads, for example) are, how plentiful labor is, how well educated the labor force is, what labor costs will be, and how well organized the unions are. There are also questions of where complementary industries (those that produce items such as glass and tires that, together with the product of a company, produce a final product, such as autos) are locating, and where the markets for a company's products are growing the most. Taxes may play a minor or a major role in such decision processes and their role varies by industry.

There are also many who argue that taxes simply are not the burden they appear to be. Many economists argue that corporations can often pass taxes along to consumers in the form of higher prices, so that the tax burden is reduced. This again varies by industry.

Finally, some politicians argue that the services governments provide (paid for by taxes) are essential for the long-term health of business. Businesses must have good road systems. It takes money to create an adequate infrastructure. Businesses also want a good labor force. They do not want illiterate workers with low productivity. Politicians argue that expenditures on education contribute to a better labor force. Imposing taxes to pay for these services may not be liked, but these services ultimately contribute to making areas more attractive.

These debates create considerable ambiguity about the impact of taxes and unease over what should be done. Despite that ambiguity, the primary instinct is to presume there is some truth to the argument that taxes are detrimental. Most northern states have been concerned in recent years about restraining taxes to make the state more competitive.

Tax level issues also play a role in the Sunbelt states. These states are experiencing economic growth and are reluctant to raise tax levels for fear of harming future growth. Yet, at the same time, officials in these states are concerned that sustaining growth will require taxes to fund better educational, transportation, and cultural services. Some southern states, for example, found that their states could not attract businesses because of limits in their education and transportation systems. The ambiguity of what to do about taxes and services is a problem for states and communities at both ends of the spectrum.

Tax Performance

Politicians may worry about the way taxes affect individuals, businesses, and economic growth, but they also worry about the way taxes perform for the government. Performance refers to whether taxes produce a stable flow of resources, how taxes respond to economic change, and how visible taxes are.

Stability

Government establishes programs that involve commitments. People must be hired to execute programs; people who are declared eligible for benefits are told they can expect to receive them for some definite or indefinite time; money is borrowed and must be repaid; projects that must be paid for are started. To fulfill all of these obligations government must be able to count on a reasonably stable flow of revenue from taxes. The best way to achieve stability is to rely on taxes whose yield does not fluctuate when economic conditions do. Revenues from income and sales taxes vary as the economy fluctuates. As unemployment rises during a recession, incomes decline and people purchase less. As a result, the state receives less in income- and sales-tax revenue. The greater government reliance on these taxes, the less stable revenue flows are. When recessions occur, revenues decline and politicians are forced to raise taxes or to cut programs. Property taxes, on the other hand, are more stable, because property values do not fluctuate as much as incomes or sales do.

Yield and Elasticity

While relying on the property tax might be a solution, such reliance has other problems. In addition to the issue of regressivity, the property tax does not tend to grow a great deal as the economy grows. It is an inelastic tax, or one in which the percentage increase in tax revenue does not correspond to the percentage increase in economic activity. Home and commercial property do increase in value over time, but not as much as income and sales activity can. For that reason, some politicians are not inclined to rely on the property tax. They prefer taxes more "responsive" to long-term economic growth.

This inclination toward an elastic tax system, though, is not shared by everyone. Indeed, to some people, this elasticity is a prime reason to oppose the income and sales tax. Income taxes in particular are bothersome to opponents. Income taxes are usually progressive to some degree. As people experience higher incomes they move into higher tax brackets and pay more taxes. Inflation pushes this pattern along. People may not have higher real incomes, but they still pay more in taxes. Since inflation persists in our society, the income tax generates more money for government without any apparent changes in tax rates. The sales tax works in a similar way.

Opponents of the income tax argue that it allows government to acquire money without having to actually raise taxes. Government grows without a political decision to do so. Critics argue that this gives liberals more money to spend while allowing them to deny that they are raising taxes. In relying on the income tax, politicians can count on more revenue without having to take noticeable action.

This pattern has led many to seek indexed taxes, or taxes formulated from tables that rise with inflation so that more revenue does not flow to government simply because of inflation. Other politicians oppose such changes because they do rely on this flow of revenue. Several states have adopted indexing, but it is not yet widespread.

Visibility

Finally, there is the issue of tax visibility, or the extent to which the public is aware that they are paying certain taxes. Politicians worry about visibility. Some want taxes to be highly visible so that everyone will fully appreciate the "pain" that government is inflicting on citizens. They believe that government should acquire revenue only if everyone is fully aware of how much they are paying. The property tax is usually regarded as visible because it is paid in periodic lump sums. The income and sales tax are regarded as less visible. Income taxes are withheld from paychecks, and individuals get used to paying without realizing what they have paid. The sales tax is also somewhat low in visibility because we generally do not think about how much money we pay in sales taxes.

Other politicians, of course, are less interested in making taxes visible. It is not that these politicians are seeking to be evasive so much as they wish to make the necessary evil of raising money as palatable as possible. Their opponents, of course, are skeptical of this argument.

The choice among taxes is not an easy one, and it is a choice with many political overtones. Many conservatives would prefer to have a stable yield, with low elasticity and high visibility, while many liberals would prefer a high yield, elastic tax that is not quite so "painful." These matters may not be of high concern to most of the public, but they do receive considerable attention from politicians who must decide among taxes.

Changes in Tax Levels

The debate about how much to tax is perpetual. While the debate continues, change continues. Levels of taxation by state and local governments have risen as state and local governments have taken on more responsibilities and provided more services.[33] As discussed earlier, the role of the state has grown more than that of local governments. This difference is reflected in the increase in tax effort since 1950 shown in Figure 4.2. Tax effort is the percent of all personal income of the population taken in taxes by state or local governments.

Total state and local tax effort has increased significantly. It rose steadily until the mid-1970s. Around that time, resistance to taxes increased, resulting in a widely discussed "tax revolt" in the late 1970s and early 1980s.[34] Since that time tax levels have been relatively stable. Over this forty-year time period, the tax effort of state governments has almost doubled, while that of local governments has increased only slightly. This difference is just another indicator of the greater role state governments have taken on in recent decades.

Paying for Government: Tax Burdens

The decision to impose taxes prompts questions about who has the money to pay (the distribution of income), who will pay, and what is fair. These issues provoke some of our most intense political debates.[35] We may know how income is distributed, but it is often difficult to anticipate what individuals and income groups will actually pay. The burden of taxes is greatly affected by tax-law provisions that specify how the law applies and what kinds of exemptions exist. There is also the issue of who receives the benefits of the expenditure financed by taxation.

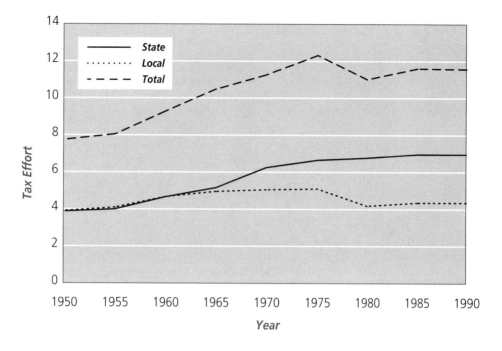

Figure 4.2
State, Local, and Total Tax Effort, 1950–1990
Source: U.S. Bureau of the Census, **Governmental Finances,** *GF 5, various years.*

The primary way of evaluating tax burdens is to assess what each income group pays. As noted earlier, a progressive tax is one that takes a larger proportion of income as income levels increase. A proportional tax is one that takes the same proportion of income regardless of the level of income. A regressive tax is one that takes a smaller proportion of income as income levels increase. Republicans are usually opposed to highly progressive taxes, while Democrats are more in favor of them. Almost no one advocates regressive taxes, but conservatives are often more willing to tolerate them. The political question that dominates many taxation debates is the question of how tax burdens will be distributed among income levels.

The simplest (and most deceptive) way to evaluate taxes is by the nominal rates listed in the laws. These nominal rates, however, neglect considerations of the exemptions allowed. Despite those limits, it is important to note the degree to which states vary their rates for the personal income tax. Table 4.6 provides some examples of differences in progressivity for the state income tax.

In Arizona and North Dakota, the personal income tax is progressive. Tax rates applied to higher levels of income increase. The highest rates, however, apply only to those with very high incomes so much of the population does not pay these

Table 4.6

Tax Schedules in the States

State	Income Subject to Tax (in dollars)	Marginal Tax Rate for Each Income Level (%)
Arizona	0–10,000	3.8
	10,001–25,000	4.4
	25,001–50,000	5.25
	50,001–150,000	6.5
	150,000 +	7.0
California	0–4,213	1.0
	4,214–9,985	2.0
	9,986–15,757	4.0
	15,758–21,875	6.0
	21,876–27,646	8.0
	27,646 +	9.3
Illinois	Taxable Net Income	3.0
Kansas	0–27,500	4.5
	27,501 +	5.95
North Carolina	0–12,750	6.0
	12,751 +	7.0
North Dakota	0–3,000	2.67
	3,001–5,000	4.0
	5,001–8,000	5.33
	8,001–15,000	6.67
	15,001–25,000	8.0
	25,001–35,000	9.33
	35,001–50,000	10.67
	50,000 +	
Oregon	0–2,000	5.0
	2,001–5,000	7.0
	5,000 +	9.0

Source: Advisory Commission of Intergovernmental Affairs, Significant Features of Fiscal Federalism *(Washington, DC, 1991), volume 1, table 22.*

higher rates. In contrast, in California and Oregon, personal income tax is less progressive. The highest rate is reached fairly quickly, and much more of the population is paying the higher rate. States such as Kansas and North Carolina have income-tax systems that are not very progressive. Only two income groups are created, and there is not much difference in rates between the top and bottom income groups. In Illinois, there is no variation in the tax level applied to different income levels, so there is no progressivity unless other provisions of tax law create progressivity.

Tax burdens are also affected by the exemptions and deductions individuals can claim before they report their taxable income. A state may allow individuals to deduct the amount paid in property taxes from their reported income, and thus reduce the income subject to taxes. The use of exemptions and deductions creates actual tax burdens different from nominal tax rates. A great deal of low-visibility legislative activity revolves around changing the technical provisions of the tax law to alter deductions and exemptions.

The primary concern with taxes is the way they actually affect taxpayers. This actual effect can be very different from the apparent effect because of individual behavior. The property tax illustrates this problem. This tax is almost always listed as a flat rate, but many argue that it ends up being regressive. This occurs for two reasons. First, as people make more money, they do not buy progressively more expensive homes. While a family that makes $20,000 might buy a $60,000 home, a person who makes $50,000 might buy only a $100,000 home. Since the property tax is applied on a flat basis, the first family pays, as an example, 4 percent of the value of the home, or $2,400. The second family also pays 4 percent, or $4,000. The first family pays 12.0 percent of the family income, while the second family pays only 8.0 percent of its income.

In addition, families benefit from being allowed to deduct the property tax paid from the total of their reported income. Since higher-income groups pay more in taxes, they are able to avoid more in taxes. Federal law also allows homeowners to deduct mortgage interest payments before determining the amount of their income subject to taxation. This deduction further reduces tax obligations.

The final effect of these practices is that the property tax tends to be regressive, a problem that causes continual political controversy. Legislators from low-income districts want to shift the burden of taxation to an income tax, while middle-class constituents are less concerned about such a shift. They may want to restrain the growth of the property tax, but they are leery of relying heavily on the income tax, which might become progressive. There is also pressure from senior citizens to reduce the impact of the property tax. Many senior citizens find themselves in a situation where they have lived in a house for a long time and it has appreciated to a high value. When they retire, their income drops, and the value of the home is not representative of their current income. They argue that taxing them on the basis of the value of their home is unfair.

One political solution to this dilemma has been to adopt what are known as "circuit breakers." Circuit breakers place a limit on the proportion of income that any individual can pay in property taxes. If the proportion goes above a certain level, they are exempt from any further obligation.

Determining the final burden of taxes involves calculating all the benefits (deductions and exemptions, among others) that different groups take advantage of and the actual taxes paid by different income groups. Once these calculations are complete, it is possible to determine the tax burden by income group, or the proportion of income that different income groups pay in taxes. One such calculation was done for all the states by the Citizens for Tax Justice.[36] The results of their analysis are shown in Table 4.7. The percentages of taxes paid are presented by quintiles, or fifths of the population, ranked from highest to lowest income. These

128   *American State and Local Politics*

Table 4.7
The Burden of State Taxes, 1991

All States	20th (%)	40th (%)	60th (%)	80th (%)	100th (%)	Difference in Taxes between the Top and Bottom Income Groups
Personal income	0.7	2.0	2.6	3.0	3.7	3.0
Property	5.4	3.7	3.2	2.9	2.5	−2.9
Sales	5.7	4.0	3.3	2.9	2.2	−3.5
All taxes	13.8	10.9	10.0	9.5	8.7	−5.1

State	20th (%)	40th (%)	60th (%)	80th (%)	100th (%)	Difference in Taxes between the Top and Bottom Income Groups
Maryland	8.0	11.5	10.9	10.6	10.0	2.0
Vermont	7.4	9.2	9.2	9.0	9.3	1.9
Hawaii	8.7	10.2	10.3	10.1	10.2	1.5
Minnesota	9.5	10.6	10.5	10.5	10.4	0.9
Oregon	9.8	11.1	10.5	10.7	10.7	0.9
Montana	7.1	7.4	7.4	7.6	7.6	0.5
Delaware	7.4	6.9	7.0	7.1	7.7	0.3
District of Columbia	10.9	11.6	11.6	11.7	11.2	0.3
New York	14.1	14.1	13.9	13.9	13.5	−0.6
Wisconsin	12.3	14.4	13.4	12.7	11.5	−0.8
North Carolina	10.6	9.8	9.7	9.7	9.3	−1.3
South Carolina	10.5	8.4	8.8	9.0	8.7	−1.8
Maine	12.4	9.7	9.4	9.9	10.4	−2.0
Alaska	5.3	3.6	3.1	3.0	2.8	−2.5
Colorado	11.0	10.0	9.3	8.8	8.2	−2.8
Virginia	11.8	10.2	9.5	9.2	8.9	−2.9
Massachusetts	13.6	11.7	11.3	11.1	10.6	−3.0
Idaho	12.8	9.4	9.6	9.7	9.5	−3.3
Kentucky	12.5	10.6	10.0	9.7	9.2	−3.3
Rhode Island	14.2	11.9	11.4	10.9	10.7	−3.5
Iowa	12.5	10.4	9.6	9.3	8.9	−3.6
Oklahoma	12.2	10.3	10.1	9.2	8.6	−3.6
Ohio	13.4	10.6	10.0	9.6	9.6	−3.8
Utah	13.7	12.0	11.2	10.8	9.9	−3.8
Georgia	13.0	10.7	10.1	9.6	9.0	−4.0
West Virginia	12.9	10.1	9.3	8.8	8.8	−4.1

Table 4.7 (continued)
The Burden of State Taxes, 1991

State	20th (%)	Percentile Groups 40th (%)	60th (%)	80th (%)	100th (%)	Difference in Taxes between the Top and Bottom Income Groups
New Mexico	13.1	10.4	9.4	9.2	9.0	−4.1
Michigan	14.3	12.2	11.4	11.1	10.3	−4.1
California	14.1	9.5	8.8	8.9	9.9	−4.2
New Jersey	15.2	11.8	10.8	10.5	10.7	−4.6
Arkansas	13.2	10.0	9.4	8.8	8.5	−4.7
Kansas	13.2	10.7	9.7	9.1	8.3	−4.9
Wyoming*	9.0	6.2	5.3	4.8	4.0	−5.0
Alabama	11.9	9.6	8.5	7.8	6.7	−5.2
Mississippi	12.9	9.4	8.6	8.1	7.6	−5.3
Missouri	13.0	10.0	9.1	8.4	7.7	−5.3
Arizona	14.3	10.7	9.6	9.0	8.3	−6.0
Nevada*	10.0	6.7	5.7	5.0	4.0	−6.0
North Dakota	13.3	9.4	8.5	7.9	7.2	−6.1
Indiana	14.8	11.0	9.9	9.3	8.4	−6.4
New Hampshire	12.7	8.2	7.6	7.2	6.3	−6.4
Louisiana	14.1	10.9	9.6	8.8	7.6	−6.5
Nebraska	16.9	13.1	11.5	10.5	9.8	−7.1
Pennsylvania	15.9	11.1	9.8	9.0	8.0	−7.9
Illinois	16.5	12.0	10.8	9.9	8.6	−7.9
Connecticut	16.5	10.7	9.5	8.9	8.4	−8.1
Florida*	13.8	9.5	7.6	6.5	5.1	−8.7
South Dakota*	16.2	10.3	8.7	7.6	6.3	−9.9
Tennessee*	15.2	9.7	7.7	6.5	5.2	−10.0
Texas*	17.1	10.7	8.4	7.3	6.0	−11.0
Washington*	17.4	11.6	9.5	8.4	6.7	−11.0

Source: Citizens for Tax Justice, A Far Cry from Fair *(Washington, DC, April 1991).*

quintiles group the population by those in the bottom 20 percent of family incomes, those in the next 20 percent, and so forth. The percent of income paid in taxes for each group is then reported.

The top part of the table presents the percent of each group's income taken by the three major taxes in all states and localities combined. The last column provides a crude indicator of how regressive taxes are. The numbers in this column indicate the difference between the percent paid in taxes by the bottom 20 percent and those in the top 20 percent. The rest of the table presents the burden of state and local tax systems for individual states. The states are arranged from the most progressive to the most regressive. Most states have regressive tax systems.

The tax systems that states set up, or allow to evolve, have consequences. People in the same income groups pay dramatically different taxes in different states.

What creates the differences shown in Table 4.7? Tax burdens by income groups depend on the kind of taxes states choose to rely on, and whether state tax law makes taxes regressive, proportional, or progressive. Some states rely heavily on the property tax, and since this tends to be regressive, it tilts the entire tax system towards being regressive. Other states rely on the income tax, but vary in how progressive it is. Some examples of how much these choices vary and their consequences are shown in Table 4.8. The table presents tax burdens by income groups for specific taxes in the four states, along with the tax burden from all taxes within the states.

Table 4.8
Tax Burdens by Income Groups in Four States

	Percentile Groups					
	20th (%)	***40th (%)***	***60th (%)***	***80th (%)***	***100th (%)***	***Difference in Taxes between Top and Bottom Income Groups***
Vermont						
Income	−1.9	1.6	2.2	2.5	3.8	5.7
Property	4.7	4.1	4.0	3.8	3.4	−1.3
Sales	2.9	2.4	2.1	1.9	1.5	−1.4
All taxes	7.4	9.2	9.2	9.0	9.3	1.9
New York						
Income	0.1	3.0	4.7	5.9	6.9	6.8
Property	6.4	5.9	4.9	4.4	3.7	−2.7
Sales	6.2	4.4	3.7	3.2	2.5	−3.7
All taxes	14.1	14.1	13.9	13.9	13.5	−0.6
Pennsylvania						
Income	3.4	3.4	3.4	3.4	3.4	0.0
Property	7.2	4.0	3.2	2.9	2.5	−4.7
Sales	4.1	3.0	2.5	2.2	1.8	−2.3
All taxes	15.9	11.1	9.8	9.0	8.0	−7.9
Texas						
Income	0.0	0.0	0.0	0.0	0.0	0.0
Property	7.6	4.2	3.3	3.0	2.7	−4.9
Sales	6.8	5.0	4.0	3.5	2.7	−4.1
All taxes	17.1	10.7	8.4	7.3	6.0	−11.0

Source: Citizens for Tax Justice, A Far Cry from Fair *(Washington, DC, April 1991).*

Vermont's overall tax system is progressive because it has a progressive income tax that offsets the effects of the property and sales tax. New York also has a progressive income tax, but because property and sales taxes are such a major source of revenue within the state, the overall system is still somewhat regressive. Pennsylvania has an income tax, but everyone pays the same percent, and the entire system ends up fairly regressive. Texas, despite several recent battles over adopting the income tax, does not have one, and the result is a very regressive tax system.

The importance of the income tax can be seen in another way. In Table 4.7 the states that do not have an income tax are noted with an asterisk next to their name. They are all states at the bottom of the list as they are the ones with the most regressive tax systems.

The crucial difference among states is the decision whether to utilize the income tax. The decision to adopt an income tax, make it progressive, and make it a primary means for raising revenue has enormous consequences. Such an income tax can affect the overall regressivity of the state tax system. Table 4.9 presents some evidence on just how important such a tax can be. The table classifies states by the extent to which the income tax is relied on for state and local tax revenue and by how progressive the income tax is. The table then presents the average difference between the top and bottom percentiles in tax burdens for the total state and local tax system (the numbers in the far right column in Table 4.7) for each group of states.

The results indicate clear differences between the groups of states. Most of the states in the upper left corner do not have a state income tax. Those that do, derive a very small percent of state and local tax revenue from the income tax, and the income tax is not very progressive. For these states, the average difference in tax burdens (proportion of income paid in taxes) for low- and upper-income groups is large. Those in the bottom one-fifth of family incomes pay 7.8 percent more of their income in taxes than those in the upper fifth. In contrast, those states that derive a large proportion of tax revenue from the income tax and have a more progressive income tax have much less regressive overall tax systems. In these states, in the lower right corner, those in the lower-income group pay only 1.6 percent more of their income in overall taxes than those in the upper income group. Decisions about income taxes have significant consequences for the equity of tax burdens.

The income-tax decision involves the two fundamental issues: how great a role the state should play, and how tax burdens should be distributed. Relying on the local property tax and local delivery of services creates more inequality in two ways. When there is inequality of tax bases among local governments, local services differ significantly. Individuals also face a more regressive tax system in such situations. The states in the upper left group derive a large percent of revenues from the property tax. That reliance creates inequalities and limits the role of the state.

The alternative is for the state to seek a greater role and to impose state taxes to finance that role. If the state is to address social problems, it must raise revenue to support its actions by imposing a sales or income tax. Those taxes, depending on how they are structured, can reduce inequalities of tax burdens.

Table 4.9

Reliance on the Income Tax and Progressivity: Average Difference in Tax Rates between Top and Bottom 20 Percent by Reliance on Personal Income Tax and Progressivity

		Progressivity of the Income Tax: Tax Difference between Top 20% and Bottom 20% Income Groups (%)	
		Low (0–3.4)	High (3.5 +)
State & Local Tax Revenue Derived from State Personal Income Tax (%)	0–14.9	−7.8* (Nine states) AK, FL, NV NH, SD, TN, TX, WA, WY	−6.0 (Six states) AZ, CT, LA MI, NM, ND
	15.00–24.9		-3.9 (Twenty states) AL, AR, CO, ID IL, IN, IA, KS ME, MI, MT, NE NJ, OK, PA, RI SC, VT, UT, WV
	25.0+		−1.6 (Fifteen states) CA, DE, GA, HI KY, MD, MA, MN MO, NY, NC, OH OR, VA, WI

*The top number in each cell is the average difference between the percent of income paid by the bottom and top income groups. The percent of the bottom is subtracted from that of the top, so a negative number indicates a regressive tax system.

Source: Derived from Citizens for Tax Justice, A Far Cry from Fair (Washington, DC, April 1991) and from government data collected by the author.

These issues—the role of the state and the kinds of tax systems in place—are the enduring concerns of politics and prompt major, usually partisan, political battles within states. In 1990, the state of New Jersey was torn by the question of how the state should respond to a court decision that its financing of schools was inequitable. In that decision the courts had ruled that it was the responsibility of the state to remedy the problem.[37] Democrats controlled both houses of the legislature and held the governorship. The issue prompted a prolonged and intense debate between the Democrats, who wanted to increase the income tax and make it more progressive, and the Republicans, who wanted far less drastic action. The Democrats eventually enacted their proposal. Prompted by a recession, they also raised the sales tax.

In the early 1990s, Texas also saw a major battle over the income tax due to a court decision that schools were inequitably financed. The issue was whether the state would increase tax revenue in order to address inequities. After a lengthy battle, no income tax was adopted because the Democrats could not muster enough votes.[38] In 1991 the Connecticut legislature adopted a state income tax after a prolonged battle. In that case, a severe recession prompted a decline in state tax revenues from other sources. Democrats provided most of the support for the progressive tax, and Republicans provided most of the opposition.[39]

These issues of what role the state should play, what taxes should be imposed, and who should pay those taxes persist in the political debates of state and local politics. In New Hampshire, groups have argued that the state needs new state taxes to offset inequalities in school financing.[40] Florida officials have argued that the state needs to adopt an income tax to meet the needs of the influx of elderly.[41]

There is, of course, intense opposition to proposals to enact new taxes. Opponents present articulate criticisms of the dangers of taxes, and politicians are reluctant to become too strongly identified with tax increases. The public does not like taxes, and politicians worry about losing elections because they acted or voted for taxes. There must be a strong imperative in order to stimulate action to make changes. The inclination to tackle tax issues often emerges only because of a fiscal crisis caused by a decline in revenues, a court order, or a significant push by a governor who wants to address a specific problem. Indeed, many of the taxes now in existence in the states were adopted during fiscal crises like the Great Depression.[42] Recessions, such as the extended one from the late 1980s and earlier 1990s, also prompt considerations of raising taxes.[43]

But problems do not always produce responses. "Crises" are not always met by solutions. What response does emerge comes from the political process. We now have some idea of the basic conflicts and concerns that may become political issues and prompt political battles. We now turn to the processes that affect what happens to these issues.

For Further Reading

The following are some studies that focus on disputes about the role of government, state–local relations, and taxes.

Citizens for Tax Justice. *A Far Cry from Fair*. Washington, DC: 1987.

Education Commission of the States. *School Finance Litigation: A Historical Summary*. Denver, 1993.

Hanson, Russell. *Governing Partners*. Boulder: West Publishing, 1994.

Hansen, Susan B., "The Politics of State Tax Innovation." In *The Politics of Taxation*, 142–174. New York: Praeger, 1983.

Lehne, Richard. *The Quest for Justice*. New York: Transaction Books, 1978.

Suggestions for Analysis in Your Own State and Locality

1. Many policy proposals result in issues about the extent of government involvement. Have there been any recent issues in your state or locality about whether government should become involved in responding to certain problems?

2. There are questions about which level of government should take responsibility for response to problems. Did any of the issues above result in disputes about whether the state or local governments should assume responsibility?

3. Has school finance and the role of the state been an issue your state? Have any lawsuits been filed? If so, what was the outcome?

4. Have taxes been an issue in your state in recent years? If so, what groups have taken positions on taxes, and what have those positions been? What has happened at the local level?

Notes

[1] Sho Sato and Arvo Van Alstyne, *State and Local Government Law* (Boston: Little, Brown, 1970), 149–308.

[2] Sidney Verba and Norman H. Nie, *Participation in America* (New York: Harper and Row, 1972); and Robert A. Dahl and Edward R. Tufte, *Size and Democracy* (Palo Alto: Stanford University Press, 1973), 239. Verba and Nie asked if larger cities promoted feelings of less political efficacy and found no significant differences. They classified cities by size and by their independence from other cities. An independent city is one that is not a suburb and does not adjoin another city. They found no differences for the tendency to vote or for the tendency to contact public officials, but they did find strong evidence that there was a greater tendency to engage in communal activity (to join and work with groups in the community).

[3] Charles Tiebout, "A Pure Theory of Local Expenditure," *Journal of Political Economy* 64 (1956), 416–435; Elinor Ostrom, "Metropolitan Reform: Propositions Derived from Two Perspectives," *Social Science Quarterly* 53 (1972), 474–493; and Robert Bish and Vincent Ostrum, *Understanding Urban Government* (Washington, DC: American Enterprise Institute, 1973).

[4] David R. Robertson and Dennis R. Judd, *The Development of American Public Policy* (Glenview, Illinois: Scott, Foresman / Little Brown, 1989).

[5] Martha Derthick, *The Influence of Federal Grants* (Cambridge: Harvard University Press, 1970), 71–97.

[6] See, for example, the articles in Donald M. Levine and Mary Jo Bane, *The "Inequality" Controversy: Schooling and Distributive Justice* (New York: Basic Books, 1975); and Jonathon Kozol, *Savage Inequalities* (New York: Crown, 1991).

[7] Michael Danielson, *The Politics of Exclusion* (New York: Columbia University Press, 1976); and Kenneth T. Jackson, *Crabgrass Frontier: The Suburbanization of America* (New York: Oxford, 1985).

[8] Robert Hanley, "The New Math of Rich and Poor," *New York Times*, 10 June 1990, E6.

[9] Roberto Suro, "Equality Plan on School Financing is Upsetting Rich and Poor in Texas," *New York Times*, 9 October, 1991, B9.

[10] "Courts Ordering Financing Changes in Public Schools," *New York Times*, 11 March 1990, 1.

[11] Thomas A. Kochan, "Correlates of State Public Employee Bargaining Laws," *Industrial Relations* 12, no. 3 (October 1973): 326; and Advisory Commission on Intergovernmental Relations, *State Mandating of Local Expenditures* (Washington, DC, July 1978), A-67.

[12] Charles Murray, *Losing Ground* (New York: Basic Books, 1984).

[13] The functions that local governments are responsible for depends on when the local government was created. Those created earlier in the country's history tend to be responsible for a wider range of activities. Roland Liebert, *Political Disintegration* (New York: Academic Press, 1976).

[14] Victor DeSantis, "County Government: A Century of Change," *The Municipal Yearbook 1989* (Washington, DC: International City Management Association, 1989), 55–85.

[15] G. Ross Stephens, "The Least Glorious, Most Local, Most Trivial, Homely, Provincial, and Most Ignored Form of Local Government," *Urban Affairs Quarterly* 24, no. 4 (June 1989), 501–512.

[16] Jeffrey M. Stonecash, "State Policies Regarding Local Resource Acquisition," *American Politics Quarterly* 9, no. 4 (October 1981), 401–425.

[17] Advisory Commission on Intergovernmental Relations, *State Mandating of Local Expenditures* (Washington, DC, July 1978), A-67.

[18] Jeffrey M. Stonecash, "Centralization in the State-Local Fiscal Relationships," *Western Political Quarterly* 34, no. 2 (June 1981), 301–309.

[19] Some have argued that this increased role is reflective of the resurgence of the states. See Ann O'M Bowman and Richard C. Kearney, *The Resurgence of the States* (Englewood Cliffs: Prentice-Hall, 1986).

[20] Martha Derthick, *The Influence of Federal Grants* (Cambridge: Harvard University Press, 1970).

[21] Jeffrey M. Stonecash, "Fiscal Centralization in the American States: Findings from Another Perspective," *Public Budgeting and Finance* 8, no. 4 (winter 1988), 81–89.

[22] For an excellent overview of this issue see John J. Harrigan, *Political Change in the Metropolis*, 5th ed. (New York: HarperCollins, 1993), 275–369.

[23] Advisory Commission on Intergovernmental Relations, *Pragmatic Federalism: The Reassignment of Functional Responsibility*, (Washington, DC, July 1976).

[24] Jeffrey M. Stonecash, "The Shifting Resources and Responsibilities of Governments in Onondaga County" (prepared for the Onondaga County Legislature, October 1991).

[25] Stephen L. Percy and Brett W. Hawkins, "Urban Counties: New Functions, New Responsibilities, and Problems of Adjustment," (presented at the Southern Political Science Association, Atlanta, Georgia, November 1990); and Joseph M. Winiski, "Counties' Role Changing as Power and Resources Expand with Population," *City and State* (July, 1986): 1, 38.

[26] Eileen Shanahan, "Going it Jointly: Regional Solutions for Local Problems," *Governing* (August 1991), 71–76.

[27] V. S. DeSantis, "County Government: A Century of Change," in *The Municipal Yearbook 1989* (Washington, DC: International City Management Association, 1989), 55–65.

[28] Peter F. Nardulli, "Misalignment of Penal Responsibility and Prison Crises: Cost Consequences and Corrective Actions," *University of Illinois Law Review* no. 2 (1984), 365–388.

[29] Advisory Commission on Intergovernmental Relations, *Significant Features of Fiscal Federalism* 2 (1991), 126.

[30] Advisory Commission on Intergovernmental Relations, *Changing Public Attiudes on Government and Taxes, 1990* (Washington DC, 1991), S–19, 4.

[31] For discussions of economic development issues and the state, see Peter Eisinger, *The Entrepreneurial State: State and Local Economic Development Policy in the United States* (Madison: University of Wisconsin Press, 1988). For the conservative argument about this issue, see the articles in Tex Lezar, ed., *Making Government Work: A Conservative Agenda for the States* (San Antonio: Texas Public Policy Foundation, 1992), 317–400.

[32] Michael Wayslenko, "Business Climate, Industry, and Employment Growth: A Review of the Evidence," (occasional paper no. 98, Metropolitan Studies Program, Maxwell School of Citizenship and Public Affairs, October 1985).

[33] Ann O'M Bowman and Richard C. Kearney, *State and Local Government* (Boston: Houghton Mifflin, 1990), 10–15.

[34] David Lowery and Lee Sigelman, "Understanding the Tax Revolt: An Assessment of Eight Explanations," *American Political Science Review* 75 (1981), 963–974; and Lee Sigelman, David

Lowery, and Roland Smith, "The Tax Revolt: A Comparative State Assessment," *Western Political Quarterly* 36 (1983), 30–51.

[35] For information and details of this debate, see Thomas B. Edsall, *The New Politics of Inequality* (New York: W. W. Norton, 1984); Frank Levy, *Dollars and Dreams: The Changing American Income Distribution* (New York: W. W. Norton, 1988); Kevin Phillips, *The Politics of Rich and Poor* (New York: Random House, 1991); Sylvia Nasar, "Even Among the Well-Off, The Richest Get Richer," *New York Times*, 5 March 1992, A1; Jason DeParle, "Democrat's Invisible Man Specializes in Making Inequity of Poor Easy to See," *New York Times*, 19 August 1991, A12; Thomas B. Edsall with Mary D. Edsall, *Chain Reaction: The Impact of Race, Rights, and Taxes on American Politics* (New York: W. W. Norton, 1991); and Sylvia Nasar, "Fed Gives New Evidence of 80s Gains by Richest," *New York Times*, 21 April 1992, A1.

[36] Citizens for Tax Justice, *A Far Cry from Fair* (Washington, DC, April 1991). For other years, see Donal Phares, *Who Pays State and Local Taxes* (Cambridge, Mass.: Oelgeschlager, Gunn, and Hain, 1980); and Citizens for Tax Justice, *The Sorry State of State Taxes*, (Washington, DC: Institute of Taxation and Economic Policy, 1987).

[37] This was not the first time that the state was faced with this decision. It had also occurred in the earlier 1970s and had resulted in the adoption of the income tax. The Democrats also held power over all branches then. See Richard Lehne, *The Quest for Justice* (New York: Longman, 1978).

[38] Robert Suro, "High Court in Texas Rules Schools in the State are Illegally Financed," *New York Times*, 3 October, 1989, A1; and William Celis, III, "School Tax Still Bedevils Lawmakers," *New York Times*, 18 November 1992, B7.

[39] Kirk Johnson, "Budget is Passed for Connecticut with Income Tax," *New York Times*, 23 August 1991, A1.

[40] Fox Butterfield, "In New Hampshire, Schools' Need Tests a Prized Feature: No Taxes," *New York Times*, 2 January 1992, A1.

[41] Larry Rohter, "In a Time of Deficits, Florida Ponders the Unpopular Idea of an Income Tax," *New York Times*, 10 December 1991, A22.

[42] Susan Hansen, "The Politics of State Taxing and Spending," in Virginia Gray, Herbert Jacob, and Robert Albritton, *Politics in the American States: A Comparative Analysis*, 5th ed. (Glenview, Illinois: Scott, Foresman/Little, Brown, 1990), 356–361; Susan Hansen, *The Politics of Taxation* (New York: Praeger, 1983).

[43] Frances S. Berry and William D. Berry, "State Lottery Adoptions as Policy Innovations: An Event History Analysis," *American Political Science Review* 84, no. 2 (June 1990), 395–417; and Michael deCourcy Hinds, "States and Cities Fight Recession with New Taxes," *New York Times*, 27 July 1991, A1.

5

Political Parties, Elections, and the Representation of Political Concerns

PREVIEW

Parties have the potential to play a significant role in representation. This chapter reviews the party role in organizing the electorate, developing electoral bases, and debating different policy options.

Much of the public distrusts parties. This distrust has led to considerable reform of the ways parties work and a movement away from strong party attachments. In addition, in many states the electoral bases were never clearly defined, and as a consequence, opposing parties in these states do not present distinctly different alternatives.

Despite these changes, parties continue to represent policy differences because areas differ in their population compositions and in their histocial (or geographical) inclination to elect Republicans and Democrats.

Political Parties and Representation: The Ideal

We live in a society with diverse concerns and need a political process that represents that diversity. The political arrangement we rely on to achieve that goal is a representative democracy. Citizens in a representative democracy generally do not directly make political decisions. Instead, they rely on elected officials to establish policies. This reliance on officials creates potential problems in our society. How do we make sure elected officials are aware of the needs of their community? Elected officials can become "out of touch" with the public that elected them. How do we determine what they have done so we can hold them accountable? These are perpetual concerns of representation.

Many observers of American politics believe that political parties have the potential to make a significant contribution to the resolution of these problems.[1] A political party is a collection of individuals who have roughly similar beliefs about public policy.[2] It is a group that seeks a broad base of support so it can try to gain control of government. The individuals agree to adopt a common designation (such as Democrat or Republican) as an indicator of their common concerns. The degree of commonality may not be very great, and the cohesion (or willingness to act together) may not be very high. As long as there is some willingness to adopt a common, publicly announced affiliation, however, we can characterize such a collection as a political party. These individuals constitute a loose organization seeking a broad base of support to achieve certain goals or to gain control of government policy.

In an ideal world, this "coming together" of party members plays a significant role in the representation process. The collective activities of individuals trying to win (and retain) offices so they can control government policy are very important. In democratic political systems, we place enormous faith in the general political benefits that follow from those activities.

There are, to be sure, anxieties about relying heavily on party politicians. Many people are troubled by the ambition of individual people to get elected and fear that the mechanism that propels political activity is not altruism, but the desire to hold office. In many cases, individual ambition is partly a desire to enact certain policies, but many individuals also desire to be important and to advance their own careers. The pursuit of office is prompted by both personal and larger concerns. We shall return to the issue of ambition later.

What is important here is the role that this pursuit of office can play. Our first concern is the *ideal* role that political parties can play, or our optimistic expectation of the ways parties can contribute to representation. We will then examine the extent to which they achieve this ideal.

Organizing and Representing Interests

The bewildering diversity of concerns in our society often makes it hard for particular interests to be heard, or for citizens to follow what all the debates are about. Parties can contribute to organizing and simplifying these concerns.

Politicians want to get elected. To do so, they must put together enough votes to win office. In American politics, our electoral rules are designed to encourage politicians to focus on winning a majority of votes. We generally favor "winner-take-all" elections and do not allocate positions according to the proportion of the vote won. There is only one victor. A politician has to attract a large, fairly broad collection of people.

To do this, politicians try to carve out policy positions that appeal to a sufficient number of voters in order to achieve a majority. They try to "organize" political interests. A Democratic candidate may try to put together a coalition of lower-income individuals who have a host of worries about jobs, health care, and food; working-class individuals and union workers who worry about the rights of unions as a means to protect their jobs and benefits; minority groups who are concerned about discrimination; and middle-class and upper-class groups who feel that more should be done to address problems of inequality in our society. These groups have a general concern about conditions of equality and can be mobilized behind a candidate (and party) to achieve an impact on public policy.

A Republican, on the other hand, might try to organize the affluent who do not want their taxes raised; middle-class people who have worked hard to raise their incomes and worry about tax revenue taken from their incomes to benefit those who they believe do not work as hard; business groups who think taxes and regulations harm their businesses; conservatives who are opposed to redistribution on philosophical grounds; and suburbanites who do not want any interference in the zoning laws that restrict who can move into suburbs. These groups share a general concern about the growing role of government and question the need for, and use of, taxes and redistribution programs.

Politicians assemble these coalitions so they can win office. They may or may not be devout believers in the principles they announce. They may support some positions only because such support will result in more votes. Regardless of what drives politicians, the positions they take affect the kinds of coalitions assembled, the issues debated, the topics that dominate public attention, and ultimately the concerns that are represented.

When politicians adopt positions, there is an indirect benefit. Politicians and parties contribute to simplifying the political process. Political issues are often complex and can fragment the public. Issue complexity can make it difficult for much of the public to follow and understand debates. The actions of politicians may simplify these issues by combining some sets of concerns into common themes.

Democrats may be able to summarize all the different concerns of their coalition by emphasizing inequality and the importance of equality of opportunity in America. Republicans may be able to capture the concerns of their coalition by stressing individualism and the importance of people being able to work hard and succeed without government threatening their success. Political parties can contribute to the representation process by organizing groups that have common concerns and by appealing to them to form coalitions. In so doing, they articulate the concerns of people in that coalition. Politicians do this to generate support and to attract enough votes to get elected, but these activities are valuable in themselves. They contribute to the representation of broad sets of political concerns. Politicians do serve as advocates of their constituents. The public feels that someone is making "their" arguments. Those angry about taxes and redistribution can rely on Republicans to make their case. Those angry about inequality can rely on Democrats to express those concerns.

Debate and Dialogues in Democracy

Democracies derive their legitimacy from the public. The public has to accept government decisions in order for the system to persist. To achieve that acceptance, we place great faith in public debate. Our hope is that if the public hears the arguments about alternatives and watches a process in which the arguments are considered, they may understand alternatives better and may also be more supportive of the choices made. The presumption is not that everyone will accept the decisions. Nor is the presumption that this dialogue of ideas will be wise and thoughtful, nor that it will produce the "right" decision. Democracies make mistakes. But if a democracy is to be a democracy, or a system in which public concerns are a fundamental basis for making decisions, then it is essential that the public feel that the process considers alternative arguments. If democracies are committed to anything, it is to the belief that all ideas ought to be considered and debated.

Political parties can play a vital role in contributing to these goals. Politicians seeking to get elected point out the merits of their ideas. They present reasons why other programs and ideas are not fair or not effective. The continual interplay creates a debate that is often not pretty but is a debate.

Symbolizing and Simplifying Political Choices

We elect many public officials at many levels of government in the United States, but much of the public is not terribly interested in politics. For a public that does not follow politics closely, it is often difficult to distinguish among all the officials and to sort out who stands for what. Parties can help the public indicate their policy preferences by providing a symbol for the public to react to.

The desire to get elected leads politicians to join with other politicians to pursue common concerns. They try to create a public identity that people will recognize and vote for if they want particular policies. Democrats may continually focus on inequities in the tax system, while Republicans may focus on waste in government and on welfare abuses. These "reputations" help the public sort out choices and then communicate their preferences through their vote. This process enhances representation.

This process also helps politicians make sense of the elections. If politicians in a party stand for particular issues, the results of an election take on considerable meaning. The politicians who emphasized particular positions and won can assume their support from the public is based on having taken those positions. They have support to enact the policies they advocated. They can also assume that the proposals of the opposing party were rejected by the majority of voters.

If parties play these roles well, then several things happen. Groups with similar concerns are brought together and their concerns are articulated by candidates. The ideas of the opposing party are critiqued, and a public debate is conducted. The public is presented with clear choices, and the results of elections indicate which views receive the support of a majority of the public. This process can promote representation and accountability, thus simplifying the entire political process.

But creating these debates is of more value to some groups than others. V. O. Key in *Southern Politics*, argues that parties are the primary means by which groups with few resources are able to obtain representation. He argued that because the upper class, business groups, and real estate interests have money, interest group resources, and a network of associations, they are consistently able to present their policy preferences to politicians. These groups obtain representation without having to create or work with political parties. Lower-income groups lack these resources and access, but if a party (or faction, in the southern states that Key studied) exists that is built around the policy preferences of this group, this party can achieve representation for this group that they otherwise might not achieve.

The importance of parties, therefore, is more than just their contribution to the overall clarity of political representation. Parties are particularly important for the representation of have-nots. Without strong political parties, have-nots are not as likely to do well in the representation process.

An Example: Politics in New Jersey

New Jersey illustrates how parties can contribute to the representation process. In 1989, James Florio, a Democrat, was elected governor. Both houses of the legislature were also held by Democrats. Florio came to office with a record as a liberal. He did not, however, suggest any need for tax increases when he campaigned for office. Events, however, soon forced him to make a decision about taxes. By 1990, the state, along with the rest of the nation, was in a recession, and revenues were dropping. The state either had to cut services or raise taxes. At the same time, the state's highest court decided a lawsuit about the financing of local schools. The court found the existing system inequitable and unconstitutional because local tax bases differed so much. The state was abruptly faced with two issues that prompted a need for more revenue.

Florio chose to cut services somewhat, but his primary choice was to raise taxes.[3] Raising taxes would provide general revenues to help the state cope with the recession and funds for more state aid to low-income school districts. Florio proposed a package that would raise the sales tax 1 percent and would also increase income tax rates on those who made more money. Some Democrats in the legislature were very worried about distributing all the additional aid only to low-income districts. They were particularly concerned about the party appearing to be concerned only with poor areas and wanted to broaden the range of school districts given consideration. After extensive negotiations, more money was distributed to working-class and lower middle–income districts, and a $2.8 billion tax package was passed by the legislature. It was the largest tax increase ever enacted in the state.

The Democrat party made choices about the way they wanted to present themselves and whom they decided to represent. First, they wanted to claim credit for being decisive and responding to two significant problems: the recession and the court case. They also wanted to make sure they presented themselves as a party concerned about the have-nots and those people living in school districts with more limited tax bases. They made these choices in the face of considerable public criticism. There were extensive protests in the state capital against these tax proposals.

Republicans also dissented. They argued that taxes were already too high, that too much of the revenues went to poor districts, and that other districts with legitimate needs were neglected. They argued that the solution to inequities in education was not just more money. They also argued that this emphasis on redistribution penalized districts that were succeeding. Republicans, with what were probably mixed motives, opposed the Democrats. Some probably were philosophically opposed to the entire tax and state-aid package. Others probably just saw the situation as a good opportunity to criticize Democrats about taxes and to gain some advantage over them. For whatever reasons, Republicans kept up a steady criticism that Democrats were too interested in raising taxes in and taking money away from the middle class.

These criticisms became the major focus of the 1991 state legislative elections and of the 1993 gubernatorial election. New Jersey holds its state elections in odd-numbered years. Republican legislative candidates promised they would reduce taxes if elected. The 1991 election provided a clear example of what can happen when parties take clear policy positions and the public reacts to those positions. Republicans won in remarkable numbers. Democrats entered the elections holding the House forty-three to thirty-seven, and the Senate twenty-three to seventeen. After the elections, Republicans held the house fifty-eight to twenty-two, a switch of twenty-one seats to the Republican side. They held the Senate twenty-seven to thirteen, an overall gain of ten seats for the Republicans. (Eleven Democratic seats were lost to Republican candidates, but one Republican seat did become Democrat.)

Perhaps more important than knowing the number of seats the Democrats lost is understanding where the Democrats lost. Republicans already held most of the seats in affluent areas. Democrats held many of the seats in less-affluent areas. Table 5.1 presents an analysis of the characteristics of the districts that did and did not shift in party control after the 1991 election. Districts are grouped by the results

---

Table 5.1

Changes in Partisan Control of Districts in New Jersey from 1991 to 1992

District Conditions	House Districts which from 1991 to 1992		
	Remained Democratic 22	*Changed from Democratic to Republican* 21	*Remained Republican* 37
Median home value in districts	$140,280	$148,087	$168,397
Black and Hispanic population (% of total)	50.6	17.1	11.8
	Senate Districts that from 1991 to 1992		
	Remained Democratic 12	*Changed from Democratic to Republican* 11	*Remained Republican* 16
Median home value in districts	$131,058	$139,347	$185,557
Black and Hispanic population (% of total)	50.2	16.3	10.4
Statewide Averages			
Median home value		$156,159	
Black and Hispanic population (% of total)		23.0	

Note: All districts except for one senate district that changed from Republican to Democrat are included. The median home value is the average of median home values for all districts in a group. The average percent of blacks and hispanics is derived from adding hispanics and blacks together and dividing by the total population. There are two house members for each district and one senate member per district. Source: Compiled by author from information obtained from the State of New Jersey.

of the 1991 election. The first set of districts remained Democrat. The last set remained Republican. The middle group changed from Democratic to Republican control.

The table indicates the traits of the groups of districts and provides a means to compare districts. Below each group of districts is the average of median home values and the proportion of black and hispanic population in those districts. At the bottom of the table is the statewide average for the same conditions.

How do these groups of districts differ? Districts that remained Democrat have relatively low median home values and relatively large black and hispanic populations. They are "traditional" Democratic districts. Districts that remained Republican are heavily white and affluent. They are "traditional" Republican districts. The remaining districts, those districts that changed, provide a means of examining the way parties and the public interact to produce representation.

The districts that changed from Democratic to Republican control are "swing" districts, changing from one party to another in response to a policy. These districts were below the statewide average for income and value of homes. They were not affluent, stereotypical Republican districts. They were working-class and lower middle–class districts. Democrats probably believed the progressive income-tax package and education-aid programs would appeal to these districts. The people in these districts, however, apparently did not like the tax increases and did not see the education-aid programs as that helpful to them. The Democrats had made a policy choice and sought to present themselves as party representatives of those less affluent. They enacted the package and in the campaigns publicly claimed credit for these changes. The difficulty is that not all of the less affluent were happy with the package. Those unhappy with the changes communicated their reactions by taking their wrath out on the Democratic party. The party label served as a symbol for the public, and the public reaction conveyed to politicians in the Democratic party that they had made a mistake. Either the policies adopted were not desired, or the party had done a poor job communicating who would benefit. Regardless, the 1991 election conveyed a clear message to politicians. The public would not support politicians who did not represent their interest. Representation had occurred.

In 1993, the representation process continued. During the gubernatorial campaign, Florio ran against the Republican candidate Christine Whitman. She relentlessly criticized Florio for his tax increases. He argued he had done the responsible thing in responding to a budget deficit and the problem of inequity in school finances. Late in a close race, Whitman proposed and promised to enact a 30 percent cut in the state personal income tax over three years. She won in a very close election by swinging moderates to her side.

By 1994, the representation process had produced two debates in which party labels were crucial in structuring the debate. Democrats defended tax increases and redistribution while Republicans stood for tax repeal. The parties gave the public clear policy alternatives. In this case the signal from the electorate was that taxes and redistribution were not terribly popular.

The Criticism of Political Parties

If parties are to play the representation roles just discussed, there are very different ways they might go about creating these relatively coherent positions and images.[4] At one extreme, party leaders might pursue a centralized strategy to create a cohesive party with clear positions. At the opposite extreme, a party might take a decentralized approach and allow party positions to emerge from the collective concerns of those who are in the party. Americans have developed a very clear preference for one of these two alternatives.

With the centralized, relatively "top-down," approach, party leaders would play a significant role in directing activities. They might develop organizations (offices with staff) to dominate recruiting, nominating, and funding candidates. They might dominate the conventions and choose party candidates and positions.

In this manner, party leaders could play a major role in the creation and perpetuation of parties.

In contrast, the process of forming party policy could be decentralized. Party officials would then play a *relatively* passive role. Party officials would be limited in the extent to which they could recruit or fund candidates. Candidates would make their own decisions about whether to run, how to raise money, and what positions to take. If party positions exist, they would emerge from the collective views of party members. The opinions of those who happen to be in the party would be the basis for policy.

The choice of most Americans has been fairly clear. They prefer the second approach. There are several reasons why.

Many people think parties can play a positive role in the representation process. But a substantial segment of the public believe that parties play a negative role in politics. There are several reasons for this belief. First, many people associate parties with corruption and abuses of power. Second, the image of political parties with cohesion imposed by party leaders strikes many as fundamentally contradictory to their notions of how democracy should work. Finally, many people believe that the emphasis of political activity should be upon what is in the interest of everyone. They argue that what parties do is focus attention on conflict, making decision making more difficult. These critics believe parties distort political debates rather than enhance them.

These criticisms have been voiced for a long time. They were particularly important at the beginning of the twentieth century at the time of the Progressive movement. These criticisms have significantly shaped the way parties now operate in most states and communities and are worth reviewing in some detail.

Party Power and Corruption

The first criticism has been that because parties acquire power, they are tempted into corruption. When a party and its leaders have clear authority over a government and the politicians who make up the party, that power can be exploited to make money for the leaders of the party and the party as a whole. Party leaders can use power to dictate the conditions under which the private sector deals with the government. For example, the party leaders can demand that construction contracts be awarded only if the chosen company bribe or "kickback" a portion of the profit to public officials. Such requirements are never stated publicly, but they are passed along privately. Since state and local governments employ the private sector for a wide variety of purposes (from supplying pencils and paper to building government offices), there are numerous possibilities for corruption of this nature. It is also possible to use this power to extract kickbacks from people appointed to government jobs by the party officials. Such a kickback usually requires that the employee return some portion of his or her government salary in return for having received the job.

This form of corruption has probably always been part of government, but it became particularly prominent during the late 1800s and early 1900s, when some cities had political "machines" notorious for such practices.[5] A machine government is generally defined as one based on the exchange of favors or services for votes.[6] Those who needed assistance from government—jobs, money, housing, neighborhood problems—received tangible assistance through a politician and in return they voted for the "machine." Businesses also participated in exchange relationships. They received preferential government service or decisions in exchange for bribes or kickbacks. To critics, the fundamental problem in this type of exchange is that there is no substantive discussion of public policies.

This corruption existed at local and state levels, though we have less evidence of state-level corruption. When this corruption existed, it was not announced as "party policy." It was usually the policy of the individuals who ran the parties. This distinction was generally unimportant to the public, however, and as stories of corruption continued to emerge during the early 1900s, much of the public became convinced that parties inevitably tended toward corruption. They wanted to reduce the roles of political parties in government.

Party Power and the Denial of Representation

The second criticism of parties has been that party leaders use their power to control elected officials, thus subverting democratic representation. In an ideal situation, the party should work to develop a set of policy proposals to bring before the public as an alternative to the other party's policies. The public should be involved in the development of party proposals, so that political parties serve to bring public concerns into the political debate.

Much of the public has felt that strong central control of the party inevitably leads leaders ("bosses") to abuse this power to serve their own interests, which are to stay in office and not be threatened by close elections.[7] The ability of party leaders to abuse the power of the party stems from the control over party processes that party leaders have. Since parties in state legislatures and city councils often rely heavily on those in leadership positions, much of the legislation supported by the party is developed and negotiated by the party officials.[8] These "deals" are then presented to the party politicians for a vote. The public feels that these deals primarily serve the needs of the leaders (and are probably very detrimental to the public). The public feels they lose representation because elected officials must vote as directed or risk losing the party nomination in the next election. Since party leaders at one time controlled local nominating committees, they could make good on these threats. This arrangement allowed party leaders to control the policy proposal process. Critics argue this entire process allows party leaders to proceed very conservatively, and to avoid issues that might be controversial and disruptive. Party leaders are seen as stifling criticism of current party policy and preventing the emergence of fresh approaches to issues.

The fundamental criticism here is that a political party is supposed to represent mass concerns, and the power to form issue positions should flow from the bottom up, not from the top down. A democratic society must have the means to allow continual infusion of new ideas and a forum for debating such ideas. To many critics, political leaders are seen as not wishing to take on "difficult" issues because they disrupt traditional, reliable bases of support. Party leaders are inclined to control the emergence of such issues. From this perspective, when a party is centrally controlled, the democratic process is abused.

The Public Interest and Party Conflict

Political parties argue for policies that benefit their constituencies. That support for segments of the population rather than for the population as a whole creates conflict. This presumption that parties should focus on their constituencies is not accepted by everyone. Much of the public believes there are policies that will benefit everyone and that there is a public interest. All states, for example, are faced with the need to improve their transportation infrastructure. Party politicians, however, do not see this as a simple issue with an obvious solution. Republicans generally want money spent on roads and bridges in cities and suburbs, while Democrats want more money spent on mass transit. These differences lead to extensive party conflict when making transportation-funding decisions. Much of the public finds this conflict distracting and wasteful. They think the parties become so concerned with seeking benefits for their constituents that nothing gets done, and the entire society is hurt. The primary concern should be maintaining the transportation system, and the public interest gets lost amid the party conflict.

E. J. Dionne, a reporter for the *Washington Post*, gives the following assessment in *Why Americans Hate Politics*. In discussing the conservative-versus-liberal debate that Republicans and Democrats have engaged in for the last two decades, he argues that

> liberalism and conservatism are framing political issues as a series of false choices. . . . liberalism and conservatism prevent the nation from settling the questions that most trouble it. On issue after issue, there is consensus on where the country should move or at least on what we should be arguing about; liberalism and conservatism make it impossible for that consensus to express itself.[9]

Responses to Criticisms

There are, of course, disputes about the validity of these criticisms of parties. In response to the criticisms that urban political parties did not focus on issues, students of urban political machines argue that voters were very rational in voting for urban ethnic bosses because party machines were responsive to the needs of urban immigrants.[10] They suggest that claims of corruption and its connection to parties have been grossly overstated. Others defend strong leadership and argue that party members often desire leadership to create some order in making decisions. They also argue that strong leaders get decisions made. Finally, defenders of parties argue that conflict is fundamental in society. Parties did not invent it. They only reflect it. Nonetheless, enough of the public has accepted the criticisms of party power to provide a basis for reforming political parties and reducing the influence of party leaders.

Reforming Political Parties: The State Level

The negative reaction toward political parties began to have some impact with the emergence of the Progressive movement around 1900.[11] The Progressive movement was concerned with changing state and local governments so that the process of reaching decisions and implementing them would be more "rational," less partisan, and more open to the general public. Some of the members of this movement, the "structural" reformers, believed that the deficiencies of the current system could be eliminated if the process were reformed so the public and politicians were put in "structures" that properly shaped their behavior. The goal of these reformers was to eliminate certain situations that encouraged undesirable traits and to create practices that would produce better behaviors.

This reform group was not composed entirely of individuals with "pure" motives. As with many attempts to institute change, some "reformers" felt that those changes would weaken the control of the groups currently in power and allow their own groups to gain power. The most significant of such groups was the middle class, which felt that it had been unjustly displaced from power by the influx of immigrants into American society in the late 1800s and early 1900s.[12]

Several groups came together during the early 1900s to initiate significant changes in the way parties operated. These groups provided the initiative, organization, and specific reforms to begin a major alteration in the way that parties worked. Almost all those changes revolved around the themes just discussed. Over the years these persistent concerns have reduced the ability of party leaders to control politicians and government employees and have increased access of the general public to the political process. Much of this reform has been motivated by a belief that partisanship in politics should be either curtailed or eliminated altogether. The presumption of many reformers has been that the democratic political process would work well only if the role of party leaders could be reduced.

A primary concern of reformers was to eliminate party-leader control of politicians. Reformers pushed for altering the mechanism by which parties choose nominees. Over the years, the nomination of party candidates has moved from the control of party caucuses (small gatherings of party leaders) to an action by a convention of party delegates (either elected or selected) to open primaries, where the public selects candidates. The progression of this change is shown in Figure 5.1. The result of this change has been a continual increase in the direct role of the public, and the resulting decrease in the role of party leaders, to influence nominations. Some states now hold "open" primaries. This arrangement allows a voter on the day of the primary to choose which party primary he or she will vote in. Open primaries greatly reduce the influence of party officials over the candidate of the party. Several states have also gone so far as to allow a voter to vote in a different party primary for each office.

Party leaders are not helpless in these situations. In some states, the party still makes endorsements of its preferred candidates. These endorsements may sway enough voters to enable the endorsed candidate to win the primary election.

Caucus: Party leaders meet to choose candidates. Process involves no involvement by the public. Dominated the 1800s and early 1900s.

Convention: Candidates chosen by party delegates, who are either elected or chosen in local areas of the state. Delegates are usually prominent, active local party members or major supporters of the party. Has been widely used as a selection method in many states for much of 1900s.

Primary: Candidates chosen by public in an election, usually involving only individuals who have declared themselves members of the party. Widely used today.

Figure 5.1
The Transformation of Party Leader Control over Nominations
Source: Adapted from Samuel Eldersveld, Political Parties in American Society *(New York: Basic Books, 1982), 94.*

The variety of state situations regarding citizen rights to participate in primaries is shown in Table 5.2. The range of situations parties have created in the states is impressive. At one extreme, there are primaries that are completely open. Voters need only declare on the day they vote which party primary they wish to vote in. Because voters can change that preference from year to year, the electorate within a party can be unstable from year to year. This change is possible in states such as Vermont, Wisconsin, and Montana. At the other extreme, some states require that voters declare their party loyalty and register as a member of that party before they can vote in that party's primary. Such states include Connecticut, Kentucky, and California. An individual can vote in the Democratic or Republican primary only if they have registered in that party.

Some states still use a nominating convention to designate the party nominee. This designation process occurs prior to the primary voters participate in. The party uses the nominating convention to indicate whom party activists prefer. Nominating conventions are used in Connecticut, Colorado, Delaware, Illinois, Massachusetts, Minnesota, New Mexico, New York, North Carolina, Rhode Island, Wisconsin, and Utah.

In convention states, there is usually a provision that someone not designated by the party can still get on the ballot in the primary if the candidate gathers sufficient signatures from state voters registered in that party. Sometimes convention designations are challenged by candidates who win.[13]

The move to reform political parties has also taken other forms. Reformers have felt that voters should not be forced to choose between complete party slates of candidates. To increase flexibility of voter choice, the major offices of states, cities, and communities are elected separately. This means that it is possible to

Table 5.2
Types of State Primary Systems by Region

| Type of Primary | Region of Country | | | | |
	Northeast	Midwest	Border	South	West
Completely closed	Connecticut Delaware Maryland New York Pennsylvania	Nebraska South Dakota	Kentucky Oklahoma West Virginia	Florida North Carolina	Arizona California Nevada New Mexico Oregon
Closed, but may enroll or change on primary day	Maine New Jersey Rhode Island	Iowa Kansas Ohio			Colorado Wyoming
Closed, but independents may shift	Massachusetts New Hampshire				
Open, but selection of party required		Illinois Indiana	Missouri	Alabama Arkansas Georgia Mississippi South Carolina Tennessee Texas Virginia	
Completely open	Vermont	Michigan Minnesota North Dakota Wisconsin			Hawaii Idaho Montana Utah
Open, blanket primary					Alaska Washington
Nonpartisan				Louisiana	

Source: Malcolm Jewell and David Olson, Political Parties and Elections in American States, 3d ed. (Chicago: Dorsey, 1988), 90.

have a Democratic governor, a Republican lieutenant governor, a Republican attorney general, and a Democratic comptroller. This practice is very common at the local level. The intent again is to allow voters to vote for the best people without regard to partisan association. Because parties often have little control over candidate nominations in primaries and because the parties may have candidates for different offices presenting very different philosophies, political parties can find it very hard to present clear images or symbols for the voters.

Finally, in a related and relatively recent development, many states have moved even further to open up the candidate selection process and remove party influence over it by establishing state funding of campaigns for major state offices.[14] The intent is to make it possible for more people who wish to run for office to do so. Funding is provided by taxpayers who agree to designate some of their tax obligation to go into a fund to be used to support candidates. This "check-off" is generally no more than a few dollars, and the candidate usually must raise a certain amount of funds or demonstrate some minimal amount of support in the public prior to receiving public funds. The rationale put forth for this change is that candidates will no longer have to go to special interests to seek funding for a campaign. While this funding may do that, it also reduces the ability of party elites to influence a candidate. When a candidate must go to traditional sources of funding, party officials can exert power over that candidate by urging contributors to support or not support him or her. This practice is used in only a few local governments. As of 1991, this funding is used in some form in twenty-three states and other states are considering adopting it.[15] Our knowledge of the impact of public funding on political parties, however, is currently very limited because no studies have been done.

Reforming Political Parties: The Local Level

The idea of reducing party influence over nominations has been even more prevalent at the local level. In many localities, there is a strong feeling that the administration of cities should be a nonpolitical matter, since managing a city has little to do with partisan issues. As it was once put, "there is no Republican or Democrat way to pave a road." Many cities have instituted nonpartisan elections. Candidates run in a general primary and party designations are not listed with candidate names. After the primary, the two candidates with the highest vote totals generally run against each other for the position. The reformers thought that, without partisan labels to rely on, the electorate would be forced to focus on the personal qualities and policies of each candidate. Their intent was to elect the best person regardless of party membership.

The tendency to use nonpartisan elections at the local level (this approach is not used at the state level for electing representatives or major officials such as the governor, attorney general, or comptroller) is shown in Table 5.3. This table shows the usage of nonpartisan elections by location of the city and by type of local government. The nonpartisan approach to elections is widespread. While we often think of politics in our society as highly partisan, 72.6 percent of all cities do *not* use partisan elections. While the tendency to use this form is strong, it is used less in

Table 5.3
Cities Having Nonpartisan Elections

	Number of Cities	Percentage of Nonpartisan Cities
Nationwide	3927	72.6
Region		
Northeast	155	21.0
North central	1,006	77.9
South	1,013	86.1
West	677	94.0
Local Government		
Council manager	2,102	81.9
Commission	118	74.6
Mayor council	1,707	61.0

Sources: Charles Adrian, "Forms of City Government in American History," 8; and Tari Renner, "Municipal Election Processes," 17, in International City Managers Association, Yearbook *(Washington, DC, ICMA, 1988).*

some categories of cities, and more in others. The nonpartisan form of election was proposed in conjunction with a set of reforms that were intended to make cities less political and run more by "objective" professionals. The whole set of proposals is called the "city-manager form of government." This form entails at-large elections (so legislators will think of and represent the whole city, not just some section of it), a city manager (a trained administrator instead of a political mayor, so political considerations in administration will be minimized), and civil service (a merit-based method of selecting administrative personnel so patronage appointments will be reduced).[16] While these proposals are put forward as a package, cities do not always adopt the entire package. Of those cities using a council-manager form of government, which relies on a city manager for administration, 81.9 percent use nonpartisan elections, while 61.0 percent of mayor-council cities use nonpartisan elections.

The movement to eliminate partisan elections did not have the same success in all areas of the country. The reformers were successful in many suburban areas where new cities were just developing.[17] But the greatest success came in those areas where the party system was least developed and therefore less resistant to nonpartisan elections. There was least resistance in the newly developing areas of the country, such as the West. In the Northeast, in contrast, parties were strongly entrenched, and the movement to nonpartisan elections was resisted.[18] Nonpartisan elections are also less common in the north central states.

The Consequences of Anti-Party Attitudes

Hostility to state and local political parties has had consequences. This hostility has produced a decline in public identification with the parties. It has also lessened the ability of parties to mobilize resources to maintain party organizations.

The Rise of Independents

Public disenchantment with parties has reduced public identification with parties. During recent decades, there has been an increase in the percent of the electorate that identifies themselves as independent. The Center for Political Studies at the University of Michigan has conducted public surveys since 1952. People are asked whether they identify with a party, and whether that identification is strong or weak. If they indicate that they regard themselves as independents, individuals are asked if they consider themselves closer to one party or another. Table 5.4 indicates

Table 5.4

Nationwide Party Identification, 1952–1988

	Percent of Public Regarding Themselves as						
	Democrats		Independents			Republicans	
			Leaning		Leaning		
Year	Strong	Weak	Democratic		Republican	Strong	Weak
1952	22	25	10	6	7	14	13
1956	21	23	6	9	8	15	14
1960	20	25	6	10	7	15	14
1964	27	25	9	8	6	11	13
1968	20	25	10	10	9	10	14
1972	15	26	11	13	10	10	13
1976	15	25	12	14	10	9	14
1980	18	23	11	13	10	8	14
1984	17	20	11	11	12	12	15
1988	17	18	12	11	13	14	14
Change:							
1952–1988	−5	−7	+2	+5	+6	0	+1

Source: Paul A. Beck and Frank Sorauf, Party Politics in America, *7th ed. (New York: HarperCollins, 1992), 88.*

the responses from 1952 to 1988. Since 1952, there has been an increase in the proportion of respondents classifying themselves as independents. The major change has involved a decline in identification with the Democratic party. Much of this change has taken place in the South and will be discussed later.

A significant proportion of the public now regard themselves as independents. The increase has been nationwide. Table 5.5 presents the data from a recent study that gives the distribution of partisan identification in each state. There is variation across the states, but a substantial percent of the electorate in all states view themselves as independents.

This decline in attachments to parties affects elections. Party candidates realize that in many communities they cannot win election just by appealing to their party supporters. As a consequence, candidates are now more prone to stress their personal characteristics and views, and not to present themselves just as a Democrat or a Republican. They realize that they must attract independents. Campaigns have become more "candidate centered."[19]

Some candidates carry the anti-party position one step further and present themselves as "outsiders" not connected to the party system. For example, in New York in 1982, Lew Lehrman was able to use his own wealth to gain the Republican gubernatorial nomination. Lehrman had never held any political office, nor did he have any prior experience working in politics. He advocated a 40 percent cut in state taxes and drastic cuts in state programs. He spent approximately $14 million (most of it his own money) in the primary and general elections before losing to Mario Cuomo. One of his main appeals was that he was not attached to party politics and would have the courage and independence to make tough decisions. In 1992, H. Ross Perot was able to attract a great deal of support as a candidate for president by presenting himself as a nonpartisan candidate.

This phenomenon of independence from partisan politics is probably more common at the local level. As noted above, nonpartisan elections are common at the local level, and this creates an environment in which politicians can present themselves as independent from politics, unconcerned with immediate political pressures, and not worried about whether they win reelection.[20]

The decline in attachment to parties and candidate-centered appeals have led to an increase in ticket-splitting.[21] Ticket-splitting occurs when an individual votes for a Republican in one race, such as the state senate, and then votes for a Democrat in the state assembly. Evidence of ticket-splitting shows up in two ways. Studies of individual voting have shown an increase in the proportion of voters splitting their ticket.[22] Evidence also comes from trends in the states. Individual split-ticket voting can create split-party control of the houses of the legislature or branches of government. There has been a steady decline since 1946 in the percent of state governments controlled by one party.[23] Figure 5.2 presents the trend in the percent of state governments in which the governorship and both legislative houses are held by one party.

The Decline of Party Organizations

The decline in public attachment to the parties appears to have coincided with a decline in public support for party organizations. It is widely agreed that during the

Table 5.5

Party Identification by State

State	Democratic	Independent	Republican
East			
Maine	32.3	38.5	26.2
New Hampshire	27.0	39.4	30.1
Vermont	20.6	54.8	18.6
Massachusetts	34.2	49.6	13.2
Rhode Island	22.2	59.6	9.7
Connecticut	32.7	42.2	20.3
New Jersey	33.1	39.9	20.6
New York	35.6	32.8	25.4
Pennsylvania	39.9	28.5	26.2
Midwest			
Ohio	35.3	35.0	24.1
Indiana	32.4	38.2	24.2
Illinois	33.4	38.0	22.8
Michigan	33.4	38.2	21.3
Wisconsin	33.1	38.2	22.3
Iowa	30.4	37.4	27.0
Minnesota	41.5	35.2	19.2
Mountain			
Colorado	30.1	41.0	25.0
North Dakota	28.1	35.0	31.1
South Dakota	43.2	19.5	34.3
Nebraska	29.2	29.6	36.3
Idaho	25.5	36.7	34.9
Montana	31.8	38.9	24.2
Wyoming	44.5	36.2	18.0
Utah	28.2	37.0	30.2
Southwest			
Arkansas	46.8	31.0	16.6
Texas	46.0	31.2	17.1
Kansas	31.6	33.9	30.4
Oklahoma	52.6	20.3	22.3
Arizona	40.2	31.6	25.0
New Mexico	44.7	32.3	20.5
Nevada	36.2	31.9	25.5
South			
Alabama	51.2	28.7	14.2
West Virginia	41.8	25.5	21.5
Delaware	37.4	42.1	16.4

continued

Table 5.5 (continued)
Party Identification by State

State	Democratic	Independent	Republican
Florida	43.2	30.0	22.4
Georgia	55.5	25.4	12.4
Louisiana	60.0	22.8	13.2
Maryland	46.2	32.1	17.0
Mississippi	50.4	25.9	17.2
Missouri	35.3	39.2	20.6
Kentucky	50.0	25.6	18.3
North California	46.4	27.8	19.4
South Carolina	41.6	31.7	19.0
Tennessee	39.8	34.2	20.7
Virginia	36.4	34.7	20.5
West			
Alaska	N/A	N/A	N/A
California	41.9	28.4	24.2
Hawaii	N/A	N/A	N/A
Oregon	38.4	30.8	27.0
Washington	32.7	45.9	17.0

Source: Gerald C. Wright, Robert S. Erikson, and John P. McIver, "Measuring State Partisanship and Ideology with Survey Data," Journal of Politics (May 1985): 476.

1960s and 1970s state and local party organizations declined. Fewer people made donations to parties or volunteered to work for them. Parties had fewer resources and played less of a role in nominating candidates and running campaigns.[24] That decline was then apparently reversed. State and local party organizations responded to the decline by raising more money and trying to rebuild their organizations.[25] Table 5.6 indicates the increase from the 1960s to 1980 in the extent to which state party organizations had certain resources or provided certain services.

State legislative party committees also emerged as new actors in state parties. These committees are organizations created by state legislators and are independent of the traditional state party organizations. Because these party committees raise their own funds and provide campaign assistance, they can play play a major role in state legislative campaigns.[26] At the local level, there is also evidence that party organizations continue to play a role in recruiting candidates, mobilizing resources, and providing volunteers.[27]

Although party organizations are still important at state and local levels and have apparently enjoyed some resurgence, political party organizations no longer

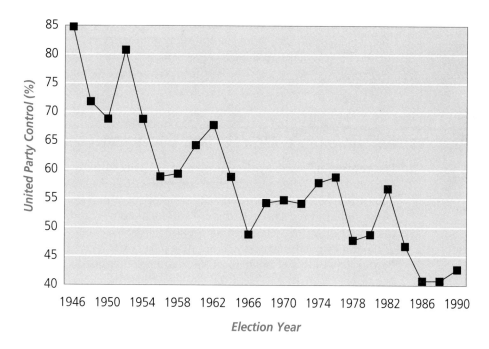

Figure 5.2

Unified Party Control in the States

Source: Morris Fiorina, "Divided Government in the States," PS 24, no. 4 (December 1991), 646.

Table 5.6

Changes in State Party Organizations: The Early 1960s and 1979 to 1980

Organizational Feature	1960–1964	1979–1980
	(%) of state parties	
Permanent state headquarters	50	91
Full-time chairman or director	63	90
Voter mobilization programs	39	75

Source: Paul A. Beck and Frank Souraf, Party Politics in America, 7th ed. (New York: HarperCollins, 1992), 88.

have a great deal of power to organize issues in states and localities. Any organization of issues emerges from the interaction of party candidates as they seek to get elected by articulating issues to represent and attract constituencies.

The Persisting Role of Political Parties: Organizing the Electorate

The reform movement has altered parties. That argument, however, must not be carried too far. While parties have lost much of the means to create policy alternatives from the top, this top-down creation of policy may never have been that important anyway. The use of state and local conventions to form party platforms filled with specific policies was probably never that significant. The determination of the policy positions that will define a party has always been done by candidates. Parties have always been to some extent a composite of candidate-articulated positions.

The interaction between candidates and party images persists. Parties and their candidates continue to be relevant to "organizing" electoral political concerns for two fundamental reasons. First, Democratic party candidates have historically supported more liberal policy positions than Republican party candidates. This difference in policy position results in separate party images, which continue to attract different groups. Second, geography still counts in politics. People who are alike continue to cluster together spatially. This creates communities whose populations have common concerns that differ from other communities, and they elect politicians from the party that best represents those concerns. Urban areas usually elect Democrats, and rural areas usually elect Republicans.

If Democrats consistently have different constituencies from those of Republicans, if Democrats consistently do better in some areas than Republicans do, and if these lead to party representation of differing concerns, then we say the parties have "organized" the electorate. They have brought those with certain common concerns together and presented their differences from those with other common concerns. The crucial matter in this "organization" is the link of voter allegiance and the issues party candidates advocate and seek to implement. The actual organizations of parties (offices, fund-raising efforts, staff and volunteers, mailing lists) are all possible means to help parties make connections with voters and mobilize them, but the heart of the"organization" of electoral concerns for political representation revolves around constituencies and party positions. A party can have an extensive organization, but not be very sharply focused on issues. Or a party can have a clear focus on issues, but be weak in formal organization. It is the connection between constituents and political positions that is important.

Continuity of Electoral Constituencies

Democrats tend to draw more of their constituency from blacks, union members, central-city residents, Catholics, Jews, and those with a liberal perspective. These groups persistently are more concerned about the broad and often messy issues of inequality and equality of opportunity. Any politician who wishes to win the votes of this constituency knows there is a relatively stable collection of groups that he or she must appeal to in order to be elected. The Democratic politician must represent their interests.

Republicans have their own traditional constituencies. The Republican party tends to draw their constituencies from professionals, protestants, suburban, small-town and rural residents, and those with higher education and higher income. These groups are less eager to engage in redistribution. Republican candidates must work to represent these constituencies.

The division of the electorate by social characteristics on a national basis is presented in Table 5.7. These figures represent national averages, and while the same distribution does not exist in each state, the figures do indicate general

Table 5.7

Social Characteristics and Party Identification

Category	Democrats (%)	Independents (%)	Republicans (%)	Advantage for Democrats over Republicans by group (%)
Education				
Eighth grade	45	34	21	24
High school	36	40	24	12
College	31	35	35	−4
Income				
Lower third	42	35	24	18
Middle third	36	36	28	8
Upper third	29	38	34	−5
Occupation				
Service	40	40	20	20
Blue collar	35	44	21	14
White collar	32	39	29	3
Professional	27	37	36	−9
Race				
Black	64	30	7	57
White	31	38	31	0
Class				
Working	43	39	19	24
Middle	30	34	37	−7

Source: Paul A. Beck and Frank J. Sorauf, Party Politics in America, *7th ed. (New York: HarperCollins, 1992), 161.*

patterns. This stability in group division creates some stability of concerns for the parties, and continuity of concerns for politicians in each party.

Surveys from individual states, such as New York and New Jersey, have shown similar divisions.[28] Studies of local parties also indicate such differences between the bases of Democrats and Republicans.[29] Table 5.8 provides an example of the way voters in Washington state identify themselves politically. People were asked whether they regard themselves as liberals, moderates, or conservatives. They were then asked whether they were Democrats, Independents, or Republicans. Liberals strongly identify with Democrats, while conservatives identify fairly strongly with the Republican party. Moderates are most likely to regard themselves as Independents.

While in some states the parties appear to have clear electoral bases, there are states where the organization is not so clear. Each state party has its own history of the groups that it attracts. Differences among the states can be seen in the data Gerald Wright and others have gathered. They used national surveys that asked people which party they identified with and whether they regarded themselves as liberal, moderate, or conservative. It was then possible to indicate the bases of parties in each state. The important matter is whether the Democratic party has a liberal-to-moderate base, and whether the Republican party has a conservative-to-moderate base. The differences in electoral bases for selected states are shown in Table 5.9.

The table is worth studying because it tells much about who comprises parties in different states and what kinds of concerns parties are likely to focus on. For each state, the composition of each party is presented. The percentages below each party sum down to 100 and indicate the percent of the party that is liberal, moderate, or conservative. An interesting variation occurs in figures for the Democratic party. In the states at the top of the table, the Democratic party is comprised primarily of moderates and conservatives. The Democratic party in these states is unlikely to be a strong advocate for liberal causes. In contrast, the states at the bottom are much more heavily dominated by liberals, and the Democratic party in these states is likely to be much more concerned with advocating liberal causes. In some states, the parties do not organize the electorate, while in other states they do.[30]

Table 5.8

Ideology and Party Identification in Washington State

Ideology	Democrat (%)	Independent (%)	Republican (%)
Liberal	54	39	7
Moderate	35	48	16
Conservative	22	41	36

Note: Percentages sum across to 100.
Source: William Mullen, The Government and Politics of Washington State *(Pullman: Washington State Press, 1978), 78.*

Table 5.9

Differing Party Bases in Selected States (Based on Self-Identification)

	Alabama (n=2053)			Idaho (n=644)			Maine (n=676)			North Dakota (n=425)		
States in which Democrats are moderate to conservative												
	R	I	D	R	I	D	R	I	D	R	I	D
				(percent of party)								
Liberal	16	14	21	10	17	18	13	25	24	6	15	20
Moderate	37	40	46	34	47	49	43	42	43	44	48	43
Conservative	48	45	33	56	36	32	44	33	33	50	37	36

	Pennsylvania (n=7522)			Vermont (n=389)			Delaware (n=396)			West Virginia (n=1301)		
States in which Democrats have a balanced base												
	R	I	D	R	I	D	R	I	D	R	I	D
				(percent of party)								
Liberal	14	25	29	10	29	32	8	21	29	14	30	25
Moderate	43	45	47	45	41	37	50	51	44	45	36	48
Conservative	44	30	25	45	30	31	42	28	27	40	34	26

	Massachusetts (n=3636)			New Jersey (n=4623)			New York (n=10,124)			California (n=12,916)		
States in which Democrats are moderate to liberal												
	R	I	D	R	I	D	R	I	D	R	I	D
				(percent of party)								
Liberal	16	27	33	17	26	35	16	28	36	11	28	35
Moderate	40	46	45	41	46	43	42	43	43	41	45	44
Conservative	44	27	22	42	28	22	43	29	21	48	27	20

Note: Read percents down. R = Republican; I – Independent: D = Democrat.
Source: Data from the files of Gerald Wright, University of Indiana. Based on surveys in each state from mid-1970s to late 1980s.

There are many reasons why the self-defined division of the electorate between the parties might not be based on class or political philosophies. As we will discuss shortly, the South has a long tradition of being heavily Democratic. Since the Democratic party included so many people, its political base included very diverse views. The political base of the Democratic Party is gradually but persistently changing. This change will be examined later.

Some observers of American politics have argued that class divisions have consistently been overshadowed by "cultural politics," or divisions dominated by disputes such as those about abortion, race, women's rights, and gay rights.[31] That is, voters will divide not along class lines, but according to their opinions about civil rights issues, or abortion. Following the 1992 elections, these cultural splits appeared to intensify in some states as the Christian right mobilized to push the Republican party to more conservative positions. In South Carolina, for example, the conservative religious right almost took over the Republican party in 1993, a situation that causd a significant split within the party. This movement may have pushed some traditional Republicans away from the party and left the party with a base defined primarily by religious views rather than by economic divisions.[32]

Unfortunately, we do not have extensive studies of the way these "other" divisions of the electorate develop at state levels. There is evidence these "other" bases of division do occur, but we need more information about their frequency and duration.

While there are situations in some states where party electoral bases are not clearly different, parties continue to play a role because, on average, Democrats take more liberal positions than Republicans. That difference results in each party attracting different constituents. This interaction between party candidates and constituents maintains the essential differences between the parties and maintains party relevance to the organization of the electorate and their issues.

Geography and Political Parties

Parties also continue to play a major role in representation because of geography. Similar populations cluster together in communities and have similar political concerns. The impact of geography is particularly evident in state legislative elections. Urban areas usually have higher concentrations of minority populations and of low-income groups. These areas tend to elect Democrats. Democrats in the state legislature and on city councils tend to share similar constituencies, resulting in their having similar political interests. The consequence is that elected officials in the Democratic party tend to work together in pursuit of the interests of similar constituents.

There are always problems in the unity of a party, of course. The Democratic party may also have elected officials from suburban areas and even a few from rural areas. They form part of the base of the party and must be incorporated into party deliberations. Their presence may force a party to be more moderate, but the Democratic party still ends up being relatively liberal.

The same issue of diversity exists for Republicans. They are more likely to be elected from rural and suburban areas, which are usually more white and affluent than urban areas. These areas are also generally more conservative than urban areas. This pattern means that Republican elected officials share similar political constituencies and policy concerns. They tend to work together to represent those interests. The Republican party in a state may contain some liberal legislators from urban areas. The presence of such liberal Republican legislators creates tensions in the party, but the Republican party still tends to be more conservative than the Democratic party in the state.

These similarities of interests in parties originate with geography. Table 5.10 presents the geographical bases of parties in several non-southern states for 1990. The table presents state legislative districts for both houses by whether they are primarily urban, suburban, or rural. The percent of elected legislators who are

Table 5.10

Geographical Bases of Political Parties in Selected Non-Southern States, 1990

	Ohio							
	House				*Senate*			
	Republican		*Democratic*		*Republican*		*Democratic*	
	(%)	*(#)*	*(%)*	*(#)*	*(%)*	*(#)*	*(%)*	*(#)*
Rural	52	(10)	47	(9)	60	(3)	40	(2)
Suburban	31	(7)	68	(15)	72	(13)	27	(5)
Urban	22	(11)	77	(37)	50	(5)	50	(5)

	New York							
	Assembly				*Senate*			
	Republican		*Democratic*		*Republican*		*Democratic*	
	(%)	*(#)*	*(%)*	*(#)*	*(%)*	*(#)*	*(%)*	*(#)*
Rural	88	(22)	12	(3)	100	(12)	0	(0)
Suburban	62	(23)	38	(14)	93	(13)	7	(1)
Urban	11	(10)	89	(78)	29	(10)	71	(25)

	California							
	Assembly				*Senate*			
	Republican		*Democratic*		*Republican*		*Democratic*	
	(%)	*(#)*	*(%)*	*(#)*	*(%)*	*(#)*	*(%)*	*(#)*
Rural	75	(9)	25	(3)	50	(3)	50	(3)
Suburban	51	(24)	49	(23)	43	(10)	56	(13)
Urban	0	(0)	100	(21)	29	(5)	90	(9)

Note: For each state, the first number in the row is the percent of legislators in an area who are Republicans or Democrats. The number of legislators in that area is in parenthesis to the right of the percent. There are two independent candidates in California who are not included in the calculations.

Sources: Compiled from legislative district maps, lists of legislators supplied by each state, and faculty in each state. [33]

Democrats or Republicans are then presented next to each type of district. In all three states, urban areas tend to elect Democrats. Rural areas tend to elect Republicans.

Elections result in party legislators from similar areas who share similar political concerns. This result has occurred across a broad array of states for some time.[34] There may be tensions in each party, but there is still considerable similarity of interests. Legislators in each party then tend to work together to form party policies that are different from the other party.

This sequence of forming party policy is not quite what we might imagine would occur in the representation process. Parties do not come together before elections to form party platforms that are presented to the public for reaction. Representation generally does not occur by having elections that are reactions to announced platforms and that produce "mandates" that give a party the authority to make changes. The situation reviewed at the beginning of this chapter, where New Jersey Republicans as a group ran on a pledge to reduce state taxes, is not typical. The more typical situation can be illustrated by a situation that occurred when New Jersey Democrats were in power. First, problems emerged. Elected party members explored the solutions party members might support and formed a consensus around the position of raising taxes on the wealthy and distributing more school aid to lower-income districts. This representative consensus occurred because individual legislators within the same party argued for their district's needs. These arguments led to some compromise and the formation of a policy position that most could accept. This ability to work together was based on their having somewhat similar constituencies and perspectives on how to respond to issues.

Conditions Affecting Party Organization of the Electorate

There are states and localities where the organization of the electorate by the legislative parties is not as distinct as just suggested. In the West, there is not as much of a tradition of strong attachments to political parties as in the East. Western states have had an enormous influx of new residents, and many of these new residents may have weak attachments to the parties in their new states. Split-ticket voting tends to be higher in states such as those in the West where parties are not clearly different.[35]

A party may also have a difficult time creating cohesion among groups even though the groups may seem to share common concerns. In a study of the Midwest states, John Fenton argued that for many years the parties in Ohio, Indiana, and Illinois were not able to get groups such as labor to focus on policy issues and provide a basis for a clear division between the parties.[36]

Factional divisions in parties also prevent the formation of any coherent policy positions.[37] Some factional fights show up inside legislative parties. At other times the division is between a governor and the legislative party. Governors may seek a different (broader) constituency than their legislative party base because they feel they must do so to get elected. In New York, for example, New York City constituted almost 60 percent of the state's population for much of the twentieth century. Republican candidates had to do well in relatively liberal and heavily Democratic New York City to be able to win. This problem resulted in Republican governors who were more liberal than, and in continual conflict with, their legislative party.[38] This divergence between governors and their legislative parties also exists in other states.[39]

The organization of the electorate in the South has been affected by southern history. As a result of the legacy of the Civil War and resulting hostility to the North and to the Republican party, the South turned completely away from the Republican party and became solidly Democratic. Although the electorate was heavily Democratic, the population was also generally very conservative, particularly on issues of civil rights, women's rights, and other social issues. Being a Democrat did not mean what it meant in the North.

That strong attachment to the Democratic party began to change during the 1960s when the conservative Republican presidential candidate Barry Goldwater won substantial votes in the South. The movement of many southern conservatives to the Republican party has continued since then. The transition that has occurred in southern states is shown in Figure 5.3. This chart presents changes in recent decades in partisan attachments among groups identifying themselves as liberals, moderates, and conservatives.

The major change has been the movement of conservatives to the Republican party.[40] But giving up one party and moving to another is not easy for many people. Many people in the South find it difficult to abandon years of attachment to the Democratic party. Older people, in particular, are less likely to make the transition. The "sorting out" of the electorate is not yet complete. The result is that the division of the electorate in the South does not yet look like the national division. It may some day, but the division is still in transition. This problem complicates the interaction between party officials and the public. Because the electorate may not yet perceive the state Republican party as the only vehicle for representing conservative views, they may not be inclined to identify with the party. If enough conservatives stay in southern Democratic parties, Democratic party candidates will be reluctant to appear too liberal.

The division of the electorate in the South (and to some degree elsewhere in the country) has been further complicated by the politics of race. Many conservative whites are unhappy with the extent of devotion of public resources to blacks. Many lower- and working-class conservative whites have left the Democratic party because they think the Democratic party is too supportive of black concerns.[41] Some argue that the primary path of success for Republicans has been to divide the lower class by appealing to the frustration of lower-class whites about race-related issues. This use of race-related issues has attracted lower-class whites to the Republican party, particularly in presidential elections, and has inhibited the development of lower-class electoral coalitions.[42]

When this happens, the role the parties play in representing the haves versus the have-nots becomes muddled. The focus of debates between the two parties may become whether too much is being done for blacks, rather than whether the haves or the have-nots are getting better treatment in society. Race often divides the electorate.

The consequence of all these factors is that the role of geography in the election of Democrats and Republicans is not as clear in the South. Urban areas do not uniformly vote Democratic, and rural areas do not always vote for Republicans. Table 5.11 presents legislative districts by whether they are primarily urban, suburban, or rural. The percent of each type of district held by Democrats or Republicans is then presented.

The electorate divides itself differently in each state. Florida has experienced a growth in Republicans, but the primary growth has come in urban areas in the southern part of the state.[43] In Florida, the Hispanic population, which is primarily from Cuba, is more conservative and votes Republican.[44] The state has historically been heavily Democratic. The rural areas, which are largely in the northern part of the state and have experienced less population growth, have remained heavily

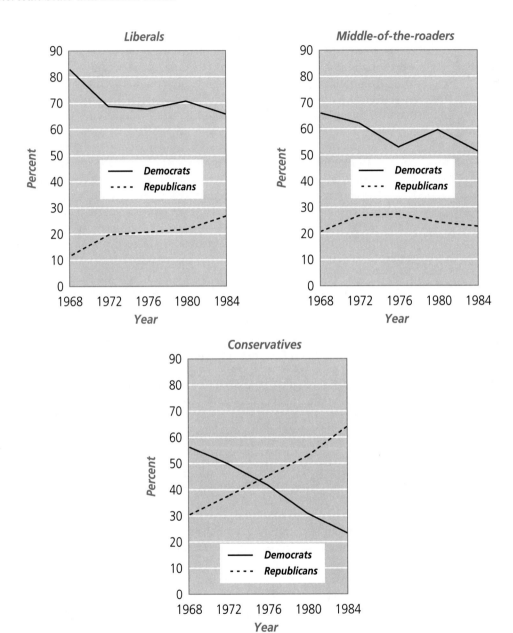

Figure 5.3

Changing Partisan Tendencies of White Southerners by Political Ideology, 1968–1984

Note: Democrats are Democratic identifiers plus independents who lean toward the Democrats; Republicans are Republican identifiers plus independents who lean toward the Republicans.

Sources: CSEP for 1968; SRC-CPS presidential election year surveys for other years; Merle Black and Earl Black, Politics and Society in the South *(Cambridge: Harvard University Press, 1987), 252.*

Table 5.11

Geographical Bases of Political Parties in Two Southern States

	Florida							
	House				Senate			
	Republican		Democrat		Republican		Democrat	
Geographical Base	(%)	(#)	(%)	(#)	(%)	(#)	(%)	(#)
Rural	0	(0)	100	(7)	0	(0)	100	(5)
Suburban	53	(20)	47	(18)	63	(5)	37	(3)
Urban	35	(26)	65	(49)	41	(11)	59	(16)
Race (% White)								
0–49.9	29	(7)	71	(17)	60	(3)	40	(2)
50–74.9	11	(2)	89	(16)	22	(1)	88	(7)
75+	47	(37)	53	(41)	44	(12)	56	(15)

	Texas							
	House				Senate			
	Republican		Democrat		Republican		Democrat	
Geographical Base	(%)	(#)	(%)	(#)	(%)	(#)	(%)	(#)
Rural	33	(7)	66	(14)	20	(2)	80	(8)
Suburban	37	(6)	62	(10)	20	(1)	80	(4)
Urban	40	(46)	59	(67)	31	(5)	68	(11)
Race (% Anglo)								
0–49.9	16	(8)	84	(42)	11	(1)	89	(8)
50–74.9	34	(14)	66	(27)	18	(2)	82	(9)
75+	59	(35)	41	(24)	36	(4)	64	(7)

Note: For each state, the first number in the row is the percent of legislators in an area or group who are Republicans or Democrats. The number of legislators in an area is in parentheses to the right of the percent.
Sources: Compiled from legislative district maps, lists of legislators supplied by each state, and suggestions from faculty in each state.[45]

Democratic. Republicans have made their greatest inroads in urban and suburban districts, where many well-to-do whites and retirees have moved.

While the political geography of the northern states may not apply to southern states, race is an important factor. In Florida, blacks have been a solid base for Democrats, while Latinos have supported Republicans. Table 5.11 also presents districts grouped by the percent white. While Democrats continue to elect legislators across a diverse set of districts (some with a low percent white and some with a high percent white), Republicans have realized almost all their success in heavily white districts. In the few districts with a low percent of whites where Republicans have won seats, Latinos have played a major role. Republicans hold three senate seats and seven house seats in areas with a low percent of white population. Hispanics average about 70 percent in those districts. Thus far, Republicans have done very well among Hispanics. Republicans are not doing well in black areas.

All these factors have created complicated electoral bases for the political parties in Florida. Democrats do well in heavily white and rural areas and in areas that are heavily black. That situation differs from the one in many northern and western states and probably makes forming party positions very complicated.

In Texas, there is also little of the association between geography and party found in non-southern states. Rural areas have a higher percent of Democrats than urban areas. Race again appears to play a major role in party bases. Table 5.11 presents the relationship between the percent of "Anglo" population of a district and the percent of the legislators from those districts who are Democrats or Republicans. Democrats elect representatives across diverse districts, but Republicans have achieved almost all their success in areas that are heavily Anglo. The Republican party has thus far built its appeal largely on conservative concerns of whites.[46] Hispanics also play a unique role in Texas. Republicans have elected state legislators in areas where the Anglo percent of population is only 50 to 74.9 and in some areas where the Anglo population is below 50 percent. In these districts the percent of Hispanics is again very high, and the percent of blacks is low. Much as in Florida, Republicans have been able to do well among Hispanics.

The party bases are also changing in Texas. The Democrats represent a party still sorting itself out. The party contains a high degree of diversity, while Republicans are more conservative and more homogeneous. Much more change is likely to occur in Texas.[47]

Changes in party situations are by no means confined to the South. Some northern states were once much more Republican than they might otherwise have been because of their reaction to the Democratic dominance of the South during the Civil War. This history has led to some "odd" political patterns. Some blue collar workers in the Northeast were Republicans because their state had a tradition of being Republican, and not because they were strong believers in Republican policy principles.[48]

The general attachment to the Republican party in the North has gradually declined over the years, however.[49] An example of this change can be seen in Figure 5.4. This graph presents party enrollments (the party indicated by voters when they register) in New York from 1920 to 1990. Over that time the major changes have been a decline in Republican enrollment and a rise in Independent enrollment. Such changes also affect who wins seats in the state legislature. Figure 5.5 presents the percent of legislative seats held by Democrats in Wisconsin from 1901 to 1991. Over that time there has been a complete shift from Republican dominance to Democratic dominance of the state legislature.

Each state has its own political history, and in many states those histories involve considerable change. This change has occurred in the South and the North. The electoral bases of state parties undergo continual change. These changes create long-term uncertainties for politicians as they adapt to changing voting patterns.

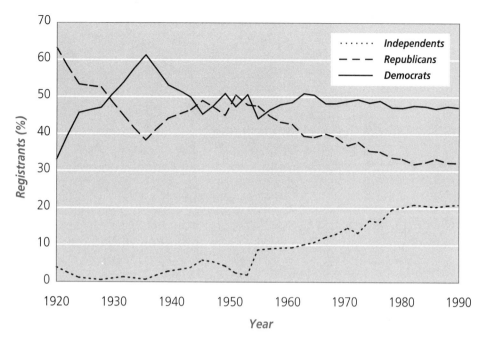

Figure 5.4
Party Enrollment in New York, 1920–1990
Source: Compiled by author.

The Unclear Role of Local Parties

The role of political parties in organizing the electorate and the issues in local politics is less clear. There is evidence that local parties do organize the electorate by class much as some state parties do, but there is also evidence that electoral divisions in cities are often dominated by ethnicity and race. Such divisions may displace class divisions. There are also reasons to suspect there are inherent limits to the kind of debate local parties can create.

There are grounds for presuming local Democratic parties attract the same groups national Democratic parties do, and that local Republican parties do the same. Images of local parties are often dominated by the positions that national political figures take. If such images dominate at the local level, then liberals and working-class individuals will be attached to the local Democratic party and conservatives and upper-income individuals will be attached to the local Republican party. There is evidence that attachments do sort out this way. In large cities across the country (Houston, Nashville, Los Angeles, and Chicago) Democrats tend to be blue-collar workers, have lower incomes, and identify themselves as liberals.

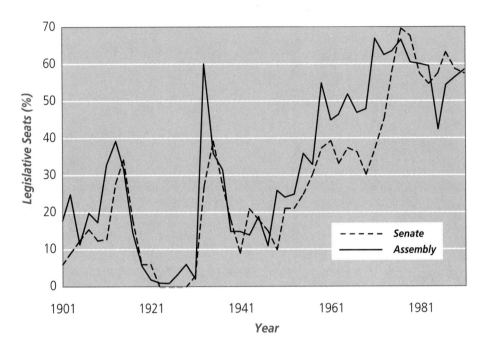

Figure 5.5
Democratic Percent of Seats in Wisconsin Legislature, 1901–1991
Source: Compiled by author.

Republicans are more likely to be white-collar workers, have higher incomes, and identify themselves as conservatives.[50]

But, much as with state parties, it is dangerous to assume that local parties just duplicate the national pattern. Each locality has its own history, and that history may produce loyalties that diverge from the pattern of lower- to middle-income groups being Democrats and middle- to upper-income groups being Republican.

Attachments may develop in different ways because of regional conflicts. As noted before, in many Northeast cities there are low-income individuals who identify with the Republican party because their family grew up in the North and identifies the Democratic party with the South. In upstate New York, the primary regional hostility has been toward New York City, and many low-income, blue-collar workers outside the city are Republicans because they are opposed to Democratic-dominated New York City.

Identification with parties and voting patterns in many communities may be based on ethnicity with class identity playing less of a role. Italians, Irish, and Poles in many areas formed their attachments to parties on the basis of which party would accept them. Italians in many northeast cities went into the Republican party for this reason, and as a result, many urban Republican parties are comprised of large groups of low-income ethnics.[51] Ethnic attachments do affect group voting patterns. Italians vote for Italian candidates, Irish for Irish, and so forth.[52] If voting is based on ethnicity, then the issues that dominate elections may not revolve around class or liberal-conservative differences.

We also have considerable evidence that racial divisions dominate many local elections.[53] This division is particularly common in mayoral races in which one candidate is black and the other is white. Such a situation occurred when black Democrat David Dinkins ran against Republican Rudy Guliani in the 1989 mayoral election in New York City. White ethnics who were enrolled in the Democratic party voted heavily for Italian Guliani, but Dinkins won.[54]

This racial division persisted in 1993, when Dinkins and Guliani ran again. Table 5.12 indicates how the electorate was divided in the polls early in 1993. The division was primarily around race (white-black). Class and income were not major sources of divisions in how people intended to vote.[55] In the 1993 race, Guliani was able to pull enough white votes to his side to win the election, even though the city had overwhelming Democratic party enrollment. The loss of an election by a minority candidate because of racial division does not mean that racial divisions in that area cannot be overcome. In some cities, minority candidates have been able to win office by assembling biracial coalitions of liberals (and minorities) around a liberal agenda.[56]

Finally, there are reasons to wonder if the ability of parties to organize political debate in many localities is constrained by the situations communities face. Many local populations in both cities and suburbs are somewhat homogeneous. Republicans do not begin elections with much of a natural electoral base in many central cities because there are not many Republicans living in city boundaries. In

---

Table 5.12

Class and Race Divisions in the Polls Prior to the 1993 New York City Mayoral Election

Race	Dinkins (D) (%)	Guliani (R) (%)
White	27	60
Black	88	7
Hispanic	45	44
Household Income		
Under $15,000	48	35
$15,000–29,999	54	34
$30,000–49,999	42	48
$50,000–75,000	38	52
Over $75,000	39	50

Source: New York Times/*CBS Poll,* New York Times, *19 May 1993, B2.*

central cities the presence of a limited electoral base with natural sympathies to Republican perspectives makes it difficult for Republican candidates to mount serious opposition to Democrats. It also makes it difficult to have much of a typical Democrat-Republican debate. Democrats have the same problem in many suburbs. It is difficult to focus party debates around issues such as class when an area has a somewhat homogeneous population.

This is much less of a problem in metropolitanwide elections for county executives or county legislative candidates. In these races, candidates from opposing parties may be able to draw on traditional constituencies and have political debates that approximate those that occur at the state level.

The nature of local political debates is also affected by the economic situation of local governments. Local governments cannot move. They must bring economic activity and residents into their cities, or face declining revenues. Focusing political campaigns on redistribution *within* a city is difficult because the taxes necessary to support redistribution may drive affluent residents out.[57] The continuing population movement out of the cities also affects political debates. Politicians in declining cities must attract new businesses. This necessity puts many central-city politicians in the position of having to focus on economic development.[58] This problem limits he kinds of political debates that might emerge.

All of these factors—regional histories, ethnicity, race, community homogeneity, and concerns with economic development—may result in electoral divisions along lines other than class. Political debates may not be about class issues, but about personalities, management issues, or ways to attract jobs into the community. The relative homogeneity of local governments limits the terms of debate. In central cities, campaigns focus on who can handle crime better and who can have the greatest impact on economic development. In the suburbs, campaigns focus on effectiveness of management and the person who can best maintain the life style of that suburb. There are debates, and campaigns do have importance, but the themes and electoral divisions that dominate are often not those that occur at the state level.

The Intrusion of National Politics

Parties struggle to create electoral bases that will endure. They seek to carve out positions that match their constituencies so that there can be some continuity to their position. But they are occasionally buffeted by the forces of national politics.

The national parties normally do not play a significant direct role in shaping state and local parties. The regulation of state and local party rules is done by state and local officials.[59] The exception occurs when delegates are selected for the national party conventions, which nominate presidential candidates. Campaign funds used by state and local officials are raised from state and local sources. In recent years the national party committees have also raised some funds to distribute to congressional candidates, but those amounts are small.[60] Campaigns themselves are conducted by state and local groups, not by national party officials. In general, state and local party organizations do run their own affairs.

While the actions of the national party have limited impact on state and local organizations, national party candidates often have significant impact on the electoral fortunes of state and local parties. Presidents and presidential candidates are the most visible symbols of their party. Their actions and statements, and to a much lesser degree Congressional positions, receive enormous media coverage. To many people, presidential (and national) politics comes to define the "party."

Occasionally the reaction to national party actions may be so strong that the electorate votes for or against all party candidates at all levels as a reaction to national issues.[61] This type of reaction happened in 1964. Barry Goldwater appeared too willing to use nuclear weapons, and he was very conservative on civil rights. The result was a major shift of votes away from Republicans at *all* levels of government in the 1964 elections. At the same time, there was a major shift in the South. Southern conservatives began to move to the Republican party. This move has affected the way parties divide and organize the electorate in the South. National politics intruded on "the solid South."

The electorate may also react to a scandal that a party candidate becomes involved in. In 1974, Richard Nixon resigned because of the Watergate scandal. Again there was a drop in votes for Republicans at all levels. The electorate may also hold a party in power at the national level responsible for the state of the economy and vote at all levels against that party.[62] These reactions occur because much of the electorate lumps all Republicans together and all Democrats together. This tendency ties party politicians together and makes state and local politicians worry about the positions and actions that national officials take.

While the impact of these reactions is significant, the reactions themselves are infrequent and generally short term. They also do not have the same impact in all states. In states like California, the attachment to parties is not as strong, and there is less of a tendency to vote for or against all party candidates. National reactions, therefore, do not play out as strongly in California. In Connecticut, on the other hand, there is less split-ticket voting, and recent "national" actions have had more of an impact because public reactions carried over to state and local voting patterns.[63]

These national reactions are called "coattail" effects. They complicate the "meaning" of state and local political results. The partisan division of control in a state might not exist because of state and local events, but because of national tides of reaction for or against a political party. Sometimes these national reactions persist, but at other times they cease to be relevant once the national event recedes from public memory.

The Persisting Role of Parties: Representing Different Concerns

Despite all of these qualifications about the clarity of party bases and the cohesion of parties, parties continue to play a major role in representing different political positions. They generally have different electoral bases, and they represent areas with different populations. Elected party officials come to decision making with different concerns. Democrats and Republicans end up pursuing different concerns, and the two parties oppose each other on a regular basis.[64] This opposition is most evident in state legislatures.

Table 5.13 presents the differences between Democrats and Republicans in the New York legislature. The situation shown here is typical of in many states. The "ratings" shown were done by two interest groups for various years. The New York Civil Liberties Union is considered a liberal group. Each year it chooses bills that it believes are important to civil liberties. It then rates legislators on whether they voted "right" or "wrong" on these bills. A score of 100 indicates that a legislator voted right on all bills and can be considered very liberal. A low score indicates a conservative position. BIPAC (Business Industry PAC) is a conservative business group. A high score from this group indicates a legislator has voted for conservative policy positions. A low score indicates a liberal voting record. The ratings for each legislator are grouped by party and then averaged to provide an idea of party voting pattern. Based on the NYCLU ratings, Democrats receive much higher (liberal) scores than Republicans in both houses, and the parties consistently oppose each other on major policy issues. BIPAC, on the other hand, gives Republicans higher scores than Democrats. The same pattern shows up in other states.[65] Parties at the state and local levels continue to represent different concerns in the political process.

While Democrats do differ from Republicans, not all Democrats across the country are the same, nor are all Republicans the same. Each state has its own political culture and history that have shaped how liberal or conservative the party in the state is. Democrats in Alabama are not the same as those in New York because the state populations differ. Democrats in Alabama may be more liberal than Republicans in Alabama, but on the whole they are more conservative than New York Democrats. Figure 5.6, based on research by Gerald Wright and others, illus-

Table 5.13

Average NYCLU and BIPAC Ratings for New York State Assembly Legislators

Year	Democrats (%)	Republicans (%)
NYCLU (Liberal)		
1979	78.4	39.8
1980	68.0	30.6
BIPAC (Conservative)		
1989	29.0	54.0

Sources: NYCLU: Howard Scarrow, Parties, Elections, and Representation in New York *(New York: New York University Press, 1983), 21; BIPAC: Jeffrey M. Stonecash, "Political Parties and Partisan Conflict," in Jeffrey M. Stonecash, John K. White, and Peter W. Colby,* Governing New York State *(Albany: SUNY Press, 1993).*

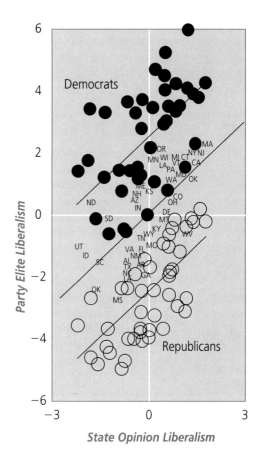

Figure 5.6
Party Elite Liberalism by State Opinion
Note: Solid dots represent Democratic elites; hollow dots represent Republican elites. State labels are placed at the midpoint between
the Democratic and Republican elite positions.
Source: From Wright APSR, September 1989, 737.

trates this. It indicates how liberal the average Democratic party leader is in each
state and how conservative the average Republican leader is. The figure also
reflects the degree of liberalism of the population of each state.

The results indicate that in the states Democrats as a group are more liberal
than Republicans as a group. But how liberal Democratic party leaders are is
dependent on which state they live in. The more liberal the population in a state, the
more liberal Democratic legislative leaders are. Similarly, the more liberal a state's
population, the more liberal Republican legislative leaders are. This variance
makes understanding parties across states complicated. It is not possible to assume
that Democrats (or Republicans) in all states will support the same positions. In

trying to understand what a party supports, it is essential to begin with the state or local history and then determine the constituency each party draws upon for its electoral base.

Party Competition in the States

All of the conditions discussed thus far affect the status and cohesion of the parties in the states. In some states, Republicans and Democrats are well organized, act as major forces in political debates, and win substantial proportions of elections. But to know the electoral bases and cohesion of the parties across fifty states requires careful case studies.[66] It is possible, however, to determine the extent to which the electorate supports Democrats and Republicans in the states. Table 5.14 presents by state the number of legislative seats held by each party in 1988 and gives the party affiliation of the state governor in that same year.

The table also presents a widely used index of interparty competition. This index attempts to capture a broader picture of the electoral success of the parties. The index averages the percentage of the popular vote for Democratic gubernatorial candidates, the percentage of seats held by Democrats in the legislature, and the percentage of time the Democrats held both the governorship and a majority in the state legislature. A value of 1.0 indicates Democratic dominance, .5 indicates balanced competition between the two parties, and 0 represents Republican domination. The index covers all elections from 1981–1988. As can be seen, there is considerable diversity among the states, though the South still tends to be more Democratic than the rest of the nation.

Summary

Parties persist in America as collections of individuals who come together to promote common concerns. Each party candidate begins with his or her own constituency and electoral base. Once elected, these candidates then attempt to find common ground with other elected officials in their own party. Most continue to find more agreement than disagreement. Their common constituencies bind them together.

In general, parties rely on different constituencies and take different positions in political debates, but parties do not always have clear constituency bases and are not always cohesive. This lack of clarity and cohesiveness has particular relevance for the have-nots. When this clarity and cohesiveness exists in the Democratic party, have-nots fare better. There are many conditions that can prevent such cohesiveness from occurring. The electorate itself may be less attached to parties, as in the West. Electoral attachments may be shifting, as in South. There may also be factional divisions within a party. For whatever reasons, political parties often do not create the strong policy debate that we might expect. We will

Table 5.14
Party Competition in the States in 1988

State	Lower House Democrats (Seats)	Republicans	Upper House Democrats (Seats)	Republicans	Governor (Party)	Interparty Competition Index (1980-1988)
East						
Maine	97	54	20	15	R	.70
New Hampshire	119	281	8	16	R	.34
Vermont	74	76	16	14	R	.53
Massachusetts	128	32	32	8	R	.74
Rhode Island	83	17	41	9	D	.72
Connecticut	88	63	23	13	I	.58
New Jersey	44	36	22	17	D	.51
New York	92	58	27	34	D	.49
Pennsylvania	104	99	23	27	D	.47
Midwest						
Ohio	59	40	14	19	R	.54
Indiana	50	50	24	26	D	.36
Illinois	67	51	31	28	R	.64
Michigan	61	49	18	20	R	.52
Wisconsin	56	43	20	13	R	.68
Iowa	61	39	30	20	R	.64
Minnesota	80	53	44	23	R	.64
Mountain						
Colorado	26	39	11	24	D	.33
North Dakota	45	61	32	21	D	.50
South Dakota	24	46	15	20	R	.26
Nebraska					D	.52
Idaho	20	64	19	23	D	.30
Montana	52	48	23	27	R	.51
Wyoming	23	41	11	19	D	.34
Utah	28	47	7	22	R	.25
Southwest						
Arkansas	88	11	31	4	D	.39
Lousiana	86	17	34	5	D	.81
Texas	93	57	23	8	D	.75
Kansas	58	67	18	22	D	.39
Oklahoma	68	32	33	15	D	.74
Arizona	26	34	13	17	R	.39
New Mexico	45	25	26	16	D	.67
Nevada	30	12	8	13	D	.49

continued

Table 5.14 (continued)
Party Competition in the States in 1988

State	Lower House Democrats (Seats)	Republicans	Upper House Democrats (Seats)	Republicans	Governor (Party)	Interparty Competition Index (1980-1988)
South						
Alabama	85	17	28	6	R	.84
West Virginia	81	19	29	5	D	.77
Delaware	18	23	13	8	R	.50
Florida	73	47	23	17	D	.74
Georgia	144	36	45	11	D	.76
Maryland	125	16	40	7	D	.76
Mississippi	112	9	44	8	D	.86
Missouri	104	58	22	12	R	.62
Kentucky	72	28	30	8	D	.77
North Carolina	74	46	37	13	R	.70
South Carolina	87	37	35	11	R	.79
Tennessee	59	40	22	11	D	.64
Virginia	59	39	30	10	D	.74
West						
Alaska	23	17	8	12	I	.47
California	46	33	24	15	R	.66
Hawaii	45	6	22	3	D	.77
Oregon	32	28	19	11	D	.60
Washington	63	35	24	25	D	.67

Note: The competition index is based on a scale of 0 to 1. A score of 1 indicating complete Democrat dominance, and a score of 0 indicating complete Republican dominance.
Source: U.S. Statistical Abstract 1991, 265; and John F. Bibby, Cornelius P. Cotter, James L. Gibson, and Robert J. Huckshorn, "Parties in State Politics," in Virginia Gray, Herbert Jacob, and Robert A. Albritton, Politics in the American States, 5th ed. (Glenview, Ill: Scott, Foresman, 1990), 92.

assess the consequences of this in Chapter 8 when we examine the ways that combinations of conditions in a state can affect representation.

For Further Reading

Browning, Rufus B., Dale R. Marshall, and David H. Tabb. *Racial Politics in American Cities.* New York: Longman, 1990.

Black, Earl, and Merle Black. *Politics and Society in the South.* Cambridge: Harvard University Press, 1987.

Davidson, Chandler, *Race and Class in Texas Politics*. Princeton: Princeton University Press, 1990.

Paddock, Joel. "Beyond the New Deal: Ideological Differences Between Eleven State Parties." *Western Political Quarterly* 43 (March 1990), 181–90.

Suggestions for Analysis in Your Own State and Locality

1. What are the electoral bases of political parties in your state and area? There are two ways to assess this.

    Individual-level data: You might first find out if any newspaper in the state does statewide polls and has current information on the differences between Democrats and Republicans. If such information is not available, the appendix of this book provides information on the differences between Republicans, Independents, and Democrats by income and by self-designated ideological position. That information is for the time period from the mid-1970s to the late 1980s. While the information is dated, most party bases do not change rapidly, so the information will give you some idea of differences in party bases. Examine that information and assess the way the electoral bases of Republicans and Democrats differ.

    For the local situation, does a local newspaper do polling? Or, is there some local politician who has done polling and would be willing to provide you with information on the differences between local Democrats and Republicans?

    Area-level data: If poll data are not available, most politicians rely on voting data by election district, neighborhood, city or town, county, or region. See what voting results are published in your state. If gubernatorial results are published, classify regions of the state by the type of population that lives there (urban, suburban, or rural; white, nonwhite; high, moderate, or low income), and then examine the percent that voted Democrat or Republican. You might also do this for a recent mayoral or countywide race.

    The same approach can be used for legislative districts. Information on income and race for all state legislative districts is contained in William Lilley III, Laurence J. DeFranco, and William M. Diefenderfer, *The Almanac of State Legislatures* (Washington, DC: Congressional Quarterly, 1994). That book may be in your school library, or your professor may have obtained a copy of it. Look at the maps of your state in that book, and determine how the districts of Democrats and Republicans differ. You can also attempt to do this for city-council and county legislative districts, using local information.

2. Party organizations can play a significant role in recruiting and helping candidates. How large of a budget do state and local party organizations have? Does each have a fulltime office that is in operation all year? Are the party organizations able to provide campaign funds and technical assistance to candidates?

3. Parties can play a crucial role in presenting and arguing for different policy choices. Did the gubernatorial candidates in your state differ much in their stands on policy matters? If so, on what policies did they differ? For local elections, choose a relatively prominent executive contest (mayor, county executive), and examine the same issues.

Do the legislative parties in your state differ much in the positions they support? You can determine that by reviewing newspaper coverage of legislative sessions, by looking at voting records on major bills, or by contacting any interest groups that create and publish ratings of state legislators.

Notes

[1] See as examples E. E. Schattschneider, *Party Government* (New York: Rinehart, 1942); and V. O. Key, Jr., *Politics, Parties, and Pressure Groups* (New York: Thomas Crowell, 1964).

[2] For other definitions, see Paul A. Beck and Frank J. Sorauf, *Party Politics in America*, 7th ed., (New York: HarperCollins, 1992), 8.

[3] Peter Kerr, "Read His Lips: More Taxes," *New York Times Magazine*, 20 May 1990, 30–33, 51–57.

[4] Malcolm Jewell and David G. Olson, *American State Political Parties and Elections* (Homewood, Ill: Dorsey, 1982), 67.

[5] On corruption, see Alexander B. Callow, Jr., *The City Boss in America* (New York: Oxford University Press, 1976), 18–22, 141–172; and Dennis R. Judd, *The Politics of American Cities*, 3rd ed. (Boston: Scott, Foresman/Little, Brown, 1988), 65–69.

[6] On the nature and development of machines, see Robert K. Merton, "The Latent Functions of the Machine: A Sociologist's View," in Alexander B. Callow, Jr., *The City Boss in America* (New York: Oxford University Press, 1976), 23–33; Martin Shefter, "The Emergence of the Political Machine: An Alternative View," in Willis D. Hawley et al., *Theoretical Perspectives on Urban Politics* (Englewood Cliffs: Prentice Hall, 1976), 14–44.

[7] For a critical portrayal of a "Boss," see Mike Royko, *Boss: Richard J. Daley of Chicago* (New York: New American Library, 1971).

[8] For a discussion of the role of legislative leaders in a strong party state, see Alan G. Hevesi, *Legislative Politics in New York State* (New York: Praeger, 1975), 26–80.

[9] E. J. Dionne, Jr., *Why Americans Hate Politics* (New York: Touchstone Books, 1991), 11.

[10] John M. Allswang, *Bosses, Machines, and Urban Voters*, rev. ed. (Baltimore: Johns Hopkins Press, 1977).

[11] Samuel J. Eldersveld, *Political Parties in American Society* (New York: Basic Books, 1982), 93–95.

[12] Richard Hofstader, *The Age of Reform*, (New York: Vintage, 1955); and Samuel Hays, "The Politics of Reform in Municipal Government," *Pacific Northwest Quarterly* 55, no. 4 (October 1964): 157–69.

[13] Malcolm Jewell and David Olson, *Political Parties and Elections in American States*, 3rd ed. (Chicago: Dorsey, 1988), 96.

[14] Ruth S. Jones, "State Public Campaign Finance: Implications for Partisan Politics," *American Journal of Political Science* 25, (May 1981): 342–61.

[15] Herbert Alexander, *Reform and Reality: The Financing of State and Local Campaigns* (New York: Twentieth Century Fund Press, 1991).

[16] John D. Buenker, *Urban Liberalism and Progressive Reform* (New York: W.W. Norton, 1973); and Michael H. Ebner and Eugene M. Tobin, eds., *The Age of Urban Reform* (Port Washington, N.Y.: Kennikat, 1977).

[17] Roland Liebert, *Disintegration and Political Action* (New York: Academic Press, 1976), 35–64.

[18] Martin Shefter, "Regional Receptivity to Reform: The Legacy of the Progressive Era," *Political Science Quarterly* 98, no. 3 (fall 1983), 459–83.

[19] Barbara G. Salmore and Stephen A. Salmore, *Candidates, Parties, and Campaigns*, 2nd ed., (Washington DC: Congressional Quarterly Press, 1989), 39–61.

[20] Kenneth Prewitt, "Political Ambitions, Volunteerism, and Electoral Accountability," *American Political Science Review* 64 (1970): 5–17.

[21] Pat Dunham, *Electoral Behavior in the United States* (Englewood Cliffs: Prentice Hall, 1991), 78–79; and Michael M. Gant and Norman R. Luttbeg, *American Electoral Behavior* (Itasca, Ill.: F. E. Peacock, 1991), 36–39.

[22] Stephen D. Shaffer, "A Multivariate Explanation of Rising Ticket-Splitting" (paper presented at the Southern Political Science Association Meetings, 1982).

[23] Morris P. Fiorina, "Divided Government in the States," *PS* 24, no. 4 (December 1991), 646–50.

[24] William Crotty, American Parties in Decline (Boston: Little, Brown, 1984), 267–77; and David E. Price, *Bringing Back the Parties* (Washington, DC: Congressional Quarterly Press, 1984), 33.

[25] Cornelius Cotter, James Gibson, John Bibby, and Robert Huckshorn, *Party Organizations in American Politics* (New York: Praeger, 1984).

[26] Anthony Gierzynski, *Legislative Party Campaign Committees in the American States* (Lexington: The University Press of Kentucky, 1992); Richard A. Clucas, "Legislative Leadership and Campaign Support in California," *Legislative Studies Quarterly* 17, no. 2 (May 1992): 265–84; and Diana Dwyre and Jeffrey M. Stonecash, "Where's the Party: Changing State Party Organizations," *American Politics Quarterly* 20, no. 3 (July 1992): 326–44.

[27] James L. Gibson, John P. Frendeis, and Laura L. Vertz, "Party Dynamics in the 1980s: Change in County Party Organizational Strength, 1980–1984," *American Journal of Political Science* 33 (1989): 67–90; James L. Gibson, Cornelius P. Cotter, John F. Bibby, and Robert J. Huckshorn, "Whither the Local Parties?" American Journal of Political Science 29 (1985): 139–60; and William J. Crotty, ed., *Political Parties in Local Areas*, (Knoxville: University of Tennessee Press, 1986).

[28] Jeffrey M. Stonecash, "Political Parties and Partisan Conflict," in Jeffrey M. Stonecash, John K. White, and Peter W. Colby, eds., *Governing New York State* (Albany: SUNY Press, 1993); Gerald Pomper, "Electoral Trends," in Richard Lehne and Alan Rosenthal, *Politics in New Jersey*, rev. ed. (New Brunswick: Eagleton Institute of Politics, 1979), 52.

[29] See Richard W. Murray and Kent L. Tedin, "Emerging Competition in the Sunbelt," 44–45, and Samuel J. Eldersveld, "The Party Activist in Detroit and Los Angeles: A Longitudinal View, 1956–1980," 94, in William Crotty, ed., *Political Parties in Local Areas* (Knoxville: University of Tennessee Press, 1986).

[30] James Gimpel, "Competition Without Cohesion," (paper presented at Midwest Political Science Association Meetings, 1989).

[31] Edward G. Carmines and James A. Stimson, *Race and the Transformation of American Politics* (Princeton: Princeton University Press, 1989); and, Nicol C. Rae, "Class and Culture: American Political Cleavages in the Twentieth Century," *Western Political Quarterly* 45, no. 3 (September 1992): 629–50.

[32] B. Drummond Ayres, Jr., "Christian Right Splits GOP in South," *New York Times*, 7 June 1993, A12.

[33] I would like to express my thanks to William K. Muir, Department of Political Science, University of California at Berkeley for helping me classify legislative districts in California. I greatly appreciate his assistance.

[34] Maureen Moakley, "Political Parties," in Gerald Pomper, *The Political State of New Jersey*, (New Brunswick: Rutgers University Press, 1986), 86; Duane Lockard, "Connecticut," in *New England State Politics* (Princeton: Princeton University Press, 1959), 236; Jack R. Van Der Silk

and Kent D. Redfield, *Lawmaking in Illinois* (Springfield: Sangamon State University Press, 1986), 57–58; Frank Bryan, *Politics in the Rural States* (Boulder: Westview, 1981), 208, 215; and John H. Fenton, *Midwest Politics*, (New York: Holt, Rinehart, and Winston, 1966).

[35] Paul T. David, *Party Strength in the United States*, (Charlottesville: University of Virginia, 1972), 22; and Robert T. Brown, "Elections and State Party Polarization," *American Politics Quarterly* 20, no. 4 (October 1992): 411–26.

[36] John Fenton, *Midwest Politics* (New York: Holt, Rinehart and Winston, 1966).

[37] See for example the discussions of factionalism in Vermont in Duane Lockard, *New England State Politics* (Princeton: Princeton University Press, 1959); and Frank Bryan, *Yankee Politics in Rural Vermont* (Hanover, N.H.: University Press of New England, 1974).

[38] Jeffrey M. Stonecash, "'Split' Constituencies and the Impact of Party Control," *Social Science History* 16, no. 3 (fall 1992): 455–77.

[39] Peter Kobrak, "Michigan," in Alan Rosenthal and Maureen Moakley, *The Political Life of the American States* (New York: Praeger, 1984), 99–128; John Fenton, *Midwest Politics* (New York: Holt, Rinehart and Winston, 1966), 148.

[40] Earl Black and Merle Black, *Politics and Society in the South* (Cambridge: Harvard University Press, 1987), 251–253.

[41] Earl Black and Merle Black, *Politics and Society in the South*, 232–56; Alexander P. Lamis, *The Two-Party South*, (New York: Oxford University Press, 1984), 212–15; and, Chandler Davidson, *Race and Class in Texas Politics* (Princeton: Princeton University Press, 1990), 221–39.

[42] Thomas B. Edsall and Mary Edsall, *Chain Reaction: The Impact of Race, Rights, and Taxes on American Politics* (New York: W.W. Norton, 1991); and Chandler Davidson, *Race and Class in Texas Politics* (Princeton: Princeton University Press, 1990).

[43] Paul Allen Beck, "Realignment Begins? The Republican Surge in Florida," *American Politics Quarterly* 10, no. 4 (October 1982): 421–438; and Susan A. MacManus and Ronald Keith Gaddie, "Reapportionment in Florida: The Stakes Keep Getting Higher," in Susan MacManus, ed., *Reapportionment and Representation in Florida* (Tampa: Intrabay Innovation Institute, 1991), 476–77.

[44] Larry Rohter, "A Black-Hispanic Struggle Over Florida Redistricting," *New York Times*, 30 May 1992, A6.

[45] I would like to express my thanks to James Carter, editor of the *Texas Journal of Political Studies* and member of the Department of Political Science, Sam Houston State University, and to Susan MacManus, Department of Political Science, University of South Florida, for helping me classify legislative districts in their states. I greatly appreciate their assistance.

[46] Chandler Davidson, *Race and Class in Texas Politics* (Princeton: Princeton University Press, 1990), 219, 246.

[47] Ibid., 240–59.

[48] Frank Munger and Ralph Straetz, *New York Politics* (New York: New York University Press, 1960).

[49] David R. Mayhew, *Two-Party Competition in The New England States*, Bureau of Government Research (University of Massachusetts, 1967).

[50] See the evidence presented in the chapters on these cities in William Crotty, ed., *Political Parties in Local Areas* (Knoxville: University of Tennessee Press, 1986).

[51] Elmer Cornwell, "Bosses, Machines, and Ethnic Groups," *Annals of the American Academy of Political and Social Science* 353, (May 1964): 27–39.

[52] For studies of the role of ethnicity, see Raymond E. Wolfinger, "The Development and Persistence of Ethnic Voting," *American Political Science Review* 59 (December 1965): 896–908; and Michael Parenti, "Ethnic Politics and The Persistence of Ethnic Identification," *American Political Science Review* 61 (September 1967): 717–26.

[53] Jeffrey R. Henig, "Race and Voting: Continuity and Change in the District of Columbia," *Urban Affairs Quarterly* 28, no. 4 (June 1993): 544–70.

[54] Asher Arian et al., *Changing New York City Politics* (New York: Routledge, 1991), 96.

[55] "New York Blacks Back Dinkins; Whites Don't," *New York Times*, 19 May 1993, A1.

[56] Rufus P. Browning, Dale R. Marshall, David H. Tabb, *Racial Politics in American Cities* (New York: Longman, 1990).

[57] Paul E. Peterson, *City Limits* (Chicago: University of Chicago Press, 1981).

[58] Dennis R. Judd, *The Politics of American Cities: Private Power and Public Policy*, 3rd ed. (Glenview, Ill.: Scott, Foresman, 1988), 371–99.

[59] Paul A. Beck and Frank J. Sorauf, *Party Politics in America* (New York: HarperCollins, 1992), 70–78.

[60] Gary C. Jacobson, *The Politics of Congressional Elections*, 3rd ed. (New York: Harper-Collins, 1992), 63–77.

[61] James E. Campbell, "Presidential Coattails and Midterm Losses in State Legislative Elections," *American Political Science Review* 80, no. 1 (1986): 45–64; and John E. Chubb, "Institutions, the Economy, and the Dynamics of State Elections," *American Political Science Review* 82, no. 1 (1988): 133–54.

[62] Gary C. Jacobson, *The Politics of Congressional Elections*, 3rd ed. (New York: Harper-Collins, 1992), 147.

[63] Jeffrey M. Stonecash, "The Intrusion of National Politics into State Politics" (paper presented at Syracuse University, Department of Political Science, the Maxwell School, 1992).

[64] Joel Paddock, "Inter-Party Ideological Differences in Eleven State Democratic Parties, 1956–1980" *Western Political Quarterly* 45, no. 3 (September 1992): 751–60.

[65] Malcolm E. Jewell, "Party Voting in American State Legislatures," *American Political Science Review* 49 (1955): 773–91; Hugh LeBlanc, "Voting in State Senates: Party and Constituency Influences," *Midwest Journal of Political Science* 13 (1969): 33–57.

[66] Jeffrey M. Stonecash, "Inter-Party Competition, Political Dialogue, and Public Policy: A Critical Dialogue," *Policy Studies Journal* 16, no. 2 (winter 1987–1988): 243–62; and Jeffrey M. Stonecash, "Observations from New York: The Limits of 50-State Studies and the Case for Case Studies," *Comparative State Politics* 12, no. 4 (August 1991): 1–9.

6

Political Participation and Representation

PREVIEW

This chapter focuses on the effect of participation on representation. Politicians listen to those who participate. There is consistent evidence that participation is greater among those with higher education and income. These individuals pay more attention to politics, vote more, and contribute more to campaigns. This activity results in overrepresentation of individuals with more education and income. Their concerns receive more attention in the political process.

Despite this advantage, lower-income groups are still able to gain considerable representation through district elections because districts are allocated representatives on the basis of population and not on the basis of voting turnout. The degree to which this offsets general participation differentials and underrepresentation for low-income groups is unclear.

The Significance of Participation

Politicians focus on public concerns because they must win votes to get elected. For politicians to know those concerns, however, the public must communicate them to politicians. The public can communicate preferences about specific policies, or they can communicate vague, general limits on policy options. Political participation is the primary means of achieving this communication. That participation can take many forms. Letters, protests, memberships in organizations, contributions, and voting are only some of the means citizens can use to communicate concerns. All of these activities contribute to expressing concerns that become part of the agendas of politicians.

But not everyone participates in politics. One of the enduring issues of politics is who participates. Politicians tend to worry about and respond primarly to those who participate. Representation in a democracy is the result of the interactions between ambitious politicians who want to win elections and the public. We have a system in which we presume politicians pay attention to people because they worry about getting elected. Politicians must continually judge how many people have what concerns and whether the groups they seek to represent will deliver enough votes to get them elected. Without sufficient support, a candidate faces a futile campaign. While politicians worry about general expressions of public opinion, they worry more about the opinions of whose who actually vote. Participation matters.

This chapter focuses on how much people participate, the ways they participate, who does and does not participate and why, and the ways these differences in participation affect representation.

Public involvement in politics is not high. Following politics is not a widespread activity.[1] Much of the public's attention is sporadic and focused on specific events.[2] The public does not spend a great deal of time reading newspapers or watching television in order to acquire political information.[3] Much of the public does not know "basic" political information, such as the name of their local representative, or how long terms of office are.[4] Much of the public also does not approach politics with a coherent, ideological set of beliefs for analyzing events.[5] While we may regularly speak highly of the importance of public involvement in American democracy, the public is clearly not intensely engaged in politics. Some individuals are, but the majority of people are not. State and local politics generally receive even less attention from the public than national politics do.[6]

Active participation in politics is low. Public engagement in different kinds of political activities is shown in Table 6.1. Activities such as joining clubs,

Table 6.1

Percentage of the Public Engaging in Political Activity

Reported Activity	Percent
Vote regularly in Presidential elections	72
Always vote in local elections	47
Active in at least one organization involved in community problems	32
Worked with others in trying to solve some community problems	30
Attempted to persuade others to vote	28
Actively worked for a party or candidate during an election	26
Contacted a local government official about some issue or problem	20
Attended at least one political meeting or rally in the last three years	19
Contacted a state or national government official about some issue or problem	18
Formed a group or organization to attempt to solve some local or community problem	14
Gave money to a party or candidate during an election campaign	13
Presently a member of a political club or organization	8

Source: Sidney Verba and Norman Nie, Participation in America *(New York: Harper and Row, 1972), 31.*

contributing money, or contacting an official are not very common. The most common form of political activity is voting.[7]

Voting frequency also varies by level of government. Turnout (the percent of eligible voters who vote) is highest for presidential elections and declines for congressional elections ("off-year" elections). Turnout is at its lowest for elections scheduled in odd-numbered years ("off–off-year" elections). These elections involve local offices. The decline in voting in nonpresidential elections is called drop-off.[8] Voting turnout is at about 55 percent for presidential elections and then declines for gubernatorial elections in off years to about 40 percent.[9] Turnout is even lower for local elections, averaging a little over 30 percent of those eligible.[10] Figure 6.1 presents voting turnout for presidential, congressional, and gubernatorial elections from 1960 to 1988. Not only is turnout not high, but it has been declining over the last thirty years.

These levels of public attention and participation have important implications for politics. Most citizens are not heavily active in politics. Politicians are generally not under heavy scrutiny. The flow of communication between citizens and public officials is not extensive. The general public is not constantly conveying its views on issues to politicians. Indeed, politicians are often in the position of trying to determine what the public thinks about issues.

While the general public does not pay great attention to politics, certain people do get involved. Given the lack of extensive scrutiny of politicians by the public at large, the issue of who does participate becomes important. Those who

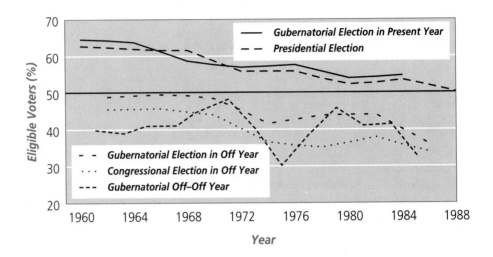

Figure 6.1
Turnout in Presidential, Congressional, and Gubernatorial Elections, 1960–1988
Source: Michael M. Gant and Norman R. Luttbeg, American Electoral Behavior (Itasca: F.E. Peacock, 1991), 110.

participate generally have greater influence. We will focus on the question of who participates after reviewing the question of why turnout and public involvement are declining.

The Reasons for Low and Declining Turnout

Democracies place great value on participation. Why, then, is such participation so low in the United States, and why is it declining? We are not quite sure. Several explanations have been proposed. While the primary concern in politics is who participates and how this affects representation, the issue of why participation, and particularly voting, is not high is also important.

The Pull of Alternatives

Participating in politics requires some interest in politics. It requires experience and comfort with political involvement, and it requires time and energy. Many people do not have the interest, experience, energy, or time. Most people are more interested in other areas of life, and they give politics a low priority. Part of the reason for low participation in politics, then, is that most people would rather allocate their free time to other activities. Some researchers suggest that the range and volume of leisure activities available to people have increased and that this change has drawn more and more people away from political involvement.[11]

Declining Trust in Politics and Politicians

The inclination not to participate is not due completely to attractive alternatives. It also stems from negative perceptions of politics. Many individuals feel that "the system" is unresponsive, and they do not participate because of that. They are alienated from politicians and believe any participation would be a waste of time. They do not trust politicians to tell the truth or to present themselves or issues honestly. They believe politics is a game of inside deals and favors to special interests. Over the last few decades, trust in government has also declined because of events like Watergate and scandals in Congress. Negative perceptions of politics and politicians combined with recent scandals have surely played a role in the decline in voting.[12]

The Decline of Political Parties

Others argue that participation has declined because political parties have declined in relevance. Parties can organize differing groups and present alternatives to the public. They can create debates that help the electorate understand issues and that present choices to the public. Some argue that parties do less and less of this. Party bases are not as clear as they once were, and the policy debates between parties are also not as clear. The disputes that party politicians engage in have less to do with the broad concerns of the public or with the broad differences in policy positions. The consequence is that public interest in politics declines and that people see voting as less relevant because the choices are not clear.[13]

It is also argued that parties now do less to mobilize people to participate in politics. In the past they conducted rallies, brought people together, and in general increased awareness of issues. The parties now engage in less of this activity. This decrease in party activity may have contributed to reduced participation.[14]

Registration Hurdles and Resulting Effects

Others take a much less benign view of the declines in turnout. They argue that low levels of participation in this country are not the result of low interest, but are a product of the dynamics of efforts to make it difficult to vote. Critics of the system argue that politicians have made it hard for political parties to mobilize the lower class. Registration requirements in the United States are more demanding than in other western countries, and the lower class is most likely to be intimidated by these requirements. Because the lower class does not vote as much, political parties have reduced their attempts to appeal to these voters. This decline in appeal to the concerns of the have-nots has resulted in a gradual decline in their political involvement.[15] This decline in explicit appeal may well be the source of much of the long-term decline in overall voting.[16]

The Media and Political Engagement

Finally, there is the crucial role of the media. The mass media (newspapers, television, and radio) play a significant role in public engagement in politics. If citizens are to participate in politics in a knowledgeable and informed manner, they must know what government does, what issues are currently under consideration, and what positions politicians are supporting. The mass media provide the means for people to gain this information. If an individual is unaware that an issue relevant to him or her is under consideration, he or she is not likely to perceive political activity as relevant or important. There is little basis for undertaking political action. There are, of course, alternative sources of information, such as interest groups, but for the bulk of the public, the media are the primary sources of political information. How the media carry out the role of informing citizens is also likely to affect participation patterns.

While the media often appear to be almost public institutions, they are private, profit-making organizations. While editors do seek to maintain a good community reputation, their primary concern is achieving an adequate profit.[17] This concern affects the allocation of media resources. Editors generally allocate their reporters to activities that will contribute to maintaining their readership, listenership, or viewing audience. Most media enterprises perceive political coverage as an important part of their activities, but not as their primary function. This assumption is particularly true of local television and radio stations, which usually do not devote many resources to provide regular coverage of state and local political events.[18]

The job of reporting state and local politics is assumed almost entirely by local newspapers. In performing this activity, editors make choices that affect citizens. Newspapers regard many community activities other than politics (sports, social events, financial information) as important. All local papers have limited staffs. This need to choose what is covered means that newspapers (except for a few in very large cities like Los Angeles, Chicago, and New York City) generally do not have staffs of sufficient size to provide extensive coverage of state and local politics.

Local newspapers also must make choices about how to use their limited resources to cover politics. First, local newspapers generally have to choose between covering state or local political events. The choice is usually to emphasize local events because newspapers presume that citizens would rather know what is happening in their own community than what happens in the state capital. State events are still covered, but not as thoroughly as local events.[19]

Second, given limited staffs, newspapers are not generally capable of producing much detailed or investigative reporting about policy areas. Newspapers usually find themselves dependent on public officials, lobbyists, state wire services, or politicians for information about government programs, budget issues, or the positions of candidates and parties. This dependence results in coverage that is often limited to quotes from interviews or to stories that present the views of one side versus another. It is difficult to find the resources for extensive research on political issues.

Newspapers also do not provide extensive coverage of politicians' ongoing activities. Newspapers only occasionally report the way local legislators vote on various bills. Newspapers also find it difficult to assess the effectiveness of programs sponsored by politicians. Analysis of how and why certain issues emerged and how they were handled is also unusual. Some of this material is covered, but newspapers cannot be looked to for thorough information about politics. The primary exceptions to this "rule" are newspapers based in state capitals. Since politics is often the big business in capitals (Albany, New York; Sacramento, California; Harrisburg, Pennsylvania; Springfield, Illinois, for example), state politics receives heavier media coverage in these cities than it does elsewhere.

Instead of pursuing in-depth information, the media, particularly television, gravitate toward coverage of events or personalities. Newspapers and television concentrate on specific confrontations or votes. When a controversial vote occurs, the media emphasize the political calculations going on and the attempts to gather votes. The constituencies involved, the policy goals at issue, or the implications of the potential outcomes usually receive less attention. A fight between the governor and the legislature, or the mayor and the police chief, for example, usually draws more attention than debates over how to allocate school aid or how to improve education in the state. The trade-off between political actions and analysis is usually not complete, but it is often sufficient to leave the reason for events and their implications unclear.

This lack of clarity has two primary causes. Journalists tend to presume citizens are more interested in controversy, personalities, and maneuvers than analysis. The life of a journalist is also hectic, and in the rush to cover politics, journalists often find themselves falling into a pattern of reacting to, and covering, immediate events, rather than engaging in thorough analysis. The constant deadlines reporters face from editors do not help.

Media critics argue that these tendencies come together to create certain ongoing journalistic practices. There is continual concern for events rather than for substantive policy issues.[20] During campaigns, journalists tend to focus on the "horse race" between candidates and on candidate controversies.[21] Rather than report the policy proposals of candidates and focus on their policy implications, the tendency is to focus on proposals as campaign strategies. Rather than let politicians speak about the pros and cons of proposals, reporters tend to focus on journalistic interpretations of the strategic reasons for the proposal.[22] Journalists also tend to be very concerned with investigations of corruption and incompetence. They serve as watchdogs to make sure that politicians do not "get away with" anything.

A significant example of the way the media affects the information the public receives comes from the House-of-Representatives "banking scandal" of 1992. The media made this a major story. They regularly conveyed the impression that members of the House of Representatives had bounced many checks in a "House bank," and that public funds were involved. That impression was inaccurate, since the "bank" was no more than a pooling of salaries to create a common fund of money from which to write checks. Members who did a poor job of handling their finances took advantage of those who did not. No federal funds were drawn on to cover bad checks. Despite that, in a national poll conducted April 2, 1992, 47 percent of the public concluded that taxpayer money was involved, while only 25 percent thought that the bad checks were covered by money of other House members.[23] The media chose to present the story as a scandal, and their watchdog mentality affected the way information was presented and the perception the public was left with.

Dissemination of information about state and local politics to citizens has also been affected by the decline in newspaper reading during recent decades. The proportion of people reporting they read newspapers has declined considerably over the last thirty years, while the proportion of people watching television news has not declined.[24] Since television does not cover state and local politics heavily, this shift in reliance on media outlets has probably led to a decline in knowledge of state and local politics over time.

All this has serious implications for citizens and their knowledge of the policy issues being considered in their state and locality. Some citizens learn about issues and policies from political parties or from interest groups. But the media remain the primary source of political news for most citizens. Citizens are likely to find it difficult to obtain thorough reviews of state and local policy options from the mass media. A great deal of political debate about policy on the state and local level occurs without extensive coverage by the media. In addition, many citizens do not make much of an effort to follow events. The extent to which this lack of interest occurs because of the poor quality of coverage in the local media is unknown, but the media surely plays some role. Regardless, the consequence is that the majority of citizens are not well informed about state and local politics.

Summary

All these conditions—increased leisure alternatives for citizens, decreased trust in government, declining parties, registration barriers, and changing media coverage—have been put forth to explain why participation is declining. Unfortunately, there is not enough research available to judge the relative impact of these changes upon participation rates. We only know that public participation in politics is not high and that turnout is declining.

Who Participates and Why

Politicians do respond to the general public, but they pay particular attention to those who vote. In most states, individuals musy register before they are able to vote, but many people do not register. Many registered voters do not vote. Perhaps more important, however, are the consistent and significant differences in participation rates among groups in the public. These differences mean that not all groups have their concerns equally represented in the political process.

Group Differences

Table 6.2 presents group voting rates in the 1988 presidential election. The factors that affect registration also affect voting, so the focus here will be on voting.[25] But it is important to keep in mind that there are two steps to voting: registration *and* voting. Since the same factors affect both, the cumulative effect of a group trait on participation is often significant. Voting is higher among those who have more

Table 6.2

Personal Characteristics and Voter Turnout in 1988 Presidential Election

Characteristics	Voters (%)
Education	
No high school degree	50
Past high school	62
Attended college	85
Income	
Low	46
Moderate	73
High	86
Race	
Blacks	60
Whites	72
Interest in campaigns	
Low	40
Medium	72
High	90
Partisanship	
Independent	50
Lean to a party	64
Weak attachment to party	68
Strong attachment to party	84
Age	
18–21	42
22–25	48
26–35	62
36–45	77
46–55	78
56–65	77
66–74	82
75+	68

Sources: *Education and race: Paul A. Beck and Frank J. Sorauf* Party Politics in America, *7th ed., (New York: HarperCollins, 1992), 218; Income: Raymond E. Wolfinger and Steven J. Rosenstone,* Who Votes *(New Haven: Yale University Press, 1980), 21; William H. Flanigan and Nancy H. Zingale,* Political Behavior of the American Electorate, *7th ed., (Washington, DC: Congressional Quarterly Press, 1991), 18; Interest and partisanship: Michael M. Gant and Norman R. Luttbeg,* American Electoral Behavior *(Itasca: F.E. Peacock, 1991), 94, 40.*

education, higher incomes, and more interest in campaigns, and among those who are older and more partisan.

Education has a very positive effect on participation. Greater education positively affects the inclination to participate. Individuals with more education find it easier to absorb information. They possess more of the skills necessary to interpret and to make sense out of political events. Their "costs" of following politics are lower. They indicate more interest in politics, and they rely on the mass media more. They are more likely to be well informed about politics.[26]

These with higher incomes also tend to participate more. They, in general, have more education. They also generally are involved in jobs that involve working with complex information and other people on a regular basis. This experience makes them more comfortable with political news and participation.

The conditions of education, income, and job status combine to form socio-economic status. Those with more years of education, higher incomes, and professional and managerial jobs have higher socioeconomic status. Those with less than a high school education, lower incomes and manual labor jobs have lower socio-economic status. The terms are not meant to be judgmental, but only to be a way to classify people for purposes of assessing differences in participation. Those of higher socioeconomic status participate more than those of lower socioeconomic status. This division is also relevant in explaining differences in turnout by race. Blacks, on average, have less education and lower incomes than whites. Their overall turnout rate is lower.

Participation is driven by more than the education and income of people, however. Some people are just more interested in politics, regardless of education. Those more interested in campaigns participate more. These people tend to have higher education and income, but not always. Those who are more attached to parties also participate more. They are more likely to see a significant difference between the parties.[27] Those perceptions prompt them to see elections as having important consequences. When people believe elections are important, they vote more.

Finally, age plays a significant role in affecting turnout. Younger people are generally not as involved in politics. They are more mobile and less attached to their communities. Their attention to, and knowledge of, politics is less, and they vote less. Older individuals are generally more attached to, and involved in, their communities. They register and vote at much higher rates than younger people.

State Cultural Norms

It also appears that participation varies because of differences in state political cultures. Political culture refers to the norms, or notions of what should be, of the role citizens should play or have a right to play. Daniel Elazar argues that states differ considerably in their norms of the proper role of citizens.[28]

In states like Mississippi and Virginia, Elazar found a "traditionalistic" culture with strong norms that politics should be left to traditional elites and that the remaining public should not expect to play a major role. In other states, such as Minnesota, Elazar found a "moralistic" culture where most people feel an obligation and a right to participate in politics. Between these two norms lie "individualistic" norms, which dominate in states like Nevada and Ohio. In these states, political activity is regarded as one activity among many in which an individual might engage. The decision of whether or not to participate is not based on deference to elites, or moral obligations, but on each individual's calculation of his or her own self-interest.

While not everyone accepts Elazar's arguments about the existence and the effects of these political cultures, his arguments have stimulated a considerable amount of research.[29] The notion that cultural norms exist and matter is plausible, and efforts to discern differences among the states continue. While some studies have not found the consequences of cultural differences that might be expected, it is the case that political participation rates are highest in "moralistic" states, lowest in "traditional" states, and in between in "individualistic" states.[30]

The Consequences of Differences in Participation

Differences in participation rates are crucial in politics because they affect who is heard and who is represented. Politicians listen more to those who participate. Some qualifications will be noted later, but, in general, differences in participation mean that the opinions of some groups are underrepresented, *relative to their proportion in the population*, while opinions of other groups are overrepresented, *relative to their proportion in the population*. Those groups that participate are "heard" more by public officials. Differences in participation are particularly important in elections because elections provide the public their primary means of punishing or rewarding politicians.

Table 6.3 provides an illustration of the consequences of differences in participation. In this case, assume 1000 people in the voting-age population are registered. Of these 1000 people, 150 are in the upper class, 400 are in the middle class, and 450 are in the lower class. The percent of the electorate in the upper class, middle class, and lower class is shown in the first column of numbers in the table. The actual number in each group is in the second column of numbers. The proportion of each group voting is shown in the third column. This proportion is called the turnout rate. If each of these groups participate at the rates shown in the third column, the number actually voting in each group will be the totals

---

Table 6.3

Effects of Differences in Participation Rates Using a Hypothetical Group (1000 Voters)

Class	Proportion of Electorate (%)	Total Number	Proportion Voting (%)	Total Voting	Proportion of Participating Voters (%)
Upper	15	150	80	120	21.4
Middle	40	400	60	240	42.9
Lower	45	450	45	200	35.7
Overall Totals	100	1000	56	560	100.0

shown in the fourth column. (These figures are found by multiplying the number of possible voters by the percent voting, or 150 × .80 = 120.) There will then be a total of 560 people actually voting. The proportion of the actual voters who are upper class will be 21.4 percent, while they actually comprise only 15 percent of the population. The proportion of the actual voters who are lower class will be only 35.7 percent, while they actually comprise 45 percent of the population. The lower class went from a relatively significant proportion of the electorate (45.0 percent) to a considerably smaller proportion (35.7 percent) of the electorate because of their lack of participation. This same table could be calculated for age or race differences.

Assuming that there are differences in opinion by class, age, or race, these differences in participation will create an active electorate with a different distribution of opinions than that in the potential electorate. As the composition of the electorate varies and as differences in participation rates vary, the actual voting electorate will vary. If the electorate in a city or state is evenly split between the middle and lower class, then lower turnout rates by the lower class will greatly affect their electoral influence. If, however, the lower class is only 15 percent of a city or state, they are likely to have limited influence regardless of their participation rate. The greater the differences in turnout between groups or classes, the greater the underrepresentaton of the lower class will be.

This argument about the effects of differences in voting also applies to letter writing, contributions, and membership in organizations. The greater the differences by socioeconomic status in engagement in these activities, the less the concerns of the lower class are heard and represented in the political process.

The Evidence of Impact

While nonvoting is much discussed and presumed to have great consequences, we do not have as many studies of the impact of nonvoting as the issue warrants. Most studies of nonvoting focus on presidential and congressional elections. The impact of participation differentials on state and local elections has been studied much less than it should be.

Evidence on the impact of nonvoting is also not as clear as we might presume it would be. Some studies of differences in opinions and voting behavior between voters and nonvoters have not found great differences between the two groups in presidential and congressional elections.[31]

Other assessments, which have focused on specific races or issues, have revealed many situations where differences between voters and nonvoters are clear and where nonvoting had a significant impact. In the 1980 presidential election, for example, those not voting were heavily in favor of Carter, not Reagan. If nonvoters had voted, Reagan would probably have lost the election.[32] On the specific issue of social security and medicare funding, there are also clear differences between younger and older people. The high levels of turnout by older people appears to have made Congress unwilling to reconsider benefits for older people during the 1980s.[33] The impact of nonvoting appears to be heavily dependent on specific situations.

Examples of Participation Differences: Local Politics

Case studies suggest just how important nonvoting can be. In 1981, Andrew Young, a prominent black, decided to run for mayor of Atlanta. His main opposition in the primary was a white liberal. Although the campaign was not explicitly fought over racial issues, race did become an implicit and subtle issue, and the two candidates found their greatest appeal, respectively, to be among blacks and whites. Blacks constituted 66 percent of the potential electorate, but, because they did not register heavily, they constituted only 53 percent of the eligible voters. Despite winning almost all the black vote, Andrew Young received only 40.9 percent of the total vote. He subsequently won the run-off election by increasing his efforts to get blacks to vote.[34] While greater representation and voting by blacks in the first election might not have given him the necessary majority to win that election, it would have greatly enhanced his chances.

A second example illustrates the more subtle effects of voting differentials.[35] In Syracuse, New York, lower-income neighborhoods, both black and white, have had much lower registration and participation rates than middle- and upper-income areas. In lower-class areas, the proportion of eligible voters who were voting has ranged from 10 to 20 percent, while in middle- to upper-income areas, that proportion ranged from 50 to 75 percent. The impact of this disproportion was that during the 1980s, despite repeated criticisms of the mayor's lack of concern for low-income neighborhoods, the Democratic mayor did not meet with representatives from these neighborhoods. He did not see them as a significant electoral threat.

Another example of the effects of nonvoting was observed by the author, who does polling and political consulting for local political candidates. A candidate facing a close race was trying to decide how to allocate his resources for a get-out-the-vote (gotv) effort. A group of spokespeople for the black community met with the candidate and made numerous requests for get-out-the-vote efforts. They also presented their expectations about jobs they wished to have if the candidate was elected. After the meeting, the candidate asked for the turnout rates in black areas. The author, who had checked the rates in those areas, told him that they were very low. The candidate then instructed his campaign manager to give the group as few resources as he could without angering them.

Examples of Participation Differences: State Politics

The same principles apply to state-level politics. In each state there is some degree of underrepresentation of those with lower incomes and less education.[36] When the lower class does not participate and vote as much as other classes, they constitute a smaller proportion of the "effective" electorate, or that group that affects electoral outcomes. In Texas gubernatorial elections, for example, the black and Hispanic populations vote less than the Anglo population. They have been significantly underrepresented among gubernatorial voters.[37] In New York, low-income voters in New York City turn out at a lower rate than other groups in the state. That turnout has put Democratic governors in a situation where they must focus their attention somewhat more on the suburbs to put together winning coalitions.[38] In the South, the effect of excluding blacks from participation for much of the twentieth century was that black concerns were completely ignored.[39]

Changing the Conditions and the Rates of Participation

Differentials in participation and their consequences have been with us for some time. Are they eternal and unvarying, or are there conditions that can change those differentials? Can turnout rates of lower-income groups be brought closer to turnout rates of those groups with high socioeconomic status?

Differences in participation by class do not appear to be fixed. They can be altered by changing the conditions under which that participation takes place. This result is particularly possible in an election, where numerous factors affect the relative tendency of groups to participate. The factors that have the biggest impact on participation differentials are the nature of registration laws, the timing of the election, the degree to which the election is partisan in nature, the competitiveness of the election, the strength of the local party organization, and the nature of the choice involved in the election. In each of these areas, there is a conventional wisdom that politicians tend to follow in order to adjust their strategy in line with these factors.

Varying these conditions alters differentials in turnout between the affluent and poor and between the young and old. The impact of these factors is illustrated in Figure 6.2. Line A shows the general tendency of individuals to participate in elections. Those of higher socioeconomic status vote more than those of lower socioeconomic status. In such situations, the lower class has less electoral significance, and politicians pay less attention to them.

If something were done to increase turnout rates, the important political question is whether it would increase the turnout of all groups equally. Since those of

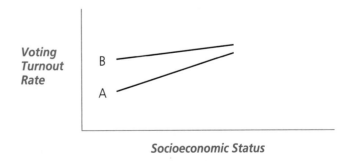

Figure 6.2
Possible Changes in Voting Rates

higher socioeconomic status already vote at fairly high rates, their turnout is not likely to increase much. The most significant change is likely to come from those of lower socioeconomic status. If their turnout increased more than other groups, the results would be similar to line B. That result would produce lower-class turnout somewhat equivalent to that of the middle class and would produce a more representative electorate.

These differences in relative turnout rates occur because of variations in voter attachment to politics. Some voters are consistent participants in politics. They consistently follow political events and vote in elections. These voters are not greatly affected by the degree of ease in participation, the excitement of the contest, or the closeness of the race. They will generally participate anyway. Other voters, the "peripheral" voters, are far more erratic in their involvement in politics. Voters in this group tend to be of lower socioeconomic status or to be young. These voters are more affected by the level of ease in participation, and by the stimulus to participate that an election presents. As these conditions vary, so will the rate of participation of this group. This variation directly affects their effective proportion in the electorate.

Registration

Before an individual can vote, he or she must register. The rules affecting registration are set at the state level (except for situations where federal intervention occurs, discussed below). States set requirements about the length of time an individual must be a resident before he or she can register, the time and place registration occurs, the frequency a citizen must vote to retain his or her registration, the number of days prior to an election an individual must register, and other such requirements. Each one of these requirements affects registration. As registration becomes more difficult, fewer individuals are likely to register, and, therefore fewer individuals are able to vote. Voting rates are accordingly reduced. While federal legislation has made state registration more similar across the states, there are still important differences between the states.

The important matter is the effect of these registration rules on relative registration and the turnout rates of groups by socioeconomic status. Table 6.4 shows the estimated effects on turnout by education level if registration laws were changed from the most restrictive to the least restrictive.[40] "Restrictive" laws are those that require registration relatively far in advance, do not allow flexible hours or locations for registration, and require regular reregistration at periodic intervals. "Easy" registration laws allow registration just before an election, allow for registration at flexible times and locations, and do not require reregistration at periodic intervals. This table assumes that very restrictive laws were in effect and indicates the likely result if these regulations were eased. For groups with an educational level of zero to four years, a change in registration laws from restrictive to easy would result in an increase in voting of 13.2 percentage points, while the same change would result in an increase of 2.8 percentage points for those with five or more years of college.

Table 6.4

Probable Increase in Participation Resulting from Change in Laws from Most Restrictive to Least Restrictive

Education (years)	Increase in Voting (%)
0–4	13.2
5–7	12.6
8	11.0
9–11	10.4
12	9.3
1–3 college	7.8
4 college	5.6
5 or more college	2.8

Source: Steven Rosenstone and Raymond Wolfinger, "The Effect of Registration Laws on Voter Turnout," American Political Science Review 72 (March 1978): 22–45.

These differentials occur because registration is a barrier to participation, and education makes it more likely an individual will overcome this hurdle. A person with more education is likely to find this procedure easier to comprehend and to feel more comfortable going through the procedure. Those with more education are likely to work in organizations and be more familiar in general with bureaucratic procedures. A more educated person is also likely to be more interested in politics and to take the time to overcome registration hurdles.

Variations in registration laws affect the composition of the electorate. For a party or candidate that relies heavily on a lower-class constituency, registration laws may be crucial to his or her chances of winning. The impact of these rules will be most pronounced in close elections where the electorate is fairly evenly divided along socioeconomic lines.

The Timing of Elections

Elections held at the same time as presidential elections draw the highest turnout. Mass media coverage of politics increases enormously during presidential elections, and people regard this election as very important. Coverage declines during off-year elections, when members of Congress, many governors, and most state legislators are elected. Turnout also declines. In local elections in odd-numbered years, the turnout reaches its lowest levels. This decline in turnout is generally greatest among independents, those who are younger, and those of lower socioeconomic status.[41] These off-year elections draw an electorate less representative of the public than the one drawn in presidential-election years. Presidential elections produce a turnout pattern similar to line B in Figure 6.2, while local elections in off–off years produce a pattern similar to line A.

Partisanship and Competition

Many local elections are nonpartisan. When that occurs, there is no party identification (Democrat or Republican, for example) listed beside the names of the candidates on the ballot. The candidates run as individuals, not as partisans or representatives of a party. Whether or not candidates announce their party affiliation during a campaign varies considerably from area to area.

The absence of party labels affects voters. Partisan elections generate higher turnout.[42] Labels provide cues to the likely positions of candidates on issues.[43] Democrats generally differ from Republicans. It can usually be assumed that Democrats are more liberal on a broad range of social-welfare issues, and that Republicans are more concerned with fiscal conservatism and are more pro-business. These cues are particularly important for marginal voters because they do not tend to follow political events closely, nor do they read newspapers extensively to gather such information. When voters rely heavily on party labels, they are likely to make errors on specific candidates because not all Democrats are liberal and not all Republicans are conservative. But party labels still help. If all citizens devoted extensive time to following politics, reliance on party cues would not be so significant, but such reliance continues to be important. Without those cues, voters with less familiarity with politics are less likely to participate. Party labels are more likely to help those of lower socioeconomic status. In partisan elections, turnout patterns are likely to approximate line B in Figure 6.2. In nonpartisan elections, participation patterns are likely to look like line A.

The competitiveness of elections also plays a major role. Voters are generally able to discern that the closer an election is, the more significant their votes are likely to be. Competitive elections also generate more media attention, which prompts more voter concern. For these reasons, competitive elections produce more overall turnout and appear to reduce class differentials in turnout.[44]

Choice and Turnout

The choice presented to voters affects how many vote and who votes. When the electorate is presented with bland, similar candidates, the election does not generate much interest. When candidates are similar, who wins has little consequence. When, however, a race is between two candidates who represent clearly different alternatives, the interest of the electorate is much greater. Such a situation occurred in the 1983 mayoral election in Chicago. This contest presented the city's first election in which a black candidate, Harold Washington, had a serious chance of success. The resulting turnout was 82 percent, one of the highest in city history. The high turnout was due to very high voter interest (both positive and negative in nature) in the possibility of having a black mayor. The greatest changes in registration came in the areas of the city that were heavily black. The changes that occurred are shown in Table 6.5. The major change from 1979 to 1983 was that the population in the black areas of the city registered and voted. No black ward had a turnout rate lower than 73 percent. Clearly the prospect of electing a black mayor (Harold Washington did win a close election) prompted greater black interest in the election.

Table 6.5

Changes in Voter Registration in Chicago, February 22, 1979 to February 22, 1983

Area	Registration Increase (%)
Predominantly black wards	29.5
All other areas	4.0
All Chicago wards	11.7

Source: Michael Preston, "The Election of Harold Washington: Black Voting Patterns in the 1983 Chicago Mayoral Race," PS (summer 1983): 487.

The Strength of Party Organizations

Local party organizations also affect turnout. They can serve to stimulate voter attention and turnout. A party can recruit volunteers to go door to door or to call residents to remind them of the election. It can send literature to prod people into voting. The party may also make numerous general appeals to constituents to make some contribution to the party. For a party to do this, it must have a well-developed organizational base. Such activity requires a committed set of leaders, numerous and loyal workers, and a clear organizational arrangement to utilize its personnel and achieve goals. If a party has such traits, it can stimulate turnout.[45]

Summary: Changing Turnout Patterns

All these conditions—registration, timing of elections, partisanship, competitiveness of elections, the choices involved, and party organizations—vary from place to place. The relative participation rates by class or age are a product of all these conditions. Table 6.6 presents the combination of conditions that are likely to minimize turnout differentials and those that are likely to maximize turnout differentials. If the conditions shown on the left prevail, the differences in turnout by socioeconomic status are likely to be small, and the number of actual voters will be fairly representative of the number of potential voters. If the conditions shown on the right exist, turnout by the lower class is likely to be at a much lower rate than other groups, and the number voting will not be as representative of the population.

Changes in Political Involvement over Time

The political involvement of groups is not stable across time. The last thirty years has seen some significant changes in the political involvement of certain groups. Four groups, in particular, have experienced changes in their participation in politics. The federal government has intervened to increase the turnout of blacks,

Table 6.6

Summary of Conditions Affecting Relative Rates of Turnout

Minimize Differentials	*Conditions That*	*Maximize Differentials*
Easy		Difficult
registration		registration
Strong party		Weak party
Candidates With		
Different policies		Similar policies
Elections		
Partisan		Nonpartisan
Competitive		Noncompetitive
Presidential year		off–off year

particularly in the South. Women have become more involved. There has been a decline in turnout among the lower class and the young.

Federal Intervention and Black Registration

Beginning in the late 1800s, southern states passed many laws to make it difficult for blacks (and whites) to register and to vote.[46] The primary target of these registration requirements was blacks. These restrictions subsequently prompted some of the most intense controversies ever experienced in Congress and eventually prompted national legislation to increase the rights of blacks.[47] Perhaps the most significant piece of Legislation was the Voting Rights Act of 1965. This act went further than existing federal law by providing federal registrars (officials responsible for registering individuals to vote) to each county where more than 50 percent of the potential voters did not vote and where local registrars were using a test to determine voter eligibility. The act also required that any changes in voting requirements that might affect minorities must first be cleared with the Justice Department.

The passage of this legislation had a significant effect on black registration. In Mississippi, the proportion of blacks registered to vote increased from 5.2 percent in 1960 to 55.8 percent in 1967. The changes in registration rates in all the southern states from 1960 to 1986 are shown in Table 6.7. These increases changed the composition of the electorate in southern states.[48] These changes have resulted in an increase in the election of black officials. The data from 1970 and the early 1990s, shown in Table 6.8, reflect that change.

Increased registration resulted in an increase in the representation of black concerns. Because there are more blacks registered, voting, and serving as elected

Table 6.7
Changes in Registration in the South

State	1990 Black Electorate (% of total)	Percentage of Group Registered to Vote			
		White Voters		Black Voters	
		1960	1986	1960	1986
Alabama	25.3	63.6	77.5	13.7	68.9
Arkansas	15.9	60.9	67.2	38.0	57.9
Florida	13.6	69.3	66.9	39.4	58.2
Georgia	27.0	56.8	62.3	29.3	52.8
Louisiana	30.8	76.9	67.8	31.1	60.6
Mississippi	35.6	63.9	91.6	5.2	70.8
North Carolina	22.0	92.1	67.4	39.1	58.4
South Carolina	29.8	57.1	53.4	13.7	52.5
Tennessee	16.0	73.0	70.0	59.1	65.3
Texas	11.9	42.5	79.0	35.5	68.0
Virginia	18.8	46.1	60.3	23.1	56.2

Sources: 1990 data: U.S. Statistical Abstract, 1991, 22; 1960 and 1986 data: Paul A. Beck and Frank J. Sorauf, Party Politics in America (New York: HarperCollins, 1992), 211.

Table 6.8
Number of Elected Black Officials by Office, 1970 and 1990, 1991

State	State Legislatures		City Councils	
	1970	1991	1970	1990
Alabama	0	24	38	409
Georgia	14	35	8	230
Louisiana	1	20	10	173
Mississippi	1	22	2	294
North Carolina	1	19	36	259
South Carolina	0	22	21	144
Texas	2	15	13	125
Virginia	3	10	21	75

Source: The New York Times, 21 July 1991, E4.

officials in the South, more attention is paid to the concerns of the black population. We will return to this topic in Chapter 8.

Women and Representation

The political involvement of women has also changed. Over the last several decades, the number of women elected to public office has increased steadily. Those changes are shown in Table 6.9. While all women politicians do not have the same political views and voting records, surveys show that women as a group consistently differ from men as a group in their attitudes about public-policy issues. Women are far more supportive than men of the right of women to have an abortion and of government intervention to solve problems. They are also more opposed than men to the death penalty and to the construction of nuclear power plants.[49] Bringing more women into office means that their views get more consideration in the political process.

Declining Participation among the Young and the Lower Class

While some groups have increased their political involvement and representation in recent decades, others have gone in the opposite direction. Two groups in particular have experienced declines in turnout. Young people participate now at lower

---

Table 6.9

Increases in the Election of Women: Number of Positions Held by Women, by Office, 1971–1991

Year	State Legislators	Mayor
1971	362	7
1973	425	12
1975	610	35
1977	696	47
1979	770	58
1981	908	78
1983	992	76
1985	1102	80
1987	1164	94
1989	1261	112
1991	1359	151

Source: New York Times, *24 May 1992, E5.*

levels than they did twenty years ago.[50] As a result the influence of older individuals in elections has increased. Politicians are acutely aware that older individuals vote more than younger people do, and the concerns of older individuals get more attention from them.

There is also considerable evidence that registration and turnout among the lower class have declined in recent decades.[51] Alienation from the political process is higher among the lower class, and it has increased more among the lower class in recent years. A comparison of the electorate in 1987 and 1990 found a general increase in the feeling that politicians "lose touch with people" when they get elected. The greatest increase in this sense of alienation from politics occurred among those with lower incomes.[52] For whatever reasons, lower-class voting has declined significantly, and, as a result, less attention is paid to their concerns.

State Turnout Differentials

All these conditions—personal traits, timing of elections, increased black voting, decreased voting among the young, the working class and the lower class—combine to affect total turnout and relative turnout by groups in the states. Differentials in turnout produce over- and underrepresentation of groups in the electorate. Table 6.10 presents turnout by state in the 1986 elections and estimates of overrepresentation of the more affluent for recent gubernatorial elections. The index of overrepresentation is first created by assessing turnout of affluent individuals (those in families with incomes of $50,000 or more) compared to their proportion of the population. The turnout of relatively poor individuals (those in families with incomes under $12,500) relative to their proportion of the population is then assessed. The ratio of these two results is then calculated. If the affluent comprise 20 percent of the voters, but only 15 percent of the population, their ratio would be 1.3 (or 20 ÷ 15). If those less affluent comprise 30 percent of voters, but 40 percent of the population, their ratio would be 0.75. If the resulting ratio of the affluent were divided by the ratio of the poor, the overall index would be 177, or (1.33 ÷ .75) × 100. If the overall index were 100, each group would be represented equivalent to its proportion in the population.

There are significant differences in turnout across the states. The overrepresentation index also indicates there are significant differences in overrepresentation across the states. There is no state in which representation in the voting is balanced. Underrepresentation of the lower class (and probably the working class) is pervasive. These two phenomena—overall turnout and overrepresentation—are also related. As overall turnout declines, the extent of overrepresentation increases.[53] It is a problem that every politician recognizes and takes into account in making judgments about possible political coalitions. If the lower class does not vote, it is difficult to build a political coalition in which they form a significant and effective proportion.

Table 6.10

Overrepresentation Indexes for the States, 1986 Elections

State	Index	Turnout	State	Index	Turnout
Alabama	139	39.3	Montana	134	62.3
Alaska	157	53.8	Nebraska	122	55.5
Arizona	163	44.2	Nevada	180	42.8
Arkansas	198	34.6	New Hampshire	153	52.5
California	153	44.7	New Jersey	107	47.1
Colorado	138	53.9	New Mexico	207	42.2
Connecticut	126	54.2	New York	141	40.6
Delaware	172	47.2	North Carolina	190	40.7
Florida	180	31.6	North Dakota	136	62.0
Georgia	200	36.4	Ohio	176	51.6
Hawaii	176	41.7	Oklahoma	166	32.4
Idaho	175	57.9	Oregon	159	48.9
Illinois	122	50.3	Pennsylvania	128	45.8
Indiana	140	51.6	Rhode Island	141	51.1
Iowa	163	56.0	South Carolina	180	39.2
Kansas	146	50.4	South Dakota	126	60.2
Kentucky	245	40.2	Tennessee	173	38.5
Louisiana	118	NA	Texas	206	39.2
Maine	172	61.1	Utah	131	57.1
Maryland	133	44.6	Vermont	156	57.1
Massachusetts	127	51.9	Virginia	187	41.4
Michigan	171	50.8	Washington	133	49.6
Minnesota	115	61.5	West Virginia	169	40.7
Mississippi	144	49.8	Wisconsin	142	56.6
Missouri	157	53.9	Wyoming	140	52.5

Sources: Overrepresentation index: Kim Q. Hill and Ian F. Leighley, "The Policy Consequences of Class Bias in State Electorates," American Journal of Political Science 36, no. 2 (May 1992): 351–366; Turnout: U.S. Statistical Abstract, 1989, p 259.

Alternative Means of Representation: Referenda, Initiatives, Polls, and Protests

Most political participation in American politics revolves around campaigns and elections. That focus troubles many people because in most situations it means engagement in partisan politics. As noted earlier, many people dislike partisan politics. Critics argue that party politicians are more interested in partisan attacks and in claiming credit for their own policies than in finding out what policies the public wants and what will "serve the public interest." In response to these concerns, some critics have proposed referenda and initiatives as ways to avoid partisan politics.[54]

Referenda and Initiatitves

A referendum allows the public to vote directly on a policy proposal. This proposal may involve imposing a tax, or borrowing money for a particular purpose. A referendum is put on the ballot by public officials (by passage by the executive and the legislature or council). The public vote then determines whether the policy is pursued. For an initiative, individuals gather signatures to have a policy proposal put directly on the ballot for a public vote. To use the initiative process, someone must first write the language for the proposal. Then some predetermined minimum number of signatures must be gathered. Both referenda and initiatives involve a public vote. The difference between the two is the way the proposition gets on the ballot.

Initiatives and referenda have been widely adopted across the United States. At the state level they have been most popular in the West, where skepticism about parties is greatest.[55] Figure 6.3 shows where the referendum and initiative are used in the states. At the local level, the pattern is different. The referendum is used in cities all across the country. The initiative, however, is not available everywhere. It tends to be available mostly in larger, central cities.[56] Table 6.11 describes the cities where the initiative and the referendum are likely to be available.

While these two mechanisms were conceived as ways to avoid partisan politics and to let "the people" speak, considerable doubt has emerged about the extent to which they do represent "the people." First, the task of gathering signatures for initiatives requires considerable resources and has evolved into a business in many states. People are hired to gather signatures. Much of the money used to pay people comes from well-financed interest groups.[57] The need to finance an initiative makes "special interests" (real-estate groups, businesses) important and detracts from the idea that these are to be tools of "the people."

Second, conducting campaigns for initiatives also costs money. Much of that money also comes from interest groups. Those with money have more capability to get initiatives on the ballot and to push for them. Interest groups are not the only ones who can get initiatives on the ballot, but they have more resources to do so. The concern that has emerged is that the haves have more resources to push for initiatives and that the initial ideal of the initiative as a tool of the mass public has been thwarted.[58]

There is also concern that class differentials are greater with referenda and initiatives. Those with lower socioeconomic status vote less on initiatives, with the result that the outcomes of initiatives are heavily influenced by the affluent. Minorities are also less likely to vote on referenda than whites, thus reducing their impact in such decisions.[59] While the initiative and the referendum may have been created to give the people a say in politics, the evidence suggests that the haves again have more of a say than the have-nots.

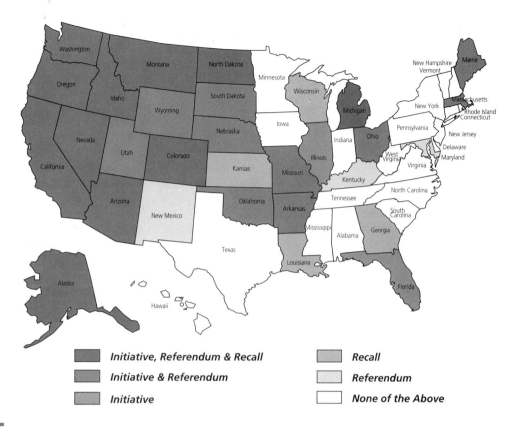

Figure 6.3

Citizen-Initiated Initiative, Referendum, and Recall at the State Level

Source: Thomas Cronin, Direct Democracy, *Twentieth Century Fund (Cambridge: Harvard University Press, 1989), 47.*

Polls and Protests

Another way of incorporating public concerns into decision making is by polling. Statewide and local polls generally seek to ask questions of a representative sample of people in the community. One difficulty, however, with assuming that polling gives "the public" a role is that the importance of who participates persists. When newspapers or politicians commission polls, they regularly screen respondents for likely voters.[60] That is, they either ask questions only of those who are likely to vote, or they break the results down by those likely and those unlikely to vote. Who votes still matters.

The second difficulty is that it is clear that polls are often heavily influenced by the ways the media cover events and by the amount of coverage events receive. If the media covers an issue in a particular way, public opinion is likely to dominated by the view the media conveys. Politicians are aware of that. They are also aware

Table 6.11
Allowance for Use of Initiative and Referendum in American Cities

City Size	Initiative (#)	Initiative (%)	Referendum (#)	Referendum (%)
500,000+	9	100.0	7	77.8
250,000–499,999	23	82.1	26	92.9
100,000–249,999	66	72.5	84	92.3
50,000–99,999	174	78.0	211	94.6
25,000–49,999	277	65.3	388	91.5
10,000–24,999	466	53.2	790	90.2
5,000–9,999	407	45.1	815	90.3
2,500–4,999	319	34.8	790	86.2
Under 2,500	88	34.1	234	90.7
City Location				
Central	224	67.1	308	92.2
Suburban	998	50.2	1,782	89.5
Independent	607	43.2	1,255	89.4

Source: Tari Renner and Victor S. DeSantis, "Contemporary Patterns and Trends in Municipal Government Structures," Municipal Year Book 1993 (Washington, DC: ICMA), 69.

that issues emerge and die and that what is prominent in one poll may disappear in a subsequent poll. That process makes decision makers much more cautious about relying too heavily on poll results. Polls are very useful as ways to assess public views, and the results often do have considerable impact. But they are still examined in partisan ways. Politicians assess how "their" constituents think before they decide to take poll results too seriously. Politicians are also often skeptical about the extent to which deeply held opinions are expressed. For all these reasons, polls have their limits.[61]

Finally, people often resort to other forms of political expression. People who feel very strongly about issues often protest. Protests can create movements that persist for some time and give groups representation they might otherwise not achieve. This route has been particularly valuable for lower-income individuals who lack the resources of money and enduring organizations.[62] These efforts are sporadic, however, and do not give the lower class enduring representation.

Representation and District Elections

All the evidence examined thus far suggests that the haves are better represented than the have-nots in American politics. There are reasons to be more specific and somewhat cautious in stating the conclusion.

Systems of Representation

The have-nots are most likely to be underrepresented in statewide or citywide elections: American elections use the plurality rule to decide elections: The candidate with the most votes wins. There is no proportional representation granted according to the percent of votes received. In situations where a diverse population exists, such as in statewide or districtwide elections, the working class and the lower class are often a a numerical minority. If these groups vote at lower levels than other groups, their influence is reduced even further. There is less attention to their concerns. In such situations, the have-nots are underrepresented.

But most state and local politicians—state and county legislators, city council members—are elected by districts. To the extent that similar groups cluster together, district-based elections means that an area will have representation even though turnout in that area is low. Indeed, the greater the number of districts for any given population, the more likely the different groups will get some representation. This result occurs at both the local and state levels.

The impact of district elections has received a considerable amount of study at the local level. In local politics, there has been a continuing debate about the effects of at-large or district elections on representation of minorities.[63] At-large elections occur when a candidate runs for office with the entire city as the electing district. In any particular year, many candidates may run; and those who receive the highest number of votes in any given election will be elected. In district elections, the city is divided into districts, and a candidate runs in one of those districts. The advocates of at-large districts believe that such districts will force candidates to consider the interests of the entire city and not just to represent the parochial and limited interests of one area in the city. Other groups support at-large districts because such districts make it harder for groups with less than 50 percent of the citywide vote to obtain representation in elections. Advocates of district elections argue that districts (and groups) differ in what they want, and each group needs to have some assurance of representation. Given the assumption that conflict exists, advocates argue that district elections should be used to achieve that representation. The compromise, a mixed system, uses a combination of at-large and district elections

Cities differ considerably in the arrangements they use, and those arrangements have a significant impact on representation. Figure 6.4 indicates the kind of representation system used by size of city in the United States. In larger cities there is usually more population diversity. Groups that find it hard to elect someone from their group in at-large elections push to have district elections in order to have a greater chance to elect someone. As a consequence, larger cities are more likely to have district or mixed systems of representation.

These electoral arrangements affect the representation of groups. In general, as a group increases its proportion in the population, their representation will increase more in a district system than in an at-large system. Table 6.12 indicates how the type of electoral arrangement affects the ability of blacks to elect local legislators. This table presents the relationship between the black proportion of the population and proportion of city council representation that is black by type of election system. The table involves *only* those cities in which the black proportion of the population is 40

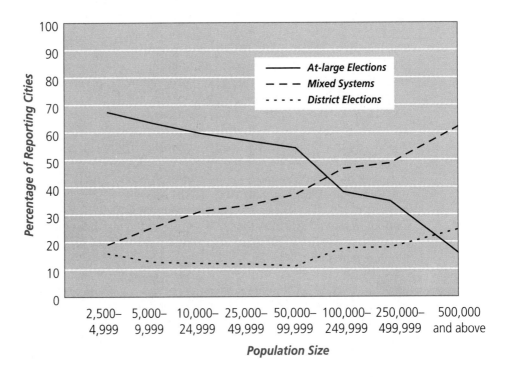

Figure 6.4

Type of Election System and City Population Size
Source: Tari Renner, "Municipal Election Processes: The Impact on Minority Representation," 1988 ICMA Yearbook (Washington, DC: ICMA, 1988), 20.

Table 6.12

Election Systems and Black Representation in Cities with 40 Percent or More Black Population

| Electoral System | Percent of Black Representatives | | |
	0–19 (%)	20–39 (%)	40 + (%)
At-large	29.4	35.3	35.3
Mixed	17.3	44.2	38.5
District	9.7	16.1	74.2

Note: Percentages sum across to 100.
Source: Tari Renner, ICMA, 15.

percent or above. Cities are then classified (on the left) by the type of election system they have. The percentages indicate how many cities in each category have 0–19, 20–39, or 40 percent black city council members. When at-large elections are used, only 35.3 percent of the cities have 40 percent or more black representatives. When district elections are used, the difference is dramatic. Seventy-four percent of cities with district elections have 40 percent or more black representatives. District election systems increase the ability of minorities to achieve representation. District systems result in representatives more reflective of the population.[64]

The same logic applies to representation in state legislatures. For any population size, the greater the number of seats (districts), the greater the chance that diverse groups in a state will obtain some representation. The presence of single-member districts (one legislator per district) in an area, instead of multi-member districts (several legislators per district), also enhances the chances of representation of minority groups because such a system allows a group's spatial concentration to serve as a basis for election.[65]

The interaction of spatial concentration of groups and district elections is important for representation. Those with less education and lower incomes participate less in politics. Less participation by a group reduces its significance in statewide or citywide elections and lessens its impact in executive (governor, mayor) elections. But districts (whether at the city, county, or state level) are drawn according to the population in a district. An area gets a representative regardless of its turnout level. Populations get representation through council and legislative elections even if they are underrepresented in citywide and statewide elections.

We must, therefore, be careful in trying to gauge how much the have-nots are harmed by their lower participation rates. The have-nots register less, contribute less, join political clubs less, and vote less than the haves. But they still send some representatives to legislative bodies when district elections are used. The extent to which the have-nots achieve representation depends on the way they are clustered and the way district lines are drawn (which we will examine next), but they still do get some representation. Whether their representation comes close to their proportion of the population is difficult to judge without examining specific cases, but some representation is achieved.

Drawing District Lines and Shaping Representation

The ability of groups to achieve representation through legislative elections is also affected by the way district lines are drawn. Apportionment refers to the drawing of legislative district boundaries in a state, county, or city. Legislators run in specific districts. Some states have more than one legislator elected per district. These are called multi-member districts. We will examine the frequency of each type of district in Chapter 10. Regardless, all legislators run from specific districts.

Apportionment plans must now result in districts of roughly equal population. The federal courts have ruled in a number of decisions, beginning in the mid-1960s, that every representative must represent roughly the same number of voters. Prior to the 1960s, many states had not changed their electoral districts in forty to fifty years, even though the bulk of the population had moved from rural to urban areas.

Because of this situation, rural districts, which constituted 50 percent of the districts, could sometimes elect the majority of state legislators, even though these districts might comprise only 15 percent of the population.[66] Beginning in the 1960s, the federal courts ruled against this practice and required reapportionment every ten years to coincide with the federal population census.[67] As the population shifts, districts must also shift. The redrawing of district plans is usually done by legislatures, with a few states using bipartisan commissions (members from both parties). These district plans are often subject to review by the courts.

Apportionment is so significant, and fought over so intensely, because it affects an individual's chances of being elected and the chances of groups or areas of obtaining representation. Individual legislators worry about apportionment because district changes may harm their reelection prospects, or may make their reelection virtually certain. Political parties, local populations, and interest groups worry about apportionment because it shapes who obtains seats and representation.[68]

Politicians try to shape outcomes by drawing on the predictability of voting in each area. Politicians know that specific areas tend to vote fairly consistently for one party or the other. This tendency is rarely totally consistent, but it is consistent enough for politicians to use past voting patterns as a guide for likely future behavior. It is also usually the case that inner-city areas are Democratic, while suburban areas are Republican. Much finer designations can be made, and experienced politicians are generally aware of these finer breakdowns. It is often possible, for example, to differentiate block by block how the residents in an area tend to vote. Politicians use this knowledge to determine the likely winner of a district election.

One way to draw district lines is for the party in power to seek to minimize the effect of the other party's voters. Assume that an area has enough population to justify having four representatives. Assume that one-half of the area is Democratic, and all Democrats live in the northern part of that area. If the Republicans are in control, they might wish to minimize the effects of Democratic votes. An example of the way this can be done is shown in the box on the left in Table 6.13. Republicans can create four districts with equal populations (100,000 residents each), and three of these four districts would have a majority of Republicans. This reapportionment would result in greater representation of Republican constituents and views, relative to their actual proportion in the electorate. Three of the four representatives would be Republican (75 percent) although only 50 percent of the entire hypothetical electorate is Republican.

Lines can also be drawn to produce the opposite effect. If the Democrats are in control, they can draw the districts as in the box on the right in Table 6.13. The Democratic lines drawn here also meet the requirement to have equal populations in each district. The difference is that the Democrats have created three districts in which Democrats constitute the majority (75,000 to 25,000), and a fourth district that they have "given" to the Republicans. The result of this would be the election of more Democrats and greater representation of Democratic concerns in the legislature. Notice that in both cases the population remains the same. Only the district lines have changed.

Table 6.13

The Consequences of Apportionment Republican and Democrat Plans (Hypothetical Case)

Population Characteristics

Total population	400,000
Number of Democrats	200,000
Number of Republicans	200,000
Number per district	100,000

Republican Plan

Democratic Plan

Democrats

Democrats

Republicans

Republicans

——— District boundary lines

Results of Republican and Democratic Plans

Republican Plan

District	Democrats	Republicans	Likely Winner
1	100,000	0	Democrat
2	25,000	75,000	Republican
3	25,000	75,000	Republican
4	25,000	75,000	Republican

Democratic Plan

District	Democrats	Republicans	Likely Winner
1	75,000	25,000	Democrat
2	75,000	25,000	Democrat
3	75,000	25,000	Democrat
4	0	100,000	Republican

The primary approach of each party to district creation is to load up one or more districts with the constituents of the opposing party in order to minimize the impact of these constituents and maximize the impact of their own constituents. When this practice involves creating odd shaped districts (drawn to encompass party constituents, even though they may be spread out in odd ways), it is known as "gerrymandering," named after the initiator of this practice in Massachusetts. The courts have put abstract limits on this practice, specifying that district components should be "contiguous" (adjoining) and that the district should be as compact as possible. The courts have found it difficult, however, to define these terms with regard to the actual practice of drawing districts, so states still have considerable freedom in state and local district creation.

The important consequence of apportionment is that it can significantly affect which interests are represented. There are limits to the effect of apportionment, to be sure. It is sometimes difficult to manipulate a state so that large areas are solidly Democratic or Republican, but a creative party can significantly affect representation.

Summary: The Effective Public

Variations in participation mean that not all political concerns are brought to the attention of politicians or become part of the political agendas and debates of a community or state. The portion of the public that actually participates is often known as the "effective" public. The groups that participate the most are generally those of higher socioeconomic status, and, because of this pattern, their concerns are likely to be relatively more prominent and important to decision makers.

These facts of political life affect every aspect of the representation process. Candidates must decide whether groups they might appeal to will vote in significant numbers. They must decide if these groups can produce sufficient volunteers and donations to help in campaigns. Political parties must decide if they can rely on their groups to appear at the polls. If participation by the have-nots is less, then they will receive less consideration at every step of the representation process. We will return to the ways participation patterns interact with political parties and interest groups to affect representation in Chapter 8.

For Further Reading

Burham, Walter Dean. *The Current Crisis in American Politics*. New York: Oxford University Press, 1982.

Cronin, Thomas E., *Direct Democracy*. Cambridge: Harvard University Press, 1989.

Piven, Frances Fox and Richard A. Cloward. *Why Americans Don't Vote*. New York: Pantheon, 1988.

Wolfinger, Raymond E. and Steven J. Rosenstone. *Who Votes*. New Haven: Yale University Press, 1980.

Suggestions for Analysis in Your Own State and Locality

1. In most states and localities, voting in state and local elections is not high and varies by type of election. Most states and localities publish official voting results. See if you can get those results and examine how much turnout varies by election (Presidential, Congress only, local elections in November, local elections at other times of the year).

2. Perhaps the most important matter in politics is who votes. To assess this, use the election results in your area. Choose areas that differ by income or class. How much does turnout vary by area? You might also compare how much this turnout varies for a presidential election and for a local election.

3. In many states and localities the public can play a direct role in decision making through the initiative process or through referenda. Does your state or locality allow these? Has either mechanism been used much? If so, what kinds of decisions have been made? How much did turnout vary by class or by area in those votes?

4. How does your local area structure local elections? Are legislators elected at large or in wards/districts? Has the approach taken appeared to affect who is elected? That is, have certain ethnic or minority groups found it difficult or relatively easy to be elected?

Notes

[1] William H. Flanigan and Nancy H. Zingale, *Political Behavior of the American Electorate*, 7th ed., (Washington, DC: Congressional Quarterly Press, 1991), 150–53.

[2] Robert S. Erikson, Norman R. Luttbeg, and Kent L. Tedin. *American Public Opinion*, 4th ed., (New York: Macmillan, 1991), 214–15.

[3] Times Mirror Center for the People and the Press, "The American Media: Who Reads, Who Watches, Who Listens, Who Cares" (Washington, DC, 15 July 1990).

[4] Donald J. Devine, *The Attentive Public* (Chicago: Rand McNally, 1970); and The Times Mirror Center for the People and the Press, "The Age of Indifference," (Washington, DC, 28 June 1990).

[5] Jon L. Pierce, Kathleen M. Beatty, and Paul R. Hagner, *The Dynamics of American Public Opinion* (Glenview, Ill.: Scott, Foresman, 1982), 162–87.

[6] Jerry Yeric and John R. Todd, *Public Opinion: The Visible Politics*, 2d ed. (Itasca, Ill.: F.E. Peacock, 1989), 198–202; and M. Kent Jennings and Harmon Zeigler, "The Salience of American State Politics," *American Political Science Review* 64, no. 2 (June 1970): 525.

[7] Robert S. Erickson, Norman R. Luttbeg, and Kent L. Tedin, *American Public Opinion*, 4th ed. (New York: Macmillan, 1991), 5.

[8] Walter D. Burnham, "The Changing Shape of the American Political Universe," *American Political Science Review*, 59, no. 1 (March 1965).

[9] John F. Bibby et al., "Parties in State Politics," in Virginia Gray, Herbert Jacob, and Robert Albritton, *Politics in the American States: A Comparative Analysis*, 5th ed. (Glenview, Ill.: Scott, Foresman/Little, Brown, 1990), 89–90.

[10] Albert K. Karnig and B. Oliver Walter, "Municipal Elections: Registration Success, Incumbent Success and Voter Participation," in *The Municipal Yearbook 1977* (Washington, DC: International City Manager's Association, 1977), 65–72.

[11] For an interesting analysis of the way the value of time has changed, see Staffan B. Linder, *The Harried Leisure Class* (New York: Columbia University Press, 1970).

[12] Michael M. Gant and Norman R. Luttbeg, *American Electoral Behavior* (Itasca: F.E. Peacock, 1991), 121–51.

[13] Everett C. Ladd, *Where Have All the Voters Gone?* 2d ed. (New York: W. W. Norton, 1982).

[14] Michael E. McGerr, *The Decline of Popular Politics* (New York: Oxford University Press, 1986).

[15] Walter D. Burnham, *The Current Crisis in American Politics* (New York: Oxford University Press, 1982), 121–65.

[16] Frances Fox Piven and Richard A. Cloward, *Why Americans Don't Vote* (New York: Pantheon, 1988).

[17] Dean E. Alger, *The Media and Politics* (Englewood Cliffs: Prentice Hall, 1989), 73–123.

[18] William T. Gormley, "Coverage of State Government in the Mass Media," *State Government* 52, no. 2 (1979): 46–51; and Phil Brooks and Bob M. Gassaway, "Improving News Coverage," *State Legislatures* (March 1985): 29–31.

[19] David Morgan, *The Capitol Press Corps* (Westport, Conn.: Greenwood, 1978).

[20] Thomas E. Patterson, *The Mass Media Election* (New York: Praeger, 1980), chap. 3.

[21] Elizabeth Kolbert, "As Campaigns Turn Negative, the Press Is Given a Negative Rating," *New York Times*, 1 May 1992, A18.

[22] Thomas E. Patterson, *Out of Order* (New York: Knopf, 1993).

[23] Adam Clymer, "Public Believes the Worst on Bank Scandal," *New York Times*, 2 April 1992, D21.

[24] Times Mirror Center for the People and the Press, "The Age of Indifference," (Washington, DC, 28 June 1990), 20.

[25] Frances Fox Piven and Richard A. Cloward, *Why Americans Don't Vote* (New York: Pantheon, 1988), 164.

[26] Raymond E. Wolfinger and Steven J. Rosenstone, *Who Votes?* (New Haven: Yale University Press, 1980), 19.

[27] Paul A. Beck and Frank J. Sorauf, *Party Politics in America* (New York: HarperCollins, 1992), 193.

[28] Daniel Elazar, *Federalism: A View from the States*, 3d ed. (New York: Thomas Crowell, 1984), 109–49.

[29] Charles A. Johnson, "Political Culture in the American States: Elazar's Formulation Examined," *American Journal of Political Science* 20 (August 1976): 491–509; David Lowery and Lee Sigelman, "Political Culture and State Public Policy: The Missing Link," *Western Political Quarterly* 35 (September 1982): 376–84; Peter F. Nardulli, "Political Subcultures in the American States: An Empirical Examination of Elazar's Formulation," *American Politics Quarterly* 18 (July 1990): 287–315; and Frederick M. Wirt, "'Soft' Concepts and 'Hard' Data: A Research Review of Elazar's Political Culture," *Publius* 21 (spring 1991): 1–13.

[30] Ira Sharkansky, "The Utility of Elazar's Political Culture: A Research Note," *Polity* 2 (fall, 1969): 66–83.

[31] Raymond E. Wolfinger and Steven J. Rosenstone, *Who Votes* (New Haven: Yale University Press, 1980), 110–14; and Stephen D. Shaffer, "Policy Differences Between Voters and Non-Voters in American Elections," *Western Political Quarterly* 35 (1982): 496–510. Others use aggregate data (voting proportions for a party) and conclude that bringing "nonvoters" into the electorate does not help Democrats in presidential elections. See James DeNardo, "Turnout and the Vote: The Joke's on the Democrats," *American Political Science Review* 74 (June 1980): 406–420; and Harvey J. Tucker and Arnold Vedlitz, "Does Heavy Turnout Help Democrats in Presidential Elections?" *American Political Science Review* 80 (December 1986): 1291–98.

[32] John R. Petrocik, "Voter Turnout and Electoral Preference: The Anomalous Reagan Elections," in Kay Scholzman, ed., *Elections in America* (London: Allen and Unwin, 1987).

[33] Gary C. Jacobson, *The Politics of Congressional Elections*, 3rd ed. (New York: HarperCollins, 1992), 106–107.

[34] Wendell Rawls, Jr., "Race Issue Emerges in Atlanta Mayoral Contest," *New York Times*, 18 October 1981, A34.

[35] Based on research of the author.

[36] Kim Q. Hill and Jan E. Leighley, "The Policy Consequences of Class Bias in State Electorates," *American Journal of Political Science* 36, no. 2 (May 1992): 351–66.

[37] Chandler Davidson, *Race and Class in Texas Politics* (Princeton: Princeton University Press, 1990).

[38] Barbara Carvello and Lee Miringoff, *The Cuomo Factor* (Poughkeepsie, New York: Marist Institute, 1986).

[39] V. O. Key, *Southern Politics* (New York: Knopf, 1949).

[40] Steven J. Rosenstone and Raymond A. Wolfinger, "The Effect of Registration Laws on Voter Turnout," *American Political Science Review* 72 (March 1978): 22–45.

[41] For evidence that the scheduling of elections has a greater effect on the turnout of the young, see Howard D. Hamilton, "The Municipal Voter: Voting and Nonvoting in City Elections," *American Political Science Review* 65 no. 4 (December 1971): 1135–40; Raymond E. Wolfinger, Steven J. Rosenstone, and Richard A. McIntosh, "Presidential and Congressional Voters Compared," *American Politics Quarterly* 9 (1981): 245–55; Jeffrey M. Stonecash, "Voting Turnout in Onondaga County: Personal Traits, Election Cycles and Variations in Turnout and Electoral Composition" (Maxwell School, Syracuse University, June 1989); and Chandler Davidson, *Race and Class in Texas Politics* (Princeton: Princeton University Press, 1990), 49–55.

[42] Robert R. Alford and Eugene C. Lee, "Voting Turnout in American Cities," *American Political Science Review* 62 (September 1968): 796–813.

[43] Willis D. Hawley, *Non-Partisan Politics and the Case for Party Politics* (New York: John Wiley, 1973).

[44] C. Richard Hofstetter, "Interparty Competition and Electoral Turnout: The Case of Indiana," *American Journal of Political Science* 17:351–66.

[45] Samuel C. Patterson and Gregory A. Caldeira, "The Etiology of Partisan Competition," *American Political Science Review* 78 (1984): 691–707; Timothy Bledsoe and Susan Welch, "Patterns of Political Party Activity among U.S. Cities," *Urban Affairs Quarterly* 23 (1987): 249–69; and John P. Frendreis, James L. Gibson, and Laura L. Vertz, "The Electoral Relevance of Local Party Organizations," *American Political Science Review* 84, no. 1 (March 1990): 225–35.

[46] J. Morgan Kousser, *The Shaping of Southern Politics* (New Haven: Yale University Press, 1974).

[47] For this debate see Theodore H. White, *The Making of the President 1964* (New York: Signet, 1965), 197–229.

[48] Earl Black and Merle Black, *Politics and Society in the South* (Cambridge: Harvard University Press, 1987), 127–51.

[49] Ruth B. Mandel and Debra L. Dodson, "Do Women Officeholders Make a Difference?" and Celinda C. Lake and Vincent J. Breglio, "Different Voices, Different Views: The Politics of Gender," in Paula Ries and Anne J. Stone, *The American Woman, 1992–93: A Status Report* (New York: W. W. Norton, 1992), 149–77, 178–201.

[50] Times Mirror Center for the People and the Press, "The Age of Indifference" (Washington, DC, 28 June 1990), 25; Frances Fox Piven and Richard A. Cloward, *Why Americans Don't Vote* (New York: Pantheon, 1988), 164; and Michael N. Gant and Norman R. Luttbeg, *American Electoral Behavior* (Itasca: F.E. Peacock, 1991), 103.

[51] Walter D. Burnham, *The Current Crisis in American Politics* (New York: Oxford University Press, 1982); Walter D. Burnham, "The Turnout Problem," in A. James Reichley, ed., *Elections American Style* (Washington, DC: Brookings Institution, 1987); and Times Mirror Center for the People and the Press, "The People, the Press and Politics Campaign '92: The Generations Divide" (Washington, DC, 8 July 1992), 4.

[52] Results from a Times Mirror surveys conducted in 1987 and 1990, and reported in Michael Oreskes, "Alienation from Government Grows, Poll Finds," *New York Times*, 19 September 1990, A26.

[53] Kim Q. Hill and Jan E. Leighley, "The Policy Consequences of Class Bias in State Electorates," *American Journal of Political Science* 36, no. 2 (May 1992): 354.

[54] David D. Schmidt, *Citizen Lawmakers: The Ballot Initiative Revolution* (Philadelphia: Temple University Press, 1989), 25–34.

[55] Thomas E. Cronin, *Direct Democracy* (Cambridge: Harvard University Press, 1989), 47.

[56] Tari Renner and Victor S. DeSantis, "Contemporary Patterns and Trends in Municipal Government Structures," in *1993 Municipal Yearbook* (Washington, DC: ICMA, 1993), 69.

[57] Charles M. Price, "Initiative Campaigns: Afloat on a Sea of Cash," *California Journal* (November 1988): 481–86.

[58] David B. Magleby, "Taking the Initiative: Direct Legislation and Direct Democracy in the 1980s," *PS* 21, no. 3 (summer 1988): 600–611.

[59] James M. Vanderleeuw and Richard L. Engstrom, "Race, Referendums, and Roll-Off," *Journal of Politics* 49, no. 4 (November 1987): 1087–89.

[60] Irving Crespi, *Public Opinion, Polls, and Democracy* (Boulder: Westview, 1989), 55–56.

[61] For a good review of these limits, see Herbert Asher, *Polling and the Public: What Every Citizen Should Know* (Washington, DC: Congressional Quarterly Press, 1988).

[62] Frances Fox Piven and Richard A. Cloward, *Poor People's Movements: Why They Succeed, How They Fail* (New York: Vintage, 1977); and Frances Fox Piven and Richard A. Cloward, *Why Americans Don't Vote* (New York: Pantheon, 1988), xi–xiii.

[63] For a review of this debate and the legal challenges to at-large systems, see Susan Welch and Timothy Bledsoe, *Urban Reform and Its Consequences* (Chicago: University of Chicago Press, 1988), xiii–17.

[64] Engstrom and MacDonald, "The Election of Blacks to City Councils: Clarifying the Impact of Electoral Arrangements on the Seats/Population Relationship," *American Political Science Review* 75, no. 2 (June 1981): 349; Susan Welch and Timothy Bledsoe, *Urban Reform and Its Consequences* (Chicago: University of Chicago Press, 1988), 12–17, 42–46; and Susan Welch, "The Impact of At-Large Elections on the Representation of Blacks and Hispanics," *Journal of Politics* 52, no. 4, (November 1990): 1050–76.

[65] Gary F. Moncrief and Joel A. Thompson, "Electoral Structure and State Legislative Representation: A Research Note," *Journal of Politics* 54, no. 1 (February 1992): 246–56.

[66] For studies of malapportionment in the 1950s, see Manning J. Dauer and Robert G. Kelsay, "Unrepresentative States," *National Municipal Review* 44 (1955): 551–75; and Gordon E. Baker, *Rural vs. Urban Political Power* (New York: Doubleday, 1955).

[66] For a history of reapportionment and a review of studies of its effects, see Timothy O'Rourke, *The Impact of Reapportionment* (New Brunswick: Transaction Press, 1980).

[68] For studies on the effects of reapportionment, see Leroy Hardy, Alan Heslop, and Stuart Anderson, eds., *Reapportionment Politics* (Beverly Hills: Sage, 1981); and Leroy Hardy, Alan Heslop, George Blair, eds., *Redistricting in the 1980s* (Claremont: Rose Institute of State and Local Government, 1993).

7

Interest Groups and Representation

PREVIEW

Interest groups play a vital role in representing concerns in the political process. Their existence also affects who gets represented. Those with more education and higher incomes are more likely to join interest groups and to have representation through such groups. These groups have resources to mobilize their members about political issues, to contribute money, and to create staffs of lobbyists to present their case to politicians.

This "bias" in the representation process troubles people, and has led to enact-
ment of policies designed to constrain the effects of interest-group campaign con-
tributions and lobbying. It has also led to efforts to give politicians more staff
resources so that they are better able to assess the arguments of lobbyists.

The Role of Interest Groups

While political parties are a vital means of representation, most people also want
their own specific concerns represented. Political parties represent combinations
of concerns. The positions taken are compromises among broad groups of people.
Groups, however, often feel they have special problems and do not want the presentation of their concerns combined with those of others. They want detailed presentation of their concerns. They want to monitor the activities of politicians closely to try to avoid legislation that they regard as unfavorable to their interests. They
mobilize their members to pressure politicians about very specific policies that may
help or hurt them.

Groups are also not satisfied with elections as means to communicate their
concerns. Elections happen only every two or four years. People can only vote for
or against a candidate. It is often difficult for groups to get attention for their distinct concerns.[1] For all these reasons, groups form political interest groups as a
means to communicate their concerns both during and after elections. To these
groups, lobbying and lobbyists are a fundamental and legitimate part of the political representation process.

But it is these same interest groups that raise fundamental concerns about
whether the representation process favors the haves over the have-nots. Defenders
of interest groups have argued over the years that there is sufficient diversity of
interest groups such that all interests receive some representation and that no
interests really dominate.[2] But critics of interest groups argue that there are more
lobbyists for the affluent and for business groups than for other groups in society.
They argue that this creates an enduring bias in what politicians hear about problems and needs.[3] As the director of one state Common Cause organization put it:
"What distorts it [the lobbying process] is the volume with which special interests
speak, and the amplifier is campaign contributions."[4] Indeed, some argue that in
American politics the formation of public policy has been overwhelmed by interest
groups and that our public policy is just a product of the efforts of powerful interest groups.[5]

While there is anxiety about the influence of interest groups, there is also considerable ambivalence about what to do about them. We have a long tradition of
supporting the right of interest groups to present their positions to politicians. To
many, interest groups are just exercising the right to free speech. If a group has concerns that they feel strongly about, they should be able to present them fully to the
powers that be. Indeed, to defenders, it is vitally important in a democracy that all
arguments about the effects of government intervention in society be considered
before adopting policies. If that consideration requires money and "lobbying," these

activities are not indications of corruption and vote buying, but are a necessary part of the representation process.

This chapter focuses on interest groups and their role in representation. We will first examine the interests that create groups, who joins these interest groups, and which interest groups have lobbyists. We will then examine the means by which interest groups seek to influence the political process. Specifically, what gives an interest group influence?

But we also need to understand why we should not overestimate the influence of such groups. Our knowledge about their impact is often more anecdotal than systematic. Certain conditions seem to constrain their influence. Some combinations of political conditions—the condition of parties, patterns of participation, the media—may affect the influence of interest groups. The fear of interest groups stems from a perception that they have enormous power. We will explore whether that presumption is always accurate. Finally, public anxieties have led to efforts to limit the influence of interest groups. We will examine those efforts.

Who Belongs to Interest Groups

Anxieties about interest groups stem from a sense that not all "interests" in society are equally represented by lobbyists. In particular, critics fear that interest groups are mechanisms of the affluent, and that only their interests are represented. That fear raises questions of who belongs to interest groups and which interests have organizations that represent them.

As we found with participation, not everyone is active in organizations. The proportion of the public involved in organizations is shown in Table 7.1. A large proportion of the public does not belong to any organization. Furthermore, we know that many of the groups that people do belong to do not get involved in politics. All groups have the potential to get involved, but many never do.

The crucial question for politics is who belongs to organizations. Is there a bias that stems from the membership base of organizations? An examination of the affect of education level and race on the tendency to belong to organizations is shown in Table 7.2. As we would expect from our information on participation

Table 7.1

Involvement in Political Organizations

Reported Activity	Proportion Reporting (%)
Belong to an organization	62
Belong to more than one organization	39
Are active in an organization	40

Source: Sidney Verba and Norman H. Nie, Participation in America (New York: Harper and Row, 1972), 176.

Table 7.2
Participation in Political Organizations

Education Level	Belong to at least one organization (%)	Active in at least one organization (%)
Not high school graduate	49	27
High school graduate	67	43
Some college	78	59
Race		
White	66	41
Black	52	30

Source: Sidney Verba and Norman H. Nie, Participation in America *(New York: Harper and Row, 1972), 181.*

patterns, individuals with more education and income are more likely to belong to an organization.[6] The differences in participation by socioeconomic status are more pronounced if we group individuals according to the number of groups they belong to. This information is shown in Table 7.3.

There are many reasons individuals join organizations. Individuals may agree with the political goals of the group, they may be seeking social or business contacts, or they may be induced by specific benefits that the group offers (low-cost insurance, information, recreational benefits, discounts on services). Usually some combination of these motives is present.[7] These reasons for joining groups present difficulties. Not all group members are firmly committed to the announced goals of the group. Leaders often struggle to find out what their members will support. They also struggle to mobilize, or activate, their members to write letters, attend meetings, or make contributions. This struggle creates a tension in interest groups that leaders must continually work at overcoming.

Table 7.3
Activity in Political Organizations by Socioeconomic Status

Membership Status	Socioeconomic Status		
	Lower (%)	Middle (%)	Upper (%)
Nonmember	56	34	20
Passive member	23	22	21
Active member in only one organization	16	28	24
Active member in more than one organization	6	16	35

Note: Percentages sum down to 100.
Source: Sidney Verba and Norman H. Nie, Participation in America *(New York: Harper and Row, 1972), 204.*

The important matter for politics is that individuals of higher socioeconomic status are more likely to belong to at least one organization and to be active in one or more organizations. Higher education and income bring more confidence in joining and working in groups, put people in situations where there is more stimulus to join organizations, and probably give people more awareness of the advantages that can come from such memberships.

All this affects representation in politics. Individuals who belong to organizations have this additional means (other than general participation) to convey their political concerns to decision makers. Their concerns are more likely to be a part of the representation process. Because of their easier access to these mechanisms for articulating their concerns, those of higher socioeconomic status gain additional representation.

Which Interests Are Organized

Since individuals with higher socioeconomic status join more organizations, there are more organizations concerned with representing the concerns of these individuals. Many interest groups have a strong self-interest in formal organization and are able to develop a membership base to sustain such an organization. This ability is true of business, agriculture, construction, labor, education, real-estate, legal, and medical groups. Business interests, in particular, are very well represented.[8]

Everyone has a lot at stake in the public policy that emerges from politics. The poor have a great deal to lose or to win, depending on the degree to which government is willing to redistribute revenue to them. The affluent can also be dramatically affected by taxes or changes in the benefits that they receive, such as mortgage-interest deductions. But not all groups have the access to the money and to the individual capabilities that the groups above have. Organized, enduring interest groups can generate considerable money from their members to create well-staffed organizations. They can draw on the skills of their members to form strong organizations. The affluent are more likely to be members of such groups, and their interests are more likely to be presented to politicians and other decision makers through enduring, well-financed organizations.

In recent years the number of interests that have formed groups has increased steadily.[9] The traditional interests of business and labor have been joined by other groups seeking to have their views heard. In particular, there has been a significant increase at the state level in public-sector unions (such as education public-employee associations) and government lobby groups.[10] There are also environmental groups, civic groups, and a whole host of groups concerned with specific issues like abortion. Police and fire personnel have formed strong lobby groups because of their concern about state rules and regulations that affect their work and pensions. Employee groups are also concerned about the amount of intergovernmental aid that the state makes available to cities because this aid will affect their pay levels. Mayors, local council members, and civil servants also have a great interest in state activities, and they have formed groups such as the Municipal League and the Conference of Mayors.[11]

In addition to these groups, which tend to focus on state-level concerns, there is a multitude of locally oriented groups. In a study of local politics, Betty Zisk found that the most active groups were the economic ones, such as the Chamber of Commerce, homeowner groups, and taxpayer groups. The full list of active groups is presented in Table 7.4.

There are also many local groups that have relatively low visibility and limited budgets, but that play an important role in cities. Neighborhood groups, usually headed by volunteers, provide organizations where people can go to find others concerned about local issues. These groups become routes of participation and vehicles for organizing people to make presentations to politicians. Such groups are often believed not to have "clout," but they are influential in communicating to politicians and in informing people about the policy decisions that are being made.[12]

The last decade has also seen the rise of a new breed of interest groups, the public-interest groups. These are groups that present themselves as concerned only with the public interest, and not with the interests of any special group. The most

Table 7.4

Groups Reported by Local Officials as Active in Local Politics

Type of Group	Times Reported (#)	Proportion of All Reported Group Activity (%)
General economic groups		
Chambers of Commerce, Jaycees, neighborhood groups, homeowners associations, taxpayer groups	445	43
General civic groups		
Service clubs, women's organizations, church groups, press	310	31
Special interests		
Merchants associations, conservationists, realtors, civil rights groups, builders and developers, veterans, unions, party clubs, senior citizens, farmers	226	23
Semiofficial and official bodies		
Planning commissions, citizens advisory committees, school committees, county commissions	25	2
Total	1006	100

Source: Betty Zisk, Local Interest Politics: A One Way Street *(New York: Bobbs-Merrill, 1973), 23.*

prominent of these is Common Cause, which was organized on the premise that no one is looking out for the general needs of the public.[13] These groups obtain their money from mass solicitations and from foundations. They seek to monitor political decisions in all branches of government and keep their membership informed of pending policy decisions.

Interest Groups and Electoral Influence

The goal of an interest group is simple. Any interest group wants decision makers to be sympathetic to its concerns. There are essentially two ways to achieve that goal. A group either must have great electoral impact, and/or it must be effective at persuading legislators of the legitimacy of its arguments.

The most obvious way for an interest group to get politicians to be responsive is for the group to have considerable electoral clout. Elections are what ultimately matter to politicians. If a group can pose an electoral "threat" to a politician, or be a source of electoral help to a politician, the group can probably expect the politician to be sensitive to its concerns. There are several resources an interest group might have that can give it electoral clout.

Membership Size

The larger the membership base of a group, the more electoral significance a group is likely to have. Teachers, unions, public-service workers, and farmers in some states have large enough membership bases to continually command attention from politicians.

Cohesion of Members

While size matters, the ability of a membership to act together also plays a significant role in whether its views are listened to. If a group can convince politicians that group members will vote as a bloc, the group will be given more respect and attention. Teachers' groups are effective because they are relatively cohesive and they vote heavily.[14] Teachers' groups can count on their members to be relatively skillful at letter writing, for example, and can often generate significant volumes of mail from their membership.

In prior years, blue-collar union members could be counted on to vote heavily Democratic. As their income levels have risen, however, many of them have started to vote for the Republican party. This change has undermined the image of unions as a cohesive voting bloc that can have a significant impact. In the language of politicians, the union leaders can no longer be counted on to "deliver" their vote, and politicians are aware of this change.

The group currently best known for its cohesion is the NRA (National Rifle Association), which has repeatedly demonstrated that when there is a possibility of gun-control legislation passing, it can be counted on to be active, united, and opposed. The group has repeatedly claimed (and delivered on the claim) that it can contact its entire membership within twenty-four hours when a threatening piece of legislation is being considered. The NRA also claims that it can count on a large proportion of its members to contact their legislators in a very short time period. The goal of such activity is simple. The group wishes to "remind" the legislator that its members are aware of a pending decision and that they are concerned about the decision. These campaigns vary in their subtlety about whether the "wrong" outcome will cost a legislator votes.

Communication Mechanisms

Even if a group has a large membership and is cohesive, the group must be able to mobilize its members. Mobilizing membership requires the ability to keep the membership informed about policy decisions and about imminent votes or bureaucratic decisions. For a group to be able to do this, it needs newsletters and the ability to communicate quickly through telegrams or telephone networks. These activities take money. It also takes money to support a staff that can keep track of all the decisions made in state and local governments that affect a group. It takes money to write, print, and distribute newsletters. It takes money to send telegrams. Groups with larger budgets and staffs have greater ability to affect legislation and to influence politicians.

Geographic Distribution

A group's influence is also affected by the spatial distribution of its members. Spatial distribution of a group affects the range of politicians and leaders likely to be sensitive to the group. If a group is spread throughout a state with a moderate-sized membership in every legislative district, then the governor and each legislator is likely to have some concern for group reactions. If a group is heavily concentrated in only one region of a state, then it is likely to be of concern only to legislators from that area. If members constitute a large group in that area, statewide politicians are still likely to be concerned about them.

Campaign Money

Campaigns are not conducted without money, and the more money a group can directly contribute, or arrange to have contributed, the more important the group is likely to become. The most prominent examples of groups that rank high on contributions are doctors (the American Medical Association) and lawyers (the American Bar Association). Teachers, business interests, unions and agricultural groups often also make large campaign donations. These groups form PACs (Political Action Committees), which raise and distribute money to candidates for their campaigns.[15] Interest-group money has also played a role in recent years outside conventional campaign channels. Interest groups have helped finance initiatives in states like California. In many cases, these initiatives, if passed, are of great value to specific interests.

Status

Finally, a group may be able to build a reputation for impartiality, such that its positive evaluation of candidate policies may be of value. The League of Women Voters, for example, has a reputation as an impartial group, and getting its approval of a proposed policy may be helpful. These traits (size, cohesion, status) affect the likelihood that a group will have sufficient electoral significance to force politicians to be sensitive to its concerns. Some groups rank high on these traits, and they consistently receive more attention in campaigns and in decision making. While union influence may not be what it once was, unions are still significant interest groups in states and localities. Business interests are regularly well represented. In most states, teacher groups have relatively large memberships, the membership is active and cohesive, the members reside in all areas of the state, the groups have large funds at their disposal, and the organizations competently watch out for their interests.

Groups representing professionals like lawyers and doctors may lack the numbers of the teachers, but they are also very well financed, active, and well organized. Doctors' and lawyers' groups in particular have considerable money at their disposal. Doctors also have more public respect than lawyers. Many people suspect or anticipate self-interest from lawyers but have been less inclined to see that behavior in doctors. Some business groups also have access to large amounts of money. Small-business associations generally have fewer funds, but they are able to build up relatively large membership bases.

Other groups rely on an image of objectivity among the electorate. The groups most dependent on image are those such as the League of Women Voters, Common Cause, and environmental groups such as the Sierra Club and the Audubon Society. These groups must convince the public and politicians that they are not seeking any personal gain from a proposed policy position.

Many groups possess few of these resources and have little electoral clout. Renters have few of the resources mentioned above. At the local level, neighborhood groups generally have very limited resources. The handicapped also have very limited resources. Senior citizens fell into this category until the mid-1970s, when they organized numerous statewide (and nationwide) groups to lobby for their interests. Since older people vote heavily, these groups are taken very seriously by politicians.

There are numerous indications that some interest groups are very "powerful," but there are also reasons to be cautious about concluding that such groups dominate policy decisions. We will discuss the reasons for that caution after reviewing the other means of interest-group influence.

Interest Groups and Persuasion

While the public generally assumes that interest-group power is based on electoral clout, most interest-group lobbyists are more concerned with personal persuasion. Indeed, legislators and lobbyists report that this approach has become more important over the years.[16] Policy issues have become more complex, and government has been drawn into more issues. Politicians need information about social conditions and the effects of government. Scrutiny of decision making by the press has made it more difficult for interest groups to use simple political pressure to produce desired outcomes. The important matter for lobbyists is to have access to legislators and bureaucrats in order to communicate with them. Having access to officials means a lobbyist will be able to present a group's case in terms of the legitimacy of its needs whenever an issue relevant to the group emerges.[17]

For example, when legislation is introduced to ban throwaway bottles, or to require a return deposit on all beverages sold in the state, the producers of throwaway bottles want to be able to present the negative impact of the legislation to the people who will vote on the bill. In such a case, there is no doubt that the unions, bottle manufacturers, beverage producers, and retail outlets have a self-interest involved in opposing the imposition of a return-deposit requirement. Such groups believe the change will mean either less business for them, or difficulties for their business in complying with the requirements. Yet, these companies are part of the economy of the state. Their economic activity generates income and tax revenue for the state. These groups believe there is the legitimate issue of whether the net effect on the economy will be negative if the new legislation is enacted. These groups argue that the overall economic health of the state is affected by their economic situation (their self-interest) and that it is perfectly appropriate for officials and politicians to listen seriously (not cynically, as if all self-interest arguments should automatically be dismissed) to their case. The goal of a lobbyist is to change the debate from one over "selfishness" of bottlers to one over the ways the overall economy (and areawide jobs) might be affected by such a policy change. Politicians are willing to listen to the latter type of argument, but they hesitate about the effect accepting the former type of argument might have on their images.

The crucial asset of lobbyists in such situations is to provide information. They have more first-hand information on the current circumstances of those who will be affected than anyone else. Lobbyists specialize in understanding and summarizing situations. Legislators recognize that lobbyists possess information and that this information is valuable to legislators as they formulate public policy.[18] While some legislators may not be comfortable relying on lobbyists for information, the dependency persists because it is difficult for legislators to acquire such detailed information through other means. Indeed, many legislators think that lobbying improves the process of decision making because more information is considered.[19]

Opponents of interest groups, of course, dismiss arguments that lobbyists just provide information and perspectives. They see inside access and "behind-closed-doors" influence. Critics argue that "sometimes lobbyists and interest groups convince public officials to support legislation that is not in the public interest."[20] Lobbyists for business groups opposed to bottle bills, however, believe that an essential part of the democratic process is a thorough discussion of the positive and negative aspects of legislation.

To achieve access to present their case, lobbyists can draw on several things. Their groups may have such electoral significance that legislators feel it is wise to listen. The lobbyist himself or herself may achieve access by building up a reputation as someone who makes credible and valid arguments and who is reasonably honest (does not slant the information too badly). The crucial matter for a lobbyist is to establish trust. Lobbyists may also spend considerable time (perhaps years) cultivating social relationships with legislators so that they are willing to interact regularly with the lobbyist. Lobbyists generally like to rely on all possible approaches, though some lobbyists simply do not have enough time to interact socially with all legislators. Regardless, lobbyists must somehow build trust and rapport with those they are trying to persuade. This trust creates access.[21]

If such access can be achieved, then a lobbyist must be prepared to make a factual and thorough presentation. Lobbyists must have the resources to present reports that will be convincing and that do not distort. In creating such presentations, the budget and staff resources of the better-financed interest groups become very important. Most lobbyists regard factual presentations and assessments of the likely impact of policies on their groups as their most important activity. Many lobbyists do this as a full-time activity.

This kind of work is often tedious and involved because it means following legislation and analyzing its impact. It means careful reports on the likely effects of legislation. It means attending hearings on legislation to present an argument, listening to opposing arguments, and preparing rebuttals. In many ways, the goal of this kind of work is to be so well prepared and knowledgeable that legislators begin to rely on the analyses of a lobbyist. If that occurs, the lobbyist has succeeded.

The key to this approach is that the effect of each new piece of legislation (such as a bottle bill) is *uncertain*. No one can be certain whether the net effect of legislation will be positive or negative. The role of the lobbyist is to *take advantage of that uncertainty* to convince legislators that the legislation should not be enacted or should be modified.

An Example: Doctors versus Nurses

An example of this persuasion struggle and the attempt to shape an issue so it is seen in terms of positive or negative effects on the public and not in terms of self-interest is illustrated by the conflict across the states between doctors and nurses. Doctors have considerable influence over deciding who can dispense health care. Decisions regarding this control are made at the state level, and doctors have lobbied long and hard to affect these decisions. In almost all states, doctors are designated as the primary, if not exclusive, dispensers of health care. They are generally the only ones who can prescribe medication and receive individual reimbursements for services from medical-insurance programs. This means that doctors control the flow of billing revenues.

Nurses can diagnose illness only under the supervision of doctors. Nurses wish to gain the right to do more of the activities legally designated "doctor only." The argument of the nurses is that allowing the nurses the right to perform certain of these activities will increase the number of medical personnel available to serve the public, will help hold down the cost of medical care, and will allow doctors to focus on major problems.

Doctors are strongly opposed to allowing nurses to operate autonomously or to receive money without doctor involvement and authority. If nurses are allowed to do these things, "we will be asking people in this country to accept second-class health care," in the words of Gerald R. Gehringer, president of the American Academy of Family Physicians.[22] The doctors argue that this change would be detrimental to the public and that legislators would be held accountable for resulting problems because they will have approved it. Legislators are willing to listen to this argument because they fear that these changes may have negative effects. They do not wish to approve changes that might lead to stories of tragic misdiagnoses. They are also willing to listen because state branches of the American Medical Association are big contributors to campaigns. The uncertainty about policy effects, the seriousness of persuasion efforts, and the need for electoral resources have left doctors with considerable ability to shape legislation in ways beneficial to their interests.

Nurses, however, are not without their arguments. Nurses' groups do not contribute large sums to campaigns, but medical costs are rising rapidly, and legislators are willing to listen in the hope that they can find a way to hold down those costs. Nurses argue that costs will be restrained, and that nurses will only diagnose minor cases, so there is very little possible harm to the public. Furthermore, they present the argument that doctors oppose the change only so that they can maintain a monopoly on the delivery of health care and keep their incomes high. As Claire M. Fagin, dean of the School of Nursing at the University of Pennsylvania, puts it, the conflict is not over the quality of health care, rather "It's a head-on clash over money and turf." The issue here may appear to be simple power politics of differing interest groups (and that is certainly present), but it is also a matter of trying to assess the consequences of making such a change in health care. It is a battle—amid uncertainty—over convincing legislators of likely outcomes.

The Validity of the Interest-Group Case

Context is crucial when lobbyists make their arguments. Lobbying is not simply a perpetual attempt to convince politicians that a certain group should receive better treatment. It involves trying to establish how important a group is for the economic health of a community or state. To make that argument, lobbyists utilize events, trends, and general information. Lobbyists will find their ability to make a case increased if other information supports the claim that their groups are undergoing economic stress, or are being hurt by current government policies. If an industry is declining, and the government data support that, it is easier to get politicians to listen. Older manufacturing industries have used evidence of their continuing decline to argue that they need tax breaks to survive or to maintain jobs in the community. The effectiveness of lobbying arguments derives from the ability of the lobbyist to document the problems of the industry, not from "power." Real change has occurred in manufacturing industries, and evidence of that change has helped lobbyists seek benefits for business.

Education groups have been particularly adept in drawing upon changing public perceptions. Education groups have tried for some time to convince state politicians that teachers are underpaid and that states now need a well educated labor force in order to develop economically. This argument was generally ignored for years. During the 1980s, it began to have an impact in the South because of the way economic change occurred. As the Sunbelt states in the West began to develop more than the southern states, many politicians in the South became receptive to these arguments. Southern governors became advocates of imposing new taxes to raise teacher salaries. Lobbying was ultimately successful because the context changed. Politicians became worried that economic development would pass their state by because of the lack of funding for education. The "clout" of teacher groups played a role, but the context in which they made their arguments also changed.

Nationwide, change has also occurred in the perceived position of teachers, and education groups have been able to take advantage of this change. Beginning in the early 1980s, reports appeared that argued that elementary and secondary schools were not effective in educating students.[23] Teachers responded to this concern by arguing that higher salaries would attract better teachers and therefore result in better education. They were able to convince state legislators to increase education budgets significantly during the latter 1980s. In California, they were successful in getting an initiative passed that dedicated 40 percent of the state budget to education, regardless of other conditions. This is an example of the credibility of an interest-group argument changing as public conditions and public concern changed.

In recent years the influence of business-interest groups in the Northeast has increased as a result of the economic decline that many northeastern states have experienced. Business interests had little influence during the 1960s and early 1970s, as state taxes and expenditure generally increased across the region. As these states began to lose jobs and tax revenues, governors and legislators became receptive to arguments that tax rates ought to be cut. During the recession of the late 1980s and early 1990s businesses again experienced difficulties and were able to get more sympathy in state capitals.

Circumstances have also contributed to more attention to the claims of environmental groups. As reports have appeared about the widespread existence of toxic-waste sites, politicians have started to listen more carefully to the arguments of environmental groups concerning the need to regulate the disposal of toxic wastes.

A Broader Approach to Communication and Lobbying

Interest groups do not communicate only with politicians. Lobbyists also spend considerable effort assessing member views. Just as politicians do, they conduct polls of their membership. With the arrival of computers, groups are now able to establish selective contact with their members so that they can communicate with members who have specific concerns. Groups are able to tap into the growing number of computer-assembled mailing lists of (probably) sympathetic people to raise funds or to prompt political activity.

Interest groups also engage in broad public lobbying. They are aware of the importance of the general and long-term image of their group. Many groups spend money on public-relations activity (advertising) in order to create a positive image. They are aware that it is difficult for a politician to appear sympathetic to a group that has a negative public image.

Finally, not all battles can be won by persuasion. Sometimes groups decide they can win only by going through the courts.[24] Groups try to find a legal basis for stopping the implementation of a policy. A lawsuit is then filed by the group. This approach is particularly useful for groups who are not "wealthy" in terms of membership or money. Environmental groups often use lawsuits as a means of political action. They seek to find a policy practice by government that violates the intent of legislation, or to find a violation in the way a policy decision was made. An environmental statement may not have been filed properly. Filing a lawsuit allows a group with few resources to have an effect they otherwise could not achieve. This approach is also used when a group objects to bureaucratic interpretations of what practices fulfill the intent of a law. A lawsuit is a way to challenge interpretations.

Some groups have found it useful to pursue "class-action" suits as a way to magnify their influence. In a class-action suit, a group files a grievance on behalf of a whole group of people potentially harmed, but who individually do not participate in actually filing or pursuing the case. If the court case is won, everyone who falls into a particular category (such as users of a medicine or a product) will receive some financial award. Needless to say, this has not been a popular tactic with businesses, which are generally the objects of the lawsuits.

Variations in Interest Groups from State to State

Thus far we have focused on the general outlines of interest groups in states and localities. While there are general patterns, the groups that are prominent in each state and city vary.[25] Much of this variation reflects economic, social, and political differences across the states.

The nature of the economy in each state plays a major role. Mining interests are more important in West Virginia and many western states because mining is a major source of economic activity in those states. Agricultural interests figure prominently in the Great Plains states. The tobacco industry is very important in North Carolina and many surrounding states. The auto industry is especially significant in Michigan. Oil concerns are important in Louisiana, Texas, and Oklahoma. The lumber industry is important in Washington and Maine. The specific groups that are prominent in any particular state—the groups around which many political controversies revolve—vary from state to state. It is necessary to examine each state's economy to know which groups are significant in that state.

Economic composition of a state is not the sole determinant of which interest groups are prominent in a particular state. Political climate also plays a role. Unions have had a very difficult time getting organized in southern states because of the dominance of conservative opinion in these states. State laws are less favorable to the formation of unions in the South, and industries have received less pressure to recognize unions there.[26] Table 7.5 presents the degree of union organization of the work force in 1988 by region of the country. While New York, Pennsylvania, Illinois, and Michigan had, on average, about 26 percent of their labor force unionized in 1988, the average in Mississippi, Texas, North Carolina, and South Carolina was around 8 percent. This proportion is changing in the nonunion states, but unions are still not a major force in politics in these states. Similarly, relatively large groups of teachers exist in each state, but teacher organizations are not aggressive in many states. Political climates affect whether groups are more or less aggressive. They

Table 7.5

Union Organization of the Workforce in the States, 1988

Region	Private Sector (%)	Public Sector (%)
Northeast	13.9	54.7
Midwest	19.0	50.0
South	9.2	24.2
Pacific	18.2	57.1
Other	10.1	31.3

Note: **Northeast:** *Connecticut, Delaware, Maine, Maryland, Massachusetts, New Hampshire, New Jersey, New York, Pennsylvania, Rhode Island, Vermont, and West Virginia;* **Midwest:** *Illinois, Indiana, Michigan, Minnesota, Ohio, and Wisconsin;* **South:** *Alabama, Arkansas, Florida, Georgia, Kentucky, Louisiana, Mississippi, North Carolina, South Carolina, Tennessee, and Virginia;* **Pacific:** *Alaska, California, Hawaii, Oregon, Washington;* **Other:** *Arizona, Colorado, Idaho, Iowa, Kansas, Missouri, Montana, Nebraska, Nevada, New Mexico, North Dakota, Oklahoma, South Dakota, Texas, Utah, and Wyoming.*
Source: *Michael A. Curme, Barry T. Hirsch, and David A. Macpherson,* Industrial and Labor Relations Review *44, no. 1 (October 1990): 22–26;*

also affect the inclination of the political system to accept such behavior. Teacher organizations (the NEA and AFT) have also been more aggressive in pursuing their goals in northern states than in southern states.

While these variations from state to state indicate diversity of interest groups in different settings, amid this diversity there is a common thread. Business concerns and the middle and upper classes are better organized than other constituencies. The specific business interests that are well organized in any particular state vary, but the general pattern holds. Table 7.6 indicates the interest groups that appear consistently significant across the states. The table presents the type of interest group along the left. The columns show the percent of states in which observers ranked the group as most effective, second most effective, or least effective, respectively.

Assessing Interest Group Influence

Interest groups are presumed to be important in the political process. Some interests are better organized and more heavily funded than others. These interests gain more of a hearing. There are more lobbyists presenting the arguments of the haves than those of the have-nots. The haves achieve more consistent representation of their concerns than the have-nots do. There are also many who argue that the regulation of interest groups does not have much impact. They argue that organizations are still somehow able to get money to the candidates that they want to support and that organized groups still have an enormous advantage over the unorganized in presenting their case to politicians.

Table 7.6

The Twenty Most Influential Interest Groups in the United States

Interest Group (Ranked by Effectiveness)	Most Effective	Second Most Effective (Number of States)	Least Effective
1. Teachers' organizations (predominantly NEA)	43	5	2
2. General business organizations (Chambers of Commerce)	31	17	5
3. Bankers associations (Savings and loan associations)	28	14	10
4. Manufacturers (Companies and associations)	23	15	18
5. Traditional labor associations (predominantly the AFL-CIO)	23	13	12
6. Utility companies and associations (Electric, gas, telephone, water)	20	17	14
7. Individual banks and financial institutions	20	12	19
8. Lawyers (predominantly state bar associations and trial lawyers)	15	15	22
9. General local government organizations (Municipal leagues)	15	18	17
10. General farm organizations (Mainly state farm bureaus)	11	23	16
11. Doctors	14	16	20
12. State and local government (Other than teachers)	16	11	23
13. Insurance companies and associations	13	14	27
14. Realtors associations	12	8	31
15. Individual traditional labor unions (Teamsters, UAW)	13	3	35
16. K-12 education interests (Other than teachers)	10	6	35
17. Health care groups (Other than doctors)	4	18	26
18. Agricultural commodity organizations (Stockgrowers, grain growers)	9	7	34
19. Universities and colleges (Institutions and personnel)	7	11	33
20. Oil and gas (Companies and associations)	7	10	34

Source: Clive S. Thomas and Ronald J. Hrebenar, "Interest Groups in the States," in Virginia Gray, Herbert Jacob, and Robert B. Albritton, Politics in the American States: A Comparative Analysis, *5th ed. (Glenview, Ill.: Scott, Foresman/Little, Brown, 1990), 144.*

Some Cautions

The conclusion that interest groups have great influence seems clear. The difficulty is that we are not sure how much influence they have. Furthermore, there are reasons for being cautious about assuming that interest groups overwhelm the political process. As Betty Zisk noted in a study of interest groups, "The actual impact of interest groups is more asserted than really measured or documented."[27] We often think lobbyists are very influential because lobbyists like to perpetuate the belief that they have great clout in order to acquire more clients. Without any information to the contrary, it is easy to assume that all the resources of interest groups translate into influence.[28]

There are reasons to be careful. The primary reason for being cautious is that interest groups, like other political actors, do not operate independently of their political contexts. Those contexts may operate to constrain the influence of interest groups. This possible constraint does not mean that they become insignificant actors in the representation of concerns, but that the seemingly obvious advantages that organized interests have in the representation process may not be quite as overwhelming as we suspect.

Many political conditions can affect the influence of interest groups. There are several, in particular, that may be very important in affecting interest-group influence.

The Inclination of Politicians to Listen

Interest group activities at their most basic are simply attempts to influence politicians. It is not always clear how amenable politicians are to these activities. Some politicians do not feel that it is proper to be influenced by "special interests." Lobbyists must approach politicians carefully because our political culture is dominated by the belief that it is somewhat improper to capitulate to such pressures. Not all politicians hold this belief, or hold it strongly, but enough do to cast some doubt on the argument that interest groups can simply use their greater resources to dominate politicians.

In a study of state legislators, for example, Harmon Ziegler found considerable variation in attitudes toward the propriety of dealing with lobbyists. After asking legislators several questions, he classified their attitudes toward lobbyists as negative, neutral, or positive. These attitudes affected the inclination of legislators to interact with lobbyists. Table 7.7 indicates the impact of these different attitudes. Legislators who have low interaction with lobbyists tend to have negative attitudes toward them.

We are not sure why these differences in attitudes exist, but one source of difference appears to be the future ambitions of politicians. Those who have aspirations for political careers appear to be somewhat more receptive to listening to interest groups. Kenneth Prewitt asked local council members a series of questions designed to determine whether they saw themselves as volunteers (amateurs, who intended to stay in office only a short time and who were concerned with doing what they felt was "right" as opposed to what was "political") or as professionals (intending to stay, seek reelection, and make a career of politics). He classified city

Table 7.7
Legislator Attitudes toward Lobbyists and Frequency of Interaction with Them

| | | Frequency | |
Attitude	Low Interaction (%)	Medium Interaction (%)	High Interaction (%)
Negative	52	30	11
Neutral	37	36	27
Positive	11	34	61

Note: Percentages sum down to 100.
Source: Harmon Ziegler and Michael Baer, Lobbying: Interaction and Influence in American State Legislatures *(Belmont: Wadsworth, 1969), 82.*

councils according to the level of member volunteerism. He also asked each member his or her perception of the way the council dealt with various interests. The results are shown in Table 7.8. In those councils where volunteerism was most present, the percent agreeing that the council listens to demands from the public and interest groups was the lowest. In those councils where volunteerism was least present (the council was dominated by people who had ambitions to remain in elective office), the percent agreeing that the council listens to demands from the public and interest groups was the greatest.

Politicians who do not think it is proper to be influenced by lobbyists and who are not as ambitious about higher office may be less likely to listen to, and be influenced by, interest groups. Those politicians who think it is proper and legitimate to listen to lobbyists and who worry about needing them in the future may be much

Table 7.8
Council Volunteerism and Perceived Level of Interaction with Interest Groups

| | Extent of Volunteerism | | |
Perceived Level of Interaction	Most Present (%)	Mixed (%)	Least Present (%)
Council listens to demands from public	29	51	73
Council views groups as politically influential	29	51	67
Council facilitates group access	35	61	60

Source: Kenneth K. Prewitt, "Political Ambitions, Volunteerism, and Electoral Accountability," American Political Science Review *64 (1970):11.*

more likely to spend time with them and listen to their concerns. This vulnerability to interest groups is particularly likely to be strong in situations where careerism is prevalent, campaigns are expensive, and candidates are largely on their own to raise funds and conduct their own campaigns, such as in California.[29]

Persuasion versus Reinforcement

There is also evidence that much of the communication and contributions go to the already persuaded.[30] Lobbyists focus most of their attention on shoring up support among those who already are inclined to support them. They then move to focusing on those who might be persuaded. They direct the least amount of attention toward those who are most inclined to oppose their interests.[31] Interest groups give contributions to those who support them.[32] The point is that much of the efforts of interest groups may not be to produce outcomes different from those that might occur anyway. The primary concern of interest groups may be to maintain the support they already have. Again, however, we do not have much clear information on this relationship.

Public Opinion and Image

The inclination of politicians to be sympathetic and responsive to interest groups is also shaped by the constituency that elected them. If interest group concerns and those of a legislator's constituency are compatible, a legislator is likely to be sympathetic. If those concerns conflict, politicians will not vote against their own constituency.[33] Even when compatibility exists, politicians must be careful because of public opinion on interest groups. Much of the public is critical of interest-group influence. The public thinks that interest groups have too much influence over politicians.[34] The public worries that special legislation will be enacted that will give generous benefits to those groups. It can be dangerous for a politician to be seen as a vehicle for "special interests." Challengers can criticize incumbents as heavily involved with, and dependent on, "the interests." Even when legislators are sympathetic to an interest group and believe that helping an interest group will be beneficial for the community or state, they must be very careful not to look as if they are simply "pawns" of some group. This problem of image makes the job of lobbyists even more difficult. Jerry Brown used the approach of attacking "special interests" in successfully running for governor in California during the 1970s. Ed Koch took a similar approach in successfully running for mayor of New York City during the 1970s and 1980s. The belief that interest groups are too powerful and greedy is widespread. The popular acceptance of this belief limits the associations politicians want to have with groups. The more pervasive these attitudes, the less power interest groups can derive from their resources.

Monitoring by the Media

Given these widespread attitudes, the media can play a significant role in limiting interest-group influence. The media can monitor and report on interactions between politicians and interest groups. Stories that make politicians appear to be too cozy with interest groups can be very damaging to political reputations. Reporters can easily make suggestions about inappropriate connections between interest-group contributions and the votes of legislators. Politicians worry about being portrayed as being "bought." The possibility of acquiring this image makes many of them careful about their dealings with lobbyists. Once the media raises the question of inappropriate connections, politicians can find it very difficult to get their side of the story into the press. It takes only one negative newspaper series to harm the reputation of a politician, and most politicians try to avoid activity that could be misinterpreted by the media.

Conflict between Interest Groups

Powerful interest groups often oppose each other.[35] When such opposition occurs, they may negate each other. The issue of medical malpractice is a good nationwide example of such opposition. Doctors argue that Americans are too inclined to sue doctors over minor matters. They argue that the increase in malpractice suits has occurred because lawyers take cases on a contingency-fee basis. That is, lawyers offer to take cases and charge as their fee a substantial percent of any award to a client. This fee might be from 25 to 50 percent. Critics characterize this as "ambulance chasing," or pursuing cases where lawyers think large settlements can be won.

Doctors argue that these lawsuits have detrimental effects on the availability and cost of medical care. Doctors are reluctant to take cases where there is any risk of a lawsuit. Delivering babies, for example, presents the possibility of many complications (and as many lawsuits), and obstetricians argue that the possibility of such lawsuits inhibits them from working and prevents residents from specializing in this area. They argue that the large settlements that some juries award has resulted in high malpractice-insurance premiums (ranging up to $100,000 a year in certain large metropolitan areas). These premiums drive up the cost of medical care. Doctors also argue that such lawsuits clog the courts with questionable cases.

Lawyers, on the other hand, have their own arguments as to why such lawsuits should be allowed and why the contingency-fee system should be preserved. They argue that many doctors make sloppy mistakes that cost people their lives or their ability to function normally in society. Lawyers argue that since the medical profession relies heavily on referrals from other doctors for their business, doctors are reluctant to criticize each other or to discipline each other when they encounter incompetence. Those doctors who are incompetent are also able to hide their mistakes because people not in medical fields generally do not have the knowledge to judge their own doctors. Finally, lawyers argue that the contingency-fee arrangement has two positive features. This arrangement prompts lawyers to turn down cases in which the evidence of malpractice is weak and there is little possibility of award. Such an arrangement also allows low-income people a chance of pursuing a legitimate case. Low-income, and even middle-class, people cannot afford lawyers' hourly rates, but they can afford to share a settlement with a lawyer. Advocates of this approach argue that it promotes equality of access to the law.

Doctors and lawyers represent well-organized and well-funded interest groups. Doctors are represented by the American Medical Association. Lawyers are represented by the American Bar Association. Faced with conflict between these two significant interest groups, most state legislatures have tried to find a compromise between the two, limiting the influence of each. When two significant interest groups oppose each other, the "power" of one interest group is often offset by the "power" of the other. The influence of any interest group is dependent on the extent of influence of the opposition.

The Political Party as an Alternative Resource

Interest groups with large memberships and well funded PACs seek to exploit those resources in order to influence politicians. The ability of interest groups to exert influence stems from the dependency of politicians upon interest-group resources. Interest groups can provide a mobilized membership (votes), money, volunteers, and phone banks for campaigns. They can also do research to help candidates. The important question for politicians is whether they can find alternative sources of these resources and thus reduce their reliance on interest groups.

One alternative source of resources for a politician is a cohesive, well-organized, and well-financed political party.[36] A political party can provide several things that may be valuable to a politician. Parties are mechanisms to mobilize large groups of voters. If a candidate can count on a party to mobilize constituencies for an election, a politician is less dependent on the promised votes of specific interest groups. The party may also have the organization to mobilize people and get voters to the polls. The party may be able to influence party members to vote their traditional loyalties, so the candidate has a better chance of obtaining votes from the traditional party base. These party activities make the resources of interest groups less necessary to the politician.

The recent emergence of legislative-party campaign committees at the state level is a particularly important case of alternative resources. State legislative parties have developed their own campaign organizations to raise money from PACs and other sources so that the party can control the way money is distributed and the way pressure is applied.[37] Parties know PACs generally give to incumbents and, particularly, safe incumbents. PACS seek to curry favor with those likely to win.[38] Parties worry that challengers will not get enough money, or that incumbents with close races may become too dependent on PAC money.

Legislative campaign committees provide an alternative source of resources to counter the influence of PACs. Campaign committees conduct polls for candidates, produce voter lists, help with writing and producing radio and television ads, write and produce direct-mail literature, and provide personnel for campaigns. The way these organizations target their money is particularly important for restraining interest-group influence. Campaign committees target their money to challengers and all candidates with close races. It is these candidates who are the most susceptible to interest groups because they need money and endorsements. This assistance from the parties helps reduce that dependence, but does not eliminate it because interest groups still represent votes.

At the local level, there is little evidence that party organizations have been able to raise much in the way of funds. They are still, however, able to help mobilize volunteers, and this mobilization does help party candidates.[39]

If parties have sufficient resources to help candidates, they may somewhat offset the power of interest groups. Assessing whether parties actually have this impact, however, has not been easy. The essential difficulty is in forming some estimate of the impact or significance of interest groups.[40] There is always the risk that estimates will be subjective. Some scholars, however, have tried to characterize the "strength" or "dominance" of interest groups in the states.[41] These characterizations are then related to the strength of parties in the state. The pattern found suggests an association between stronger parties and decreased dominance of interest groups.[42]

But we are still not sure that there is a causal relationship involved. That is, the conditions of parties and interest groups may only reflect the broader conditions of the economy and society in the states. Luttbeg argues that interest groups are less likely to be dominant when the economy of the state is complex. When an economy is complex, there are more conflicts, and strong political parties develop as a reflection of those social conflicts. In diverse economies, there are more conflicts and more opposing interest groups, meaning none can be dominant.[43]

These differing conclusions about the relationship of parties and interest groups are important. They indicate how little we know about lobbyists and their organizations. We *think* that strong parties can affect the amount of influence interest groups have, but our evidence to support that argument is not as clear as we might like.

Alternative Sources of Information

Finally, there is one other factor in the political process that may lessen interest group influence. That factor is the presence of alternative sources of information for politicians. One of the primary resources of interest groups is information and analysis. If a group is well-funded and well-managed, it should be able to hire good research staffs that can produce detailed information on the likely impact of legislation or bureaucratic regulations. If a legislator has no alternative sources of such information, dependency on lobbyists develops. A legislator may not wish to have such dependency, but making decisions without information is unsettling, so the tendency to listen to lobbyists emerges. This tendency is greater when legislators are only part-time or when they do not have staffs of their own to do independent research. Without time to do such work on their own and no one to draw on, interest-group information becomes invaluable.

In response to this situation, many groups have urged that legislatures should be more professional. Legislators should work full-time, and legislatures should have large staffs so they can conduct their own analyses.[44] Legislators should also be encouraged to stay longer so that they build up expertise and will not be easily swayed by lobbyists. For legislators to work full-time, they need to be paid higher salaries. During the last two decades, there have been efforts to increase both staff and salaries in many state legislatures.[45] Most local councils, though, have generally remained part-time with limited staffs.

In many state legislatures, salary levels have increased over the years, and more legislators are staying longer.[46] Even with these increases, however, salaries are still not equivalent to those many middle-class individuals make. Most legislators hold other jobs. In local governments, most salaries are even lower—less than $5,000—and very few council members are full-time.

The other crucial matter is staff availability. The larger the staff available, the less dependency, we presume, on lobbyists and their analyses.[47] When legislatures are populated by full-time legislators and have large staffs, we presume that the impact of lobbyist information is limited. Table 7.9 classifies states by the salaries of legislators and the size of staffs in the states. States like California and New York pay high salaries to their legislators and hire large staffs. In those states, lobbyists have to be careful in making their arguments because many legislators have considerable experience in issues and their staffs have the capacity to check the information used.[48]

An incident in New York illustrates how the emergence of staff can affect lobbyists. In the early 1980s, the legislature was giving serious consideration to a bottle bill. The lobbyists for the bottlers consistently claimed that the bill would cause great harm to their industry. In the legislature, these claims were regularly regarded as significantly exaggerated. In response, the speaker of the assembly directed the staff to refuse even to meet with the existing lobbyists. The staff were directed to do their own research on the issue. The bill subsequently passed.

Following this passage, questions emerged about whether bottlers were holding unclaimed deposits, or deposits not returned because consumers did not return their bottles. The governor claimed that millions of dollars were held in unclaimed deposits, while the bottlers claimed that overall they were losing money because of the costs of buying equipment and trucks to comply with the new legislation. Faced with the prospect that the bottlers would lose on this new issue, the soft-drink bottlers association replaced their executive director with a former staff member of the legislature. The new director recognized the importance of credibility and eventually talked his members into opening their accounting books to an independent auditor so that the association could establish (with some credibility) the amount of money they actually made and the degree to which compliance with the legislation had increased their costs. The existence of a critical and well informed legislative staff forced the interest group to produce more acceptable (and credible) documentation. The existence of a staff large enough to research the issues around legislation has forced the lobbyist to do more than just argue.

In other states, such as New Hampshire and New Mexico, salaries for legislators are low, and staffs are not large. Legislators in such situations are less likely to have years of experience with issues, and they have little in the way of staff to assist them. At the local level, few councils nationwide have research staffs for city council members. This lack of support staff increases the importance of information from interest groups.

Table 7.9
Salary and Staff Levels in State Legislatures

Yearly Salary	Staff Size 0–300	Staff Size 301–700	Staff Size 701–3600
Per diem Basis	Kansas Kentucky Montana Nevada New Mexico North Dakota Rhode Island Utah Wyoming	Alabama	
$ 0–15,000	West Virginia Vermont South Dakota South Carolina Oregon North Carolina New Hampshire Nebraska Mississippi Maine Indiana Idaho Arkansas	Georgia Alabama	Texas
$15,000–30,000	Alaska Colorado Delaware Iowa Hawaii Tennessee Virginia	Connecticut Louisiana Maryland Minnesota Missouri Washington	Florida Massachusetts
$31,000–$45,000	Oklahoma	Ohio Wisconsin	Illinois Michigan New Jersey
$46,000+			California New York Pennsylvania

Source: Council of State Governments, Book of the States, 1992–1993, *151–52.*

Summary

All of these conditions affect the ultimate impact of lobbyists. The haves have more lobbyists and are able to communicate more regularly and thoroughly with politicians. But when certain combinations of these conditions exist, the impact of interest groups may well be less than we expect. Legislators may feel uneasy about being susceptible to such influence, and the media may be vigilant in searching for suggestions of corruption. Political parties may help politicians find other resources. Under those circumstances, the haves may be well represented, but their actual impact may be somewhat constrained. On the other hand, if the dominant feeling is that interest groups are legitimate, if politicians face weak parties with no resources for campaigns, and if the media devotes little attention to the relationships between politicians and lobbyists, the haves are likely to acquire a significant advantage in representation in the political process.

All of these conditions have a cumulative impact on the influence of interest groups. Hrebener and Thomas have assessed the results of studies of interest groups in all the states and have classified states as to whether interest groups are dominant, complementary, subordinate, or some combination of these conditions. Their assessment of the situations in specific states is shown in Table 7.10. In general, those states with weaker parties and less professional legislatures, primarily in the South, are the ones with the most-dominant interest groups. In the states with stronger, more competitive parties and more professional legislatures (many of them in the Northeast and Midwest) interest groups have a complementary or subordinate impact on the political process.

Public Efforts to Restrain Interest Groups

While there are reasons to be cautious about attributing too much influence to interest groups, most of the public is worried about their degree of influence. Most people regard interest groups as fairly powerful and detrimental to the democratic political process. The general presumption is that interest groups use money and resources in ways that make politicians feel indebted to them. Political campaigns are becoming more and more costly at all levels of government, and this increase in the need for campaign funds raises the possibility that the money of interest groups will become even more important as a source of leverage. As Herbert Alexander puts it, "Most candidates seeking statewide and state legislative office cannot fund their own campaigns, and their pursuit of wealthy individuals and special-interest lobbies is creating a perception that the financing system is corrupt."[49]

This perception was reinforced by events in the early 1970s. Investigative stories found cases of large sums of money being transferred from private interests to politicians in ways which made tracking the money to the original source difficult. Because most interest-group contributions go to incumbents, there are concerns that politicians are deaf to new ideas and reluctant to enact policies that threaten existing interests.[50] Public anxieties about interest groups have prompted efforts to limit their influence. Many states have enacted laws to try to contain the influence of interest

Table 7.10

Classification of the Fifty States According to the Overall Impact of Interest Groups

	Overall Impact of Interest Groups			
Dominant (9)	Dominant/ Complementary (18)	Complementary (18)	Complimentary/ Subordinate (5)	Subordinate (0)
Alabama	Arizona	Colorado	Connecticut	
Alaska	Arkansas	Illinois	Delaware	
Florida	California	Indiana	Minnesota	
Louisiana	Hawaii	Iowa	Rhode Island	
Mississippi	Georgia	Kansas	Vermont	
New Mexico	Idaho	Maine		
South Carolina	Kentucky	Maryland		
Tennessee	Montana	Massachusetts		
West Virginia	Nebraska	Michigan		
	Nevada	Missouri		
	Ohio	New Jersey		
	Oklahoma	New Hampshire		
	Oregon	New York		
	Texas	North Carolina		
	Utah	North Dakota		
	Virginia	Pennsylvania		
	Washington	South Dakota		
	Wyoming	Wisconsin		

Source: Clive S. Thomas and Ronald J. Hrebenar, "Interest Groups in the States," in Virginia Gray, Herbert Jacob, and Robert B. Albritton, Politics in the American States: A Comparative Analysis, 5th ed. (Glenview, Ill.: Scott, Foresman/Little, Brown, 1990), 147.

groups, or to at least increase public awareness of their role. These efforts have been the greatest in states where the legislature is more professional (higher salaries, more staff, and longer legislative sessions) and in states where the political culture has historically placed more emphasis on the importance of morality in politics.[51] The efforts to control these groups have followed several lines of attack.

Registration and Disclosure

The first concern of reformers has been to make the contributions and activities of interest groups more visible. Reformers believe that a primary way to limit the influence of lobbyists is to expose their activities to the glare of public scrutiny. They argue that interest groups achieve power because no one realizes how much their money is important in politics, or how much politicians depend on their funds. Given this logic, the best solution is make the activities of lobbyists public.

One way to expose lobbying relationships is to require candidates to report the sources of their funds. Some states also require that public officials disclose whether they hold stock or part ownership in any private-sector business. Table 7.11 indicates how many states require that candidates file reports on their funding sources. Perhaps the most important thing about that reporting is its timing. For disclosure to work, candidates must report funding sources prior to elections. Such timing allows opponents and the press time to review a candidate's sources of contributions and to make their assessment of such sources public. The logic of having public preelection reports is that candidates will not take contributions that will look inappropriate if they are made public. Contributions will be assessed in terms of whether they will result in embarrassing revelations later.

The limitation on these reports is that they are often difficult to analyze in short periods of time and that they often do not receive much publicity in the press. Despite those limitations, it is clear that many candidates have become sensitive about the way such reports can create an impression that they are highly dependent on "special interests." The presence of these reports may well prompt many candidates to decline contributions from some groups, or to limit the amount they take so that no large sums will be prominent.

Reformers have also pushed for registration of lobbyists along with disclosure of their activities. Such laws usually require that a lobby group register with the state, regularly report how much money they spend, to whom they contribute, and how they spend their total lobbying budget. There is usually a fine for noncompliance. Table 7.12 presents the number of states that require interest groups to report total expenditures and the number that require them to report their expenditures by the categories of expenditure. While these requirements often appear significant, the penalties for noncompliance are usually mild. Furthermore, the

---

Table 7.11

State Preelection Reporting Requirements for Candidates

Preelection Filings (Primaries Included)		
Number of Reports	*Required by*	*Number of States*
None		1
1		14
2		20
3		2
4		6
5 or more		3
Total number of states requiring preelection reports		46

Source: Council of State Governments, Book of the States, 1992–1993, *294–302.*

Table 7.12
Regulation of Interest Groups across States

Interest Group Reporting Requirements	Yes	No
		(# of States)
Expenditures	35	15
Categories of expenditures	35	15
Candidate disclosure and monitoring by independent election agency	30	20

States Setting Contribution Limits for Specific Groups	No Limit	Specific Amount	Prohibited
Corporations	10	19	20
Labor Unions	17	22	10
PACs	22	27	0

Source: Herbert E. Alexander, Reform and Reality: The Financing of State and Local Campaigns *(Twentieth Century Fund Paper, 1991), 110, 112; Council of State Governments,* Book of the States, 1992–1993, *317–25.*

enforcement of the reporting requirements are rarely pursued energetically. Even when it is, organizations often understate the amount of money they spend on direct lobbying.

Limits on Contributions and Expenditures

A second major approach to limiting the influence of interest groups is to impose limits on interest-group contributions or on campaign expenditures. Contributions from some sources might be banned altogether, or a maximum dollar amount might be imposed. Some states, however, continue to set no limits on contributions. Table 7.12 presents the number of states that constrain corporations, labor unions, and PACs with specific limits or prohibitions, and the number that set no limits on these groups. As with the other attempts at regulation, there is little information on the effectiveness of these limits. Even when there are limits or prohibitions, organizations are capable of getting money to candidates by channeling smaller contributions through various committees. They also can channel money through individuals who contribute money to the candidates on behalf of organized interests. We do not know the extent to which interest groups are able to evade regulations, but we suspect such evasion does go on.

Table 7.13

Public Finance of Campaigns and Limits on Campaign Expenditures across States

Spending limits on		
Organizations	30	20
Candidates	39	11
Public financing	*Yes*	*No*
	23	27
Source of Public Funds		
Check-off	11	
Add on	9	
Both	1	
Other	4	

Source: Herbert Alexander, Reform and Reality: The Financing of State and Local Campaigns *(New York: Twentieth Century Fund, 1991).*

Another approach to limiting the role of private money in campaigns is to limit the amount of money that can be spent in campaigns. Table 7.13 indicates the number of states that have limits on campaign expenditures. As with previous matters, we have no systematic information on these systems at the local level. The top of Table 7.13 indicates the number of states that limit the total amount of money spent during campaigns. These limits usually vary with the size of the population and number of votes cast in an election. Such limits have met with considerable opposition, and after their initial adoption in the 1970s, a number of states using these limits dropped them. Groups with large financial resources have opposed them on the grounds that they indirectly limit the right of candidates to present themselves to the public. Advocates of more competition in elections have also become uneasy with these limits because they believe that challengers need to spend larger sums of money than incumbents in order to establish name recognition and to communicate their views and their criticisms of incumbents.

Public Funding

The third way to control the role of money is to establish programs to raise public funds to provide campaign money to candidates for public office. In almost all cases, the elections funded are only the major statewide ones, such as the election for governor. The funds for these programs are raised by allowing taxpayers to check off on their income tax returns if they wish to contribute to a state fund for this purpose. In most cases, this contribution does not cost the taxpayer any additional money since the amount contributed is subtracted from the tax obligation. In a few states, a taxpayer must add the amount on to his tax obligation. The amounts contributed and the rate of participation is much higher when there is no additional tax obligation.[52] The number of states having such programs is shown in Table 7.13. Some of these programs give money only to qualifying candidates, while others have tried to strengthen the role of political parties by giving money directly to the parties for distribution to their candidates.

The impact of these funding programs is uncertain at this point. The amounts raised are not sufficient in most cases to fund full campaigns, so they have little impact on campaign practices. Many funding programs prohibit candidates from accepting more money, so some candidates have declined to participate. As of now, we have no studies on whether public funding reduces overall expenditure levels, or whether it reduces responsiveness to interest groups.

Furthermore, there are significant arguments that all these limits and controls are not legitimate, or healthy for the exchange of political ideas. Groups with significant resources argue that to limit the amount of money they can spend to promote an idea is to limit their free speech, and the courts have accepted some of these arguments. Others argue that limiting the amount of money spent in campaigns prohibits challengers from mounting the large campaign that is usually necessary to unseat an incumbent. Public funding of campaigns with limits of expenditures, in this view, is a program designed to protect incumbents. The effects of public funding remain to be assessed.

Regardless of all these ambiguities about the actual impact of interest groups, efforts to constrain their role continue. The impact of these constraints, however, is not clear, but it is clear that lobbyists are now more cautious in the ways they use money than they were thirty and fifty years ago. Scandals involving legislators taking bribes or direct cash from lobbyists still occur, but these cases are not the norm. Our political culture now makes politicians reluctant to engage in such practices. Getting caught in this type of scandal is generally an automatic end to a political career. Requirements that contributions be reported and the scrutiny by opponents and by the press limit the impact of contributions.

Summary

Interest groups are not representative of all interests in American politics. While some observers have argued that pluralism reigns and that many groups play a role in representation, as E. E. Schattschneider put it, "the flaw in the pluralist heaven is that the heavenly chorus sings with a strong upper-class accent."[53] There is continual concern that politicians hear more from the affluent than from other groups. That concern has led to continual efforts to constrain the influence of interest groups.

Despite these public anxieties about their "power," the influence of interest groups is not unchecked. Strong political parties and public scrutiny play a significant role in limiting politician dependency on interest groups. Interest-group influence remains strong, but is not unlimited. Perhaps their most significant role continues to be persuasion, rather than the provision of money.

For Further Reading

Rosenthal, Alan. *The Third House.* Washington, DC: Congressional Quarterly Press, 1993). A general book on interest groups in the states.

Ronald J. Hrebenar and Clive S. Thomas have prepared a series of books that present studies of interest groups in different regions of the country. For those interested in profiles of interest groups in each state, see works in their series. The following works have been published.

Interest Group Politics in the West. Salt Lake City: University of Utah Press, 1987.

Interest Groups Politics in the Southern States. Tuscaloosa: University of Alabama, 1992.

Books on other regions may now have been published. Look for books by Hrebenar and Thomas in your library.

Suggestions for Analysis in Your Own State and Locality

1. Much interest group activity is done quietly and does not get reported in the press. Of all political activities, interest group activity is probably the hardest to track. There are, however, ways to find out about their activities.

    Many states require that interest groups register and indicate the amount of money they spend on lobbying activities. See if there is such a requirement in your state. You can call the office of your local board of elections or your state legislators and they should be able to tell you. If such a requirement exists, request a copy of any report they issue.

    Another way to determine the activities of interest groups is to talk to the object of their lobbying—politicians. You might request interviews with local politicians or with your state legislators and ask them whom they hear from and how often they are contacted by these groups. You might also ask what kind of presentation lobbyists make—the degree of political threat and the degree of persuasion.

    Finally, you might contact lobbyists for a prominent group, such as the education lobby in your area or at the state level, and ask them what kinds of information (brochures, newsletters, press releases, studies) they have and request copies. These samples will give you some idea of the materials lobbyists put together to make their case to politicians.

2. States try to regulate the influence of interest groups by limiting the amount of money they can contribute to candidates. What limitations, if any, exist in your state? Are politicians required to file reports with a local office indicating the amounts they receive? If so, request copies of reports for a recent election and compare candidates. What differences do you find in funding

sources? In amounts of contributions? Examine the report filed by the candidate who eventually won. Did the bulk of funding come from private individuals, public campaign funds, or interest groups and PACs? If time permits, obtain the recent voting record of this politician. Does his or her voting pattern seem to support the interests of the groups that contributed money to his or her campaign?

Notes

[1] Clive S. Thomas and Ronald J. Hrebenar, "Interest Groups in the States," in Virginia Gray, Herbert Jacob, and Robert B. Albritton, *Politics in the American States: A Comparative Analysis*, 5th ed. (Glenview, Ill.: Scott, Foresman/Little, Brown, 1990), 125.

[2] David Truman, *The Governmental Process* (New York: Knopf, 1951).

[3] L. Harmon Ziegler and Hendrik van Dalen, "Interest Groups in State Politics," in Herbert Jacob and Kenneth Vines, *Politics in the American States*, 3rd ed. (Boston: Little, Brown, 1976), 110; Jeffrey Berry, *The Interest Group Society* (Boston: Little, Brown, 1984), 219; Clive S. Thomas and Ronald J. Hrebenar, "Interest Groups in the States," in Virginia Gray, Herbert Jacob, and Robert B. Albritton, *Politics in the American States: A Comparative Analysis*, 5th ed. (Glenview, Ill.: Scott, Foresman/Little, Brown, 1990), 126.

[4] Quoted in Alan Rosenthal, *The Third House* (Washington, DC: Congressional Quarterly Press, 1993), 138.

[5] Theodore J. Lowi, *The End of Liberalism*, 2nd ed. (New York: W.W. Norton, 1979).

[6] Kay L. Schlozman and John T. Tierney, *Organized Interests and American Democracy* (New York: Harper and Row, 1986), 60.

[7] Ronald J. Hrebenar and Ruth K. Scott, *Interest Group Politics in America* (Englewood Cliffs: Prentice Hall, 1982), 18–25; and Jack L. Walker, "The Origins and Maintenance of Interest Groups in America," *American Political Science Review* 77, no. 2 (June 1983): 390–406.

[8] Kay L. Schlozman and John T. Tierney, *Organized Interests and American Democracy* (New York: Harper and Row, 1986), 70; and Kenneth G. Hunter, Laura Ann Wilson, and Gregory G. Brunk, "Societal Complexity and Interest-Group Lobbying in the American States," *Journal of Politics* 53, no. 2 (May 1991): 493.

[9] Clive S. Thomas and Ronald J. Hrebenar, "Interest Groups in the States," in Virginia Gray, Herbert Jacob, and Robert B. Albritton, *Politics in the American States: A Comparative Analysis*, 129.

[10] Clive S. Thomas, "Understanding Interest Group Activity in Southern State Politics," 25 and Jack D. Fleer, "Interest Groups in a State of Transition," 118, in Ronald J. Hebrenar and Clive S. Thomas, eds., *Interest Group Politics in the Southern States* (Tuscaloosa: University of Alabama Press 1992).

[11] Suzanne Farkas, *Urban Lobbying: Mayors in the Federal Arena* (New York: New York University Press, 1971); and Donald H. Haider, *When Governments Come to Washington* (New York: Free Press, 1974).

[12] Jeffrey M. Berry, Kent E. Portney, and Ken Thomson, *The Rebirth of Urban Democracy* (Washington, DC: Urban Institute, 1993).

[13] For a study of a "good-government" group, see Andrew S. McFarland, *Common Cause* (Chatham: Chatham House Publishers, 1984).

[14] Maurice R. Berube, *Teacher Politics: The Influence of Unions* (New York: Greenwood, 1988), 1–17.

[15] Frank S. Sorauf, *Money in American Elections* (Glenview, Ill.: Scott, Foresman/Little, Brown, 1988), 72–120; and Ruth Jones and Thomas J. Borris, "Strategic Contributing in Legislative Campaigns: The Case of Minnesota," *Legislative Studies Quarterly* 10 (1985): 89–105.

[16] John Syer, "Political Giants in a Megastate," in Ronald J. Hrebenar and Clive S. Thomas, *Interest Group Politics in the American West* (Salt Lake City: University of Utah Press, 1987), 38;

Alan Rosenthal, *The Third House*, 121–22; Clive S. Thomas and Ronald J. Hrebenar, "The Wheeler Dealer Lobbyist: An Endangered Species in State Capitals?" in Thad Beyle, *State Government, 1992–93*, (Washington, DC: Congressional Quarterly Press, 1992), 106–111; and Keith E. Hamm and Charles W. Wiggins, "The Transformation from Personal to Informational Lobbying," in Ronald J. Hrebenar and Clive S. Thomas, eds., *Interest Group Politics in the Southern States* (Tuscaloosa: University of Alabama Press, 1992), 152–80.

[17] Alan Rosenthal, *The Third House*, 123–26, 135–39.

[18] Clive S. Thomas and Ronald J. Hrebenar, "Interest Groups in the States," in Virginia Gray, Herbert Jacob, and Robert B. Albritton, *Politics in the American States: A Comparative Analysis*, 126, 144.

[19] Gary Moncrief, "Idaho: The Interests of Sectionalism," 70 and Walfred Peterson, "Washington: The Impact of Public Disclosure Laws," 129, in Ronald J. Hrebenar and Clive S. Thomas, *Interest Group Politics in the American West* (Salt Lake City: University of Utah Press, 1987); Jack D. Fleer, "Interest Groups in a State in Transition," in Ronald J. Hrebenar and Clive S. Thomas, eds., *Interest Group Politics in the Southern States* (Tuscaloosa: University of Alabama Press, 1992), 120.

[20] Arthur English and John J. Carroll, "Arkansas: the Politics of Inequality," in Ronald J. Hrebenar and Clive S. Thomas, eds., *Interest Group Politics in the Southern States* (Tuscaloosa: University of Alabama Press, 1992), 189.

[21] Alan Rosenthal, *The Third House*, 121–22.

[22] Milt Freudenheim, "Doctors Battle Nurses Over Domains in Care," *New York Times*, 4 June 1983, A1.

[23] For examples, see the National Commission on Excellence in Education, *A Nation at Risk* (Washington, DC, 1983); and Diane Ravitch, *The Troubled Crusade: American Education, 1945–80* (New York: Basic Books, 1983).

[24] Kim Lane Scheppele and Jack L. Walker, Jr., "The Litigation Strategies of Interest Groups," in Jack L. Walker, Jr., *Mobilizing Interest Groups in America* (Ann Arbor: University of Michigan Press, 1991), 157–83.

[25] For studies of the situations in specific states, see Ronald J. Hrebenar and Clive S. Thomas, eds., *Interest Group Politics in the American West* (Salt Lake City: University of Utah Press, 1987); and Ronald J. Hrebenar and Clive S. Thomas, eds., *Interest Group Politics in the Southern States* (Tuscaloosa: University of Alabama Press, 1992).

[26] Thomas A. Kochian, "Correlates of State Public Employee Bargaining Laws," *Industrial Relations* 12, no. 3 (October 1973): 322–35.

[27] Betty Zisk, *Local Interest Politics: A Two-Way Street* (Indianapolis: Bobbs-Merrill, 1973), 1.

[28] Alan Rosenthal, *The Third House*, 205, 215.

[29] John Syer, "Political Giants in a Megastate," in Hrebenar and Thomas, *Interest Group Politics in the American West*, 36.

[30] Diana M. Evans, "PAC Contributions and Roll-Call Voting: Conditional Power," in Allan J. Cigler and Burdett A. Loomis, *Interest Group Politics*, 2d ed., (Washington, DC: Congressional Quarterly Press, 1986), 126; and Kay L. Schlozman and John T. Tierney, *Organized Interests and American Democracy* (New York: Harper and Row, 1986), 255–56.

[31] Alan Rosenthal, *The Third House*, 138.

[32] Philip M. Stern, *Still the Best Congress Money Can Buy* (Washington, DC: Regenry Gateway, 1992), 71.

[33] Alan Rosenthal, *The Third House*, 211.

[34] Ibid., 5–8.

[35] Ibid., 149–154.

[36] Sarah M. Morehouse, *State Politics, Parties and Policy* (New York: CBS Publishing, 1981), 305; Clive S. Thomas and Ronald J. Hrebenar, "Interest Groups in the States," in Virginia Gray, Herbert Jacob, and Robert B. Albritton, *Politics in the American States: A Comparative Analysis*, 127.

[37] Diana Dwyre and Jeffrey M. Stonecash, "Where's the Party: Changing State Party Organizations," *American Politics Quarterly* 20, no. 3 (July 1992): 326–344; and Anthony Gierzynski,

Legislative Party Campaign Committees in the American States (Lexington: University Press of Kentucky, 1992).

[38] Joel A. Thompson and William Cassie, "Party and PAC Contributions to North Carolina Legislative Candidates," *Legislative Studies Quarterly* 17, no. 3 (August 1992): 412–13.

[39] William Crotty, *Political Parties in Local Areas* (Knoxville: University of Tennessee Press, 1986).

[40] Charles W. Wiggins, Keith E. Hamm, and Charles G. Bell, "Interest Group and Party Influence Agents in the Legislative Process: A Comparative State Analysis," *Journal of Politics* 54, no. 1 (February 1992): 82–100.

[41] Clive S. Thomas and Ronald J. Hrebenar, "Interest Groups in the States," in Virginia Gray, Herbert Jacob, and Robert B. Albritton, *Politics in the American States*, 147.

[42] Sarah M. Morehouse, *State Politics, Parties and Policy* 117.

[43] Norman R. Luttbeg, *Comparing the States and Communities* (New York: HarperCollins, 1992), 186.

[44] The Citizens Conference on State Legislatures, *The Sometimes Governments: A Critical Study of the 50 American Legislatures* (Kansas City: Citizen Conference on State Legislatures, 1973), 101–119.

[45] Advisory Commission on Intergovernmental Relations, *State and Local Capacity*, (Washington, DC, 1985), 65–126; and Alan Rosenthal, "The Legislative Institution," in Carl Van Horn, *The State of the States* (Washington, DC: Congressional Quarterly Press, 1989), 71–78.

[46] David Ray, "Membership Stability in Three State Legislature: 1893–1969," *American Political Science Review* 68 (1974): 106–112; Alan Rosenthal, "The Legislative Institution: Transformed and at Risk," in Carl E. Van Horn, ed., *The State of the States* (Washington, DC.: Congressional Quarterly Press, 1989), 69–101; and Jeffrey M. Stonecash, "Careerism in the New York Legislature" (paper delivered at the New York State Political Science Association Meetings, New York City, April 1989).

[47] L. Harmon Ziegler, "Interest Groups in the States," in Virginia Gray, Herbert Jacob, and Kenneth Vines, 4th ed. (Boston: Little, Brown, 1983), 126.

[48] William K. Muir, *Legislature: California's School for Politics* (Chicago: University of Chicago Press, 1982).

[49] Herbert Alexander, *Reform and Reality: The Financing of State and Local Campaigns* (New York: Twentieth Century Fund Press, 1991), 10.

[50] Bruce B. Mason, "Arizona: Interest Groups in a Changing State," in Hrebenar and Thomas, *Interest Group Politics in the American States*, 28; Gary C. Jacobson, *The Politics of Congressional Elections*, 3d ed. (New York: HarperCollins, 1992), 66–71; and Herbert Alexander, *Reform and Reality: The Financing of State and Local Campaigns* (New York: Twentieth Century Fund Press, 1991), 24.

[51] Cynthia Opheim, "Explaining the Differences in State Lobby Regulation," *Western Political Quarterly* 44, no. 2 (June 1991): 415–416. States with high regulation are New Jersey, Washington, Wisconsin, California, Maryland, Massachusetts, and Connecticut. Those with low regulatory efforts are Delaware, North Carolina, Illinois, Vermont, Wyoming, and Arkansas (409).

[52] Ruth Jones, "Financing State Elections," in Michael J. Malbin, ed., *Money and Politics in the United States: Financing Elections in the 1980s* (Chatham: Chatham House Publishers, 1984), 189–90; and Herbert E. Alexander, *Reform and Reality, The Financing of State and Local Campaigns* (New York: Twentieth Century Fund Press, 1991), 88–90.

[53] E. E. Schattschneider, *The Semi-Sovereign People* (New York: Holt, Rinehart and Winston, 1960), 35.

8

Representation: The Effects of Political Conditions

PREVIEW

Whose interests get represented is the product of the activities of party politicians, interest groups, and public participation. It is the combination of these means of representation that affects whose interests get heard in the representation process and what policies are enacted in response to those interests.

This chapter first discusses the combination of conditions that would enhance representation of the haves, and the combination that would benefit the have-nots. The second half of this chapter reviews the evidence available on how political conditions and arrangements affect who is heard and then examines the effects of representation on the enactment of policy.

Political Processes and Differences in Representation

Representation is the process that brings issues to the attention of politicians. It is not a neutral process. Some concerns are better represented than others. Some concerns get more attention from politicians than other concerns do.

Thus far we have focused on single aspects of the process, but no single part of the process determines the outcome of the representation process. Whose interests—those of the haves or those of the have-nots—receive more attention from politicians depends on the *combination* of representation conditions that exist in that particular city or state. We now need to consider the cumulative effect of representation practices.

There are many combinations that might, and do, exist. To give our review some coherence, we will focus on two contrasting combinations that might exist. We will then examine the evidence we have about the effects of different combinations.

Restating Key's Argument

Key argued that the enduring political battles are between the haves and the have-nots. Battles persist over equality of opportunity, tax burdens, state intervention to address inequities, and numerous related matters. Key argued that the have-nots need political organization to bring their interests together and to articulate them to achieve representation. The haves already possess much of society's wealth, and most of them do not seek to change society. The haves also begin the political process with representation advantages. They participate more, and they have more resources and means of getting their concerns expressed. The have-nots lack these advantages and need some means to get their concerns articulated and included in the political process.

Key focused on the role of political parties in helping the have-nots achieve representation of their concerns because he was reacting to their widespread inability to do so in the South. The situation that prompted his concern, the dominance of one-party politics in the South, has declined over time, but his general argument about the ways the political process can affect who wins and loses in politics is still very relevant. The approach in this text has been to broaden the consideration of those aspects of the process that affect representation, but the concern is still how the entire process enhances or diminishes the representation of different segments of society.

An Example: Two Contrasting Combinations

There are many combinations of conditions that might, and do, occur. To simplify our review, we will contrast two very distinct and opposite combinations. The combinations shown in Table 8.1 present two hypothetical political processes that might exist at the state or local level, but which do not always occur. These combinations indicate those conditions most likely to maximize the representation of one group over another. The first set of conditions, situation A, represents those that should be most favorable to the haves. The second set of conditions, situation B, represents those that should be most favorable to the have-nots. The contrast is valuable in clarifying differences in the way representation processes can work.

In situation A, the electoral bases of the parties do not differ much by class. Lower-income individuals are as likely to vote for Republicans as for Democrats, so Democrats have no distinctive electoral base. It may be that social or cultural issues divide the electorate more than class issues. In this situation, Democrats will not be preoccupied with class issues. Because politicians in situation A have limited access to party resources and to staff resources, they are more dependent on interest-group contributions and information. If the lower class does not participate (vote) as much as others, there will be less attention to their concerns. Politicians will not be able to count on the lower-class vote, and they will not worry about retaliation from this part of the electorate.

The result should be that the electorate is not clearly organized along class lines. Voters may be organized (divided) along other lines, but there will be no clear division of the electorate. Politicians from opposing parties will not differ much in

Table 8.1

The Consequences of Two Possible Combinations of Political Conditions on the Representation Process

Conditions	Situation A	Situation B
Difference between parties in electoral bases (by class or income)	low	high
Cohesion of politicians in parties	low	high
Party resources	low	high
Role of interest groups	dominant	restrained
Participation differentials by class	high	low
Consequences		
Organization of conflict	muddled	clear
Articulation of contrasting views and presentation of differing policies	limited	high
Pressure on Republicans (party of the haves)	low	high
Politicians sensitive to	the haves	the have-nots

the views they articulate. Democrats will not devote their attention to bashing Republicans for being "heartless and uncaring" about the problems of working people. Democrats and Republicans may end up sounding very much alike. As a consequence of all these conditions, politicians and the political process in situation A will be somewhat more sensitive to the haves than to the have-nots.

Situation B presents a set of conditions favorable to the representation of the have-nots. Party bases differ, and that difference has important consequences. Democrats have a strong base among lower- to middle-income groups, who are concerned about the economic issues that affect them. Democrats will work to represent those concerns. This emphasis should leave Republicans with a clear base of middle- to upper-income individuals, and they will focus on lower taxation and less redistribution. If the parties have their own resources, party candidates (and particularly those supported by the have-nots, the Democrats) should be less dependent on interest groups and PACs for contributions and information on policy issues. Finally, if the lower class participates (votes) as much as other groups, politicians will be able to count on that voting base, and they should be more attentive to that group. All these conditions should make politicians more concerned with lower-income concerns.

Situation B should result in a fairly clear class organization of the electorate. Politicians from each party will devote considerable energy to presenting alternative views of public policy issues. Democrats will be inclined to argue for the need to redress inequities, while Republicans will argue for the need to encourage individual initiative and to pursue economic development so that benefits trickle down. Democrats will be inclined to criticize Republicans regularly for being uncaring. This criticism should create some pressure on Republicans not to look too insensitive to those less well off.

Equality of opportunity is a highly valued condition in American society, and arguments calling attention to a lack of opportunity create pressures on politicians either to argue that there is opportunity, or to respond to the apparent unfairness. In our political system, this situation usually means putting pressure on Republicans. If equality of opportunity can be made a prominent issue in society, it leads to more concern among all politicians about not looking unsympathetic to those less well-off and should result in more public concern for the have-nots. The crucial matter in this representation process is the presence of a group of politicians who consistently articulate the concerns of the have-nots and attempt to portray the other party as uncaring. This activity should have political consequences.

Again, combinations like those in situation A and those in situation B may not be present in their entirety in many cities and states. We suspect most cities and state have some mix of these conditions, with the resulting situations somewhere in between the two examples presented here. There is not as much research on such conditions in states and cities as we might like. This lack of research makes it difficult to anticipate in specific states or localities exactly how, and with what effect, the representation process will work. The combinations contrasted here provide a base to help form expectations about the effects of the representation process.

The Difficulty of Forming Expectations
of the Impact of Different Processes

If political processes differ then we might expect that these differences will affect which concerns politicians hear about and pay attention to, and which constituents they worry about. If the haves are faring better in the representation process, we would expect politicians to listen more to their concerns and to worry about responding to them. If the have-nots fare well in the representation process, we would expect their policy concerns to receive more attention when decisions are made.

Although we may be able to form expectations about such differences, it is not always easy to detect them. The problem we face is that it is difficult to acquire evidence about what politicians are thinking. Politicians are generally reluctant to reveal their thoughts about such matters.

As a result, we are generally forced to *infer* from their behavior, and their policy choices, whom they pay attention to. If there are differences in the representation of the haves and the have-nots, then those differences should affect which policies are adopted and what resources are committed to different programs. If the have-nots do not fare as well in representation, the commitment of resources to programs beneficial to them should be less.

To make this kind of assessment, we first classify certain policy commitments (progressive and higher taxes, more funding for food stamps, higher welfare benefits, public housing subsidies, redistributive school-aid programs, more higher-education funding for the less affluent) as more beneficial to the have-nots than to the haves. The have-nots are the recipients of such programs, and the haves pay the bulk of the costs of these programs. We should see higher levels of resource commitments to these policies in states where the have-nots achieve better representation. These differences between states should persist over time if there are enduring differences in whom the representation process favors.

Figure 8.1 presents an illustration of the policy differences that would emerge under these conditions. The lines represent the level of some policy such as tax effort. We assume that for the have-nots to do well, tax effort must be higher to create the ability to establish more programs. In situation A, the have-nots do not do well in the representation process, and tax effort is lower. Situation B is one where they do better, and tax effort is higher.

The next section examines the evidence that we have about these theoretical expectations. There are not as many comprehensive studies as we might wish. There are few studies that try to assess the cumulative effect of party systems, participation patterns, interest groups, and the role of the media. It is a very demanding task to capture all of these phenomena in even one state or locality over any period of time. To do all this for several states or cities is even more difficult. Much of our information is based on research involving only parts of the political process. Despite these limitations, the evidence that we do have provides some valuable insights.

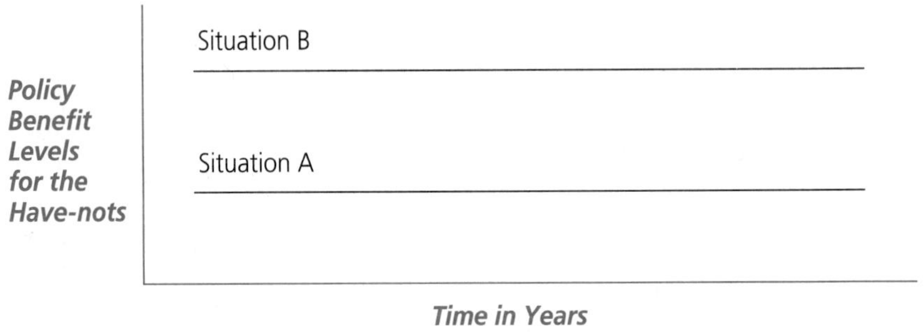

Situation B
_____

*Policy
Benefit
Levels
for the
Have-nots*

Situation A
_____

Time in Years

Figure 8.1
The Effects of Differences in Representation

Whose Concerns Get Attention: Evidence from the States

The Effects of Participation

Participation is of fundamental importance in the representation process. The issue of who votes and who does not vote matters in a democracy, and it affects how groups are treated. To find the effects of differences in voting, it is first necessary to find situations in which significant differences in participation between groups exist. We need a situation in which lower-class turnout is much less than upper-class turnout. We also need to find a contrasting situation in which the differentials in voting by class are very limited. Then, in comparing these two situations, we need to examine carefully the issues presented by politicians as their concerns and the issues that become the objects of debates among politicians.

Changes in Black Registration

Changes in black registration provide situations where we can assess the effects of differences in voting. Black involvement in politics in the South has changed considerably in recent decades. As reviewed in Chapter 6, from the mid-1960s to the late 1970s, black registration and voting changed from being virtually prohibited to reaching levels very close to that of whites. As a result, the composition of the electorate in the South changed dramatically. This change should have affected the level of attention devoted to concerns of blacks and whites.

As the registration rates of blacks increased, their electoral importance increased. In a democracy, electoral importance breeds respect among politicians fairly quickly. As Andrew Young, a black southern politician, put it:

> It used to be Southern politics was just "nigger" politics, who could "outnigger" the other—then you registered 10 to 15 percent in the community and folk would start saying "Nigra," and then you get 35 to 40 percent registered and its amazing how quickly they learned to say "Nee-grow," and now that we've got 50, 60, 70 percent of the Black

votes registered in the South, everybody's proud to be associated with their Black brothers and sisters.[1]

This dramatic rise in participation by blacks did more than just change the respect accorded them. It also changed the themes that dominated southern elections. Politicians had to respond to a (new) group that was not doing well economically. This group wanted job development in the South so that they would have a chance to improve their standard of living. This increase in black registration also meant that conservative whites no longer dominated the electorate and that their concerns should no longer have dominated political debates. A study by Earl Black indicates just how much change can take place when the composition of the electorate changes. He tracked the content of southern gubernatorial campaigns during this time of transition.[2] Earl Black examined the campaign stances and appeals of southern gubernatorial candidates from 1960 to 1969 (when the major changes in registration were taking place) for the positions they took on segregation. He classified governors as militant segregationists (who were completely or strongly opposed to allowing integration), moderate segregationists (who were opposed to integration, but did not wish to make it a major issue of the campaign or to fight a court decision that ruled against segregation), and nonsegregationists (who avoided the issue, giving no support to segregationist views, perhaps even welcoming black support). He then grouped the candidates who won (since his concern was the circumstances that surrounded being able to win an election) by the black-white differences in registration rates for that state. If blacks were registered at 30 percent and whites at 70 percent, the difference in registration rates would be 40 points. If registration rates were about the same, the differences would be close to 0. Table 8.2 groups gubernatorial campaigns by stance on segregationist issues and

---

Table 8.2

Southern Gubernatorial Campaign Stances on Racial Segregation and Differences between White and Black Registration Rates, 1960–1969

Differences between Black-White Registration Rates			
Segregationist Position during Campaign	**High (%)**	**Medium (%)**	**Low (%)**
Militant	70	27	10
Moderate	20	55	0
None	10	18	90
Number of campaigns	10	11	10

Note: Definitions of differences: High equals 30 percentage points or more; medium equals 15–29.9, low equals fewer than 15 percentage points. Percents sum down. Each column presents the percent of campaigns in which the winner took a militant stance, a moderate stance, or no stance on the issue.
Source: Earl Black, "Southern Governors and Political Change: Campaign Stances on Racial Segregation and Economic Development, 1950–69," Journal of Politics 33 (August 1971): 703–734.

by whether those campaigns took place in situations with high, medium, or low differences in registration rates.

The important matter is the way campaign stances varied as the registration advantage of whites declined. When whites registered at much higher rates than blacks, 70 percent of winning candidates took strong segregationist stances, and segregation concerns dominated those campaigns. When the differences in registration rates were low, 90 percent of the candidates took nonsegregationist positions. In these situations, blacks received more attention, and campaign support for segregationist positions declined. As registration varied, campaign debates varied accordingly. Candidates responded to changes in the composition of the electorate by changing the issues they emphasized.

The effects of increased black registration did not stop with the kinds of concerns discussed. The kinds of policies adopted also changed. As the composition of the electorate changed, counties in the South that had resisted providing social programs for blacks began to provide them.[3] These changes in registration in the 1960s did change the concerns that were discussed during campaigns, and it changed the policies adopted by politicians. The overall change was particularly important to those whose concerns and needs had been neglected, the have-nots.

The Entrance of Women

The addition of women to the electorate provides another example of how a significant change in political involvement by a particular group changed the concerns of politicians. With the ratification of the Nineteenth Amendment to the Constitution in 1920, women obtained the right to vote. As a result of the registration of women, the political parties devoted considerable effort to recruiting women to their side. They appointed women to political positions and worked to pass laws that protected the rights of women. The eventual impact of this amendment proved to be less than expected because a high percentage of women did not register. Women were not as active in politics as expected, but their initial entrance did create much greater concern among politicians about issues important to women.[4]

Summary

These examples indicate the ways in which representation can change attention to groups in society. We also have systematic evidence—across the states—of the effects of low participation. The lower class, in general, is underrepresented relative to the affluent. Underrepresentation varies across states, and these variations have an impact. The evidence indicates that states with greater underrepresentation of the lower class have lower welfare and medicaid benefits. States where such underrepresentation is less have higher benefits for these programs.[5]

The Effects of Parties and Process

Political parties can play an important role in affecting whose interests dominate political agendas. If parties have clear electoral bases and play a central role in decision making, they serve as vehicles to make sure the interests of their constituents are heard. We can see the ways parties affect the concerns that dominate agendas in several situations.

Democrats and Issue Advocacy

We can see evidence of the effect of political parties when party control in a single state changes hands. In New Jersey, the Democrats held the governor's office and the legislature in 1990 and 1991. During that time one of their primary concerns was responding to rising local taxes and inequities in school expenditures across the state. The party made these concerns central to policy debates. After the 1993 elections, Republicans held both the legislature and the governor's office. Their agenda reflected their sense of their own constituency. They focused on tax cuts and lowering expenditures.[6] Democrats, of course, criticized the tax cuts on the grounds that those cuts would result in less revenue for state aid to schools to address inequities.

What is important for the representation process is the way the Democrats in New Jersey shaped the debate that emerged, and the issues that dominated agendas. Regardless of who controlled government, Democrats continued to serve as advocates for their own constituency. Battles went back and forth over redistribution versus tax cuts, with the Democrats keeping the issue of inequality high on the agenda. The Democrats lost control of the legislature after 1991 elections and lost the gubernatorial election in 1993, but their actions had placed issues on the agenda that would otherwise have been ignored.

Parties and Process: Two Examples

The role of political parties is also affected by the way the process works. Sometimes the political process allocates them a significant role, and sometimes it does not. A comparison of the ways New York and California handled debates about tax levels illustrates this. Taxes rose in most states from the 1960s to the 1970s. Those increases led to considerable complaints about rising tax levels. In New York and California, this led to efforts to cut taxes. In both states, those seeking cuts sought to make this issue a priority in the political process. The decision-making processes in the states, however, differed. This difference affected how the issue was handled and how effectively the have-nots were able to make their argument during the process of deciding on tax issues.[7]

In New York, the issue was handled through negotiations between parties in the legislature. The issue was initially pressed by the Republicans, who controlled the senate. The Democrats, who controlled the assembly, felt compelled to respond to the issue because the state was losing jobs and because critics were blaming this loss on high taxes. Democrats did not want to be blamed for not responding to a problem. The Democrats, however, also wanted to protect their constituency base in urban areas during any process of change. Their constituency made less money and were less capable of paying taxes, at least in the eyes of the Democrats. The Democrats argued long and hard for the importance of equity considerations as a part of any change. Democrats, then, played a vital role in representing the interests of their constituents. As a consequence of their focus and cohesion, they were able to negotiate an even greater reduction in tax rates for lower-income individuals as a part of a general reduction in taxes. They gave the Republicans some of what they wanted—lower overall rates—but they also got something for their own constituency. In this case, the Democratic legislative party played a crucial role in making sure the interests of the lower and working classes were considered.

In California, the process of change was very different, and this difference affected the ability of lower-income interests to be a part of the debate about taxes. California law provides for making decisions by initiative and referendum. Citizen groups can get an issue on the ballot by collecting a specified number of signatures. The initiative is then voted on by the general public. In California, this process was used during the late 1970s and 1980s to put proposals on the ballot to cut property taxes and income taxes. These cuts were generally more beneficial to the affluent.

Although the initiative process has the potential to be equally accessible to all groups, it tends to be more amenable to use by well financed groups and those of upper socioeconomic status. It takes money to pay to have petitions gathered. It takes money to create and distribute brochures, and to create and pay for television and radio ads. The need for funding makes it difficult for lower-income interests to be able to participate in this public debate. Lower-income groups are also less likely to vote on such issues because these issues are difficult to follow. In California, several of these initiatives to cut taxes passed, and they resulted in far fewer resources for government and a more regressive tax system. These debates and changes bypassed the legislature because the initiative process does not require legislative involvement. Use of a decision-making process in which legislative parties were excluded resulted in less representation of lower-income groups and proved detrimental to their interests.

Whose Concerns Get Attention: Evidence from Local Politics

Differences in Participation and Involvement

Just as changes in political involvement have changed state agendas, changes in who participates in local politics have shaped local concerns. In the past, ethnic groups, such as the Italians and the Irish, increased their involvement in local politics and found that the attention to their concerns increased. This attention can vary from symbolic responses, such as appointments to office, to serious responses to their concerns about the right to participate in American society.[8]

The rise of black participation has also increased the attention to local black concerns. Studies of southern cities indicate much more concern for black issues after the Civil Rights movement increased black registration and voting.[9] The same transition is now under way for the gay population in many cities. During the 1980s, the gay population in cities like San Francisco, Houston, and New York City became more politically active. Once those groups demonstrated that they were capable of acting as a relatively cohesive electoral group, politicians began to take them seriously and to sponsor legislation to protect their rights to housing and jobs.

The Role of Structure and Process

While participation itself matters, this participation takes place within specific electoral and decision-making arrangements. Such arrangements can thwart or help a group. The weakness or strength of local political parties and the effects of party reform are particularly important.

Reform in Atlanta

In a study of Atlanta, Clarence Stone found a pattern in which the black population had a difficult time getting politicians to listen to their concerns.[10] He focused on urban renewal and building public housing. The former was a matter of high priority to the middle class and the business segments of the community. They wanted slums torn down, and they wanted civic projects (a stadium and a general performing-arts center, for example) built in their place. The black community was more concerned with the building and placement of public housing.

The political process in Atlanta had been largely reformed, with weak political parties. City council members could live anywhere, but they had to run in designated districts. The parties did little to mobilize voters, and most council members lived in middle- and upper-class neighborhoods. This situation meant that blacks had no representatives in government. Blacks were not a significant proportion of the registered electorate, and they also had no well-developed local groups to press their demands to the mayor. The local papers only sporadically raised the issue of the treatment of the lower class in the process of urban renewal. Mayors who were elected were generally sympathetic to the interests of the middle class and business (as should be expected, given their electoral base), and they were generally convinced that urban renewal should receive top priority. The mayors tended to pay much more attention to the well-organized interest groups of their constituents and saw those concerns as the most prominent on the city agenda.

The formal structure of local government contributed to stifling the representation of the conflict that existed in the city. The concerns of the low-income groups got less attention because of the way representation worked. Atlanta presents an example of why structure matters.

Comparing Representation across Cities

We also have broader evidence of the effects of formal political arrangements across local governments. Cities vary in their use of partisan labels in elections. This variation should affect the outcomes of the representation process. One way to assess this effect is to examine concurrence at the city level. Concurrence is defined as the extent of agreement between decision makers and the public about which issues are regarded as important. In general, we place our faith in politics as the means to achieve concurrence. Not everyone agrees with that approach. As discussed earlier, many reform groups have been uneasy about this faith in politicians. In particular, reformers have often argued that politicians are too wrapped up in partisan positions and political maneuvering to gain an objective sense of the concerns of the public. Politicians may know the views of the groups that elected them, but they are unlikely to know the views of other groups.

Reformers believe that changing political structures would improve political behaviors. Changing from ward to at-large elections for example, would make politicians think about what is good for everyone, rather than just what is good for their particular neighborhoods. Reformers have pursued such concerns most effectively at the local level, and it is at that level that there are interesting variations in political conditions. Susan Hansen was interested in whether differences in political arrangements affect the extent to which politicians and the public agree about what the important issues are. She constructed an index of concurrence for local governments. She did this by asking the public what the major problems of the area were, and then asking heads of local government the same question.[11] The more heads of government who agreed with the public, the higher the index of concurrence. Hansen then compared the concurrence scores for different kinds of political arrangements. The results of one of her comparisons are shown in Table 8.3.

The reformers want to play down partisan politics. Some also want to remove decision makers from direct connections with the electorate so that they would have more freedom to make the "right" decisions. But Hansen's results show that the degree of concurrence is higher when elections are partisan, and the politician must appeal directly to the public. Furthermore, she found that concurrence was highest when there were frequently contested elections with high public turnout. These findings suggest that the process of partisan politics, with officials appealing to the public, produces more concurrence than a political process that is less partisan and somewhat more removed from the public.

Table 8.3

Political Structure and Concurrence between the Public and Heads of Local Government

Political Structure	Average Concurrence Score
Political arrangement	
Partisan elections	22.4
Nonpartisan	16.2
Method of election of all local executives	
Direct (by popular vote)	19.6
Indirect (chosen by membership of elected council)	11.4
Method of electing mayors only	
Direct	21.8
Indirect	11.5

Note: Maximum scores equal 100, meaning leaders and the public were in complete agreement.
Source: Susan B. Hansen, "Participation, Political Structure, and Concurrence," American Political Science Review 69, no. 4 (December 1975): 1188.

What Policies Are Enacted: Evidence from the States

Key argued that political parties are the most important source of representation for the have-nots. Parties bring together people and politicians with similar concerns. Party politicians act to represent specific groups of people. Elected officials from the party can enact policies favorable to their constituents. Much recent research has focused on trying to understand the impact of parties on policy levels in the states. It is also in this area that the greatest research frustrations have occurred. Scholars generally presume that parties affect the policies enacted. But the evidence about their effect is very mixed.

The difficulty with relying on existing research to understand the role of parties is that there are disputes over the validity of much of the research conducted. The problem for scholars in this field is that we rarely have sufficient information about the electoral bases and the cohesion of parties. Researchers generally must *assume* that Republicans are different from Democrats, that Republicans are conservative, and that all Republicans share essentially the same views. They must *assume* that Democrats are different from Republicans, that Democrats are more liberal than Republicans, and that all Democrats share essentially the same views. Early studies of the role of parties made these assumptions and presumed that the closer the total vote proportions for Democrats and Republicans in a state, the greater and more focused the competition between Democrats and Republicans. It was assumed that greater party competition reflected a clear political debate between two parties with different agendas and that this debate produced more benefits for the lower class. Numerous studies have been conducted based on these assumptions. The results, however, did not suggest much of an impact due to party competition.[12]

As discussed in Chapter 5, all these assumptions are very questionable.[13] This approach to research involves *assuming* situations rather than *examining* states to see what conditions exist. Accepting the problems with assuming these conditions has come reluctantly. As two scholars of state politics, who have struggled with trying to measure the impact of parties, put it:

> Scholars of state politics may have to face the fact that it is next to impossible to study the impacts of political parties on public policies in either longitudinal [over time] or cross-sectional [across states at one time] quantitative research that relies on the standard measures [using just the information] of which party controls the various institutions of government. The detailed information necessary to understand the nature of the party or parties that control a state's government may not be feasible to collect in any large sample.[14]

The alternative has been to turn to case studies. Case studies of one, two, or several states make it possible to acquire information about the electoral bases, political agendas, and cohesion of political parties. It is also sometimes possible to assess participation patterns, the clout of interest groups, and other important political conditions. These studies provide some important evidence about the role of parties in shaping policy enactments.

Case Studies

Texas since 1950

Chandler Davidson conducted an analysis of Texas politics from the 1950s to the 1980s. He found that the representation process can affect whose interests get heard. He found significant differences in political needs by class within the state. Despite those differences, concerns of the working class (such as job safety) received limited attention because of the cumulative nature of the representation process. Unions were not strong, blacks and Hispanics voted at lower levels than Anglos, political contributions from the wealthy played a major role in campaigns, and the Democrats were struggling to sort out their electoral base amid conflict in Democratic primaries and the emergence of the Republican party. The representation process did not work to make the concerns of the working class a part of political debates, and there was less policy established to help them.[15]

New Hampshire and Vermont

Other studies have focused on comparing two states. As discussed in Chapter 1, New Hampshire and Vermont differ considerably in their tax efforts (see Figure 1.1). Winters found that in New Hampshire the actions of the editor William Loeb had made it difficult for anyone to discuss taxes.[16] In Vermont there had been no such intimidation of politicians who proposed raising taxes and providing more services. The consequence was that programs that required public expenditure got less attention and funding in New Hampshire, and tax effort has consistently been lower in New Hampshire. The state still plays less of a role in providing services in New Hampshire than in Vermont (see Table 4.6) and the heavy reliance on the property tax in New Hampshire results in a more regressive tax system in that state than in Vermont (see Table 4.9).

Louisiana and Virginia

Louisiana and Virginia provide another example of how states can differ.[17] From the 1930s through the 1960s Louisiana consistently enacted policies more favorable to the have-nots than did Virginia.

This difference stemmed from the relative political concern with class issues and policies in the two states during that era. In Louisiana, Huey Long made the issue of helping the poor a fundamental issue of political debate. He represented the liberal faction in the Democratic party at a time when all the political battles in the state took place in the Democratic party. By giving the poor so much emphasis, the Long faction mobilized groups who wanted more welfare and more education benefits. They also presented these groups with a set of policies that, if elected, they promised to implement. This faction made welfare benefits an issue that other politicians had to deal with.

In Virginia, a quite different situation prevailed from the 1930s to the 1960s. The state had a traditional political culture, which stressed that the elites should run politics. The Democratic party was dominated by a group headed by then Senator Harry Byrd. This group felt the primary obligation of government was simply to maintain existing conditions and to, above all else, operate on a "pay-as-you-go" basis. The party never pushed higher welfare benefits as a policy issue. In addition, most of the black population, which was poor and would have benefited from such policies, was excluded from the voter registration process. The interest groups of business and agriculture were well organized and adamantly pushed their shared concern that taxes and government expenditure not increase. The result was that in Virginia the issue of welfare programs was not prominent, and politicians felt little need to concern themselves with this issue.

In Louisiana, the Long faction derived much of its support from the lower and working classes, and, as a result, made class benefits a prominent issue. When an issue is prominent, more attention is given that policy area, and more politicians feel inclined to respond to the issue.

That increase in attention and politician response translates (roughly) into more policy. In this case, the difference in concern translated into a major differ-ence in expenditures in welfare between the two states. The differences in the two states for the 1930s through the 1960s are shown in Figure 8.2. This figure indicates "real" welfare (with the effects of inflation eliminated) per capita in the two states over time. Louisiana consistently spent more per person on welfare benefits for the have-nots because this concern was considered fundamental by the Long faction. This faction kept up intense scrutiny of actions by Long's opponents, the Reform faction. This scrutiny kept that group from cutting these benefits. Huey Long served as a spokesperson for working class concerns. In this case, a party (faction) with a clear electoral base pushed an issue and got more resources devoted to benefits that helped its constituency. In Virginia this advocacy group did not exist, and much less was spent on welfare benefits.

The Midwest

Situations in other states provide evidence of the ways differences in policy enact-ments can endure. John Fenton studied six states in the Midwest during the late 1950s and early 1960s.[18] Fenton found that in Wisconsin, Michigan, and Minnesota, the political system was organized around political parties that had very clear class differences. The Democratic party had a constituency that wanted more money devoted to lower- and working-class concerns and to welfare. The Republican party had a constituency generally more concerned with holding down taxes and keeping welfare expenditures low. These issues dominated campaigns and political argu-ments between the governor and the legislature. Issues such as public welfare pro-grams, education, and unemployment compensation generally were explicitly or implicitly a part of political dialogues.

On the other hand, in the states of Ohio, Indiana, and Illinois, there was much less stress on such issues in the political process. In those states, the parties tend-ed to organize around the more limited concerns of distributing government jobs to party supporters and obtaining benefits for politicians. In these states, the Demo-cratic party was usually fragmented and was not capable of organizing the lower and working class into a party opposing the Republicans. The political cultures of each state were also important to this situation. The southern parts of each state were settled by conservative southern Democrats who had migrated there after the Civil War. These Democrats were not sympathetic to providing welfare benefits, and

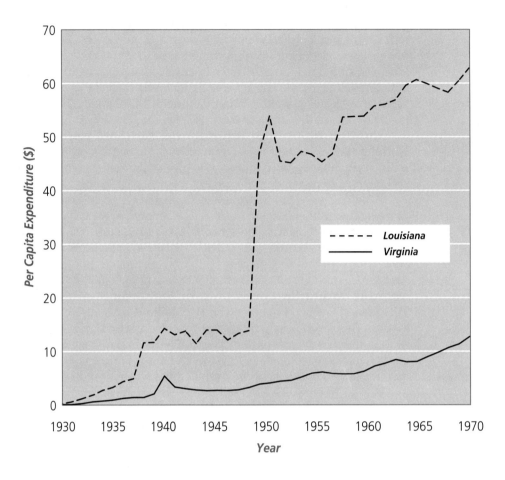

Figure 8.2

Per Capita Welfare Expenditures in Louisiana and Virginia, 1930–1969
Note: The numbers used are per capita welfare expenditures in each state for each year. They are determined by taking total welfare expenditure and dividing it by the total population of the state. The figures are then adjusted for inflation, or expressed in constant-purchasing-power dollars.

their influence made it difficult to create a cohesive party base with a clear focus on have-not issues.

The difference between these two groups of states is that in the first group, have-not issues were advocated by the Democratic party, while in the second group, no such advocacy occurred. More attention and resources were given to raising tax revenue in Minnesota, Wisconsin, and Michigan in order to provide welfare programs than was given to such programs in Ohio, Indiana and Illinois.[19]

That study was conducted over thirty years ago and examined policy in only one year. To see if these patterns have persisted, we need to examine more recent

data. Table 8.4 presents tax effort in the six states from 1953 to 1990. As noted earlier, tax effort is the amount of total taxes divided by the total income of the population. Tax effort indicates the willingness of politicians to take income from residents for government programs. The consistency of differences is impressive. The
states of Illinois, Indiana, and Ohio consistently have tax efforts below that of Minnesota, Wisconsin, and Michigan. There is no way to be certain that this continuity
of differences in tax effort is due entirely to the differences Fenton found. We need
another in-depth study to determine that. Despite that necessary caution, the continuing difference is intriguing. It suggests that some differences in political conditions may persist for some time.

Other Studies

Other researchers have found similar effects in different party systems. Jennings
explored the differences in party systems in several states over time and assessed
their effects on policy. He first classified states as to whether the parties were class-
based. He then compared welfare benefit levels in the class-based and non–class-
based states. The non–class-based state had welfare benefit levels considerably
below the other states.[20]

An analysis of New England states also found that in those states with parties
that had different electoral bases, welfare and unemployment benefits were higher
than in those states in which Democrats and Republicans had similar electoral
bases.[21]

Altering Party Bases

The situations reviewed thus far suggest fairly stable differences between states,
but states also experience change. Louisiana and Virginia provide an example of

---

Table 8.4

Tax Effort in Midwest States, 1953–1990

States	1953	1965	1981	1990
		Tax Effort		
Minnesota	9.38	12.72	12.00	13.00
Wisconsin	8.91	12.55	12.24	12.60
Michigan	7.31	10.67	11.57	11.80
Average	8.53	11.98	11.94	12.46
Illinois	6.37	8.89	11.05	10.90
Indiana	7.08	10.24	9.23	10.20
Ohio	5.87	8.64	9.20	10.90
Average	6.44	9.26	9.82	10.60

*Source: Advisory Commission on Intergovernmental Relations, Significant Features of Fiscal Federalism, 1981–1982
and 1991 eds.*

how change can occur. Virginia in particular has changed. Beginning in 1965, several changes occurred. The black population was given the right to vote by the Voting Rights Act of 1965. In 1960, the black population represented 10.3 percent of those actually voting. At that time, 23.1 percent of blacks and 46.1 percent of whites were registered. By 1982, 53.6 percent of blacks and 60.8 percent of whites were registered, and blacks constituted 17.6 percent of those voting, an increase of more than 5 percent. It is also likely that more poor whites registered to vote during this change.

The situation involving political parties also changed considerably. Democrat Mills Godwin, somewhat of a moderate, was elected to the governor's position in 1966. He was a more liberal Democrat than those elected previously. Most Democrats in Virginia had been conservative.[22] In 1970, Linwood Holton, a moderate Republican was elected governor. These two governors, and those who followed, recognized that the composition of the electorate was changing, and that the dominant issues were changing. They moved their parties' campaign positions to a more moderate stance, and they paid more attention to welfare needs and educational needs. By the end of the 1980s, Virginia's parties divided the electorate much as the national parties did.[23]

The change in the commitment to welfare benefits in Louisiana and Virginia during that time is shown in Figure 8.3.[24] Per capita (average) "real" welfare expenditure in the state increased enormously from the mid-1960s to the early 1970s. The change occurred because the workings of the political process thrust a previously buried issue to the forefront.

At the same time, class organization of the electorate was declining in Louisiana.[25] As discussed earlier, parties in the South experienced considerable change in party attachments beginning in the early 1960s, and this change disrupted the factional division that had existed in Louisiana. The consequence was that the pressure to do more for the lower class declined. Federal programs continued to provide aid for welfare programs, but the pressure to increase benefits was not as strong. By the early 1980s, the welfare expenditure in two states was not that dissimilar.

The change in Virginia provides an example of the consequences of a (new) segment of the population becoming politically active. Blacks desired public policies that were different from those desired by the population that had dominated the state until the 1960s. The change in composition of the electorate altered the "average" opinion in the state and made state and local politicians change their political response. The record of the South over the last thirty years presents the most dramatic example in our society of the way the issues that dominate politics can change as the composition of the electorate changes.

What Policies Are Enacted: Evidence from Local Politics

Most local-politics studies have focused on differences in cities at one particular time. Some of these studies have pursued the same questions as those asked in this text. That is, does the nature of the political process affect whose interests are

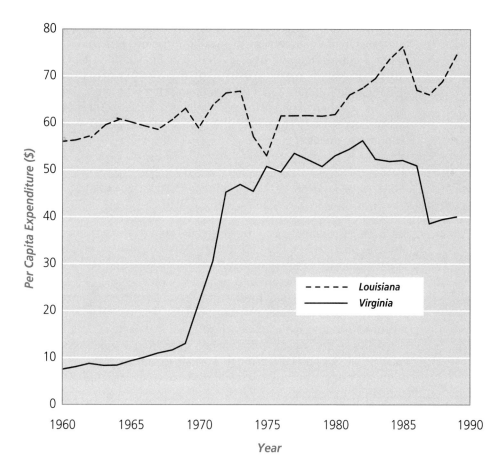

___
Figure 8.3

Per Capita Welfare Expenditures in Louisiana and Virginia, 1930–1969
Note: The numbers used are per capita welfare expenditures in each state for each year. They are determined by taking total welfare expenditure and dividing it by the total population of the state. The figures are then adjusted for inflation, or expressed in constant-purchasing-power dollars.

responded to and what policies are enacted? This question has particular relevance in comparing reformed and unreformed cities. Do cities with partisan and district elections tax and spend more than those without such political arrangements?

The evidence is that these differences do occur. In cities that deemphasize partisan elections, "organizing" the electorate is more difficult. In cities that elect council members at large, the representation of lower-class neighborhoods is likely to be diminished. In these cities, taxes and expenditures are lower, even after taking into account the differences in poverty across cities. If cities with similar proportions of poverty are compared, those with nonpartisan elections and at-large elections tax and spend less.[26]

There are few studies of cities across time. Those that exist indicate that increases in black involvement in southern cities resulted in more responsiveness to black concerns about housing and jobs, but that political response was still significantly affected by the dominant political culture. There was more resistance to such change in older cities with well-entrenched whites than in newer communities.[27] Though the change in policy concern in these cities did not involve variation in the degrees of reformism, the nature of the political process did affect the response to change.

Summary

Measuring the way that political systems convey the attitudes of the public into the political process is a difficult matter. Nonetheless, several things are clear. Variations in political involvement, in political parties, and in overall political processes affect the ability of groups to get their views articulated as part of the political process. The concerns of the lower class are registered more often when they participate heavily in politics. Lower-class groups, and other groups with low resources, do relatively better when a political party is organized around their concerns. These groups are helped when the media is vigilant in monitoring the influence of special-interest groups. Formal institutional arrangements and informal political conditions can also result in greater participation by them and representation of their concerns.

Well-to-do interests in our society have less trouble achieving representation. It usually takes a specific set of political conditions to offset those tendencies. As noted years ago by E. E. Schattschneider, politics is a game of "mobilizing biases," or of creating political arrangements that help some interests and harm others.[28]

For Further Reading

The following are examples of studies that focus on the way representation can affect the political agendas that emerge in state and local politics.

Black, Earl. *Southern Governors and Civil Rights: Racial Segregation as a Campaign Issue in the Second Reconstruction.* Cambridge: Harvard University Press, 1976.

Davidson, Chandler. *Race and Class in Texas Politics.* Princeton: Princeton University Press, 1990.

Dwyre, Diana, Mark O'Gorman, Jeffrey M. Stonecash, and Rosalie Young. "Disorganized Politics and The Have-Nots: Taxes and Politics in New York and California." *Polity* (1994).

Jennings, Edward T. "Some Policy Consequences of the Long Revolution and Bifactional Rivalry in Louisiana." *American Journal of Political Science* 21, no. 2 (May 1977): 225–46.

Stone, Clarence. *Economic Growth and Neighborhood Discontent*. Chapel Hill: University of North Carolina Press, 1976.

Winters, Richard. "Political Choice and Expenditure Change in New Hampshire and Vermont." *Polity* 12, no. 4 (summer 1980): 598–621.

Button, James W. *Blacks and Social Change*. Princeton: Princeton University Press, 1989.

Suggestions for Analysis in Your Own State and Locality

1. The sum of representation activities come together to affect the representation of different interests. In some political processes, party politicians will have very different electoral bases and represent different constituent concerns. In this situation, politicians will take different policy positions and create debates about different choices. In other settings, there will not be much difference in the concerns of politicians in opposing parties. Political debate will be fairly limited and a consensus may even appear to prevail.

    One way to see the effects of the representation process in a particular state or locality is to listen to what politicians talk about and what they advocate. What issues dominate exchanges between politicians? How much do politicians from opposing parties or groups disagree with each other?

    If you can find newspaper stories about politics in your state and locality, review the kinds of issues that are discussed, and the kinds of disagreements that emerge. Do Democrats take different positions from Republicans? Do Democrats agree with each other and disagree with Republicans in the policies they support and oppose? Or, is there little disagreement between the parties?

2. Newspaper stories may not always be a good guide to party policy because journalists may not devote much attention to reporting party differences even when they do exist. Another way to determine the way the parties differ is to ask politicians in each party. You might call the local state legislators, or members of the city or town council and ask them what they see as the differences between parties.

3. Finally, another way to assess the way the representation process is working is to examine the issues that dominate political debate. If liberal interests are dominating agendas, then the focus is likely to be on improving equal opportunity, on women's rights, on providing more school aid for low-income school districts. If conservative interests dominate, the focus is likely to be on welfare reform, on lowering taxes, on reducing the size of government, and on introducing more efficiency into government. What kind of issues have recently dominated public attention in your state and locality?

Notes

[1] Walter Bass and Jack DeVries, *The Transformation of Southern Politics*, 47.

[2] Earl Black, *Southern Governors and Civil Rights: Racial Segregation as a Campaign Issue in the Second Reconstruction* (Cambridge: Harvard University Press, 1976), 145–61.

[3] M. Elizabeth Sanders and Richard F. Bensel, "The Impact of the Voting Rights Act on Southern Welfare Systems, in Benjamin Ginsberg and Alan Stone, eds., *Do Elections Matters?* 2nd ed. (Armonk, New York: M.E. Sharpe, 1991), 96–114.

[4] J. Stanley Lemons, *The Woman Citizen: Social Feminism in the 1920s* (Urbana: University of Illinois Press, 1973), 63–116.

[5] Kim Hill and Jan Leighly, "The Policy Consequences of Class Bias in State Electorates," *American Journal of Political Science* 36, no. 2 (May 1992): 358–61.

[6] Jerry Gray, "GOP Plans on Surpluses to Make Up for Tax Cuts," *New York Times*, 1 February 1994, B5.

[7] Diana Dwyre, Mark O'Gorman, Jeffrey M. Stonecash, and Rosalie Young, "Disorganized Politics and The Have-Nots: Taxes and Politics in New York and California," *Polity*, 1994.

[8] Robert Dahl, *Who Governs: Democracy and Power in an American City* (New Haven: Yale University Press, 1966), 38; and Theodore J. Lowi, *At the Pleasure of the Mayor* (New York: Free Press, 1964).

[9] James W. Button, *Blacks and Social Change: Impact of the Civil Rights Movement in Southern Communities* (Princeton: Princeton University Press, 1989).

[10] Clarence Stone, *Economic Growth and Neighborhood Discontent* (Chapel Hill: University of North Carolina Press, 1976).

[11] Susan B. Hansen, "Participation, Political Structure, and Concurrence," *American Political Science Review* (December 1975).

[12] For examples of these studies, see Thomas R. Dye, *Politics, Economics, and the Public* (Chicago: Rand McNally, 1969); Michael S. Lewis-Beck, "The Relative Importance of Socioeconomic and Political Variables for Public Policy," *American Political Science Review* 71 (1977): 559–66; and Robert D. Plotnick and Richard F. Winters, "A Politicoeconomic Theory of Income Redistribution," *American Political Science Review* 79 (1985): 458–73.

[13] Jeffrey M. Stonecash, "Inter-Party Competition, Political Dialogue, and Public Policy: A Critical Review," *Policy Studies Journal* 16, no. 2 (winter 1987–1988): 243–62.

[14] Frances Stokes Berry and William D. Berry, "Tax Innovation in the States: Capitalizing on Political Opportunity," *American Journal of Political Science* 36, no. 3 (August 1992): 735.

[15] Chandler Davidson, *Race and Class in Texas Politics* (Princeton: Princeton University Press, 1990).

[16] Richard Winters, "Political Choice and Expenditure Change in New Hampshire and Vermont," *Polity* 12, no. 4 (summer, 1980): 598–621.

[17] Edward T. Jennings, "Some Policy Consequences of the Long Revolution and Bifactional Rivalry in Louisiana," *American Journal of Political Science* 21, no. 2 (May 1977): 225–46.

[18] John Fenton, *Midwest Politics* (New York: Holt, Rinehart and Winston, 1966).

[19] Ibid., 229–30.

[20] Edward T. Jennings, "Competition, Constituencies, and Welfare Politics in American States," *American Political Science Review* 73, no. 2 (June 1979): 419–21.

[21] Duane Lockard, *New England State Politics* (Princeton: Princeton University Press, 1959), 326–37.

[22] Alexander P. Lamis, *The Two-Party South* (New York: Oxford University Press, 1984), 146.

[23] Scott Keeter, "Virginia's Party System: from 'Museum Piece' to Mainstream," in Maureen Moakley, ed., *Party Realignment and State Politics* (Columbus: Ohio State University Press, 1992), 134–36.

[24] I wish to thank Edward T. Jennings, University of Kentucky, for letting me use his data on state welfare expenditures for this graph.

[25] Alexander P. Lamis, *The Two-Party South*, (New York: Oxford University Press, 1984), 108; and James Bolner, ed., *Louisiana Politics* (Baton Rouge: Louisiana State University Press, 1982).

[26] Robert L. Lineberry and Edmund P. Fowler, "Reformism and Public Policies in American Cities," *American Political Science Review* 61, no. 3 (September 1967): 701–716; and Paul D.

Schumaker and Russell W. Getter, "Responsiveness Bias in 51 American Communities," *American Journal of Political Science* 21, no. 2 (May 1977): 247–81. On the other hand, Gerald C. Wright finds very mixed evidence for this proposition. See "Linear Models for Evaluating Conditional Relationships," *American Journal of Political Science* 20, no. 2 (May 1976): 349–73.

[27] James W. Button, *Blacks and Social Change*, 206–41.

[28] E. E. Schattschneider, *The Semi-Sovereign People* (New York: Holt, Rinehart and Winston, 1961).

Overview *II*

Institutions and Decision Making

Political Control and Policy Impacts

Political Control and Expectations of Change

The representation process is ongoing; it never ends.[1] It shapes which interests dominate during policy debates. Who gets represented affects the long-term policy commitments of states and localities. Who wins and loses in the long run is of fundamental importance, but politics also revolves around short-term concerns. Elections determine which politicians win and acquire power. Those who acquire power must decide what agendas, if any, to pursue. Events and crises occur that no one expected. The economy changes. Those in power must decide if and how to respond to such events.

The question of the next several chapters is whether politicians do anything once they acquire power. Do politicians respond to their political constituencies in the subsequent public-policy decisions that politicians make? Is there a connection between elections and policy? Do politicians who promised changes deliver on those pledges? Do liberal Democrats pursue and enact liberal agendas? Do conservative Republicans pursue and enact conservative agendas?

Institutional Arrangements in American Democracy

Elections are often presumed to be of some consequence. But the acquisition of power may not bring about any change. Critics have expressed concern that elections and changes in control of government do not have much impact. They argue that politicians lack courage, that they are so interested in getting reelected that they wish to avoid tough decisions and controversy.[2] Government is paralyzed.[3] There may or may not be reluctance within the political process to pursue certain questions. We will address that issue in the following chapters.

But it is important to note that some of this paralysis is by design.[4] Most American government institutional arrangements are designed to make change difficult. Our system of government is built on a belief in having power divided among institutions.[5] In most state and local governments power is divided between executives and legislatures. Within state legislatures (except in the unicameral Nebraska legislature) power is further divided between two houses. Each body of government is elected directly by the people. Each body can claim a mandate from the people to make policy decisions. The institutional arrangement in the states that creates separation of powers is shown in Figure 1. Each body can act as a check on the ability of any other body of government to act without the agreement of others. If one institution balks, no policy changes can be made.

The courts can complicate the decision-making process even more. They retain the right to decide whether to intervene over questions of due process and of constitutionality of process and decisions.

This system of separation of power derives from a long-standing belief that in a democracy no single governmental body should have too much power. Numerous political actors must agree to a change before such change occurs. This arrangement restrains government and slows down the decision-making process. It creates an institutional situation in which change is difficult.

The separation-of-powers principle is also used in many general-purpose local governments. Many local governments have some form of an executive (mayor, county executive, or supervisor) and a legislature or council. The legislatures that exist in cities, counties, and local governments are all "one-house" legislative bodies. In cases where there is an executive and a legislative body, the names applied to the local government may vary, but the structure fits the separation-of-powers pattern. In these cases, any policies adopted must be accepted by both branches of government.

The specific form of this arrangement varies across local governments. Many cities have adopted the mayor-council form of government. In this arrangement, the mayor and the council members are separately elected. This arrangement conforms to the separation-of-powers structure. When the system is a strong-mayor form, the mayor is directly elected by the public and has control over administrative agencies. When it is a weak-mayor form, the mayor is often elected from the council by the existing council members, and the mayor does not directly control agencies.[6]

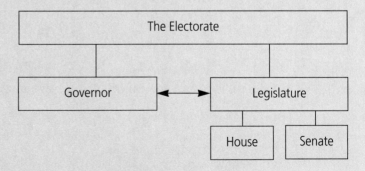

Figure 1
Separation of Powers: State Government

Counties have similar variations. Some counties have a county executive or supervisor and a county legislature. Each is separately elected by the public. If the county executive has the power to appoint agency heads and prepare a budget, this arrangement is a strong-executive form of government. If the executive does not have these powers, or if the executive is a supervisor elected by other supervisors, the arrangement is a weak-executive form of government. These "weak" forms of government involve minimal separation of powers, but there is some separation.

There are, however, very significant exceptions to this general pattern of separating and fragmenting power. At the state and local levels, many governments have established public authorities, or special-district governments. These agencies or boards are set up to handle policy in very specific (and limited) areas. The authority may be responsible for maintaining harbors, bridges, roads, and water systems. A board or individual presides over the authority. The agencies often raise very large sums of money through the fees that they charge for use of their facility or services. Many also may spend large sums of money.

The important matter is that these public authorities are generally set up to be free from political interference. Individuals are appointed to direct the authority. Their appointments are usually reviewed by the state legislature or a local legislature. Once they assume office, these executives are usually free from political accountability during their term of office. The presumption with these arrangements is that appointed individuals should handle policy problems without political interference. In these cases, appointees have no direct connection to the electorate, and there is generally no one to interfere with the decisions made. In some cases, the courts may be used to oppose a decision.

Many critics have argued that these organizations have too much power and that they make too many decisions and allocate too many resources without scrutiny.[7] They have control over many significant public-policy decisions and over large budgets, and there is continual debate about whether there should be more political control of them.

There is also a lack of separation in many local general-purpose governments. Many local governments have only one branch, and all power is consolidated in that branch. Some local governments—generally those over small populations—use the commission form of government. In this arrangement, commissioners are elected almost as council members, and each directly manages a department. This system was first created in Texas in 1900 to respond to a crisis. Efficiency and the ability to respond quickly were chosen over fragmentation. This arrangement was used in only 148 cities in 1992.[8]

The council-manager form of local government also creates less separation. The public elects the council, which in turn chooses a manager to execute decisions made by the council. There may be disagreements within the council, but there is no other elected body to restrain actions of the council. Figure 2 illustrates the nature of these arrangements. The public elects officials, but there is only one branch of government. The council then appoints a manager, who has direct control over local departments.

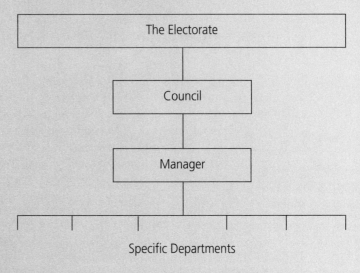

```
┌─────────────────────────────────────────┐
│               The Electorate              │
└─────────────────────────────────────────┘
                     │
            ┌─────────────────┐
            │     Council      │
            └─────────────────┘
                     │
            ┌─────────────────┐
            │     Manager      │
            └─────────────────┘
                     │
```

Specific Departments

Figure 2
Nonseparation of Powers: Council-Manager Form of Local Government

School districts also lack separation of powers. The school board is elected by the public, and there is no other branch to restrain action by the board.

With arrangements of nonseparation of powers, there is still a direct connection to the electorate with the commission and council-manager institutional arrangements, but there is no restraint on the ability of the legislative body to act once a majority is created. There has generally been a strong fear of such concentrations of power. The rationale for these cases of nonseparation of powers was that they would be more efficient. Many people regard local governments as more involved with technical policy administration and management, and they are more supportive of consolidations of power in such situations.

Questions About the Politics-Policy Connection

It is generally recognized that the commitment to the separation-of-powers principle makes it harder to change public policy. Critics of American politics are willing to acknowledge the impact of separation of powers, but they still have doubts about the connection between campaigns, elections, and policy choices. They are skeptical that politicians really stand for any clear policy commitments. As noted before, there is concern that legislators are too preoccupied with staying in office. They argue that parties are in decline, that campaigns are individual-centered affairs in which the emphasis is on character. Every politician is independent of others, and few of them are willing to work together.

Critics also argue that political decision making is so entangled with vested interests that nothing really happens when control of government changes hands. Even when politicians wish to make a change, it is virtually impossible to do so because of the strength of opposition to change. For all these reasons, there is considerable skepticism that campaigns and elections produce any changes. It is widely commented that "they all promise a lot but nothing really changes when they get into office." The implication is that elections are of little consequence, and who acquires power makes little difference.

The next several chapters will address these concerns. Does change occur when partisan control over government changes? We first need to consider each branch of government separately. Politicians in each institution form their own goals. Because of the separation-of-powers practice, we then need to consider the negotiations between the branches if we are to understand whether politicians can change policies when they acquire power. Changes emerge from combinations of political conditions.[9]

Two broad sets of conditions shape what politicians and institutions are likely to do: their priorities about what policies to pursue and their power to enact those policies. The first matter, their pursuits, are shaped by their beliefs, the electoral coalitions that put them in office, and their future ambitions.

But pursuing goals does not guarantee achievement of them. The second determinant of what politicians are likely to do is the extent of power (formal and informal) that they have to influence others. Does the constitution grant the governor the right to make certain decisions, or is that power shared with the legislature? Does the governor have the ability to use informal power to persuade others to follow? Is the majority party in the legislature capable of acting as a cohesive group to pursue its policy goals? These and many other conditions affect which actors dominate in the process.

Again, it is how these conditions combine in specific situations that shapes what happens. A governor may have clear and ambitious goals, but be completely constrained by the legislature and the condition of the economy. A governor may have a limited agenda but be prompted to make choices by a changing economy that legislators are very concerned about. The courts may force decisions that politicians would rather avoid.

The concerns of the following chapters will be to sort out how combinations of conditions affect what happens after elections are over or when events intrude upon politicians to pressure them to act. The concern is *if* and *how* representation concerns are translated into policy. As with the earlier chapters, the concern is not just whether anything happens, but whether constituency concerns are responded to when decisions are made. Do battles between the haves and the have-nots become part of policy decisions? If a governor campaigns on appeals to the have-nots and obtains a largely lower- to middle-class electoral base, does he or she pursue policies favorable to that constituency? If those goals are pursued, how do formal and informal power affect the ability to achieve those goals? If the majority party in a legislature is dominated by liberal-to-moderate interests, are members able to act cohesively to enact policies responsive to their constituency? Or do these electoral appeals and bases have little connection to policy once people acquire power?

Policy decisions result from interactions among executives, legislatures, and the courts. We begin this assessment with a focus on executives.

Notes

1. Benjamin Ginsberg and Martin Shefter, *Politics by Other Means* (New York: Basic Books, 1990).

2. Alan Ehrenhalt, *The United States of Ambition* (New York: New York Times Books, 1992).

3. This concern has been persistent in American politics. For examples, see James McGregor Burns, *The Deadlock of Democracy*, (Englewood Cliffs: Prentice-Hall, 1963) and John E. Chubb and Paul E. Peterson, *Can the Government Govern?* (Washington DC: Brookings Institute, 1989).

4. The importance of these principles is explained in James Madison, Federalist paper no. 47, in Isaac Kramnick, *The Federalist Papers* (New York: Penguin, 1987), 302–308; and David F. Epstein, *The Political Theory of the Federalist* (Chicago: University of Chicago Press, 1984), 126–146.

5. For a history of the debates that led to the separation-of-powers situations in the states, see Gordon S. Wood, *The Creation of the American Republic, 1776–1787* (New York: W. W. Norton, 1969), 138–159, 197–255.

6. Dennis R. Judd and Todd Swanstrom, *City Politics: Private Power and Public Policy* (New York: HarperCollins, 1994), 92–97.

7. For an excellent study of politics and the ways of structuring power in a democracy, see Robert Caro, *The Power Broker* (New York: Knopf, 1974).

8. John J. Harrigan, *Politics and Policy in States and Communities*, 5th ed. (New York: HarperCollins, 1994), 169.

9. Donald A. Gross, "The Policy Role of Governors," in Eric B. Herzik and Brent W. Brown, *Gubernatorial Leadership and State Policy* (Westport, Conn.: Greenwood, 1991), 10–11.

9

Executives and Policy Pursuits

PREVIEW

Governors and mayors have enormous potential to shape the public policy decisions that are made. They can define an agenda and use their influence to get legislators to adopt that agenda. The agendas that executives form are a product of their personal beliefs and of the electoral coalition that put them in office. As politicians, they must also decide whether they aspire to be reelected or to seek another office. Such aspirations affect the agenda they pursue.

Once an agenda has been settled upon, the ability to achieve that agenda is shaped by the formal power associated with the office. The informal power of an executive, the power to influence and persuade others, also affects their ability to have an impact.

It is the combination of formal and informal power that determines the impact a politician has. An executive with a clear agenda, but very little power, may achieve very little. An executive with no clear agenda may have significant power, but also achieve very little. To have an impact, an executive must have a clear agenda, significant power, and the desire and ability to exercise that power.

Governors and Mayors: Defining and Pursuing Agendas

Executives—governors and mayors—have the potential to play a very significant role in the political process. Political debates and decision making are messy and often hard to follow. They involve numerous public figures competing to express their views. Amid the disorder that exists, executives have the potential to provide a focal point and to lead. The person holding an executive position is presumed to be able to make things happen, to have some control over events, and to be able to provide leadership. The public focuses on the person occupying this position. This public attention gives executives the potential to bring coherence and leadership to public concerns. To take advantage of this potential, an executive needs some sort of agenda. It is necessary to focus public attention on some concerns, devoting less attention to others.

The agendas of politicians stem from, and are affected by, several factors. The relative impact of these factors is not always clear, but we know that together they shape the priorities that emerge. These factors are personal beliefs, the nature of the campaign, the electoral base of the candidate, the future ambitions of the individual, conditions while in office, and press portrayal of proposals.

Personal Beliefs

Governors and mayors come to office with their own beliefs, and these beliefs shape their policy choices. Politicians come from all kinds of backgrounds, but backgrounds do not always determine what people believe.[1] What is important are the beliefs they hold. Most politicians form strong beliefs about the proper role of government in society, the role of individual responsibility, the possible solutions to problems, and many other issues. These beliefs do not go away once a politician is in office. It may appear that politicians are always calculating how to change their policy stances to look better to the public, but most also have concern for doing what they believe is the "right" thing. Some have more concern for this than others, but this concern seems to play some role for most of them. During the civil-rights turmoil and transition in the South in the 1960s, for example, some governors, such as Fritz Hollings of South Carolina, tried to moderate the intensity of racial hostilities. Hollings felt it was his duty to maintain some order during a time of stressful change.[2]

Each politician brings his or her own beliefs to office. Some are liberals. Jim Florio, former governor of New Jersey, came to office with a long record of commitment to liberal policy positions. That commitment did not change when he got into office, and it affected how he reacted to events. Ronald Reagan held strong conservative beliefs before he became governor of California in the 1960s, and those beliefs stayed with him when he became president. Others come in as moderates and take that approach to policy issues. Politicians may calculate how to modify their positions to survive politically, but they start with their own beliefs, and those beliefs affect their reactions to events that occur while they hold office.

The Nature of the Campaign

To become governor or mayor, an individual usually must first run a campaign and win an election. The campaign process involves raising enough money to run the campaign and making commitments to various groups in order to win their votes. Those financial obligations and policy commitments do not go away once power is acquired, and they may shape what policies executives pursue.

Campaigns are expensive. Gubernatorial campaigns regularly cost several million dollars, and, in states like California and Texas, candidates have spent a combined total of $30,000,000.[3] Mayoral campaigns, even in medium-sized cities, can cost $500,000. We suspect that donations from major groups, such as real-estate interests, labor unions, and teachers, create obligations. The difficulty with understanding the role of campaign finance, however, is that many times the commitment of the candidate to a group has been made before the question of funding arises. In addition, many groups contribute to a candidate because they think that candidate is the one most sympathetic, or perhaps least hostile, to their concerns. Regardless, candidate policy inclinations may precede contribution patterns. This possibility means that we cannot assume that large contributions always cause or create policy obligations for a candidate.

While the influence of money may not be entirely clear, the impact of electoral blocs in campaigns seems more certain. Candidates need to build coalitions to win. That process means making policy commitments, either explicitly, or with vague assurances of concern about particular groups. Conservatives may make strong statements about the importance of reducing taxes in order to appeal to the middle class, who feel taxes are too high. Liberals may promise to do something about inequality of opportunity and poverty in order to appeal to lower-income groups. Campaign stances create support among some electoral groups and diminish support among other groups.[4] Even when events change, it is difficult for an to elected official to walk away from the commitments made to groups during the campaign. A Democrat may need the support of labor unions, teachers' unions, and public-employee unions. Campaign promises to be sympathetic to those groups create subsequent policy obligations to them and shape political agendas. These promises create inclinations to support legislation for the groups that supported the candidate.

Electoral Bases: Governors

Once in office, every politician must assess how he or she got there and where to go in the future. The result of that assessment affects the position that a politician takes on policy issues. Some governors and mayors win with a largely conservative-to-moderate constituency because they express beliefs compatible with that constituency and are personally inclined to approach policy from that perspective. For many executives, this compatibility between their constituency and their personal beliefs is probably very simple. Liberal Democrats do well in liberal areas and focus on the concerns of that constituency. Conservative Republicans do well in conservative areas and focus on the concerns of that constituency.

Tables 9.1 and 9.2 present examples of the way electoral bases coincide with the concerns of candidates. Census data and the results of gubernatorial elections are available at the county level. These data can be used to determine the percent of each county that is urban, nonwhite, or below the poverty level. In Tables 9.1 and 9.2, these

Table 9.1

Electoral Bases of Winning Governors: Percent of Vote Won by County and Characteristics of Counties

Urban	Nonwhite	Proportion (%) New York, 1990 Election Cuomo Vote	Cuomo's Total Vote
0–49	4	35	9.1
50–69	7	42	5.0
70–89	10	51	15.9
90+	31	62	70.0

Urban	Nonwhite	New Jersey, 1989 Election Florio Vote	Florio's Total Vote
0–49	3	42	2.1
50–69	9	55	2.9
70–89	16	60	29.8
90+	25	64	65.2

Urban	Nonwhite	California, 1990 Election Wilson Vote	Wilson's Total Vote
0–49	10	54	2.6
50–69	21	55	3.8
70–89	23	51	18.6
90+	29	46	75.0

Source: America Votes *Various Years;* and 1990 census reports.

Table 9.2

Electoral Bases of Winning Governors: Percent of Vote Won by Counties and Characteristics of Counties

		Proportion (%) Connecticut, 1990 Election	
Won by Dukakis, 1988	*Weicker Vote*	*Vote for Republican Candidate*	*Vote for Democratic Candidate*
0–39	32	52	16
40–49	44	33	21
50+	50	27	21

		Texas, 1990 Election	
Nonwhite	*Richards Vote*	*Poverty*	*Richards Total Vote*
0–7	41	14	3.6
8–15	46	17	10.3
16–23	48	19	26.8
24+	50	21	59.2

		Florida, 1990 Election	
Nonwhite	*Chiles Vote*	*Poverty*	*Chiles Total Vote*
0–7	52	14	8.3
8–15	53	16	38.2
16–23	56	20	29.4
24+	61	23	24.0

Source: America Votes *Various Years; and 1990 census reports.*

data were used first to classify counties according to the percent urban and the percent nonwhite. Table 9.1 presents data from three different gubernatorial elections in three different states. The vote for the winning candidate is broken down by counties grouped by percent of urban population. The percent of nonwhite population for each grouping is presented in the second column. The third column gives the percent of the vote the winner received in each grouping. The final column gives the percent of the overall vote for the winner coming from each grouping.

In 1990, Mario Cuomo, essentially a liberal Democrat, won his third term as governor of New York. The differences by areas in votes he won indicate his primary bases of support. He won his highest percent of the vote (62) in the heavily urban areas of the state. Those areas also have a high proportion of nonwhites. He received his lowest percent of the vote (35) in the upstate rural areas, which have low proportions of nonwhites and tend to be conservative.[5] The column on the right in Table 9.1 indicates the proportion of Cuomo's total vote that came from each area. He got 70 percent of his vote from heavily urban, nonwhite counties. These areas formed his primary electoral base.

In New Jersey, James Florio, another fairly liberal Democrat, had a similar pattern in his 1989 election. He also did very well in urban, nonwhite areas and received the bulk of his electoral support from those areas. In both these cases, the candidates had reputations of being relatively liberal. Their support was high in urban areas where the presence of nonwhites and the level of poverty were also greater. Their support dropped off significantly in more rural, predominantly white areas. When candidates take clear positions, they are likely to do well in areas sympathetic to those concerns and drive away those in areas not sympathetic to their concerns.[6]

Republican Pete Wilson, who ran as a moderate in 1990, faced a different situation. Most of the population in California lives in urban areas, and much, but not all, of that population is liberal. To win, he had to avoid losing badly in urban areas. He took moderate positions and was able to do reasonably well in traditionally Democratic urban areas. He was able to win 46 percent of the vote in heavily urban, nonwhite areas. A moderate can win by reducing the loss of votes in normally hostile areas. Not only was Wilson able to reduce that loss in urban areas, but he eventually drew most of his electoral base from those areas.

Situations can more complicated. In Connecticut, Lowell Weicker ran as an independent gubernatorial candidate. He had been a liberal Republican U.S. Senator for a number of years. Where and in which areas did he do well? Table 9.2 presents the 1990 results for Weicker by the way areas voted for Dukakis, the Democratic presidential candidate, in 1988. Weicker got his strongest vote in 1990 in areas that had voted heavily for Dukakis in 1988. Since Weicker had been developing a reputation as a liberal over the years, his appeal in liberal areas made sense.[7] The table also presents how the other two candidates did. The Democratic candidate did not experience an increase in votes as Dukakis' vote increased, indicating that Weicker probably pulled that vote away from the Democratic candidate.

Electoral situations in southern states differ from those in the North and the West. In many southern states, much of the nonwhite population, which usually votes Democrat, lives in rural areas. If a Democrat appeals to nonwhites, the sources of electoral support for that Democrat will not be in urban, but in rural areas. Many whites with long-standing attachments to the Democratic party also live in rural areas. This point is relevant in understanding electoral bases of governors in Texas and Florida. Table 9.2 presents the results from the 1990 gubernatorial elections in Texas and Florida. Governor Ann Richards of Texas, with a reputation as a relatively liberal Democrat, ran against a conservative Republican.[8] She won, and the relative success she had by area shows her base of support. She got her greatest support in areas with high proportions of nonwhites and individuals living below the poverty line. In Florida, Lawton Chiles, a Democrat who won by a larger proportion than Richards, had a similar pattern of support. The difference was that his support was more diverse and he received considerable levels of support all across the state. The race in Texas polarized the electorate. This polarization did not occur in Florida.

These cases present fairly clear situations. Liberals do well in urban areas or areas with large nonwhite populations. Moderates generally do well across all groups. But this is not always the case. Candidates often pursue and achieve electoral bases different from the typical base for a Democrat or Republican. A Republican may conclude there are not enough registered Republicans to run as a typical Republican and move to the middle to try to do well in liberal areas as a means to winning.[9] Likewise, a Democrat may have to do well in conservative areas to win. This necessity may reduce the clarity of electoral bases for candidates. It is not uncommon to have campaigns where there are limited differences between the candidates and where the electoral divisions between the candidates are also limited. Winners may not come to office with clear mandates. Such a situation makes it difficult to anticipate the policy positions a governor or mayor will support while in office. Politics then becomes less predictable, and we must devote more attention to determining electoral bases and not assume their nature.[10]

Regardless of what happens, winning candidates must interpret elections. They must make a connection between what they argued for during the campaign, who voted for them, and the policies they should pursue. Ronald Reagan was elected in California in 1966 on a promise to cut government, and he saw that as his mission.[11] In 1982, Richard Celeste ran for governor of Ohio (a state with chronic budget deficit problems at that time) with a campaign theme that he would not rule out raising taxes as a way to solve problems. He interpreted his election as giving him that option to deal with the fiscal situation of the state. These connections are not always clear, but candidates do seek to discern them.

Electoral Bases: Mayors

Mayors face the same political realities as governors. As candidates, they decide what groups they want to appeal to in order to get elected. Once elected, they must determine who voted for them and whether there is a sufficiently clear connection to pursue policies that respond to those groups. Harold Washington was elected mayor in Chicago in 1983 on a platform of "good government" and of reform of the political machine. He interpreted the election results to indicate that he had support for that platform. Ed Koch won mayoral elections in New York City in 1981 and 1985 with conservative appeals to whites, and he pursued policies favorable to those groups after those elections.[12]

In the early 1990s, many Republicans were elected as mayors in cities such as Los Angeles and New York City.[13] These cities are generally held by Democrats. The Republicans were able to build electoral coalitions by appealing to concerns about efficiency in managing government, crime, and "deviant" behavior. They were able to get elected by winning the votes of moderates and conservatives worried about these issues.

Rudy Guliani, elected as the Republican mayor of New York City in 1993, illustrates how coalitions and campaign themes can translate into agendas. His campaign focused on better management of government and on crime problems. He received no support from labor unions. When he proposed his first budget, he proposed significant increases in expenditures on police and cuts in social services and schools. He also proposed significant cutbacks in union employment unless he received concessions from unions to make the workforce more productive.[14]

The Role of Future Ambitions

Politicians are driven by more than past electoral coalitions. The future is also relevant. Many executives want to, and do, run for reelection.[15] This concern for reelection has increased in recent years because more state laws have been changed to allow governors to run for reelection. Table 9.3 presents the number of governors prohibited from seeking reelection, the number who could run for one more term, and those who could run for an unlimited number of terms for 1960, 1982, and 1992. Over the last thirty years, the number who are allowed to run for more than one term has greatly increased.[16] Many governors have taken advantage of these changes to seek and win reelection for several terms.[17]

Running for reelection affects agenda formation. Governors or mayors who want to run for reelection or for another office have to think about how to position themselves for the future. Will specific issue positions help or harm them? Governors and mayors do lose reelection bids, and they need to think about their images and positions.[18] Executives must be careful unless they want to become one of the losers.

Concern with the future impact of policy positions has always been with us. But the importance of this concern and the ability to anticipate impacts may have changed in recent years. As noted in earlier chapters, the electorate is now comprised of more independent voters, and there is more ticket-splitting and volatility

Table 9.3
Governors' Reelection Limits 1960–1992

		Years	
	1960	1982	1992
Four-Year Term			
No restraint on reelection	12	18	17
One consecutive reelection allowed	7	24	27
No consecutive reelection allowed	15	4	3
Total	34	46	47
Two-Year Term			
No restraint on reelection	14	4	3
One reelection allowed	2	0	0
Total	16	4	3

Source: 1960 and 1992: Book of the States; *1982: Advisory Commission on Intergovernmental Relations,* The Question of State and Government Capability, *A-98, (Washington, DC, January 1985), 130.*

in voter loyalties. To governors and mayors, this volatility creates the possibility of an electorate that can be won over, but that may desert them at any time. They worry about their ratings and the stability of their electoral standing.

At the same time, the rise of polling makes it possible for politicians to assess how they are doing with different constituent groups, and which groups like or dislike certain policy choices.[19] Polling gives politicians the possibility of anticipating when policy choices will be detrimental to them. Such anticipation does not mean that an executive will simply choose the most popular policy. Politicians have personal beliefs that affect them. They may also believe that the public will reward them for making the "right" choice if enough time passes that the benefits of the policy emerge. Or they may believe they can persuade enough voters that they did the right thing. Regardless, the availability of polling does mean that a politician is more likely to be aware of public opinion when making policy choices about important issues. This "political intelligence" may make it easier to win reelection.[20]

While more politicians may be concerned with the future, this concern does not always make their policy stances easier to predict. Concern with future aspirations leads politicians in very different directions. Each politician faces different situations, and each politician makes different calculations about the way to respond to his or her situation. A politician must decide where the primary threat of losing may come from.

The greatest threat to an executive may come from within a particular wing of his or her own party. Pete Wilson was elected governor of California in 1990 as a moderate Republican. His main opposition once in office, however, came from conservative Republicans who felt he was betraying the Republican party. Thus, while his personal inclinations may have been moderate, he had to support some conservative policies to reduce sustained opposition from the conservative wing of the party.[21] He felt he had to become less moderate. Otherwise, conservatives might threaten his chances to win the Republican nomination and to pursue reelection in 1994.

On the other hand, the threat may come from the middle. A Republican may face difficulty in winning independents and Democrats and may have to move to the moderate middle. Nelson Rockefeller, governor of New York from 1959 to 1973, continually faced the difficulty that he had to draw well among independents and among New York City residents, who were heavily Democratic. He began almost every campaign trailing in those groups and had improve his status with those groups in order to win. That need forced him to put more emphasis on urban programs.[22]

James Florio, the former Democratic governor of New Jersey, faced a similar situation after enacting an increase in taxes in 1990. His decision to increase income and sales taxes hurt his standing with working- and middle-class constituents. His primary concern in preparing for reelection was to focus on winning back those groups by emphasizing his moderate policies.[23] But Florio lost. In these last two cases, politicians from opposite parties faced essentially the same situation. Each had to win the middle to have a chance at reelection.

The calculations of politicians are made more difficult because their electoral bases can never be presumed to be constant. Events and conditions change, and politicians have to adjust their agendas and appeals accordingly. Changes in the economy often shape the popularity of governors. When the economy is growing and unemployment is low, their popularity rises. When the economy slides, so does their popularity.[24] They may not ultimately lose, but their popularity erodes.

The situation of Mario Cuomo, governor of New York since 1983, illustrates this. Cuomo won a close contest in 1982. He then won in 1986 with the largest proportion of the vote ever in New York state. His personal ratings were high. His success in 1986 came essentially from increasing his vote proportions in the suburbs around New York City and in the upstate urban counties.[25] Both of these areas have tended to be "swing" areas in statewide contests. Changes in his electoral support by areas of the state are shown in Table 9.4. His proportion of the vote in the New York City suburban area increased from 49 to 57 percent from 1982 to 1986, and from 49 to 66 percent in the upstate urban counties. But that change did not hold. By 1990, with the economy sliding badly, continued large deficits in the state budgets, persistent delays in enacting the state budget, and suggestions that his personal style was wearing thin on the electorate, that support had shifted again. His vote proportion decreased from 57 to 50 percent in the New York City suburbs and from 66 to 48 percent in the upstate urban areas. His concern for the 1994 election was to improve his status in those swing counties. In response, he began to shift his emphasis to his record of being fiscally responsible and to his efforts to enact a balanced state budget without resorting to borrowing.

The Importance of Conditions

Politicians may devote considerable attention to formulating and preparing policy changes. Those plans, however, are constrained and shaped by the conditions that politicians face when they acquire office. Perhaps the most significant constraint that they face is the accumulation of past choices made by prior politicians. These choices create programs and groups with a vested interest in maintaining at least the status quo in those programs. These groups fight hard to resist change. This

Table 9.4

Changes in Electoral Base for Mario Cuomo, Governor of New York, 1982–1990

	Cuomo Proportion of Vote		
	Years		
Area	*1982*	*1986*	*1990*
New York City	66	70	73
NYC suburbs	49	57	50
Upstate urban	49	66	48
Upstate rural	35	35	43

Source: Legislative Manual, *various years.*

resistance often puts a governor or mayor in the situation of being able only to propose marginal changes from the existing priorities.[26]

They also may find their ability to pursue their own agendas curtailed because changes in budget conditions limit their ability to engage in new programs. The most intrusive and demanding issue for executives is whether the economy is declining. If decline occurs, revenues from income, sales, and property taxes decline, and states and cities must decide whether to cut services or raise taxes in order to bring in more revenue. A declining economy also creates more demand for social services such as welfare, medical services, and unemployment compensation. Revenues decline, but demands increase.

It is not clear whether executives can affect the economy. It also is not clear whether governors are held accountable by the electorate. The relationship between the condition of the economy and the percentage of the vote governors receive is not clear.[27] But governors continually worry about being blamed for the economy, or for their party's management of it. Most governors and mayors think they will be held responsible for the economy. They also feel pressure to look as though they are making an effort to respond to economic conditions.[28] Many seemingly popular midwestern Republican governors chose to resign in 1982 because of the national recession presided over by a Republican president. They felt they could not control the economy, and that their incumbency status as Republicans would be a detriment, not an asset.

It is not just the economy that executives must deal with. Issues get pushed on the agenda for many reasons. The federal government may cut program funding to state and local governments, as it did during the 1980s.[29] During the 1980s, education reform and funding were also prominent issues because studies showed that many students were not doing well in school. Economic development became an issue as manufacturing jobs disappeared. Other issues like consumer protection, environmental protection, and tax relief may rise to prominence and then fade away once some conflict is resolved.[30] If a politician is to maintain the goodwill of the public, he or she must attempt to respond to these short-term public concerns. The need to respond to these events often means they have to change their agenda.

Even if an executive tries to be ready, events sometimes emerge suddenly and overwhelm an executive. Michael Bilandic was a relatively low-key and apparently safe mayoral successor to Richard Daley in Chicago until a sudden snowstorm struck the city prior to the primary. His administration did not handle the cleanup well, and he happened to be in Florida on vacation. His opponent, Jane Bryne, capitalized on his absence and the inefficiency of the administration, and he lost the primary. In a similar vein, Kathy Whitmire, the first female mayor in Houston's history (elected in 1981), was criticized for her handling of the cleanup after a hurricane, and for a time some observers thought she might be in trouble in 1983. She survived the 1983 election, but the incident indicates the way uncontrollable events can harm an incumbent.

These events and conditions create pressure on governors and mayors to react. It is then that the personal beliefs, political coalitions, and career aspirations of politicians become very important. These affect how a politician responds. Democrats and liberals are more likely to respond to economic decline by placing more emphasis on raising taxes than on cutting services.[31] They may propose cuts, but they are more likely than conservative Republicans to fight for some increases in revenue as part of the solution.[32] Conservative Republicans, on the other hand, are more likely to argue for reductions in service obligations. William Weld, a conservative Republican, ran for governor of Massachusetts in 1990. When he took office in 1991, the economy, and state tax revenues, were still sliding. His conservative inclinations affected how he reacted to that situation. While Democrats wanted to combine tax increases and spending cuts to deal with the problem, he pursued severe spending cuts as the sole solution.[33]

Sometimes politicians feel very constrained in the ways they can respond. It has been argued that mayors, in particular, face limited options. They face the reality that people can move out of a city at any time, and that their concern must be to bring people and economic activity into their city.[34]

When black politicians Coleman Young and Andrew Young became mayors of Detroit and Atlanta, respectively, they were each faced with the necessity of retaining old businesses and of attracting new business to the city so that the tax base would be sufficient to support government expenditures. Each mayor was liberal and black and had relied heavily on black votes to win office. It was presumed their agenda would not be pro-business. Their pursuit of business surprised and angered many of their supporters, but both mayors felt that they had no choice if they were going to be able to successfully manage their cities.[35]

The most enduring and most difficult decisions for executives revolve around taxes. Many programs, though not all, require money. A governor may want to allocate more money to increase education funding, aid to local governments, welfare benefits, or to provide broader coverage for health programs. To get that revenue, taxes or fee increases are necessary. Declines in the economy may change the decision. The issue may become whether to raise taxes just to maintain programs, though the decision still involves taxes. The difficulty is that tax increases are often detrimental to reelection prospects. Proposing and presiding over a tax increase does not doom an incumbent to defeat, but those who propose taxes win reelection at lower rates than those who do not.[36] Those who survive do suffer declines in their percentage of the vote.[37]

Many politicians believe that they can create an image of a progressive leader who raised taxes and provided better government services. During the 1980s, there were executives who advocated tax increases and believed they could portray themselves as courageous leaders who did what was necessary to remedy terrible financial situations. Ohio and Michigan, for example, were experiencing declines in revenues in 1982 due to a declining state economy and a national recession. Each state was unable to pay its bills or meet its payroll obligations. In the 1982 gubernatorial races, each state elected Democrats, who then pushed through a sharp tax increase to solve the state's problem. By late 1983, both governors had little public support in the polls. Nonetheless, the hope of these governors was that they would be able to go before the electorate in 1986 and claim that they had successfully managed to preserve the fiscal solvency of the state. But even the most optimistic politicians are leery of raising taxes. Raising taxes is politically dangerous. Many governors appear to avoid this problem by proposing tax increases early in their term.[38]

It is not always easy to time such changes, however, as changes in the economy and other events may make taxes an issue later in their terms.

Anticipating Press Portrayals

Finally, no politician can formulate an agenda without considering how the press will portray a proposal. The press is autonomous and makes its own decisions about the way to present a story. All politicians must try to anticipate how their ideas will be covered. A governor might be worried about the long-run reliance on the automobile. The state may import large volumes of oil, and residents may have heavy reliance on the automobile. The latter could be troubling because such heavy use creates problems with air pollution. One approach to this problem might be to raise the gasoline tax in order to encourage long-term shifts away from dependence on the automobile. The difficulty lies in trying to influence how the proposal will be covered by the media. Will headlines read "Governor Seeks to Reduce Automobile Pollution," or will they read "Governor Seeks Tax Increase on Suburban Commuters"? A governor might get credit for the first coverage, but find it difficult to counteract the effects of the latter. A governor who anticipates detrimental coverage may be inhibited from making a desired proposal.

Similarly, a mayor may want to reassess city residential properties because studies show that there are inequities in the fairness of assessment patterns. Will the story be "Mayor Seeks Fairness in Tax Assessments," or will it be "Mayor's Proposal Will Raise Taxes on West and South Side"? Politicians seek to work with journalists in order to influence how a story will be presented, but a politician's ability to shape coverage is often very limited. The intent of proposals may be lost in the headlines. All of this affects and often alters the proposals politicians are willing to present.

Policy Agendas: The Haves and the Have-Nots

The important issue is whether all this affects the policy positions taken and whether it affects how the haves and have-nots fare in the decision-making process. The answer, unsatisfying as it may seem, is that it all depends. Governors and mayors start with their own beliefs and electoral bases. Some Democrats are elected by liberal, urban constituencies, and they push those concerns once elected. Some Republicans are elected by rural and suburban conservatives, and they push those concerns.

But every politician worries about the "swing" vote. They worry about alienating the middle class, about watching their ratings and political clout drop, and about losing reelection. As discussed in Chapter 1 the important question is whether the have-nots can achieve representation and have a large enough voice in the decision-making process to have an impact on policy. Concern about the swing vote and the volatility of the electorate creates particularly important problems for those seeking to represent the have-nots. Liberals worry that they will drive away the swing vote if they are seen to support the have-nots. Furthermore, not only is there greater volatility of the electorate, but more and more of the population have moved to the suburbs, and lower-class registration and voting have declined. All these conditions may make forming and pursuing a redistributive agenda difficult.

The example of Jim Florio, former governor of New Jersey, is again important. He came to office in 1989 with a liberal record. He reacted to a budget deficit and to a court order about inequality in the schools with a tax increase and a plan to distribute more money to low-income school districts. He was successful in securing his policy goals, but, as discussed in Chapter 5, his policies alienated the middle-income districts. Democratic legislators in those districts lost in the next election (see Table 5.1). He did pursue an agenda largely favorable to the have-nots, but this agenda was not seen as positive by all working-class districts. This problem led him to focus on restoring his image with moderates. It led him to temper his advocacy of redistributive programs. The shift helped his ratings improve over a two-year time period, but the improvement was not enough to prevent his losing a close election in 1993.

The need to maintain support among moderates is a problem common to many governors and mayors. There are those who suggest that governors who have survived to win reelection bids did so only by moving to the middle and assuming moderate positions on issues before their opponents could can do so.[39] If so, it suggests that it may be difficult for any governor or mayor to sustain attention to the have-nots. It suggests that if they want to stay in office, they need to restrain their focus on lower-class concerns. We will return to this question in Chapter 12.

Pursuing Agendas: The Formal Power of Governors and Mayors

If governors or mayors form agendas, can they achieve them? Again, the answer is that it depends. The person holding office must have the power to be able to make things happen. Power refers to the ability to get others to do something the executive desires. Power is also often defined as the ability to get others to do something they might not otherwise be inclined to do. Much of the power of the executive comes from formal authority, authority granted by the constitution of the state, the charter of the local government, or laws passed by government. "Informal" political power, which is not explicitly granted, is also important. Informal power involves the ability to persuade or pressure others to go along with a policy proposal. Such power stems from such conditions as having good rapport with state legislators, good relations with the press, or large electoral margins.

The executive power we will discuss here is only potential. Whether this potential power actually results in change depends on the power of institutions like the legislature. Legislatures have also changed in recent decades, and their changes may limit the power of executives. But in this section, we will discuss only the formal power of executives.

The Nature of Formal Power

Formal power refers to the legally granted authority to play specific roles in government. Formal power is granted to a particular office, regardless of who controls that office. Formal power involves the ability to influence government officials, such as other state officials and state legislators. Formal power makes a governor or a mayor an actor who cannot be avoided and who must be responded to in the decision-making process. Bureaucrats and legislators cannot assume that if they can ignore a governor, there will be no consequences.

The formal powers that appear to be most important are those that make the governor or mayor the dominant elective official, give executives the authority to appoint individuals to other positions in government, give them the authority to construct the initial or proposed budget for government, and define their rights to veto legislation. Each of these powers can make it possible for an executive to use his or her legal authority to affect outcomes. The greater the formal power granted a position, the greater the ability of the executive to achieve that agenda.

Changes in the Power of Governors

For much of our history, Americans have been reluctant to grant significant power to executives. The early political experiences of this country affected not only the creation of federalism, but also the formal power given to executives. The negative experience with English colonial governors convinced Americans that executives should be weak and that the primary power should be given to legislatures, which directly represent the people. In the early 1800s, governors had little control over their budgets, could not affect the appointments of many agency heads, and were limited to short, single terms of office.[40]

By the early 1900s, attitudes toward legislatures and governors changed significantly. The reputation of legislatures had declined because of repeated scandals. The Progressive movement, which stressed the need to have a single individual take a coherent overview of budgets and policies, began to advocate changes in the role of the governor. For many years, agencies had made direct appeals to the legislature. Reformers advocated the establishment of an executive budget. Such a budget meant that all requests for funding had to be presented to the governor and that the governor was then to arbitrate among them and present an overall budget to the legislature.[41] The goal was to make the governor more of a central actor in the decision process.

This change is part of a general change in our expectations about government. During the twentieth century, Americans have increased their expectations of how active government should be. As these expectations have risen, there has been a corresponding rise in the acceptance of and the desire for stronger leadership and administrative control.[42] This change has affected attitudes toward executives. The result has been a strengthening of the office of governor. We have very little information about such changes in the situation of mayors.

Table 9.3, discussed earlier, provides one indication of the recent changes that affect governors. The initial fear of executive power resulted in limited terms of office and constraints on reelection. Citizens feared that leaders who stayed in office would accumulate too much power. Over the last several decades, there has been increased acceptance of four-year terms of office and of the possibility of reelection. These changes have also increased the formal power of governors.

The Importance of Being the Primary Elected Official: The Gubernatorial Situation

A governor is the most prominent elected official in the state. When a governor is the only elected official, other officials may be somewhat subordinate to him or her. When there are numerous other elected officials, each may legally claim to have an independently elected position and have no responsibility to the governor.

Because of our long history of distrusting concentrated political power, there is a widespread practice in states and localities of having many officials elected separately from the governor or mayor. Advocates of this practice argue that it creates a government whose prominent officials have independent bases of authority. These contesting bases insure some competition among officials. Such competition can limit abuses of power.

In most states, governors have the right to appoint the heads of agencies that are concerned with agriculture, banking, the budget, civil rights, commerce, consumer affairs, corrections, economic development, energy, environmental affairs, insurance, labor, the handicapped, parks and recreation, public utility regulation, transportation, and welfare. The lieutenant governor, the secretary of state, the attorney general, and the treasurer are often independently elected. The positions of auditor and superintendent of education are fairly evenly divided between being appointed and elected positions.[43]

The political centrality of governors appears to have increased. Over the last thirty years, there has been a reduction in the number of officials elected separately from the governor, along with a reduction in the number of independent state agencies, and in the number of such agency heads appointed independently from the governor.[44]

These changes are significant for understanding the position of executives in the political process. Executives serve as the focal point of the political process. The changes of recent decades suggest a greater willingness on the part of the public and other politicians (for it is often legislatures that must pass these laws) to have the governor play this enhanced role. The pattern has been to strengthen the office and to increase the formal powers of the office.

Appointment and Removal Powers: The Governors

Executives have more power if they can appoint and remove administrative officials. Although an executive may be the only elected official, he or she may not have any authority to appoint the people who head government agencies.[45] Officials who hold those positions may be career civil servants, or people who work in the bureaucracy and are protected by rules that buffer them from political pressures. This protection may give them considerable autonomy from a governor. If governors are to be able to impose their policies on organizations, it is vital that they place people in office who are sympathetic to their views. If the power of appointment does not exist, an official may be able to publicly disagree with the governor or deliberately stall the studies and the goals desired by the governor.

Similar to the increase in other powers in recent decades, governors have acquired greater control over appointments.[46] Table 9.5 provides one assessment of gubernatorial appointment powers. The states are grouped by the percent of administrative officials appointed by the governor. The results show a remarkable diversity of appointment powers. The figures show the proportion of major positions in each state that can be filled by the governor. New York ranks high, in that the governor can appoint 89 percent of all positions. In South Carolina, the governor can appoint only 21 percent of all positions. Governors in states like South Carolina are automatically limited in the extent that they can change administrative practices.

Power over Local Agencies: The Mayors

Mayors experience fragmentation of formal authority over government. Table 9.6 presents the percent of mayors who have control over budget preparation and the power to appoint department heads. Mayors have been given surprisingly little formal power in these areas. In smaller cities, there is even less such formal power. Mayors may still be able to informally influence budgets and the length of time a department head survives, but explicit formal power in these areas is limited.

The move to make city agencies independent of the mayor was pushed by the Progressives, who believed that such independence would result in better management. They also wanted to fragment power in the wake of the machines of the turn of the century, because they thought machine "bosses" created too much concentrated (and corrupted) power in the hands of a few people. As we noted in reviewing the existence of partisanship in local governments, the Progressives

Table 9.5

States Grouped by Percent of Administrative Officials Appointed by Governor

70% or more
  New York, Virginia, Hawaii, Illinois, California, Iowa
60 to 69%
  Minnesota, Pennsylvania, Louisiana, New Hampshire, Indiana
50 to 59%
  New Jersey, Vermont, Massachusetts, Nebraska, New Mexico, Ohio, Connecticut, Delaware, North Carolina, Rhode Island, South Dakota
40 to 49%
  Utah, West Virginia, Colorado, Maryland, Tennessee, Idaho, Wisconsin, Wyoming, Montana, Arizona, Arkansas, Mississippi, Kansas, Kentucky, Alabama, Washington
Less than 40%
  Oklahoma, Maine, Nevada, Michigan, Florida, North Dakota, Alaska, Oregon, Missouri, Georgia, Texas, South Carolina

Source: Coleman Ransone, The American Governorship, *(Westport, Conn.: Greenwood, 1982), 35.*

Table 9.6

Mayors and the Power to Influence Budgets and Appoint Department Heads

City Size	Mayors with Control over Budget Development (#)	(%)	Mayors with Power to Appoint Department Heads (#)	(%)
500,000+	6	60.0	7	70.0
250,000–499,999	10	32.2	10	33.3
100,000–249,999	20	20.2	28	29.2
50,000–99,999	57	22.8	60	27.4
25,000–49,999	81	15.9	102	22.4
10,000–24,999	156	14.2	227	23.7
5,000–9,999	147	12.4	256	26.0
2,500–4,999	206	16.2	315	31.7
Under 2,500	40	10.8	55	20.5
City Location				
Central	114	30.4	123	36.8
Suburban	333	12.9	523	24.0
Independent	276	14.8	414	27.6

Source: Tari Renner and Victor S. DeSantis, "Contemporary Patterns and Trends in Municipal Government Structures," Municipal Year Book 1993, (Washington DC: ICMA, 1993), 62–63.

were most successful in affecting newly formed governments in the West and in the suburbs.[47]

In many cities, service agencies are not under the control of city officials. Table 9.7 presents the variations in responsibilities for services across cities. Cities are grouped by region. The proportion of cities in each region responsible for specific services are then reported. The most significant variations across regions involves welfare, education, and judicial matters. Cities in the Northeast are generally responsible for these activities, while cities in the West are not. In the West, these policies may be handled by counties, by special districts, or by the state. When city officials do not control these activities, their ability to affect changes in these areas is greatly diminished.

This fragmentation of responsibilities is often confusing to the public, as well as to other politicians. Most of us presume that mayors have responsibility for the services delivered in their cities. But in those cities affected by the movement to create independent agencies, the mayor now has little influence. The perception, however, may still be that mayors have considerable influence. This perception is illustrated by the testimony of the former mayor, of Los Angeles, Sam Yorty, before a Congressional committee. In the testimony excerpted in the box, members of Congress were questioning Yorty about what he was going to do about particular

Table 9.7

Cities and Responsibility for Different Functions, by Region

	New England (%)	Middle Atlantic (%)	East Border (%)	Deep South (%)	West Border (%)	Northwest Territory (%)	Midcontinent Highlands (%)	Far West (%)
Welfare, Federal aid	55	7	32	0	1	1	2	1
Judicial affairs	100	2	32	1	1	0	2	1
Hospitals	25	12	35	15	15	9	11	2
Education	98	37	59	4	4	13	2	0
Welfare, general assistance	100	43	56	1	16	9	10	1
Health	97	80	88	60	84	69	73	32
Parks and recreation	92	91	82	96	90	79	92	95
Sanitation	56	77	94	94	84	73	67	47
Sewers	47	52	79	70	77	54	79	48
Number of cities	64	97	34	84	73	154	63	99

Note: **New England:** *Maine, New Hampshire, Vermont, Massachusetts, Connecticut, Rhode Island;* **Middle Atlantic:** *New Jersey, New York, Pennsylvania, Maryland, Delaware;* **East Border:** *Virginia, West Virginia, Kentucky, Tennessee;* **Deep South:** *Louisiana, Alabama, Mississippi, Florida, Georgia, North Carolina, South Carolina;* **West Border:** *Texas, Oklahoma, Kansas, Missouri, Arkansas;* **Northwest Territory:** *Ohio, Indiana, Illinois, Michigan, Wisconsin;* **Midcontinent Highlands:** *Minnesota, Iowa, North Dakota, South Dakota, Nebraska, Montana, Idaho, Colorado, Utah, Wyoming, New Mexico;* **Far West:** *California, Oregon, Washington, Nevada.*
Source: Roland Liebert, Disintegration and Political Action *(New York: Academic Press, 1976), 50.*

problems facing him. Yorty continually responded that he had no jurisdiction over these problems and that he could do nothing about these problems.

In contrast, mayors in many Northeast cities are the primary elected officials and have a great deal of control over what happens in various city agencies. In New York City, for example, the mayor is a very powerful figure. He has a large number of agencies under his control, and he is able to appoint a large number of the officials who control those agencies.

The power to remove officials is important for all executives. If an executive does not have the potential to remove administrators who fundamentally disagree with policies being pursued, the governor loses considerable influence. Much as with the other powers examined, the power to remove officials has been increasing in recent decades. This power also varies considerably across the states. Some governors have broad discretion to remove officials, while in other states this power is very restricted.[48] Those governors with this power have more ability to impose their agenda on government and to prevent sustained dissent.

Budget Preparation Powers: The Governors

The most significant and coherent statement of an executive's priorities is the budget. Budgets create an initial agenda for discussion by others. They provide the

The Power of the Mayor: Testimony Given by Sam Yorty, Mayor of Los Angeles, 1966

Senator Kennedy: But are you not mayor of all the people in Los Angeles?

Mayor Yorty: Of the people of the city of Los Angeles, yes.

Senator Kennedy: Then if they have a problem, do they not look to you for some leadership?

Mayor Yorty: Yes. They get leadership, too, evidenced by the last election. But whether or not I can solve a problem may depend upon my jurisdiction.

Senator Ribicoff: As I listened to your testimony, Mayor Yorty, I made some notes. This morning you have really waived authority and responsibility in the following areas: schools, welfare, transportation, employment, health, and housing, which leaves you as head of the city basically with a ceremonial function, police, and recreation.

Mayor Yorty: That is right, and fire.

Senator Ribicoff: And fire.

Mayor Yorty: Yes.

Senator Ribicoff: Collecting sewage?

Mayor Yorty: Sanitation, that is right.

Senator Ribicoff: In other words, basically you lack jurisdiction, authority, responsibility for what makes a city move?

Mayor Yorty: That is exactly it.

Senator Ribicoff: I would say that the city of Los Angeles right now, from your testimony, does not stand for a damn thing.

Mayor Yorty: Well, it stands for a lot.

Senator Ribicoff: I believe that there will be federal programs that will be initiated in the next two years that will really put America on the road to start doing something about the cities in America . . . The one city that won't be able to take advantage of any of these programs will be Los Angeles, because you are not organized to do so.

Mayor Yorty: The only way we can organize is . . . to . . . do it by a joint powers agreement with the other jurisdictions that are involved, so at that point we can work together. When you get to solving the problems of the cities, in our community we probably have to work countywide.

Source: Excerpted and adapted from U.S. Senate Subcommittee on Executive Reorganization, The Federal Role in Urban Affairs, 1966, 775–777, In Roland Liebert, Disintegration and Political Action: The Changing Functions of City Governments in America *(New York: Academic Press, 1976), 9.*

opportunity to capture public and legislative attention by proposing what should be done with public funds. A budget proposed by the governor may be rejected or totally altered by the time it is enacted, but the opportunity to dominate debate still exists.

For this opportunity to mean anything, an executive must have control over the budget preparation process. If the budget is not prepared by the executive, but it must be done in conjunction with other officials, the executive loses the power to create his or her own budget and to present it as his or her set of goals or priorities. In most states, the governor has considerable authority to prepare the budget. In other states, the governor has to share this activity with someone such as a budget director, but the governor still usually has considerable authority over this official. There are a few states, such as Texas, where the governor has to share this power with other executive-branch officials and with a legislative committee. This process considerably weakens the ability of the governor to present a set of priorities to the state.

Budget Preparation Powers: The Mayors

Control by mayors over the budget is limited to larger cities. This power is also affected by the form of government that exists in the city. In city-manager governments, the city manager has responsibility for preparing the budget, and, if a mayor exists in such a city, he or she is largely just another commentator on the proposed budget. In mayor-council governments, the mayor is the chief executive officer of the city and either prepares the budget or has one of his or her agency heads prepare it.

Veto Power: The Governors

Finally, there is the formal authority to veto legislation passed by a state legislature (or a city council). When an executive vetoes legislation, that piece of legislation is formally rejected and usually does not become law. This power is one of the most effective powers that an executive can possess. Veto power has gradually increased over the course of American history.[49] It gives executives the ability to threaten particular programs during bargaining over budgets and legislation. There are two aspects of the veto power that determine just how much power the executive has. The first is whether the veto power can be used for specific parts of legislation (an item veto) or whether it can only be used to reject an entire piece of legislation (a blanket veto). The more specific the veto power, the greater the power an executive possesses. When only a blanket veto exists, opponents of an executive can seek to create a package that includes both desired and undesired legislation, but with just enough desired legislation to induce an executive to accept the legislation. The goal is to create a package that presents a dilemma to the executive. If the executive rejects the package, he or she may be rejecting legislation that he or she wishes to support and that various groups in society want. When an item veto exists, a governor can remove the parts that he or she does not want. The executive's opponents know this, and this knowledge makes it more difficult to write such items into the legislation.

The other important aspect of the veto power is the provision for overriding it. No veto power is absolute. The belief has always been that if an intense majority wishes a policy, they should be able to get it. Legislatures always have the authority to override (to enact legislation over the objections of an executive) if enough legislators are willing to vote for an override. The power of the governor stems from the requirements for an override. The greater the proportion of the legislature that must vote for an override, the more difficult it will be to get an override, and the more power a governor has. Some states make an override easy by requiring only 50 percent of legislators to support it. Others require voting proportions of three-fifths or two-thirds. The ability to override is also affected by requirements as to the proportion of the legislature that must vote on the override. If it is necessary to have all elected legislators in attendance in order to vote on an override, it is more difficult than if the vote does not have to involve all elected legislators.

Finally, the amendatory veto has become important. In many states, governors have the power to change specific language in legislation after the legislature passes it. This power enables the governor to change the substance of legislation in addition to challenging the amount of money allocated to a program.[50]

There are quite different veto-power situations across the states. If a governor has an item veto that can be overridden only if three-fifths of the entire legislature votes to do so, that governor has considerable power. This situation exists in states such as New York. On the other hand, in states such as Texas, the governor has only a blanket veto, and it can be overridden by a simple majority of the legislature. This situation makes the governor in Texas a weaker political actor than the governor in New York. Table 10.12 on page 351 summarizes veto powers.

The veto can be a powerful weapon if a governor makes a commitment to reject legislators' plans in order to force them to deal with a gubernatorial plan. Lowell Weicker's use of the veto in Connecticut illustrates this. In 1992, the state was facing a shortfall in revenue. The state did not have an income tax on wages and salaries. There were repeated discussions about adopting one, particularly because the sales tax was already very high. Weicker proposed an income tax and a cut in the sales tax rate. A majority in the legislature did not want to adopt an income tax and sent to the governor several budget packages that raised several other taxes, cut certain programs, and avoided an income tax. He vetoed every one of them and indicated he would continue to do so. There were not enough votes to override the governor, a situation which enhanced his power. As the budget deadline passed and threats of layoffs of government workers became more serious, the pressure on legislators grew. Finally, enough legislators changed their votes, and the tax was passed.[51] The veto was the governor's crucial weapon because it gave him the power to reject legislative proposals and to force legislators to deal with his proposal.

Veto Power: The Mayors

While all governors have some sort of veto power, this principle has not carried over to city governments. Table 9.8 presents information on the number of mayors who do have veto power. The distrust of giving executives too much power seems to be particularly strong at the local level, and most mayors are without veto power.

Indexes of the Formal Powers of Governors

For a governor or mayor to be powerful, he or she must be able to run again for office. If an executive can be reelected, other politicians see him or her as a force

Table 9.8

Veto Power and Mayors

City Size	Mayors Having Veto Power	
	(#)	(%)
500,000+	8	80.0
250,000–499,999	14	43.8
100,000–249,999	35	35.0
50,000–99,999	86	34.5
25,000–49,999	160	31.6
10,000–24,999	327	30.6
5,000–9,999	397	34.5
2,500–4,999	361	29.5
Under 2,500	80	21.9
City Location		
Central	171	45.5
Suburban	714	28.4
Independent	583	32.1

Source: Tari Renner and Victor S. DeSantis, "Contemporary Patterns and Trends in Municipal Government Structures," Municipal Year Book 1993, *67.*

to be reckoned with in the future. Mayors must be able to control the budget preparation process so that they can propose their own policies as a starting point for discussion of policy alternatives. Governors must be able to appoint agency heads. The ability to control a number of situations can give a governor or mayor a great deal of power. With less ability to control these processes, governors and mayors have very limited power.

In an attempt to summarize these matters, we can create a scale to represent the variations across the states. Situations of high power (those with an item veto and a three-fifths override provision) can be given a high number, and situations of low power (those with a blanket veto and a majority override provision), a low number. This scale can be created for the power of a governor to run for reelection, the power of appointments, the control over budget preparation, and the power to veto. These scales can then be added to produce a very rough indication of the levels of power that exist. There are many problems with these indexes. They neglect certain aspects of power. They only provide an indication of variations across the states and are not good at assessing absolute increases in the power of governors over time.[52] Nonetheless, such scales provide crude ideas of variations among the states. Table 9.9 presents the states grouped by one such index. It indicates the relative formal powers that governors have in different states. The same index might be created for mayors, though less information is available.

Table 9.9

States Grouped by Formal Powers of Governors

Formal Power

High

   Maryland, Massachusetts, West Virginia, New York, Minnesota, Arkansas, Connecticut, Hawaii, Kansas, Nebraska, New Jersey, Oregon, Tennessee, Utah

Moderate

   Alaska, Delaware, Illinois, Louisiana, Michigan, North Dakota, Ohio, Pennsylvania, South Dakota, Virginia, California, Colorado, Georgia, Mississippi, Montana, Washington, Wisconsin, Wyoming, Arizona, Florida, Idaho, Kentucky, Missouri, Indiana

Low

   Alabama, Maine, Nevada, New Mexico, Oklahoma, New Hampshire, South Carolina, Vermont, North Carolina, Texas, Rhode Island

Source: Thad Beyle, "Governors," in Virginia Gray, Herbert Jacob, and Robert Albritton, Politics in the American States, *5th ed. (Glenview, Ill.: Scott, Foresman/Little, Brown, 1990), 228.*

In states such as New York, the governor has considerable power in numerous areas and can potentially become a dominant figure. In Texas, on the other hand, the governor has relatively little formal power. If a governor uses power skillfully, it should be easier to achieve an agenda in New York than in Texas.

Pursuing Agendas: The Informal Power of Governors and Mayors

Formal power is not the only means of influence that executives have. There is also informal power. Again, this power lies in the ability to get others to do what they might not otherwise do. The difference is that informal power is not based in law. It is derived from the ability of a governor or mayor to persuade or politically pressure others.

This power is important. In a study of the most important powers that a governor can have, informal powers occupied a significant position.[53] Legislators and administrators at the state level were asked what they thought gives the governor the most power. The results are shown in Table 9.10. The rankings indicate that, to those involved in state government and politics, informal power is just as important as formal power for the influence of a governor.

In the broadest sense, informal power over others exists when a governor has some resource that makes some other political actor inclined to go along with the governor. That resource might be the support of the public, the ability to persuade other political actors, the support among significant interest groups, party loyalty, or the ability to distribute benefits. The influence of all of these resources can lead to a situation where others are more inclined to go along with a governor. They may

Table 9.10

Rankings by Legislators and Administrators of Sources of Gubernatorial Power

Power	Type of Power	Rank	Total Mentions
Budget formation	F	1	127
Popular support	I	2	107
Administrative control	I	3	104
Veto	F	4	103
Mass media	I	5	90
Prestige of office	I	6	81
Personal conferences with legislators	I	7	72
Party leader	I	8.5	61
Personal characteristics	I	8.5	61
Public relations	I	10	58
Patronage	F	11	46
Bargaining skills	I	12	43
Legislative message	F	13	40
Administration of programs in districts	F	14	36

Note: The (F) and (I) refer to formal and informal power, respectively.
Source: E. Lee Bernick, "Gubernatorial Tools: Formal and Informal," Journal of Politics 41, no. 2 (May 1979):660.

go along reluctantly or enthusiastically, but they go along. This kind of power is fundamental in politics, but it is the hardest power to measure.

Breadth of Electoral Support

Perhaps the most important base of power for an executive is his or her electoral margin. A governor who wins with a large margin sends a clear signal to others that he or she has a strong following among the public.[54] Public opinion polls that indicate the governor or mayor has a high job approval rating also contribute to the feeling that he or she should be listened to. That respect from other political actors can be used in many ways. Such respect can be used to claim a mandate to implement the policies that the candidate campaigned for. In an era of ambiguity of party images, this popularity can be more important than a "party" mandate. The mandate created by the popularity of a candidate is attached to that candidate.

This popularity can be used in positive or negative ways to influence other politicians. A popular governor might publicly endorse others to increase their chances of being elected. A popular mayor might appear at another candidate's fund-raiser to help raise money. These actions create gratitude among those helped. These actions, of course, can be useless or even detrimental if the mayor is unpopular. Popularity can also be used to threaten other politicians in order to influence them to go along with the governor. A popular governor can campaign against a state legislator and may sway the attitudes of voters who are not sure of the record of the legislator. Such an action can cause an election loss. Executives have to be selective in their use of this power to avoid charges of meddling. They can take a more subtle approach by passing the word that it is legitimate to attack or oppose someone.

Trying to capitalize on popularity is not always easy in this era of ambivalence about partisan politics. In 1983, Republican Thomas Kean was a relatively popular governor in New Jersey. He sought to change Democratic control of the legislature by raising funds and conducting a general campaign against Democrats. He was unsuccessful, however, and Democrats actually gained seats.[55] He tried to stretch his influence too far. Many executives worry that such unsuccessful efforts may harm their appearance of being "powerful," so they avoid such general attempts at influence, or they choose their battles very carefully to avoid damaging their reputations. Candidates who barely win, of course, lack such a starting base. They must somehow convince other politicians that there is some support for their policy positions. It is not a good position from which to start trying to influence others.

Persuasion and the Press

Governors and mayors have one enormous advantage over other politicians. They are generally regarded (whether or not they have the corresponding formal power) as the primary political actors in the system. The press looks to them for initiatives, for policy leadership, and for political leadership. A skillful politician can exploit this position to dominate the issues that emerge by defining what is important. Ronald Reagan was skillful at doing this as governor of California and as president. When he entered office, he was able to define the dominant issues deserving attention as the reduction of government waste and the cutting back of government. Reagan stuck to relatively simple themes and repeated these themes again and again. He also sought to be relatively cordial and personable in his dealings with the press so that he would be treated well and would come across well to the public. A shrewd politician seeks to dominate the attention of the public and to take away attention from other politicians who want to push other issues or who wish to attack the governor. For mayors, this ability can be particularly important. If a mayor can remain on friendly terms with the editors of local newspapers, he or she may be able to avoid negative editorials and investigative stories. A skillful mayor may also be able to obtain front-page coverage of policy announcements. This ability to manipulate the press can be useful as a means to dominate public attention and overshadow other politicians so that the mayor's ideas dominate public discussions. This attention puts pressure on other politicians (city council members and legislators) to at least discuss the mayor's proposals. Press coverage can be used to cultivate an image of concern, activeness, and leadership with the public. Politicians who wish to pursue other agendas may find themselves on the defensive because they have not responded to the mayor's proposals. A mayor who does not cultivate this channel of influence may find his or her ideas ignored. Getting all this attention increases informal power.

To create this kind of power, a politician has to show some sympathy for the needs of the media. An executive has to be willing to meet with editors and reporters, to hold regular press conferences, meetings, or interviews and to be able to be somewhat dynamic, engaging, and responsive. Such activity requires a personality trait that some politicians simply do not have.

Building Bases of Support

Another route to influence is to seek support from groups, encouraging members of those groups to communicate that support to legislators. To do this, an executive must meet with groups to indicate his or her respect for their political importance. Politics is an art of getting others to accept your policy proposals, and showing political respect for groups is one means of cultivating such support. Some politicians find this an easy activity to engage in and are forever conducting meetings with groups throughout the city and state. Others find it a demeaning, exhausting, and distracting activity and try to keep such activity to a minimum.

The practice of meeting regularly with various groups may not always produce support, but it may at least create the belief among members of the group that its opinions are considered important. This activity creates a continuing dialogue with groups and recognizes the legitimacy of their concerns and their right to be heard. It also gives the executive an opportunity to make his or her case to the groups. If done well, such meetings can reduce the extent of opposition from a group that a governor feels he cannot please. The democratic process is an ongoing exchange over what is right to do. That activity continues after elections, and effective politicians use their position to shape that dialogue.

The Legislative Party

There is one other major source of power that an executive might draw on. Politics in states and in most localities takes place in a partisan context. Commonality of partisan allegiances can create loyalty among politicians. An executive can draw on this loyalty to get politicians from the same party to go along with him or her on policy disputes. The appeal can be very simple: "We are all Republicans (Democrats), and we should stick together to pursue the programs our party wants." Commonalities of perspective and goals may serve to soften minor differences among politicians of the same party members to work together for common purposes.

These appeals are often effective. A governor or a mayor can argue that the electorate will distrust their party if they cannot work together to solve problems. Commonality of political constituencies and policy interests, of course, makes it easier for a governor and his or her legislative party to work together. These appeals, however, do not have the effect they used to.[56] Governors no longer have clear control over state party committees, and legislators have developed their own campaign organizations. The rise of split-ticket voting has also made legislators think more about their own images and less about their unity with a governor.

Not only are the effects of these appeals for "party unity" uncertain, but there are reasons it might be unwise to make them. A governor, and particularly a mayor (local politics are often nonpartisan officially and in spirit), may have campaigned on his or her independence from partisan politics. It may be detrimental to alter that image by making strict appeals to partisanship the basis for passing legislation.

It may also be that despite the presumed commonality of interests between an executive and his or her legislative party, the executive may have a constituency considerably different from that of the party.[57] A governor may wish to avoid being linked with the constituency of the legislative party. Governors and mayors must run "at large" in their state or city, and they must be able to attract a large enough constituency to win at least 50 percent of the electorate. If a legislative party has most of its support concentrated in one area of the state and does not have much support elsewhere in the state, the legislative party base may not be sufficient to elect a governor. In such a situation, a governor who becomes too clearly identified with the legislative party may find it difficult to build beyond that base.

Finally, there is one other very important reason governors may wish to avoid a strong association with their own party. Governors must contend with legislatures, and it is more and more common for there to be divided control of government.[58] If governors wish to achieve anything, they must often obtain backing from a majority of members in both houses. If they appeal to partisan loyalties when their party does not control the legislature, governors are likely to alienate the opposition party and make the opposition more inclined to oppose them. Such governors are likely to accomplish very little and to be regarded as ineffective when they run for reelection. This situation often discourages governors from making partisan appeals.

City councils have just one house. Mayors must worry about which party controls the council. If the opposition party is in control, mayors also have an incentive to avoid a partisan approach.

The Mix of Constituencies and Power

Policy Changes

Constituencies and executive agendas and powers come together to affect the kinds of concerns executives pursue and the possibilities of achieving their goals. Past and hoped-for constituencies shape political goals. Power creates the ability to achieve those goals. Formal and informal power can reinforce each other. A governor with strong formal power is more likely to be able to persuade others. A governor with a large margin of victory is more likely to be able to have a veto respected by legislators. It is when clear policy agendas combine with effective use of high formal and informal powers that potential for change exists.[59] Whether that change actually occurs depends on how other actors—the legislature in particular—react to executive efforts. But we can discern particular combinations that make certain changes more likely.

Liberal Policy Changes

Policy concerns begin with the beliefs of elected politicians and the constituencies that put them in office. The pursuit of a liberal agenda is most likely to occur when a liberal Democrat who ran on liberal campaign themes is elected by virtue of a strong vote in liberal areas of the state. The same conditions apply to mayors. The potential to achieve that agenda is the greatest when the executive also has considerable formal powers, is skilled at using the media, cultivates support among groups, and uses selective penalties and incentives to create the support necessary to pass legislation.

Conservative Policy Changes

Other conditions make it more likely that conservative policy changes will be pursued and implemented. Conservative Republican candidates who emphasize conservative themes and draw their electoral base from Republican areas and voters are more likely to pursue conservative agendas. Their ability to do so will be greater if they also have formal powers and the political skills to build support for their programs.

The Ambiguous Cases

Many executives do not fit into these simple cases. Some Democrats are more conservative than others. Some Republicans are more liberal than others. Other politicians come to office as moderates or without clear agendas. It is very difficult to anticipate what an executive without a clear agenda is likely to pursue. But an executive with a clear agenda might also have little formal power or be uneasy or unskilled at exercising informal power. Such lack of power, or the inability to use it, makes it hard for any executive to have much impact.

For all these reasons, it is frequently difficult to anticipate what executives are likely to pursue, and whether they are likely to be successful at achieving whatever they do pursue. The outcomes of such cases is very difficult to predict without detailed understanding of the situation in the specific state or locality.

Case Studies of Policy Pursuits

These general possibilities are reflected in countless real situations in states and localities. The following summaries provide examples of the way the constituencies, the concerns, and the influence of governors interact to produce policy agendas and impacts across the states.

Liberal Democrats

When Bill Clinton won his second term of office as governor of Arkansas, one of his primary concerns was improving the quality of education in the state. He articulated and pursued the relatively liberal agenda of raising the level of funding for local education. He proposed an increase in the sales tax to finance that change. To claim that he was getting something in return, he also sought testing of teachers to insure they met minimal competency levels. With a clear agenda in mind, he used numerous means of influence. Clinton used the media to present his proposals statewide. He called the legislature into a special session. He met with legislators and lobbyists to press his case. After he won the increase in the sales tax, the teachers balked at the competency testing. He then used the media to portray them as reluctant to carry through on their part of the deal. He was able to present them as selfish after a commitment had been made to them. As he increased the pressure, teachers relented, and he was able to achieve the rest of his agenda. Clinton pursued his beliefs about the role of government and used formal and informal power to be successful.[60]

In other cases, a governor may not have campaigned promising a liberal agenda, but may respond as a liberal when events occur. The response of Jim Florio, former governor of New Jersey, illustrates that. When presented with a decline in the economy and a court order to address inequities in school finance, he did not avoid these problems. Instead, he proposed raising taxes and redistributing aid. He worked hard to persuade his party that they would be able to claim credit for solving the problems. That argument prevailed, and he was able to achieve these goals.

In other cases, a governor may have liberal concerns, but few formal powers, and may need to be careful in choosing the agenda to pursue. Ann Richards, a Democratic governor of Texas, took over at a time when there was continuing controversy and pressure from the courts to do something about inequities in school finance. When the legislature was considering a referendum that would redistribute some school finance funds, Richards' primary source of influence was limited to a promise to campaign for any program that would raise and distribute funds for schools.

Conservative Democrats

Not all Democrats are liberal. Some Democrats come to office by virtue of their appeals to moderates in swing district areas. Democrat Ella Grasso did well in Republican areas that other Democrats had not been able to win.[61] There were times during her tenure as governor when Democrats held the legislature and promoted consideration of an income tax. She resisted such efforts and pursued a more conservative course that would not alienate moderates.[62] Her resistance created a situation where the gubernatorial and legislative wings of the party were in conflict.

Conservative Republicans

Ronald Reagan became the Republican governor of California in 1967. He took a conservative approach to issues.[63] Reagan opposed tax increases, believed government was too large, and tried to reduce the size of government while in office. His agenda and policy pursuits fit his campaign. Governor William Weld of Massachusetts also fit this pattern. He appealed for a more limited government during his campaign and pursued that objective once in office.

Liberal Republicans

Nelson Rockefeller was first elected governor of New York in 1958. He faced the dilemma that he had to do well in New York City to win reelection. That situation compelled him to adopt relatively liberal policy positions regarding state aid and urban development programs.[64] Rockefeller, as New York state governor, had very strong formal powers, and he carefully and thoroughly worked to increase his informal power. His governorship was characterized by continual efforts to cultivate support with the press, local officials, and a broad coalition of state legislators. He was willing to meet with and curry the favor of the press. Rockefeller frequently met with, consulted, and listened to local officials and heads of local organizations. He continually did favors for legislators, kept track of every favor done, and expected legislators to reciprocate when he needed legislation passed. He worked closely with the party, but tried to mold it to his needs and goals. He created a large executive staff that answered only to him, and he used that staff continually to generate ideas that would put him at the center of attention and initiative in the state. Rockefeller was also willing to spend money for programs that various groups wanted. As a result, his power in the state was enormous.[65]

Ambiguous Cases

Finally, there are those executives who do not have a clear agenda and who may not be very effective at building the power they need in order to achieve whatever agenda they may create. Francis Sargent, governor of Massachusetts from 1969 to 1974, had not previously held an elective office. Prior to being governor, he was an engineer who rose through the ranks in the state department of transportation. Sargent was appointed acting governor in 1969 when John Volpe left the governorship to serve as a cabinet officer in the Nixon administration. Sargent inherited a position with almost as much formal power as the governorship in New York.

Once in office, however, Sargent used his office in a way that gave him very little informal power and perhaps even diminished the significance of his formal power. He seemed to have little taste for political maneuvering. He did little to create the dynamic staff that he needed in order to dominate issue discussions. He relied largely on reports from state agencies. He did not like to use the press much, did not like to spend his time traveling to meet with various groups, and did not like to bargain with them. He did not think in terms of doing favors for legislators to cultivate their loyalty, and he did little to twist their arms to adhere to his goals. When asked which legislators his office had done favors for, he replied that his office did not even keep track of such matters. Finally, he did not work well, if at all, with the party. Sargent set up his own campaign organization and did nothing to help other candidates or the party organization raise money. His background was that of an administrator, and he approached his position as if he was uncomfortable with being a "political animal." The result was that he was not popular with other political figures in the state, and he was largely ineffective in achieving his policy goals.[66]

The Mayors

All the variations in agendas and power situations discussed here for governors also exist for mayors. Their formal powers vary considerably as do their ability to develop informal powers. Much as with governors, they are also constrained by the amount of formal power granted them. The experience of Mayor Harold Washington of Chicago illustrates this. The mayoral position in Chicago has always been perceived as a strong position, but in reality the formal powers of the position are very limited. The city council has considerable power. When Washington became mayor there were high expectations of what he would be able to accomplish. By late 1983, early in his tenure in office, Washington became quite aware of the limits of his power. The city council blocked a great number of his activities, and

Washington had to begin bargaining with individual council members to create support for policies that he wanted to adopt.

Summary

The policy pursuits of governors and mayors are not always predictable. What executives pursue depends on electoral bases, personal beliefs, future ambitions, and many other factors. There is some predictability, to be sure. Democrats tend to be more liberal than Republicans. But it is always necessary to consider the specific political position of each politician before presuming what his or her agenda will be. Each political context—each state and locality—needs to be assessed on its own terms.

There are also no automatic assumptions we can make about politicians. Understanding what drives them requires careful study. There are no simple generalizations we can rely on, and there is much information we need to know. What any particular governor or mayor is likely to pursue (and why he or she does so) is a complicated matter. Even if we do figure out an executive's agenda our study of decision making has only begun. An executive's agenda is presented to the legislature or the local council, which may drastically alter it. In the next chapter, we will discuss the nature and the role of state and local legislatures.

For Further Reading

Benjamin, Gerald. "The Diffusion of Gubernatorial Power in American State Constitutions: Tenure and Tenure Limitations." *Publius* 15, no. 2 (fall 1985). A discussion of the changes in the powers granted to governors.

Beyle, Thad ed. *Governors and Hard Times.* Washington DC: Congressional Quarterly Press, 1992. Studies of situations faced by governors in specific states, with their responses.

Liebert, Roland. *Political Disintegration and Political Action.* New York: Academic Press, 1976. A discussion of the sources of current municipal administrative structures.

Miringoff, Lee M., and Barbara L. Carvalho. *The Cuomo Factor.* Poughkeepsie, New York: Marist Institute, 1986. An excellent study of a governor's electoral base.

Suggestions for Analysis in Your Own State and Locality

1. An executive begins with an electoral coalition. Find the election results of the current governor of your state and see how support varied by area. How would

you characterize the electoral coalition the governor put together? Analyze the same data for the mayor.

2. Executives who can run for reelection also to have worry about being able to retain their electoral coalition. Did the current governor win by attracting areas that are not certain to support his or her party? If so, what will the governor have to do to retain those areas? Consider the same questions for the mayor.

3. The constitution spells out the powers of the governor. Does the constitution of your state give the governor considerable power? Are there limits on the ability to run for reelection, to prepare the budget, and so forth? A local charter defines the power of the mayor or county executive. See if you can get a copy of it and review the powers granted to the local executive.

4. How skilled is your governor in using informal power? Does he or she define an agenda that is easy to grasp? Is that agenda kept prominent through news stories? How much success has the governor had in achieving the agenda? Again, consider the same questions for the mayor.

Notes

[1] Larry Sabato, *Goodbye to Good-Time Charlie* (Washington, DC: Congressional Quarterly Press, 1983), 25–45.

[2] Jack Bass and Walter DeVries, *The Transformation of Southern Politics* (New York: Basic Books, 1976), 63.

[3] Thad Beyle, "Governors," in *Book of the States, 1992–1993* (Lexington, Kentucky: Council of State Governments, 1992), 35.

[4] For interesting studies of the relationship between campaign stances and electoral bases, see the state studies in John Fenton, *Midwest Politics* (New York: Holt, Rinehart and Winston, 1966); and Earl Black, *Southern Governors and Civil Rights* (Cambridge: Harvard University Press, 1976), 48–141.

[5] Jeffrey M. Stonecash, "Political Cleavage in Gubernatorial and Legislative Elections: The Nature of Inter-Party Competition in New York Elections, 1970–1982," *Western Political Quarterly* 42, no. 1 (March 1989) 69–81.

[6] Dennis Hale, "Massachusetts: William F. Weld and the End of Business as Usual," in Thad Beyle, ed., *Governors and Hard Times* (Washington, DC: Congressional Quarterly Press, 1992), 131–35.

[7] Russell D. Murphy, "Connecticut: Lowell P. Weicker, Jr., A Maverick in the 'Land of Steady Habits,'" in Thad Beyle, *Governors and Hard Times*, 64–65.

[8] Richard Murray and Gregory R. Weiher, "Texas: Ann Richards, Taking on the Challenge," in Thad Beyle, ed., *Governors and Hard Times*, 179–188.

[9] Jeffrey M. Stonecash, "'Split' Constituencies and the Impact of Party Control," *Social Science History* 16, no. 3 (fall 1992): 455–477.

[10] Jeffrey M. Stonecash, "Inter-Party Competition, Political Dialogue, and Public Policy: A Critical Review," *Policy Studies Journal* 16, no. 2 (winter 1987–88): 243–262.

[11] James E. Jarett, "Gubernatorial Control of State Government Workforces," *State Government* 54, no. 3 (1981): 90.

[12] Asher Adrian et al., *Changing New York City Politics* (New York: Routledge, 1990), 28–38.

[13] Rob Gurwitt, "Indianapolis and the Republican Future," *Governing* (February 1994): 24–28.

[14] See Steven L. Myers, "Guliani Outlines a Budget to Cut Government Size," and Alison Mitchell, "Taking on the Unions," *New York Times*, 3 February 1994, A1.

[15] Larry Sabato, *Goodbye to Good-Time Charlie*, 2d ed. (Washington, DC: Congressional Quarterly Press, 1983), 104; and Thad Beyle, "Governors," in Virginia Gray, Herbert Jacob, and Robert Albritton, ed., in *Politics in the American States*, 5th ed. (Glenview, Ill.: Scott, Foresman/Little, Brown, 1990), 243.

[16] While the right to run for at least one additional term has increased, the support for unlimited pursuit of office has not increased. Over the last 200 years the proportion of executives who could run for as many terms as possible first increased but has been gradually declining for most of the last 100 years. See Gerald Benjamin, "The Diffusion of Executive Power in American State Constitutions: Tenure and Tenure Limitations," *Publius* 15, no. 4 (fall 1985): 78–80.

[17] William W. Lammers and David Klingman, "Durable Governors as Political Leaders: Should We Limit Tenure," *Publius* 16, no. 2 (spring 1986): 54–55.

[18] J. S. Turret, "The Vulnerability of American Governors, 1900–1969," *Midwest Journal of Political Science* 15 (1971): 108–132; Mark E. Thompkins, "The Electoral Fortunes of Gubernatorial Incumbents: 1947–1981," *Journal of Politics* 46, no. 2 (May 1984): 524; and Thad Beyle, "Governors," in Virginia Gray, Herbert Jacob, and Robert Albritton, ed., in *Politics in the American States*, 243.

[19] Barbara G. Salmore and Stephen A. Salmore, *Candidates, Parties and Campaigns*, 2d ed. (Washington, DC: Congressional Quarterly Press, 1989), 63–74.

[20] Irving Crespi, *Public Opinion, Polls and Democracy* (Boulder: Westview, 1989), 18–28.

[21] Richard W. Gable, "California: Pete Wilson, a Centrist in Trouble," in Thad Beyle, *Governors and Hard Times*, 52–57.

[22] James E. Underwood and William J. Daniels, *Governor Rockefeller in New York* (Westport, Conn.: Greenwood, 1982), 62–64.

[23] Peter Kerr, "Florio's Gamble," *New York Times*, 8 January 1992, A1.

[24] John Chubb, "Institutions, the Economy, and the Dynamics of State Elections," *American Political Science Review* 82, no. 1 (March 1988): 149; and Alan Rosenthal, *Contending Powers* (Washington, DC: Congressional Quarterly Press, 1990), 29–34.

[25] Lee M. Miringoff and Barbara L. Carvalho, *The Cuomo Factor* (Poughkeepsie, New York: Marist Institute, 1986).

[26] See the studies in Edward C. Lynch and Thomas P. Lauth, *Governors, Legislatures, and Budgets: Diversity Across the American States* (New York: Greenwood, 1991).

[27] Patrick J. Kenney, "The Effect of State Economic Conditions on the Vote for Governor," *Social Science Quarterly* 64 (1983): 154–161; and John E. Chubb, "Institutions, the Economy, and the Dynamics of State Elections," *American Political Science Review* 82, no. 1 (March 1988): 148–49.

[28] Dennis Grady, "Managing the State Economy: The Governor's Role in Policymaking," in Eric B. Herzik and Brent W. Brown, *Gubernatorial Leadership and State Policy* (Westport, Conn.: Greenwood, 1991), 109.

[29] Saundra Schneider, "Governors and Health Care Policy in the American States," *Policy Studies Journal* 17, no. 4 (1989): 909–926.

[30] Eric Herzik, "Policy Agendas and Gubernatorial Leadership," in Eric B. Herzik and Brent W. Brown, *Gubernatorial Leadership and State Policy* (Westport, Conn.: Greenwood, 1991), 31–32.

[31] Susan B. Hansen, *The Politics of Taxation: Revenue Without Representation* (New York: Praeger, 1983), 154.

[32] Elmer E. Cornwell, Jr., "Rhode Island: Bruce Sundlun and the State's Crises," in Thad Beyle, ed., *Governors and Hard Times*, 167.

[33] Dennis Hale, "Massachusetts: William F. Weld and the End of Business as Usual," in Thad Beyle, *Governors and Hard Times*, 131–135.

[34] Paul E. Peterson, *City Limits* (Chicago: University of Chicago Press, 1981).

[35] Clarence Stone, *Regime Politics: Governing Atlanta, 1946–1988* (University of Kansas Press, 1989), 77–134.

[36] Theodore Eisemier, "Votes and Taxes: The Political Economy of the American Governorship," *Polity* 15 (spring 1983): 368–79.

[37] Susan L. Kane and Richard F. Winters, "Taxes and Voting: Electoral Retribution in the American States," *Journal of Politics* 55, no. 1 (February 1993): 22–40.

[38] John Mikesell, "Election Periods and State Policy Cycles," *Public Choice* 20: 49–58; and Frances S. Berry and William D. Berry, "Tax Innovation in the States: Capitalizing on Political Opportunity," *American Journal of Political Science* 36, no. 3 (August 1992): 715–742.

[39] William W. Lammers and David Klingman, "Durable Governors as Political Leaders: Should We Limit Tenure," *Publius* 16, no. 2 (spring 1986): 62.

[40] L. Ray Gunn, *The Decline of Authority: Public Economic Policy and Political Development in New York, 1800–1860* (Ithaca: Cornell University Press, 1988), 62–66.

[41] New York State Division of the Budget, *The Executive Budget in New York State* (Albany: New York State Division of the Budget, 1981); and Edward J. Lynch and Thomas P. Lauth, "Budgeting in the American States: Important Questions about an Important Activity," in Edward J. Lynch and Thomas P. Lauth, *Governors, Legislatures, and Budgets: Diversity Across the American States* (Westport, Conn.: Greenwood, 1991), 1–4.

[42] Advisory Commission on Intergovernmental Relations, *The Question of State Government Capability,* (Washington DC: 1985), A-98, 127–41.

[43] Lee Sigelman and Nelson Dometrius, "Governors as Chief Executives," *American Politics Quarterly* 16 (1988): 157–170; and *The Book of the States*, 1992–1993 (Lexington, Ky.: The Council of State Governments, 76–81.

[44] Thad Beyle, "Governors," in Virginia Gray, Herbert Jacob, and Robert Albritton, *Politics in the American States*, 221–222.

[45] Dennis Grady, "Managing the State Economy: The Governor's Role in Policymaking," in Eric B. Herzik and Brent W. Brown, *Gubernatorial Leadership and State Policy* (New York: Greenwood, 1991), 114–116.

[46] Thad L. Beyle and Robert Dalton, "Appointment Powers: Does It Belong to the Governor?" *State Government* 54, no. 1 (1981): 2–12.

[47] Roland Liebert, *Disintegration and Political Action* (New York: Academic Press, 1976), 53.

[48] Thad Beyle, "Governors: The Power of Removal," *Policy Studies Journal* 17, no. 4 (summer, 1989): 805–827.

[49] Gerald Benjamin, "The Diffusion of the Governor's Veto Power," *State Government* 55, no. 3 (October 20, 1982): 99–105.

[50] Irene S. Rubin, Jack King, Steven C. Wagner, and Ellen M. Dran, "Illinois: Executive Reform and Fiscal Condition," in Edward C. Lynch and Thomas P. Lauth, *Governors, Legislatures and Budgets: Diversity Across the American States* (New York: Greenwood, 1991), 20–21.

[51] Kirk Johnson, "Quick Rebuff for New Weicker Tax Plan," *New York Times*, 15 August 1991, B1; and Kirk Johnson, "Hartford Offers Sobering Lessons as More States Face Tax Troubles," *New York Times*, 26 August 1991, A1.

[52] Nelson C. Dometrius, "Changing Gubernatorial Power: The Measure vs. Reality," *Western Political Quarterly* 41, no. 2 (1988): 319–328.

[53] E. Lee Bernick, "Gubernatorial Tools: Formal and Informal," *Journal of Politics* 41, no. 2 (May 1979): 656–64.

[54] Sally McCally Morehouse, *State Politics, Parties, and Policy* (New York: Holt, Rinehart and Winston, 1981), 251.

[55] Joseph F. Sullivan, "Control of Legislature is Prize in Jersey Election," *New York Times*, 7 November 1983, B1; and Joseph F. Sullivan, "Jersey Democrats Keep Control of Legislature," *New York Times*, 9 November 1983, B4.

[56] Alan Rosenthal, *Governors and Legislatures: Contending Powers*, (Washington, DC: Congressional Quarterly Press, 1990), 17–20.

[57] Jeffrey M. Stonecash, "'Split' Constituencies and the Impact of Party Control," 455–77.

[58] Morris Fiorina, *Divided Government*, (New York: Macmillan, 1992), 24–41.

[59] Lee Sigelman and Nelson C. Dometrius, "Governors as Chief Administrators: The Linkage Between Formal Powers and Informal Influence," *American Politics Quarterly* 16, no. 2 (April 1988): 161–65.

[60] Dan Durning, "Education Reform in Arkansas: The Governor's Role in Policymaking," in Eric B. Herzik and Brent W. Brown, ed. *Gubernatorial Leadership and State Government* (New York: Greenwood, 1991), 121–39.

[61] Jeffrey M. Stonecash, " 'Split' Constituencies and the Impact of Party Control" (paper presented at the American Political Science Association Meetings, 1984).

[62] Joseph I. Lieberman, *The Legacy* (Hartford: Spoonwood, 1981), 188–98.

[63] James E. Jarett, "Gubernatorial Control of State Government Workfaces," *State Government* 54: 87–92.

[64] Jeffrey M. Stonecash, " 'Split' Constituencies and the Impact of Party Control," *Social Science History* 16, no. 3 (fall 1992): 455–477.

[65] Robert H. Connery and Gerald Benjamin, *Rockefeller of New York: Executive Power in the Statehouse* (Ithaca: Cornell University Press, 1979), 40–108; and James Underwood and William J. Daniels, *Governor Rockefeller in New York* (Westport, Conn.: Greenwood, 1982).

[66] Martha W. Weinberg, *Managing the State* (Cambridge: Massachusetts Institute of Technology, 1977), 43–73.

10

Legislatures and Policy Pursuits

PREVIEW

Just as with governors and mayors, the policy pursuits that emerge from legislatures at the state and local levels are shaped by electoral coalitions. The important electoral groups are those that serve as the base of the majority party in each legislature body. To understand policy pursuits, we first must focus on these electoral bases.

The next, and biggest, challenge legislatures face is trying to forge a compromise among the different concerns that legislators have. Legislatures rely on a series of formal and informal practices to reconcile these differences.

Legislatures must also negotiate with governors and mayors. Just as with governors, the more formal power granted to legislatures and the more informal cohesion and power they can create, the more power legislatures have in negotiations with governors.

The Role of State and Local Legislatures

Legislatures embody the hopes and frustrations of democracy. While executives seek to represent majorities and provide policy coherence, legislatures embody diversity. They are an arena where the diverse concerns of the public can be represented. Legislators are generally elected from specific geographic areas because there has always been recognition that areas differ and that these different concerns should be represented. Legislators from these differing constituencies serve as the means to make sure their district's needs and views are fully presented.

Legislatures at the state and local level provide a setting where group concerns can be presented and debated before policy choices are made. This debate contributes to the democratic goal of a full airing of diverse views. If democracies are to be mechanisms by which "the people" have a role, legislatures are the prime arena for that to take place. Expectations for the rule of legislatures in democracy are considerable.

But legislatures also present frustrations. There are inevitably conflicts over desired policies. Legislators focus on district needs and are often considered parochial. District needs differ, legislators disagree, and sometimes it is difficult to reach any agreement on policies. Those agreements that are made often involve lengthy negotiations and compromise. This process is frustrating to the public. They regard legislators as self-serving and too preoccupied with reelection. Much of the public believes that there is a public interest. They believe there are public policies that are good for society. Politicians should "get on with it" and make the decisions. The public does not like much of the haggling involved.

Although it may sometimes seem that disorder prevails, legislatures play a coherent role in shaping decisions. Our concerns in this chapter are similar to those pursued in the preceding chapter. What affects the policy choices legislatures pursue? Does which party controls a legislature matter? If control of a legislature changes from one party to another, does this mean different policies will be enacted? What affects the ability of legislators to create coalitions cohesive enough to enact policies? And what affects the ability of the legislature to affect other political actors, such as the governor?

These roles are, of course, carried out in conjunction with those of governors and mayors. We will consider the interaction of executives and legislators in Chapter 12. For now, however, we will focus primarily on the workings of legislatures.

Political Representation: Careerism and the Issue of Motivations in State Legislatures

Legislators are the mechanisms of representation. It is they who must articulate and fight for the concerns of constituents. Legislators form the basis for the coalitions that pass or that block legislation. Legislators bring perspectives to office, and the more one perspective dominates, the more it is likely to shape the agenda pursued in a legislature. Our first concern then is to understand what shapes the concerns of legislators.

In a simple world, legislators would just "represent" their districts. There has been considerable concern, however, about whether representation can ever be this simple. Several questions about representation have received attention. Are legislators typical of the electorate? Does campaign money distort their concerns? Does preoccupation with reelection affect representation? These are serious questions that deserve attention. They raise the question of what assumptions we can make about the concerns, motives, and goals of legislators.

The Typicality of Representatives

One of the primary matters that might affect the concerns of legislatures is the background of legislators. Representation might occur because legislators are very typical of the populations in their districts. If our legislators are like us, then we can trust that our views will be expressed. If legislators are not like us, then we must trust that they are sufficiently aware of, or concerned about, our views to represent them.

The reality is that legislators are not like the general public. They are generally of higher socioeconomic status than the rest of the population.[1] Most legislators have more education than the general public.[2] They are more likely to be from white-collar occupations like law and business. They are also more likely to be white and male.

The reasons for this "overrepresentation" of some groups is related to our earlier discussions of differences in participation. Individuals with more education are more skilled at working in political organizations, they are more skilled at presenting themselves to various groups during campaigns, and they are more likely to have access to the resources (money and organizational support) necessary to run for office. Occupations also matter. Those individuals with jobs in law and business have more-flexible time schedules. People in these positions can more easily campaign and serve in legislatures.

Women and minorities have held fewer legislative positions because parties have not been eager to recruit them, and the public has not been willing to vote them into office. There has been change in the composition of state legislatures during the last decade, with more minorities and women gaining office.[3] Despite those gains, women and minorities are still underrepresented relative to their proportion in the population.

In general, legislators are not like their constituents. The evidence suggests we are not likely to obtain representation simply because legislators are like their constituents. Any representation that does occur must come from the way legislators approach their job, from their ambitions to remain in office, and from their sense of what they must do to stay in office.

Role Conceptions

Role conceptions refer to the way legislators approach their positions and what they conceive their responsibilities to be. One of the long-standing concerns of democratic theorists has been the attitudes that legislators hold about the proper relationship between constituents and themselves. Some legislators believe their role is to be somewhat independent of the passions or parochial views of their constituents and to focus on making the best decisions based on their own judgment. In such a view, the legislator is elected to draw on his or her wisdom and should take a reasonably detached view of which policies are best. These legislators hold what we call a "trustee" role conception.[4] The alternative role for a legislator is to serve as an instructed delegate of his or her constituents. In this view, a legislator should find out the views of his or her district, and then serve as a conveyer of those views to other legislators and decision makers. Such a legislator should not be independent, but should be closely tied to the needs and concerns of his or her constituents. This role is called that of the "delegate."

While these role models might be fine in the abstract, there is also the possibility of a middle ground between these two alternatives. Some legislators may feel that under certain circumstances it is appropriate to be independent, but that in others, they must vote with the desires of their constituents. The term usually applied to this type of legislator is "politico."

Are these role conceptions relevant to the way legislators approach the task of representation of their districts? When asked their conception of their role, most legislators (about 60 percent) viewed themselves as trustees.[5] About 30 percent defined themselves as politicos, and about 10 percent as delegates. Most legislators do not approach their role with the belief that they should serve as delegates. This expectation might produce a situation in which legislators are not very aware of the needs and concerns of their constituents. Indeed, there is evidence that self-described delegates are a little more aware of opinions in their districts than those who think of themselves as trustees.[6] This evidence that many legislators think of themselves as trustees creates anxiety about how well they represent their constituents.

Campaign Money

There are also worries about the effects of campaign donations on legislators. It is argued by many that money determines the outcome of elections. The cost of elections has increased, and upper-income individuals and PACs contribute large proportions of the funds raised. There is concern that reliance on these sources of funds makes politicians more responsive to PAC concerns and less responsive to district constituents.[7]

Electoral Competition

Finally, there are anxieties about a decline in electoral competition. Many argue that the primary way to make legislators worry about their constituents is to have them face competitive races. The more competitive the race, the more likely a legislator will be concerned about being representative. The concern of critics is that most legislators do not face close elections. Most areas of a state tend to be dominated by one party. That dominance almost insures that the candidate of that party wins by a relatively large margin. If a close election is defined as one in which the winner and loser are separated by less than 10 percent of the vote, few elections are close.[8] There is also evidence that electoral competition is declining,[9] and that the proportion of uncontested elections is rising.[10]

These phenomena—legislators who are not typical of their constituents, who think they should do what is right, who rely heavily on campaign donations, and who do not have close elections—raise serious questions about how well legislators represent their constituents.

The Sources of Representation

Despite these anxieties, there is considerable evidence that legislators do represent their constituents. First, most state legislators are elected from districts. Table 10.1 presents a summary of the use of districts in state legislatures. Most state legislators are elected from single-member districts. That is, only one legislator is elected from any district. Some legislators are elected from multimember districts, or ones in which the top two or three vote getters assume office, with all of them representing the same area. But even these legislators are representing fairly limited geographic areas.

Election from districts is important for representation. People of similar backgrounds tend to cluster together, and districts tend to differ in their population

Table 10.1

Use of Single-Member and Multimember Election Districts for State Legislators

Legislature State House	Single Member Districts (#)	(%)	Multimember Districts (#)	(%)
Districts	4,034	88	563	12
Legislators	4,034	74	1,418	26
State Senate				
Districts	1,833	97	62	3
Legislators	1,833	93	148	7

Source: State legislatures: Samuel G. Patterson, "State Legislators and the Legislatures," in Virginia Gray, Herbert Jacob, and Robert B. Albritton, eds., Politics in the American States, 5th ed. (Scott, Foresman, 1990), 166.

composition. The legislators who come out of these districts tend to be somewhat typical of the population of their districts. Rural districts with conservative white populations tend to elect conservative whites. Urban districts with liberal minority populations tend to elect liberal minority legislators. Suburban districts, which often embody a diverse electorate, elect legislators who are moderate. There are exceptions to be sure, but the pattern is that districts elect legislators who are fairly typical in their political views of the population they represent.[11] If they are typical of their district, then doing what they think is the "right" thing is likely to produce positions not very different from what the district wants. A Republican elected from any district is likely to be more conservative than a Democrat elected from that same district, but neither of them is likely to diverge much from the nature of the district.

The tendency to be aware of and sensitive to constituent concerns may also be increased by the ambitions of politicians. State legislators who wish to run for reelection and who view themselves as professionals are more likely to be willing to meet with, listen to, and interact with groups in their districts.[12] This desire to run for reelection has increased over the years. The proportion of legislators running for reelection has increased steadily in Congress and in many state legislatures.[13] Many legislators do quit, but it appears that approximately 80 percent now regularly seek reelection at the state level.[14] Even in years after reapportionment, such as in 1992, when many legislators found they had to campaign in new districts, 80 percent still sought reelection.[15] Interest in staying in office is also indicated by the length of legislative careers. More legislators are staying in office longer.[16]

The consequence of this concern with reelection is fundamental to representation. Legislators who want to stay in office are more likely to be attentive to their district. The desire not to be out of touch with their constituency drives legislators to pay more attention to their districts. Even those who appear to be safe are still likely to worry about losing their position and work hard to represent their district.[17]

There are also more legislators who treat their position as full-time. They spend more time in their districts just meeting people and listening to their concerns.[18] The homogeneity of most districts makes it easier for legislators to use this time to develop a good idea of district concerns. Legislators continually attend local meetings and luncheons. They receive letters and calls from constituents. All this activity adds to their knowledge of public opinion. On many issues, legislators have a very good sense of constituency opinion. This knowledge is usually greatest when an issue has received considerable public attention.[19]

Legislators whose opinions are typical of their districts, who are concerned about reelection, and who have been in office for several years are likely to be concerned about representing their districts and knowledgeable of district concerns. While there are reasons to worry about pressures—particularly campaign money—that might make legislators less representative of districts, the focus of most legislators is to represent their districts. One need only attend a legislative session in which some controversial legislation is being voted on to see how much they worry about the way legislation will affect their districts.

Legislators may respond, when asked, that they regard their own judgment as primary, but they also indicate they place primary reliance on district concerns

Table 10.2

*Decision Referents for Legislators: Should and Actual,
Ranked from Most to Least Important*

Should Use	Actually Use
Conscience	District
State	Conscience
District	Party
Party	State
Governor	Group
Group	Governor

Source: Ronald Hedlund, "Perceptions of Decision Referents in Legislative Decision Making," American Journal of Political Science 19, no. 3 (August 1975): 527–542.

when actually making decisions. Table 10.2 presents the results from one study that asked legislators what concerns they believe they should use and what concerns they actually do use. District concerns dominate their actual decision making.

Not everyone agrees with this assessment. Critics of the rise of career politicians think that legislators have become too professional. They argue that career legislators get out of touch with the electorate, or that they want to stay in office so badly that they avoid controversial issues. This criticism and others will be taken up at the end of this chapter.

Political Representation: Careerism and the Issue of Motivations in Local Legislatures

Local legislators and legislatures present somewhat more of an unknown than those at the state level. We know some things, but not others. In some ways, local legislators are very similar to state legislators. Local city councilors and county legislators are also not typical of the public they represent. They have higher incomes and more education.[20] They also differ in whether they believe their job is to do what they believe is right, or to do what constituents want, although most do believe that they should function as trustees.[21]

In other regards, however, there are differences between state and local situations. At the local level, the most common arrangement for electing legislators is at-large districts, or districts combined with at-large districts. Table 10.3 indicates the types of election districts used in cities and counties of different sizes. Most local legislators are not elected from specific districts.

It also appears that there may be differences in motivations to continue in office. Most local legislators do not stay in office very long. We do not have

Table 10.3

Use of At-Large and District Arrangements for Election to Local Legislatures

Type and Size of Local Government	At-large (#)	At-large (%)	District (#)	District (%)	Mixed (#)	Mixed (%)
Cities, by population						
500,000+	2	15.4	3	23.1	8	61.5
100,00–499,999	43	37.0	28	24.1	53	45.6
25,000–99,999	385	55.0	70	10.0	236	33.7
2,500–24,999	1924	62.7	396	12.9	747	24.3
All Cities	2354	60.4	497	12.8	1044	26.8
Counties, by population						
500,000+	9	24.3	15	40.5	13	35.1
100,00–499,999	57	34.1	70	41.9	40	23.9
25,000–99,999	88	23.0	176	46.0	118	30.8
Under 24,999	152	22.7	310	46.4	206	32.9
All Counties	306	24.4	571	45.5	377	30.1

Source: Tari Renner, "Municipal Election Processes: The Impact on Minority Representation," The Municipal Year Book (1988) (Washington DC, 1988), 13.

thorough analyses of career patterns at the local level. But the evidence that we do have indicates that most do not stay very long, and that those who leave do so because they quit rather than because they are defeated.[22] While careerism appears to be increasing at the state level, there is no evidence of this trend at the local level.

The differences at the local level are potentially very important. Legislators who represent homogeneous districts are more likely to know their district and to be able to speak for it knowledgeably. Legislators from at-large districts may be less aware of constituent needs and opinions. City councilors who aspire to win reelection pay more attention to their constituents.[23] When there are situations in which legislators operate with trustee conceptions of their roles, have diverse districts, and are not worried about reelection, the connection between constituents and legislator representation may be more erratic.[24] We do not know, however, whether this is actually the case. Indeed, critics of legislatures argue that the representation process works better when legislators are not preoccupied with reelection. But the concern of these critics is whether problems are responded to, not whether representation occurs.

The important point is that the evidence indicates that local legislatures are dominated less by careerism. This situation may mean that legislators spend less time on their jobs and less time interacting with constituents. That situation has the potential to affect representation. Theory tells us that it should make a difference, but our systematic evidence is limited.

Policy Pursuits: Legislators and Political Coalitions

The election of individual legislators only begins the process of deciding on policy agendas. The next step is to find sufficient commonalities among legislators such that they can agree on what policies to support. Although a governor may listen to many, he or she ultimately can choose what agenda to pursue. Decision making in legislatures, however, involves many people. Legislators must explore commonalities and try to work out an agreement among diverse members on what agenda will be pursued. That exploration begins once legislators are elected to office.

The search for potential agreement usually starts with those of the same party. Democrats come to office with some minimal agreement on values with other Democrats. Party members also would like to avoid having to rely on the other party to reach decisions. This point is particularly true when applied to members of the majority party. Members of the majority party want to avoid relying on members of the minority party. The first place to start, then, in trying to understand what legislatures are likely to do is with the majority party in each house. Table 10.4 presents party control of each house in the state legislatures for 1992.

In 1992, Democrats controlled the bulk of houses in the states. There were only six legislatures where the Republicans were the majority party in both houses. In eleven states, party control was divided between the two parties.

While Democratic or Republican party control provides some indication of the likely policies a legislature may pursue, it is only a crude indicator. Shared party labels often suggest common agendas among legislators when there is considerable diversity of views within a party. Legislators may be from the same party, but they may not share the same constituency. Republicans, for example, are elected from different areas of a state or city, and the party may contain members with different constituencies. The Democratic legislative party may also contain members with diverse constituencies.

Table 10.4

Partisan Control of State Legislatures, 1992

Majority Party in Senate	Majority Party in House	
	Democratic	*Republican*
Democratic	AL, AR, CA, CT, FL, GA, HI, IL, IA, KY, LA, ME, MD, MA, MN, MS, MO, MT, NM, NC, OK, RI, SC, TN, TX, VA, WV, WI	AZ, DE, ND, OR
Republican	IN, KS, MI, NY, OH, PA, WA	CO, NH, NJ, SD, UT, WY

Note: States where seats are evenly distributed between two parties: Alaska, Idaho, Nevada, Vermont; Nebraska has a one house, nonpartisan legislature.
Source: Book of the States, 1992–1993.

Table 10.5 presents the electoral bases for legislative parties in three non-southern states. These are the same three non-southern states examined in Chapter 5. In this case, however, the information is presented somewhat differently. The concern here is the composition of each party, or the proportion of each party that comes from urban, suburban, or rural areas. In California in 1990, Democrats were the majority party in each house. The Democratic party is more than an urban party in California. In the House, only 45 percent of the legislators come from urban areas. In the Senate, only 36 percent are from urban areas. These proportions suggest that the Democratic party in California is not likely to be concerned only with policies helpful to urban areas. A large part of the party is based in suburban areas. Proposals to distribute more school aid to urban areas and away from suburbs are likely to have little chance with such a party base.

Table 10.5

Geographical Bases of Political Parties in Selected Non-Southern States, 1990

	House/Assembly				Senate			
Area	Republican		Democrat		Republican		Democrat	
	(%)	(#)	(%)	(#)	(%)	(#)	(%)	(#)
Ohio								
Rural	36	10	15	9	14	3	17	2
Suburban	25	7	25	15	62	13	42	5
Urban	39	11	61	37	24	5	42	5
Total		28		61		21		12
New York								
Rural	40	22	3	3	34	12	0	0
Suburban	42	23	18	14	37	13	4	1
Urban	18	10	82	78	29	10	96	25
Total		55		95		35		26
California								
Rural	27	9	6	3	17	3	12	3
Suburban	73	24	49	23	56	10	52	13
Urban	0	0	45	21	28	5	36	9
Total		33		47		18		25

Note: For each state, the numbers in the right-hand columns for each party represent the actual number of legislators in that house. The numbers in the left-hand columns give the percent of the party's seats which come from each area. The total number of members in each party is shown below each column. Percents sum down.
Source: See Chapter 5.

Republican parties also have their tensions. The Republican party held the senate majority in New York and in Ohio in 1990. Most of the members of both parties came from suburban and rural areas. But each party also obtained its majority because of members elected from urban areas. Those urban-based Republicans are not likely to have the same concerns as Republicans from rural and suburban areas. That difference creates tensions in the party.

Every party has some of these tensions. The diversity of party bases can make it difficult to anticipate the policies that a party will be willing to support when it holds a majority in a house. But there is certainly some predictability. In states like Ohio, New York, and California, the Republican party has most of its base in suburban and rural areas. The party is more likely to be conservative to moderate. The Democratic party in these states is primarily based in urban and suburban areas and is more likely to be liberal to moderate.

The situation in southern states is somewhat more complicated. In states like Florida and Texas, the parties are still in transition, and the electoral bases of the parties are not as clear. Table 10.6 presents the bases of the legislative parties in those states in 1990. The Democratic party held the majority in each house in those two states in 1990. The Democratic party derives much of its support from urban and heavily nonwhite areas in each state. But the Democratic party also has a significant proportion of its members in rural areas and in heavily white areas. It is a party with a very diverse base. Such diversity will affect the way a party responds to policy proposals.

These party bases establish the policy inclinations of the parties. But they only define general possibilities. Campaigns tend to be individual in nature. It is very unusual for a statewide legislative party to propose general party policies during campaigns as a means for their candidates to get elected.[25] The individual legislators who are elected have preferences, and they bring these preferences to the legislature. After each election, each party begins again to explore the possibilities of support for different policies.

The greater the predominance of one group in a party, the more the policy inclinations of the party will be clear. If the Democrats acquire power and if most of their legislators are from urban areas, support for redistribution of school and mass-transit aid to urban areas will be high. If Republicans with a rural and suburban base acquire power, support will be high for more aid to their schools and for spending money on roads rather than on mass transit.

These inclinations are affected, of course, by the party's reading of the current political climate, or current conditions and events. Similarly to governors, legislators must deal with the setting that exists when they acquire power. If Democrats acquire power when businesses are leaving the state because they say taxes are too high, it is unlikely that Democrats will use their power to enact higher taxes. Some times legislators do feel that they have a mandate. When Republicans acquired power in New Jersey in 1992, they felt they had a mandate to cut taxes because that proposal had been the theme of the preceding campaign. Republicans had taken seats from Democrats in areas that were angry about taxes proposed and passed by Democrats.

Once again, what politicians do with power depends.

Table 10.6

Geographical Bases of Political Parties in Two Southern States, 1990

	House				Senate			
Area	*Republican*		*Democrat*		*Republican*		*Democrat*	
	(%)	*(#)*	*(%)*	*(#)*	*(%)*	*(#)*	*(%)*	*(#)*
Florida								
Rural	0	0	9	7	0	0	21	5
Suburban	43	20	24	18	31	5	13	3
Urban	57	26	66	49	69	11	67	16
Total		46		74		16		24
Race (% white)								
0–49.9%	15	7	23	17	19	3	8	2
50–74.9%	4	2	22	16	6	1	29	7
75 + %	81	37	55	41	75	12	63	15
Total		46		74		16		24
Texas								
Rural	12	7	15	14	25	2	35	8
Suburban	10	6	11	10	13	1	18	4
Urban	78	46	74	67	63	5	48	11
Total		59		91		8		23
Race (% Anglo)								
0–49.9%	14	8	46	42	13	1	35	8
50–74.9%	24	14	30	27	25	2	39	9
75 + %	59	35	26	24	63	5	30	7
Total		59		91		8		23

Note: For each state, the numbers in the right-hand columns for each party represent the actual number of legislators. Numbers in the left-hand columns give the percent of the party's seats which come from each area. The total number of members in each party is shown below each column. Percents sum down.
Source: See Chapter 5.

Organizing to Act: The Formal Process of Enacting Legislation

The political bases of legislative parties shape what policies are likely. The challenge facing legislatures is to turn that political base into policy decisions. It is a long and demanding task, with many steps and conditions affecting how that happens and what is possible. One of the first conditions that is important is the formal process of passing legislation.

Legislators must set up a formal process for making decisions. Legislators come from different districts with different needs, and they differ in desired policies. The dilemma for legislators is how to organize their decision-making process in a way that protects the rights of legislators to be heard, while also creating the means to allow legislators to resolve conflicts. Legislators want to be heard, but they want an organized process that will allow decisions to emerge.

The Formal Process

To accommodate these needs, legislatures have established formal processes that must be adhered to before a decision can be made. Getting people with different views to agree is never easy. But there is agreement that majorities should be able to enact policy when a majority can agree about a policy. To make sure that there is an organized review and a debate of legislation, legislatures have an agreed-upon set of rules that all proposals must go through. If that process is known, members can at least anticipate the steps a proposal must pass through. This anticipation makes the process orderly and routine. All legislators involved in the process can anticipate when they must make persuasive arguments if they are going to have a chance to change minds about legislation. This process provides minimal protection for minority views, but it does make it possible to enact majority preferences.

The primary goal of these procedures is not efficiency. Democracies have always been uneasy about making it too easy for majorities to act quickly. Therefore there are steps in the process where objections can be raised and where extended debate can be conducted. The result is that legislatures are generally orderly but slow. This slowness often leaves the public frustrated. Many expect that efficiency and order should prevail. But the emphasis on deliberation creates rules that slow down quick action.

Rules of Procedure

The bulk of legislative procedures revolve around the way bill proposals are handled. A bill is a proposed law that will determine policy in some area, whether it be in civil rights, tax practices, or eligibility for a government program. There is variation among legislatures, but the general procedure is to require a series of steps that a bill must go through before it can be adopted. The general sequence is as follows:

Bill writing and introduction (either house)   Interest groups, individuals, governors, and legislators get ideas for legislation. That idea is then worked over by someone with experience in legal language, and that person prepares a bill for consideration by the legislature. The bill is filed with the clerk or the presiding officer of either house. The bill is given a number and referred to the committee that considers that area of public policy (transportation, welfare, property taxes). At this stage, bills are printed so that they are available to others.

Public hearings and committee review   Bills that are considered particularly important may be reviewed at a public hearing where all interested parties can speak about the bill. Normally, however, the bill is considered by the legislators and staff who make up the committee. The staff will do whatever research they can to understand the effects of the bill. The staff will usually consult with interest groups and receive statements and reports from other parties interested in the bill. Other legislators will also be consulted.

Committee consideration   The members of the committee (legislators accompanied by their staff) will then meet to decide whether to pass the bill out of the committee for consideration by the entire legislature. In general, the majority party will decide which bills will come out of committee, since the majority party has more members on each committee. A report may accompany the bill. The report usually reviews the rationale and the consequences of the proposed legislation and makes a suggestion of action. The committee may also "hold" a bill in committee. This is what happens to most bills. Committee members may regard a proposal as unwise, not sufficiently developed, or too politically dangerous to handle yet. The majority party on the committee may simply be opposed to the bill because of the way it harms their constituents. A held bill cannot be considered by the legislature unless a special appeal is made to discharge the bill from the committee. If the bill has fiscal implications or affects another policy area, it may also have to go through a fiscal committee or another policy committee. The leadership of the legislature may play a dominant role at this stage by trying to pressure members to accept or reject the legislation.

Calendar placement   The bill is then placed on the calendar, or schedule, for formal consideration. A bill can sometimes get on the calendar even if a committee holds it, but that is not the norm. The calendar is made public so that all interested parties will know when the bill is likely to be voted on. A bill usually has to be put on a calendar several days before it is actually voted on. This delay gives everyone time to prepare for the debate and vote.

Floor debate, amendment, and vote   The bill is then considered by the entire legislature, at which time individual legislators may propose changes. There are significant variations across legislatures in when amendments are allowed and what the procedures are for creating them. A vote is finally taken on the bill unless there is agreement that the legislation is not desired as is. Such a decision on a bill might result in its being sent back to committee for reconsideration. In some cases, this vote may be considered only the preliminary vote, and it may be necessary to take a final vote shortly thereafter.

Action in the second chamber   In all states but Nebraska, which has a unicameral (one-house) legislature, this procedure must then be repeated in the other house. City councils also have just one legislative body, so the steps just reviewed finish initial action for them, and passed legislation is sent to the chief executive of the city or county.

Conference committee   If the other house passes a different version of the legislation, in some states a conference committee is formed from members of both houses, and they seek to produce a compromise bill. The compromise bill must then go back to each house to be voted on. If there is no provision for a conference committee, an identical bill must be submitted to and passed by each house. This may entail lengthy negotiations to decide which bill should prevail.

Executive action   The legislation is then sent to the governor or mayor who may accept or reject the legislation. If the executive explicitly rejects the bill, or refuses to sign by a required deadline, the bill does not become law.

Legislative override   If the legislation is rejected, it is returned to the legislature, but it may be overridden according to the terms discussed in Chapter 9.

Parliamentary Rules

This legislative procedure is also accompanied by a set of procedural rules known as parliamentary rules. These rules define the way this legislative process must take place and the way it can be altered. These rules include requirements as to what proportion of committee members must be present to take a vote, whether a minority can take action on its own, how a step can be avoided, how long a bill must be in everyone's possession before it can be voted on, and other such requirements.

Together, these rules are intended to create an orderly process for considering legislation and to make it possible for large groups of diverse legislators to handle different concerns. Though we have no firm evidence, it appears that these rules are more formally developed in state legislatures than in city councils. Councils are much smaller in size, and some argue that with smaller numbers it is possible to be more informal in procedure. Although that may be true, city councils still have such rules on the books, and those rules may be invoked as legislators desire.

Committees

Bills are reviewed in committees. Legislatures face a considerable volume of proposed legislation each year. In some states, 400 to 500 bills are introduced each year, while in the larger states, the number can be as high as 16,000. Even if the number of bills introduced were small, legislatures would still face the problem of acquiring information on, and understanding the many different legislative proposals. Legislatures must find a way to cut down the number of bills being considered.[26]

The solution is to establish committees that specialize in various subject areas and to have these committees do the bulk of the work of evaluating and shaping legislation. In this way, legislators develop in-depth knowledge of specific areas, and the legislature in turn has someone to turn to in order to assess the merits and effects of proposed legislation.[27]

Committees exist because the legislators cannot be expected to know all the issues considered by the legislature. Members can focus on areas of interest and relevance to them and delegate consideration of other issues to members on other committees. It would be impossible for most legislatures to proceed without this committee system.

The Role of Leadership

In addition to relying on procedural rules, legislatures also rely on leaders to direct activities. As with any organization, there is generally a desire to place someone in charge. This leadership role is handled by the speaker or president of each house. Members of the legislature elect a leader, who is given responsibility for organizing activity and "directing traffic." Leaders are usually given the power to appoint the chairs of committees, along with the other members of the committee. He or she is also empowered to interpret many rules and to assign bills to committees. In states without strong leadership, committee heads are selected by a caucus (an informal gathering of political party members, meeting prior to the start of the session), by a committee on committees, or by election by the house. In such systems, the leadership has less influence over the committee process.

Strong leadership often emerges for several reasons. There may be a tradition of strong leadership that is difficult to change, but the primary factor affecting the power of leadership is the inclination of members to want it. If the leadership is able to convince members that they are listened to and that policy compromises are fair to most members across a range of issues, the inclination to grant leadership authority is greater.[28] If a leader can fulfill this role well, the members can rely on the leadership to keep the legislative process moving along. This reliance on the leader will allow members to pursue other legislative and political concerns that they have. Houses that have larger memberships usually grant more power to leadership because it is more difficult to coordinate action among a larger body of people.

Strong leadership is not well regarded by the public. Criticism has emerged because of stories about powerful leaders who dictate committee decisions and who remove committee members who do not go along with leadership wishes. In other cases, the press may create an image of a powerful boss even when that person's power may not be so great. The press often portrays politics in terms of personalities, and it is not unusual for a speaker to have a reputation for more power than he or she actually has. These stories serve as catalysts to mobilize public sentiment against strong leadership. Much as with political parties, strong leadership often clashes with the public's notion of the way the democratic process should work. Many people believe decisions should emerge from lengthy debate and serious consideration of issues. If this process is done properly and thoroughly, then the public interest should emerge. Leaders are often seen as self-interested and inclined to distort the legislative process for personal or partisan purposes.

Despite these criticisms, legislators usually find some virtues in having strong leadership. The leadership can move the process along and curtail stalling by the minority party or a faction in the majority party that is holding out for a better deal. The leadership can be given the power to negotiate a settlement with the other house or with the governor. Leadership can contribute to reaching some decision. This process does not mean that the members just surrender power to the leadership. Most members are willing to grant authority to a leader as long as that power is not abused. Leadership power is derived from the members, and it persists only so long as the leader is somewhat restrained in using it.[29]

Organizing to Act: Staff and the Professional Legislature

Reviewing legislation is a demanding task. It is a job that requires some expertise and time enough to consider the nature and effects of legislation. Faced with multiple demands on their time, many legislators have come to rely on staff to do much of this work. Staff members provide a means to develop policy proposals, to review proposals made by other legislators, to review gubernatorial proposals, and to oversee executive behavior. They provide help to individual legislators. They also give the legislature more capacity to be equal to the governor in developing and responding to policy proposals.

There have been significant increases over the last two decades in the size of legislative staffs. Thirty years ago, many legislatures had limited staffs, and they were not in session for many days during the year. That situation has changed. In the larger states, legislatures now have large, often well paid, staffs working for them. These legislatures are also in session for longer periods of time.[30] There are, however, legislatures where there has not been much change in staff resources. Table 10.7 summarizes differences in the size of legislative staffs across the states. It also groups states by legislator salaries.

In states like California and New York, there are large legislative staffs available to critique and to develop policy proposals. Legislator salaries are also high. In other states, such as Montana and North Dakota, there are far fewer staff members available for such tasks, and legislator salaries are much lower. The tendency is for legislatures with high legislator salaries to also devote more money to staffs. Those legislatures high on both of these are the ones we call professional legislatures.

Table 10.7

Legislative Staffs and Legislator Salaries in the States

| Staff Size | Per Diem | Legislator Salary Levels | | |
		$0–14,999	$15,000–29,999	$30,000 +
0–300	MT, NE, ND, NE RI	ID, ME, MS, NH, SD	CO, DE, TN	
301–499	AL, KY, KS, NM	AR, AK, IN, NC, SC	IA	OK, WV
500–800		CT, GA, OR	AK, HI, LA MD, MO, VA	OH, MA, WI
801–4000		TX	FL, MN, WA	CA, IL, MI NY, PA, NJ

Sources: The Book of the States, 1992–1993, and National Conference of State Legislatures, Legislative Staff Services, 50 Staff Profile (1988).

For city councils and county legislatures, staff resources are generally very limited. The amount of time that these bodies meet is also very limited. Sessions are usually held once a month, every two weeks, or once a week, and often only at night. Meetings may go on at other times, but formal meeting times are limited.

What difference does the existence of staff make? Its greatest impact is on the capability of the legislature to play a role in decision making. Larger staffs result in legislators having more information, generated by their own staff.

Information alone, however, does not change the concerns that legislators bring to office. It is unlikely to make Democrats agree with Republicans. Democrats from urban areas still want aid for urban areas. Conservative Republicans still want welfare restrained and taxes cut. The coalitions that dominate legislatures are still the primary determinant of the policy directions likely to be pursued.

What has changed is that legislatures now have more resources to research, articulate, and pursue the agendas legislators want. Legislature capacity to research information and to conduct analyses has increased.[31] Legislators who want to formulate an agenda now have the resources to present that agenda. They have the staff to challenge the revenue estimates of the governor. They have the staff to review, critique, and propose alternatives to the governor's budget.[32] The legislature has changed from having to accept gubernatorial information to researching its own.[33] Legislatures have developed to such an extent that many of them are engaged in oversight activities, or attempts to monitor what the governor is doing. This change has been accompanied by an increase in the number of legislators who remain in the legislature for consecutive terms. These legislators, with more experience in issues and more knowledge of government, and with more staff, are now more capable of playing an effective role in policy debates.

Much as with other changes, the rise of professional legislatures has drawn considerable criticism. Critics argue that it creates too many career politicians who are too preoccupied with staying in office. They argue that larger staffs, paid for with public dollars, are used to do constituency work for voters, an act that creates gratitude among constituents.[34] At the same time, legislators still avoid controversial issues in order not to alienate voters.[35] All this makes legislators safer in office, but important policy issues are not resolved.[36]

These are important criticisms. As with the previous ones regarding legislatures, these criticisms involve basic questions of whether legislators are representing their constituents and whether the institution is responding to political concerns. Such criticisms have led some to propose a limit on the number of terms legislators can serve. We will return to these criticisms at the end of the chapter.

Organizing to Act: Informal Practices for Reaching Decisions

The formal procedures of legislatures are important. They provide a continuing and known process for making decisions. Understanding these procedures is important, but it is of limited value for understanding how legislatures work. It neglects the informal processes that legislators use to reach agreements about policies.

Informal processes refer to practices that legislatures adhere to, but that are not written down. These practices evolve over time and acquire a tradition and a base of support among the members such that most members come to rely upon them. The most significant informal practices revolve around the mechanisms that legislators use to get members to agree to legislation that they may not be completely in favor of. Such practices are the means to achieve minimal consensus among a majority.

Accommodating Each Other

Legislatures are institutions where differing political concerns are represented. They are also social institutions where people must learn to work together. Legislators with one set of concerns must continually interact with legislators who have other policy preferences. Some of these policy differences involve intensely held views, such as those involving pro-choice and pro-life views on abortion. Somehow legislators must find a way to make decisions amid this diversity of needs. They would also probably prefer to work together in a reasonably cordial way. The primary means of doing this in legislatures has been to rely on a set of practices that emphasize accommodation and reciprocity. The intent is to find a way to mediate conflict. The general principle pursued is: I will do something for you (support your legislative needs) if you will do something for me (support my legislative needs).

There are several general norms that legislators adopt to help the environment of decision making. They strive not to allow policy arguments to become personal. Legislators may not like each other, but they try to respect each other. They also try to respect (though not necessarily accept) each other's district needs whenever possible. If someone else needs specific legislation for his or her district and such legislation affects only that district or an individual in that district ("local" bills), then that legislator should be able to get the bill through without opposition.

The fundamental informal practices for trying to smooth the process of decision making are compromise, logrolling, and pork-barreling. These are mechanisms by which legislators seek to resolve conflicts so that decisions can be reached.

Compromise

Compromise is perhaps the most enduring and essential practice that legislators rely upon. Legislation that addresses a particular policy problem is regularly proposed. Schools need more resources, so legislation is proposed to increase state aid to local school districts. Central-city legislators are likely to propose that, because funding is limited, the bulk of the increase should go to their districts, which have lower tax bases and more disadvantaged students. That proposal draws opposition from suburban and rural legislators who argue that their school districts also need funding assistance. Unless the urban legislators have a majority in a house, they lack the votes to pass their proposals. The only way to get enough votes is to compromise with legislators from other areas and to increase the number of districts that will receive funding. It may be necessary to change a formula to distribute more of the money on a simple per-student basis so that all districts get some money. The essential matter is to change who benefits from the legislation so that more legislators will vote for it.

Sometimes compromising is difficult, as with abortion policies. Some groups want the right to abortions guaranteed and others want the activity banned. It appears to be an either-or proposition. But legislators often find ways to forge a compromise. A state law that recognizes the right to abortion and even allows state funds to be used to pay for them might be passed. But it might also be declared that local hospitals have the option to decide whether or not to conduct them. This latter provision creates the likelihood that abortions may be difficult to obtain in certain local areas. To many citizens, this compromise does not clearly resolve the right of individuals to have abortions. In some areas of the state, abortions will be possible, while in other areas of the state, they will not be. There will be no "state" policy. To legislators, this compromise gives the pro-choice group a positive outcome, but creates the possibility for intense opponents to continue to work against abortions in specific jurisdictions. It is a compromise that none of the parties may like, but it does produce a policy. This type of compromise is fundamental to the decision process.

Legislators also engage in logrolling, or promising to vote for someone else's legislation now, with the understanding that the other legislator will vote for your piece of legislation later. An urban legislator may be asked to vote for legislation that is very important for someone else (say, dairy farmers), but that is of marginal interest to the legislator from the urban district. The dairy bill may impose some costs on the urban consumers, but those costs are slight. An urban legislator may vote for the bill if the rural legislator promises to vote for a bill to encourage urban development later. This vote trading makes it possible to acquire enough votes to pass legislation that otherwise might not pass.

Finally, "pork-barreling" is a common practice. This practice involves creating legislation that distributes diverse, unrelated benefits to many legislative districts. The leadership may need to create a coalition among diverse members to get sufficient support to pass certain legislation. The member may not want any change in the proposed policy, but he or she may need funding for a particularly expensive local bridge repair. Another legislator may want funding for a local senior-citizen center. The leadership may respond to these diverse requests by adding "local projects" to a piece of legislation in order to draw support from more legislators and bring in more votes.

All these practices stem from the desire to build political coalitions in legislatures in order to resolve conflict and to get decisions made. The practices of compromise, logrolling, and pork-barreling are not popular among much of the public, who feel that "rational" policy making should prevail. But legislators find these practices useful as a means of bridging differences.

Political Parties and Building Majorities

The formal process structures the steps that must be taken to reach a decision. Informal practices serve to bring legislators together. But it is political parties that drive this process. Parties must work with these practices to forge a majority to pass legislation.

The process of building a majority begins with the political base of the party. A legislative party may have members elected from urban, suburban, and rural areas. It may have members elected from heavily white areas and from areas with a large minority population. Party leaders must work with these diverse legislators and their electoral bases to determine what policies are possible. They must find or create a coalition. This pursuit of a coalition begins inside their own party. When that fails, nothing may happen, or a coalition of Democrats and Republicans may be created. We will first focus on the problems of creating coalitions in parties.

Every party has tensions within it. Democrats may control a house and have most of their members from urban areas. But they may also have members from suburban areas. The interests of legislators from the two areas are likely to clash. Republicans may control a house, but have members from urban, suburban, and rural areas. These members are likely to seek different policies and there will be conflict in the party.

Each party has a core of legislators who represent its enduring electoral base. For Democrats, this core is usually urban legislators. For Republicans, they are usually from suburban and rural areas. The party faces its primary difficulty with legislators who represent areas with constituencies different from that core. These are legislators in "swing" districts, or areas with a very mixed constituency that might vote either Republican or Democratic. The pressures of a mixed constituency or a close election create a tendency for legislators from a party to deviate from their party.[37] The more a district differs from the core constituency of a party, the more the legislator is likely to deviate from the party. A study from Massachusetts indicates the pattern. Democrats from districts with large proportions of renters were most likely to be loyal to their party. In this situation, renters were more likely to have less money. As the proportion of homeowners increased—presumably signifying more fiscally conservative middle-class individuals—the tendency of legislators to vote with the party declined. The pattern is shown in Figure 10.1. It indicates a decline in party loyalty as homeowners increased.

The opposite pattern prevailed in the Republican party. The primary base of the Republican party was in areas with high proportions of homeowners. As the proportion of homeowners declined, Republicans were more likely to deviate from the party.

The electoral fortunes of legislators and their personal beliefs also affect party loyalties. The closer their last election, the more legislators worry about their images and about appearing too attached to the party. An example of this comes from the Republicans in Wisconsin. Legislators were classified into party regulars (usually voting with party) and mavericks (disagreeing with party frequently) and then grouped by their margin of victory. The results are shown in Table 10.8. Almost all mavericks had won close elections.

Ideology also affects legislator behavior. In the same study, legislators were grouped according to their ideological orientation—conservative, moderate, or liberal. Republican mavericks were more likely to be moderates and liberals, and Republican party regulars more likely to be conservatives. The combination of

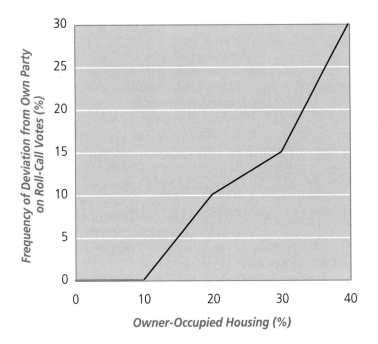

Figure 10.1

Party Loyalty among Massachusetts Democratic Legislators and Proportion of Owner-Occupied Housing in Their Districts

Source: Duncan MacRae, "The Relationship Between Roll Call Votes and Constituencies in the Massachusetts House of Representatives," American Political Science Review 46, no. 4 (December 1952):1046–1055.

Table 10.8

Legislator Margin of Victory, Ideology, and Party Loyalty in Wisconsin

Legislator	Margin of Victory (%)		Ideological Orientation (%)		
	Safe	Close	Conservative	Moderate	Liberal
Maverick	12	88	0	88	12
Party regular	58	42	88	12	0

Note: The numbers here are percents. They sum across to 100 within the categories of electoral situation and ideological orientation. That is, within the category electoral situation, 12 percent of mavericks had safe elections and 88 percent had close elections.
Source: Samuel Patterson, "The Role of the Deviant in the State Legislative System: The Wisconsin Assembly," Western Political Quarterly 14, no. 2 (June 1961): 460–462.

these traits is important. Republican "regulars" are more likely to come from safe districts and to take a conservative position on issues. Republican mavericks are moderates who faced close elections.

Election pressures and personal beliefs make it difficult to bring some legislators into a majority. Legislators in a party who have different constituencies and who face close elections are less likely to support their party. They are most likely to seek moderate policies and compromises that spread benefits across a broader array of districts. This tendency creates problems for the rest of the party and for the leadership.

The Resources of Parties

Parties are not without resources in trying to overcome these tensions and create cohesion. Leaders can try to negotiate compromises. They can distribute "pork," or funding for projects that help individual districts, in order to win the support of legislators. They can arrange vote trading across a range of bills to develop support. Skilled leadership can use all these tactics to create a majority.

When parties create a cohesive party, they can also help legislators outside the formal legislative process. The goal of a party is to get members sufficiently committed to the party such that members have some concern about the party and are willing to work together to produce some party policy. The goal is not to create blind loyalty such that a legislator will vote against his or her district. It is to create a greater inclination than otherwise might exist to go along with the party on legislation.

There are many activities that parties engage in to create this inclination to work together. The party may shape legislative loyalties by playing a role in beginning a legislator's career. In many states, party organizations play a significant role in recruiting legislators. This role is affected by state laws that define the role parties may play in recruitment. Table 10.9 presents the results of a study of four states that had different nominating practices. Connecticut had a party nominating convention, Pennsylvania had a closed (party members only) primary, Minnesota had a nonpartisan primary (anyone of any party could participate and there were no party labels attached to any candidates), and Washington had a blanket primary (party was indicated, but everyone could participate and could vote for anyone). The differences in the activity levels of the parties are shown in the table. Parties in Connecticut and Pennsylvania were legally given a greater role in determining who their nominees would be. In those two states, the party was more likely to have prompted some interest in running and to have contacted candidates before an election. Candidates in those states were also more likely to have received the party endorsement. This greater party role in these states did not mean legislators were "indebted" to the party. It is more likely that the sense of commitment to "party" in the broad sense was greater as a result of the help the party provided.

It is difficult to obtain detailed information on the extent to which states play a role in recruiting legislators, but there is some information. Table 10.10 presents evidence about the role parties in selected states played in the recruitment of candidates for legislative office. These figures may not reflect current levels of party

Table 10.9

Party Roles in the Nomination Process

	Type of Nominating Process			
	Closed		Open	
Activity	Connecticut	Pennsylvania	Minnesota	Washington
First source of interest in running for office:				
Political party	37.5	42.7	22.5	25.6
Other: family, job, friends, personal	62.5	57.3	77.5	74.4
Talked to party prior to election				
Yes	83.0	74.8	63.4	69.4
No	17.0	25.2	36.6	30.6
Received party endorsement				
Yes	79.1	64.3	45.1	26.5
No	20.9	35.7	54.9	73.5

Source: Richard Tobin and Edward Keynes, "Institutional Differences in the Recruitment Process: A Four State Study," American Journal of Political Science 19, no. 4 (November 1975): 671, 674, 676.

Table 10.10

Party Recruitment of State Legislative Candidates, Selected States

State	Candidates Recruited by Party (%)
Connecticut	83
Pennsylvania	75
New Jersey Democrats	74
Washington Republicans	69
New Jersey Republicans	66
Minnesota	65
Iowa	56
Oregon	50
California Democrats	42
Georgia Republicans	37
Tennessee Republicans	28
Ohio Republicans	24
California Republicans	22
Tennessee Democrats	15
Wisconsin	13
Ohio Democrats	12
Georgia Democrats	6

Source: Malcolm Jewell and David Olson, American State Political Parties and Elections (Homewood: Dorsey, 1978), 87.

activity, but they are probably accurate as indications of the relative level of party activity across the states. As discussed in Chapter 5, in some states, anti-party attitudes and reform have reduced the role of the party. In other states, party organizations are still very important. These differences emerge in this list. In Connecticut and New Jersey, party organizations play an important role in recruiting candidates. In California, the party organizations play much less of a role. These relative differences across states probably persist.

As politics has changed, party organizations have continued to play a role, but in new ways. As discussed in Chapter 5, in many states, state legislative campaign committees have emerged to play a crucial role in recruiting candidates, raising money for their campaigns, directing their campaigns, and providing technical assistance during campaigns.[38] These organizations tend to focus their resources on those who have close races. To the extent that parties are responsible for getting legislators into office, legislators are likely to feel an obligation to help the party when possible.

Parties also play a vital role in helping legislators during the legislative process. Party leaders distribute staff budgets and make committee appointments. Leaders may use their control over these resources to reward loyal legislators and to neglect those who resist working with the party. In states where the commitment to party is strong, such as in Wisconsin, leaders appoint committee members based on loyalty to the speaker and agreement with his or her political philosophy.[39] In Montana, on the other hand, party loyalty is not regarded as of primary importance. Committee appointments are based on prior experience, personal desires, area of residence in the state, and other such matters. When parties work to reward loyal members, members are more likely to be inclined to work with their party. If parties make no such efforts, more members will act independently.

Leaders must be careful how they use such powers. A leader who pushes legislators too hard is likely to alienate them and to incline them to resist leadership pressures. It takes a skilled leader to know how far to push. The power of a leader of a legislative body is ultimately derived from the members who elect the leader. If they are to maintain the loyalty of the bulk of the legislative members, they must act roughly in accord with majority wishes. If leaders are abusive of members, or of the necessity of legislators to have some independence, they are likely to create dissent and rebellion. For most legislative bodies, the task of leadership is to serve the members and help them achieve their individual goals while leading them to support party issues. Most legislators recognize the need to have someone push and prod members so decisions get made. Yet, they do not want that person to be coercive. The task of a legislative leader is to work within those confines and skillfully create voting unity. In legislatures organized around partisan divisions, the members expect the leader to push for party goals.

Partisan Conflicts in Legislatures

The cumulative effect of all these conditions affects the extent of partisan conflict in legislatures. When states have enduring traditions of parties representing significantly different concerns, parties can be expected to regularly oppose each other on policy questions. In some states, there is a long history of extensive partisan conflict in the legislature. In these legislatures, many issues get drawn into the partisan struggle. When legislators perceive themselves as distinct groups with different needs, a lot of the issues that emerge are treated as partisan issues that result in party votes. A party vote is defined as one in which a majority of each party votes against a majority of the other party. More than 50 percent of Democrats vote for a bill, while more than 50 percent of Republicans vote against it.

Party voting is very common in state legislatures.[40] Table 10.11 provides an indication of the extent of party voting for selected states. Bills in which the majority of one party opposed the majority of the other party were selected. These bills involved significant differences between parties. Legislators were then assessed in terms of the proportion of times they voted with their own party. On these kinds of bills, the tendency is for party members to stick together. In most situations, at least 75 percent of party members will vote with their own party. The results indicate the extent to which partisan conflict dominates legislative sessions in some states. In northeastern states like New Jersey, New York, and Connecticut, partisan conflict is pervasive. In these states, building a coalition to pass legislation begins with the

Table 10.11

Tendency of Party Members to Vote with Their Own Party on Selected Bills In State Senates, Selected States

State and Party	Proportion Voting with Their Own Party (%)
Delaware	
Democrats	82.8
Republicans	75.6
Maryland	
Democrats	59.2
Republicans	62.1
North Carolina	
Democrats	78.5
Republicans	74.6
Ohio	
Democrats	92.1
Republicans	89.4
Virginia	
Democrats	79.4
Republicans	73.3

Source: Thomas H. Little, "The Effect of Objective Vulnerability, Subjective Vulnerability, and Roll Call Behavior: Revisiting the Marginality Hypothesis AGAIN" (paper presented at the 1993 Midwest Political Science Association Meetings, Chicago, Illinois), 19.

political party. Legislation sponsored by the majority party has a much better chance of passage than legislation sponsored by the minority party. Many northern states have long histories of such partisan conflict.[41]

In states where there was once not much partisan conflict, there is evidence that partisan conflict is now developing. In southern states, the Republican party is becoming more of a factor in the legislature, and partisan conflict is increasing.[42] In other states, it is the Democratic party that is growing. For many years, Iowa was predominantly a Republican state. During the 1950s, this changed, and, by the mid-1960s, politics had become more competitive, and more issues were treated in a partisan fashion. Since the 1950s, the proportion of party votes has steadily increased in both Iowa houses, reflecting the growth of the Democratic party.[43]

Many states have experienced these changes as one-party states have declined. The South was once heavily Democrat, but is now more balanced. Many northern states were once heavily Republican, but the two parties are now more competitive in the legislatures. This change has increased the extent of partisan conflict in these legislatures.

While partisanship shapes the way many issues are handled, not all issues get caught up in partisanship. Indeed, most legislation flows through legislatures without being treated as a partisan issue. Legislation becomes partisan when it involves matters that are fundamental to each party's constituencies. When legislation focuses on welfare benefits, the distribution of education aid, civil rights, labor laws, and tax burdens, it is likely to become partisan. The inclination to close ranks then increases, and legislators vote as a party.[44]

What happens when there is not a clear partisan division of the electorate and of the legislators? These situations involve states where one party dominates or where politics is formally nonpartisan (such as in Nebraska and in many cities across the United States). In these situations, there is less coherence to the coalitions that make decisions. In such situations, for example, urban legislators do not necessarily join with other urban legislators against rural legislators. The absence of party labels appears to reduce the connection between constituencies and voting patterns.[45] There may be no pattern to voting in the legislature. Coalitions are fluid and unstable.

Cross-Party Coalitions

Finally, there are times when partisanship breaks down and parties do not serve as the basis for decisions. Sometimes legislative leaders and governors recognize that support for an issue cuts across party lines and that they must recruit Democrats and Republicans to have enough votes to achieve a majority. This situation may happen when suburban Republicans and urban Democrats find themselves having similar interests (such as more school aid for growing districts, or more money for urban transportation needs) and they band together. It may also happen when an issue involves regional interests, and legislators from opposite parties in the same region join together to pass legislation.

An example of such a coalition took place in New York during the 1960s when Republican Nelson Rockefeller was governor. His goals were to build a reputation as a problem solver. He was particularly concerned with addressing problems in New York City, because he had to do well there to win reelection. He needed revenue to pursue many of his goals. He generally faced a Republican-controlled legislature that was relatively conservative. When the Democrats took control of the legislature briefly in the 1960s, Rockefeller sought support from Democrats *and* Republicans in New York City and other urban areas. He put together a cross-party coalition of urban Democrats and Republicans and was able to get a sales tax adopted.[46]

Case Studies of Legislative Agendas

All these conditions come together to affect the way issues get handled in legislatures. Again, the intriguing questions are whether the political process represents the concerns of the haves and the have-nots and whether those concerns are considered during the decision-making process. To restate the arguments of Key, the have-nots are likely to do well only when a political party has a clear base among these interests and when that party is cohesive. Such a party will advocate the interests of the have-nots and pursue legislation to help their interests. When this cohesive party has sufficient size, it should be possible to enact changes favorable to the have-nots or to prevent changes unfavorable to them. When these conditions do not prevail, the have-nots will not do as well.

Despite the importance of this argument, we do not have as many studies of this question as one might expect. In part, this deficiency is due to the difficulty in obtaining all the information necessary to characterize a state legislative party. There is, however, some information that indicates how state legislative parties vary in their electoral bases and cohesiveness and how these situations affect decision making.

New York parties have a long history of having different concerns and of being cohesive. The Democratic party, which is based in New York City and other urban areas in the state, has controlled the assembly since 1975. It is a cohesive party that relies on strong leadership. The Republican party, which has controlled the senate for most of the twentieth century, is based primarily in rural and suburban areas. It also relies on strong leadership and is cohesive. The cohesion of the Democratic party became very important in the 1980s. The federal government had just revised the federal income tax law, making more income subject to taxation, but lowering the percent of income taxed. States were faced with the question of whether to revise their definitions of taxable income and the tax rates applied to income. Because most states require that taxpayers use information from their federal returns to fill out state returns, states have tended to use the federal definition of income. The federal change in definition presented states with the issue of whether to change the state definition. Republicans saw this as an opportunity to push for lower state tax rates. The cohesiveness of the Democrats in New York was decisive during negotiations over this definition issue. Democrats agreed to change the tax system and to lower rates, but only if this change was accompanied by changes that made the tax system somewhat more progressive and completely removed many lower-income individuals from the tax rolls. They were successful in advocating the interests of their constituency because they were able to function as a cohesive party. As a consequence the have-nots fared relatively well during the decision-making process.[47]

In the New York situation, the legislative party took the initiative to create and pursue a policy goal. In other situations, a relatively cohesive Democratic legislative party can provide a base for a governor to work with legislators in order to seek legislation favorable to the have-nots. In Connecticut in 1991, the new independent governor Lowell Weicker wanted to enact an income tax to deal with the shortage of state revenue. He was able to turn to the Democratic party for support. Democrats wanted to replace reliance on the sales tax, which tends to be regressive, with the income tax, which tends to be more progressive. The Democratic party was able to generate considerable party unity to provide the votes needed to adopt the income tax.[48]

A similar situation prevailed in New Jersey in 1990 when the state was faced with a shortfall of revenue and the state was under a court order to address inequities in school finance. The Democratic governor James Florio turned to the Democratic party, which bargained with the governor. Eventually both an increase in the sales and income tax and a new program for distributing school aid that favored low-income areas were adopted.

In these situations, Democratic parties with primarily liberal and urban bases served as vehicles for representing the interests of the less affluent. The results were changes in the way money was raised (which groups paid taxes) or in the way money was distributed (which groups got state revenues).

When there is not a clear liberal electoral base for the Democratic party and when that party is not cohesive, the have-nots do not fare as well. This situation prevails in many states. As discussed in Chapter 5, in many states the Democratic party draws its support in the electorate from liberals, moderates, and conservatives, and its legislative parties comprise representatives from urban, suburban, and rural areas. The result can be legislative parties with no cohesive focus on issues of the have-nots. The "center" of these parties is more moderate, and there is less concern for representing the have-nots.

In Texas, for example, Democrats have dominated the legislature for years. The Democratic party comprises numerous factions, and there is not a cohesive party focusing on have-not issues.[49] This lack of a cohesive liberal Democratic party has made it very difficult to derive a solution to court decisions that the current distribution of school resources is inequitable in the state.

This situation prevails in other states. When there is no party to represent the interests of the have-nots, policy changes that respond to their concerns are less likely to occur, and the status quo is more likely to prevail. Legislatures bring together the different interests of society. When there is no clearly dominant group, or when there is no cohesion among those of seemingly similar interests, clear policy choices are not likely to emerge from the legislature. Indeed, in those situations, there is likely to be considerable squabbling and delay in making decisions, reflecting the lack of a dominant group or of any consensus on what to do.

Legislative Agendas and Power

Once legislators are able to reach some sort of agreement and pass legislation, they then face the issue of gubernatorial power and interests. The ability of a legislature to translate its policy agenda into enacted policy depends on the formal power the legislature has relative to the governor. If the legislature and the governor are of the same party and have the same concerns, the issue of relative power will not be significant. But that situation is increasingly not the case in the states.

The important issue for the legislature involves provisions for overrides. If the governor vetoes legislation, all legislatures have the legal right to override him or her. The requirements to override the governor can favor the governor or the legislature. In some states, the number of votes necessary for an override is based on the actual number of elected members of the legislature. In those states, it may be necessary to have two-thirds of that number of legislators vote to override. This requirement makes it more difficult to override the governor. If, for example, there are 100 legislators in a house and two-thirds must vote for an override, then 66 legislators are needed to override. If only a majority of all elected legislators must vote for an override, then, in this example, only 51 votes are necessary to override. It is even easier to override a governor if only two-thirds of the legislators *present* need to vote for the override. The number of votes necessary for the override can drop even lower in such cases.

Table 10.12 presents the provisions for overriding governors in the states. In many states, it is relatively difficult to override a governor. These states are shown in the upper left part of the table. In Arkansas, the number of votes necessary for the override is two-thirds of all elected legislators. In other states it is much easier to override the governor. In New Mexico, it is only necessary to have two-thirds of those present vote for the override. Official action can still be taken even if some legislators happen to be absent. This enhances the relative power of the New Mexico legislature.

Since all legislators know these rules, the rules affect how the legislature deals with the governor. When it is difficult to override a gubernatorial veto, legislators are inclined to compromise with the governor on legislation before it leaves the legislature. By doing so, legislators have a chance of getting most of what they want. When it is easier to override a governor, the legislators are less likely to compromise because they think they can avoid doing what the governor wants.

It is also important whether a governor has a line-item veto or a blanket veto. Most governors have the line-item veto. This veto allows them to selectively delete parts of legislative actions. This type of veto limits the power of the legislature and prevents legislators from packing legislation with programs a governor does not want.

Informal power is as relevant to the effectiveness of the legislature as it is to the effectiveness of the governor. With legislatures, the crucial matter is whether the coalition that passed legislation is sufficiently cohesive to hold together when faced with gubernatorial opposition. The greater that unity, the more the legislators will be successful when confronting a hostile governor.

Table 10.12

Provisions for Legislature to Override Gubernatorial Veto

Who Must be Present (Legislators Who Must Participate for Override Vote to Occur)

Required Vote for Override Breadth of Veto Power	All Those elected			Only Those Present		
	2/3	3/5	Majority	2/3	3/5	Majority
Line-Item Veto	AK	DE	AL	ID		
	AZ	IL	AR	MA		
	CA	MD	KY	OR		
	CO	NE	TN	SC		
	CT	OH		TX		
	GA			UT		
	IA			VA		
	LA			WA		
	MI			WV		
	MN			WI		
	MS			FL		
	MO			KS		
	HI			LA		
	NJ			MT		
	NY(a)			NM		
	ND					
	OK					
	PA					
	SD					
	WY					
Blanket Veto	NE		IN	ME	RI	
	NH			VT		

Note: a: Governor has item veto over appropriations.
Source: Book of the States, 1992–1993, (Lexington: The Council of State Governments, 1992).

The same principles are relevant for local governments. Each local government has a charter. This charter is like a constitution, in that it specifies the rules for the operation of government and defines the powers held by each branch. The more formal power a city council or a county legislature has, the greater the chances of its winning a political battle with a local executive. The more cohesive a local council, the greater its ability to prevail in a confrontation.

The Public and Legislatures

The path from initial concern with an issue by legislators to their adopting a policy to deal with it is a long one. Some proposals take a very long time to get through the legislature. Although many of these proposals sound reasonable, at least based on initial summaries of them, many of them never make it through the process at all, or they are heavily compromised before they are enacted into law. Political party leaders may oppose many of them and prevent their passage.

This process frustrates much of the public. They think that decisions should be made sooner and that merit—how "good" a policy proposal is—should determine whether legislation passes. Citizens may feel their own legislator is doing a good job representing district concerns, but they are frustrated with the inability of the legislature to resolve issues.[50] This frustration is often not confined to constituents and interest groups. Many legislators are also unhappy with the performance of the legislature.[51]

Much of the blame for this situation has been directed at professional legislators and the professional legislature. Critics argue that legislators are too concerned with reelection. They charge that legislators use their staff to promote their accomplishments and to do favors for constituents, all of which helps them to be reelected and increases their margins of victory.[52]

While it may seem appropriate to blame legislators for conflicts and delays, this blame may be a case of "killing the messenger." Problems in passing legislation stem from the extent of conflict in society. As long as districts contain different populations and legislators represent different concerns, conflict will persist. One of the enduring problems of a democracy is to find some way to work out these differences. But these conflicts, and respect for differences, are also the reason for having a democratic process, which is slow and emphasizes compromise. The democratic process presumes that legitimate differences exist, that no one has the right answers, and that the emphasis must be on a process that represents interests and works out compromises among groups so that no one feels completely left out.

But the belief that legislators are too entrenched and that they are the source of the "real" difficulty persists. To many critics, the goal should be to elect legislators who are less interested in being reelected and more interested in doing "the right thing." As a consequence, considerable effort has gone into trying to impose term limits on state legislators.[53] These efforts have been prominent in states where the right of initiative exists. In 1990, fourteen states passed initiatives limiting the number of terms legislators can serve.[54]

Despite these efforts, there are grounds for doubting whether such changes will reduce the extent of conflict in legislatures. As long as legislators come from districts with different concerns, they will articulate different perspectives and will argue over what policies should be adopted. Legislatures will continue to struggle with conflict and will experience lengthy delays in enacting policy. The public will continue to be frustrated by the length of time it takes to enact change and by the number of compromises that must be made to enact policy.

In Chapter 12, we will consider how legislatures work, or do not work, with governors in order to affect legislation and policies. Before doing that, however, there is a third branch of government, the courts, that we need to examine.

For Further Reading

Muir, Edward. *Legislature: The California School of Politics*. Berkeley: University of California Press, 1982. An analysis of a relatively decentralized legislature, with emphasis on the way this decentralization contributes to educating members and to public policy debates in the institution.

Stonecash, Jeffrey M. "The Legislature: The Emergence of an Equal Branch." In Jeffrey M. Stonecash, John K. White, and Peter W. Colby, *Governing New York State*, 3d ed. 149–163. Albany: SUNY Press, 1994. A discussion of the rise of the professional legislature, the reasons it continues to rely on a strong leadership system, and the impact of these two conditions on the ability of the legislature to bargain with the governor.

Benjamin, Gerald, and Michael J. Malbin. *Limiting Legislative Terms*. Washington DC: Congressional Quarterly Press, 1992. A review of current criticisms of legislatures and the proposals to limit terms in office as a solution.

Stonecash, Jeffrey M. "The Pursuit and Retention of Legislative Office in New York, 1870–1990: Reconsidering Sources of Change." *Polity* 26, no. 2 (winter 1993): 301–15. An argument that success at reelection is not at all new, and that critics may be in error.

Suggestions for Analysis in Your Own State and Locality

1. Information on income and race for all state legislative districts is contained in William Lilley III, Laurence J. DeFranco, and William M. Diefenderfer, *The Almanac of State Legislatures* (Washington, DC: Congressional Quarterly, 1994). That book may be in your school library, or your professor may have obtained a copy of it. Look at the maps of your state in that book, and determine where Democrats and Republicans in the legislature come from. What is the composition of each party in the legislature?

2. You can also attempt to do this for city-council and county legislative districts, using local information.

3. What is the institutional condition of your state legislature? How much do legislators get paid? Do they have offices in the state capitol? Do they have staff? How many legislators treat their work as a full-time job? Does the legislature have a staff devoted just to researching issues for legislators? You might pursue the same questions for the city council.

4.   How cohesive is the legislative party? Do members vote together on issues, or are there splits within the majority party that make it difficult for members to work together?

5.   Parties can play a crucial role in presenting and arguing for different policy choices. Do the legislative parties in your state differ much in the positions they support? You can determine that by reviewing newspaper coverage of legislative sessions, by looking at voting records on major bills, or by contacting interest groups that create and publish ratings of state legislators.

Notes

[1] Malcolm E. Jewell and Samuel C. Patterson, *The Legislative Process in the United States*, 3d ed. (New York: Random House, 1977), 62–68; and William J. Keefe and Morris S. Ogul, *The American Legislative Process: Congress and the States*, 6th ed. (New York: Prentice-Hall, 1986), 109–114.

[2] Jewell and Patterson, *The Legislative Process in the United States*, 3d ed., 71.

[3] Malcolm E. Jewell and Samuel C. Patterson, *The Legislative Process in the United States*, 4th ed. (New York: Random House, 1986), 50–51; and see Chapter 6 of this text.

[4] John C. Wahlke, Heinz Eulau, William Buchanan, and Leroy Ferguson, *The Legislative System* (New York: Wiley, 1962).

[5] Robert S. Erikson, Norman R. Luttbeg, and Kent L. Tedin, *American Public Opinion*, 3d ed. (New York: Macmillan, 1988), 287–90.

[6] Donald J. McCrone and James H. Kuklinski, "The Delegate Theory of Representation," *American Journal of Political Science* 23, no. 2 (May 1979): 278–300.

[7] Anthony Gierzynski and David Breaux, "Money and Votes in State House Elections," *Legislative Studies Quarterly* 16, no. 2 (May 1991), 203–218; and Herbert Alexander, *Reform and Reality: The Financing of State and Local Campaigns* (New York: The Twentieth Century Fund Press, 1991).

[8] See the work by Craig Grau, cited in Samuel C. Patterson, "Legislators and Legislatures in the American States," in Virginia Gray, Herbert Jacob, and Kenneth N. Vines, *Politics in the American States*, 4th ed. (Boston: Little, Brown, 1983), 149; and Malcolm E. Jewell and David M. Olson, *Political Parties and Elections in American States* (Chicago: Dorsey, 1988), 214–17.

[9] David Ray and John Havick, "A Longitudinal Analysis of Party Competition in State Legislative Elections," *American Journal of Political Science* 25, no. 1 (February 1981), 119–28.

[10] Malcolm Jewell and David Breaux, "The Effect of Incumbency on State Legislative Elections," *Legislative Studies Quarterly* 13 (1988): 495–514.

[11] Alan Rosenthal, *Legislative Life* (New York: Harper and Row, 1981), 100–102.

[12] John W. Soule, "Future Political Ambitions and the Behavior of Incumbent State Legislators," *Midwest Journal of Political Science* 13 (August 1969), 439–54.

[13] Samuel Kernell, "Toward Understanding 19th Century Congressional Careers: Ambition, Competition, and Rotation," *American Journal of Political Science* 11 (1977): 669–93; Robert Struble, Jr., "House Turnover and the Principle of Rotation," *Political Science Quarterly*, 94 (1979–1980): 649–67; David Ray, "Voluntary Retirement and Electoral Defeat in Eight State Legislatures," *The Journal of Politics* 38 (1976): 426–33; and Jeffrey M. Stonecash, "The Pursuit and Retention of Legislative Office in New York, 1870–1990: Reconsidering Sources of Change," *Polity* 26, no. 2 (winter 1993): 301–315.

[14] Jerry Calvert, "Revolving Doors: Volunteerism in State Legislatures," *State Government* 52, (autumn 1979): 175.

[15] Michael deCourcy Hinds, "Elections Change Face of Lawmaking Bodies," *New York Times* 5 November 1992, B9.

[16] Kwang Shin and John Jackson, "Membership Turnover in U.S. State Legislatures, 1931–1976," *Legislature Studies Quarterly* 4 (1979): 95–104; and Jeffrey M. Stonecash, "Careerism in the New York State Legislature, 1890–1990;" (paper presented at the 1990 New York State Political Science Association Meetings).

[17] Richard F. Fenno, *Home Style: House Members in Their Districts* (Boston: Little, Brown, 1978), 35–36.

[18] Alan Rosenthal, *Legislative Life* (New York: Harper and Row, 1981), 100–106.

[19] Robert S. Erikson, Norman R. Luttbeg, and William V. Holloway, "Knowing One's District: How Legislators Predict Referendum Voting," *American Journal of Political Science* 19, no. 2 (May 1975): 231–246; and James H. Kuklinski with Richard C. Elling, *American Journal of Political Science* 21, no. 1 (February 1977): 135–147.

[20] Timothy Bledsoe, *Careers in City Politics: The Case for Urban Democracy* (Pittsburgh: University of Pittsburgh Press, 1993), 51.

[21] Heinz Eulau and Kenneth Prewitt, *Labyrinths of Democracy* (New York: Bobbs-Merrill, 1973).

[22] Bledsoe, *Careers in City Politics*, 116–146.

[23] Kenneth Prewitt, "Political Ambitions, Volunteerism, and Electoral Accountability," *American Political Science Review* 64 (1970): 11; and Kenneth Prewitt and William Noulin, "Political Ambitions and the Behavior of Incumbent Politicians," *Western Political Quarterly* 22 (June 1969): 298–308.

[24] Stephen L. Elkin, *City and Regime in the American Republic* (Chicago: University of Chicago Press, 1987), 76–77; and Bledsoe, *Careers in City Politics*, 145–46.

[25] Joseph Schlesinger, "On the Theory of Party Organization," *Journal of Politics* 46, no. 2 (May 1984): 369–400.

[26] Alan Rosenthal, *Legislative Performance in the States: Explorations of Committee Behavior* (New York: The Free Press, 1974), 36–65.

[27] Edward Muir, *Legislature: California's School for Politics* (Berkeley: University of California Press, 1982).

[28] Malcolm E. Jewell and Samuel Patterson, *The Legislative Process in the United States*, 4th ed. (New York: Random House, 1986), 118–21.

[29] Alan Hevesi, "The Renewed Legislature," in Peter W. Colby and John K. White, *New York State Today* 2d ed. (Albany: State University of New York Press, 1989), 170–173.

[30] Advisory Commission on Intergovernmental Relations, *The Question of State Capability*, A-98, (Washington, DC, January 1985), 65–126.

[31] Joel Thompson, "State Legislative Reform: Another Look, One More Time, Again" *Polity* 19, no. 1 (1986/1987): 27–41.

[32] For examples of this change, see Thomas Lauth, "Shared Power and Fiscal Conservatives," 55; and Gloria A. Grizzle, "Florida: Miles to Go and Promises to Keep," 94–95, and other chapters in Edward J. Lynch and Thomas P. Lauth, *Governors, Legislatures, and Budgets* (New York: Greenwood, 1991).

[33] Gerald Benjamin and Robert T. Nakamura, *The Modern New York State Legislature: Redressing the Balance* (Albany: Rockefeller Institute, 1991).

[34] Gary C. Jacobson, *The Politics of Congressional Elections*, 3d ed. (New York: Harper-Collins, 1992), 25–60.

[35] Morris Fiorina, *Congress: The Keystone of the Washington Establishment*, 2d ed. (New Haven: Yale University Press, 1989).

[36] Alan Rosenthal, "The Legislative Institution: Transformed and at Risk," in Carl Van Horn, ed., *The State of the States* (Washington, DC: Congressional Quarterly Press, 1989), 69–101.

[37] Thomas R. Dye, "A Comparison of Constituency Influences in the Upper and Lower Chambers of a State Legislature," *Western Political Quarterly* 14 (1961), 473–481.

[38] Diana Dwyre and Jeffrey M. Stonecash, "Where's the Party?" *American Politics Quarterly* 20, no. 3 (July 1992): 326–344; and Anthony Gierzynski, *Legislative Campaign Committees in the American States* (Lexington: University of Kentucky Press, 1992).

[39] Douglas C. Chaffee and Malcolm E. Jewell, "Selection and Tenure of State Legislative Party Leaders: A Comparative Analysis," *Journal of Politics* 34 (November 1972): 1278–1286.

[40] David Leuthold, "The Legislature in Missouri's Political System," in Samuel Patterson, ed., *Midwest Legislative Politics* (Iowa City: University of Iowa Institute of Public Affairs, 1967), 78.

[41] See such studies as Malcolm Jewell, ""Party Voting in American State Legislatures," *American Political Science Review* 49 (September 1955): 773–91; Thomas Flinn, "Party Responsibility in the States: Some Causal Factors," *American Political Science Review* 58 (March 1984): 60–71; and Hugh L. LeBlanc, "Voting in State Senates: Party and Constituency Influences," *Midwest Journal of Political Science* 13 (February 1969): 33–37.

[42] Robert Harmel and Keith E. Hamm, "Development of a Party Role in a No-Party Legislature," *Western Political Quarterly* 39, no. 1 (March 1986): 79–92; Robert Harmel and Keith E. Hamm, "Political Party Development in State Legislatures: The Case of the Texas House of Representatives" (paper presented at the 1991 Midwest Political Science Association Meetings, Chicago, Illinois); and Thomas H. Little, "The Effect of Objective Vulnerability, Subjective Vulnerability and Roll-Call Behavior: Revisiting the Marginality Hypothesis *AGAIN* (paper presented at the 1993 Midwest Political Science Association Meetings, Chicago, Illinois).

[43] Charles W. Wiggins, "Party Politics in the Iowa Legislature," *Midwest Journal of Political Science* 11 (February 1967): 86–97; and Jonathan P. Euchner, "Partisanship in the Iowa Legislature, 1945–1989" (paper presented at the April 1990 Midwest Political Science Association Meetings, Chicago, Illinois).

[44] Glenn T. Broach, "A Comparative Dimensional Analysis of Partisan and Urban-Rural Voting in State Legislatures," *Journal of Politics* 34 (1972): 905–921.

[45] Susan Welch and Eric H. Carlson, "The Impact of Party on Voting in a Nonpartisan Legislature," *American Political Science Review* 63 (September 1973): 854–67.

[46] Jeffrey M. Stonecash, "'Split' Constituencies and the Impact of Party Control," *Social Science History* 16, no. 3 (fall 1992), 455–477.

[47] Diana Dwyre, Mark O'Gorman, Jeffrey M. Stonecash, and Rosalie Young, "Disorganized Politics and The Have-Nots: Politics and Taxes in New York and California," *Polity* (1994).

[48] Russell D. Murphy, "Connecticut: Lowell P. Weicker, Jr., A Maverick in the 'Land of Steady Habits'," in Thad Beyle, *Governors and Hard Times* (Washington, DC: Congressional Quarterly Press, 1992):70.

[49] Chandler Davidson, *Class and Party in Texas Politics* (Princeton: Princeton University Press, 1990), 158–162.

[50] Richard F. Fenno, Jr., "If, as Ralph Nader Says, Congress is 'The Broken Branch,' How Come We Love Our Congressmen So Much?" in N. J. Ornstein, ed., *Congress in Change*, 277–87; and Glenn R. Parker and Roger Davidson, "Why Do Americans Love Their Congressman So Much More than Their Congress, *Legislative Studies Quarterly* 4, (1979): 53–62.

[51] Keefe and Ogul, *The American Legislative Process*, 32–34.

[52] David Mayhew, *The Electoral Connection* (New Haven: Yale University Press, 1974); and Morris Fiorina, *Congress: Keystone of the Washington Establishment*, 2d ed. (New Haven: Yale University Press, 1989).

[53] Mark P. Petracca, "Rotation in Office: The History of an Idea," in Gerald Benjamin and Michael J. Malbin, eds., *Limiting Legislative Terms* (Washington, DC: Congressional Quarterly Press, 1992), 19–52.

[54] Robert Reinhold, "Move to Limit Terms Gathers Steam After Winning in 14 States," *New York Times* 5 November 1992, B8.

11

Courts and the Agendas of Politicians

PREVIEW

Courts are political institutions. They are somewhat removed from politics because of concerns that they remain neutral, but they are often drawn into disputes about issues of process and fairness in society. This involvement of the courts is sometimes direct. Courts are asked to directly rule on disputes in the political process. But the courts can also indirectly become a political issue. How cases are treated and how different groups get treated often generate publicity, which prompts politicians to respond to claims that the courts are arbitrary, give "soft" treatment to criminals, or discriminate against women, minorities, or the poor.

The issue of how responsive the courts should be has led to different proposals for the selection of judges. Some states favor election, and others favor appointment.

Ultimately, the courts have the potential to push issues onto the agendas of politicians. There are strong reasons for the courts to avoid ruling on controversial issues, but there are times when the courts are willing to make such rulings.

The Argument for the Third Branch

Most public policy decisions in our society are made through executives and legislatures. These institutions receive the bulk of political attention, and they are seen as our primary "political" institutions. But we have not placed complete trust in these two institutions. Courts play a crucial role as the third branch of government. The rationale for a judicial system is to have a branch of government that is somewhat, if not completely, removed from politics. This branch can serve as a politically independent assessor of whether the rules and the laws of society have been adhered to.

The commitment to this role stems from the same concerns that affected the creation of American democracy. There has always been a strong fear of rule by the individual in American politics. Human beings are subject to partisan views, to passions of the moment, and to long-standing prejudices. Individuals, with their own prejudices, are unlikely to accord equal treatment to everyone. The desire of the founders of our country was to avoid such variability of treatment, and to create a "rule by laws, not by men." Law was intended to embody society's sense of the rules that should apply to everyone. Once expressed as laws, these rules would provide a clear set of norms known to everyone and reduce the extent to which arbitrary rules could be applied to different groups or individuals.

The courts exist to serve as an independent institution for judging whether the norms of society are violated. Judges (and juries) hear allegations of the violation of norms. The judicial process is presumed independent of partisan politics and of personal prejudice.

The Courts and Political Agendas

While it is presumed that the courts are independent, it is not presumed that the courts are apolitical. The courts have considerable "political" importance because they distribute costs and benefits. They certify certain practices as acceptable and others as unacceptable. They make judgments about the violations of social norms by individuals. They issue rulings about the legality of broad public policy practices. The courts respond to political issues. They also create political issues because of decisions they make and the practices they engage in. Their actions and the assessments of their actions become part of the political process.

The effects of the courts on the political process are both direct and indirect.[1] They can rule on whether political actors are adhering to required procedures in the political process. They arbitrate disputes between executives and legislatures about what practices must be followed in making decisions. They handle citizen complaints that the rules of the political process are not being adhered to. They determine if candidates have fulfilled requirements to remain on ballots. These rulings are direct judgments about the political process.

Courts also have direct effects by making decisions about the propriety of existing public policy practices. They can determine if abortion rights have been unduly infringed on, if school finance practices are illegal, if women are paid significantly less than men, or if prisons are overcrowded. A ruling against current practices could place the issue on the agenda of politicians, who may or may not deal with it.

Practices of the courts also lead to political issues in more indirect ways. The way cases and individuals are treated can become a public issue and create pressure on politicians to respond. Do women receive the same treatment as men? Do blacks and whites receive equal treatment?

The impact of the courts stems from the way they handle cases. Courts cannot initiate consideration of issues. Judges cannot formulate and pursue an agenda. They must wait on cases to be brought before the courts. The processing of cases creates political issues. The way cases are treated and the kinds of judgments that are rendered often come to the attention of politicians or the public.

The process from case initiation to court consideration to final ruling to the impact on the political process is a long one. This chapter focuses on this process and on the way court cases can affect the agendas of politicians. This chapter follows the flow of legal activity and issues that emerge during the process of considering cases: the way cases get initiated, the courts—state or federal—that take up a case, the relationship between federal and state law, the structure of the courts, the nature of judges and the way they are chosen, the decisions issued, and, finally, the impact of court rulings.

As with the preceding chapters on other political institutions, the concern here is the way the practices of the court system affect whose concerns get on political agendas and what kinds of decisions are made. We will focus on the way variations in court practices affect what interests fare well in society. With the courts, these connections to group interests may be more indirect, but they still exist.

Arbitrating Disputes Over the Political Process

Most cases that we will examine involve disputes between individuals or accusations by the government against individuals. But sometimes there are accusations brought by individuals or by branches of government against the government that the political process is not being conducted properly. Citizens may argue that boundaries for legislative districts are not drawn fairly. Governors and legislatures often disagree about what practices must be adhered to during the political process. Legislators may challenge a governor for not including in budget proposals details that the legislators believe should be there. Governors may challenge legislators for trying to amend state laws in ways that governors believe are not allowed. Legislators may argue that a governor has an obligation to fulfill agreed-upon spending levels for specific programs. Legislators may argue that details of federal programs cannot be altered without legislative approval. Governors and legislators may disagree about the way to interpret language in the constitution concerning the required procedure for vetoing legislation.

All of these disputes must be taken somewhere for resolution. These are not the typical cases that courts consider, but they are very important cases. The courts have the power of "judicial review," or the right to review the legality of actions of other branches, and have become the arena to resolve these disputes.[2] They provide a check on the behavior of each institution relative to others.

In some cases, the courts try to avoid these issues. Judges like to stay out of disputes between branches that involve explicit "political" allocations of benefits. For example, when the majority party assumes control in a legislature, it may allocate the bulk of the available staff to itself and leave the minority party with limited resources. Since there is no constitutional or statutory specification of the way these resources should be allocated, the courts are reluctant to intervene or to decide what the required allocation of benefits should be. The courts regard this as a political decision, or one that is the product of the political process.

On the other hand, the courts do arbitrate some "political" questions. Beginning in the 1960s, the courts ruled that legislative districts should have essentially the same number of residents so that areas of the state have equal representation.[3] Judges have increasingly become involved in questions of how legislative districts should be drawn in order to fairly represent minorities. During the 1980s, the courts became heavily involved in reviewing reapportionment plans to see if minorities received adequate representation.

These cases involve questions of the fairness of the process and, in some ways, are relatively safe cases for the courts. But they also present difficulties. The courts must decide if it is wise for them to get involved in an issue that many people see as a political dispute. Getting drawn into deciding political disputes can create the impression that the courts are just another political institution. This impression may undermine respect for the courts as a neutral institution arbitrating legal disputes.

The Role of Cases: Issues of Access and Representation

The bulk of court activity involves handling accusations against individuals by the state, or resolving disputes between individuals by rendering decisions about specific situations or cases. This is not a role the courts can actively pursue. Judges and juries cannot seek cases of inappropriate or unjust behavior. Rulings emerge from the courts only because a case is brought to the courts. That case may be initiated by a district attorney, an individual, or a corporation. Consideration by the courts begins with a case. Once a judge decides to accept a case, he or she issues a ruling that focuses on the circumstances of that case. Sometimes a ruling may have implications beyond the specific case, but most rulings are relevant only for the specific set of circumstances brought before the court. The grist of courts, then, is cases, and the process of bringing cases to court is one of the prime matters of concern in the judicial process.

Initiating Cases

To initiate a case, there must be an accusation that a specific injustice has been done. Cases arguing that the general state of society is not proper or that a potential problem is likely to occur in the future cannot be filed. There must be some specific incident or situation, and some specific individual or entity must claim that it has been wronged.

Criminal cases involve alleged violations of state and federal laws. These are cases where a crime has been committed against "the state."[4] The initiation of these cases is done by a representative of the state. A district attorney (representing local or state governments) or a U.S. attorney (representing the federal government) concludes that an individual or a corporation has committed a crime. A case is then brought to court accusing that individual or corporation of a crime. The accused party then seeks to have a lawyer defend him or her.

A civil case involves a dispute between two private parties. The state court system is used to resolve the dispute, but the accusation is made by an individual who argues that a contract was violated or was not fulfilled, that he or she was deprived of a right, or that some damage was done that the individual wishes remedied. In this situation, the individual obtains a lawyer who handles the complaint. The person filing the case is called the plaintiff, and the person charged is called the defendant.

The Adversarial Nature of Proceedings

Once a case is initiated, it is argued by opposing lawyers. American law presumes that the best way to have full consideration of all aspects of a case is to proceed through an adversarial approach. Lawyers for each side—plaintiff and defendant—present all the evidence and arguments possible to make one side of the case as strong as possible. They also try to create doubts about the arguments and evidence of the opposition. A decision is then reached by a judge or judge and jury as to whether there is evidence for the accusation. The presence of competent lawyers on both sides of the case is crucial. Given this approach to handling cases, a participant without a competent lawyer has less chance of doing well during the process. We will return to that issue later.

Heading Off Court Cases

There has been considerable concern in recent years about the volume of cases brought to the courts. The number of cases has been steadily rising.[5] This growth has led to proposals for alternative means of handling disputes, particularly in civil cases. Dispute resolution is one approach.[6] This process involves having the two parties involved in the dispute appear before a professional mediator. Lawyers are not necessary, and most people present their own cases. The mediator listens to both sides present their cases and then works with the two parties to resolve the dispute and to achieve a formal settlement. If either party regards the final settlement as unfair, they can still take the case to court.

Questions of Bias in Case Initiation and Access

Most cases, however, end up in the adversarial process. These cases constitute the raw material of the courts. Cases are what eventually prompt reactions from judges and juries. Someone must initiate these cases. There are continuing controversies in our society about whether the process of initiating cases is biased. These controversies ultimately create policy issues. Our society has a general commitment to equality of treatment and opportunity. To the extent that there is evidence that some people are more likely to be prosecuted and that inequalities of access to our institutions exist, there are arguments by liberals that such inequality should be corrected.

In criminal cases, the judicial process begins with police arrests and a decision by a prosecutor to pursue the case. These individuals are state district attorneys or U.S. attorneys. State district attorneys are generally elected, and U.S. attorneys are appointed.[7] There has been a continuing accusation that these attorneys at both levels are more likely to initiate cases for lower-income crimes such as robbery, assault, and drug cases and less likely to initiate cases for violations of civil rights, rape, spouse abuse, child neglect, and white-collar crimes. The accusation is that arrest and case initiation are more likely against low-income individuals and minorities, even when the characteristics of cases are essentially the same.[8]

These accusations have led to numerous studies to assess the validity of these charges. The studies in some cases have indicated considerable evidence for these accusations. Defenders of the courts, on the other hand, have argued that the presence, or lack, of certain cases is not reflective of bias, but of the state of our society. Prosecutors do little but react to that reality. The evidence, however, indicates that prosecutors probably reflect the values of society and regard some crimes as more important and devote more attention to prosecuting crimes of violence than white-collar crimes such as fraud.[9]

In civil cases, there have also been arguments that lower-income individuals do not have the money to hire lawyers. They have a hard time using the courts to resolve their legal problems. When faced with rental contract problems or disputes about product quality, a lawyer is often needed to resolve the dispute.

These criticisms have had their effects. In the criminal area, district and U.S. attorney offices have created divisions that focus on civil-rights violations, crimes against women and children, and white-collar crimes. Whether these divisions always proceed with sufficient resources and whether the activities of these divisions have high priority are subjects of continuing controversy. It is regularly charged, for example, that rape occurs far more regularly than it is prosecuted, and that this gap reflects the unwillingness of district attorneys to devote resources to prosecution of such acts. Divisions have been created to prosecute these crimes, but it is not clear whether creation of these divisions has really changed the priorities of the kinds of crimes governments prosecute.

In the area of civil litigation, the concern about inequality of access to legal assistance has also had an effect. Several proposals have been made to respond to these accusations of inequality of access. One response has involved the creation of small-claims courts. In some civil disputes between two individuals involving damages or money owed, the amount in dispute may be so small that it does not pay to hire a lawyer to handle the case. To make it possible for such cases to be resolved, the small-claims court was created.[10] Individuals make their own arguments to judges, who issue rulings about who is responsible or who must pay. The intent is to make the courts accessible to individuals who have limited disputes and to reduce the volume of cases coming to the courts.

Despite the ideals behind small-claims courts, this mechanism has not worked out as many thought it would. Studies have found that these courts tend to be used by businesses to collect debts from working-class individuals.[11] Businesses become very familiar with the way the process works and repeatedly use the courts to pursue debts. The courts have not emerged as a place for "common people" to resolve conflicts.

The consistent problem for low-income individuals over the years has been the inability to afford to hire lawyers to pursue disputes they have with others. This issue has not gone unrecognized. In response to this argument, during the 1960s, Congress created the Legal Services Corporation, which provides federal grants to states. The funds are to support legal services for low-income individuals. States must also provide a proportion of funding in order to qualify for the grants. The state can, of course, provide separate and additional funds for the defense of low-income individuals.

This program has generated considerable controversy. Conservatives argue that too much of the money goes to support suits on such issues as government hiring practices and landlord practices. The business community has strongly opposed the use of public funds to sue over private-sector disputes.[12] This opposition has led to limited budgets for the Legal Services Corporation and limits on the types of suits that can be pursued. Much as with other federal grant programs, some states have drawn on this federal money more than others. Some states have established extensive programs, and others have established only minimal programs. This program currently does not provide extensive services to low-income individuals.

Filing and pursuing cases costs money. This cost inhibits many people who have a complaint from filing a suit. An individual may have a complaint about a product, but not be inclined to pursue a suit because of costs. A woman may feel she is discriminated against in wages, but not file a suit because of costs. One way of reducing the costs associated with a suit is to file a class-action suit.[13] In this suit, a group (class) of individuals sues collectively. Not everyone who has experienced a problem need be a part of the suit (and usually only one or a few people actually file the suit).

For such a suit to take place, the courts must grant the right for the suit. Traditionally, an individual was allowed to file a suit only if that particular individual had experienced an injury. The individual had to have what is called "standing" to sue. Each individual had to file his or her own suit. The courts generally will not allow an individual to sue on behalf of another. Although class-action suits have a long history, for many years the courts restricted their use. During recent years, the courts have moved from a restrictive use of such mechanisms to a more lenient use of them on the grounds that it may be the only feasible way for the parties involved to obtain a fair settlement.[14] The advantage of such suits is that they lower the cost of pursuing a legal remedy to a dispute. This process makes it possible for the average individual to pursue a grievance involving major appliances, bad cars, and wage discrimination.

Interest groups also play a role in getting cases brought before the courts for consideration. They do this by searching for a "test" case that presents the court with a very specific situation that involves a clear inequity. That situation was present in *Brown v. Board of Education* (1954). The case involved two school systems (one black, one white) that were ostensibly equal, but that really provided unequal educations. The goal was to confront the court with a test of its doctrine that "separate but equal" facilities were constitutional.[15] The courts ruled that having separate facilities was unconstitutional.

Interest groups often provide the resources to find test cases that they think will present the court with a troubling consequence of an allegedly legal situation, or that will prompt the court to consider whether some existing situation should be seen as illegal.[16] This process involves providing resources to find specific situations, to marshall evidence, and to put together cases to file. These suits have served as a means of getting many issues onto the public agenda. Such suits have been used to register complaints about defective cars, wage differentials between men and women, overcharging on airfares, and many other concerns.[17]

Interest groups also try to "lobby" the courts about their viewpoint by filing amicus, or "friends of the court," briefs. Such briefs are legal arguments about why a particular viewpoint should be adopted. These briefs can be filed by anyone interested in a case. They are filed by all types of groups.

Certain practices of lawyers also facilitate access to legal services regardless of income. In civil suits, an individual may claim that he or she has suffered extensive personal injury, but cannot afford to hire a lawyer to pursue the issue. A lawyer may also think that the case has merit and recognize that the client cannot afford to pay for services on an hourly basis. The solution is to bill for services on contingency-fee basis. The lawyer agrees to take on the case with no fees except a fee *contingent* upon winning the case. That fee may be as much as 40 percent of the amount awarded by a judge or jury. Much of the public disparages lawyers who do this, and such lawyers are often called "ambulance chasers." The name derives from the public image of lawyers following ambulances in search of someone who has suffered personal injury and then urging that person to sue. Critics argue that this practice encourages too many lawsuits. In fact, many lawyers decline to handle most claims of personal injury because the evidence available for a case may not indicate that the case is winnable. Lawyers also argue that this is a system that promotes more equality of access to the courts than would exist if only hourly-rate fee systems were used.

All of these mechanisms increase the access to the court system for those without the personal resources to hire their own lawyer. But it is clear that these mechanisms do not result in equality of access to the courts. They are not equivalent to having funds to hire a lawyer to pursue a case. These mechanisms are also not well suited for the pursuit of appeals, which are often crucial in the ultimate resolution of cases. Their effect is to reduce inequity of access, but those with more money still enjoy a considerable advantage in initiating and pursuing cases.

Issues of Access: Bias in Case Defense

In an adversarial process, a lawyer defends an individual. One of the fundamental concerns of observers of the court system has been that many individuals cannot afford legal assistance. This assistance is particularly important in criminal cases. That issue eventually came before the U.S. Supreme Court. In *Gideon v. Wainwright* (1963), the courts ruled that free legal counsel must be provided in felony cases for defendants who cannot afford to hire a lawyer. This requirement applies to anyone, regardless of whether the case goes to state or federal court.

This requirement has been satisfied in many communities by instituting a public-defender program. State or local funds are used to hire lawyers whose sole job is to defend those who cannot afford a lawyer. Localities also attempt to fulfill this responsibility by calling on lawyers to provide pro bono work, or work donated to the community.

These mechanisms do provide some coverage for those without funds, but they do not provide complete coverage. Public-defender programs are usually funded at low levels, and donation of time for defense work is not extensive. While there may be court rulings that low-income individuals are entitled to defense, the Supreme Court has been reluctant to define what adequate legal representation is, and the legal assistance available to low-income individual defendants is generally minimal.[18]

Summary: Access to Legal Resources and the Bias Issue

Much as with other political institutions, there have always been questions of whether equality of access exists.[19] Critics have charged that not everyone has the same capability to initiate cases, or to receive defense when charged.[20] Evidence of inequities in the ability to gain access to the courts and legal defense has existed for some time.[21] Such inequity has also been a continuing issue for politicians. It is widely acknowledged that low-income individuals do not have the same access to the courts that well-to-do individuals have.

These disputes often become partisan issues. Liberals argue that more resources should be allocated to programs like Legal Services and public defenders, while conservatives have often opposed extensive funding for these programs. Conservatives argue that using public monies to support private lawsuits is inappropriate. They also are less sympathetic to providing assistance to those accused of crimes. This disparity of belief often results in partisan battles over funding levels for these programs.

Structures, Jurisdictions, and Process

The Relationship between Federal and State Law

If a case is to be pursued, a decision must be made as to which court should hear the case. Where is the case to be filed? Should a case go to state courts or to federal courts? Federal and state courts exist side by side as two very separate organizations. There are federal judges and courts, and state judges and courts. The former are selected at the national level, and the latter are selected at the state level. Deciding where a case goes involves questions of court jurisdictions. It also raises the question of whether federal and state law differ and what the relationship between the two is. This last question is perhaps primary.

Federal law is the supreme law of the land. That is, federal law prevails over state law. But this dominance is not as simple as it may seem. Federal law is primary, but only in cases in which federal law applies. Most of the criminal law in the United States is written by state politicians, so most violations of criminal law involve state statutes. Much of civil law, such as product-liability law, is also of this nature. Second, even though federal law is primary, there is still reliance on state courts and judges to interpret and apply these laws to specific cases. This situation gives state courts interpretive latitude over federal law and creates situations where there may be disparity between federal law and state applications. State courts can go beyond federal law in providing for individual rights or penalties for environmental pollution. Such interpretation can result in divergences between federal and state laws. We will return to how state courts use their autonomy later.

State court systems also developed earlier than federal court systems, and there is a continuing tendency to rely on state courts to process most cases. Cases can always be appealed from state courts to the federal courts on the principle that a federal law or procedure is involved and has been violated, but most cases start in state courts.

Federal law may be supreme, but state courts handle most cases. If a federal law is involved, as in interpretation of antitrust legislation or interstate commerce issues, a case goes directly to federal courts. Otherwise, a case goes to state courts. When a case goes to a state court, it is initially filed in some lower-level court. The next issue in filing a case is determining which court has jurisdiction over the case. In some states, this determination is not difficult because the state has established general jurisdiction courts, or ones that may hear all types of cases. In other states, there may also be specialized courts, such as family court, bankruptcy court, criminal court, or traffic court. In situations where a case can go to several courts, the decision may depend on a lawyer's sense of where the case has the best chance, based on perceptions of the sympathies of different judges.[22]

The existence of specialized courts has drawn criticism from reform groups, who would like to see local courts consolidated into a unitary system.[23] A unitary court system is a court system in which all cases go into one court rather than into diverse courts. The argument is that a consolidated court system is more efficient and is easier for citizens to understand. These reform efforts have had success in some states, but it is difficult to change existing systems.[24] Local judges and court workers seek to preserve their positions and autonomy, and they tend to resist such changes.[25] As a consequence, many states still have courts of specialized jurisdiction.

The Progress of Cases

Assuming a case is heard by a court, some decision is reached. It is always possible to appeal that decision. An appeal involves a reconsideration of a case to see if a legal error (improper procedure, a misreading or misapplication of the law) has occurred. In some states, these appeals go directly to the highest court, the supreme court or the court of appeals. In other states, there is an intermediate court of appeals, which hears cases before they go to the final court. Decisions by a state's highest court are not necessarily final. Someone can always appeal to the federal courts on the grounds that a federal law has been violated and that the state court has ignored that violation.

A composite picture of a typical state court system is shown in Figure 11.1. Cases start in some lower court. If appealed, they may go to an intermediate appellate court, or directly to the state's highest court.

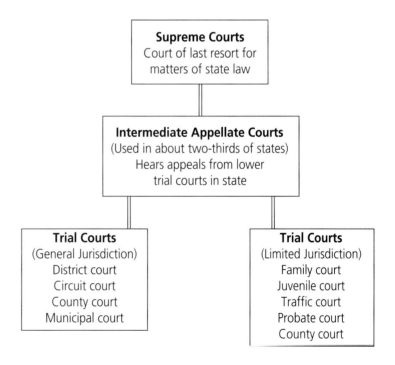

Figure 11.1

A Typical State Court System

Sources: Adapted from John J. Harrigan, Politics and Policy in States and Communities *(Boston: Little, Brown, 1980), 175; and Henry Glick,* Courts, Politics, and Justice, *2d ed. (New York: Macmillan, 1988), 22.*

Processing Cases

Prosecutors and courts face an enormous volume of criminal cases. Their number has been growing.[26] The number of civil suits has also been growing. This volume creates pressure on the courts to dispose of cases. The way cases are handled also creates political issues for politicians.

With the large volume of cases before the courts, delays in hearing cases are common. Many felony criminal cases are dismissed at a preliminary hearing. The prosecution may be unable to produce the necessary witnesses, or the judge may feel that the evidence is not sufficient to justify proceeding. Other cases are settled before they go to trial. In civil suits, the parties may agree to avoid the costs of a trial, or they may be uneasy about placing their case before a judge or a jury, and they accept a negotiated settlement before the case goes to trial.

In criminal cases, one or both parties (prosecutor or defendant) may be uneasy about a case. A defendant may be worried about being convicted of a severe charge, which carries a lengthy sentence. A prosecutor may worry that existing evidence is so weak that the defendant will be acquitted of all charges. In those situations, prosecutors may plea-bargain. Plea bargaining involves getting a defendant to plead guilty to a lesser charge. This bargaining guarantees the prosecutor of a conviction and allows him or her to move on to the next case. For defendants, this bargaining may result in some sentence, but it may also avoid a more severe penalty.

These actions—delays, dismissals, and plea bargains—can create political issues. Delays create stories about the lack of "swift" justice. Plea bargains create concerns about leniency.[27] A charge of murder in a prominent case may be dismissed or a plea bargain agreed to that does not involve a lengthy sentence. Press coverage may create an impression that prosecutors and the courts are "soft" on crime. The press may follow this initial coverage with a series on what happens to cases in the courts.

These situations result in pressure on legislators. Delays and dismissals create demands for more resources for criminal investigators, prosecutors, and judges. These demands require budgetary allocations. Plea bargains create demands to limit the use of plea bargains. Lenient sentences create demands to mandate the sentences imposed on people convicted of certain crimes.

Politicians often respond to these pressures by passing laws mandating certain practices. But it is not clear that any of these mandates significantly alter court practices. Judges have considerable autonomy in running their courts, and they have their own norms of work-load expectations and the way justice should be meted out.[28] Plea bargaining has been banned in some communities. Such banning appears to lengthen the time needed to process cases, but the conviction rate remains about the same.[29] Jail time has been mandated for those convicted of DWI, but judges often find ways to ignore the mandate.[30] "Speedy" trials have been required, but that requirement has had very mixed impact.[31] Despite this evidence of the limited effects of mandates, such efforts are likely to continue. Practices in the courts often receive extensive press coverage, and politicians are likely to continue to feel pressure to change court practices.

Selecting Those Who Preside
Anxieties over Bias in Selection Methods

When cases are processed, there is always concern about the nature of those who preside over the process and the way these individuals treat cases. There are significant differences of opinion about the way these individuals should be selected. Opinion differs over the extent to which judges should be accountable to the "general" beliefs of society and over who is best qualified to choose judges.

People want judges to be competent and fair, but they also want them to reflect and enforce the dominant norms of the society. They may want judges to be independent and enforce "the law," but they do not want them to be too independent. Many people fear that the subjective perspectives of judges may intrude into the process. Others want judges to be given more independence so that they can interpret the law without yielding, however slightly, to public pressure. Protection of civil liberties and civil rights, for example, might not occur if judges worry too much about public opinion. There is also the question of the length of time that judges should serve. Should judges be appointed for short terms so that they stay in touch with social norms, or should they have long terms so that they can be more independent of public opinion?

There is then the question of who should do the choosing. Is the public competent to make these judgments? Critics argue that judicial elections are too hard to follow and that the public does not know candidates well.[32] Others argue that while the general public does not follow judicial elections, those who do are sufficiently informed to make decisions.[33] If the public is to elect judges, should those elections be partisan or nonpartisan? Or should judges be appointed? And, if they are to be appointed, who should do the nominating? Who should do the appointing?

These debates over how to choose judges have resulted in different processes for selecting judges across the states. In some states, judges are elected, with some states using partisan and others nonpartisan elections. In other states, judges are appointed. Proponents of appointment have pushed for having merit serve as a basis for selection. This idea has led to the "Missouri" plan. In the Missouri plan, a commission of prestigious lawyers, judges, and laypersons review prospective candidates and then make recommendations to the governor. The governor is usually presented with three candidates and must choose one of them. After the judge has served in office for some time, the judge is usually put before the public in an election. No opponent is on the ballot, and the only issue is whether that particular judge should be retained. Few judges lose such elections. Such approaches to appointment do not go unopposed. Many people believe it is important to keep judges responsive and do not want to do away with selection by elections.

There are strong vested interests who oppose changing systems that already exist. In many states, judges have patronage powers. They appoint law clerks and court personnel. Political parties have not been eager to give up the influence they have over such appointments through the judges' links to the parties. In addition, relying on the bar to appoint judges has been resisted by many who suspect that an appointment process dominated by the bar will result in upper-class nominations. Because of all these reasons, reform efforts have failed in many states.[34]

There is considerable variation across the states in methods used for selecting judges. Table 11.1 presents the variations among the states. Some states retain a system in which judges run as party candidates, while others have gone to a system in which the link of the courts to the political process is more indirect.

There is also the issue of the length of appointment. Anxieties over autocratic rule by judges have resulted in relatively short limits on the length of time judges can serve. While U.S. Supreme Court judges are appointed for life, such appointments seldom occur in the states. Table 11.2 shows the average length of appointments for the different levels of courts across the states. Appointment for life is rare. The intent of fixed terms of appointment is to insure that judges do not become distant and removed from society.

Selection Procedures and the Nature of Judges

Debates about selection processes occur because people believe the method of selection affects who becomes judges and what kinds of decisions might emerge because of who sits on the bench. Do some systems result in more Republicans or conservatives, and do those loyalties and beliefs affect the decisions made?

Table 11.1

Major Methods of Selecting Judges for State Courts, All States

Partisan Election	Nonpartisan Election	Gubernatorial Appointment	Legislative Election	Merit (The Missouri Plan)
Alabama	California	Connecticut	South Carolina	Alaska
Arkansas	Florida	Delaware	Virginia	Arizona
Georgia	Idaho	Maine		Colorado
Illinois	Kentucky	Maryland		Hawaii
Indiana	Louisiana	Massachusetts		Iowa
Mississippi	Michigan	New Hampshire		Kansas
New Mexico	Minnesota	New Jersey		Missouri
New York	Montana	Rhode Island		Nebraska
North Carolina	Nevada			South Dakota
Pennsylvania	North Dakota			Utah
Tennessee	Ohio			Vermont
Texas	Oklahoma			Wyoming
West Virginia	Oregon			
	Washington			
	Wisconsin			

Source: Henry Glick, Courts, Politics, and Justice *(New York: Macmillan, 1988), 85.*

Table 11.2

Average Length of Appointment to State Courts, All States

Length of Term (Years)	State Supreme Courts (# of States)	Intermediate Appellate Courts (# of States)	Major Trial Courts (# of States)
Life (or to age 70)	3	1	3
14–15	1	0	2
10–12	17	8	3
6–8	29	25	36
4–5	0	2	9
Less than 4	0	0	0

Source: John J. Harrigan, Politics and Policy in States and Communities, *4th ed. (New York: HarperCollins, 1991), 320.*

Much as with other officials in the political process, judges are not typical of the public. The people who are selected as judges tend to be white, well-educated, affluent males. The evidence suggests this result occurs regardless of the type of selection process used.[35]

When there are differences in who is selected, they appear to be primarily a function of the population from which judges are selected and who does the selection. When a state or locality has higher proportions of some groups, those groups do better in the selection process. When judges are selected locally and that area has a high proportion of minorities, there are more minorities on the bench.[36] When a state has a high proportion of Democrats (or Republicans), people who are Democrats (or Republicans) end up getting more appointments. Table 11.3 presents one study of the proportion of Democratic supreme court judges according to whether states are primarily Democrat or Republican in their voting patterns. States that vote Democrat tend to have more Democratic judges, and states that vote Republican tend to have more Republican judges, regardless of the selection process used.

The nature of judges is also affected by who does the selection and what their preferences are. In many selection processes, politicians or party committees make appointments. Selection through appointment is a very important route to the bench for certain groups. A politician, for example, may be concerned about responding to minorities and stress their appointment. Most blacks who become judges get the position through appointment.[37] Politicians with different priorities who have the appointment power can generate very different appointments.

When Jerry Brown [a liberal Democrat] was governor of California, he placed 86 blacks, 73 Hispanics, 33 Asians, and 132 women in judicial positions. Overall, minorities and women constituted about 40 percent of Brown's judicial appointments. In

Table 11.3

Partisan Affiliations of Judges and Party Dominance in State

Party Dominance in State	Proportion of Judges Democratic (%)
One party, Democratic	100.0
Democratic-dominant	89.1
Two-party competitive	44.6
Republican-dominant	11.5

Source: Henry R. Glick and Kenneth N. Vines, State Court Systems *(Englewood Cliffs: Prentice-Hall, 1973), 50.*

contrast, Texas Governor Bill Clements [a conservative Republican] appointed a total of just 10 Hispanics and no blacks to the state bench during his two terms as governor.[38]

Judge Characteristics and Decisions

Does the presence of males, whites, or Democrats affect the kinds of decisions rendered? Might a predominance of Democratic state judges mean that justice is "Democratic" in nature in that state? There is some evidence that this does occur. Democrats tend to be more favorable to those seeking unemployment-compensation claims than to employers. Democrats tend to be more sympathetic to tenants in landlord-tenant disputes.[39] Black judges were found to send blacks and whites to jail at the same rate, while white judges sent more blacks to jail.[40] Judges from working-class backgrounds in Pittsburgh tend to give out less harsh sentences than judges in Minnesota from upper-income backgrounds.[41] It is generally presumed that judges appointed by liberal Democrats will produce different rulings than judges appointed by conservative Republicans.[42]

But other studies do not provide clear evidence that who makes decisions matters. Women bring different attitudes about social issues to the bench, but there is no clear evidence they make decisions that are different from those made by men.[43] Other studies have found that black judges and white judges do not appear to handle cases involving black defendants and white defendants differently.[44] There is clearly much more research to be done in order to understand if, and when, the characteristics of judges affect decisions.

Any assessment of the impact of judges is complicated by variations in state laws about criminal standards. States with a large population of liberals are more likely to pass liberal laws than states with a large proportion of conservatives. Laws about divorce, drinking, and minimum criminal penalties are stricter in states that are dominated by conservative groups, such as fundamentalists.[45] Individuals in different states may receive different penalties for similar criminal behavior, but these differences may stem from the values and laws of the state, and not because

Democrats (or Republicans) control judicial positions and make only Democratic (Republican) interpretations.

Treatment of Cases

Issues of Fairness

What matters ultimately is the way cases are handled. Is the law applied equally to all? Do some groups get treated better or worse in the legal process? The concern is how *categories* of cases get handled. A court decision in a specific case may attract a great deal of attention for a short period of time, but it is the systematic treatment of cases that can prompt public concern and complaint and that can put an item on the agenda of politicians.

Some differences in treatment have great political significance. Political values of American society stress that everyone should be treated equally. The suspicion that everyone is not treated equally has prompted extensive research into whether this is true. Sometimes that evidence is clear, and sometimes it is not.

Treatment by race has been extensively researched, and much of the evidence indicates that minorities fare less well than others in the legal process.[46] But others have disputed this conclusion and argued that once the conditions of cases are considered, there is not much difference in the treatment of racial groups.[47] In other words, some studies conclude that minorities are convicted more, get sent to jail more, and get longer sentences. Others argue that case conditions, such as the number of previous offenses, should be considered. If cases are grouped so that defendants with the same number of previous offenses are considered (for example), studies indicate that within similar groups, there are no significant differences by race in the sentences imposed. The difficulty lies in the way of handling previous offenses. Minorities are more likely to have more previous offenses, and those with more previous offenses get more severe sentences. Those with several previous offenses get similar sentences, and race has no impact. Statistically, that conclusion is correct. The difficult question for debates about race and the legal process, however, is why so many minorities fall into certain categories, such as the category of many previous offenses. Is it because minorities are more likely to commit many offenses (a possible answer from a conservative), or is it because minorities are poorer and driven to crime, or because minorities are arrested more, prosecuted more, and get poorer legal counsel so that they end up with more prior convictions (possible liberal answers)?

There is no definitive answer to this question. In our society, there are many perspectives on this question. These perspectives become part of political debates, and the treatment of racial groups in the legal system has been an enduring political issue for politicians and for those involved in the court system.

Women also argue that the legal system provides them with unequal treatment. They point to studies that conclude that women receive lower awards than men when a spouse dies and there is a settlement in a wrongful death suit.[48] They argue that the movement to no-fault divorce proceedings has disadvantaged women.[49] Advocates for the poor also argue that low-income individuals generally do not fare well in the courts.[50]

Whether these accusations are true cannot be settled here. What is crucial for the political process is that many participants in the process believe and argue that there are differences in the way groups are treated and that politicians should address this issue. These arguments put an item on the public agenda that some politicians will be concerned about responding to, while others will feel little pressure to do so.

State Traditions and Decision Patterns

It appears that different decisions and penalties occur because of who individuals are. Differences also emerge across the states because of differing state traditions in interpreting the law. The "law" is not a rigid body of specifications about proper behavior and arrangements. There are considerable grounds for ambiguity, and considerable room for interpretation. As noted earlier, much of law in the United States is state law. This situation leaves room for state autonomy. Even when federal law applies to a decision made in the states, state judges have the freedom to interpret what that federal ruling means for a specific case. These conditions allow state judges to make their own interpretations. Each state constitution is also different from the federal constitution, and judges have the right to reach decisions based on the state constitution as long as that decision does not override federal law.[51] All these conditions create possibilities for state judges to make their own interpretations and rulings.

When judges make decisions that disrupt the status quo, they are accused of becoming policymakers, or of usurping the function that is assigned by the Constitution to executives and legislatures. In recent years, several state courts have ruled that existing systems of financing local schools (which rely heavily on unequal property tax bases) are unconstitutional, that abortion is a right of women, that certain legislative district-drawing patterns are illegal, that public and low-income housing must be allowed in the suburbs, and that variation in local assessment practices are illegal, among many other decisions. Such decisions are controversial and receive a considerable amount of publicity.

The law relevant to school finance provides an example of the way interpretation takes place. Many state constitutions (but not all) say that the education of children is a state responsibility and make reference to the obligation of the state to provide an "efficient" education system. The constitution may also indicate or imply that the state may delegate this power, but that educating children is ultimately a state responsibility. Elsewhere the constitution may also say or imply that the state is to insure that there be equality of opportunity for the residents of the state. These statements contain some ambiguity and also provide an opportunity for judicial interpretation.

What does it mean to say that a state has responsibility? How far does that go? Does it mean that the state is responsible for the educational activities taking place in all the districts of the state? And what does it mean that everyone should have equal opportunity? Does it mean that everyone should receive a chance for an education, or does it mean that all citizens should have equitable educations, whatever that means? If the state is responsible, does it mean that it is the state's "fault" that children go to schools in districts with enormous variations in tax bases, equipment, and teacher salaries? In the state of California, the state courts in *Serrano v. Priest* (1971) decided that it did mean this and that the entire educational finance system of the state had to be changed. The same decision was reached by the New Jersey courts in *Robinson v. Cahill* (1974). The law provides the opportunity for such interpretations, and school finance situations have been ruled illegal in several states.

Not all state courts are equally inclined to respond to that opportunity. While some state courts have issued many "innovative" rulings over the last decade, others have been inclined to follow a more conservative approach. During the 1980s, the Supreme Court became dominated by more conservative appointees of Presidents Reagan and Bush. The Court issued many rulings that reflected a more conservative interpretation of the law. Many state courts adopted those rulings as their own over the 1980s, while others did not.[52]

Tort-law decisions provide an indication of the way state courts differ in their inclination to issue "innovative" rulings. Tort law involves the legal obligations between the parties involved in an exchange. For many years, the courts were largely sympathetic to producers and unwilling to infringe on their rights in the marketplace. In recent years, the courts in some states have taken considerable initiative to redefine those rights and to give consumers more rights.[53] But not all states have been equally active. Table 11.4 ranks the states according to the extent to which they have been inclined to adopt new doctrines of tort obligations. There are considerable differences across the states.

What motivates some courts to act and others not to? For a judge to be willing to rule that unequal spending matters, there must be a perception that variations in district spending create variations in education that create variations in opportunities. This idea is relatively recent in American society. As discussed in Chapter 2, for many years the predominant idea in our society was that individual initiative, not government spending, determined how students did. A motivated individual would learn regardless of the circumstance. Therefore, differentials in spending could not be regarded as an indication of state-sanctioned (legal) inequality of opportunity.

As the idea spread that education is part of an individual's environment and that environment affects opportunity, some people began to believe that variations in education do violate equality of opportunity. That idea has become a widely (if not unanimously) accepted idea in our society. It has become a common concern in our society, and many judges are likely to hold these ideas. When judges read a constitution holding the state responsible for the delivery of education, some of them may conclude that heavy reliance on local finance is unconstitutional.[54] To do so is to take a very activist position as a judge. A passive approach would be to simply accept the existing situation as a politically derived situation that is best changed by politics.

We do not know a great deal about what makes some judges more active than others, but we do know that some state courts have traditionally been activist, and

Table 11.4

Rankings of State Supreme Courts in Propensity to Tort-Law Activism in the Postwar Years

State	Rank of Average Tort-Innovation Adoption	State	Rank of Average Tort-Innovation Adoption
1. New Jersey	12.6	26. Florida	27.9
2. Michigan	14.5	27. Delaware	28.1
3. Kentucky	15.1	28. Arkansas	28.4
4. California	16.7	29. South Carolina	28.6
5. Louisiana	18.1	30. Maryland	29.8
6. Pennsylvania	19.8	31. Mississippi	31.0
7. New York	19.9	32. North Dakota	31.3
8. Washington	20.4	33. South Dakota	31.5
9. Ohio	21.7	34.5 Idaho	31.6
10.5 Minnesota	21.8	34.5 Nebraska	31.6
10.5 New Hampshire	21.8	36. Nevada	31.7
12. Connecticut	22.0	37. Arizona	31.8
13. Illinois	22.3	38. North Carolina	34.5
14. Oklahoma	23.0	39. Rhode Island	35.0
15. Oregon	23.1	40.5 Kansas	35.8
16. Texas	23.3	40.5 West Virginia	35.8
17. Iowa	24.0	42. Alaska	36.1
18. Wisconsin	24.7	43. Hawaii	36.3
19. Colorado	24.9	44. Montana	37.0
20. Indiana	25.0	45. New Mexico	37.4
21. Tennessee	25.5	46. Vermont	37.7
22. Georgia	25.8	47. Virginia	38.6
23. Utah	27.0	48. Massachusetts	41.1
24. Alabama	27.1	49. Wyoming	44.7
25. Missouri	27.2	50. Maine	46.6

Note: Rankings are based upon the adoption of fourteen innovations in tort doctrine. A court was given a rank of 1 if it was the first adopter of an innovation, a 2 if the second adopter, and so on. A court was not ranked for an innovation if it was precluded from acting by the adoption of a statute. Courts not adopting an innovation are ranked 50 (or slightly lower if one or more courts were not ranked). The average ranks shown in the table are means of all ranks for individual innovations.
Source: Lawrence Baum and Bradley Canon, "State Supreme Courts as Activists," in Mary C. Porter and G. Alan Tarr, State Supreme Courts Policy Makers in the Federal System (Westport, Conn. Greenwood, 1982), 83–108.

they perceive it as appropriate and legitimate to be so.[55] In one study of four states, judges were asked whether they saw themselves as law interpreters (who apply law to facts of case), lawmakers (who arrive at a ruling that responds to the situation), or as pragmatists (who try to balance the need to follow the law with the possibility that some innovation may be necessary to handle unique situations). The judges in New Jersey were most inclined to see themselves as pragmatists who needed to be innovative to deal with new situations. Judges were also asked how much importance they attached to following precedent (doing what has been decided before—*stare decisis*—so that the continuity of the law is maintained). Again, New Jersey judges put much less emphasis on precedent.[56]

It is not easy to explain why some state courts develop such patterns of activism. It is clear that some state courts do have a tradition of being more active and of being more inclined to make "broader" interpretations of the law. The New Jersey court regularly falls into that category. Its record over the last twenty years illustrates how significant such a role can be. In the early 1970s and late 1980s, the court ruled that the heavy reliance on local property taxes as a means of financing schools was unconstitutional. During the 1980s, the court also ruled that, since the state was legally responsible for land use in the state, it was unconstitutional for the state to allow local governments to use their zoning powers to keep out low- and moderate-income housing. In a case involving Mt. Laurel, the court ruled that such cities had to allow more diversity of housing. In 1983, the court became frustrated with the inaction of cities on the matter and demanded positive action on the issue. This activism has been greeted with considerable political criticism from conservatives, but there have been no suggestions that the rulings of the court should be repudiated or defied. Some have suggested changing the constitution, or passing new laws, but the respect for the court and its interpretation of the law has not been fundamentally challenged. There are other states where such rulings would probably not even be made and so easily accepted by the public.

Judicial Activism and Restraint in Handling Cases

While "innovation" occurs, judges are also aware that whenever they appear to be explicitly political or exercising their personal view of the way society should be, they run the risk of undermining their credibility as judges interpreting the law. Judges realize that public acceptance of decisions and adherence to the law is contingent upon the perception that a decision reflects the law and not the personal opinion of judges. People are likely to respect decisions based on the law, but not those based on personal opinions. Judges must seek to maintain the belief that they are interpreting, not "making it up." To maintain that position, judges must generally stay roughly (and only that) within the confines of precedent.

Courts make very basic judgments as to whether actions in our society are right or wrong. The courts must ultimately rely on the legitimacy of their position if society is to accept their judgments. We accept court decisions primarily because we regard it as appropriate that there be a third branch making decisions based on the law. This situation is so commonplace that we often do not even think about it. But when a court rules that abortions are legal, that desegregation is illegal, and that local finance of schools is illegal (in certain states), we accept such a decision because we accept the courts as legitimate. Maintaining that legitimacy requires convincing the public that the courts are independent from politics.

The 1992 decision of the Supreme Court about abortion contains a blunt statement by Justice David Souter about the importance of this credibility before the public. In *Roe v. Wade 1973*, the Court ruled that women had a right to abortion.

That decision generated enormous opposition from many conservatives. During the 1980s Presidents Reagan and Bush appointed judges who they thought would be sympathetic to overturning this decision. In 1992, the Court was presented with a case involving a Pennsylvania statute that was very restrictive about abortion rights. The case of *Planned Parenthood of Southeastern Pennsylvania v. Casey* was seen by many as the vehicle for the courts to overturn *Roe v. Wade*. The Court could have affirmed the Pennsylvania statute and thereby overturned the precedent that women had a right to abortion. The Court did not do so, much to the surprise of many. In a section of the decision, written largely by Justice David Souter, he explained why:

> Our analysis would not be complete, however, without explaining why overturning *Roe*'s central holding [principle] . . . would seriously weaken the Court's capacity to exercise the judicial power and to function as the Supreme Court of a Nation dedicated to the rule of law. To understand why this would be so, it is necessary to understand the source of this Court's authority, and its relationship to the country's understanding of itself as a constitutional Republic.
>
> The Court . . . cannot independently coerce obedience to its decrees. The Courts' power lies, rather, in its legitimacy, a product of substance and perception that shows itself in the people's acceptance of the Judiciary as fit to determine what the Nation's law means. . . .
>
> The court must take care to speak and act in ways that allow people to accept its decisions on the terms the Court claims for them, as truly grounded in principle, not as compromises [due to] social and political pressures.
>
> There is a point beyond which frequent overruling would overtax the country's belief in the Court's good faith. The legitimacy of the Court would fade with the frequency of vacillation.[57]

Judges must also be careful about being somewhat reflective of the context of public opinion in which they operate.[58] During the 1960s, for example, prosecutors in the South "saw" few violations of civil rights, and courts did not convict many individuals for alleged violations.[59] If the courts had recognized violations, they would have directly conflicted with dominant local political attitudes. In the area of abortion, public opinion polls reveal that most Americans support the right to abortion, and this support may have affected the Court in its 1992 decision.

Although critics of the courts argue that judges make too much policy, judges, in general, try to constrain such involvement. Why they do so tells us a lot about the nature of law in our society and the way judges perceive their position. The law is respected in our society because almost everyone regards it as legitimate and appropriate to have and to obey laws. Judges who make decisions wish to have them respected and obeyed on the presumption that they are simply interpretations of the existing law. Judges have little ability to actually force anyone to accept their decisions. They must rely on deference from other decision makers and from the mass public on the basis that they, as judges, are essentially applying existing law. The mystique of "the law" is powerful in our society, and people will honor decisions that are part of the law. If the public begins to believe that the decisions being made are only the personal (political) opinions of the judges involved, then the legitimacy of the opinions breaks down. The "rule of law" would be replaced by the "rule of men," and the entire basis for deference to the opinions of judges and acceptance of their decisions would be gone.

The Effects of Court Practices and Rulings: Shaping Agendas and Altering Policy

Shaping Agendas

Court practices are of concern to society and can create political issues for politicians. General perceptions of inequities in access to the courts, or of bias in sentences awarded, can result in public concern and political pressure to correct those problems.

Issues also come before politicians as a result of specific court cases over inequities. Court decisions can force governors and legislators to deal with issues they might otherwise choose to ignore. In Texas, the courts ruled in the early 1970s in *Rodriquez v. San Antonio* that school finance funds were too inequitably distributed and that the existing situation was unacceptable. Texas legislators have tried several modest redistribution schemes to satisfy the courts. Each time the courts have ruled that the proposed solution was unacceptable. The governor and the legislature tried in 1993 to get a public referendum passed that would have allowed the redistribution of local property taxes, which the constitution forbids. The failure of that referendum has forced the governor and the legislature to search for another solution.

In 1993 in Connecticut, a lawsuit was filed arguing that racial and class segregation were the consequence of state grants of authority to municipalities to incorporate and to zone property. While that lawsuit, *Sheff v. O'Neill,* worked its way through the courts, Governor Lowell Weicker tried to head off the lawsuit by proposing legislation that would consolidate some school districts around urban areas so that greater racial integration and more sharing of tax bases would be possible.[60] This legislation and the concern over this issue would probably not have emerged without the threat of the lawsuit.

Getting an issue on the agenda, however, does not guarantee its resolution. Funding for public defenders remains limited. Legal services for low-income individuals are not extensive. The controversy over inequities in school finance in Texas has gone on for at least twenty-five years without a resolution, and the lawsuit in Connecticut may ultimately not generate any difference in response from the state.

What, then, is the impact of court decisions? That impact is not easy to sort out. Court decisions often receive a great deal of publicity when they are first announced. Whether court decisions led to different public policies, however, is often in the hands of other political institutions. The essential power of the courts is to rule that something is illegal. They are generally reluctant to rule what is legal.

There are important reasons for making negative, not affirmative rulings. The courts have limited abilities to actually "make" anything happen. In issues such as school finance, they cannot direct anyone to impose taxes and redistribute money. That power belongs to the governor and to the legislature, and the courts cannot usurp that power. Furthermore, if the courts did get involved in allocating funds, they would be engaging in political decisions and would soon be seen as a political institution. That image would erode public support for court decisions. Courts would no longer be deciding matters of the law, but making what are essentially political decisions.

Since the courts cannot decide what should be, their approach must be to declare a current situation unconstitutional or in violation of a statute and then hope that other political actors will respond. Courts can prod, but they still cannot decide what should replace the existing arrangement. Whether or not others respond depends on which party controls the governorship and the legislature and on the electoral base of that party.

The way school finance was handled in New Jersey and Texas illustrates how important the response of politicians is. On February 13, 1970, the case of *Robinson v. Cahill* was filed in a lower level trial court of New Jersey.[61] Kenneth Robinson was a sixth grader in Jersey City, a city with a relatively poor tax base. Only 28 percent of the school budget came from the state. A lawsuit was filed contending that this arrangement was unfair. It was filed against Governor Cahill, on the grounds that the governor should be held responsible for this situation.

On April 3, 1973, the New Jersey supreme court, the highest court in the state, declared the existing system of school funding unconstitutional. The court did not specify what had to be done to remedy the situation. By June 1973, no response had occurred, and the courts set a deadline of December 31, 1974, for a response. That deadline passed and the court set another deadline of October 1, 1975. That deadline also passed without any changes. There were proposals and bills in the legislature, but nothing changed. Finally, on May 13, 1976, the court ruled that it was illegal for any further funds to be spent on the school system, and they ordered the schools to close on July 1, 1976, if no response was forthcoming. While this suggests the court was being very intrusive by issuing this closing order, the schools would not be open in July, so the real impact would be limited. The symbolic effect, however, was significant. The governor and the legislature finally agreed on July 9, 1976, to pass an income tax to provide the revenue to remedy the school funding issue.

The governor and the legislature did eventually respond. That response was surely helped along by the fact that the governor and the majority party in the legislature were Democrats. They reacted to this controversy with considerable sympathy toward the issue of inequality. The legislative party bargained very hard to make sure that the benefits of increased state aid to schools were spread out as much as possible, but the party as a whole was not opposed to doing something about the issue. But even with this relatively sympathetic response, it took three years and considerable prodding by the courts for a response to occur.

In contrast, the situation in Texas illustrates how limited the powers of the courts can be when there is no sympathetic response from politicians. In 1968, a factory worker in San Antonio filed a lawsuit against the city on behalf of his son, claiming that the child was being discriminated against because he went to a school with a limited tax base. That suit led to a 1971 state supreme court ruling that school finance in Texas was inequitable. That ruling was appealed to the U.S. Supreme Court, which overturned the ruling. The state court, however, has kept up its pressure, with further rulings that inequality existed, and the governor and the legislature have responded by passing different state aid programs that added some money to school districts with limited tax bases.[62] The courts have ruled that these efforts are inadequate. The essential problem facing the state is that there is no income tax. Such a tax is probably necessary to provide the magnitude of revenue needed for equitable funding. There is tremendous political opposition in the state to the income tax. The legislature has tried several ways to resolve the issue without imposing an income tax. In 1993, they put before the voters a plan to consolidate school districts so that local property tax revenues could be shared. The voters rejected that proposal, and there was considerable speculation that the court would resort to closing the schools to force a decision.[63] In response, the legislature and the governor agreed to a plan in which wealthy school districts would transfer their tax bases to lower-income districts within regions. It is clear that the agenda of politicians has been altered by the "near-constant political headache" of these court rulings.[64] Politicians in Texas have avoided change, but school finance has remained on the agenda.

There are other ways in which court activities can contribute to getting an item on the public agenda. Even when the courts do not rule in favor of a group alleging injustice, the lawsuits surrounding a court case may serve as stimuli to mobilize groups of plaintiffs to pursue their political interests through conventional channels. There is evidence, for example, that some of the lawsuits about wage discrimination against women served to make women more aware of their common situation, created more public attention about the issue, and led to more collective action to address the issue.[65]

Altering Policy

The major concern about court activism is whether judges have actually become decision makers. Many critics have argued that judges have usurped the rights of executives and legislatures and that they are dictating what public policy should be.[66] The question is, do court decisions directly affect public policy?

The evidence is mixed.[67] School prayer has been ruled unconstitutional, but many schools still begin the day with prayers. On the other hand, school prayer is not as widespread now as it was thirty years ago. Abortion has been ruled to be a fundamental right of women, but there are many areas of the country where it is not easy to obtain an abortion. Abortion is, however, much more available legally than it was twenty-five years ago. The court rulings clearly had some impact, but it is not a simple impact. For many court rulings, the issue of the extent to which state and local officials will comply is of major concern.

Several conditions affect whether a ruling has an effect.[68] The ruling must be clear as to meaning. Many times the meaning of a ruling is intentionally not clear. The courts realize that they have limited means of enforcement, and they may issue rulings with some ambiguity. The courts generally do not make it clear what, if any, policy should be implemented to replace an existing practice. This practice avoids a confrontation with other public officials. There also may be little communication of a ruling to the local officials who would be responsible for implementation.

Even when a ruling is clear and it is communicated to the appropriate officials, there is again the inevitable interaction with the predispositions of those receiving the ruling. Some officials are likely to be sympathetic to the ruling and pursue implementing it as best they can. Others may be hostile to the ruling and resist implementation as much and as long as they can.

It is worth repeating the lessons from the school finance situations in Texas and New Jersey. In Texas, there has been little change because the politicians holding the governorship and the legislature have been hostile to that change. In New Jersey, prodding in the mid-1970s resulted in some change after three years. Another court ruling in New Jersey of inadequate financing in the early 1990s was met with a response in 1991 by a Democratic governor and legislature.

The importance of the dispositions of public officials shows up in other areas. The courts have issued numerous rulings about overcrowding in prisons. The rulings do not uniformly result in greater expenditures. They appear to result in more expenditure when facilities are old and the local governments have developed a plan to respond to this problem.[69] These plans are probably more likely to exist in local governments, which are more amenable to doing something about their problems. Court rulings can be issued, but their reception does depend on the attitudes of those receiving them.

For Further Reading

Baum, Laurence. "State Supreme Courts: Activism and Accountability." In Carl Van Horn, *The State of the States*. Washington DC: Congressional Quarterly Press, 1989.

"Developments in the Law: Race and the Criminal Process." *Harvard Law Review* 101, no. 7 (May 1988): 1472–1641.

Lehne, Richard. *The Quest for Justice: The Politics of School Finance Reform*. New York: Longman, 1978.

McCann, Michael. *Rights at Work: Law and the Politics of Pay Equity*. Chicago: University of Chicago Press, 1993.

Weitzman, Leonore J. *The Divorce Revolution*. New York: Free Press, 1985.

Suggestions for Analysis in Your Own State and Locality

1. Court actions generally receive little public attention. They can become an issue when some actions receive public attention. This attention can occur because of the way the courts resolve a certain case. An unpopular resolution or ruling can lead to charges that the courts are not doing their job well. Have there been court cases in your state or locality that received enormous

attention because of the decision that resulted? Have there been any local studies released publicly that claimed that the courts were not doing their job?

2. Court actions can also become an issue if the courts rule on a controversial issue such as school finance, pay equity, open housing, or the siting of community centers or waste dumps. Have there been such cases in your state or locality? If so, what kinds of public responses resulted?

3. There are continuing disagreements in American politics about the way to choose judges. How are judges chosen in your state and locality? Are they appointed or elected? How much of a role does partisanship play in selecting judges?

Notes

[1] Mary C. Porter and G. Alan Tarr, "Introduction," in Mary C. Porter and G. Alan Tarr, *State Supreme Courts: Policymaking in the Federal System* (Westport: Greenwood, 1982), xvi–xviii.

[2] For a review of this development, see Charles H. Sheldon, "Judicial Review and the Supreme Court of Washington, 1890–1986," *Publius* 17, (winter 1987): 69–90.

[3] Reapportionment involved a series of decisions. Beginning in 1962 with *Baker v. Carr*, the U.S. Supreme Court ruled that legislative districts had to represent roughly equal numbers of people.

[4] Norman R. Luttbeg, *Comparing States and Communities* (New York: HarperCollins, 1992), 291.

[5] Wesley G. Skogan, "Crime and Punishment," in Virginia Gray, Herbert Jacob, and Robert Albritton, *Politics in the American States*, 5th ed. (Glenview Ill.: Scott, Foresman/Little, Brown, 1990), 387–406.

[6] Harry P. Stumpf and John H. Culver, *The Politics of State Courts* (New York: Longman, 1992), 164–166.

[7] David Neubauer, *America's Courts and the Criminal Justice System*, 2d ed. (Pacific Grove: Brooks/Cole, 1984), 104–107.

[8] Douglas A. Smith and Christy A. Visher, "Street-Level Justice: Situational Determinants of Police Arrest Decisions," *Social Problems* 29 (1981): 184.

[9] Lawrence M. Friedman, *Crime and Punishment in American History* (New York: Basic Books, 1993), 290–293.

[10] Eric H. Steele, "The Historical Context of Small Claims Courts," *American Bar Foundation Research Journal* 293 (1981).

[11] Marc Galanter, "Why the 'Haves' Come Out Ahead: Speculations on the Limits of Legal Change," *Law and Society Review* 9, no. 1 (fall 1974): 95–160; and Barbara Yngvesson and Patricia Hennessey, "Small Claims, Complex Disputes: A Review of the Small Claims Literature," *Law and Society Review* 9, no. 2 (winter, 1974): 219–74.

[12] Stumpf and Culver, *The Politics of State Courts*, 78–79.

[13] Henry R. Glick, *Courts, Politics, and Justice*, 2d ed. (New York: McGraw-Hill, 1988), 149.

[14] Henry R. Glick, *Courts, Politics, and Justice*, (New York: McGraw-Hill, 1983), 138–39.

[15] Harvard Sitkoff, *The Struggle for Black Equality* (New York: Hill and Wang, 1993), 18–22.

[16] Clement E. Vose, "Litigation as a Form of Pressure Group Activity," *Annals of the American Academy of Political and Social Science* 319 (1958): 20–31.

[17] "Developments in the Law—Class Actions," *Harvard Law Review* 89 (1976): 1318–1644; and Michael McCann, *Rights at Work: Law and the Politics of Pay Equity* (Chicago: University of Chicago Press, 1993).

[18] Stumpf and Culver, *The Politics of State Courts*, 76–78.

[19] Herbert Jacob, *Justice in America*, 4th ed. (Boston: Little, Brown, 1984), 69–75; and Christopher E. Smith, *Courts and the Poor* (Chicago: Nelson-Hall, 1991).

[20] John J. Harrigan, *Empty Pockets, Empty Dreams: Class and Bias in American Politics* (New York: Macmillan, 1993), 268–291.

[21] Herbert Jacob, *Justice in America*, 3d ed. (Boston: Little, Brown, 1978), 185–86.

[22] Glick, *Courts, Politics, and Justice*, 133.

[23] Herbert Jacob, "Courts," in Virginia Gray, Herbert Jacob, and Kenneth N. Vines, *Politics in the American States*, 4th ed. (Boston: Little, Brown, 1983), 224–30.

[24] Stumpf and Culver, *The Politics of State Courts*, 32–34.

[25] Doris M. Provine, *Judging Credentials: Nonlawyer Judges and the Politics of Professionalism* (Chicago: University of Chicago Press, 1986); and Glick, *Courts, Politics, and Justice*, 46–49.

[26] Glick, *Courts, Politics, and Justice*, 143.

[27] Herbert Jacob, *Justice in America*, 4th ed. (Boston: Little, Brown, 1984), 188–196.

[28] Peter F. Nardulli, *The Courtroom Elite: An Organizational Perspective* (Cambridge: Ballinger, 1983).

[29] Malcolm D. Holmes et al., "Plea Bargaining Policy and State District Caseload," *Law and Society Review* 26, no. 1 (1992): 139–59.

[30] H. Laurence Ross and James P. Foley, "Judicial Disobedience of the Mandate to Imprison Drunk Drivers," *Law and Society Review* 21, no. 2 (1987): 315–23.

[31] Thomas B. Marvell and Mary Lee Luskin, "The Impact of Speedy Trial Laws in Connecticut and North Carolina," *Justice System Journal* 14, no. 3, and 15, no. 1 (1991): 343–55.

[32] Anthony Champagne and Greg Thelmann, "Awareness of Trial Court Judges," *Judicature* 74, no. 5 (February-March 1991): 271–76.

[33] Nicholas P. Lovrich et al., "Citizen Knowledge and Voting in Judicial Elections," *Judicature* 73, no. 1 (June-July 1989): 28–33.

[34] Philip L. Dubois, "Voter Responses to Court Reform: Merit Judge Selection on the Ballot," *Judicature* 73, no. 5 (February-March, 1990): 238.

[35] Bradley Canon, "The Impact of Formal Selection Processes on Characteristics of Judges—Reconsidered," *Law and Society Review* 13 (May 1972): 570–93; Craig F. Emmert and Henry R. Glick, "The Selection of State Supreme Court Judges," *American Politics Quarterly* 16 (October 1988): 445–65; and Nicholas O. Alozie, "Black Representation on State Judiciaries," *Social Science Quarterly* 69, no. 4 (December 1988): 979–86.

[36] John Paul Ryan, Allan Ashman, Bruce D. Sales, and Sandra Shane-Dubow, *American Trial Judges: Their Work Styles and Performance* (New York: Free Press, 1980), 124–30; and Richard Engstrom, "When Blacks Run for Judge," *Judicature* 73, no. 2 (August-September 1989): 87–89.

[37] Barbara L. Graham, "Judicial Recruitment and Racial Diversity on State Courts: An Overview," *Judicature* 74, no. 1 (June-July 1990): 28–34.

[38] Stumpf and Culver, *The Politics of State Courts*, 48.

[39] Stuart Nagel, "Political Party Affiliation and Judges' Decisions," *American Political Science Review* 55 (1961): 843–51.

[40] Susan Welch, Michael Combs, and John Gruhl, "Do Black Judges Make a Difference?" *American Journal of Political Science* 32, no. 1 (February 1988): 126–36.

[41] Martin A. Levin, *Urban Politics and the Criminal Courts* (Chicago: University of Chicago Press, 1977).

[42] Malcolm M. Feely, "Another Look at the 'Party Variable' in Judicial Decision Making: An Analysis of the Michigan Supreme Court," *Polity* 4 (1971): 91–104.

[43] Elaine Martin, "Men and Women on the Bench: Vive la Difference," *Judicature* 73, no. 4 (December-January 1990): 204–208.

[44] Cassia Spohn, "The Sentencing Decisions of Black and White Judges: Expected and Unexpected Similarities," *Law and Society Review* 24, no. 5 (1990): 1197–1216.

[45] John Fairbanks, "Religious Forces and 'Morality' Policies in the American States," *Western Political Quarterly* 26 (1973): 411–17.

[46] For an extensive review, see "Developments in the Law: Race and the Criminal Process," *Harvard Law Review* 101, no. 7 (May 1988): 1472–1641.

[47] James L. Gibson, "Race as a Determinant of Criminal Sentencing: A Methodological Critique and a Case Study," *Law and Society Review* 12 (1978): 455; and Cassia Spohn et al., "The Effect of Race on Sentencing: A Reexamination of an Unsettled Question," *Law and Society Review* 16 (1981–1982): 71–88.

[48] Jane Goodman et al., "Money, Sex, and Death: Gender Bias in Wrongful Death Damage Awards," *Law and Society Review* 25, no. 2 (1991): 261–85.

[49] Leonore J. Weitzman, *The Divorce Revolution* (New York: Free Press, 1985). For conflicting evidence, see Herbert Jacob, "Another Look at No-Fault Divorce and the Postdivorce Finances of Women," *Law and Society Review* 23, no. 1 (1989): 95–115.

[50] Stanton Wheeler et al., "Do the 'Haves' Come Out Ahead Winning and Losing in State Supreme Courts, 1870–1970?" *Law and Society Review*, 21, no. 3 (1987): 403–45; and Karl Monsma and Richard Lempers, "The Value of Counsel: Twenty Years of Representation Before a Public Housing Eviction Board," *Law and Society Review* 26, no. 3 (1992): 648–55.

[51] Stanley H. Friedelbaum, "Independent State Grounds: Contemporary Invitations to Judicial Activism," in Mary C. Porter and G. Alan Tarr, *State Supreme Courts* (Westport: Greenwood, 1982), 23–53.

[52] Barry Lanzer, "The Hidden Conservatism of the State Court 'Revolution'," *Judicature* 74, no. 4 (December-January 1991): 190–97.

[53] Laurence Baum, "State Supreme Courts: Activism and Accountability," in Carl Van Horn, *The State of the States*, 2d ed. (Washington, DC: Congressional Quarterly Press, 1993): 103–130.

[54] Bill Swinford, "A Predictive Model of Decision Making in State Supreme Courts: The School Financing Cases," *American Politics Quarterly* 19, no. 3 (July 1991): 336–52.

[55] For an excellent study of such differences in traditions, see G. Alan Tarr and Mary C. Porter, *State Supreme Courts in State and Nation* (New Haven: Yale University Press, 1988).

[56] Henry Glick, *Supreme Courts in State Politics* (New York: Basic Books, 1971), 41.

[57] *Planned Parenthood v. Casey* (1992), 22–24.

[58] William Mishler and Reginald S. Sheehan, "The Supreme Court as a Countermajoritian Institution: The Impact of Public Opinion on Supreme Court Decisions," *American Political Science Review* 87, no. 1 (March 1993): 87–101.

[59] Kenneth N. Vines, "Federal District Judges and Race Relations Cases in the South," *Journal of Politics* 26 (1964): 337–57; and Kenneth N. Vines, "Southern State Supreme Courts and Race Relations," *Western Political Quarterly* 18 (March 1965): 5–18.

[60] George Judson, "Marketing Integration in the Schools," *New York Times* 23 May 1993, 34; and George Judson, "Regional Approach Urged to Help Troubled Schools," *New York Times* 29 May 1993, 24.

[61] Richard Lehne, *The Quest for Justice: The Politics of School Finance Reform* (New York: Longman, 1978).

[62] Eugene W. Jones et al., *Practicing Texas Politics*, 7th ed. (Boston: Houghton Mifflin, 1989), 311–14.

[63] Sam Howe Verhovek, "Texans Reject Sharing School Wealth," *New York Times* 3 May 1993, A12.

[64] Sam Howe Verhovek, "Poor Would Tax the Rich in Texas Plan for Schools," *New York Times* 28 May 1993, A10.

[65] Michael McCann, *Rights at Work: Law and the Politics of Pay Equity* (Chicago: University of Chicago Press, 1993).

[66] Nathan Glazer, "Towards an Imperial Judiciary," *The Public Interest* 41 (1975): 104–123.

[67] Mark Kessler, "Legal Mobilization for Social Reforms: Power and the Politics of Agenda Setting," *Law and Society Review* 24, no. 1 (1990): 121–43; and Gerald Rosenberg, *Hollow Hopes: Can Courts Bring About Social Change?* (Chicago: University of Chicago Press, 1991).

[68]

[69] William D. Duncombe and Jeffrey D. Straussman, "The Impact of Courts on the Decision to Expand Jail Capacity," *Administration and Society* 25, no. 3 (November 1993): 267–92.

12

Political Control and Public Policy Decisions

PREVIEW

Campaigns are conducted as if who controls government matter. This chapter first summarizes the impacts we might expect if control over government changes from one party to another, and then reviews what we know about the impact of control.

As with most political situations, the impact of changes in party control depends on many factors. The electoral bases and commonality of bases for executives and legislatures play a significant role. When parties have unified control and clear constituencies, we expect to see impacts from party control. There is evidence impact does occur. When unified control exists and parties do not have different constituencies, we should not see much consequence of who controls government.

When party control is divided, as is increasingly the case, the situation becomes more complicated. The constituency base of each branch and their power relative to each other affect what policies are adopted.

Expectations of Impacts

Elections bring people to power. They give people control of institutions and give them the potential to make decisions that change public policy. Does the acquisition of power make any difference? Does it change policy? Or, are the skeptics right who believe it doesn't matter who is elected, because all politicians do essentially the same thing?

It may help to first clarify what kinds of expectations we might have about change. That involves two basic concerns. First, if changes are possible, what conditions are likely to bring about change? What conditions are likely to bring about little change? Second when change is discussed, just what kinds of changes are involved? What impacts might elections or events have on the direction of public policy?

Parties, Agendas, and Cohesion: Restatements

There are essentially two possible sources of changes in public policy. Change may occur because politicians initiate it. Or change may occur because events prompt a response from politicians. For politicians to be inclined to seek to change public policy, several conditions need to exist. As Key argued, the crucial matters are the electoral bases of politicians and the willingness of politicians to work together.[1] He argued that the only way for the have-nots to get policies favorable to them is to have a cohesive party with a lower-income base advocating its concerns. It is only when that situation exists that we can expect to see a change in policy when Democrats acquire power.

Political parties are the primary means of organizing politicians in American society. Agreements to change public policy are most likely when the same party holds the executive branch and the legislature, whether at the state or local level. Politicians are most likely to agree on policy principles when they share the same electoral bases and policy concerns.[2] When the legislative party has a relatively clear electoral base and one that is very similar to that of the governor, the cohesion of party members is likely to be high. Arriving at a consensus on policy should be easier in that situation. Finally, the inclination to pursue change also depends on the agenda that politicians pursued during elections. If, during a campaign, a party presented a relatively coherent set of proposals that they promised to enact, the likelihood of change is considerably higher. In these situations, politicians take the initiative to change policy.

Politicians, however, often find themselves reacting to events rather than pursuing their own agendas. The economy changes, federal policy options shift, and the courts sometimes push issues onto their agenda that they may not have anticipated. Recessions compel politicians to decide whether to cut services or to raise taxes. A growth in revenues may prompt politicians to decide whether to increase program funding, or to cut taxes and return revenues to the public. The federal government may reduce the amount of money made available to the states. Such a cut may prompt state officials to decide whether to maintain their own level of policy commitment by raising state taxes, or to cut the level of services in order to avoid raising taxes. Change can come about not because a particular party acquires power but because events prompt a decision regardless of who is in office. Partisanship shapes the direction taken, but the decision to act does not always occur because a party acquired power and had a predetermined plan.[3]

In contrast, there are many conditions under which change is less likely to occur. The same party may hold both branches of government, but the electoral bases of the legislative party and of the governor may differ, and they may not be able to agree on policy changes. Even if they do share electoral bases, the party may not have made change a part of their campaign and may feel no pressure to pursue change. Control of government may be divided, making change much less likely.

Furthermore, events may also make it unnecessary for politicians to explicitly deal with change. Liberals may acquire power at a time when revenues are flowing into the state or local treasury, and they may be able to put more money into programs without having to enact any changes in tax laws. Change occurs, but without politicians having to make painful choices to raise taxes or fees.

Finally, there is the crucial matter of institutional power. Changes (or no change) come about because of negotiations between executives and legislatures. One branch may have considerably more formal or informal power than the other. The governor may be able to dominate policy negotiations such that he or she is more successful in achieving goals. The relative power of the branches of government also needs to be considered.

Formalizing Expectations

If the expectation is that change may occur, just what form might that change take? What is it that we might expect to see? It may help at this point to provide several illustrations of the kinds of changes possible.

Party Control and Net Increases

If liberal and cohesive Democrats acquire power and do what we think they do, then we should see certain consequences. Assume they acquire power from Republicans. They should be more inclined to raise taxes, and to raise them on higher-income individuals. They should devote more resources to programs that help low-income groups. This inclination might show up as "permanent" increases in taxes or policies. Figure 12.1 presents an example of an increase in taxes that is enduring.

Net Decreases

If our expectations about conservative and cohesive Republicans are correct, then when they acquire power, we should see the opposite activity. Assume they acquire power from Democrats. We should see reductions in taxes, and, specifically, reductions on higher-income individuals. They should cut back programs that help lower-income individuals. Their constituencies are more capable of providing these things on their own and are less in need of explicit government help. They may also seek indirect benefits for their constituents, such as tax deductions, but the direct provision of government assistance should be less. Figure 12.2 presents an example of a "permanent" reduction in taxes or policies.

No Net Change

If two parties battle back and forth and alternate control of government, policy could change with each shift in control. Democrats might enact tax increases and provide greater funding to programs they favor. They might be followed by Republicans, who repeal those tax increases and the programs these revenues fund. The effect could be considerable change, but no "net" change over time. The changes ultimately cancel each other out. Figure 12.3 provides an illustration of this situation. Taxes go up, come back to their initial level, are lowered, return to their initial level, increase, and then finally return to their initial level. Changes occur, but the net effect is no change.

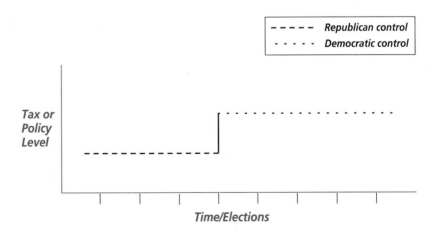

Figure 12.1
An Enduring Increase in Taxes or Policy

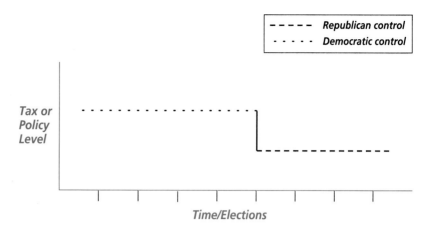

Figure 12.2
An Enduring Decrease in Taxes or Policy

No Change

Finally, there is a host of situations that might provide no change. Control may be unified, but there may not be the electoral base necessary or any sense of obligation to enact change. Or control may be divided and a stalemate may exist. Or it may be that the critics are correct—that elections or events produce no change, and that taxes or public policy do not vary across time. Figure 12.4 presents an example of

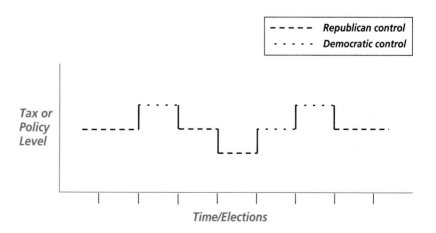

Figure 12.3
No Net Change in Taxes or Policy

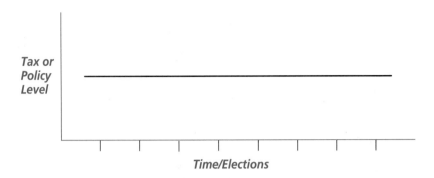

Figure 12.4

No Changes at All in Taxes or Policy: Divided Control or Similar Party Electoral Bases

such a situation. In this case, elections and events come and go, but there are no changes in tax levels and policy levels.

These are just four possibilities. They by no means capture all the changes that might occur. Many political debates are not about levels of taxes or policies, but about the distribution of tax burdens or policy benefits. The major change in policy may involve who pays taxes while the overall tax rate stays the same. Or the overall level of services may remain the same, but the relative allocation of funds among programs may change. The possibilities are endless. These figures provide only some illustrations of what is meant by "change".

The Significance of Party Control

History

We presume political parties have the potential to have a significant impact on public policy when they acquire control over government. The relevance of these expectations, however, depends on the frequency of unified party control in local and state governments. Parties may have theoretical importance, but there may be few cases where they actually have the impact we might expect.

We have remarkably little information about party control at the local level. No organization collects that information, and there are no studies on the way parties play a role in local decision making. Party control and party variations have been tracked at the state level, however, and these data provide an indication of the frequency of unified party control. Unified party control over the governorship and both houses of the legislature was very common fifty years ago, but there has been a steady decline over time in its presence.[4] Figure 12.5 indicates the proportion of unified governments in the states from 1946–1990.

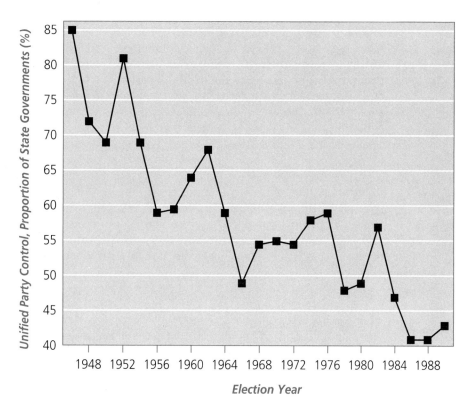

Figure 12.5

Unified Party Control in the States, 1946–1990
Source: Morris P. Fiorina, "Divided Government in the States," Political Science 24, no. 4 (December 1991), 646.

This decline is in part a function of shifting party allegiances in the United States. The South was once solidly Democrat. As Republicans have made inroads in the area, the proportion of unified Democratic governments has declined.[5] The Northeast and Midwest, which were once solidly Republican, have also changed. Democrats have improved their situation in many of these states, and the proportion of Northeast and Midwest governments controlled by Republicans has declined. The proportion of unified Republican governments overall has declined steadily and reached less than 10 percent by 1990.[6]

This decline of unified party control is also a result of the general decline in attachment to parties in the electorate. As noted earlier, there is considerable evidence that split-ticket voting has increased. These conditions have resulted in more and more situations where control of the governorship and the legislature is divided.

The Evidence

Unified party control is no longer the dominant situation in state politics, but there are still many states in which such control occurs. The question is whether instances of unified party control have any impact. Does it matter whether one party controls government rather than another? While party control is often presumed to be of some policy significance, the evidence is not clear that it always is. Numerous studies have examined the impact of political parties upon policy. The results of these studies are important. They suggest certain things that we need to know in order to assess whether who controls government matters.

In some ways, the results are very mixed. A study of the states for the 1970s found that states with Democratic control do not engage in more redistribution than states with Republican control.[7] An analysis of party control in the states from 1950 to 1980 found that in more than half of the states controlled by Democrats, such control did not produce higher welfare payments or greater expenditure on education.[8] Spending levels did not appear to change when party control changed.[9]

On the other hand, there is also evidence that party control often does have the effects we expect. Enactment of a state income or sales tax was more likely to occur when Democrats controlled government than when Republicans did.[10] Democrats were more likely than Republicans to pass civil-rights legislation during the 1960s.[11] Legislation to establish Fair Employment Commissions or to establish fair housing statutes have fared better when Democrats controlled legislatures than when Republicans did. Democrats tended to vote for such legislation while Republicans tended to vote against it.[12] Democratic control was also found to result in higher welfare expenditures than when Republicans had control. As might be expected, party control did not result in the same impact on transportation spending.[13] Case studies also provide evidence of the significance of party. When Republicans gained control of the legislature and the governorship in Connecticut during the early 1970s, they were able to stop the growth of state government employment.[14] Republican control of government in Washington resulted in significant cuts in state programs.[15]

These divergent, often contradictory, results are in some ways puzzling. Does party control have policy significance, or doesn't it? Do all these battles over which party will control government have any consequences? Sometimes they do, and sometimes they don't. Although that is an accurate statement, it does not provide much information for understanding how (and if) party control affects public policy and what prompts politicians to take action.

The reason for such puzzling findings lies in the nature of assumptions made in analyses. Some research has *assumed* that political parties have different electoral bases, so that alternation of control should produce politicians with different sets of concerns. As discussed earlier, this is a questionable assumption.[16] We have considerable evidence that the bases of political parties are not the same across the states. The composition of the Democratic party, for example, is not the same in all states. The interest of Democrats in pushing for more resources being devoted to welfare, job training, housing, medical care, and equalization of school finance varies across the states.

Party control is likely to have consequences if parties have clear electoral bases and those bases are distinct from each other. The difficulty for research, as noted before, is finding thorough information about these matters. In the studies we have commented on, no attempt was made to determine the electoral bases of the parties. The research was done based on the assumption that Democrats desire a more active government that helps the have-nots and that Republicans are less sympathetic to those interests. It is not surprising that in these studies, the assessments of the impact of party control show mixed results.

The interesting studies are those in which some attempt was made to determine the nature of party bases. When states in which the party bases differ are examined, the evidence indicates that party control affects the policy directions taken.[17] Again, it is the case studies in which it is possible to acquire detailed information on politics in a state that provide valuable insights into the way parties can make a difference.

Edward Jennings has done studies that address these questions. In Chapter 8, we reviewed his comparison of Louisiana and Virginia, with a focus on the way the two states differed in levels of welfare expenditure. Louisiana spent more because the Long faction represented the have-nots and continually argued for their interests in the political process. They kept up continual pressure for their constituency, and this pressure resulted in more resources devoted to welfare. In Chapter 8, we dealt with the long-term consequences of representation, but in this chapter, we are concerned about the impact of the acquisition of power by factions. From 1929 to 1960, the Long faction and the Reform faction alternated control of state government. The Long group was committed to a more active state government, specifically to more benefits for lower-income individuals. Table 12.1 indicates how policy changed depending on which faction controlled government.

Prior to 1929, the political world in Louisiana was not divided between the Long and Reform factions. Per capita expenditure on government in general and welfare in particular was low. When the Long faction acquired power in 1929, they raised total expenditure by 81.4 percent and welfare expenditure by 172.2 percent. But that still left welfare at a low level. They then raised welfare by 1866.6 percent in their next term, from 1937–1940. The Reform faction then acquired power, and for the next term, only a small increase occurred. The following term, the Reform faction lowered expenditures. That pattern of increases under the Long faction and little or no change under the Reform faction continued through 1960. When the Long faction held power, the average annual per capita percentage increase in welfare per term was 563.5. When the Reform faction held power, that average change was −9.4 percent. By the end of 1960, total government and welfare expenditures had increased dramatically. The actions of the Long faction when they were in power were very different from the Reform faction, and the cumulative impact of those actions was significant.

Jennings then followed this study with an analysis of northern states from 1950 to the mid-1970s. He examined states in which the parties differed in their electoral bases. He found a consistent pattern of increases in welfare and education expenditures when Democrats controlled government.[18]

Table 12.1
Policy Changes in Louisiana Under Long-Faction and Reform-Faction Control 1929–1960

Budget Years	Faction in Control	Change Per Capita Expenditure (%)	Change Per Capita Welfare (%)	Per Capita Expenditure	
				Total	Welfare Only (dollars)
1927–1928	pre-Long			20.27	.11
1929–1931	Long	81.4	172.2	36.77	.30
1937–1940	Long	55.4	1866.6	57.16	5.90
1941–1944	Reform	1.4	3.2	58.01	6.09
1945–1948	Reform	−1.1	−16.5	57.40	5.09
1949–1952	Long	81.7	202.9	103.34	15.42
1953–1956	Reform	12.6	−15.0	116.40	13.11
1957–1960	Long	29.2	12.4	150.47	14.74
Average changes per faction	Long	61.9	563.5		
	Reform	9.8	−9.4		

Note: Data were not available for 1932–1936.
Source: Edward T. Jennings, "Some Policy Consequences of the Long Revolutions and Bifactional Rivalry in Louisiana," American Journal of Political Science 21, no. 2 (May 1977):225–246.

Changes in Connecticut, a state included in his analysis, illustrate the way partisanship affects policy. Parties in the state were policy oriented, with the Democratic party having more of an urban, blue-collar, minority base than the Republicans. The Democratic party during that time was dominated by John Bailey, who worked hard to produce a cohesive party. The party was issue oriented and concerned with responding to the constituents of the party. The Republican party also was issue oriented (with a suburban, white, middle-class, professional constituency) and relatively cohesive.

During the years Jennings studied the state, Democrats controlled the governorship and the legislature a total of four years (1959 to 1960 and 1967 to 1968). When Democrats assumed power, they significantly increased expenditures in the areas of welfare and education, policy areas directly relevant to their constituency. The party served to organize a set of concerns in the state, and party control became a means to implement policies that dealt with those concerns.

When the Republicans controlled government, they either slowed the rate of growth of government or held it constant. Their acquisition of control in 1971 presented a particularly difficult situation for the party. The general trend of public opinion was that government should do more. Republicans wanted to have an impact on government, but they could not completely reverse the direction of government. In 1971, Thomas Meskill took over as a Republican governor with a Republican legislature. He wanted to slow the growth of government, and he focused on the growth of government employment. In the year prior to his administration, the number of state employees grew by 4.5 percent. In the subsequent years, total employment grew by 1.3, −2.2, and 1.2 percent.[19]

In California, partisan control has also resulted in policy changes. Throughout the late 1940s and 1950s, the parties lacked coherence and meaning because of the reform movement. Candidates often ran with endorsements from both parties, and it was difficult for the parties to sustain clear policy differences. By the mid-1960s, the parties were becoming more coherent, and Democratic and Republican candidates were sorting themselves out, taking policy positions similar to their national parties. The candidate who probably did the most to make party differences mean something was Ronald Reagan. Before Reagan became president, he was governor of California. Even as governor he had a strong conviction about limiting the growth of government. During the early 1960s, the state government was controlled by a Democratic legislature and a Democratic governor, Pat Brown, who was supportive of liberal programs. Reagan ran for governor as a conservative Republican, with a pledge to cut government. He was elected in 1966 and served through 1974. During his first several years, he faced a Democratic legislature, which he fought continually.

In 1971, a Republican legislature was elected. With that legislature behind him, Reagan set out to shrink the size of government. Reagan was able to actually turn around the pattern of expenditure and reduce the real level of expenditure on program areas of interest to the Democrats. When he left office in 1975, Democrat Jerry Brown (the son of Pat Brown) took office, and, in conjunction with a Democrat-controlled legislature, the growth in government expenditure resumed. These changes are shown in Figure 12.6. Reagan was able to work with the Republican legislature to reduce government expenditures, but Jerry Brown and a Democrat-controlled legislature adopted policies which resulted in increased expenditures.

Factors Affecting Party-Control Impact

Negotiating Party Policies and Building Coalitions

Even when executive and legislative parties are in relative agreement, the process of arriving at policy is never easy. The perpetual problem for executives is the diversity of concerns that exist in legislative parties. No legislative party is completely uniform. Democratic legislative parties may be primarily urban, but they always have members from suburban areas. Republican legislative parties may be primarily rural and suburban, but they almost always have members from urban areas. This diversity must be responded to, and this diversity often means that executives and legislators must negotiate policy agreements.

The critical question is how much must an executive compromise? If compromise is necessary, then how does it proceed? Executives are regarded as strong when they win by large margins, have high ratings in the polls, and have considerable formal and informal powers. Such governors are likely to receive more support from the legislative party.[20] The ability of a governor to capitalize on that popularity is heightened by the pattern of party loyalty in the legislature. The greater the

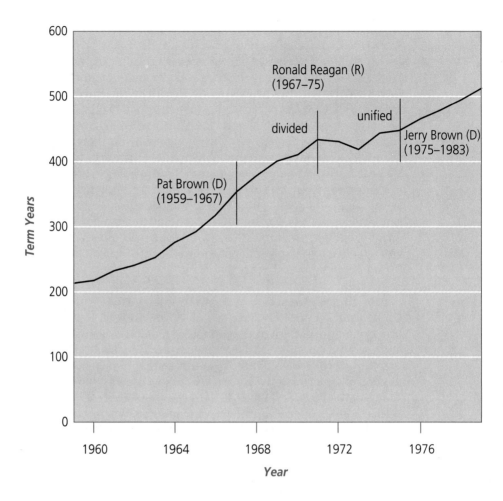

Figure 12.6
Per Capita Government Spending California, 1959–1979
Note: Figures are per capita spending by state government in California. All general expenditures by the state are considered.

tradition of party loyalty and high party cohesion, the greater the ability of the governor to generate support in the majority party in the legislature and the less the need to compromise. These situations also create the greatest opposition from the minority party.[21]

But even when parties are in general agreement, there is always the need for compromise between the branches. Governors and mayors, just as presidents, may begin with programs that focus resources in very specific ways, but they often must cope with legislators who want that focus changed to accommodate the needs of their districts before they will vote for the proposal.

How a governor or mayor goes about creating a supportive coalition depends very much on the structure of authority in the legislature. When the leadership is weak and does not organize, and preside over, the decision-making process, the governor cannot turn to the leadership to negotiate agreements. In those situations, the governor may have to meet with legislators individually to try to generate support for proposals. When the leadership is strong, the governor can bargain with the legislative leaders, who will work with their party to create a coalition large enough to pass legislation.[22]

The ability of executives to work with the legislature also depends on their willingness to compromise and to bargain. Some executives do not mind consulting in advance with legislators. They are willing to "massage" egos by listening to and responding to the individual needs of the legislators. They are willing to attend numerous meetings in which compromises are worked out. Other executives clearly dislike the entire process and are very reluctant to engage in sustained bargaining. Those in the latter group often find themselves very unsuccessful.[23]

The enactment of tax changes in New Jersey illustrates how executives sometimes must accommodate legislative party interests in order to get legislation passed. This process of accommodation repeated itself across two different governors. When the courts first ruled in 1973 that the existing system of financing schools was unconstitutional, Brendan Byrne, the Democratic governor, proposed an income tax to the Democrat-controlled legislature in order to resolve the problem. This tax would provide more revenue and allow distribution of more money to poorer school districts. The assembly, generally dominated by liberals, passed his proposal in the 1974 session. The senate, however, presented him with a major problem. Some senators did not like the idea of an income tax, or of a progressive tax. Others did not like the formula for distributing the new funds. The senate responded after a delay of one year and passed a different package. Their package provided for a flat-rate income tax that would yield one-half the revenue of Byrne's proposal. Negotiations then ensued with the house, and Byrne's proposal was changed. Liberal-Democrats wanted some progressivity, but conservative-Democrats wanted none. Agreement was reached on a limited amount of progressivity. Conservatives also wanted limits on expenditure increases so that the result of new taxes would not just be more expenditure. Finally, it was agreed that the tax would expire in two years unless renewed by the legislature. Throughout the process, conservatives in the party sought changes, and the governor and the more liberal house had to compromise to win passage of the legislation.[24]

In 1990, the state was again confronted with a school finance issue. The courts had ruled that there was too much inequity in the schools. In response, Jim Florio, the Democratic governor, proposed an income-tax increase that would apply only to higher-income people and a sales-tax increase. The key to his success in getting passage of this proposal was his willingness to make sure that working-class legislative districts would receive a considerable increase in school funding. Legislators in those districts indicated that they had to see some benefit to their districts (and not just to poor inner-city districts) if they were going to vote for the package.[25] Florio made those compromises and secured passage of the tax increase and the formula for distributing school aid.

Democratic control of state government had consequences. The party had acquired power in 1966, 1974, and 1990. The party used that unified power to enact significant changes in taxes. Those taxes increased the revenue flowing to the state and increased the role of the state in providing services at all levels in the state. The state became a bigger actor in providing aid to local governments in order to address questions of inequality of tax bases in the state. The consequence of these changes is shown in Figure 12.7. This figure presents the proportion of all state and local tax revenue raised by the state over the last three decades. There were three major shifts. The first change was in 1966, when Democrats enacted a sales tax.[26] The next two changes are the ones just discussed. In 1977, the income tax enacted under the Byrne administration took effect, and in 1991, the increased taxes of the Florio administration took effect. Unified party control in New Jersey has had a significant impact on taxes and on the role of the state. There has been compromise throughout, but the Democrats did produce change.

In New Jersey, compromise led to solutions because there was some basic sympathy for responding. When that sympathy is lacking, as it has been in Texas, no amount of compromise will help. A majority of Texas Democrats have been opposed to an income tax for a long time. The governor has limited powers to push for change, and no one has yet found an acceptable compromise. The resistance is too widespread.

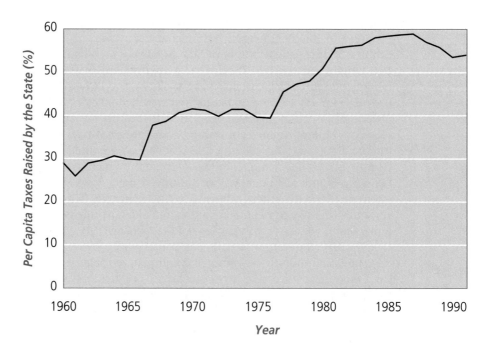

Figure 12.7
Percent of All Taxes Raised by the State, New Jersey 1960–1990

Shifting Political Climates and Party Control

Even if party bases differed and both wings of a party were in agreement, there are conditions that might inhibit a party from taking the actions we might expect. Politicians do respond to broad changes in their immediate environment. Perhaps the most significant factors disrupting the "predictability" of Democratic goals during the last decade have been the general decline in economic growth in the United States, several severe recessions, and the shift of jobs and employment from the Northeast to the Sunbelt. In recent years, many Democratic governors in the Midwest and Northeast acquired power at a time when their states have had deficit budgets and declining economies. These governors were faced with the conventional wisdom that the way to revive the economy was to cut taxes in order to make the state more attractive to business. Many Democratic governors dampened their enthusiasm for expenditures and became advocates of fiscal restraint. Changing conditions prompted some Democrats to alter their goals from the traditional Democratic position. In 1983, for example, the state of Connecticut witnessed a Democratic governor opposing his Democrat-dominated legislature over enactment of a state income tax, a traditional Democratic goal. He argued that a state in the Northeast could not afford to start down the road to greater taxation, and that the lack of an income tax had encouraged a lot of businesses from New York to move into Connecticut. He was successful in his arguments.

Unified Party Control and No Impact

There are other reasons why party control may have no impact. As discussed in Chapter 5, the parties may not divide and organize the electorate. Democrats may not be that different from Republicans. In such situations, there is little reason to expect that changes in party control will produce an inclination by a party to set off in new and bold policy directions.

It may also be that the governor and the legislature have divergent electoral bases and find it difficult to agree. As discussed in Chapter 9, a Republican governor may be more liberal than the Republican legislative party. This situation occurred in New York from 1959 to 1973 when Nelson Rockefeller was governor. During the 1950s and most of the 1960s, the Republican party controlled both houses of the state legislature. The Republican legislative party was (and still is) based in upstate areas and in the suburbs around New York City. The Republican legislative party was much more conservative than the Democratic legislative party, which was (and still is) based in New York City and the large urban areas of the state.

Rockefeller had enormous visions of reshaping government and of spending money to make New York State a progressive state. His goals clashed with those of his legislative party, which wanted to constrain the growth of government. Rockefeller proceeded to actively seek to create urban legislative coalitions (regardless of the partisan designation of the legislators) to build support for his programs. He took his support where he found it and did not worry about formal partisan alignments.

Because his programs required funds, Rockefeller had to raise taxes. He often had to rely on Democrats for votes to pass his tax increases. Table 12.2 indicates

Table 12.2
Party Support for an Income Tax Increase in the Republican-Held Senate New York , 1968

		Vote on Increase		
		Yes		No
Republicans	*(#)*	*(%)*	*(#)*	*(%)*
New York City	4	100.0	0	0
Other areas	19	67.9	9	32.1
Democrats				
New York City	18	85.7	3	14.3
Other areas	1	33.3	2	66.7
Totals	42	75.0	14	25.0

Source: Jeffrey M. Stonecash, "'Split' Constituencies and the Impact of Party Control," Social Science History 16, no. 3 (fall 1992):471.

where support came from in the Republican-controlled senate for increasing the state income tax in 1968. He could not get enough (only twenty-three) votes from his own party. He needed thirty-one votes to pass the bill. Rockefeller turned to the relatively liberal Democrats from New York City. He was able to get eighteen of the twenty-one New York City Democrats to vote for the tax increase, and the legislation passed. His own relatively liberal agenda frequently put him at odds with his own party.[27] That agenda also resulted in an outcome that we would not have expected if we presume all Republicans are moderate to conservative. In New York, Rockefeller consistently forged a coalition with the more liberal groups in the legislature, and state taxes and expenditures in New York increased most of the years he held office. Such situations complicate what we can expect from party control.

This partisan situation, of course, could be reversed. A governor could share control over government with his legislative party, but be much more conservative than the party. In this situation, a governor might continually engage in battle to limit the ability of his legislative party to enact moderate or liberal policy changes.

The situation of Democrat Dan Walker and the legislative Democrats in Illinois provides an example of this. In 1974, Walker took over as governor. Walker was not a typical Democratic governor. He was a former corporation lawyer who had gained publicity by walking the length of the state and pledging "good government" to the people. He was not an urban liberal, and his election did not sit well with the Democratic legislative party, which took control of both houses of the legislature in that election. In this case, it was very difficult to tell what it meant for "Democrats" to take control of government. It was not clear just what policy Walker would pursue. He had built his reputation on not being a part of the "bosses" in the Democratic party. His goals proved to be much more conservative than those of the legislative party, and during his first several years, he and the legislative leaders engaged in a great deal of fighting over legislation. His record of achievement was rated by some political scorekeepers as no more than 25 percent for the first two years. He was preoccupied with reforming government, and the legislative Democrats were concerned with traditional Democratic programs of aid for their urban constituents.[28]

Diverging Constituencies and Institutional Power

Electoral constituencies for executives and legislatures may differ such that party control cannot represent unified goals. In such situations, the formal powers of each branch become very important.[29] The branch of the party that has the greatest formal power has the advantage in any negotiations. An example from the local level indicates the extent to which formal powers matter in such situations.

Democrat Harold Washington, the first black mayor of Chicago was elected in 1983. Washington came to office firmly committed to reforming Chicago politics. Though the city was almost all Democrat, there might as well have been two parties. Washington's goal was to make the political process more accessible to minorities and to reduce the grip of white ethnics on everything from nominations to office to the budget. This goal put him in opposition to established politicians, who constituted the "machine" in Chicago. Many people did not believe him. They thought he would use power to give more positions to blacks, not to dismantle power. The word soon got out that Washington was serious. He wanted to fill most positions in the city with civil service employees and to cut the number of patronage positions to between 1200 and 1500. The number of patronage positions in the city had been variously estimated as anywhere from 10,000 to 30,000. All these positions had been controlled by the machine (aldermembers and their supporters), and they were used to reward loyal party workers and to make government responsive to the needs of the machine. The machine was also accused of using these positions to guarantee kickbacks while the people they appointed were in office. Needless to say, the prospect of Washington being successful did not sit well with members of the machine.

When Washington submitted his first proposals on reorganizing government to the city council, he discovered that the machine had more supporters than he thought. The machine had 29 of 50 councilors, while Washington had only 21 allies. The machine councilors ignored Washington's proposals and his attempts to get them considered at meetings. The opposition leader, "Fast Eddie" Vrdolyak, repeatedly adjourned meetings, using his majority on the council to do so. Washington, who had campaigned against the machine, refused to compromise and filed a lawsuit claiming that the mayor had a right to run the meetings and to have his proposals considered. The court ruled that a majority of councilors could control meetings and conduct affairs as they saw fit. Washington lost, and he was in a difficult situation because he had campaigned hard against a group he could not control. He quickly realized that the position of mayor in Chicago carried limited formal power. He could not dictate any outcomes. The city charter specified a "weak-mayor" form of government, making the council dominant. Anything he wanted to change had to be approved by the city council.

Alternating Party Control: Long-Term Effects?

Throughout this text, a central theme has been the effects of the organization of the electorate on the fate of the haves and the have-nots. Those groups are not always clearly distinct, and much of our society does not think of itself in those terms. But the issues of treatment of the lower and working class appear regularly during the decision-making process. How do these battles over party control play a role in responding to these differences?

This chapter began with a series of graphs that presented hypothetical consequences that might occur. Some of those graphs do capture the consequences of party control. Figure 12.4 presents the possibility of no change. Studies indicate that there are situations where no change occurs. We suspect that no change occurs when parties do not differ. There may be gradual changes in public opinion that push the level of government up, but in these situations changes do not appear to come about because of party control.

In other states, it appears that party control has other effects. The question to be addressed here is whether the change is like Figure 12.1 or Figure 12.2 or Figure 12.3. Does control by Democrats followed by control by Republicans result in shifts up and then down in policy levels, as shown in Figure 12.3? If so, there are no net changes in public policy over time. Or does party control produce permanent shifts up or down? The evidence suggests that when parties differ, Democrats play a significant role in raising the level of government activity. The evidence suggests the impact in this situation is similar to Figure 12.1. Democrats appear to raise the level of government activity and, in particular, the devotion of resources to welfare and education. Republicans, at least in the post-World-War-II era, appear to slow or stop the rate of growth. They do not appear to reverse these levels.

In Louisiana, the Long faction produced a long-term rise in general government spending and in the resources devoted to welfare. Much of this, of course, was probably pushed along by federal welfare programs that provided significant matching funds for states establishing such programs. But it was the Long faction that took advantage of those funds, and the Reform faction that was less interested in doing so. The presence of the Long group in the state was crucial in making these choices. The Reform group stopped growth, but it did not reverse state spending or return it to the levels that prevailed before the Long group changed policy.

In California, Democrats raised state expenditures. When Republican Ronald Reagan had a Republican legislature, he stopped growth, but he did not lower expenditure levels. In New Jersey, Republicans also stopped growth in the role of the state. They did not reverse that growth.

These are only a limited number of case studies, but they suggest something important about the long-term consequences of the presence of Democrats who have a commitment to increased state activity. Their increases were not reversed, and the net effect was that state activity continued at a substantially higher level.

This result suggests a fundamental connection between the concerns of this chapter and those of Chapter 8. In that chapter, the concern was how parties with clear bases among the lower and working classes can affect the long-term level of government services. The argument was that in states where parties have such bases there is a group that makes a steady effort to present the concerns of their constituents. That situation produces pressure on Republicans. The concern in this chapter is how Democrats use their control of government to take the steps to actually bring about change. The situations discussed here in Louisiana, Connecticut, California, and New Jersey provide some idea of the way this change proceeds. Democratic control appears to produce an increase in certain policy commitments, in taxes, and in the role of the state. That change tends to persist when Republicans get into office and results in a relatively enduring greater role for government. Over the long run, states where Democrats took such actions probably have higher levels of taxes, services, and activity by the state.

Unified party control by Democrats, of course, is not the only means by which the levels of taxes and services increase. There have been long-term general increases in support for government activity in the last fifty years, and this support has resulted in a general trend toward greater government activity. Recessions prompt politicians to raise taxes. Sometimes those taxes become permanent, and, as a result, there is more revenue and more government activity. But there still appears to be a distinct and separate impact from Democratic control. When Democrats with a clear electoral base come into power, they make changes.

The interesting matter is why Republicans do not reverse the changes made by Democrats. Only careful analyses of many situations can answer that, but the changes in New Jersey may suggest an answer. These changes also may provide more evidence of the argument V. O. Key made about the impact of organized groups in creating political dialogues and critiquing their opponents.

After the 1991 elections, Republicans took control of both houses of the legislature in New Jersey. They won so many seats that their majorities were "veto-proof," or sufficient to override Jim Florio, the Democratic governor. As the 1992 session began, the Republicans drew up their own budget, ignoring the governor's. They made bold statements about repealing all of the Democrats' tax increases, which totalled $2.8 billion. As the session wore on, Florio kept up steady criticism of them. The Democrats in the legislature did the same because they sought to protect new programs that had just been allocated to their constituents. They also argued that Republicans were going to cause cuts in school aid and in medical programs to help the poor. They kept up a steady drumbeat of criticism that Republicans did not care about people. The Democratic legislative party paid for television ads that said that homeowners would lose the property-tax relief payments just enacted by Democrats. The criticisms took their toll. By the end of the session, Republicans scaled back their cuts to only a one billion dollar cut in the sales tax and some reductions in the state budget.[30]

The Democratic party behaved as a relatively cohesive group presenting a simple but persistent criticism that Republicans were harming the middle class. Republicans tried to counter that by pointing out they were cutting the regressive sales tax, not the progressive income tax, but they were still wary as a result of the criticism. Key argued that a cohesive party with a clear base will use public criticism as a political weapon. The Democrats were cut back largely to their urban lower- to middle-income districts in the 1991 elections. With that clear base, they continually attacked. It made the Republicans hesitant. As Key argued, the presence of this pressure made it more difficult for conservatives to enact their changes.

But why does this work? Why doesn't a conservative party claim a mandate and cut significantly? Several matters play a role. Groups who have won benefits are reluctant to give them up. The American belief in equality of treatment surely restrains actions that might look like a party is clearly catering to upper-income interests. The presence of swing districts also constrains some Republicans from voting too conservatively. Those who take seats from Democrats in working-class districts worry that the steady criticisms of Democrats will stick and that the electorate will turn on them. As a consequence, the decisions of Democrats to raise government services appear to have stuck in many states.

Divided Party Control

A common situation in state politics is that the control of government is divided between two parties. Again, we do not know much about local situations. This division could be a situation where the governor is of one party and both houses of the legislature are controlled by the other party. It might also be a situation where only one house of the legislature is controlled by the other party. Both situations result in divided control. For any legislation to pass and become law, it must be approved by both houses. If an opposition party controls one house and the party leaders in that house are unwilling to compromise, they can stop a governor's program by refusing to pass anything.

What are the consequences of divided control? First, it should be noted that we do not know very much about divided control. The concern with the effects of unified party control has received so much attention that divided control has not been studied much. Second, as with everything else in politics, it all depends on the conditions. When the two parties, each holding a branch of government, represent concerns significantly different from each other, there is likely to be greater conflict between the two branches. Support for the governor from the opposing party will be less, and the parties in the legislature are more likely to vote against each other.[31] Decision making is likely to involve more conflict. Governors are likely to veto more legislative proposals.[32] When the differences between the parties are less, the extent of conflict between the branches should be less.

Fundamental Conflicts

The crucial matters in these situations are whether the governor has a clear agenda and whether he or she uses the powers of the office to pursue that agenda. It appears from many of the case studies we have that the most serious conflicts emerge when a conservative Republican governor encounters a liberal Democratic legislature. In Massachusetts, William Weld came in as a conservative Republican determined to reduce the size of government. He made it clear he would veto any budget that the Democrats put forth, and eventually he got a smaller budget.[33]

Ronald Reagan was also able to be effective in this way when he became governor of California. State expenditures and the number of state employees had been steadily rising. Reagan wanted to cut the size of state government.[34] He indicated his strong resistance to increases and his willingness to veto any increases. He was also able to slow the growth of government employment. Figure 12.6, earlier in this chapter, indicates how the rate of expenditure slowed when divided government prevailed. Table 12.3 presents the annual rate of change in the number of government employees for California for 1965 to 1972. The two years before Reagan became governor, state employment grew by 5.2 percent each year. After Reagan became governor, the rates of growth for the years of divided control dropped to −1.8, 2.4, .1, and 1.3. Reagan had clear goals, and he was willing to use his formal powers to significantly lower the rate of growth of government. He repeated that impact when he was elected president and faced a Democratic Congress.[35]

A similar pattern occurred in 1983 when George Deukmejian, a Republican, became governor of California and faced a Democratic legislature. He also faced a recession and a budget shortfall. Deukmejian had campaigned on the promise that he would oppose any new taxes as a way to solve the deficit. He insisted that the budget had to be cut.

Deukmejian confronted Democratic leaders and informed them that expenditure programs would have to be cut and that he would veto anything that did not conform to the cuts he thought necessary. The Democratic legislature took up his challenge and passed budget proposals that Deukmejian believed too large. Using the line-item veto, Deukmejian repeatedly vetoed these proposals. By the end of the first year, he had vetoed more than one billion dollars in proposed expenditure increases and a one-billion-dollar proposed increase in the sales tax. He was able to play this game of confrontation because he possessed formal power.[36]

Table 12.3

The Impact of Republican Governor Ronald Reagan on Government-Employment Growth in California, 1965–1972

Year	Total Employment Change (%)
1965	5.2
1966	5.2
1967	−1.8
1968	2.4
1969	.1
1970	1.3
1971	−2.0
1972	2.9

Source: James E. Jarrett, "Gubernatorial Control of State Government Work Forces, State Government 54, no. 3, 90.

These situations represent the interaction of conservative executives with Democratic legislatures. Conservatives were able to use their powers to slow the growth of government. Presumably conservative legislatures could also stop liberal Democratic governors from achieving their agendas.

Finding Coalitions

Governors do not always seek just to confront legislatures. There are problems that must be dealt with, and governors need to find a group in the legislature which they can work with if they are going to respond to problems. When control is divided, a governor may have to work with the opposing party to find a coalition to pass legislation.

During some of the years Republican Nelson Rockefeller was governor of New York, the legislature was controlled by Democrats. When he wanted to enact programs that required revenue, he worked with the Democratic party to find supporters for an increase in taxes. Eventually he got the programs he wanted, and his support came from the Democratic party.[37] In his case, building this coalition was not distasteful because Rockefeller was a liberal Republican.

Lowell Weicker, the Independent governor of Connecticut, also found a way to work with a coalition from the "opposing" party when he sought to deal with a budget shortfall. The legislature was controlled by Democrats. Weicker, a former Republican with a liberal record, felt strongly that the way to address the chronic revenue problems of the state was to enact an income tax. Republicans would not help him. He got enough support from Democrats to adopt an income tax. Table 12.4 presents the vote for the income tax by party in the Connecticut legislature.

Negotiated Settlements

Divided control does not always mean that conflict will dominate the decision-making process. Sometimes the parties do not differ much. In those situations, conflict will be less. It is also probably easier for the branches to reach accommodation and to compromise on policy in those situations.[38]

Table 12.4

Party Support for an Income Tax Vote in the Connecticut Legislature, 1992

	House		Senate	
	Yes (%)	No (%)	Yes (%)	No (%)
Democrats	87	13	80	20
Republicans	17	83	13	87

Source: Russell D. Murphy, "Connecticut: Lowell P. Weicker, Jr., A Maverick in the 'Land of Steady Habits'," in Thad Beyle, Governors and Hard Times, (Washington, DC: Congressional Quarterly Press, 1992), 70.

Even when the parties do differ, it is quite possible for each branch to lower the level of partisan attacks and to focus on negotiating policy settlements. Differences will occur, but compromise is possible.

An example from New York indicates how compromise works when control is divided. The change in the federal tax law in 1985 presented the states with the issue of whether to change state tax laws. Many states allow taxpayers to use their federally defined income to determine state tax obligations. In New York, the Republicans, who controlled the senate, seized on this issue as an opportunity to lower taxes. They thought taxes were too high and argued that while changes were being discussed, overall reductions should be considered. Democrats, who controlled the assembly and the governorship, wanted a more progressive tax system. They were willing to give Republicans what they wanted, but only if the tax system were made more progressive.

After lengthy negotiations, each side got some of what it wanted. The overall rates were lowered. But there was a price for the change. The reductions were phased in over several years. Democrats were worried about losses of revenue and cuts in programs, and they thought that gradual growth in the economy would allow the replacement of revenues. The initial cuts went to low-income individuals, and the affluent would get their reductions last. The system was also made somewhat more progressive. Divided control did not produce a stalemate. The separate parties recognized the need to bargain in an orderly fashion and they were able to reach an agreement, even though they argued from very different political perspectives.[39]

We have much to learn about what happens when divided control exists. Outcomes become dependent on such conditions as the level of cohesion a party has and the relative institutional power of the branches that are under divided control. Being able to predict outcomes hinges on understanding the conditions under which the divided control takes place, and this requires a thorough analysis of a particular city or state.

Public Involvement in Decision Making

Not everyone likes having decisions made by politicians, and not all decisions are made by them. There is considerable support for having the public directly make certain decisions. Table 12.5 presents results from one survey on public opinions on the different ways of making decisions. The table shows strong support for using the initiative, and the public has positive views about its effects on the political process.

Many decisions are made through public voting. Some states, particularly in the West, allow citizens to get issues on the ballot through the initiative process. In addition, many referenda are put before the public at the initiative of the governor and the legislature, or the mayor and the local council. These mechanisms have been used to have the public vote on taxes, the death penalty, environmental regulations, campaign-finance laws, and many other issues.[40] Public voting also occurs when changes in state constitutions and local charters are being considered. The

Table 12.5

Public Opinion on Means of Making Decisions

Survey Statements	Agree	Disagree	No Answer
The state legislature should decide all state issues instead of having initiative elections on issues.	9	86	5
Voting on state candidates (governor, attorney general, etc.) is generally more important to me than voting for initiatives.	28	59	13
The public ought to be able to vote directly on issues.	78	17	5
If people could vote on issues, they would become interested in politics and participate in government.	82	14	4

Source: Thomas E. Cronin, Direct Democracy *(Cambridge: Harvard University Press, 1989), 79, 233.*

public must vote on such changes. It is also often required that increases in public debt be approved by the public. Public voting may not be a primary means of making decisions, but it does occur regularly and does involve important concerns.

The Bias Issue

The essential concern with making decisions through public voting is whether this process is biased against certain interests. Petition drives take considerable organization and there is concern that the better-educated and more affluent are more adept at utilizing this process. Initiatives and referenda often involve public campaigns in which large sums of money are necessary for brochures and radio and television ads. The more affluent have greater abilities to generate these funds. Finally, the lower class understands these propositions less and votes less, resulting in an electorate comprised more of middle- and upper-income voters.[41]

Table 12.6 indicates the extent to which voters for propositions differ from the general public and from those who vote in general elections. The table presents the composition by self-identified social class of those who do not vote, those who vote, but only for elected officials, and those who also vote on ballot issues. The pool of individuals who do not vote at all is heavily working class. Of those who vote for officials only, about 45 percent (36 + 9) of that group is middle and upper class. Of those who vote on ballot propositions, that percent increases to 52.

Critics argue that lower-income groups lose when initiatives are relied on for decision making. Not only are there the differences just discussed, but critics argue

Table 12.6

Class Characteristics of Nonvoters and Initiative and Referendum Voters

Social Class Self-Identification	Nonvoters (%)	Voted Only for Elected Officials (%)	Voted on Ballot Issues (%)
Working class	67	55	48
Middle class	28	36	36
Upper middle class	5	9	16

Note: Percents sum down.
Source: Thomas E. Cronin, Direct Democracy (Cambridge: Harvard University Press, 1989), 76.

that it is difficult to have coherent debates about public policy options. Debates are dominated by newspaper headlines and television commercials. Informed exchanges are very difficult, and compromise is impossible since propositions require yes or no votes. Legislative parties lose the ability to bargain and to represent the concerns of their constituents.[42]

Changes in California and New York illustrate the way different means of decision making can affect outcomes. During the 1970s, California experienced dramatic population growth. Property values skyrocketed, as did taxes. Government spending also increased dramatically. There was considerable grumbling among the public, but most of the major state politicians assumed that it was "normal" complaining that did not mean much. At the same time, the real income of the public was no longer growing. In the face of no response from politicians to requests for tax relief, some private citizens led a movement to get propositions on the ballot to cut taxes and to slow government growth. Most of the state politicians did not believe that the public really wanted to face a cut in government services, and they assumed that the first of the propositions, Proposition 13, would fail. They misjudged badly, and in short order, two major propositions were enacted.

The changes enacted were significant. Proposition 13 (1978) amended the state constitution to sharply reduce property taxes and to curtail their future growth. Proposition 4 (1979) limited how much state and local appropriations could grow in the future. The public was able to force changes that politicians either did not want, or did not believe that the public really wanted. The public imposed a broad across-the-board cut in property taxes. Most of those benefits went to business and those with more expensive pieces of property.[43]

In New York, the same sentiment against taxes rose during the 1970s. The state was losing jobs, and taxes were close to the highest in the nation. The initiative process is not allowed in New York. The Democratic party, which held the assembly, recognized the shifting public sentiment. Democrats were able to engage in protracted negotiations and obtain some protection for their lower-income constituents while negotiating a cut in taxes. The absence of the initiative made this possible.

Unfortunately, we have few studies that compare these two mechanisms of decision making, but the way change was handled in these two states illustrates the concerns of critics of the initiative process. They argue that with initiatives there is little room for negotiation and compromise and that lower-income voters do not fare well. Low-income groups lose any leverage that they might have in the normal bargaining process. Others have argued that tax changes through initiatives have not produced outcomes that are different from normal executive-legislative interactions. Studies have compared tax levels, changes in taxes, and spending in states with and without referenda and concluded that there is not much difference in impacts.[44] The conclusion of these studies is that politicians in non-initiative states saw the evidence of hostility to taxes in other states and lowered taxes in their state, with the result that outcomes were similar. This situation still suggests, however, that the presence of referenda enabled people to "send a message" that might not have been heard otherwise.

These studies are limited, however, in that they address overall tax levels, not the distribution of tax burdens among groups. One of the primary criticisms of initiatives has been their effect by class. We will not be able to address that question until we have more studies that compare different means of making decisions.

Summary

Elections put politicians in charge of decision making. But political control of government does not always result in change. There are many situations in which politicians enter office and there is little change in public policy. At other times, there are significant changes in policy.

The reasons for these differences in outcomes are many, but a few important ones stand out. Many elections result in divided control of government. The parties may differ, and their differences may result in no ability to agree on changes. Sometimes change may occur under such circumstances, but only if one branch is dominant or if the parties controlling separate branches or houses can successfully negotiate to achieve change.

The crucial matter, however, is the nature of the parties that acquire control. If party control changes hands, changes in policy are likely if the party coming to power has a clear electoral base that differs from that of the party that previously held power. It is then that constituency bases translate into clear policy agendas and decisions. Clear, distinct electoral bases for the two parties do not exist in all states and localities, so often we get little change. When parties have similar electoral bases, change does not occur because politicians feel no mandate to enact significant changes.

For Further Reading

Dye, Thomas R. "Party and Policy in the States." *Journal of Politics* 46, no. 4 (November 1984). An attempt to classify states as to whether party control has had an impact.

Fiorina, Morris. *Divided Government.* New York: Macmillan, 1992. A study of the extent of divided control in the states.

Hansen, Susan B. *The Politics of Taxation.* New York: Praeger, 1983, 142–174. An analysis of the role of parties in the adoption of major state taxes.

Jennings, Edward T. "Some Policy Consequences of the Long Revolutions and Bifactional Rivalry in Louisiana." *American Journal of Political Science* vol. 21, no. 2 (May 1977): 225–246. A discussion of the role of factions in Louisiana in changing taxes and spending.

Murphy, Russell D. "Connecticut: Lowell P. Weicker, Jr., A Maverick in the 'Land of Steady Habits'." In Thad Beyle, *Governors and Hard Times.* Washington: Congressional Quarterly Press, 1992. A discussion of the role of gubernatorial beliefs and legislative parties in adoption of income tax in Connecticut.

Stonecash, Jeffrey M. "'Split' Constituencies and the Impact of Party Control." *Social Science History* 16, no. 3 (fall 1992): 455–477.

Suggestions for Analysis in Your Own State and Locality

1. The clue to understanding whether party control has consequences is to put together a number of conditions. In previous chapters, it was suggested that you explore the electoral bases of the parties in your state. That information should tell you if the parties begin with different constituencies.

    What party controls each branch of government in your state? Is control of the legislature unified? When was the last time control of government changed? How much has control over government changed during the last ten years?

    If party constituencies differ and party control has changed hands, there should be some consequences. Is there any evidence of such changes? If there are no differences in party bases, changes in control should have little impact.

    If your state has divided control, as many do, then the important question is which branch has the clearest agenda, and the power to achieve their goals? What prevails in your state?

2. Repeat the same analysis for the major local government in your area. Has change in party control occurred, and has such change had an impact?

Notes

1 V. O. Key, Jr., *Southern Politics in State and Nation* (New York: Knopf, 1949).

2 Donald A. Gross, "The Policy Role of Governors," in Eric B. Herzik and Brent W. Brown, eds., *Gubernatorial Leadership and State Policy* (New York: Greenwood, 1991), 3–6.

3 For a study of this at the national level, see David R. Mayhew, *Divided We Govern: Party Control, Lawmaking, and Investigations, 1946–1990* (New Haven, Yale University Press, 1991).

4 Morris P. Fiorina, "Divided Government in the States," *PS* 24, no. 4 (December 1991): 646–650; and Morris P. Fiorina, *Divided Government* (New York: Macmillan, 1992), 26–43.

[5] Fiorina, *Divided Government*, 31.

[6] Fiorina, *Divided Government*, 34.

[7] Brian Fry and Richard Winters, "The Politics of Redistribution," *American Political Science Review* 54, no. 2 (June 1970): 550–567; Richard Winters, "Party Control and Policy Change," *American Journal of Political Science* 20, no. 4 (November 1976): 597–636; and Richard D. Plotnick and Richard F. Winters, "Party, Political Liberalism, and Redistribution," *American Politics Quarterly* 18, no. 4 (October 1990): 430–458.

[8] Thomas R. Dye, "Party and Policy in the States," *Journal of Politics* 46, no. 4 (November 1984): 1112.

[9] E. Terrence Jones, "Political Change and Spending Shifts in the American States," *American Politics Quarterly* 2 (1974): 414–429; and Tom Rice, "The Effects of Changing Party Control on Economic Policy in the American States" (paper presented at the Northeast Political Science Association Meetings, 1983).

[10] Susan B. Hansen, *The Politics of Taxation: Revenue Without Representation* (New York: Praeger, 1983), 142–174.

[11] Robert S. Erickson, "The Relationship Between Party Control and Civil Rights Legislation in the American States," *Western Political Quarterly* 24 (1971): 178–182.

[12] Duane Lockard, *Toward Equal Opportunity* (New York: Macmillan, 1968), 46–57.

[13] Sung-Don Hwang and Virginia Gray, "External Limits and Internal Determinants of State Public Policy," *Western Political Quarterly* 44, no. 2 (June 1991): 277–298.

[14] James E. Jarrett, "Gubernatorial Control of State Government Work Forces," *State Government* 54, no. 3 (1981): 90.

[15] Hugh Bone, "Legislative Party Upheaval in Washington," *Comparative State Politics Newsletter* 2, no. 3 (1981): 8–9.

[16] James A. Garand, "Partisan Change and Shifting Expenditure Priorities in the American States," *American Politics Quarterly* 13 (October 1985): 355–391; and Jeffrey M. Stonecash, "Inter-Party Competition, Political Dialogue, and Public Policy: A Critical Review," *Policy Studies Review* 16, no. 2 (winter 1987–1988): 243–262.

[17] Garand, "Partisan Change and Shifting Expenditure Priorities in the American States," 355–391.

[18] Edward T. Jennings, "Competition, Constituencies, and Welfare Policies in American States," *American Political Science Review* 73 (1979): 414–429.

[19] James E. Jarret, "Gubernatorial Control of State Government Work Forces," *State Government* 54, no. 3 (1981): 90.

[20] Sarah P. McCally-Morehouse, "The Governor and His Legislative Party," *American Political Science Review* 60 (1966): 923–942; and Sarah P. Morehouse, *State Politics, Parties and Policy* (New York: Holt, Rinehart and Winston, 1981), 246–252.

[21] Sarah Morehouse and Malcolm E. Jewell, "Divided Government and Legislative Support for the Governor's Program" (paper presented at the November 1992 Southern Political Science Association Meetings, Atlanta, Georgia).

[22] Alan Rosenthal, *Governors and Legislatures: Contending Powers* (Washington: Congressional Quarterly Press, 1990), 67–94.

[23] Rosenthal, *Governors and Legislatures*, 72–82.

[24] Richard Lehne, *The Quest for Justice: The Politics of School Finance Reform* (New York: Longman, 1978), 90–163.

[25] Peter Kerr, "Florio Urges Taxing Rich," *New York Times* 20 March 1990, B4; and Peter Kerr, "Florio Woos A New Kind of Coalition," *New York Times* 13 June 1990, B1.

[26] Alan Rosenthal, "The Governor, the Legislature, and State Policymaking," in Alan Rosenthal and John Blydenburgh, eds., *Politics in New Jersey* (New Brunswick: Rutgers University Press, 1975), 141–174.

[27] Jeffrey M. Stonecash, " 'Split' Constituencies and the Impact of Party Control," *Social Science History* 16, no. 3 (fall 1992): 455–477.

[28] Rosenthal, *Governors and Legislatures*, 60.

[29] Gross, "The Policy Role of Governors," 4–16.

[30] Jerry Gray, "GOP Details Sweeping Cuts in New Jersey," *New York Times* 11 June 1992, B1.

[31] Morehouse and Jewell, "Divided Government and Support for the Governor's Program."

[32] James J. Gosling, "Wisconsin Item-Veto Lessons," *Public Administration Review* 46 (July-August 1986): 297–298.

[33] Dennis Hale, "William F. Weld and the End of Business as Usual," in Thad Beyle, *Governors and Hard Times* (Washington DC: Congressional Quarterly Press, 1992), 127–150.

[34] Richard B. Harvey, *The Dynamics of California Government and Politics*, 2d ed. (Monteray: Brooks/Cole, 1985), 22–23.

[35] See the studies in John L. Palmer and Isabel V. Sawhill, eds., *The Reagan Record* (Cambridge: Ballinger, 1984).

[36] Harvey, *The Dynamics of California Government and Politics*, 124–126.

[37] Stonecash, " 'Split' Constituencies and the Impact of Party Control," *Social Science History* 16, no. 3 (fall 1992): 455–477.

[38] Morehouse and Jewell, "Divided Government and Legislative Support for the Governor's Package," 14.

[39] Diana Dwyre, Mark O'Gorman, Jeffrey M. Stonecash, and Rosalie Young, "Disorganized Politics and the Have-Nots: Politics and Taxes in New York and California," *Polity* (1994).

[40] Cronin, *Direct Democracy*, 196–200.

[41] Cronin, *Direct Democracy*, provides a review of these issues.

[42] Dwyre et al., "Disorganized Politics and the Have-nots."

[43] Ibid.

[44] David Lowery, Thomas Kanda, and James C. Garand, "Spending in the States: A Test of Six Models," *Western Political Quarterly* 37 (1984): 48–66; and Susan B. Hansen, "The Politics of State Taxation," in Herbert Jacob, Virginia Gray, and Robert Albritton, *Comparative State Politics*, 5th ed. (Boston: Little, Brown, 1990).

13

Trying to Change Social Conditions: The Design and Impact of Public Policy

PREVIEW

The decision for government to do something about policy problems leads to decisions about how policy efforts should proceed. Should government deliver services, and which level of government should take action? Or should the private sector be relied on in some fashion? These questions have prompted major battles in American politics. Debates about these choices have led to long-term increases in public delivery of many services.

There are widespread public policy efforts to affect society. There are also continual disputes about the impact of public policy efforts. Some of these disagreements stem from disputes about what we expect public policy to achieve. Other disputes revolve around how to assess the impact of public policy. Assessments are also affected by the ideological perspectives of those who assess.

Finally, there are reasons why policies sometimes do not have the impacts expected. Government cannot "control" the organizations which policies are directed at, nor can they "make" people behave differently. Government inability to mandate the behavior of individuals and, generally, the implementation of policy by local organizations limits the impact of government programs.

Introduction

The prominent battles in politics are about the role government should play. How much should government intervene to respond to social conditions? Should government provide welfare? Should school aid be redistributed? Should affirmative action programs be required? Have-nots generally want these policies, and the haves generally resist them. Should government give tax breaks to businesses to try to generate jobs? Haves tend to favor those programs and have-nots are skeptical about them. These battles involve broad issues of the responsibility of government.

Sometimes advocates of government action win, and headlines trumpet the arrival of some new policy. At other times, proponents of limited government win, and program cuts are announced. The decision to enact a public policy, however, ends only one battle in politics. A decision is made to try to change social conditions. The focus then shifts to *how* to achieve a policy goal. Attempts to use government to affect society are complicated. There are many different ways that policies might be pursued, and prolonged battles revolve around what approach to take to achieve policy goals. It is never clear just how programs should be designed.

Efforts to affect society are also frustrating because achieving desired outcomes is often difficult. There are doubts that programs really are effective. Concern with *how* to pursue policy and with the impact of policies has become more widespread in recent decades.[1] Critics have become more adamant in their questions about whether programs have the impacts expected.

This chapter focuses on the two issues of the means of pursuing policy goals and of the impact of public policy. How does government go about trying to affect society, and what impacts do policies have?

Politicians and bureaucrats, of course, seek to design programs that work, that have the impact sought. But there is no consensus about the best way to design programs. Should state government directly handle a program, or should it use local governments to administer programs? If government does not provide a service, should government contract with someone in the private sector? Should government try to induce the private sector to provide benefits? Or should government simply regulate the private sector? These disputes are accompanied by broad differences of opinions about whether government programs can work to change society at all.

These disputes about the way to pursue policy goals are not just technical disagreements. Although some policy analysts may assess policies just in terms of *whether* they "work," advocates for different interests are concerned with *the way* implementation affects who wins and who loses. Advocates of the haves and the have-nots continually ask if the method of implementation affects the treatment of their constituencies. For example, if civil rights complaints are handled in a decentralized manner, does that mean enforcement will be more varied and more unequal? If education is to be improved, is it best to provide more money to local school districts and trust them to know what is best to do with the money, or should the state mandate how money is used? If autonomy is granted, school districts may decide to use the money for salaries rather than for smaller classes. The former may or may not help students, but it will clearly help teachers, many of whom are middle class. Is this ultimately good or bad for the have-nots, or does it just help teachers? There are prolonged disputes about the way to go about improving education. Who will benefit from each approach is fundamental to those debates. Will education vouchers given to parents to allow them to choose schools benefit the affluent or the poor?

This chapter is not a comprehensive review of all the policies that states and local governments pursue. Such efforts are valuable, but they inevitably must be cursory when attempting to cover fifty states and their local governments. There is a vast literature available that provides detailed reviews of the many public policies that states and local governments pursue.[2] The focus here, however, is on the enduring issues that emerge when government tries to affect society: How does government go about trying to have an impact? Do those efforts have an impact?

Pursuing Public Policy: Alternative Methods of Achieving Policy Goals

There are many different ways government might seek to achieve policy goals. Government might decide to directly provide a benefit. The choice must then be made as to whether the state should directly provide benefits or whether local governments should be responsible for programs. If local governments are relied on, the state might provide them with intergovernmental aid, or they might mandate that local governments provide the program.

Alternatively, government might rely on the private sector to provide some service, but seek to influence how that activity occurs. Government might try to induce the private sector to provide a policy. Government might also contract with the private sector to provide the service. Or the private sector might already be providing the service, and government might act only to regulate the activity of the private sector.

Each of these approaches is a product of the political process. Liberals tend to trust government handling of programs more than private-sector control of programs. Liberals fear that profit motives rather than the desire to help people will dominate. They also feel that if government handles programs, politicians will retain more control over the way they are implemented. Conservatives, on the other hand, tend to prefer private-sector execution whenever possible. They think the private sector will be more efficient and that activity through the private sector may generate other tax-generations private-sector jobs. Amid all this, interest, groups devote enormous time to trying to shape the way programs are implemented so that their interests are protected. Groups present arguments that regulations and intrusions will be harmful in some way. In this section, we review these different ways of pursuing policies and the accompanying debates about who will be responsible for implementation.

We then consider the debates about the efficacy of public-policy programs. There has been considerable dispute over the impact of public policy. Critics argue that government actions often do not achieve the goals desired and do not make situations any different. For example, governments regularly try to influence the amount of economic activity in their borders. There are many who argue that government intervention cannot really change the way private markets work. There are also consistent efforts to get people out of poverty. There are general efforts to get people to change their behaviors. Government has programs to motivate teachers and programs to encourage people to generate less garbage. There are critics who doubt that these government policies have much impact. There are, of course, those who argue that policies have real and significant impacts on social conditions.

These differences about the way to do things and the effects of government efforts are in many ways just further reflections of differences between liberals and conservatives. Liberals are generally more likely to believe that it is possible to change people and society, while conservatives are more likely to be skeptical about the prospects for significant change. These general attitudes reflect differences in concern for the haves and the have-nots. We will review these debates as we proceed.

Government Provision of Services

Direct Provision

Many services are now provided directly by government that were once provided almost entirely by private-sector organizations. Private-sector provision was ultimately regarded as inadequate, and the responsibility for these activities was assumed by government. State and local governments, for example, now spend large amounts on welfare, education, and transportation. There have also been times when government spending on housing was significant. All these were once private-sector activities. The transition from private-sector dominance to public-sector dominance indicates much about the way the political battles over public policy have evolved. They also reveal the successes and failures of different groups in society.

Welfare

In the late 1800s and early 1900s, welfare was largely locally provided. Substantial funds came in the form of private charitable contributions. Many private individuals made voluntary contributions to local organizations that, in turn, helped out those in need. Local groups or governments then determined who needed assistance and how much they received.[3] This process resulted in relatively low benefit levels and wide divergences across communities in who was eligible for benefits and in the benefits they received.[4] In some states, the state government reacted to this situation and created state programs or provided funding for local-level programs. As a consequence, there was considerable diversity across states and localities in types of programs and levels of benefits.

The persistent high levels of unemployment during the Great Depression (the 1930s) and changes in our sense of individual responsibility (see Chapter 2) led to proposals for federal welfare programs for single mothers and unemployment compensation for workers laid off work. The decision whether to participate in these federal programs led to lengthy battles in the states.[5] There were also prolonged debates over whether the programs would be delivered by state or local governments. Liberals advocated adoption of state programs because they felt those without income, food, or health insurance should receive some assistance from government. They also supported state administration of the programs so that there would be uniform eligibility and benefits in the state. Conservatives resisted these programs. They saw charity as a valid and effective way to respond to these programs and felt that the emphasis should be on individual initiative, not on government support. They were also reluctant to have state governments assume the financial obligations accompanying uniform welfare benefits across a state.

States eventually adopted these programs and, after long battles, state governments assumed responsibility from local governments for programs. From the 1930s to the early 1970s, welfare made a transition from being a largely local program to a largely state-administered program.

The federal government pushed along these changes through persistent pressures on the states to adopt uniform practices in each state. All states now provide welfare assistance, though states still vary in the benefits given recipients. Within a state, uniform rules generally prevail in determining eligibility for welfare. Local discretion surely continues to play some role, but it is no longer a major role.

The 1960s saw the emergence of a health insurance program directed at low-income individuals. Medicaid began in 1966 as a joint state-local financed program, and by the early 1990s, most states had assumed complete responsibility for financing. Liberals were again able to keep up sustained criticism of the inequities accompanying local administration, and uniform state standards were adopted.

The political debates discussed earlier were fundamental in pushing these changes. Critics continually opposed relying on local charity programs and autonomous local administration of government welfare programs. Criticisms of local administration of government welfare programs were particularly important. Advocates of state administration presumed that there should be equal treatment of similar cases, and they consistently argued that local determination of eligibility and benefits were unfair to lower-income groups. States became involved in the direct provision of these programs because it was finally concluded that neither charity nor local fund raising and local administration would be adequate. Debates about what political values should prevail had long-term effects.

Considerable sums are now spent by the national, state and local governments on income-assistance programs. These programs provide direct benefits to individuals. The funding and administering of these programs is a complicated combination of national, state, and local efforts. Table 13.1 presents a summary of the major programs that provide assistance to people. The table presents the number of recipients in each program, the level of government that funds the program, the level that administers it, and the total amount of money spent on each program. Some of these programs, such as Medicare and Medicaid, involve relying on the private sector. Others, such as social security, are the responsibility of the national government. The latter are presented here only to allow comparison with state and local programs.

The major state and local programs are AFDC (Aid for Families with Dependent Children), food stamps, unemployment compensation, and workers' compensation. Together these programs provide income and food-purchasing capabilities to those below the poverty level. They also provide funds to unemployed and disabled workers.

Table 13.1

Major Social Welfare and Social Insurance Programs 1986

Program	Number of Recipients (millions)	Who Funds	Who Administers	Total Expenditures (millions of dollars)
Direct cash transfers				
AFDC	11.1	National, state	State, local	9.9
SSI	4.6	National	National	12.8
General assistance	1.2	State, local	State, local	35.0
In-kind program				
Food stamps	20.6	National	State, local	12.8
Medicaid	23.3	National, state	State, local	43.9
Social insurance				
Social security	26.2	National	National	272.0
Medicare	32.4	National, state	National, state	75.9
Unemployment compensation	2.4	State, private	State	18.5
Worker's compensation	87.2	State, private	State	24.4

Source: Adapted from Ann O'M Bowman and Richard C. Kearney, State & Local Government *(Princeton: Houghton Mifflin, 1990), 66; and from U.S. Bureau of the Census,* Statistical Abstract of the United States, *1989.*

We can assess the impact of these programs by comparing the extent of poverty without such programs and then with them. Table 13.2 presents such an assessment. The percent of individuals below the poverty level before transfer payments (funds transferred directly to individuals) are considered. The poverty line is the amount of money the U.S. government concludes a family has to have to meet basic needs. This level changes from year to year. Then the effects of cash payments (for example, Aid For Dependent Children) are considered. Finally, benefits that do not involve cash (food stamps, medicaid, and housing) are considered. The inclusion of all these benefits results in a poverty rate that is considerably less than it would be without these programs.

The impact of these programs can be seen more clearly across time. As discussed earlier, there has been a gradual growth in the belief that something should be done to assist those in poverty. Liberals have fought to devote money to such programs. Conservatives have worried more about keeping taxes down and maintaining an emphasis on individual initiative and responsibility. Over the long run, liberals have had some success, and funding for these programs has grown considerably since World War II. During the last two decades, the growth has been fairly limited because conservatives have argued that welfare is not doing what we want. Nonetheless, the long-term growth has resulted in a gradual but persistent decline in the percentage of the population in poverty. Figure 13.1 indicates how much these various poverty rates have declined. The top line of the graph represents the latent proportion of poverty, or that before any government benefits of any kind (such as welfare and social security) are considered. The official poverty rate is the proportion of people whose cash income (from their own earnings or some government program) is below the poverty level. The net poverty proportion is the proportion after all transfers (housing, food stamps, and medical assistance) have been considered. From the 1950s to the early 1990s, there was a decline in the percentage of the population in net poverty. Much of this decline is due to government programs in various forms. These programs have not eliminated poverty, and they have drawn considerable criticism. But government funding of these programs has

---

Table 13.2

Impact of Antipoverty Programs 1987

Situation	Number in poverty (millions)	Poverty Rate (%)
Before transfers	49.7	20.6
Plus social insurance	34.4	14.3
Plus cash welfare	32.5	13.5
Plus food and housing	29.0	12.0
Minus federal taxes	30.4	12.6

Source: Sar A. Levitan, Programs in Aid of the Poor *(Baltimore: Johns Hopkins University Press, 1990) 36; and Data from the House Ways and Means Committee.*

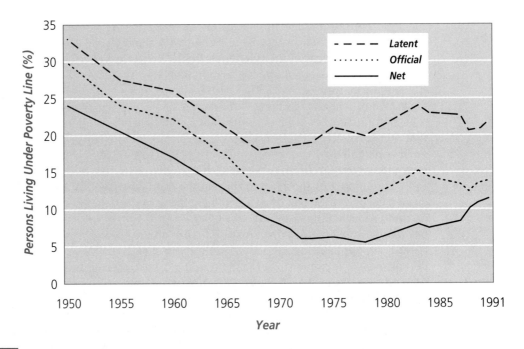

Figure 13.1

Alternative Definitions and Levels of Poverty, 1950 to early 1990s
Source: Thomas R. Dye, Politics in States and Communities, 7th ed. (Englewood Cliffs: Prentice-Hall, 1991), 462.

reduced poverty levels. This is a policy area where we see a clear change in attitudes towards the poor, and a significant change in their treatment.

There are still, however, criticisms of these programs. There continue to be significant disparities across the states in the benefits provided.[6] Debates continue about the efficacy of existing programs, with ideology heavily influencing the conclusions reached. Liberals argue that these programs do not really help the poor, but are meant only to placate them. These liberal critics argue that funding rises only during difficult economic times and that the programs are designed to appease lower-income groups and to quell dissent in American society.[7] Critics think that funding should be at higher levels and that those receiving funding should not be treated as if it is their fault that they need such benefits.

Conservatives are also critical of these programs. They argue that these subsidies undermine the inclination to work and that they slow the movement of people off welfare.[8] They argue that recipients stay on welfare too long. Critics propose that recipients be required to take part-time jobs or undergo training or education so that they will be able to get jobs in the future. In response, many states have imposed "workfare" requirements, or requirements that some work be engaged in as a condition of receiving public assistance.

There have been significant changes in welfare policies over time in the United States. Government has become the primary source of programs, and funding and responsibility have shifted from local governments to the federal government and the states. The increase in the number of programs and the funding of these programs has lowered the amount of poverty. The debate, however, goes on, and will continue to go on, about whether existing programs are the best way to address the problem of poverty.

Education

Government has also assumed direct responsibility for providing education, at both the elementary and secondary level and at college level. In the case of education, government has not so much replaced activities being done in the private sector as it has expanded the provision of publicly provided education.

Elementary and secondary education began as a local government activity, and it has remained so. State involvement with local education began when states started to mandate common curriculums and to provide state aid. Over time, state governments have become more and more involved in local education.[9] Some of this involvement began because groups turned to state government to seek the imposition of mandates on local schools. Advocates of the handicapped did not believe local governments would provide assistance to the handicapped unless forced to by state mandates. Minority groups wanted mandatory curriculums that stressed respect for diversity in society. Groups living in areas with limited tax bases also turned to the state to seek state aid to reduce inequities among districts. Teachers sought greater aid from the state so that salaries could increase.

Debates between liberals and conservatives, Democrats and Republicans, have again played a role in these changes. Democrats have been the primary advocates of greater state aid to address inequities. Republicans, with constituencies in rural and suburban districts, have been much less supportive of state taxation and redistribution programs. Only lawsuits and increasing costs for suburban schools have reduced Republican opposition. Liberals have been able to achieve some success. In 1960, states provided 39.5 percent of funding for local schools. In 1990, states provided 47.2 percent. Education continues to be a locally delivered activity, but many state governments now provide a large proportion of the funding for local school districts and mandate many education practices.[10]

There is still, however, considerable diversity in the role states play in funding local schools. The argument that states should play a major role has not been accepted everywhere. Table 13.3 indicates how much the states differ in their role. In states like Hawaii, Washington, and New Mexico, the state has come to play a major role in funding schools. In other states, such as New Hampshire, Oregon, and Nebraska, the state role is limited. New Hampshire has even considered eliminating state minimum education standards to weaken the claim that the state is obligated to provide more funding support.[11] The battle over who should be responsible for local schools has been a long one, and it will continue.

Public education has become available to everyone. There are, to be sure, clear differences in the quality of education offered to everyone. The funding available across school districts, discussed in Chapter 4, are significant and have real consequences. There are also continuing criticisms of the general quality of educa-

Table 13.3

State Funding of Local Education, 1990

Funding from State Sources (%)				
Less than 40%	**40–49**	**50–59**	**60–69**	**70+**
Colorado	Arizona	Arkansas	Alabama	Hawaii
Illinois	Connecticut	Florida	Alaska	New Mexico
Maryland	Iowa	Georgia	California	Washington
Michigan	Kansas	Indiana	Delaware	
Nebraska	Missouri	Minnesota	Idaho	
New Hampshire	Montana	Mississippi	Kentucky	
New Jersey	New York	Oklahoma	North Carolina	
Oregon	North Dakota	South Carolina	West Virginia	
South Dakota	Ohio	Utah		
Vermont	Pennsylvania	Wyoming		
Virginia	Rhode Island			
	Tennessee			
	Texas			
	Wisconsin			

Source: *Advisory Commission on Intergovernmental Relations,* Significant Features of Fiscal Federalism, 1992, *vol. 2 (Washington, DC, September 1992), M-180-II, 9, 265.*

tion provided in local schools. Beginning in the early 1980s, arguments have also emerged that the local education system has not been doing a good job preparing students for adult life.[12] These arguments have generated numerous suggestions for reforming schools. We will return to the issue of the performance of schools later.

Although there was early support in American society for the widespread provision of elementary and secondary education, support for higher education came later. Most college education was initially provided by private colleges. By the mid-1800s, there was considerable population growth in the Midwest, where there were fewer private schools. This growth led to pressures to establish public state colleges in the Midwest and other areas outside the East. The initial efforts were limited, but there was gradual growth in the size of these public colleges by the end of World War II. The 1950s produced dramatic changes. There was a large population of veterans seeking access to colleges. The federal government provided the GI bill, which paid for veterans to attend college. The average income of Americans also increased, making it possible for more people to afford education. In addition, by the late 1960s, the post-World-War-II baby boom was beginning to seek admission to colleges. The 1950s and 1960s saw a vastly increased demand for admission to college.

The decision of whether and in what way to respond became a state government decision. There were no national universities, and few local governments had the resources to respond. In eastern states, the decision was complicated because of the presence of private colleges. Many private colleges were worried about competition from public universities and sought state subsidies for students to attend private schools.[13] The primary issue that emerged was who would provide education. This issue was tied to the question of how accessible schools would be in terms of tuition costs. Would education be provided privately, and cost more, or would state governments provide education at a relatively low tuition, making it accessible to a broader range of people. The decision during the early 1950s was generally to expand state public universities so that education would be accessible to more students. With low tuition, states became heavy subsidizers of higher education costs.

The arrival of the postwar baby boom prompted greater demands for access to higher education. States responded in two ways. They created branch universities throughout each state so that more students would have access to higher education. They also devoted more money to creating and to supporting community colleges so that there would be greater equality of opportunity of access to education.[14] Students could attend college and live at home. In most states, local governments pay a part of the costs of community colleges in order to keep tuition low.

Similar to the decisions about welfare, these decisions about the way education would be provided were shaped by larger public debates about equality of opportunity in society. Liberals wanted to expand these opportunities and became prime advocates of devoting more resources to higher education. Conservatives did not express intense opposition because they saw education as providing opportunities, not giveaways. The result has been a consistent expansion of community-college facilities across the country.[15] Education is now more available than it was thirty years ago. More students can attend schools in their local area, and the costs of tuition remain relatively low at public universities. There are, to be sure, criticisms of the quality of education at community colleges, but education is now more widely available. Again, debates about opportunity led to more resources being devoted to education.

Transportation

Transportation systems were originally provided through a mixture of private and public efforts. Government built many roads in the 1700s and 1800s, but many roads were also built by private contractors, who then charged tolls. Many of the mass transit (bus and rail) systems of the early 1900s were also provided by private contractors. Eventually the responsibility for roads was transferred to government. Users of toll roads complained of excessive charges, and these complaints led to government regulation. This regulation made many roads less profitable, and private owners sold or transferred these roads to government. Private transit systems declined even more because increasing reliance on the automobile reduced ridership and made private transit companies unprofitable. Local governments then took over the companies and created public bus and rail mass transit systems.[16] States began to provide much more aid. The federal government started programs to provide large sums of money to states and localities for road maintenance. As a consequence of all these changes, transportation systems are now a government responsibility, and considerable sums are spent to maintain roads and bridges.

The move to have government play a larger role has evolved differently across the states. Just as in other policy areas, state histories and politics shape the role each state plays. In states such as Kentucky, Ohio, Oklahoma, and Arkansas, the state provides over 60 percent of all funding for highways. In other states, like Georgia, New York, and Rhode Island, the state provides only 30 percent of funding.[17] The latter situation creates enormous potential for differences across the state in the level of maintenance for roads.

Regardless, there is now a substantial ongoing government expenditure to support roads. These expenditures have had a direct effect on people's lives. Public investment in roads has made the automobile easier and cheaper to use as a mode of transportation. Major investments of money have created interstate highways and networks of highways throughout metropolitan areas, all of which make it easier for people to rely on automobiles for transportation.

While welfare expenditures have made the lives of the lower class somewhat better, expenditure on roads appears to have made the lives of the middle class somewhat better. Much of the money spent on transportation in American society has gone to roads, and investment in mass transit has been considerably less. Over the last forty years, the response of government to traffic congestion has been to build more roads. That response encouraged more people to rely on cars, and use of mass transit systems has declined dramatically since the 1950s.[18] Only in the last two decades, with greater concern about energy consumption and air pollution from cars, have there been significant efforts to shift more money to mass transit. We remain, however, a society that relies primarily on cars for transportation.

Fire and Police

Government also provides all fire and police services. As with the policy areas just reviewed, there were early efforts to provide these services through private contractors. The perception that these services are generally of benefit to everyone led to government assumption of these activities in many local governments. The belief that there should be a minimal level of professional fire protection across all localities, however, has not developed. Many, local communities still rely on volunteer fire departments. Local governments are still able to get volunteers, and the cost of full-time, professional fire departments is one that most local communities are not yet prepared to bear.

Market Failures and Changing Attitudes

The changes in these policy areas represent situations in which a mixture of local public and private delivery of services was gradually transformed into public delivery alone. In areas like transportation and higher education, the impetus for change was that the public was not completely satisfied with private provision of services. In other cases, private entrepreneurs no longer found it attractive to provide a service and gradually withdrew from provision. There was public support for continuing the service provided, and government became that provider. In some policy areas, responsibility for programs or services was assigned to state governments, and in others local, or state and local, governments are responsible. Regardless of which level of government took responsibility, the important transition was from private to public responsibility.

In areas like health care, this transition is by no means complete. Health insurance has traditionally been provided by private employers, who have discretion in the benefit package they provide. Employers also have some discretion in which of their employees receive insurance. Large companies tend to provide insurance, while small companies do not.[19] Part-time employees and full-time temporary employees usually do not receive insurance. Over the last several decades, there has been an increase in the proportion of workers who work for employers who do not provide insurance, or who are part-time and do not receive insurance. There is also now a growing number of employers who eliminate full-time positions (carrying benefits) and farm out the work that those employees would have done to freelance workers who receive no benefits. Many workers now do not have insurance. This situation has prompted more debates about whether government should intervene to somehow correct this problem. Governments could provide insurance for those not covered, or for everyone. Or it could impose regulations on the private sector. As of yet, however, there is no consensus about what should be done, so health insurance still remains largely a private-sector activity. The transition from private- to public-sector provision may eventually occur, but there will be intense debates before that occurs.

Working through Local Governments

If government decides to provide a service, there is still the question of which level of government should be responsible for that service. There may be resistance to having the state assume certain responsibilities. Rural areas may not wish to have services such as welfare be a state responsibility because they think urban poor populations will create heavy statewide taxation burdens. State officials may not want to be involved in the intricacies and the often emotional battles of local zoning. Local officials and residents are also likely to resist giving up this power.[20]

As a result, state governments often do not assume direct responsibility for policies, but rely on local governments to provide the service. States can still have influence over local practices through the provision of state resources and the use of state authority. State can supply state aid to support local activities. When local governments are not inclined to provide some policy, the state can provide aid contingent on the local government using the money to provide the service. State governments can provide aid to induce local planning and cooperation among local governments. Many programs involve a pledge of state aid if local governments will pursue sharing of facilities or duties, such as in the joint telephone systems used to receive emergency calls and to dispatch police.

Finally, the state can mandate that a policy be pursued. State mandates in education are quite common.[21] State legislators are subject to heavy lobbying by education groups seeking to have specific curricula (music, physical education, special education, the number of science or other courses) required by the state. These groups generally presume it will be difficult to convince school boards in each district to adopt the policies that they desire. If advocates of specific policies get them mandated by the state, there is a greater chance of some policy uniformity across the state. This approach has resulted in mandates about specific topics that must be covered in the schools.

State mandating is used to influence many local government activities. State governments mandate local working conditions, local contributions to employee retirement systems, exemptions of local property from local property taxes, safety standards for fire departments, and many other conditions.[22]

States seek to assure mandates are implemented by requiring local governments to file reports about their activities. Many local officials complain that state officials impose mandates, but do not provide accompanying state aid. The evidence, however, suggests that more mandates are usually accompanied by more aid. States that are more liberal tend to provide more state aid and also to impose more mandates.[23] States like New York, Wisconsin, and Minnesota impose many mandates, while states like Rhode Island, West Virginia, and Alabama issue few mandates.[24]

Some mandates are indirect in nature. The state may not require an outcome, but change the rules that shape what happens at the local level. This indirect route is commonly used to help local-government employee groups. State politicians may not want to mandate that a union exist, or that certain benefits be granted. They may, however, want to assure that local governments give serious consideration to local employee groups trying to form a union or to negotiate contracts with local governments. Many states have also passed laws that require employers to recognize votes by employees to form local unions. State laws creating rules that local employers must follow in negotiating contracts also exist.[25] Such laws still leave as a local option which shape the labor agreement resulting from local negotiations will take and whether there will be a union. These laws, however, give government employees more leverage during the bargaining process because they require governments to bargain. The more favorable these laws are to local employee groups, the higher the wages the workers receive.[26] By using these indirect mandates, pro-union politicians have been able to contribute to the success of unions in achieving their goals.

These same laws affect teacher contract negotiations. State governments can require that administrations recognize and bargain with teacher unions. State laws can significantly shape the ability of teacher groups to win benefits. State laws can define what aspects of school budgets citizens are allowed (or not be allowed) to vote on. In some states, teachers have successfully lobbied the state to exempt much of the budget (including their salary obligations) from citizen voting. Such an exemption gives citizens less ability to have an impact on budgets.

Overall, it is very common for state officials to accept the continuation of local delivery, but to impose numerous mandates and rules that affect the way local governments may proceed in delivering services.

Regulating Private-Sector Practices and Behaviors

Contracting with the Private Sector

If politicians decide to use government to try to shape society, that decision does not necessarily mean that services will be provided directly by government. In many cases, the public expresses concern about the way a service is distributed, but the service is currently provided by the private sector. Those providers often have no interest in having the government displace them. As noted before, there is considerable concern in our society about the cost and delivery of health care. There has, however, been tremendous resistance among doctors to having the government play any role in providing health services. Doctors have consistently fought government intrusion into their right to set fees and control their practices.[27]

Because of this resistance, government has chosen to accept the basic principle of private delivery of services. Politicians have created programs in which government has in effect contracted with the private sector for the provision of medical services. At the national level, government created the medicare program. This program provides for government payment of the costs of medical care for senior citizens. Private doctors provide the service, but the government pays.

The same approach is used for medicaid. This program provides medical services to low-income individuals. The federal government provides substantial intergovernmental fiscal aid for medicaid programs to the states, which decide what package of services they will support for low-income individuals.[28] Contracting with the private sector puts government in the situation of negotiating with private providers and trying to influence private-sector practices through negotiations over what will be paid for and how much will be paid. Government is in a difficult situation because private providers (doctors) may not find certain reimbursement terms attractive and may reduce their provision of services. This possibility reduces the direct control government has and makes achieving objectives more difficult.

Government contracting with the private sector is relied on for other services. In many suburban and rural areas, private companies have traditionally provided garbage collection. As long as private companies make a profit, they do not want government to replace them. The public also may find the existing arrangement quite satisfactory. But the public may still want government to monitor or review private haulers so that homeowners and renters can be sure providers are operating properly. Government then becomes the agent that reviews haulers, but the service remains private.

Government contracting with the private sector is widely used. The private sector provides supplies, materials, and consultants. In all these cases, there are efforts to apply regulations to make sure providers fulfill minimum requirements.

Shaping Behaviors in the Private Sector

Much of the effort to shape policy outcomes does not involve purchasing anything from the private sector. Policy proposals often originate because citizens believe conditions in the private sector are not appropriate and need to be influenced by government. In these cases, people want government to change rules or policies to induce different behaviors. They desire to have government shape what the private sector does. The presumption is that private-sector actors will respond differently if government specifies what practices can and cannot prevail. If the right guidelines, rules, or whatever exist, then behavior in the private sector may more closely approximate what the public wants.

Partisan views play a significant role in the debates over how much government should intrude through regulations. Democrats in many states are more inclined to intervene in the private market to try to alter its workings. They are also more inclined to try to remedy inequalities in society through government action. Republicans are generally less inclined to intervene and to regulate the private market. They may not always regard the workings or outcomes of the private sector as desirable, but they worry about the effects of government intrusions. As a consequence of these debates, many regulations have emerged that seek to shape private-sector behaviors.

Private-Sector Union Rules

Similarly to employees in the public sector, employees in the private sector have turned to government to get changes in the rules that govern employer-employee relations. If unions can obtain passage of laws establishing the right of employees to form a union and the right of that union to bargain with employers, labor has a better chance to negotiate more favorable wages and working conditions. Government does not dictate the terms of contracts, but it can change the nature of interactions in the private sector.

Democrats have traditionally been more receptive to passing these laws. They believe in helping working people, and they also wish to help out the constituents who have helped put them in office. Republicans have been less favorable to such legislation.

Consumer Legislation

Governments have devoted considerable attention to trying to broadly shape interactions between sellers and purchasers in the private sector. Laws have been passed about consumers' rights to return bad cars, or "lemons," and about the terms under which such cars can be returned. Laws have also been passed giving consumers the right to see their credit records and the right to withdraw from certain agreements within specified time periods.

Democrats have tended to be more supportive of consumer legislation than Republicans. This greater support occurs because Democrats again are more likely to think that big business has an advantage over the consumer and that the consumer should have some leverage against business. Republicans have gradually come to accept consumer legislation, but they tend to worry that such legislation harasses business during times when job growth is limited.

Economic Development

There is probably no area that has received as much attention in the last decade as economic development. During the 1970s, state and local governments became aware of significant shifts in their economic bases. Older manufacturing industries with older plants were dying off all across the country because of the availability of cheaper labor in third world countries and because newer plants were more cost-efficient. The changes were most significant in the Northeast and the Midwest because those areas had a larger number of older factories. As their economic bases declined, states and cities realized that they needed to make their locales attractive, both to retain existing businesses and to attract new ones.

Partisan politics again became relevant. As job growth slowed, Republicans were quick to argue that businesses find it difficult to start and grow when there are many regulations and limited help from government. Republicans argued for help in borrowing money or acquiring land. Democrats have reluctantly gone along, but worry about too many giveaways to business. Out of those debates, states and localities have formed economic development policies.

Attempts to help businesses have led to a whole set of policies that have the purpose of inducing businesses to invest in an area.[29] States and localities have programs that forgive property taxes so that land will be cheaper, that subsidize borrowing so that the cost of capital will be less, and that make direct grants to pay for infrastructure for new or existing plants. States also pass laws allowing reductions in corporate taxes, or credits against tax obligations for those companies that invest in equipment or in the retraining of workers. Finally, many groups continually seek to lower tax levels to make a state or locality a more "attractive" place to do business.

Despite all the attention devoted to trying to promote economic development, it is not clear what affects business activity. It does not appear that tax levels,[30] or attempts to reduce the costs of doing business, have a great impact on business decisions.[31] Businesses appear to locate in places because of the size of markets, the access to other markets, transportation costs, and many other factors that governments cannot easily control. On the other hand, there is evidence that state assistance to specific industries can help improve economic growth in the states.[32] There is also evidence that helping retain industries can have secondary benefits. Businesses that stay often provide economic benefits through their purchases from other firms and their payments for necessary infrastructure.[33] Unfortunately, however, there is considerable ambiguity about the effects of state economic development programs.

Divorce Rules

Policy changes often produce ambiguous effects, and sometimes these changes produce impacts considerably different than expected. Changes in divorce laws in the last twenty years vividly illustrate this problem. Government has long taken an interest in the private institution of the family. For many years, the policy of government was to establish rules to encourage the stability of the family by making it difficult for marriages to end. Advocates for women also argued it was important to protect women, who were likely to have stayed home and, on average, made less money. Rules were established to determine fault and to require awards based on fault, on the presumption such rules would protect women. Table 13.4 presents a summary of these "traditional" rules. The category of "Traditional Divorce" indicates the norms that prevailed before the 1970s.

Beginning in the early 1970s, a movement to adopt "no-fault" divorce rules began. Liberals were the prime advocates of changing the rules of divorce. They felt that government did not treat women as equals and that the law should be changed to make them equal. The intent was to treat spouses as equals and to avoid lengthy and bitter court battles determining fault. These battles were seen as destructive to the individuals and to their children. This pressure led to a set of new rules, or norms. These are presented under "No-Fault Divorce" in Table 13.4.

Much to the surprise of many, these changes did not have the impact expected. It was presumed that the courts would divide assets evenly and that both parties

---

Table 13.4
Changes in Divorce Law in the States

Traditional Divorce	No-Fault Divorce
Restrictive law	Permissive law
To protect marriage	To facilitate divorce
Specific grounds	No grounds
Adultery, cruelty, and others	Marital breakdown
Moral framework	Administrative framework
Guilt vs. innocence	Neither responsible
Fault	No fault
One party caused divorce	Cause of divorce irrelevant
Consent of innocent spouse needed	No consent needed
Innocent spouse has power to prevent	Unilateral divorce
or delay divorce	No consent or agreement required
Gender-based responsibilities	Gender-neutral responsibilities
Husband responsible for alimony	Both responsible for self-support
Wife responsible for custody	Both eligible for custody
Husband responsible for child support	Both responsible for child support
Financial awards linked to fault	Financial awards based on equality and need
Alimony for innocent spouse	Alimony based on need
Greater share of property to innocent spouse	Property divided equally
Adversarial	Nonadversarial
One party guilty, one "innocent"	No guilty or innocent party
Financial gain in proving fault	No financial gain from charges
	Amicable resolution encouraged

Source: Leonore J. Weitzman, The Divorce Revolution *(New York: Free Press, 1985), 40.*

would fare equally well. The courts, however, tended to favor men. Women apparently fared much worse after the enactment of no-fault divorce.[34] Table 13.5 shows how men and women, married for less than ten years, fared after divorce. The most remarkable differences occurred among the affluent. In those families in which the income had been the highest, women made 51 percent of their predivorce income, while men made 195 percent. When marriages lasted longer, women did even less well. These results were not expected. When new policies are adopted, it is never certain they will be interpreted as originally intended. The change in divorce rules is just one example of that.

Regulating Private Sector Behavior

The policy areas just reviewed—labor, economic development, divorce—represent examples of indirect approaches to shaping outcomes. Government in these examples did not mandate specific outcomes, but created rules and policies that encouraged specific outcomes. Sometimes such indirect routes do not achieve the goals desired. Government may seek to improve worker safety in the workplace by encouraging unions in the hope that they will negotiate better conditions. Unsafe conditions, however, may persist and may lead some politicians to seek more direct action. They may then choose the more coercive route of specifying the minimum conditions that must prevail in the workplace. For example, direct regulations set the minimum age workers can be, the maximum hours that can be worked in a week (without overtime), and the minimum wage that must be paid. These regulations exist because workers pressured politicians to impose conditions that they did not think they could get from employers on their own.

Direct regulations are used in numerous policy areas. In many professions, governments require that a person must be licensed to practice and that minimum training requirements must be met in order to be licensed. Government did not

Table 13.5

Pre and Postdivorce per Capita Incomes for Couples Married Less Than Ten Years

Predivorce Yearly Family Income	Predivorce per Capita Family Income	Postdivorce per Capita Income		Postdivorce per Capita Income as Percentage of Predivorce Family per Capita Income	
		Wife	Husband	Wife	Husband
under $20,000 (n = 41)	$ 6,050	$ 7,000	$10,450	116	172
$20-29,999 (n = 24)	$11,000	$ 8,900	$18,050	81	164
$30-39,999 (n = 19)	$17,500	$13,050	$27,000	75	154
40,000+ (n = 21)	$23,500	$12,000	$45,700	51	195

Source: Leonore J. Weitzman, The Divorce Revolution *(New York: Free Press, 1985), 328.*

trust the private market to generate these requirements, so they were imposed. Concerns about the environment have also generated regulations. To force the consideration of the environmental effects of new developments, companies that wish to build new factories, shopping malls, or housing developments must first file an environmental impact statement.

Direct regulation has been particularly important in the regulation of utilities. Utility services—power, telephones, water—originated as private companies. They quickly became vitally important to communities. As consolidation of local companies occurred, many of the utility companies became monopolies, or near monopolies, in that they were the only providers in an area. This monopoly power gave companies considerable freedom to set rates, and some took advantage of that situation to set relatively high rates. That misuse of power led to statewide regulation of utilities in every state. Regulators set rates and determine what rate increases will be granted from year to year.

Issues of equality of access have played a significant role in these debates.[35] The elderly and the poor have argued that everyone should have access to utility services and that companies should be required to provide minimal services at some relatively low rate. As a consequence, many utilities are required to provide "lifeline" services for telephones. Power companies that provide heat must have programs to help low-income people spread out their payments and in many states are not allowed during the winter months to disconnect service for nonpayment.

Summary

There are many ways in which government seeks to influence society. Each of these is a product of social and economic change and political battles over how to respond, if at all, to change. Sometimes government acts as a direct provider. At other times, government works with the private sector, either by contracting with private suppliers, shaping the rules under which they operate, or directly regulating their activities.

All these battles become entangled with broad debates about the role government should play. The decision about how to intrude is intertwined with the issue of who will benefit from one approach versus another. Groups who do not trust government and who need government less want limited state action and local responsibility for any actions taken. Groups who see themselves as more reliant on government action are more likely to want state government intrusion as a means to insure that similar policies exist across areas. Political differences do not cease when policy-design issues emerge. Groups just move their battle to other arenas.

The Impact of Policy: The Expectations Problem

The important question is whether these programs make a difference. Do they change social conditions in the ways expected? Do they help the groups they are intended to help? Over the last thirty years, many different programs have been established by federal, state, and local governments. In particular, billions of dollars have been devoted to programs designed to provide help to lower-income individuals in our society. While some assessments provide a positive view of these programs, some very critical assessments of these programs have also been offered. In the 1960s, for example, many programs were passed as a part of the "Great-Society" program of the Lyndon Johnson presidency. The general conviction was that these programs would make our society better. By the mid- to late 1970s, a steady barrage of criticism of these programs had started. The essential theme was that these programs had not worked. The election of Ronald Reagan as president in 1980 signified considerable support for that view. He consistently expressed the belief that government programs do not work well, that they are too costly, and that we would be better off letting the private sector operate on its own. Views like Reagan's were dominant for much of the 1980s.

In 1992, those views took another turn. Bill Clinton was elected for many reasons, but one clear reason was that he supported programs to promote jobs and economic development, to reform the health care system, and to change the welfare system. Many people felt existing approaches were not working. It was not clear that Clinton's answers were the right answers, but it appears that people were at least willing to give his proposals a chance. Over the years, we have gone from a belief in programs, to disbelief, to a desire to believe.

Amid all this change, the question persists of whether, and for whom, government programs work. The answer obviously varies by program. Some programs have had more effect than others. But the answer also depends on the expectations that people bring to their assessments. At the simplest level, we might assess programs on the basis of what happened after the program was adopted. If a program involves job training and is intended to reduce unemployment, then we can assess whether unemployment increases, remains the same, or decreases after the program is established. We could then track unemployment rates before and after the program is adopted to assess whether it had the desired impact.

Figure 13.2 presents a graph illustrating possible trends in unemployment levels. The left side of the graph presents a line indicating some level of unemployment. In the middle of the graph, there is a vertical line representing the adoption of a policy to provide training for the unemployed. In the right side of the graph are lines that represent different levels that might exist after the program is established. We can use these postprogram levels to evaluate the program. Line A indicates an increase in unemployment, suggesting the program did not work. Indeed, it may have made the situation worse. Line B represents no change, also suggesting the program had no effect. Line C represents a decline in unemployment, suggesting that the program was effective.

Unfortunately, it is not that simple to evaluate programs. There is one fundamental problem that always occurs when trying to evaluate policy. Other conditions also change, and we can never be sure how much the pattern we see is due to those changes, and not to the program. Other conditions can intrude in at least two ways that can make assessment difficult. First, an apparent positive effect of a program can really be due to these other changes. A government program to retrain workers to reduce unemployment might be launched at just the time the economy begins to recover from a recession. The increased sales accompanying the recovery

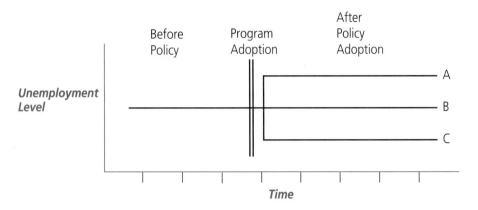

Figure 13.2

Possible Changes in a Policy Indicator

may lead to more hiring, lowering the unemployment rate. The job training program may have had no effect on the unemployment level, but its timing may make it look as though it had an effect. In Figure 13.2 line C may be due to the general improvement of the national economy. We may be deceived about apparent positive impacts of a policy.

Other conditions may also lead to an apparent situation of no impact or a negative impact, when in fact the program had a positive impact. A program to retrain workers might be launched at the very time the economy is sliding into a recession, or when industries that might employ retrained workers are declining. The job retraining program may successfully help many workers make a transition from one job to another, but the decline in the economy may result in a net increase in unemployment. It will appear that the program had no impact. It may well be, however, that unemployment would have been worse without the program.

Figure 13.3 presents this possibility. Line B represents the actual pattern of unemployment that developed across time after a retraining program was adopted, suggesting that the program had no impact. But it may be that without the program, unemployment would have gone to line A. The presence of the program prevented conditions from getting worse than they otherwise would have been. This argument has been made about many of the programs that operated in the 1970s. The economy was undergoing tremendous changes. Manufacturing employment was dropping steadily. Job training programs may have helped prevent unemployment from getting any worse.[36]

It is difficult to form simple assessments of programs. A job training program may appear to have a positive effect, but the change may be due to changing economic conditions. A program may appear to have no effect, but the program may have prevented conditions from getting worse. It is possible, of course that no complicating conditions intrude, and the effects of programs may be seen in an obvious and simple

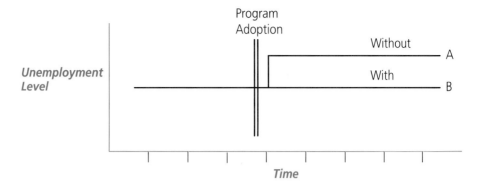

Figure 13.3
Possible Changes in Policy Indicator With and Without Government Policy

way. Unfortunately, there is always the possibility of other conditions playing a role, and program assessments and expectations are complicated accordingly.

Problems of Policy Impacts

The goal in enacting public policy is to affect society. The intent is to produce outcomes that would presumably not occur without the policy in effect. Many programs have been directed at very specific groups as a result of political debates. More money has been put into welfare to try to reduce the effects of poverty. Money has been spent on public housing to help the poor. More money has been spent on education to improve the general performance of the education system and to help students from low-income families. Despite all these programs, the poverty rate has not declined.[37] The persistent question about these programs is whether they work.

Devoting money to some programs clearly makes a difference. Spending more money on welfare gives welfare recipients more cash to spend. Increasing expenditures on transportation results in better roads. Providing more state aid to support community colleges results in more opportunities for students to attend these institutions. But these "successes" do not please everyone, nor do they address the concerns of some groups. Many of the programs that state and local governments adopt have been severely criticized on the grounds that they ultimately do not change peoples' lives, and change was the original reason for devoting money to the policy area.

Critics of welfare argue that our existing welfare programs do not really solve the more serious problem of getting people off welfare and back into the job market so that they can become self-sufficient (for their own sake) and become contributing members of society (for the benefit of the larger society). Liberals argue that the programs do not work because the actual efforts in these areas are fairly limited. They argue that despite public perceptions about growing welfare, direct transfers to individuals have not really increased much over the last several decades.[38] They also argue that although many programs appear to fail, the real problem is that the private sector does not generate sufficient jobs and that minorities are often discriminated against when they apply for the jobs that exist.[39] Conservatives argue that perhaps too much has been done. They argue that the rise of the welfare state has provided an incentive for people to remain on welfare and avoid returning to the labor force.[40]

Critics of subsidizing of higher education argue that giving students more credentials should not be the point of education. What is important is that students are well trained in the skills the economy needs. Critics of spending on local education argue that it does no good to funnel more money to education if that money does not produce better-adults.[41]

There are also numerous frustrations with economic-development policy. Critics worry that tax abatements and low-interest loans do not really generate more jobs; they just move jobs from one location to another as businesses exploit government offers of support.[42] Liberals worry that these programs do not generate more jobs, but are just giveaways to business and that the government simply subsidizes the costs of business activities.[43] Conservatives, on the other hand, worry that the private market is not being allowed to weed out unprofitable companies.

The list of frustrations with public policy is long. There are many areas in which there are doubts that policy achieves what it should. In some cases, these doubts stem from differences in original expectations. In other cases, however, doubts stem from legitimate skepticism about policy impacts.

States and localities, for example, have devoted vast sums of money to local education over the last decade because they wanted to improve the educational achievement of students. There are legitimate disagreements about expectations and the way we should measure achievement. Should achievement be defined by standardized test scores or by critical-thinking skills? But even if we resolve those disagreements, there is still a sense that the money spent on education has not achieved what we might have hoped. The same concern exists in other policy areas. It does appear that government programs do not always achieve what is desired. Efforts to change society run into real problems. There are several major obstacles to policies having the impacts expected.

Working through "Other" Organizations

Once policy has been agreed on, it is necessary to implement that policy through some organization. State governments regularly rely on local governments, school districts, and nonprofit organizations to handle the actual execution of policies. Policy execution is generally not in the hands of those who create the policy. This situation inevitably gives implementers some discretion in deciding how to use resources or in determining what practices fulfill the original policy goals. Local organizations do acquire some control, and their values and goals shape what finally happens.

Changes in education illustrate this process. In 1983, concern about the effectiveness of education increased with the publication of *A Nation at Risk*, a report arguing that the education system was not working well.[44] The report argued that teachers were not doing a good job and that students were not learning. This report generated support for providing more resources for education. State governments increased their aid to local school districts. Local governments raised local property taxes. These increases in resources came at a time when there were significant disagreements about what should be done to change the performance of schools. There were separate advocates for tougher standards,[45] smaller class sizes, and higher pay for teachers. While these arguments about direction continued, politicians responded to the general concern about education by directing more money to schools.

Those in the school system had their own priorities about the way additional money should be used. During the 1970s, inflation and low raises eroded teacher salaries. Teachers wanted to bring salaries back up. They argued that low salaries were not attracting new teachers and were resulting in the more experienced ones quitting for better jobs. Teacher groups at the local level were able to bargain for devoting additional funds to salary increases. At the same time, they generally were able to avoid the creation of merit-based salary increase systems. Teachers argued that such systems would promote unhealthy competition among teachers. Critics argued they were trying to avoid accountability.[46] Teachers were able to make sure that greater state funding led primarily to higher teacher salaries, not reduction in class sizes, and that there were no attached stipulations for accountability arrangements.[47] Whether this has improved student performance is difficult to tell. The expectations issue is relevant here. If salaries had not increased, performance might have declined because good teachers might have left the field. What is clear, however, is that resource usage was heavily influenced by the goals of local teacher groups, which saw the increased funding as an opportunity to raise salaries. State officials and the general public may have wanted to see more money go into lowering class size or some other objectives. Local organizations, however, shaped the way the resources were actually used.

This "mismatch" of goals is common when policies are pursued. Local organizations have their own goals and try very hard to shape the specifics of what practices must be pursued and how resources are used. Past efforts to provide greater federal and state aid to local police departments to combat crime have run into this problem. While policymakers wanted more money devoted to putting more police on patrol, or funding neighborhood police stations, many police departments used these funds to buy more equipment (patrol cars, radio systems, guns).[48] Police departments may care more about using funding for equipment, and they decide how funding is actually used. Results of implementation of policy by local organizations often differ from goals intended by those passing the legislation. Local organizations find ways to pursue their own goals despite attempts by policymakers to shape what they do.

This tension between state objectives and local preferences is ongoing in state-local relations. Much as the national government worries about the way states implement programs funded with national grants, states worry that local governments and organizations will deviate from the intent of state policymakers. As a consequence, states require reports from funded organizations and regularly audit their financial records to see if funds are used as intended. Even when deviations are found, however, the state may still have difficulty making local governments or organizations do what the state desires. Most of the time, local delivery does follow what states want, but there are enough exceptions to make achieving policy goals through these routes frustrating.

Unanticipated Consequences

Even when government creates very specific policies in an attempt to have a precise effect, there can be effects that no one anticipated that create further problems. These other problems may even lead to doubts about continuing the original policy. Governments have struggled for years over what to do about crime.[49] There is continual frustration that sentencing policies do not work to deter criminals. One proposal has been to announce tougher penalties for repeat offenders. Some states have imposed "3-strikes-and-you're-out" rules. Under this policy, commission of three felonies would result in lifetime imprisonment of the offender. Washington state implemented this policy, but soon found that created its own problems. Felons facing their third arrest proved to be particularly violent, since they faced life imprisonment. Those accused of crimes were less inclined to plea-bargain if it meant a felony conviction. Instead, they demanded time-consuming (and costly) trials. Finally, there are crimes that, although they fall into the felony category, are not seen as threatening to society. People who commit three of these felonies would also be sentenced, perhaps unfairly, to lifetime imprisonment.[50] As a result of these consequences, there is concern that this proposal will produce more problems than it might solve.

Others have proposed that we need specific and definite penalties attached to crimes so that there is greater certainty of punishment. Many states implemented a policy of determinant sentences, or fixed lengths of imprisonment for specific crimes, along with limits on parole. This policy apparently has worked, but with the consequence that states needed vastly greater prison capacities. States built many more prisons during the 1980s and early 1990s. Despite the new prisons, however, states found themselves with overcrowded prisons and numerous lawsuits about unhealthy prison conditions.[51] Determinant sentencing may or may not have had some impact on crime, but it has increased budgetary demands at a time when budgetary needs for education and infrastructure are already high.

There are many policy areas where such unintended consequences of program implementation occur. When such consequences do occur, there is often a tendency to conclude that the program does not work and a desire to abandon the original policy. The program itself may have the expected positive effect, but other consequences may be so undesirable that the original program is considered a failure.

Trying to Change People

Government ability to change social conditions is also limited by its lack of control over people. As discussed throughout this text, many of the major battles in politics revolve around conflicts between the haves and the have-nots. In response to these conflicts government has established programs to help minorities and the poor. Affirmative-action programs have been established that require employers to consider candidates of both sexes and all racial and ethnic backgrounds. Training programs have been established to help the poor make the transition into the job market. Nutrition programs have been established to educate young unwed mothers about the nutritional needs of their children.

There is considerable frustration that these programs do not achieve everything intended. A fundamental difficulty is that government programs cannot make people behave differently. Individual behaviors can thwart government objectives. Employers may have to be conscious of (keep track of and report) the race and sex of their applicants, but this awareness does not necessarily translate into hiring more minorities and women. Training programs may be made available, but people do not necessarily take the initiative to enroll in those programs.[52] Even if the unemployed do complete training programs, the job market may not provide jobs for newly trained people, or employers may discriminate against newly trained applicants on the basis of class, race, or sex. Young mothers do not necessarily enroll in subsidized nutrition classes, read brochures, have the money to eat better, or desire to change their nutrition habits or those of their children. Individual behaviors ultimately decide what happens to programs, and sometimes those behaviors result in programs that work, and sometimes in programs that do not.[53]

The fact that programs do not always change the situation of the lower class or minorities in ways expected generates significant debate about why this nonresult occurs. Conservatives argue that the problem is a "poverty of culture." They argue that the lower class, as a group, has attitudes and habits that make it unlikely that government programs will have any impact. Edward Banfield, a political scientist, generated enormous controversy in the early 1970s when he articulated the view that the lower class lacks the ability to engage in deferred gratification.[54] He argued that these programs have no effect because of the desire of the lower class for immediate gratification. That argument has been repeated by others over the years, who assert that the lower class are dependent on handouts and are not interested in doing much about it.[55] Some of these arguments about culture and attitudes as a source of problems are supported by evidence, while others are primarily simple assertions that this is the case. Regardless, such arguments appeal to many in American society because of our cultural emphasis on individualism and individual responsibility.

Liberals, of course, dispute the argument that lower class people lack motivation and discipline. They argue that most people do not stay on welfare for extended time periods. They do seek jobs, but are often very discouraged by rebuffs in the job market because of their limited skills. Liberals also argue that the funds provided for most programs have been inadequate to really help the poor escape poverty. Some of the failure of programs is not surprising.[56]

No single explanation of why programs do not achieve all their objectives is completely right. Some people do lack the motivation to escape poverty. But others work very hard to escape poverty, but encounter enormous difficulties. Regardless of the completeness of these arguments, however, they do illustrate why government programs often have limited impact. Job training programs may be provided, but some potential beneficiaries do not take advantage of them because of their attitudes. Others may take advantage of them, but still find employers reluctant to hire them. Other participants do escape unemployment and poverty. The variability of impact is often difficult to convey in political arguments, and reports on policies tend to simplify the data and report policy effects as either positive or without any effect.

Shifting Societal Conditions

Finally, programs are often frustrated because social conditions shift while the program is being pursued. At an individual level, job training efforts may not result in jobs for many graduates of these programs because the economy is declining as people leave programs. Unexpected economic changes may render programs ineffective.[57]

Efforts to shape business development at the state and local level also face problems of shifting economies. A state may spend considerable amounts of money to retain a company, but find that ultimately its efforts are thwarted by long-term shifts in markets and labor prices that put the assisted company out of business. Declines in the national economy may also undermine government assistance efforts.[58]

The Persistence of Efforts to Affect Social Conditions

Some programs work, and some do not. Some organizations and local governments are effective at achieving policy goals, and others are not. Some people respond, and others do not. These discrepancies between goals and desired effects are an enormous source of frustration. Critics regularly attack programs and argue that they must be made more effective or terminated. Supporters defend programs and characterize critics as uncaring.

The search for greater effectiveness is perpetual, but such effectiveness is difficult to achieve. We are never quite sure how to design programs to make them effective. There is also considerable resistance to giving government more power to achieve results. Local governments consistently seek more autonomy to adapt programs to their own sense of priorities and of proper ways of doing things. Liberals resist giving government more power to intrude upon the lives of the poor, even if it would make government efforts more effective. To return to the issues discussed in earlier chapters, there is great suspicion in American society about giving government more power. To many, it is better to have programs with limited effectiveness than to grant too much power to government bureaucrats. Autonomy of local governments and of individuals is highly valued in American society, even if it constrains the effectiveness of programs.

Given all the apparent limitations of government programs, why do so many efforts continue? Why do so many politicians fight so hard to increase funding of existing programs and to establish new ones? There are several important reasons.

Many people have strong beliefs that people are affected by their environment. They also believe that we have an obligation to try to affect the environment of people in order to ensure equality of opportunity in society. Many conservatives, of course, disagree. While that debate persists, liberals have continued their efforts to get more programs. They persist in their efforts not only because of their beliefs, but also because their political constituencies support their efforts. As long as there are politicians with electoral bases that support such efforts, the fight for such programs will continue.

There are also differences in assessments of the efficacy of programs. Critics argue that poverty has not gone away and that, therefore, programs do not work. As discussed earlier, they expect to see poverty levels decline significantly or disappear. Supporters, however, often see things very differently. They argue that without food stamps, day care, public housing, public welfare, job training, and counseling services, conditions for the poor would be much worse.

To return to the themes of V.O. Key, these programs represent the end point of the battles between the haves and the have-nots. In most states and communities, Democrats have been the primary supporters of these programs. Sometimes that support is weak because of the composition of electoral bases of the party. But over time, Democrats have argued for expansion of programs to help the have-nots. Republicans have been less enthusiastic, but they have also been uneasy about complete opposition because of concern about being seen as indifferent to equality-of-opportunity values in American society. Pressure from Democrats has led to expansion, and opposition from Republicans has led to constraint. Although there will continue to be ebbs and flows of support, it is likely that our society generally will continue to support such programs and to seek new ways to have an impact on social conditions. These programs are products of the political battles between the haves and the have-nots and will persist as long as there are parties with electoral bases who support these programs.

For Further Reading

Below are some analyses that deal with some policy areas of major concern. Each author brings a different perspective and set of biases, and the works are interesting for the information and for the perspective on what the problem is.

Brint, Steven, and Jerome Karabel. *The Diverted Dream: Community Colleges and the Promise of Educational Opportunity in America, 1900–1985*. New York: Oxford University Press, 1989.

Chubb, John E., and Terry M. Moe. *Politics, Markets, and America's Schools* Washington DC: Brookings Institute, 1990.

Lehman, Nicholas. "The Myth of Community Development." *New York Times* 9 January 1994.

Murray, Charles. *Losing Ground*. New York: Basic Books, 1984.

Piven, Frances Fox and Richard C. Cloward *Regulating the Poor: The Functions of Public Welfare*. New York: Vintage Books, 1971.

Starr, Paul. *The Social Transformation of American Medicine*. New York: Basic Books, 1982.

Suggestions for Analysis in Your Own State and Locality

1. What major programs exist in your area to try to affect poverty and economic development? How much funding is devoted to them, and which level of government is responsible for them? Have efforts in these areas increased or decreased in recent years? In particular, what has happened to funding for schools in your state?

2. Have there been any public reports about these programs, or any newspaper series about them? If so, try to get them in order to see what public perceptions of programs exist. What kinds of expectations do the reports assume?

3. Have economic conditions in your area that might affect the effectiveness of these programs changed? What has happened to the local population that might alter the efficacy of schools?

Notes

[1] For an example of this concern, see David Osborne, *Reinventing Government* (Reading, MA.: Addison-Wesley, 1992)

[2] For good reviews of policy practices in states and localities, see Jeffrey R. Henig, *Public Policy and Federalism: Issues in State and Local Politics* (New York: St. Martin's, 1985); Virginia Gray et al., *Politics in the American States*, 5th ed. (Glenview: Scott, Foresman/Little, Brown, 1990); and John J. Harrigan, *Politics and Policy in States and Communities*, 4th ed. (New York: HarperCollins, 1991).

[3] William Trattner, *From Poor Law to Welfare State* (New York: Free Press, 1974).

[4] Martha Derthick, "Intercity Differences in Administration of the Public Assistance Program: The Case of Massachusetts," in James Q. Wilson, *City Politics and Public Policy* (New York: J Wiley, 1968), 243–66; and Martha Derthick, *The Influence of Federal Grants* (Cambridge: Harvard University Press, 1970).

[5] Theda Skocpol, *The Politics of Social Policy in the United States*, (Princeton: Princeton University Press, 1988).

[6] Robert Albritton, "Social Services: Welfare and Health," in Virginia Gray, Herbert Jacob, and Robert Albritton, *Politics in the American States*, 5th ed. (Glenview: Scott, Foresman/Little, Brown, 1990), 423–70.

[7] Frances Fox Piven and Richard A. Cloward, *Regulating the Poor: The Functions of Public Welfare* (New York: Vintage, 1971).

[8] Charles Murray, *Losing Ground: American Social Policy, 1950–1980* (New York: Basic Books, 1984).

[9] Frederick Wirt and Sam Gove, "Education," in Virginia Gray, Herbert Jacob, and Robert Albritton, *Politics in the American States*, 5th ed. (Glenview: Scott, Foresman/Little, Brown, 1990), 448–54.

[10] Frederick M. Wirt, "Institutionalization: Prison and School Policies," in Virginia Gray, Herbert Jacob and Kenneth N. Vines, *Politics in the American States, A Comparative Analysis*, 4th ed. (Boston: Little, Brown, 1983), 303–328.

[11] Fox Butterfield, "In New Hampshire, Schools' Need Tests a Prized Feature: No Taxes," *New York Times* 2 January 1992, A1; and William Celis, III, "Furor in New Hampshire, on Vote to Cut Standards," *New York Times* 26 August 1992, B7.

[12] National Commission on Excellence in Education, *A Nation at Risk* (Washington, DC, 1983).

[13] Jeffrey M. Stonecash, "Politics and the Development of the SUNY System: The Persisting Issue of the Privates," (paper presented at the Department of Political Science, Maxwell School, Syracuse University, 1992).

[14] Steven Brint and Jerome Karabel, *The Diverted Dream: Community Colleges and the Promise of Educational Opportunity in America, 1900–1985* (New York: Oxford University Press, 1989).

[15] Brint and Karabel, *The Diverted Dream.*

[16] David R. Goldfield and Blaine A. Brownell, *Urban America: A History*, 2d ed. (Boston: Houghton Mifflin, 1990), 259–74; and Kenneth T. Jackson, *Crabgrass Frontier* (New York: Oxford University Press, 1985), 157–71.

[17] Robert S. Friedman, "The Politics of Transportation," in Virginia Gray, Herbert Jacob, and Robert Albritton, *Politics in the American States*, 5th ed. (Glenview: Scott, Foresman/Little, Brown, 1990), 537.

[18] For studies of this, see Michael N. Danielson, *Federal-Metropolitan Politics and the Commuter Crisis.* (New York: Columbia University Press, 1965); George M. Smerk, *Urban Mass Transportation,* (Bloomington: Indiana University Press, 1974); and Robert Caro, *The Power Broker* (New York: Vintage, 1975), 755–919.

[19] Erik Eckholm, "Double Sword for President," *New York Times* 23 August 1993, A1, A9.

[20] Michael Danielson, *The Politics of Exclusion* (New York: Columbia University Press, 1976).

[21] Frederick M. Wirt, "Institutionalization: Prison and School Policies."

[22] Advisory Commission on Intergovernmental Relations, *State Mandating of Local Expenditures* (Washington, DC, July 1978).

[23] Jeffrey M. Stonecash, "State Policies on Local Resource Acquisition," *American Politics Quarterly* 9, no. 4 (October 1981).

[24] Advisory Commission, *State Mandating*, 44–45.

[25] Thomas A. Kochan, "A Theory of Multilateral Collective Bargaining in City Governments," *Industrial and Labor Relations Review* 27, no. 4 (1974): 525–542; and Jeffrey S. Zax and Casey Ichniowski, "Bargaining Laws and Unionization in the Local Public Sector," *Industrial and Labor Relations Review* 43, no. 4 (April 1990): 447–462.

[26] Thomas A. Kochian and Hoyt N. Wheeler, "Municipal Collective Bargaining: A Model and Analysis of Bargaining Outcomes," *Industrial and Labor Relations Review* 29, no. 1 (1975): 46–66; and Richard B. Freeman and Robert G. Valetta, "The Effects of Public Sector Labor Laws on Labor Market Institutions and Outcomes," in Richard B. Freeman and Casey Ichniowski, *When Public Sector Workers Unionize* (Chicago: University of Chicago Press, 1988), 81–103.

[27] Paul Starr, *The Social Transformation of American Medicine* (New York: Basic Books, 1982).

[28] For a thorough study of the initial choices made by states, see Robert Stevens and Rosemary Stevens, *Welfare Medicine in America: A Case Study of Medicaid* (New York: Free Press, 1974).

[29] For a comprehensive review of these efforts, see Peter Eisenger, *The Rise of the Entrepreneurial State* (Madison: University of Wisconsin Press, 1988).

[30] Michael Wasylenko, "Empirical Evidence on Interregional Business Location Decisions and the Role of Fiscal Incentives in Economic Development," in Henry W. Herzog Jr. and Alan M. Schlottmann, *Industry Location and Public Policy* (Knoxville: University of Tennessee Press, 1991), 13–30.

[31] Peter Eisinger, "State Economic Development in the 1990s: Politics and Policy Learning," (paper presented at the Conference on New Perspectives on State Government, Policy, and Economic Development, Chicago, Illinois, May, 1993).

[32] David Lowery and Virginia Gray, "Holding Back the Tide of Bad Economic Times: The Compensatory Impact of State Industrial Policy," *Social Science Quarterly* 73, no. 3 (September 1992): 483–495.

[33] Edward G. Goetz, "Type II Policy and Mandated Benefits in Economic Development," *Urban Affairs Quarterly* 26, no. 2 (December 1990): 170–90.

[34] Leonore J. Weitzman, *The Divorce Revolution: The Unexpected Social and Economic Consequences for Women and Children in America* (New York: Free Press, 1985).

[35] William T. Gormley, Jr., *The Politics of Public Utility Regulation* (Pittsburgh: University of Pittsburgh Press, 1983).

[36] John E. Schwarz, *America's Hidden Success*, rev. ed. (New York: W. W. Norton, 1988).

[37] Robert Pear, "Poverty in U.S. Grew Faster Than Population Last Year," *New York Times* 5 October 1993, A20.

[38] Theodore R. Marmor, Jerry Mashaw, and Philip L. Harvey, *America's Misunderstood Welfare State* (New York: Basic Books, 1990), 82–127.

[39] Gordon Lafer, "Minority Unemployment, Labor Market Segmentation and the Failure of Job Training Policy in New York City," *Urban Affairs Quarterly* 28, no. 2 (December 1992): 206–235.

[40] Charles Murray, *Losing Ground: American Social Policy, 1950–1980.* (New York: Basic Books, 1984).

[41] William Celis, III, "10 Years After a Scathing Report, Schools Show Uneven Progress," *New York Times* 26 April 1993, A19.

[42] Dennis R. Judd, *The Politics of American Cities*, 3d ed. (Glenview: Scott, Foresman/Little, Brown, 1985), 371–97.

[43] Richard C. Feiock, "The Effects of Economic Development Policy on Local Economic Growth," *American Journal of Political Science* 35, no. 3 (August 1991): 643–55.

[44] National Commission on Excellence in Education, *A Nation at Risk.*

[45] Edward B. Fiske, "Pressure Mounts for Standards," *New York Times* 20 January 1984, C1.

[46] William E. Schmidt, "Teachers Up in Arms Over Arkansas Skills Test," *New York Times* 17 January 1984, A16.

[47] The Public Policy Institute of New York State, *The $11 Billion Mystery* (Albany: Public Policy Institute of New York State, 1992).

[48] Herbert Jacob, *The Frustration of Policy: Responses to Crime in American Cities* (Boston: Little, Brown, 1984), 83–118.

[49] Lawrence M. Friedman, *Crime and Punishment in American History* (New York: Basic Books, 1993).

[50] Timothy Eagan, "A 3-Strike Penal Law Shows It's Not as Simple as It Seems," *New York Times* 15 February 1994.

[51] Wesley G. Skogan, "Crime and Punishment," in Virginia Gray, Herbert Jacob, and Robert Albritton, *Politics in the American States*, 5th Edition (Glenview: Scott, Foresman/Little, Brown, 1990), 387–406.

[52] Peter T. Kilborn, "U.S. Study Says Job Training is Not Effective," *New York Times* 15 October 1993, A1.

[53] Sheldon H. Danziger and Daniel H. Weinberg, *Fighting Poverty: What Works and What Doesn't* (Cambridge: Harvard University Press, 1986).

[54] Edward Banfield, *The Unheavenly City* (Boston: Little, Brown, 1970).

[55] Charles Murray, *Losing Ground* (New York: Basic Books, 1984).

[56] David T. Ellwood, *Poor Support: Poverty in the American Family* (New York: Basic Books, 1988).

[57] Schawrz, *America's Hidden Successes.*

[58] Paul Brace, "Isolating the Economies of States," *American Politics Quarterly* 17, no. 3 (July 1989): 256–276; and Paul Brace, *State Government and Economic Performance* (Baltimore: Johns Hopkins University Press, 1993).

Appendix A

Electoral Allegiances and Party Composition

The next pages present information on party allegiances in each state. The information is based on CBS/*New York Times* surveys conducted during the 1970s and 1980s in the United States. The results from those national surveys were combined by Gerald Wright at the University of Indiana. Robert Brown, a graduate student at Indiana, now teaching at the University of Mississippi, updated them in the late 1980s.

Participants in the surveys were asked three questions that are drawn on for these tables. They were asked if their income was low, high, or moderate. They were also asked if they regarded themselves as liberal, moderate, or conservative. Finally, they were asked if their party identification was Republican, Independent, or Democrat.

The table that follows presents that information in two ways. The left half of the table presents, for each state, the electoral allegiances of those with different incomes and ideological identifications. It suggests which party people choose as their personal situations change. The percents sum down to 100 for each income or ideological group, indicating the distribution of those with low, medium, and high incomes and of those having liberal, moderate, conservative beliefs. The first column, for example, presents the percent of those who are low income who are Republicans, Independents, or Democrats. The next two columns present the distribution of party choices for those who are of moderate income and of high income. The next three columns present the distribution of party choices for those who have liberal, moderate, and conservative beliefs.

This first set of tables is of value to indicate whether people who differ in income or ideological belief differ in their party allegiances. Each state differs in the extent to which those of different income levels and ideological beliefs differ in party choice. To compare states, compare how much income affects the party allegiances in different states, or compare how much ideology affects which party individuals choose in different states.

The right half of the table then presents the information in another way. It presents the consequences of individual party allegiances for the composition of parties. It indicates for each party what percent of the party has low, moderate, and high incomes and what percent of the party is liberal, moderate, and conservative. In this case, the percents sum across to 100. Again, to compare states, compare how parties in different states differ in the proportions of their party who are liberals, moderates, or conservative, or who have low, moderate, or high incomes.

| | Electoral Choices (Percents sum down to 100) | | | | | | Party Composition (Percents sum across to 100) | | | | | |
| | Income | | | Ideology | | | Income | | | Ideology | | |
	Low	Medium	High	Lib.	Mod.	Conserv.	Low	Medium	High	Lib.	Mod.	Conserv.
Alabama												
Republican	17.2	22.1	34.7	21.4	20.8	27.7	14.0	58.6	27.5	15.6	36.8	47.6
Independent	23.7	34.5	32.7	28.1	32.3	37.3	14.1	66.9	19.0	14.5	40.3	45.2
Democrat	59.1	43.4	32.7	50.6	46.9	35.1	25.4	60.9	13.7	20.6	46.0	33.5
Arizona												
Republican	28.8	32.4	44.3	19.4	30.6	50.6	11.2	55.9	32.9	10.3	37.1	52.6
Independent	25.9	30.9	28.9	34.0	31.6	25.7	11.9	62.7	25.4	21.7	46.1	32.2
Democrat	45.3	36.7	26.8	46.6	37.9	23.7	17.5	62.7	19.8	26.0	48.2	25.8
Arkansas												
Republican	20.0	19.9	22.9	15.3	18.1	27.1	21.0	60.5	18.5	13.8	38.4	47.9
Independent	25.2	34.3	36.8	37.8	32.6	29.7	16.4	65.1	18.5	21.9	44.4	33.7
Democrat	54.7	45.9	40.1	46.9	49.4	43.1	24.9	61.0	14.1	18.9	47.0	34.1
California												
Republican	22.9	32.0	40.3	14.7	31.6	51.9	8.00	56.7	35.2	11.0	40.5	48.4
Independent	27.8	28.0	25.5	30.0	28.1	22.7	12.0	60.7	27.3	28.2	45.3	26.6
Democrat	49.3	40.0	34.2	55.3	40.3	25.4	14.7	60.0	25.3	35.5	44.3	20.3
Colorado												
Republican	29.1	31.7	36.4	18.5	29.3	50.3	9.90	61.1	29.1	12.7	40.7	46.6
Independent	35.0	39.7	37.9	41.3	41.2	31.3	10.0	64.6	25.5	24.7	50.0	25.3
Democrat	36.0	28.7	25.7	40.2	29.5	18.4	13.8	62.9	23.3	32.2	47.9	19.9
Connecticut												
Republican	19.1	23.1	29.1	13.2	21.6	40.0	8.60	54.1	37.3	13.4	39.6	46.9
Independent	40.2	43.2	44.1	41.8	45.9	39.5	10.3	57.6	32.1	24.5	48.6	26.8
Democrat	40.6	33.7	26.9	44.9	32.5	20.5	13.9	60.0	26.2	35.3	46.1	18.6
Delaware												
Republican	17.8	28.4	37.1	11.4	28.7	36.8	8.50	58.5	33.1	8.20	50.0	41.8
Independent	40.3	39.6	42.2	44.3	43.8	36.8	13.9	58.9	27.2	21.2	50.9	27.9
Democrat	41.9	32.1	20.7	44.3	27.6	26.4	19.1	63.2	17.7	28.9	43.8	27.3

continued

| | Electoral Choices (Percents sum down to 100) | | | | | | Party Composition (Percents sum across to 100) | | | | | |
| | Income | | | Ideology | | | Income | | | Ideology | | |
	Low	Medium	High	Lib.	Mod.	Conserv.	Low	Medium	High	Lib.	Mod.	Conserv.
Florida												
Republican	25.1	31.6	41.1	22.3	29.1	44.4	10.2	60.5	29.4	13.3	37.5	49.2
Independent	23.9	28.7	27.6	28.9	30.3	24.4	11.5	65.2	23.3	20.7	46.9	32.5
Democrat	51.1	39.7	31.3	48.8	40.7	31.2	17.5	63.8	18.7	25.0	45.2	29.8
Georgia												
Republican	14.8	20.7	26.8	15.5	19.8	28.7	10.7	60.0	29.3	13.4	39.9	46.7
Independent	21.6	31.5	35.4	28.2	31.9	33.4	10.7	62.7	26.6	17.1	44.9	38.0
Democrat	63.5	47.8	37.8	56.3	48.3	37.9	20.4	61.4	18.3	23.4	46.9	29.7
Idaho												
Republican	27.3	38.2	43.1	24.2	29.5	49.3	12.9	64.2	22.9	9.60	33.9	56.5
Independent	47.7	37.8	34.0	45.3	42.2	32.1	21.6	61.0	17.4	17.4	47.0	35.6
Democrat	25.0	24.0	22.9	30.5	28.4	18.6	18.4	62.6	19.0	18.4	49.4	32.3
Illinois												
Republican	26.1	27.4	33.2	15.0	26.4	42.5	10.7	58.9	30.4	11.7	41.1	47.2
Independent	27.8	36.9	39.1	39.7	37.9	31.0	9.00	62.8	28.2	24.9	47.4	27.7
Democrat	46.2	35.7	27.7	45.3	35.7	26.5	15.7	63.4	20.9	29.3	46.2	24.5
Indiana												
Republican	29.6	32.3	38.0	22.8	29.8	43.8	12.8	64.9	22.3	13.1	39.9	47.0
Independent	31.8	36.6	36.3	37.1	37.4	33.3	12.6	67.8	19.6	20.0	46.6	33.4
Democrat	38.6	31.1	25.7	40.1	32.8	22.9	17.7	66.3	16.0	25.3	47.9	26.9
Iowa												
Republican	30.9	31.9	35.3	20.6	31.4	43.2	15.3	62.8	21.9	12.2	45.1	42.7
Independent	35.1	39.5	35.6	37.6	37.8	38.6	14.8	66.3	18.9	19.5	47.3	33.3
Democrat	34.0	28.7	29.1	41.8	30.9	18.1	18.4	61.8	19.8	28.5	50.9	20.6
Kansas												
Republican	37.9	38.6	38.3	25.6	36.6	49.2	13.5	65.0	21.5	13.7	40.3	46.1
Independent	26.8	33.0	35.2	36.0	32.3	30.4	11.2	65.5	23.2	23.0	42.8	43.2
Democrat	35.4	28.4	26.5	38.4	31.1	20.3	16.7	63.5	19.8	27.8	46.5	25.8

Kentucky												
Republican	27.7	23.4	31.8	19.4	22.5	32.9	19.4	58.8	21.8	15.8	40.9	43.3
Independent	25.2	25.6	20.5	25.6	23.5	26.8	18.4	67.0	14.6	21.1	43.2	35.7
Democrat	47.1	51.0	47.7	55.0	54.0	40.3	17.0	66.1	16.9	22.9	50.1	27.1
Louisiana												
Republican	12.3	18.2	31.6	16.7	16.1	26.5	10.5	54.4	35.1	14.0	34.0	52.0
Independent	18.8	25.1	27.5	26.8	27.0	23.0	13.1	61.7	25.1	18.0	45.7	36.2
Democrat	68.8	56.8	40.9	56.5	56.9	50.5	21.4	62.1	16.6	17.7	45.1	37.2
Maine												
Republican	23.8	26.7	33.0	17.4	28.5	34.8	16.7	66.7	16.7	13.0	42.7	44.3
Independent	41.5	43.1	48.1	50.0	42.7	39.3	18.1	66.9	15.1	24.7	42.3	33.0
Democrat	34.7	30.2	18.9	32.6	28.8	25.8	22.3	69.1	8.70	24.4	43.0	32.6
Maryland												
Republican	21.2	23.4	27.5	13.0	24.6	31.7	8.60	57.3	34.2	13.6	46.3	40.1
Independent	22.9	29.9	30.1	31.2	28.6	29.5	7.70	61.1	31.2	26.4	43.4	30.1
Democrat	55.9	46.7	42.5	55.9	46.8	38.8	11.9	60.3	27.8	29.9	45.0	25.1
Massachusetts												
Republican	13.0	14.9	19.9	9.50	14.4	25.0	9.60	57.9	32.5	16.1	40.3	43.6
Independent	43.6	51.1	49.7	49.4	51.8	48.0	10.4	63.5	26.1	26.9	46.3	26.8
Democrat	43.4	34.0	30.5	41.1	33.8	27.0	15.0	61.6	23.4	33.1	44.6	22.3
Michigan												
Republican	25.0	29.2	34.4	17.3	27.2	42.5	11.9	60.0	28.1	13.3	41.6	45.1
Independent	32.7	39.2	39.0	38.5	40.5	35.9	12.2	62.9	24.9	22.8	47.8	29.4
Democrat	42.3	31.7	26.7	44.2	32.3	21.6	18.8	60.8	20.4	31.9	46.6	21.6
Minnesota												
Republican	23.0	26.7	32.5	13.5	23.0	41.2	12.7	59.7	27.6	10.1	39.8	50.1
Independent	30.9	36.4	36.6	35.9	36.8	34.3	13.3	62.7	24.1	20.4	48.1	31.4
Democrat	46.1	36.9	30.9	50.7	40.2	24.5	19.1	61.4	19.6	27.8	50.5	21.7
Mississippi												
Republican	14.7	28.5	38.2	17.0	26.0	31.4	11.4	65.5	23.1	10.2	41.6	48.3
Independent	20.7	31.1	32.2	31.4	28.0	31.2	15.0	66.8	18.2	16.8	40.2	43.0
Democrat	64.7	40.3	29.6	51.6	45.9	37.4	31.2	57.6	11.1	19.1	45.4	35.6

continued

| | Electoral Choices (Percents sum down to 100) | | | | | | Party Composition (Percents sum across to 100) | | | | | |
| | Income | | | Ideology | | | Income | | | Ideology | | |
	Low	Medium	High	Lib.	Mod.	Conserv.	Low	Medium	High	Lib.	Mod.	Conserv.
Missouri												
Republican	25.5	26.0	32.0	15.3	22.6	38.2	17.0	62.0	21.0	10.9	39.8	49.3
Independent	33.6	39.5	39.8	42.0	41.2	35.2	15.8	66.0	18.2	20.3	49.0	30.8
Democrat	40.9	34.5	28.2	42.7	36.2	26.6	21.3	64.3	14.4	23.7	49.5	26.8
Montana												
Republican	20.0	29.4	29.8	13.7	24.8	41.4	10.7	71.0	18.3	11.4	38.3	50.3
Independent	40.0	37.5	49.0	48.4	40.0	37.6	15.0	63.8	21.3	27.3	41.8	30.9
Democrat	40.0	33.1	21.2	37.9	35.2	21.0	18.7	70.0	11.4	28.3	48.8	22.9
Nebraska												
Republican	34.9	39.7	45.4	24.9	34.4	52.4	13.1	63.2	23.7	11.8	38.7	49.5
Independent	29.6	30.0	25.2	30.7	33.1	24.6	15.5	66.3	18.2	19.3	49.7	31.0
Democrat	35.5	30.3	29.4	44.4	32.5	22.9	17.3	62.8	19.9	26.5	46.2	27.3
Nevada												
Republican	20.7	31.9	37.1	24.0	29.0	43.4	7.70	62.8	29.5	22.4	38.1	39.6
Independent	24.1	33.2	29.0	30.4	33.5	30.3	9.20	67.1	23.7	28.4	44.0	27.6
Democrat	55.2	34.9	33.9	45.6	37.5	26.2	17.7	59.1	23.2	36.8	42.6	20.7
New Hampshire												
Republican	27.7	30.8	38.6	16.8	29.5	43.4	12.7	62.3	25.0	11.4	41.4	47.1
Independent	42.9	48.1	42.4	51.8	47.1	43.4	13.6	67.3	19.0	23.7	44.6	31.7
Democrat	29.5	21.1	19.0	31.5	23.4	13.1	19.8	62.3	18.0	31.3	47.9	20.8
New Jersey												
Republican	24.9	26.6	30.9	17.2	26.2	38.8	8.20	58.7	33.1	16.6	41.3	42.1
Independent	32.6	39.8	42.0	39.6	41.8	37.4	7.50	61.2	31.3	26.3	45.6	28.0
Democrat	42.5	33.7	27.2	43.2	32.0	23.8	12.0	63.3	24.8	35.2	42.9	22.0
New Mexico												
Republican	22.3	24.5	35.7	16.7	23.2	39.9	12.0	59.1	28.9	12.4	36.6	51.0
Independent	33.1	31.6	30.2	35.3	30.4	29.5	15.0	64.4	20.6	23.5	42.9	33.6
Democrat	44.6	43.9	34.1	48.0	46.4	30.6	15.2	67.3	17.5	24.1	49.5	26.4

New York												
Republican	30.5	28.9	31.8	17.1	29.0	41.8	12.8	60.9	26.3	15.8	41.7	42.5
Independent	26.8	32.6	35.1	34.0	32.9	31.9	10.3	63.0	26.7	28.3	42.5	29.2
Democrat	42.7	39.5	33.1	48.9	38.1	26.3	14.2	64.2	21.7	35.6	43.2	21.2
North Carolina												
Republican	24.0	27.3	33.2	19.6	25.6	35.0	14.4	64.2	21.4	12.0	41.2	46.8
Independent	22.3	27.3	22.7	27.0	26.5	25.7	14.5	69.7	15.9	17.6	45.6	36.8
Democrat	53.7	45.3	44.2	53.4	47.9	39.3	19.2	63.7	17.1	20.1	47.5	32.4
North Dakota												
Republican	38.6	35.1	38.0	16.1	34.7	42.6	12.3	66.5	21.2	6.00	44.4	49.7
Independent	35.1	35.7	40.0	41.1	38.9	33.0	11.1	66.9	22.1	14.7	48.1	37.2
Democrat	26.3	29.2	22.0	42.9	26.4	24.4	11.0	72.8	16.2	20.3	43.2	36.4
Ohio												
Republican	26.6	29.6	38.2	18.3	29.4	43.6	11.9	60.1	28.1	13.1	42.3	44.6
Independent	30.0	34.7	32.6	35.6	34.0	31.5	12.3	65.5	22.2	23.9	45.9	30.2
Democrat	43.6	35.8	29.2	46.0	36.6	24.9	17.1	64.0	18.9	29.6	47.4	23.0
Oklahoma												
Republican	18.9	30.1	39.2	19.2	24.5	41.2	10.6	62.0	27.4	9.21	34.7	56.1
Independent	19.2	19.1	19.5	20.3	19.4	18.9	16.9	61.8	21.3	15.4	43.7	40.9
Democrat	61.9	50.8	41.3	60.5	56.0	39.9	20.7	62.2	17.1	17.8	48.8	33.4
Oregon												
Republican	27.0	31.1	35.3	18.5	26.5	47.2	15.5	63.2	21.3	14.7	36.0	49.3
Independent	25.9	31.9	28.9	33.0	33.3	25.3	15.4	66.7	17.9	26.9	46.1	27.0
Democrat	47.2	37.0	35.8	48.5	40.3	27.5	21.9	60.7	17.4	31.6	44.8	23.6
Pennsylvania												
Republican	31.7	34.2	39.4	21.3	33.3	46.6	13.9	64.4	21.7	13.6	42.5	43.8
Independent	23.8	27.3	27.2	30.1	27.3	25.0	13.6	66.9	19.5	24.9	44.8	30.4
Democrat	44.5	38.5	33.4	48.6	39.4	28.4	17.6	65.7	16.7	28.8	46.5	24.7
Rhode Island												
Republican	13.4	16.4	14.4	7.80	15.1	24.7	11.5	70.8	17.7	13.1	42.9	44.1
Independent	54.9	54.7	62.7	59.9	58.8	51.3	13.0	65.6	21.4	28.2	46.4	25.5
Democrat	31.7	28.9	22.9	32.4	26.1	24.0	15.0	69.4	15.6	31.9	43.1	25.0

continued

Electoral Choices (Percents sum down to 100) / Party Composition (Percents sum across to 100)

| | Electoral Choices (Percents sum down to 100) | | | | | | Party Composition (Percents sum across to 100) | | | | | |
| | Income | | | Ideology | | | Income | | | Ideology | | |
	Low	Medium	High	Lib.	Mod.	Conserv.	Low	Medium	High	Lib.	Mod.	Conserv.
South Carolina												
Republican	15.4	27.6	26.6	19.1	24.6	35.5	9.00	62.9	28.1	12.5	36.4	51.1
Independent	28.1	33.0	37.6	32.8	34.6	33.7	13.6	62.4	24.0	17.8	42.2	40.0
Democrat	56.5	39.4	25.8	48.1	40.8	30.8	23.1	63.0	13.9	23.2	44.3	32.5
South Dakota												
Republican	41.7	38.1	36.1	30.3	33.7	48.7	20.9	66.4	12.6	11.3	40.6	48.1
Independent	14.4	22.0	27.8	24.7	21.2	22.5	13.1	69.3	17.7	16.2	44.9	39.0
Democrat	43.9	40.0	36.1	44.9	45.1	28.8	21.1	66.8	12.1	16.8	54.6	28.6
Tennessee												
Republican	23.0	26.5	32.4	19.1	24.5	33.6	15.3	61.7	23.0	14.2	39.8	46.0
Independent	27.9	34.7	37.6	37.4	32.0	37.3	14.5	64.6	20.9	21.2	39.8	39.0
Democrat	49.1	39.3	29.9	43.6	43.5	29.1	22.2	63.4	14.4	22.7	49.5	27.9
Texas												
Republican	15.9	24.6	34.8	16.1	22.1	35.6	7.50	57.1	35.4	10.5	35.3	54.1
Independent	30.7	34.3	35.9	35.1	35.8	34.0	11.1	61.0	27.9	17.4	43.3	39.3
Democrat	53.4	41.0	29.3	48.9	42.1	30.4	16.8	63.3	19.9	22.0	46.2	31.8
Utah												
Republican	31.3	42.7	47.3	22.1	35.2	55.7	10.0	66.0	24.0	8.20	33.7	58.2
Independent	38.9	33.2	30.4	37.4	34.6	32.3	15.7	64.8	19.4	17.1	41.1	41.8
Democrat	29.8	24.1	22.2	40.5	30.2	12.1	16.5	64.1	19.4	26.4	51.2	22.4
Vermont												
Republican	23.3	30.6	27.4	11.8	32.3	38.5	18.8	68.0	13.3	9.60	45.2	45.2
Independent	45.6	47.5	53.2	57.0	46.6	40.7	21.9	62.8	15.4	29.0	41.0	30.1
Democrat	31.1	21.8	19.4	31.2	21.1	20.7	30.2	58.5	11.3	31.9	37.4	30.8
Virginia												
Republican	27.0	28.7	32.7	16.9	25.7	40.6	12.4	60.2	27.4	11.1	38.4	50.5
Independent	32.2	38.6	38.8	34.6	41.5	36.8	11.5	63.1	25.4	17.5	47.6	35.0
Democratic	40.9	32.7	28.5	48.5	32.8	22.6	16.9	61.6	21.5	19.3	44.9	25.8

Washington												
Republican	19.1	23.0	30.4	12.6	22.7	37.8	11.1	59.0	29.9	11.9	43.5	44.7
Independent	45.6	44.1	42.6	43.5	45.6	41.3	14.6	62.3	23.1	23.1	49.3	27.6
Democrat	35.3	32.8	27.1	43.9	31.7	20.9	15.7	64.0	20.3	32.6	47.9	19.5
West Virginia												
Republican	29.0	27.7	32.8	17.4	28.5	35.4	19.5	60.8	19.7	14.5	45.4	40.2
Independent	19.1	23.0	25.1	29.6	18.9	24.8	16.4	64.4	19.2	29.7	36.3	34.0
Democrat	52.0	49.3	42.1	53.0	52.6	39.8	20.8	64.3	15.0	25.5	48.4	26.1
Wisconsin												
Republican	24.0	26.0	33.2	14.0	24.3	40.2	13.4	62.2	24.4	11.7	40.6	47.7
Independent	34.9	38.9	40.2	41.0	41.1	35.7	13.8	65.4	20.8	23.5	47.3	29.2
Democratic	41.1	35.1	26.6	44.9	34.6	24.1	18.2	66.4	15.5	30.1	46.8	23.1
Wyoming												
Republican	26.2	36.7	31.3	18.8	33.6	43.4	9.60	73.0	17.4	12.4	37.8	50.0
Independent	38.1	32.8	42.2	39.1	31.8	39.8	13.6	63.6	22.9	23.8	33.3	48.9
Democratic	35.7	30.6	26.6	42.2	34.6	16.8	14.7	68.6	16.7	32.1	45.2	22.6

Appendix B

The Constitution and the States

Interpreting the Constitution

The Constitution is often turned to for guidance as to the relative powers of the national government compared to state governments. The Constitution, however, does not always provide clear answers. Remember that the document is the product of political compromises at the Constitutional Convention. It is full of ambiguities and contradictions. It contains some sections that could be taken as supporting a strong national government and other sections that could be taken as supporting the rights of states to be autonomous. As with any such document, people often cite the sections that support their own political position and interpretation.

The Constitution did not seek to provide definitive answers. As discussed in Chapter 2, it set up a political system that faced the task of addressing the question of relative powers as a regular part of the process. In defining that political system, the Constitution addresses some matters precisely, but leaves others ambiguous.

The Constitution is reprinted at the end of this commentary. What follows is a brief commentary on what the constitution has to say about national and state powers. The intent is not to review the entire constitution or to discuss subsequent interpretations of the document. There have been numerous court decisions affecting federalism and the position of the states. For reviews of subsequent cases and commentaries on the constitution, see Louis Fisher *American Constitutional Law*, (New York: McGraw-Hill, 1990), pp. 371–463 in particular; and, Otis H. Stephens, Jr., and John M. Scheb, II, *American Constitutional Law*, (Minneapolis: West Publishing Co, 1993), particularly pp. 385–462.

The review that follows is organized around specific topical questions. This review is not in the order topics appear in the constitution, but in a topical order that may help clarify some issues about the position of the states within federalism.

The States as Basic Representation Units

There is one issue that is very clear in the Constitution. The states and their sub-jurisdictions are the basic units of representation. National politicians must work within a system in which the focus of representation is built around states. Any changes in the Constitution must be approved by states. As noted in Chapter 2, this role of states as bases of representation is crucial for giving state populations a means to thwart or to influence the formation of national policy. These specifications emerge from several sections in the Constitution.

- Elections for members of Congress must take place within states or their sub-jurisdictions. Each state is guaranteed two Senators and at least one Representative. The representation units of Congress are the states. (Article I, Sections 2 and 3)
- The electoral college formally elects the President. This system is also built around the states. Each state gets a number of electors equal to the number of its Senators and Representatives. The vote of these electors is first taken in the state, which results in a winner-take-all system of awarding state electoral votes. This places a high premium on not just doing well, but on winning the state. This means that Presidential candidates must focus on state concerns in an attempt to win a majority in a state. This gives states (or more precisely, state populations) considerable power in the representation process of electing the President. (Article II, Section 1)
- States are the units that must ratify Constitutional Amendments. Changes require a positive vote of ¾ of the states. Note that this is *not* a requirement for ¾ of the public vote. (Article V)

The States as Protected, Unalterable Government Units

The Constitution also specifies that states cannot be altered without their permission. This guarantee appears in the following way:

- New states cannot be formed within the boundaries of existing states. No new state can be formed from the merger of two states or from parts of existing states without the consent of the legislatures of the states concerned. (Article IV, Section 3)

Ambiguities of State Powers

The Constitution is clear that the states are the basic units of representation and that their boundaries cannot be altered. When it comes to which level has what powers, however, the Constitution is not so clear. There is no specification in the document as to which level should do what. That is, there is no formal division of responsibilities provided as a guide. Some responsibilities are mentioned, and those specifications will be discussed here. But there is no overall blueprint for responsibilities. Indeed, there are some parts that are ambiguous. Again, the political process is the means of deciding many of these responsibility questions.

- The section that sounds most definitive in allocating power to the states is the 10th Amendment, which was ratified several years after the original Constitution was adopted. This Amendment specifies "All powers not delegated to the United States by the Constitution; not prohibited by it [the Constitution] to the States, are reserved to the States respectively, or to the people." This appears to reserve extensive powers to the states, but it also contains an ambiguous phrase, "or to the people." Since members of Congress represent the people, these Representatives, acting for the people, could make the national government responsible for some activity it had previously not been responsible for. This is a case of ambiguity in the document. (Amendment X)

Prohibitions of State Powers

While parts of the Constitution are ambiguous, there are parts of the Constitution that expressly prohibit the states from involvement in certain activities:

- The states are prohibited from establishing treaties with other countries. They cannot impose tariffs on goods from other countries or from other states. They cannot maintain troops and they cannot enter into wars. (Article I, Section 10)

Specific Grants of Power to the National Government

While prohibiting the states from doing certain things, the Constitution specifically grants the national government the power to operate in some areas. The following sections of the Constitution contain specific grants of authority to the national government:

- The states are allocated the responsibility for determining "The Times, Places and Manner for holding Elections for Senators and Representatives." But at the same time, the Constitution says "the Congress may at any time by Law make or alter such Regulations, except as to the Places of chusing Senators." In this case, an apparent allocation of power to the states also specifies that Congress has the right to intervene if it wishes to act on that potential. It is left to the political process in Congress to decide whether to act on that potential. (Article I, Section 4)

- The Constitution allocates specific powers to Congress. Section 8 of Article I allocates to Congress a broad array of responsibilities. Congress has the power, for example, to declare war, coin money, establish post offices and post roads, and to borrow money. (Article I, Section 8)

Broad Grants of Power to the National Government

The most intriguing aspect of the Constitution involves the broad grants of powers to the national government. These grants suggest the national government has the potential to take action in numerous areas as it deems necessary. What constitutes necessity, of course, is not specified. This is defined by the political process. This ambiguity is what has been very frustrating for many. Some people seek a precise definition and allocation of powers in the document. The broad grants of power to the national government are contained in several places in the Constitution. Each of these sections contains phrases that are subject to very different interpretations in the context of the overall document.

- Congress shall have power to "provide for the common Defence and general Welfare of the United States." The general welfare can be seen as a responsibility of broad scope, depending on one's political perspective. (Article I, Section 8)
- Congress shall have power "To regulate Commerce . . . among the several States." The issue of what is commerce can also differ considerably. (Article I, Section 8)
- Congress shall have the power "To make all Laws which shall be necessary and proper for carrying into Execution the foregoing Powers, and all other Powers vested by this Constitution in the Government of the United States." This again is a potentially broad grant of power. (Article I, Section 8)
- Finally, there is what is referred to as the Supremacy clause. "This Constitution, and the Laws of the United States which shall be made in Pursuance thereof . . . shall be the supreme Law of the Land." This also has the potential to grant the national government broad dominance. Notice again, however, that the political process must first produce these laws. There is the potential for national power, but it must be taken advantage of by politicians. (Article VI)

Implications of an Integrated Nation and Uniform Rights

Finally, there are suggestions in the Constitution that we are a unified nation. That suggests, but does not require, that state variations are unacceptable. Some provisions indicate that citizens' rights extend across states. Amendments suggest that citizens have rights across the United States, not just within specific states.

- The Constitution specifies that actions within one state must be honored in other states. It states "Full Faith and Credit shall be given in each State to the public Acts, Records, and judicial Proceedings of every other State." (Article IV, Section 1)
- There is also a reference to the idea that citizens have rights that extend across the states. The Constitution states "The Citizens of each State shall be entitled to all Privileges and Immunities of Citizens in the several States." (Article IV, Section 2)
- Finally, there have been numerous Amendments to the Constitution that suggest there are some minimal rights every citizen has. None of these Amendments make the possession of these rights contingent on place of residence. In fact, most were adopted as a result of disagreement with varying individual rights across the country. These Amendments clearly limit the powers of the states to create differing laws. The Amendments adopted, their concern, and the year they were adopted are as follows:
  - Amendment I–X (1791)   A national Bill of Rights
  - Amendment XIII (1865)   The abolition of slavery
  - Amendment XIV (1868)   A statement that everyone has the right to "the equal protection of the laws"
  - Amendment XV (1870)   The right to vote regardless "of race, color, or previous condition of servitude [slavery]"
  - Amendment XIX (1920)   The right to vote regardless of sex
  - Amendment XXIV (1964)   The abolition of the poll tax as requirement before voting
  - Amendment XXVI (1971)   The establishment of 18 as the age at which a citizen has the right to vote

Summary

The Constitution contains material that gives the states a clear and important role in the political process and in delivering policy. It also, however, contains language that allows the national government to play a very significant role. It gives national politicians the potential to impose national laws, but only if the political process produces support for taking such actions. As noted at the beginning, those who oppose and those who support a strong national government can find phrases in the Constitution to support their position.

The Constitution of the United States of America

We the People of the United States, in Order to form a more perfect Union, establish Justice, insure domestic Tranquility, provide for the common Defence, promote the general Welfare, and secure the Blessings of Liberty to ourselves and our Posterity, do ordain and establish this Constitution for the United States of America.

Article. I.

Section. 1.

All legislative Powers herein granted shall be vested in a Congress of the United States, which shall consist of a Senate and House of Representatives.

Section. 2.

The House of Representatives shall be composed of Members chosen every second Year by the People of the several States, and the Electors of the most numerous Branch of the State Legislature.

No Person shall be a Representative who shall not have attained to the Age of twenty five Years, and been seven Years a Citizen of the United States, and who shall not, when elected, be an Inhabitant of that State in which he shall be chosen.

Representatives and direct Taxes shall be apportioned among the several States which may be included within this Union, according to their respective Numbers, which shall be determined by adding to the whole Number of free Persons, including those bound to Service for a Term of Years, and excluding Indians not taxed, three fifths of all other Persons. The actual Enumeration shall be made within three Years after the first Meeting of the Congress of the United States, and within every subsequent Term of ten Years, in such Manner as they shall by Law direct. The Number of Representatives shall not exceed one for every thirty Thousand, but each State shall have at least one Representative; and until such enumeration shall be made, the State of New Hampshire shall be entitled to chuse three; Massachusetts eight; Rhode Island and Providence Plantations one; Connecticut five; New York six; New Jersey four; Pennsylvania eight; Delaware one; Maryland six; Virginia ten; North Carolina five; South Carolina five; and Georgia three.

When vacancies happen in the Representation from any State, the Executive Authority thereof shall issue Writs of Election to fill such Vacancies.

The House of Representatives shall chuse their Speaker and other Officers; and shall have the sole Power of Impeachment.

Section. 3.

The Senate of the United States shall be composed of two senators from each State, chosen by the Legislature thereof, for six Years; and each Senator shall have one Vote.

Immediately after they shall be assembled in Consequence of the first Election, they shall be divided as equally as may be into three Classes. The Seats of the

Senators of the first Class shall be vacated at the Expiration of the second Year, of the second class at the Expiration of the fourth Year, and of the third Class at the Expiration of the sixth Year, so that one third may be chosen every second Year; and if Vacancies happen by Resignation, or otherwise, during the Recess of the Legislature of any State, the Executive thereof may make temporary Appointments until the next Meeting of the Legislature, which shall then fill such Vacancies.

No Person shall be a Senator who shall not have attained to the Age of thirty Years, and been nine Years a Citizen of the United States, and who shall not, when elected, be an Inhabitant of that State for which he shall be chosen.

The Vice President of the United States shall be President of the Senate, but shall have no Vote, unless they be equally divided.

The Senate shall chuse their other Officers, and also a President pro tempore, in the Absence of the Vice President, or when he shall exercise the Office of President of the United States.

The Senate shall have the sole Power to try all Impeachments. When sitting for that Purpose, they shall be on Oath or Affirmation. When the President of the United States is tried, the Chief Justice shall preside: And no Person shall be convicted without the Concurrence of two thirds of the Members present.

Judgment in Cases of Impeachment shall not extend further than to removal from Office, and disqualification to hold and enjoy any Office of honor, Trust of Profit under the United States: but the Party convicted shall nevertheless be liable and subject to Indictment, Trial, Judgment and Punishment, according to law.

Section. 4.

The Times, Places and Manner of holding Elections for Senators and Representatives, shall be prescribed in each State by the Legislature thereof, but the Congress may at any time by Law make or alter such Regulation, except as to the Places of chusing Senators.

The Congress shall assemble at least once in every Year, and such Meeting shall be on the first Monday in December, unless they shall by Law appoint a different Day.

Section. 5.

Each House shall be the Judge of the Election, Returns and Qualifications of its own Members, and a Majority of each shall constitute a Quorum to do Business; but a smaller Number may adjourn from day to day, and may be authorized to compel the Attendance of absent members, in such manner, and under such Penalties as each House may provide.

Each House may determine the Rules of its Proceedings, punish its Members for disorderly Behaviour, and with the Concurrence of two thirds, expel a Member.

Each House shall keep a Journal of its Proceedings, and from time to time publish the same, excepting such Parts as may in their Judgment require Secrecy; and the Yeas and Nays of the Members of either House on any question shall, at the Desire of one fifth of those Present, be entered on the Journal.

Neither House, during the Session of Congress, shall, without the Consent of the other, adjourn for more than three days, nor to any other Place than that in which the two Houses shall be sitting.

Section. 6.

The Senators and Representatives shall receive a Compensation for their Services, to be ascertained by Law, and paid out of the Treasury of the United States. They shall in all Cases, except Treason, Felony and Breach of the Peace, be privileged from Arrest during their Attendance at the Session of their respective Houses, and in going to and returning from the same; and for any Speech or Debate in either House, they shall not be questioned in any other Place.

No Senator or Representative shall, during the Time for which he was elected, be appointed to any civil Office under the Authority of the United States, which shall have been created, or the Emoluments whereof shall have been increased during such time; and no Person holding any Office under the United States, shall be a Member of either House during his Continuance in Office.

Section. 7.

All Bills for raising Revenue shall originate in the House of Representatives; but the Senate may propose or concur with Amendments as on other bills.

Every Bill which shall have passed the House of Representatives and the Senate shall, before it become a Law, be presented to the President of the United States; if he approve he shall sign it, but if not he shall return it, with his Objections to that House in which it shall have originated, who shall enter the Objections at large on their Journal, and proceed to reconsider it. If after such Reconsideration two thirds of that House shall agree to pass the Bill, it shall be sent, together with the Objections, to the other House, by which it shall likewise be reconsidered, and if approved by two thirds of that House, it shall become a Law. But in all such Cases the Votes of both Houses shall be determined by yeas and Nays, and the Names of the Persons voting for and against the Bill shall be entered on the Journal of each House respectively. If any Bill shall not be returned by the President within ten Days (Sundays excepted) after it shall have been presented to him, the Same shall be a Law, in Manner as if he had signed it, unless the Congress by their Adjournment prevent its Return, in which Case it shall not be a Law.

Every Order, Resolution, or Vote to which the Concurrence of the Senate and House of Representatives may be necessary (except on a question of Adjournment) shall be presented to the President of the United States; and before the Same shall take Effect, shall be approved by him, or being disapproved by him shall be repassed by two thirds of the Senate and House of Representatives, according to the rules and Limitations prescribed in the Case of a Bill.

Section. 8.

The Congress shall have Power to lay and collect Taxes, Duties, Imposts and Excises, to pay the Debts and provide for the common Defence and general Welfare of the United States; but all Duties, Imposts and Excises shall be uniform and throughout the United States.

To borrow Money on the credit of the United States;

To regulate Commerce with foreign Nations, and among the several States, and with the Indian Tribes;

To establish an uniform Rule of Naturalization, and uniform Laws on the subject of Bankruptcies throughout the United States;

To coin Money, regulate the Value thereof, and of foreign Coin, and fix the Standard of Weights and Measures;

To provide for the Punishment of counterfeiting the Securities and current Coin of the United States;

To establish Post Offices and Post Roads;

To promote the Progress of Science and useful Arts, by securing for limited Times to Authors and Inventors the exclusive Right to their respective Writings and Discoveries;

To constitute Tribunals inferior to the supreme Court;

To define and punish Piracies and Felonies committed on the high Seas, and Offences against the Law of Nations;

To declare War, grant Letters of Marque and Reprisal, and make Rules concerning Captures on Land and Water;

To raise and support Armies, but no Appropriation of Money to that Use shall be for a longer Term than two Years;

To provide and maintain a Navy;

To make Rules for the government and Regulation of the land and naval Forces;

To provide for calling forth the Militia to execute the Laws of the Union, suppress Insurrections and repel Invasions;

To provide for organizing, arming, and disciplining, the Militia, and for governing such Part of them as may be employed in the Service of the United States, reserving to the States respectively, the Appointment of the Officers, and the Authority of training the Militia according to the discipline prescribed by Congress;

To exercise exclusive Legislation in all Cases whatsoever, over such District (not exceeding ten Miles square) as may, by Cession of particular States, and the Acceptance of Congress, become the Seat of the Government of the United States, and to exercise like Authority over all Places purchased by the consent of the Legislature of the State in which the Same shall be, for the Erection of Forts, Magazines, Arsenals, dock-Yards, and other needful Buildings;—And

To make all Laws which shall be necessary and proper for carrying into Execution the foregoing Powers, and all other Powers vested by this Constitution in the Government of the United States, or in any Department or Officer thereof.

Section. 9.

The Migration or Importation of such Persons as any of the States now existing shall think proper to admit, shall not be prohibited by the Congress prior to the Year one thousand eight hundred and eight, but a Tax or Duty may be imposed on such Importation, not exceeding ten dollars for each Person.

The Privilege of the Writ of Habeas Corpus shall not be suspended, unless when in Cases of Rebellion or Invasion the public Safety may require it.

No Bill of Attainder or ex post fact Law shall be passed.

No Capitation, or other direct, Tax shall be laid, unless in Proportion to the Census or Enumeration herein before directed to be taken.

No Tax or Duty shall be laid on Articles exported from any State.

No Preference shall be given by any Regulation of commerce or Revenue to the Ports of one State over those of another: nor shall Vessels bound to, or from, one State, be obliged to enter, clear, or pay Duties in another.

No Money shall be drawn from the Treasury, but in Consequence of Appropriations made by Law, and a regular Statement and Account of the receipts and Expenditures of all public Money shall be published from time to time.

No Title of Nobility shall be granted by the United States: And no Person holding any Office or Profit or Trust under them, shall, without the Consent of the Congress, accept of any present, Emolument, Office, or Title, of any kind whatever, from any King, Prince, or foreign State.

Section. 10.

No State shall enter into any Treaty, Alliance, or Confederation; grant Letters of Marque and Reprisal; coin Money; emit bills of Credit; make any Thing but gold and silver Coin a Tender in Payment of Debts; pass any Bill of Attainder, ex post facto Law, or Law impairing the Obligation of Contracts, or grant any Title of Nobility.

No state shall, without the Consent of the Congress, lay any Imposts or Duties on Imports or Exports, except what may be absolutely necessary for executing its inspection Laws: and the net Produce of all Duties and Imposts, laid by any State on Imports or Exports, shall be for the Use of the Treasury of the United States; and all such Laws shall be subject to the Revision and Control of the Congress.

No State shall, without the Consent of Congress, lay any Duty of Tonnage, keep Troops or Ships of War in time of peace, enter into any Agreement or Compact with another State, or with a foreign Power, or engage in War, unless actually invaded, or in such imminent Danger as will not admit of delay.

Article. II.

Section. 1.

The executive Power shall be vested in a President of the United States of America. He shall hold his Office during the Term of four Years, and together with the Vice President, chosen for the same Term, be elected, as follows:

Each State shall appoint, in such Manner as the Legislature thereof may direct, a Number of Electors, equal to the whole Number of Senators and representatives to which the State may be entitled in the Congress: but no Senator or Representative, or Person holding an Office of Trust or Profit under the United State, shall be appointed an Elector.

The Electors shall meet in their respective States, and vote by Ballot for two Persons, of whom one at least shall not be an Inhabitant of the same State with themselves. And they shall make a List of all the Persons voted for and of the Number of Votes for each; which List they shall sign and certify, and transmit sealed to the Seat of the Government of the United States, directed to the President of the Senate. The President of the Senate shall, in the Presence of the Senate and House of Representatives, open all the Certificates, and the Votes shall then be counted.

The Person having the greatest Number of votes shall be the President, if such Number be a Majority of the whole Number of electors appointed; and if there be more than one who have such Majority, and have an equal Number of Votes, then the House of Representatives shall immediately chuse by Ballot one of them for President; and if no Person have a Majority, then from the five highest on the List the said House shall in like Manner chuse the President. But in chusing the President, the Votes shall be taken by States, the Representation from each State having on Vote; A quorum for this Purpose shall consist of a Member or Members from two thirds of the States, and a Majority of all the States shall be necessary to a Choice. In every Case, after the Choice of the President, the Person having the greatest Number of Votes of the Electors shall be the Vice President. But if there should remain two or more who have equal Votes, the Senate shall chuse from them by Ballot the Vice President.

The Congress may determine the Time of chusing the Electors, and the Day on which they shall give their Votes; which Day shall be the same throughout the United States.

No Person except a natural born Citizen, or a Citizen of the United States, at the time of the Adoption of this Constitution, shall be eligible to the Office of President, neither shall any Person be eligible to that Office who shall not have attained to the Age of thirty five Years, and been fourteen Years a Resident within the United States.

In Case of the Removal of the President from Office, or of his Death, Resignation, or Inability to discharge the Powers and duties of the said Office, the Same shall devolve on the Vice President, and the Congress may by Law provide for the Case of Removal, Death, Resignation or Inability, both of the President and Vice President, declaring what Officer shall then act as President, and such Officer shall act accordingly, until the Disability be removed, or a President shall be elected.

The President shall, at stated Times, receive for his Services, a Compensation, which shall neither be encreased nor diminished during the Period for which he shall have been elected, and he shall not receive within that Period any other emolument from the United States, or any of them.

Before he enter on the Execution of his Office, he shall take the following Oath or Affirmation:—"I do solemnly swear (or affirm) that I will faithfully execute the Office of President of the United States, and will to the best of my Ability, preserve, protect and defend the Constitution of the United States."

Section. 2.

The President shall be Commander in Chief of the Army and Navy of the United States, and of the Militia of the several States, when called into the actual Service of the United States; he may require the Opinion, in writing, of the principal Officer in each of the executive Departments, upon any Subject relating to the Duties of their respective Offices, and he shall have Power to grant Reprieves and Pardons for Offences against the United States, except in cases of Impeachment.

He shall have Power, by and with the Advice and Consent of the Senate, to make Treaties, provided two thirds of the Senators present concur; and he shall nominate, and by and with the Advice and Consent of the Senate, shall appoint

Ambassadors, other public Ministers and Consuls, Judges of the supreme Court, and all other Officers of the United States, whose Appointments are not herein otherwise provided for, and which shall be established by Law; but the Congress may by Law vest the Appointment of such inferior Officers, as they think proper, in the President alone, in the Courts of Law, or in the Heads of Departments.

The President shall have Power to fill up all Vacancies that may happen during the recess of the Senate, by granting Commissions which shall expire at the End of their next Session.

Section. 3.

He shall from time to time give to the Congress Information of the State of the Union, and recommend to their Consideration such measures as he shall judge necessary and expedient; he may, on extraordinary Occasions, convene both Houses, or either of them, and in Case of disagreement between them, with respect to the Time of Adjournment, he may adjourn them to such Time as he shall think proper; he shall receive Ambassadors and other public Ministers; he shall take Care that the Laws be faithfully executed, and shall Commission all the Officers of the United States.

Section. 4.

The President, Vice President and all civil Officers of the United States, shall be removed from Office on Impeachment for, and Conviction of, Treason, Bribery, or other high Crimes and Misdemeanors.

Article. III.

Section. 1.

The judicial Power of the United States, shall be vested in one supreme Court, and in such inferior Courts as the Congress may from time to time ordain and establish. The Judges, both of the supreme and inferior Courts, shall hold their Offices during good Behaviour, and shall, at stated Times, receive for their Services, a Compensation, which shall not be diminished during their Continuance in Office.

Section. 2.

The judicial Power shall extend to all Cases, in Law Equity, arising under this Constitution, the Laws of the United States, and Treaties made, or which shall be made, under their Authority;—to all Cases affecting Ambassadors, other public Ministers and Consuls;—to all Cases of admiralty and maritime Jurisdiction;—to Controversies to which the United States shall be a Party;—to Controversies between two or more States;—between a State and Citizens of another State,— between Citizens of different States,—between Citizens of the same State claiming Lands under Grants of different States, and between a State, or the Citizens thereof, and foreign States, Citizens or subjects.

In all Cases affecting ambassadors, other public Ministers and Consuls, and those in which a State shall be Party, the supreme Court shall have original Jurisdiction. In all the other Cases before mentioned, the supreme Court shall have appellate Jurisdiction, both as to Law and Fact, with such Exceptions, and under such Regulations as the Congress shall make.

The Trial of all Crimes, except in Cases of Impeachment, shall be by Jury; and such Trial shall be held in the State where the said Crimes shall have been committed, but when not committed within any State, the trial shall be at such Place or Places as the Congress may by Law have directed.

Section. 3.

Treason against the United States, shall consist only in levying war against them, or in adhering to their Enemies, giving them aid and Comfort. No Person shall be convicted of Treason unless on the Testimony of two Witnesses to the same overt Act, or on confession in open Court.

The Congress shall have Power to declare the Punishment of Treason, but no Attainder of Treason shall work Corruption of Blood, or Forfeiture except during the Life of the Person attainted.

Article. IV.

Section. 1.

Full Faith and Credit shall be given in each State to the public Acts, Records, and judicial Proceedings of every other State. And the Congress may by general Laws prescribe the Manner in which such Acts, Records and Proceedings shall be proved, and the Effect thereof.

Section. 2.

The Citizens of each State shall be entitled to all Privileges and Immunities of Citizens in the several States.

A Person charged in any State with Treason, Felony, or other Crime, who shall flee from Justice, and be found in another State, shall on Demand of the executive authority of the State from which he fled, be delivered up, to be removed to the State having Jurisdiction of the Crime.

No Person held to Service or Labour in one State, under the Laws thereof, escaping into another, shall, in Consequence of any Law or Regulation therein, be discharged from such Service or Labour, but shall be delivered up on Claim of the Party to whom such Service or Labour may be due.

Section. 3.

New States may be admitted by the Congress into this Union; but no new State shall be formed or erected within the Jurisdiction of any other State, nor any State be formed by the Junction of two or more States, or Parts of States, without the Consent of the Legislatures of the States concerned as well as of the Congress.

The Congress shall have Power to dispose of and make all needful Rules and Regulations respecting the Territory or other Property belonging to the United States; and nothing in this Constitution shall be so construed as to Prejudice any Claims of the United States, or of any particular State.

Section. 4.

The United States shall guarantee to every State in this Union a Republican Form of Government, and shall protect each of them against Invasion; and on Application of the Legislature, or of the Executive (when the Legislature cannot be convened) against domestic Violence.

Article. V.

The Congress, whenever two thirds of both Houses shall deem it necessary, shall propose Amendments to this Constitution, or, on the Application of the Legislatures of two thirds of the several States, shall call a Convention for proposing Amendments, which, in either Case, shall be valid to all Intents and Purposes, as Part of this Constitution, when ratified by the Legislatures of three fourths of the several States, or by Conventions in three fourths thereof, as the one or the other Mode of Ratification may be proposed by the Congress; Provided that no amendment which may be made prior to the Year One thousand eight hundred and eight shall in any Manner affect the first and fourth Clauses in the Ninth Section of the first Article; and that no State, without its Consent, shall be deprived of its equal Suffrage in the Senate.

Article. VI.

All Debts contracted and Engagements entered into, before the Adoption of this Constitution, shall be as valid against the United States under this Constitution, as under the Confederation.

This Constitution, and the Laws of the United States which shall be made in Pursuance thereof; and all Treaties made, or which shall be made, under the Authority of the United States, shall be the supreme Law of the Land; and the Judges in every State shall be bound thereby, any Thing in the Constitution or by Laws of any State to the Contrary notwithstanding.

The Senators and Representatives before mentioned, and the Members of the several State Legislatures, and all executive and judicial Officers, both of the United States and of the several States, shall be bound by Oath or Affirmation, to support this Constitution; but no religious Test shall ever be required as a Qualification to any Office or public Trust under the United States.

Article. VII.

The Ratification of the Conventions of nine States, shall be sufficient for the Establishment of this Constitution between the States so ratifying the Same.

Done in convention by the Unanimous Consent of the States present the Seventeenth Day of September in the Year of our Lord one thousand seven hundred and Eighty seven and of the Independence of the United States of America the twelfth. In witness whereof We have hereunto subscribed our Names,

George Washington, President and deputy from Virginia
Attest: William Jackson, Secretary

New Hampshire—John Landon, Nicholas Gilman

Massachusetts—Nathaniel Gorham, Rufus King

Connecticut—Wm. Saml. Johnson, Roger Sherman

New York—Alexander Hamilton

New Jersey—Wil. Livingston, David Brearley, Wm. Paterson, Jona. Dayton

Pennsylvania—B. Franklin Thomas Mifflin, Robt. Morris, Geo. Clymer, Thos. FitzSimons, Jared Ingersoll, James Wilson, Gouv. Morris

Delaware—Geo. Read, Gunning Bedford Jr., John Dickinson, Richard Bassett, Jaco. Broom

Maryland—James McHenry, Daniel of Saint Thomas' Jenifer, Danl. Carroll

Virginia—John Blair, James Madison Jr.

North Carolina—Wm. Blount, Rich'd. Dobbs Spaight, Hugh Williamson

South Carolina—J. Rutledge, Charles Cotesworth Pinckney, Charles Pinckney, Pierce Butler

Georgia—William Few, Abraham Baldwin

Amendments to the United States Constitution

(The first ten amendments are collectively known as the Bill of Rights.)

Amendment I

Congress shall make no law respecting an establishment of religion, or prohibiting the free exercise thereof; or abridging the freedom of speech, or of the press; or the right of the people peaceably to assemble, and to petition the Government for a redress of grievances.

[effective December 15, 1791]

Amendment II

A well regulated Militia, being necessary to the security of a free State, the right of the people to keep and bear Arms shall not be infringed.

[December 15, 1791]

Amendment III

No Soldier shall, in time of peace, be quartered in any house, without the consent of the Owner, nor in time of war, but in a manner to be prescribed by law.

[December 15, 1791]

Amendment IV

The right of the people to be secure in their persons, houses, papers, and effects, against unreasonable searches and seizures, shall not be violated, and no Warrants shall issue, but upon probable cause, supported by Oath or affirmation, and particularly describing the place to be searched, and the persons or things to be seized.

[December 15, 1791]

Amendment V

No person shall be held to answer for a capital or otherwise infamous crime, unless on a presentment or indictment of a Grand Jury, except in cases arising in the land or naval forces, or in the Militia, when in actual service in time of War or public danger; nor shall any person be subject for the same offence to be twice put in jeopardy of life or limb; nor shall be compelled in any criminal case to be a witness against himself, nor be deprived of life, liberty, or property, without due process of law; nor shall private property be taken for public use, without just compensation.

[December 15, 1791]

Amendment VI

In all criminal prosecutions, the accused shall enjoy the right to a speedy and public trial, by an impartial jury of the State and district wherein the crime shall have been committed, which district shall have been previously ascertained by law, and to be informed of the nature and cause of the accusation; to be confronted with the witnesses against him; to have compulsory process for obtaining witnesses in his favor, and to have the Assistance of Counsel for his defence.

[December 15, 1791]

Amendment VII

In suits at common law, where the value in controversy shall exceed twenty dollars, the right of trial by jury shall be preserved, and no fact tried by a jury, shall be otherwise reexamined in any Court of the United States, than according to the rules of the common law.

[December 15, 1791]

Amendment VIII

Excessive bail shall not be required, no excessive fines imposed, nor cruel and unusual punishments inflicted.

[December 15, 1791]

Amendment IX

The enumeration in the Constitution, of certain rights, shall not be construed to deny or disparage others retained by the people.

[December 15, 1791]

Amendment X

The powers not delegated to the United States by the Constitution; nor prohibited by it to the States, are reserved to the States respectively, or to the people.

[December 15, 1791]

Amendment XI

The Judicial power of the United States shall not be construed to extend to any suit in law or equity, commenced or prosecuted against one of the United States by citizens of another State, or by Citizens or Subjects of any foreign State.

[February 7, 1795]

Amendment XII

The Electors shall meet in their respective States and vote by ballot for President and Vice-President, one of whom, at least, shall not be an inhabitant of the same State with themselves; they shall name in their ballots the person voted for as President, and in distinct ballots the person voted for as Vice-President, and they shall make distinct lists of all persons voted for as President, and of all persons voted for as Vice-President, and of the number of votes for each, which lists they shall sign and certify, and transmit sealed to the seat of the government of the United States, directed to the President of the Senate;—The President of the Senate shall, in the presence of the Senate and House of Representatives, open all the certificates and the votes shall then be counted;—The person having the greatest number of votes for President, shall be the President, if such number be a majority of the whole number of Electors appointed; and if no person have such majority, then from the persons having the highest numbers not exceeding three on the list of those voted for as President, the House of Representatives shall choose immediately, by ballot, the President. But in choosing the President, the votes shall be taken by states, the representation from each state having one vote; a quorum for this purpose shall consist of a member or members from two-thirds of the states, and a majority of all the states shall be necessary to a choice. And if the House of Representatives shall not choose a President whenever the right of choice shall devolve upon them, before the fourth day of March next following, then the Vice-President shall act as President, as in the case of the death or other constitutional disability of the President.—The person having the greatest number of votes as Vice-President, shall be the Vice-President, if such number be a majority of the whole number of Electors appointed, and if no person have a majority, then from the two highest numbers on the list, the Senate shall choose the Vice-President; a quorum for the purpose shall consist of two-thirds of the whole number of Senators, and a majority of the whole number shall be necessary to a choice. But no person consitutionally ineligible to the office of President shall be eligible to that of Vice-President of the United States.

[June 15, 1804]

Amendment XIII

Section. 1.

Neither slavery nor involuntary servitude, except as a punishment for crime whereof the party shall have been duly convicted, shall exist within the United States, or any place subject to their jurisdiction.

Section. 2.

Congress shall have power to enforce this article by appropriate legislation.

[December 18, 1865]

Amendment XIV

Section. 1.

All persons born or naturalized in the United States, and subject to the jurisdiction thereof, are citizens of the United States and of the State wherein they reside. No State shall make or enforce any law which shall abridge the privileges or immunities of citizens of the United States; nor shall any State deprive any person of life, liberty, or property, without due process of law; nor deny to any person within its jurisdiction the equal protection of the laws.

Section. 2.

Representatives shall be appointed among the several States according to their respective numbers, counting the whole number of persons in each State, excluding Indians not taxed. But when the right to vote at any election for the choice of electors for President and Vice-President of the United States, Representatives in Congress, the Executive and Judicial officers of a State, or the members of the Legislature thereof, is denied to any of the male inhabitants of such State, being twenty-one years of age, and citizens of the United States, or in any way abridged, except for participation in rebellion, or other crime, the basis of representation therein shall be reduced in the proportion which the number of such male citizens shall bear to the whole number of male citizens twenty-one years of age in such State.

Section. 3.

No person shall be a Senator or Representative in Congress, or elector of President and Vice-President, or hold any office, civil or military, under the United States, or under any State, who, having previously taken an oath, as a member of Congress, or as an officer of the United States, or as a member of any State legislature, or as an executive or judicial officer of any State, to support the Constitution of the United States, shall have engaged in insurrection or rebellion against the same, or given aid or comfort to the enemies thereof. But Congress may by a vote of two-thirds of each House, remove such disability.

Section. 4.

The validity of the public debt of the United States, authorized by law, including debts incurred for payment of pensions and bounties for services in suppressing insurrection or rebellion, shall not be questioned. But neither the United States nor any State shall assume or pay any debt or obligation incurred in aid of insurrection or rebellion against the United States, or any claim for the loss or emancipation of any slave; but all such debts, obligations, and claims shall be held illegal and void.

Section. 5.

The Congress shall have the power to enforce, by appropriate legislation, the provisions of this article.

[July 28, 1868]

Amendment XV

Section. 1.

The right of citizens of the United States to vote shall not be denied or abridged by the United States or by any State on account of race, color, or previous condition of servitude—

Section. 2.

The Congress shall have power to enforce this article by appropriate legislation.

[March 30, 1870]

Amendment XVI

The Congress shall have power to lay and collect taxes on incomes, from whatever source derived, without apportionment among the several States, and without regard to any census or enumeration.

[February 25, 1913]

Amendment XVII

The Senate of the United States shall be composed of two Senators from each State, elected by the people thereof, for six years; and each Senator shall have one vote. The electors in each State shall have the qualifications requisite for electors of the most numerous branch of the State legislatures.

When vacancies happen in the representation of any State in the Senate, the executive authority of such State shall issue writs of election to fill such vacancies: Provided, That the legislature of any State may empower the executive thereof to make temporary appointments until the people fill the vacancies by election as the legislature may direct. This amendment shall not be so construed as to affect the election or term of any Senator chosen before it becomes valid as part of the Constitution.

[May 31, 1913]

Amendment XVIII

Section. 1.

After one year from the ratification of this article the manufacture, sale, or transportation of intoxicating liquors within, the importation thereof into, or the exportation thereof from the United States and all territory subject to the jurisdiction thereof for beverage purposes is hereby prohibited.

Section. 2.

The Congress and the several States shall have concurrent power to enforce this article by appropriate legislation.

Section. 3.

This article shall be inoperative unless it shall have been ratified as an amendment to the Constitution by the legislatures of the several States, as provided in the Constitution, within seven years from the date of the submission hereof to the States by the Congress.

[January 29, 1919; repealed December 5, 1933]

Amendment XIX

The right of citizens of the United States to vote shall not be denied or abridged by the United States or by any State on account of sex.

Congress shall have power to enforce this article by appropriate legislation.

[August 26, 1920]

Amendment XX

Section. 1.

The terms of the President and vice-President shall end at noon on the 20th day of January, and the terms of Senators and Representatives at noon on the 3d day of January, of the years in which such terms would have ended if this article had not been ratified; and the terms of their successors shall then begin.

Section. 2.

The Congress shall assemble at least once in every year, and such meeting shall begin at noon the 3d day of January, unless they shall by law appoint a different day.

Section. 3.

If, at the time fixed for the beginning of the term of President, the President elect shall have died, the Vice-President elect shall become President. If a President shall not have been chosen before the time fixed for the beginning of his term, or if the President elect shall have failed to qualify, then the Vice-President elect shall act as President until a President shall have qualified; and the Congress may by law provide for the case wherein neither a President elect not a Vice-President elect shall have qualified, declaring who shall then act as President, or the manner in which one who is to act shall be selected, and such person shall act accordingly until a President or vice-President shall have qualified.

Section. 4.

The Congress may by law provide for the case of the death of any of the persons from whom the House of Representatives may choose a President whenever the right of choice shall have devolved upon them, and for the case of the death of any of the persons from whom the Senate may choose a Vice-President whenever the right of choice shall have devolved upon them.

Section. 5.

Sections 1 and 2 shall take effect on the 15th day of October following the ratification of this article.

Section. 6.

This article shall be inoperative unless it shall have been ratified as an amendment to the Constitution by the legislatures of three-fourths of the several States within seven years from the date of its submission.

[January 23, 1933]

Amendment XXI

Section. 1.

The eighteenth article of amendment to the Constitution of the United States is hereby repealed.

Section. 2.

The transportation or importation into any State, Territory, or possession of the United States for delivery or use therein of intoxicating liquors, in violation of the laws thereof, is hereby prohibited.

Section. 3.

This article shall be inoperative unless it shall have been ratified as an amendment of the Constitution by conventions in the several States, as provided in the Constitution, within seven years from the date of the submission hereof to the States by the Congress.

[December 5, 1933]

Amendment XXII

No person shall be elected to the office of the President more than twice, and no person who has held the office of President, or acted as President, for more than two years of a term to which some other person was elected President shall be elected to the office of the President more than once.

But this Article shall not apply to any person holding the office of President when this Article was proposed by the Congress, and shall not prevent any person who may be holding the office of President, or acting as President, during the term within this Article becomes operative from holding the office of President or acting as President during the remainder of such term.

[February 27, 1951]

Amendment XXIII

Section. 1.

The district constituting the seat of Government of the United States shall appoint in such manner as the Congress may direct:

A number of electors of President and Vice President equal to the whole number of Senators and Representatives in Congress to which the District would be entitled if it were a State, but in no event more than the least populous State; they shall be in addition to those appointed by the States, but they shall be considered, for the purposes of the election of President and Vice President, to be electors appointed by the State; and they shall meet in the district and perform such duties as provided by the twelfth article of amendment.

Section. 2.

The Congress shall have power to enforce this article by appropriate legislation.

[March 29, 1961]

Amendment XXIV

Section. 1.

The right of citizens of the United States to vote in any primary or other election for President or Vice President, or for Senator or Representative in Congress, shall not be denied or abridged by the United States or any State by reason of failure to pay any poll tax or other tax.

Section. 2.

The Congress shall have power to enforce this article by appropriate legislation.

[January 23, 1964]

Amendment XXV

Section. 1.

In case of the removal of the President from office or of his death or resignation, the Vice President shall become President.

Section. 2.

Whenever there is a vacancy in the office of the Vice President, the President shall nominate a Vice President who shall take office upon confirmation by a majority vote of both Houses of Congress.

Section. 3.

Whenever the President transmits to the President pro tempore of the Senate and the Speaker of the House of Representatives his written declaration that he is unable to discharge the powers and duties of his office, and until he transmits to them a written declaration to the contrary, such powers and duties shall be discharged by the Vice President as Acting President.

Section. 4.

Whenever the Vice President and a majority of either the principal officers of the executive department or of such other body as Congress may by law provide, transmit to the President pro tempore of the Senate and the Speaker of the House of Representative their written declaration that the President is unable to discharge the powers and duties of his office, the Vice President shall immediately assume the powers and duties of the office of Acting President.

Thereafter, when the President transmits to the President pro tempore of the Senate and the Speaker of the House of Representatives has written declaration that no inability exists, he shall resume the powers and duties of his office unless the Vice President and a majority of either the principal officers of the executive department or of such other body as Congress may by law provide, transmit within four days to the President pro tempore of the Senate and the Speaker of the House of Representatives their written declaration that the President is unable to discharge the powers and duties of his office. Thereupon Congress shall decide the issue, assembling within forty-eight hours for that purpose if not in session. If the Congress, within twenty-one days after receipt of the latter written declaration, or, if Congress is not in session, within twenty-one days after Congress is required to assemble, determines by two-thirds vote of both Houses that the President is unable to discharge the powers and duties of his office, the Vice President shall continue to discharge the same as Acting President; otherwise, the President shall resume the powers and duties of his office.

[February 10, 1967]

Amendment XXVI
Section. 1.

The right of citizens of the United States, who are eighteen years of age or older, to vote shall not be denied or abridged by the United States or by any State on account of age.

Section. 2.

The Congress shall have power to enforce this article by appropriate legislation.

[July 1, 1971]

Amendment XXVII

No law, varying the compensation for the services of the Senators and Representatives, shall take effect, until an election of Representatives shall have intervened.

[May 7, 1992]

Index

Abortion
  availability of, 62
  compromise on, 340
  court rulings on, 374, 377–78, 381
  education and, 77
  federal involvement in, 72
  interest groups and, 225
  party affiliation and, 161–62
  religious differences on, 2
  women's support for, 205
Acid rain, 48
Advisory Commission on Intergovernmental Relations, 18n, 120
African Americans
  in Atlanta, Ga., 265
  Democratic party and, 165
  district elections and, 211–13
  issues of equality and, 51, 53
  group identity of, 80–81, 86
  political agendas of, 72, 79
  politicians and, 104
  poverty and, 85
  voter registration and, 39–40, 198, 201–5, 260–62, 264, 272
  voter turnout and, 193–94, 197
  See also Race and racism
Age
  voter turnout and, 193–94, 198–200, 203, 205–6
Agnew, John, 67n
Aid to Families with Dependent Children (AFDC)
  Massachusetts and, 41
  recipients and funding of, 422
  state reimbursement rates for, 35–36, 37
AIDS, 48

Alabama
  high poverty levels in, 30
  party politics in, 174
  state mandates in, 430
Alaska, 31
Alexander, Herbert E., 180n, 245, 254n, 354n
Allswang, John M., 180n
American Bar Association, 228, 241
American Medical Association (AMA), 228, 232, 241
Amicus briefs, 364
Antitrust laws, 47
Appointments
  by executives, 299–302, 307
  of judges, 369–72
Apportionment
  court rulings on, 60–61, 360
  process of, 213–16
  reelection percentages and, 326
Arizona, 31, 125
Arkansas
  gubernatorial policy in, 313–14
  high poverty levels in, 30
  highway funding in, 428
  Social Security disability programs and, 40
  state versus local government in, 116
  veto power in, 350–51
Articles of Confederation, 22
Asher, Herbert, 220n
Atlanta, Ga., 265
Audubon Society, 229

Bachrach, Peter, 98n
Bailey, John, 396

484 *Index*

Banfield, Edward, 18n, 443, 448n
Baratz, Morton S., 98n
Bass, Walter, 275n, 317n
Baum, Laurence, 385n
Beck, Paul A., 180n, 182n
Beer, Samuel, 66n
Bell, Charles G., 254n
Benjamin, Gerald, 99n, 318n, 319n, 320n, 355n
Bensel, Richard F., 276n
Bernick, E. Lee, 319n
Berry, Frances S., 136n, 276n, 319n
Berry, Jeffrey M., 252n
Berry, William D., 136n, 276n, 319n
Beyle, Thad, 317n, 318n
Bibby, John F., 181n, 217n
Bilandic, Michael, 295
Bills, legislative, 333–35
Black, Earl, 66n, 182n, 219n, 261, 276n
Black, Merle, 66n, 182n, 219n
Bledsoe, Timothy, 219n, 220n, 355n
Boise, Idaho, 104
Borris, Thomas J., 252n
Boston, Mass., 92
Bottle laws, 72, 83, 230, 243
Bowman, Ann O'M., 135n
Brace, Paul, 448n
Breaux, David, 354n
Brown, Jerry, 239, 371, 397, 398
Brown, Pat, 397, 398
Brown, Robert, 449
Browning, Rufus P., 182n
Brown v. Board of Education, 61, 364
Bryan, Frank, 99n
Budgets, 303–5, 307
Burnham, Walter D., 217n, 218n, 219n
Bush, George, 30
    centralized government and, 57, 58–59
    Supreme Court appointments of, 375, 378
Businesses
    economic development plans and, 433, 440, 444
    interest groups and, 225, 228–29, 233, 235, 248
    small-claims courts and, 363
    taxes and, 120–22
Button, James W., 276n, 277n
Byrd, Harry, 268
Byrne, Brendan, 399–400
Byrne, Jane, 295

California
    campaign costs in, 287
    federal farm policy and, 31
    federal fuel policy and, 31
    federal land ownership in, 31
    government employees in, 407
    gubernatorial elections in, 288, 290, 291, 293, 314
    interest groups in, 239
    judicial appointments in, 371
    Latino immigration to, 92
    legislator salaries in, 243, 337

long-term effect on spending in when alternating party
        controls, 404
    personal income tax in, 126
    political parties in, 163, 173, 330–31, 344–45, 397, 398, 405
    primaries in, 149
    school funding in, 233, 375
    tax levels in, 263–64
    tax revolt in, 411
    unemployment in, 31
    urban-rural conflicts in, 84
    water issues in, 85–86
Calvert, Jerry, 354n
Campaigns
    character emphasis in, 282
    endorsements in, 309–10
    for initiatives, 208
    interest groups and, 228, 245–50, 324
    media coverage of, 191
    policy agendas and, 287
    public funding of, 151, 249–50
    See also Elections; Fund raising
Canon, Bradley, 384n
Careerism, 323–28
Carlson, Eric H., 356n
Caro, Robert, 284n
Carter, Jimmy, 33, 196
Cassie, William, 254n
Celeste, Richard, 291
Chaffee, Douglas C., 355n
Chamber of Commerce, 226
Chicago, Ill.
    black political success in, 92, 201–2
    mayoral elections in, 291, 295
    mayoral power in, 315–16
    political reform in, 403
Chiles, Lawton, 289, 290
Christian Right, 162
Chrysler Corporation, 47
Chubb, John, 318n
Cities
    apportionment and, 60–61
    black political involvement in, 265, 274
    conflicts within, 86–90
    Democratic party and, 158, 162–63, 214, 287–91
    district elections in, 211–13, 327–28
    ethnic voting in, 81–82
    federal aid for, 33
    government types for, 280–82
    initiatives and referenda in, 208, 210
    interest groups in, 226
    legislators from, 93, 326
    mayoral elections in, 291–92
    nonpartisan elections in, 151–52, 273
    school funding in, 88
    services provided by, 302–3
    suburban flight from, 90–93
    urban-rural conflicts and, 84–85
Citizens for Tax Justice, 136n
City-manager form of government, 152, 305
Civil cases, 361–63, 368

Civil rights
  court rulings and, 378
  enforcement of, 419
  federal government and, 45
  local government control and, 104
  party affiliation and, 161, 394
  politicians and, 286
  Southern electorate and, 94, 264
Class-action lawsuits, 363–64
Class status
  access to courts and, 362–65, 374, 379
  criminal prosecutions and, 362
  government centralization and, 109
  inequitable school funding and, 107
  initiatives and referenda and, 208, 264,
      410–12
  interest groups and, 223–25, 235, 250
  judges and, 371
  V. O. Key on, 6–8, 141
  party affiliation and, 161–62, 169–72
  personality characteristics and, 443–44
  policy decisions and, 283, 406
  political role of, 8–9, 257–60, 271, 274
  protests and, 210
  self-definitions of, 75–76
  self-interest and, 73–77
  suburban flight and, 87–88, 298
  support for democracy and, 97
  support for federal programs and, 78–79
  tax rates and, 121, 263–64
  transportation spending and, 428
  utility regulations and, 436
  voter registration and, 189, 197, 200, 298
  voter turnout and, 193–99, 201–3, 206, 260
Clements, Bill, 372
Clinton, Bill
  activist national government and, 60, 437
  gubernatorial policies of, 313–14
  NAFTA and, 33
  votes for by state, 29, 30, 32
Cloward, Richard A., 218n, 219n, 220n, 446n
Clucas, Richard A., 181n
Coattail effects, 173
Colorado, 30, 149
Combs, Michael, 384n
Common Cause, 227, 229
Concurrence, 265–66
Conference of Mayors, 225
Congress, U.S.
  AFDC and, 41
  black voting rights and, 203
  budget debates and, 38
  civil rights laws and, 45
  deficit reduction and, 60
  diversity among states and, 26, 30–37, 49, 53
  federal regulatory activity and, 58, 59
  federalism and, 23–26
  House banking scandal and, 191
  local policy implementation and, 42, 63
  policy goals and, 39

  pork-barreling and, 33
  senior citizens and, 196
Connecticut
  gubernatorial elections in, 290
  political parties in, 173, 343–44, 346–47, 396–97, 405
  primaries in, 149
  school segregation in, 88, 379
  state income tax in, 133, 306, 349, 401, 408
  state government employment in, 394
  welfare payments in, 30
Connery, Robert H., 320n
Connor, ``Bull,'' 53
Conservatives
  access to courts and, 365
  campaign promises by, 287, 313
  class status of, 78
  criminal law and, 372
  Democratic party and, 314
  diversity among states and, 32
  economic decline and, 296, 440
  education issues and, 427
  government centralization and, 57, 109, 110
  government pricing policies and, 119–20
  philosophy of, 2, 420
  private sector and, 419–20
  public consensus and, 147
  ratings of, 174
  Republican party and, 160–61, 175, 201, 314
  by state, 449–57
  taxation and, 124, 125
  welfare and, 30, 421, 423–24, 440, 443
Constitution, U.S., 22–24
Consumer groups
  corporate tax hikes and, 120
  government regulations and, 83, 432
  tort law and, 375
Corporations
  See Businesses
Corruption, 145–46, 147
Cotter, Cornelius, 181n
Council-manager governments, 281–82
County governments
  consolidation efforts and, 117
  duties of, 110
  types of, 281
Courts
  access to, 360–65
  appeal process of, 367
  campaign spending limits and, 150
  centralization and, 60–62
  divorce laws and, 434–35
  inequitable school funding and, 108, 374–75
  interest groups and, 233–34
  political role of, 15, 280, 358–65, 379–82
  redistricting and, 213–14, 216, 360, 374
  relationship between federal and state law and, 366–67, 374
  selection of judges and, 369–73
  on state superiority over local governments, 102
  treatment of cases in, 373–79

Crime
    prosecution of, 362
    public opinion shifts on, 94–95
    sentencing laws and, 442
Criminal cases, 361–62, 368
Cronin, Thomas E., 220n
Culture
    class status and, 443
    party affiliation and, 161–62
    political attitudes and, 81–82
Culture, political
    black involvement and, 274
    definition of, 8
    lobbyists and, 237, 246, 250
    voter turnout and, 194–95
Culver, John H., 383n
Cuomo, Mario, 154, 288, 289–90, 294

Daley, Richard, 295
Daniels, William J., 318n
Danielson, Michael N., 99n, 447n
Danziger, Sheldon H., 448n
Davidson, Chandler, 16, 182n, 219n, 268, 276n, 356n
Decentralization
    Articles of Confederation and, 22
    federalism and, 21
    movement away from, 46–55
    political parties and, 25, 144–45
    state involvement in local government and, 103–4, 105,
        109, 110
Delaware, 115, 149
Democracy
    debate and dialogue in, 140, 146–47
    institutional arrangements in, 279–82
    interest groups and, 222–23, 245
    judicial role in, 358
    legislatures in, 322, 324, 333
    political participation and, 186, 188
    public belief in, 97
    public policy and, 69
    social diversity and, 138, 352
Democratic party
    apportionment and, 214–16
    central cities and, 92, 214
    coalition building by, 139–41, 341
    conservatism in, 314
    constituency of, 158–64, 176, 287, 290, 297
    consumer legislation and, 432
    control of state legislatures by, 329–32, 389–406
    decline in, 154
    economic decline and, 295–96, 433
    economic regulation and, 432
    education issues and, 425
    electoral bases for, 288–91
    labor unions and, 227, 432
    liberalism and, 158, 175, 201, 312–13
    local level of, 169–72
    members of by state, 155–56
    mobilization of have-nots and, 6, 257–58, 297–98, 348–49,
        445

progressive income taxes and, 102, 125
    selection of judges and, 371–72
    spends more money for government programs than
        Republicans, 404
    state mandates and, 109
    support for by state, 176–78, 449–57
    transportation issues and, 147
    unity appeals and, 311
Deregulation, 56
Derthick, Martha, 66n, 105, 446n
Desegregation
    See Civil rights; Education; Segregation
Deukmejian, George, 407
DeVries, Jack, 275n, 317n
Diamond, Martin, 66n
Dilger, Robert J., 67n
Dillon's rule, 102
Dinkins, David, 171
Dionne, E. J., 147
Diversity
    local government control and, 104
    representative democracy and, 138, 322
    among states, 26–33, 53, 57
    tax rates and, 121
Divorce laws, 433–35
Doctors
    and conflicts with nurses, 231–32
    government involvement in health care and, 431
    interest groups and, 225, 228–29
    medical malpractice and, 82, 240–41
Dometrius, Nelson C., 319n, 320n
Dukakis, Michael, 289, 290
Dwyer, Diana, 181n, 253n, 276n, 355n, 415n
Dye, Thomas R., 17n, 355n, 414n

Economy
    business taxes and, 121–22
    centralized government and, 46–48
    constraints on politicians and, 295, 389, 401
    government intervention in, 420, 433, 440, 444
    popularity of governors and, 293–94
    See also Businesses
Edsall, Thomas B., 136n
Education
    Bush administration and, 58
    congressional aid for, 32
    costs of, 119
    desegregation and, 61–62, 87–88
    government involvement in, 425–27, 440–41
    interest group membership and, 223–25
    of legislators, 323, 327
    liberalism and, 76–77
    public opinion shifts on, 94–95
    reform of, 295, 441
    school prayer and, 62, 381
    state mandates in, 429–30
    support for federal programs and, 78–79
    teacher lobbying groups and, 232–33
    voter registration and, 199–200
    voter turnout and, 193–94, 197
    See also School funding

Ehrenhalt, Alan, 18n
Eisemier, Theodore, 319n
Eisenger, Peter, 447n
Eisenhower, Dwight David, 54
Elastic tax systems, 123
Elazar, Daniel, 17n, 194–95
Eldersveld, Samuel, 66n
Elections
    competition in, 325
    district-based, 211–13, 325–28
    funding reports and, 247
    impact of, 279–84, 388–92
    interest groups and, 227–29
    of judges, 369–70
    nonpartisan, 151–52, 154, 201, 273
    plurality rule for, 211
    presidential, 25, 32, 187–88, 196, 200
    reform of, 13, 14, 148–49, 152, 265–66
    timing of, 200
    turnout for, 187–207, 260–62, 410–11
    See also Campaigns; Fund raising
Electoral bases
    of governors, 288–91
    of mayors, 291–92
    political change and, 388–89, 394–95, 401, 405,
        412, 445
Electoral college, 25
Elkins, Stanley L., 355n
Ellwood, David T., 448n
Engstrom, Richard L., 220n
Environmental concerns
    congressional action on, 32
    education and, 77
    government mandates and, 56, 59, 72, 436
    interest groups and, 225, 229, 233–34
Environmental Protection Agency (EPA), 58
Equality of opportunity
    early beliefs about, 50
    industrialization and, 50–51
    V. O. Key on, 4
    political process and, 3, 5–6, 256, 258, 406, 444–45
    socioeconomic factors and, 51–53, 56, 375
    See also Inequality
Equal Rights Amendment (ERA), 77
Equity Center, 107
Erickson, Robert S., 414n
Ethnicity
    political attitudes and, 81–82, 86–87
    political involvement and, 264
    political machines and, 147
    political parties and, 169–71
Eulau, Heinz, 355n
Executives
    coalition building by, 397–406
    constituencies of, 312–16
    formal power of, 298–308
    informal power of, 308–12
    political agendas of, 15, 72, 286–98
    See also Governors; Mayors
Expenditures
    long-term effect on of alternating party control, 404

    by national government, 44–45, 63–64
    for state facilities and services, 118–20
Exports, 26

Fagin, Claire M., 232
Fairbanks, John, 384n
Farmers, 83, 225, 227–28
Farm production, 28–29, 31
Federal agencies, 38–42
Federal aid
    expansion of, 55–56
    Reagan administration and, 58
    state dependence on, 44–45, 63
Federalism
    congressional policy and, 26–37
    diversity among states and, 26–33
    formation of, 20–24, 50, 299
    national government activism and, 14, 42–62
    politicians and, 23, 24–26
    state leverage and, 38–42
Federal land ownership, 28–29, 31
Federal Trade Commission (FTC), 47
Fenno, Richard F., 355n
Fenton, John H., 164, 182n, 269, 271
Fiorina, Morris P., 181n, 319n, 355n, 356n, 413n
Firefighters, 82, 428
Flinn, Thomas, 356n
Florida
    gubernatorial elections in, 289, 290
    high poverty levels in, 30
    Latino immigration to, 92
    political parties in, 165, 167–68, 331–32
    tax debates in, 133
Florio, James, 141–42, 144, 287, 288, 290, 293, 298, 314, 349,
        399–400, 405
Formula grants, 112
Fowler, Edmund P., 276n
Frendeis, John P., 181n
Friedman, Lawrence M., 383n
Fry, Brian, 414n
Fuel production, 28–29, 31
Fund raising
    congressional candidates and, 25
    interest groups and, 228, 245–47
    political parties and, 151, 345

Gable, Richard W., 318n
Gaddie, Ronald Keith, 182n
Garand, James A., 414n
Garand, James C., 415n
Garbage collection, 431
Garcia v. San Antonio Transit Authority, 61
Gays, 92, 104, 264
Gehringer, Gerald R., 231
General Motors Corp., 47
Geography
    interest groups and, 228
    party affiliation and, 158, 162–64
    political attitudes and, 83–90

Georgia, 30, 428
Gerrymandering, 216
    See Apportionment
Gibson, James L., 181n
Gideon v. Wainwright, 365
Gierzynski, Anthony, 354n
Gimpel, James, 181n
Glick, Henry R., 383n
Godwin, Mills, 272
Goldwater, Barry, 165, 173
Gormley, William T., 218n, 448n
Government, national
    cuts to local and state programs by, 295, 389
    increasing activism of, 42–60
    local policy mandates and, 20–21
    See also Federalism
Governors
    agendas of, 286–87, 292–98, 314–16, 329
    coalition building by, 397–406
    divided government control and, 406–9
    electoral bases of, 288–91
    formal power of, 298–301, 303–8, 389
    informal power of, 308–12
    lawsuits filed by, 359–60
    legislation and, 333
    legislative agendas and, 350–51
    legislative staffs and, 337–38
    See also Executives
Grady, Dennis, 319n
Grasso, Ella, 314
Great Depression, 52, 421
Grodzins, Morton, 26, 66n
Gross, Donald A., 284n, 413n
Group identities, 80–83
Gruhl, John, 384n
Guliani, Rudy, 171, 291–92

Hale, Dennis, 317n
Hamm, Keith E., 253n, 254n, 356n
Handicapped
    civil rights campaigns of, 53
    education of, 425
    federal government and, 45
    interest groups and, 229
Hansen, Susan, 136n, 266, 276n, 318n, 414n
Harmel, Robert, 356n
Havick, John, 354n
Hawaii
    school funding in, 425, 426
    state versus local government in, 115–16
Hawley, Willis D., 219n
Health care
    class issues and, 3
    communicable diseases and, 48
    conflicts between doctors and nurses and, 231–32
    government involvement in, 429, 431
    medical malpractice and, 240–41
Herzik, Eric, 318n
Hill, Kim Q., 219n, 276n

Hispanics
    party politics and, 167–68
    politicians and, 104
    voter turnout of, 197
    See also Race and racism
Hofstader, Richard, 18n
Hollings, Ernest F. ``Fritz,'' 286
Holton, Linwood, 272
Home rule, 102
Housing
    in Atlanta, Ga., 265
    court rulings on, 374
    Democratic party and, 394
    federal expenditures on, 63
    federal standards for, 49
    local regulations for, 87
Houston, Texas
    gays in, 104, 264
    mayoral elections in, 295
    population growth and political conflict in, 91–92
Hrebenar, Ronald J., 245, 252n, 253n
Huckshorn, Robert, 181n

Idaho, 31
Illinois
    air pollution in, 48
    federal farm policy and, 31
    labor unions in, 234
    nominating conventions in, 149
    personal income tax in, 126
    political parties in, 164, 269–71, 402–3
    prison overcrowding in, 119
    school funding in, 105–6
    school segregation in, 88
    unemployment in, 31
    urban-rural conflicts in, 84
    See also Chicago, Ill.
Immigration, 3
Income taxes
    inflation and, 123
    by state, 125–26, 128–32
    visibility of, 124
Independents, 153–54
    electorate volatility and, 292
    voter turnout of, 200
Indexed taxes, 123
Indiana, 164, 269–71
Individualism
    federal economic aid and, 73–74, 75
    industrialization and, 50–51
    social science views and, 51–52
Industrial Revolution, 46, 47, 50–51
Inequality
    in access to civil courts, 362–65
    distribution of wealth and, 52
    government's role in addressing, 2–3, 5, 14, 103, 104–8, 256
    V. O. Key on, 4, 5
    political parties and, 6
    See also Equality of opportunity

Inflation, 123
Initiatives, 208–10
  in California, 264
  interest groups and, 228
  public support for, 409–12
  on term limits, 352
Insurance companies, 83
Interest groups
  apportionment and, 214
  influence of, 227–34, 235–45
  initiation of court cases by, 364
  initiatives and, 208
  legislation and, 333–34
  membership of, 223–27
  policy implementation and, 420
  political conflict and, 69
  public restraint of, 245–50, 274
  role of, 15, 222–23
  by state, 234–35
  See also Lobbyists
Interstate Commerce Commission (ICC), 47–48
Iowa
  federal farm policy and, 31
  political parties in, 347
  unemployment in, 31
  urban-rural conflicts in, 84–85

Jackson, Andrew, 51
Jackson, John, 355n
Jackson, Kenneth, 99n
Jacob, Herbert, 384n, 385n
Jarett, James E., 317n, 414n
Jennings, Edward T., 271, 276n, 395–96, 414n
Jewell, Malcolm E., 17n, 66n, 354n, 355n, 356n, 414n
Jews
  group identity of, 82, 86
  liberalism of, 79
Johnson, Charles A., 218n
Johnson, Lyndon Baines, 437
Jones, Charles, 66n
Jones, Ruth S., 180n, 252n, 254n
Judd, Dennis R., 17n, 134n
Judges
  activism of, 375–82
  selection of, 369–73
Judicial review, 360

Kanda, Thomas, 415n
Kane, Susan L., 319n
Kansas, 40, 126
Kean, Thomas, 310
Kearney, Richard C., 135n
Kennedy, John Fitzgerald, 54
Kentucky, 149, 428
Kett, Donald F., 66n
Key, V. O., 4–9
  democratic conflicts and, 69

  on political parties and have-nots, 141, 256, 267, 348, 388, 405, 445
  on taxation and welfare, 13
Keynes, John Maynard, 54
Kickbacks, 145–46
King, Mel, 92
Klingman, David, 318n
Koch, Ed, 239, 291
Kochan, Thomas A., 134n
Kozol, Jonathon, 17n

Labor unions
  campaign contributions by, 287
  government guarantees for, 432
  group identity of, 82
  as interest groups, 225, 227–29, 248
  political positions of, 79, 83
  public employees and, 108, 430
  Southern organizing of, 234–35
  strikes by, 47, 48–49
  working conditions and, 435
Lamis, Alexander P., 276n
Lammers, William W., 318n
Lauth, Thomas P., 318n
Lawyers, 82–83
  contingency fees and, 364
  interest groups and, 225, 228–29
  medical malpractice and, 240–41
  public defender programs and, 365
League of Women Voters, 228–29
LeBlanc, Hugh L., 356n
Legal Services Corporation, 363
Legislatures, state
  agendas of, 338, 348–51
  careerism and motivations in, 323–27
  district representation in, 213
  divided control of, 279–80, 406–9
  executive veto power and, 305–6
  informal practices in, 338–40
  initiatives and, 411
  interest groups and, 228
  lawsuits filed by, 359–60
  leadership of, 336, 340, 343, 345, 399
  legislative process in, 332–36
  lobbyists and, 230–31, 237–39, 242–43, 245, 250
  party campaign committees and, 241–42
  party politics in, 156, 162–64, 174–78, 311–12, 329–32, 340–48, 389–409
  population movements and, 93
  public and, 352–53
  redistricting and, 213–14
  role of, 322
  staffs for, 337–38
  tax laws and, 127
Lehn, Richard, 136n, 385n
Lehrman, Lew, 154
Leighley, Jan E., 219n, 276n
Levy, Frank, 136n
Lewis-Beck, Michael S., 276n

Liberals
    access to courts and, 365
    campaign promises by, 287, 312–13
    criminal law and, 372
    Democratic party and, 158, 160–61, 175, 201, 287–91
    diversity among states and, 32
    divorce laws and, 434
    economic decline and, 295–96, 440
    education issues and, 425, 427
    education of, 76–77
    government centralization and, 109, 110
    government pricing policies and, 119–20
    philosophy of, 2, 420
    private sector and, 419–20
    public consensus and, 147
    ratings of, 174
    Republican party and, 314–15
    by state, 449–57
    state mandates and, 430
    taxation and, 123, 124
    welfare and, 30, 421, 423–24, 440, 443
Liebert, Roland, 135n, 319n
Lineberry, Robert L., 99n, 276n
Little, Thomas H., 356n
Livingston, William S., 66n
Lobbyists
    effectiveness of, 232
    information provided by, 230, 242
    legislators and, 230–31, 237–39, 242–43, 245, 250
    polling by, 233
    registration of, 247–48
    See also Interest groups
Local bills, 339
Lockard, Duane, 181n, 276n, 414n
Loeb, William, 9–10, 268
Logrolling, 33, 339–40
Long, Huey, 268–69, 395, 404
Los Angeles, Calif., 302–4
Louisiana
    class politics in, 268–70, 271–72, 395, 405
    federal fuel policy and, 31
    long-term effect on spending in when alternating
        party controls, 404
    oil interests in, 234
Lowery, David, 135n, 218n, 415n
Lowi, Theodore J., 252n, 276n
Luttbeg, Norman R., 242, 254n
Lynch, Edward C., 318n

McFarland, Andrew S., 252n
MacManus, Susan A., 182n
Madison, James, 23
Magleby, David B., 220n
Maine, 234
Marshall, Dale R., 182n
Massachusetts
    gubernatorial power in, 315, 406
    nominating conventions in, 149
    political parties in, 341–42
    Social Security disability programs and, 40

    unemployment in, 31
    welfare in, 41, 105
Mayhew, David R., 66n, 182n, 356n, 413n
Mayor-council governments, 280, 305
Mayors
    agendas of, 286–87, 292–99
    coalition building by, 397–406
    electoral bases of, 291–92
    formal power of, 301–7, 315–16
    informal power of, 308–12
    See also Executives
Media
    civil rights coverage and, 53
    competitive elections and, 201
    coverage of courts by, 368, 379
    coverage of executives by, 310–11
    coverage of legislatures by, 336
    initiatives and, 411
    interest groups and, 229, 239–40, 245, 247, 250, 274
    political agendas and, 297
    polling and, 209–10
    presidential campaigns and, 173, 200
    public opinion and, 80, 189–92, 194
    See also Newspapers
Mediators, 361–62
Medicaid
    government control of, 431
    lower class under representation and, 262
    purpose of, 46
    reasons for creation of, 421–22
    state reimbursement rates for, 35, 36, 37
Medicare, 422, 431
Merton, Robert K., 180n
Meskill, Thomas, 396
Michigan
    auto industry interests in, 234
    economic decline in, 296
    labor unions in, 234
    political parties in, 269–71
    school segregation in, 88
    urban-rural conflicts in, 84
Minnesota
    federal farm policy and, 31
    nominating conventions in, 149
    political culture in, 194, 269–71, 343–44
    state versus local government in, 116, 430
Mississippi
    AFDC payments in, 36
    black voter registration in, 203
    high poverty levels in, 30
    labor unions in, 234
    political culture in, 194
    rural-urban conflicts in, 85
Missouri Plan, 369–70
Moakley, Maureen, 181n
Moncrief, Gary F., 220n, 253n
Montana
    legislator salaries in, 337
    national speed limits in, 40, 42
    natural resource interests in, 86
    open primaries in, 149

party loyalty in, 345
rural-urban conflicts in, 85
state versus local government in, 116
Morehouse, Sarah P. McCally, 253n, 319n, 414n
Morgan, David, 218n
Mosquito abatement, 111
Muir, William K., 254n, 355n
Municipalities, 110
Municipal League, 225
Murphy, Russell D., 317n
Murray, Charles, 67n, 446n

Nakamura, Robert T., 355n
Nardulli, Peter F., 99n, 384n
Nathan, Richard P., 68n
National Rifle Association (NRA), 227–28
A Nation at Risk, 441
Natural resources, 85–86
Nebraska
    conservatism in, 32
    federal farm policy and, 31
    legislature in, 334, 347
    school funding in, 425, 426
    unemployment in, 31
Nevada, 31, 194
New Federalism, 34
New Hampshire
    legislator salaries in, 243
    school funding in, 425, 426
    state versus local government in, 115, 116
    taxation debates in, 9–11, 133, 268
New Jersey
    gubernatorial elections in, 288, 290, 293, 298
    judicial pragmatism in, 376–77
    long-term effect on spending in when alternating party
        controls, 404
    political parties in, 141–44, 164, 263, 310, 331, 344–47, 405
    school funding in, 105–6, 108, 132–33, 141–42, 314, 349,
        375, 377, 380, 382, 399–400
    school segregation in, 88
    welfare payments in, 30
New Mexico
    legislator salaries in, 243
    nominating conventions in, 149
    population growth in, 30
    school funding in, 425, 426
    state versus local government in, 115
    veto power in, 350–51
Newspapers
    political coverage of, 190–92
    political influence of, 9–10, 268, 310
    polling by, 209
New York
    acid rain and, 48
    AFDC payments in, 36
    gubernatorial elections in, 288, 289–90, 293, 294
    gubernatorial power in, 301, 306, 308, 314–15, 347–48,
        401–2, 408
    highway funding in, 428
    interest groups in, 239

labor unions in, 234
Latino immigration to, 92
legislator salaries in, 243, 337
liberalism in, 32, 314–15
mayoral elections in, 291–92
mayoral power in, 303
nominating conventions in, 149
political parties in, 163, 164, 168–69, 170–71, 174, 330–31,
    346–49, 409
population stagnation in, 30
school funding in, 105–6
school segregation in, 88
Social Security disability programs and, 40
state versus local government in, 116, 430
tax burdens in, 130–31, 263–64, 409, 411
urban-rural conflicts in, 84
voter turnout in, 197–98
welfare payments in, 30
Nie, Norman H., 134n
Nie, Verba, 134n
Nixon, Richard M., 173, 315
North American Free Trade Agreement (NAFTA), 33
North Carolina
    high poverty levels in, 30
    labor unions in, 234
    nominating conventions in, 149
    personal income tax in, 126
    Social Security disability programs and, 40
    state versus local government in, 116
    tobacco interest in, 234
North Dakota
    conservatism in, 32
    legislator salaries in, 337
    personal income tax in, 125
Nurses, 231–32

Occupation, 82–83, 323
O'Gorman, Mark, 276n, 415n
Ohio
    air pollution in, 48
    economic decline in, 296
    gubernatorial elections in, 291
    highway funding in, 428
    political culture in, 194
    political parties in, 163, 164, 269–71, 330–31
    state versus local government in, 116
Oil production, 31
Oklahoma
    federal fuel policy and, 31
    highway funding in, 428
    oil interests in, 234
Olson, David M., 66n
O'Neill, Tip, 25
Opheim, Cynthia, 254n
Oregon
    federal land ownership in, 31
    personal income tax in, 126
    school funding in, 425, 426
    state versus local government in, 115
Orfield, Gary, 99n

Organizational affiliations, 82–83

O'Rourke, Timothy, 220n

Osborne, David, 446n

Ostrom, Elinor, 134n

Parks, 119

Parliamentary rules, 335

Participation, political

    changes in, 198–206

    consequences of, 195–98, 260–62, 264

    decline in, 187–92

    reasons for, 192–95

    significance of, 186–88

    by state, 206–7

Partisanship

    criticism of, 207–8, 265–66

    executive power and, 311–12

    judicial process and, 358

    Progressivism and, 148

    in state legislatures, 345–47

    voter turnout and, 201

    See also Political parties

Party voting, 346

Patronage, 13

Patterson, Samuel C., 354n

Patterson, Thomas E., 218n

Pennsylvania

    labor unions in, 234

    liberalism in, 32

    population stagnation in, 30

    recruitment of legislators in, 343–44

    school segregation in, 88

    tax burdens in, 130–31

Perot, H. Ross, 154

Peterson, Paul E., 66n

Petracca, Mark P., 356n

Pittenger, John C., 68n

Piven, Frances Fox, 218n, 219n, 220n, 446n

Plea bargains, 368, 442

Plotnick, Richard D., 414n

Pole, J. R., 67n

Police officers

    See Public employees

Political action committees (PACs), 228, 241, 248, 324

Political parties

    appeals to women by, 262

    apportionment and, 214–16

    criticism of, 144–47, 207–8

    decline of, 153–58, 189, 282

    democratic conflicts and, 69–70

    divided control of government by, 406–9

    electorate organizing and, 158–68

    ideal of representation and, 138–41, 146

    interest groups and, 241–42, 245, 250

    judicial appointments and, 369

    long-term effects on spending with alternating control of, 404

    mobilization of have-nots and, 6, 7, 176, 256, 267, 274, 348, 388

    political process and, 262–72

    public funding of candidates and, 150

    public policy and, 267–74

    recruitment of legislators and, 343–45

    reform of, 13, 14, 148–52, 158

    state legislatures and, 156, 162–64, 174–78, 340–48

    unified control of government by, 392–406

    voter turnout and, 201–2

    See also Democratic party; Republican party

Political process, role of, 3

Politicians

    agendas of, 286–98, 388–89

    appointment of judges and, 371–72

    apportionment and, 214

    blacks and Hispanics and, 104, 261

    coalition building by, 139–41

    constraints on, 294–97

    court rulings and, 359, 369, 373–74, 379, 389

    distrust of, 138, 189, 322, 327–28, 336, 338, 340, 352

    federalism and, 23, 24–26

    gays and, 92, 104, 264

    interest groups and, 222, 225–35, 237–43, 245–50

    media coverage of, 297

    moderation of conflict by, 97

    political change and, 388–89, 401

    political participation and, 186–87, 192, 195–96, 206, 216

    political parties and, 25, 154

    political processes and, 256–60

    polling and, 209–10

    reelection positioning of, 292–94, 326, 341

    reform and, 265–66

    tax increases and, 133

    tax visibility and, 123–24

    See also Legislatures, state

Polling, 209–10

    by lobbyists, 233

    policy decisions and, 293

Pollution

    federal standards on, 45, 48, 49

    state courts and, 366

Population change

    diversity among states and, 26–30

    political conflict created by, 90–93, 172

    tax rates and, 121

Populism, 94

Pork barreling, 33, 339–40, 343

Porter, Mary C., 385n

Portney, Kent E., 252n

Poverty

    diversity among states and, 27–28, 30

    impact of welfare programs on, 423–25, 437, 439, 443–45

    perceptions of, 85, 108–9

    socioeconomic factors and, 52–53

    support for federal aid and, 74–75

Power, formal

    diverging constituencies and, 403–6

    of governors, 299–301, 303–8, 389

    of mayors, 301–8, 351

    nature of, 298–99, 312–13

Power, informal

    breadth of electoral support and, 309–11, 312

legislatures and, 311–12, 350
  media coverage and, 310–11
Pressman, Jeffrey, 66n
Prewitt, Kenneth, 181n, 237–38, 355n
Pricing policies, 118–20
Prisons
  overcrowding of, 119, 382
  sentencing laws and, 442
Private sector, 418–20, 425, 427–29, 431–36
Progressivism, 145, 148, 299, 301–2
Project grants, 112
Property taxes
  criticism of, 120
  regressive nature of, 127, 130
  stability of, 123
  and tax revolt, 411
  visibility of, 124
Protests, 210
Provone, Doris M., 384n
Public authorities
  See Special-purpose governments
Public employees
  appointment process for, 300–301
  interest groups and, 225, 227
  kickbacks and, 145
  salaries of, 82
  state mandates and, 108, 430
Public opinion
  informal power of executives and, 309
  on interest groups, 239, 245
  judges and, 369, 377–79
  on legislators, 322, 352
  shifts in, 94–96

Race and racism
  class issues and, 9
  district elections and, 211–13
  gubernatorial elections and, 290
  initiatives and referenda and, 208
  interest group membership and, 223–24
  judicial process and, 359, 371–73
  legislators and, 323
  perceptions of, 108–0
  political attitudes and, 80–81
  political parties and, 165, 167–68, 169, 171
  public opinion shifts on, 95–96
  suburban flight and, 87–88
  voter turnout and, 193–94, 197–98
  See also Civil rights; Desegregation
Ravitch, Diane, 253n
Ray, David, 254n, 354n
Reagan, Ronald
  centralized government and, 57–58, 59
  conservatism of, 287, 314, 397, 398, 437
  election mandates for, 291
  government employees and, 407
  and government spending in California, 404
  logrolling and, 33
  media coverage of, 310
  New Federalism and, 34
  Social Security disability programs and, 40

supply-side economics and, 96
  Supreme Court appointments of, 375, 378
  unemployment and, 55
  voter turnout and, 196
Redistricting
  See Apportionment
Referenda, 208–10, 409–12
Reform
  in Atlanta, Ga., 265
  of education, 295, 426
  of executive power, 299, 301–2
  of interest groups, 245–50
  of judicial selection process, 370
  local consolidation battles and, 116–17
  of political parties, 13, 14, 148–52, 158
  of political processes, 94, 265–66
  of specialized courts, 366–67
Regulations, federal
  on business, 47
  increase of, 63
  private sector and, 431–36
  of roads, 427
Religion
  abortion and, 2
  political attitudes and, 81–82
Republican party
  apportionment and, 214–16
  central cities and, 92, 171–72
  coalition building by, 139–41, 341
  conservatism and, 160–61, 175, 201, 313–14
  constituency of, 158–64, 176, 297
  consumer legislation and, 432
  control of state legislatures by, 329–32, 389–406
  economic decline and, 295–96, 433
  economic regulation and, 432
  education issues and, 425
  electoral bases for, 288–91
  labor unions and, 227, 432
  liberalism and, 314–15
  local level of, 169–72
  members of by state, 155–56
  progressive income taxes and, 102, 125
  rural areas and, 158, 162–63, 214
  selection of judges and, 371–72
  spends less money for government programs than
    Democrats, 404
  state mandates and, 109
  support for by state, 176–78, 449–57
  transportation issues and, 147
  unity appeals and, 311
  Watergate and, 26, 173
Restaurant owners, 83
Revolutionary War, 21–24
Rhode Island
  ethnic voting in, 82
  federal farm policy and, 31
  highway funding in, 428
  liberalism in, 32
  nominating conventions in, 149
  population stagnation in, 30
  state mandates in, 430

Richards, Ann, 289, 290, 314
Robertson, David R., 134n
Robinson, Kenneth, 380
Roche, John P., 66n
Rockefeller, Nelson, 293, 314–15, 347–48, 401–2, 408
Roe v. Wade, 377–78
Roosevelt, Franklin Delano, 53, 60
Rosenstone, Steven J., 218n, 219n
Rosenthal, Alan, 252n, 253n, 254n, 319n, 354n, 355n, 414
Rural interests
    and conflicts with urban interests, 84–85, 429
    legislators and, 326
    redistricting and, 213–14
    Republican party and, 158, 162–63

Sabato, Larry, 317n
Sales taxes, 123, 124
Salmore, Barbara G., 181n
Salmore, Stephen A., 181n
Sanders, M. Elizabeth, 276n
San Francisco, Calif., 104, 264
Sargent, Francis, 315
Savings and loan bailouts, 47
Schattschneider, E. E., 17n, 250, 274, 277n
Schlesinger, Joseph, 355n
Schmidt, David D., 219n
School funding
    basis for distribution of, 112
    court rulings on, 108, 374–75, 379–81, 382
    state role in, 115, 132–33, 339–40, 419, 425–27, 441
    tax bases and, 4–5, 88, 105–8
School prayer, 62, 381
Schwartz, John E., 67n, 448n
Segregation
    political conflict and, 2
    Southern gubernatorial campaigns and, 261–62
    suburban flight and, 87–88
Senior citizens
    interest groups and, 229
    Medicare and, 431
    property taxes and, 127
    voter turnout of, 196, 206
Sexual preference, 80–81
Sharkansky, Ira, 218n
Shefter, Martin, 180n
Shinn, Kwang, 355n
Sierra Club, 229
Sigelman, Lee, 135n, 218n, 319n, 320n
Sitkoff, Harvard, 383n
Skocpol, Theda, 446n
Skogan, Wesley G., 383n
Social scientists, 51–53
Social Security, 40, 422
Socioeconomic status
    government policy and, 56
    individual responsibility and, 51–53
    initiatives and referenda and, 208, 264
    interest group membership and, 224–25
    legislators and, 323, 327
    voter turnout and, 194, 196, 198–202, 216

Soil conservation districts, 111
Sorauf, Frank J., 180n
Souter, David, 377–78
South
    black voter registration in, 39–40, 94, 198, 203–5, 260–62,
        264, 272
    civil rights violations in, 378
    class issues in, 6, 8
    Democratic party in, 154, 161, 164–68, 176, 290, 331
    interest groups in, 245–46
    labor unions in, 234–35
    Republican party in, 164–68, 173, 347, 393
    taxes and services in, 122
    teacher salaries in, 232–33
    welfare payments in, 30
South Carolina
    gubernatorial appointment power in, 301
    labor unions in, 234
    religious right in, 162
Southern Politics (V. O. Key), 4, 7, 141
Special-purpose governments, 111, 281
Speed limits, 40, 42
Starr, Paul, 447n
Stephens, G. Ross, 135n
Stone, Clarence, 265, 318n
Stonecash, Jeffrey M., 17n, 68n, 135n, 181n, 182n, 253n,
        276n, 317n, 354n, 355n, 414n, 415n
Strong-executive governments, 280–81
Stumpf, Harry P., 383n
Suburbs
    Democratic party in, 172
    election reform in, 152
    legislators from, 326
    local consolidation battles and, 116–17
    political conflicts and, 87–93
    Republican party and, 162, 214
    state aid to, 103, 112
Swanstrom, Todd, 17n

Tabb, David H., 182n
Tarr, G. Alan, 385n
Taxation
    Articles of Confederation and, 22
    burdens of, 124–33, 256, 392
    court rulings on, 374
    Democratic party and, 389–90, 394
    economic growth and, 121–22, 433
    economic self-interest and, 73, 75
    executive decisions on, 296
    exemptions from, 83, 124–25, 127
    increasing federal government activism and, 43–45
    inequality and, 2, 4, 14
    V. O. Key on, 7
    Republican party and, 390–91
    state control of local governments and, 111–15
    in suburban areas, 91
    and tax revolts, 124, 411–12
    types of, 120–21
Tax bases
    differences in, 2, 102, 131

population stagnation and, 30, 92
school funding and, 4–5, 88, 105–8, 425
suburban flight and, 90
Tax effort
class status and, 259–60
definition of, 10
differences across states, 12
increase in, 124–25
in the Midwest, 271
in New Hampshire and Vermont, 10–11, 268
welfare and, 11–12
Teachers
campaign contributions by, 287
education reform and, 441
interest groups and, 82, 227–29, 232–35
state control of school funding and, 419, 425, 430
Term limits, 13, 338, 352
Texas
campaign costs in, 287
commission government in, 281
federal farm policy and, 31
federal fuel policy and, 31
gubernatorial elections in, 289, 290
gubernatorial power in, 305, 306, 308, 314
judicial appointments in, 372
labor unions in, 234
Latino immigration to, 92
oil interests in, 234
political parties in, 167–68, 268, 331–32, 349
population growth in, 30
school funding in, 105–7, 133, 314, 379, 380–81, 382
state income tax proposals in, 400
state versus local government in, 116
tax burdens in, 130–31
voter turnout in, 197
Theistic beliefs, 50
Thomas, Clive S., 245, 252n, 253n
Thompkins, Mark E., 318n
Thompson, Joel A., 220n, 254n, 355n
Thomson, Ken, 252n
Ticket-splitting, 154, 164, 292, 311, 393
Tiebout, Charles, 134n
Tort law, 375–76
Townships, 110–11
Transportation
government involvement in, 427–28
party differences on, 147, 394
state role in funding, 116
usage costs of, 119
Trattner, Walter I., 67n
Truman, David, 252n
Turret, J. S., 318n

Underwood, James E., 318n
Unemployment
declining economies and, 295
diversity among states and, 27–28, 31
government responsibility for, 54–55, 421
Great Depression and, 52, 54

impact of government programs on, 437–39, 443–44
tax revenue and, 123
Universities
government support for, 426–27
state legislatures and, 83
subsidized tuition at, 5, 427
Utah
conservatism in, 32
federal land ownership in, 31
nominating conventions in, 149
Utility companies, 83, 436

Value choices, 3
Vermont
open primaries in, 149
rural-urban conflicts in, 85
tax burdens in, 130–31
taxation debates in, 9–11, 268
Vertz, Laura L., 181n
Veto power, 305–7, 350–51
Vietnam War, 55
Virginia
political culture in, 194, 268–70, 271–72
state versus local government in, 116
Volpe, John, 315
Voter registration
requirements for, 189, 192, 199–200
of Southern blacks, 39–40, 202–5, 260–62, 264, 272
of women, 262
Voter turnout
See Elections
Voting, frequency of, 187–95
Voting Rights Act of 1965, 40, 203, 272
Vrdolyak, Edward ``Fast Eddie,'' 403

Walker, Dan, 402–3
Washington, Harold, 92, 201, 291, 315–16, 403
Washington State
criminal sentencing in, 442
lumber interests in, 234
party identification in, 160
recruitment of legislators in, 343–44
school funding in, 425, 426
state program cuts in, 394
Water districts, 111
Watergate
negative views of government and, 55, 189
Republican party and, 26, 173
Water quality, 56
Weak-executive governments, 280–81
Weicker, Lowell, 289, 290, 306, 349, 379, 408
Weinberg, Daniel H., 448n
Weinberg, Martha W., 320n
Weisbrot, Robert, 67n
Weitzman, Leonore J., 385n
Welch, Susan, 219n, 220n, 356n, 384n
Weld, William, 296, 314, 406

Welfare
  criticisms of, 439–40
  declining economies and, 295
  Democratic party and, 394
  federal expenditures on, 63
  government involvement in, 420–25
  impact of government programs and, 423–25, 437, 439,
    443–45
  local versus state control of, 5, 113, 116
  lower class under representation and, 262
  in Louisiana, 268–70, 272–73, 395–96
  in Massachusetts, 41, 105
  nationalization of, 41
  New Federalism and, 34
  public support for, 74–75, 78–79, 94–95
  Reagan administration and, 57
  Southern conservatism and, 30
  tax effort and, 11, 12
  in Virginia, 268–70, 272–73
West Virginia
  mining interests in, 234
  Social Security disability programs and, 40
  state versus local government in, 115–16, 430
Wheeler, Stanton, 385n
Whitman, Christine, 144
Whitmire, Kathy, 295
Why Americans Hate Politics (E. J. Dionne), 147
Wiggins, Charles W., 253n, 254n, 356n
Williams, Oliver, 87
Wills, Gary, 67n

Wilson, James Q., 18n
Wilson, Pete, 288, 290, 293
Winters, Richard F., 9–10, 268, 276n, 319n, 414n
Wirt, Frederick M., 218n, 446n
Wisconsin
  open primaries in, 149
  political parties in, 168, 170, 269–71, 341–43, 345
  state mandates in, 430
Wolfinger, Raymond E., 182n, 218n, 219n
Women
  civil rights campaigns of, 53, 381
  divorce laws and, 433–35
  judicial process and, 359, 372, 373–74
  political attitudes of, 80–81
  political involvement of, 205, 262, 323
Wood, Gordon S., 66n
Wright, Deil, 49
Wright, Gerald C., 16, 160, 174, 277n, 449
Wyoming, 31, 32

Yorty, Sam, 302–4
Young, Andrew, 197, 260, 296
Young, Coleman, 296
Young, Rosalie, 276n

Ziegler, Harmon, 237
Zimmerman, Josepg F., 67n
Zisk, Betty, 226, 237, 253n

Copyrights and Acknowledgments

The author is indebted to the following for permission to reprint from copyrighted material:

V. O. Key Estate. For the excerpts from *Southern Politics* by V. O. Key. Reprinted by permission of estate.

The Urban Institute Press. For *Natural Resources and the Environment* by Paul Portney. Reprinted by permission of the publisher.

Louis Harris and Associates, Inc. For material from the Louis Harris Polls of 21 September 1981 and 17 August 1981. Reprinted by permission.

American Political Science Association. For excerpts from "Participation, Political Structure, and Concurrence . . ." by Susan B. Hansen, which originally appeared in *American Political Science Review* (December 1975). Reprinted by permission.

American Political Science Association. For excerpts from "The Election of Harold Washington" by Michael B. Preston, which originally appeared in *Political Science* (Summer 1983). Reprinted by permission.

American Political Science Association. For excerpts from "The Effect of Registration Laws on Voter Turnout" by Steven Rosenstone and Raymond Wolfinger, which originally appeared in *American Political Science Review* (March 1978). Reprinted by permission.

American Political Science Association. For excerpts from "Political Parties, Public Opinion, and State Policy in the U.S." by John O. McIver and Robert S. Erikson, which originally appeared in *American Political Science Review* (September 1989). Reprinted by permission.

Newsweek. For statistical material from *Newsweek*, 6 May 1991, © 1991, Newsweek, Inc. All rights reserved. Reprinted by permission.

Newsweek. For statistical material from *Newsweek*, 2 March 1992, © 1992, Newsweek, Inc. All rights reserved. Reprinted by permission.

Simon & Schuster. For excerpts from *Local Interest Politics* by Betty Zisk. Reprinted with the permission of Simon & Schuster from the Macmillan College text. Copyright © 1973 by Bobbs Merrill Company.

Simon & Schuster. For the tables from *American Public Opinion*, Fourth Edition, by Robert S. Erickson, Norman Luttberg, and Kent L. Tedin. Reprinted with the permission of Simon & Schuster from the Macmillan College text. Copyright © 1991 by Macmillan College Publishing Company, Inc.

Gallup Poll Service. For excerpts from Gallup Opinion Index (December 1969). Reprinted by permission.

New York Review of Books. For excerpts from "Playing the Racial Card" by Andrew Hacker, which appeared originally in the *New York Review of Books*, 24 October 1991. Reprinted by permission.

Gary Orfield. For excerpts from "The Growth of Segregation in American Schools: Changing Patterns . . ." (December 1993) by Gary Orfield. Reprinted by permission of the author.

Greenwood Publishing Group, Inc. For excerpts from *Trends in Public Opinion* by Richard G. Niemi et al. Copyright © 1989. Reprinted with permission of Greenwood Publishing Group, Inc., Westport, CT.

HarperCollins Publishers, Inc. For excerpts from *Urban Politics and Public Policy*, Third Edition, by Robert Lineberry and Ira Sharkansky. Copyright © 1978 by Robert L. Lineberry and Ira Sharkansky. Reprinted by permission of HarperCollins Publishers, Inc.

University of Texas Press. For excerpts from "How Citizens Think About National Issues" by Shanto Iyengar in *American Journal of Political Science* Vol. 33:4 (November 1989) pp. 878–900. Reprinted by permission of the author and the University of Texas Press.

Wadsworth Publishing Co. For excerpts from *American State Political Parties and Elections* by Malcolm Jewell and David Olson. Copyright © 1978 by Dorsey Press. Reprinted by permission.

International City/County Management Association. For excerpts from "Contemporary Patterns and Trends in Municipal Government Structures" by Tari Renner and Victor S. DeSantis, which appeared in *The Municipal Year Book* 1993 (Washington, D.C.: The International City/County Management Association, 1993). Reprinted by permission.

International City Management Association. For excerpts from "Municipal Election Processes: The Impact on Minority Representation" by Tari Renner, which appeared in *The Municipal Year Book 1988* (Washington, D.C.: The International City Management Association, 1988). Reprinted by permission.

International City Management Association. For excerpts from "Forms of City Government in American History" by Charles Adrian, which appeared in *The Municipal Year Book 1988* (Washington, D.C.: The International City Management Association, 1988). Reprinted by permission.

HarperCollins Publishers. For excerpts from *Party Politics in America*, Seventh Edition, by Paul Allen Beck and Frank J. Sorauf. Copyright © 1992 by HarperCollins Publishers, Inc. Reprinted by permission of HarperCollins Publishers, Inc.

HarperCollins Publishers. For excerpts from *Politics and Policy in States and Communities*, Fourth Edition, by John J. Harrigan. Copyright © 1991 by John J. Harrigan. Reprinted by permission of HarperCollins Publishers, Inc.

American Political Science Association. For excerpts from "Divided Government in the States" by Morris P. Fiorina, which originally appeared in *Political Science* (December 1991). Reprinted by permission.

New York University Press. For excerpts from *Parties, Elections, and Representation in New York* by Howard Scarrow. Copyright © 1983. Reprinted by permission.

University of Chicago Press. For excerpts from *Participation in America* by Sidney Verba and Norman Nie. Copyright © 1972. Reprinted by permission.

F. E. Peacock Publishers. For excerpts from *American Electoral Behavior* by M. Gant and N. Luttbeg. Copyright © 1991. Reproduced by permission of the publisher, F. E. Peacock Publishers, Inc., Itasca, Illinois.